EARLY LITERACY INSTRUCTION AND INTERVENTION

Also from Donna M. Scanlon

Comprehensive Reading Intervention in Grades 3–8:
Fostering Word Learning, Comprehension, and Motivation
Lynn M. Gelzheiser, Donna M. Scanlon,
Laura Hallgren-Flynn, and Peggy Connors

Early Literacy Instruction and Intervention

The Interactive Strategies Approach

THIRD EDITION

Donna M. Scanlon
Kimberly L. Anderson
Erica M. Barnes
Joan M. Sweeney

THE GUILFORD PRESS
New York   London

Library of Congress Cataloging-in-Publication Data

Names: Scanlon, Donna M., author. | Anderson, Kimberly L., author. |
  Barnes, Erica Marie, author. | Sweeney, Joan M., author.
Title: Early literacy instruction and intervention : the interactive
  strategies approach / Donna M. Scanlon, Kimberly L. Anderson, Erica M.
  Barnes, Joan M. Sweeney.
Other titles: Early intervention for reading difficulties
Description: Third edition. | New York, NY : The Guilford Press, [2024] |
  Includes bibliographical references and index.
Identifiers: LCCN 2023054188 | ISBN 9781462553662 (hardcover) |
  ISBN 9781462553655 (paperback)
Subjects: LCSH: Reading—Remedial teaching. | BISAC: EDUCATION / Teaching /
  Subjects / Reading & Phonics | EDUCATION / Schools / Levels / Early
  Childhood (incl. Preschool & Kindergarten)
Classification: LCC LB1050.5 .S228 2024 | DDC 372.43—dc23/eng/20231129
LC record available at *https://lccn.loc.gov/2023054188*

About the Authors

Donna M. Scanlon, PhD, is Professor Emeritus in the Department of Literacy Teaching and Learning at the University at Albany, State University of New York, where she served as director of the Child Research and Study Center. Dr. Scanlon has spent most of her career studying children's reading difficulties and helping families and schools address the needs of students who struggle with literacy development. Her research contributed to the emergence of response to intervention as a process for preventing reading difficulties and avoiding inappropriate and inaccurate learning disability classifications. In recent years, her work has focused on the development of teacher knowledge and teaching skill to help prevent reading difficulties in young children and remediate reading difficulties among older children. Dr. Scanlon has served on the Literacy Research Panel, Response to Intervention Task Force, and Response to Intervention Commission of the International Literacy Association.

Kimberly L. Anderson, PhD, is Associate Professor in the Department of Literacy Studies, English Education, and History Education at East Carolina University. Her research focuses on improving teacher preparation for early literacy instruction and on the development of literacy tutoring protocols that can be used by tutors with limited expertise. Dr. Anderson contributed to research on the Interactive Strategies Approach (ISA) in her past role as a research associate and director of professional development at the Child Research and Study Center, University at Albany, State University of New York. Dr. Anderson has a particular interest in the role of strategy instruction in word solving and has studied the differential impact of professional development that emphasizes the combination of alphabetic decoding and meaning-based strategies, one of the main tenets of the ISA.

Erica M. Barnes, PhD, is Associate Professor in the Department of Literacy Teaching and Learning at the University at Albany, State University of New York. Her research investigates teacher–child interactions in preschool and early elementary classrooms that promote language and literacy growth, with an emphasis on the developmental trajectories of children with varying levels of language abilities from underserved populations. Dr. Barnes is interested in how language facilitates literacy development, and how teachers may differentiate instruction for students to prevent literacy-learning difficulties. She has worked as a special education teacher, a teacher consultant, and a progress monitoring consultant in K–12 settings.

Joan M. Sweeney, MSEd, is a reading specialist in a Capital District public school in New York State. Previously, she was a research associate in the Child Research and Study Center, University at Albany, State University of New York, where she provided intervention for struggling readers, supervised intervention teachers, and coached classroom teachers utilizing the ISA to support children's literacy development.

Preface to the Third Edition

This text is an update and revision of *Early Intervention for Reading Difficulties, Second Edition*. The first two editions of this book (Scanlon, Anderson, & Sweeney, 2010, 2017) provided detailed information on an approach to early literacy instruction and intervention that we call the Interactive Strategies Approach (ISA). This approach has been found to be successful in reducing the number of children who experience early and longer-term reading difficulties when implemented in classroom, small-group, and one-to-one instructional contexts (Scanlon, Vellutino, Small, Fanuele, & Sweeney, 2005; Scanlon, Gelzheiser, Vellutino, Schatschneider, & Sweeney, 2008; Vellutino et al., 1996). The original version of the approach was developed by drawing on theoretical explanations of early literacy development, the findings from basic research on the skills that contribute to early literacy success/development, extensive observational work in classroom and remedial/ intervention settings, and our own work as literacy/reading specialists and educational and research psychologists. Subsequent iterations of the approach, across the many years since the first iteration was evaluated in a longitudinal early intervention study (Vellutino et al., 1996), reflect continual refinement based on additional research—both our own and that of others pursuing the goal of preventing long-term difficulties—and feedback from teacher educators, practicing teachers, and students pursuing teaching degrees.

The revised title of the current edition reflects our thinking that, while the prevention of reading difficulties among primary-grade learners remains an important focus, much of the text offers evidence-based guidance for teaching primary-grade literacy learners more generally. The text is intended to help teachers and prospective teachers develop and refine their knowledge and skills related to early literacy development so as to enable them to effectively promote literacy development, especially among those who experience difficulty in the primary grades.

Like the first two editions, this edition describes the ISA (Vellutino & Scanlon, 2002; Scanlon & Anderson, 2020), an evidence-based instructional approach developed and tested in a series of large-scale, longitudinal studies that investigated ways to prevent and remediate early reading difficulties. Also, like the first two editions, this edition is largely structured around a set of instructional goals for early literacy learners, particularly students who struggle with literacy acquisition, and how to help children accomplish those goals.

Given that it has been several years since we completed the last of our studies focused at the primary level (see Scanlon et al., 2008; Vellutino, Scanlon, Zhang, & Schatschneiderm, 2008), one might wonder why we elected to develop a third edition of the book. In fact, when Craig Thomas, Senior Editor at The Guilford Press, originally suggested a new edition, we were reluctant to agree. However, upon further consideration, we identified several major reasons for producing a third edition, which we detail below, along with a description of what is new in this edition.

• First and foremost, in the last several years, there has been a great deal of discussion about how instruction for early literacy learners should be organized and delivered. One frequently articulated concern has been that the development of phonics/decoding skills was not being sufficiently addressed in the primary grades. Having spent decades prior to writing the first edition of this text investigating the differences between children who learned to read with relative ease and those who experienced difficulty, we have always been acutely aware of the important role that phonics skills (and phonological skills more generally) play in early literacy success. A listing of some of our early studies can be found on the book's companion website (see the box at the end of the table of contents). Explicit, systematic, and responsive instruction to develop phonics skills was a central feature in our early intervention studies and was described in detail in the first two editions of this text. However, in the last several years, new research related to the development of foundational phonological skills has emerged, and we felt it was important to align the guidance we provide to better reflect what has been recently learned through research. We have done that in the current edition, primarily in Part II of this text.

• Concerns have been raised in recent years regarding the guidance children receive about identifying unfamiliar printed words they encounter while reading. As we will touch on repeatedly throughout this text, the vast majority of words that proficient readers can read are learned through effective word solving while reading. Comprehension, the end goal of reading instruction, requires that readers be able to effortlessly read the vast majority of the words they encounter in printed text. While estimates vary, the lowest estimate is that proficient readers can effortlessly (automatically) read at least 40,000 distinct words. Obviously, this is far too many words for teachers to explicitly teach. Teaching children to decode unfamiliar words when they are encountered in meaningful text seems an obvious solution. Indeed, there has been quite a bit of advocacy recently for teaching children to rely *exclusively* on using phonics skills to determine the identities of unfamiliar words encountered while reading. However, unlike several other alphabetic languages, English does not have strict and reliable one-to-one correspondences between some of the letters and the sounds they represent (especially for vowels). For this reason learners need to make sure that their attempts at unknown words make sense in the context in which they are encountered. If not, learners may need to be a bit flexible in their decoding attempts by trying different sounds for some of the letters until they identify a real word that *does* make sense. This flexibility with decoding has always been an important element of ISA word-solving instruction. Research by several research groups in the last couple of years has provided strong support for the utility of being able to "correct" a mispronunciation of a word. This skill is referred to as having a "set for variability." This important (and now better understood) relationship between the strength of children's set for variability and their reading growth led us to place greater emphasis on this aspect of the ISA in the current edition.

• There was also a call for more information on teaching linguistically diverse students, a need that has been addressed more extensively in the current volume.

• Teacher educators, teacher leaders, teachers, and students in undergraduate and graduate teacher education courses who used previous editions of the book provided feedback that we felt needed to be addressed. While people have been generally positive about the content and presentation of the material in the first two editions, many have offered useful suggestions for improvement. A number of the suggestions called for more examples of explicit instructional language, such as the sample instructional scripts included in the first two editions. Several have been added to this edition.

• Over the years, we received multiple inquiries about the order in which certain decoding skills should be taught and about how those skills relate to other aspects of literacy learning. Across many of the chapters in the current edition, we have clarified relationships between explicit, systematic, and responsive instruction on decoding skills and how these skills relate to the development of other foundational skills such as print concepts and phonemic awareness and to the guidance provided to children as they attempt to figure out unfamiliar words encountered while reading. These relationships are concisely summarized in the "decision tree" that appears in the introduction to Part II of this book (see p. 100) and are an important focus of the word-solving process described in Chapter 12.

• While earlier editions represented reading and writing as language skills and included a chapter on vocabulary and language more generally, none of the authors of the earlier editions had particular expertise related to child language development. We viewed this as an important weakness of the earlier editions and regard it as a strength of the third edition, as the new member of the author team (Dr. Erica Barnes) has extensive experience in researching and writing/teaching about child language development and the relation of language skills to reading and writing development. She is the primary author of the extensively revised chapter on vocabulary and language in the current edition and has contributed her expertise throughout the text.

• Finally, research on reading and reading development and instruction continues to evolve on many fronts. Developing a third edition gave us the opportunity to update the entire text. Much has been learned about early literacy development and literacy learning difficulties in the years since the second edition was submitted for publication, and we have accordingly updated the research reviewed in many of the chapters throughout the book.

We should also note that the third edition includes a detailed glossary at the end of the text. In addition, the companion website, which includes many online resources, is better organized than the one provided for the second edition.

Contents

Introduction

Reading and writing skills are critical foundations for virtually all school learning. Success during the early stages of developing these skills generally bodes well for long-term educational success. The primary purpose of this text is to develop and/or enhance primary-grade teachers' understanding of early literacy development and how to:

- design and deliver instruction that is responsive to children's current knowledge and skills, and
- accelerate literacy development among children whose skills are limited in relation to grade-level expectations.

Responsiveness involves considering both the focus of instruction (which would be guided by what children know and are able to do) and the intensity of instruction needed by children who are at different points in developing their literacy skills. In this text, we place particular emphasis on ways to accelerate literacy learning among children with more limited preparation so as to increase the likelihood that all primary-grade learners will attain the level of literacy proficiency expected for their grade level.

Our purpose in this text is to help teachers gain insight into the complexity of early literacy learning processes by summarizing some of the theory and much of the research that informs the field. In addition, we provide a detailed description of the Interactive Strategies Approach (ISA), a successful approach to early literacy instruction and intervention that we developed and tested across a series of three large-scale federally funded longitudinal studies (Scanlon, Gelzheiser, Vellutino, Schatschneider, & Sweeney, 2008; Scanlon, Vellutino, Small, Fanuele, & Sweeney, 2005; Vellutino et al., 1996; Vellutino & Scanlon, 2002; Vellutino,

Scanlon, Zhang, & Schatschneider, 2008) and a smaller-scale study that compared the effects of two of the major components of the ISA (Anderson, 2009). In the process of describing the ISA, we have also drawn on research that has emerged in the last several years so as to ensure that the information we share with teachers is as current as possible.

Structure of the Book

The book is divided into five main parts, each of which is composed of multiple chapters that address differing but related aspects of early literacy development and instruction that supports that development. The majority of the chapters (Chapters 3–16) describe goals that are important foci for early literacy learners and how children can be helped to accomplish those goals.

In Part I, "Theoretical and Practical Understandings of Early Literacy Learning and Instruction" (Chapters 1–3), we describe the complexity of the reading process and the corresponding need for instruction to attend to this complexity, to be responsive to children's current knowledge and skills in relation to literacy development, and to promote enthusiasm for and interest in literacy learning in the primary grades. In Part II, "Understanding Print and the English (Alphabetic) Writing System" (Chapters 4–11), we focus on the development of alphabetic and orthographic knowledge and the understanding of how printed language relates to spoken language.

Part III, "Word Learning" (Chapters 12 and 13), focuses on the development of sight vocabulary (i.e., words that can be identified effortlessly and automatically) through explicit teaching of and practice with high-frequency words and through the application of word-solving strategies that enable readers to effectively identify unfamiliar words encountered in context.

Part IV, "Meaning Construction," focuses on the purpose of reading: meaning making—or making sense of what is read. Chapters 14–16 focus on oral reading fluency, language skills, and active construction of the meaning of texts that children listen to and read.

In Part V, "Integration of the Goals," Chapter 17 illustrates how instruction provided in small-group contexts, which involve children who are at similar points in their literacy development, provides one of the most responsive and productive vehicles for moving children forward in their literacy learning. The chapter discusses the five or six segments that would be included in an ISA-based small-group lesson and discusses how instruction might differ for children at earlier and later points in literacy development. Part V concludes with a chapter (Chapter 18) that prompts reflection across the content discussed in the entire text and reminds readers to, once again, consider the general principles for prevention of reading difficulties, which are initially introduced in Chapter 2 and are revisited in various ways throughout the text.

Our goal in writing this book was to address a fairly broad audience spanning the range from undergraduate education students taking one of their first courses in literacy instruction to highly experienced and knowledgeable teachers seeking to learn (more) about the scientific research that can help to inform approaches to early literacy instruction and intervention. Given this broad audience, the content of the book may be variably perceived as dense or repetitive. Chapters 1 and 2 may be perceived as dense by most of our readers. In those chapters we present a broad range of content on early literacy development and instruction in general and on the Interactive Strategies Approach more specifically. Our purpose is to help our readers develop an organizational schema for what is to come. These chapters "set the stage" for the rest of the book. We will revisit (most of) the content and concepts in subsequent chapters as we break down the complex process of reading/learning to read into its component parts. The sense of repetitiveness is apt to emerge more or less strongly as readers read through the goals chapters. In some contexts, the chapters will not be read in the order in which they are presented. Therefore, concepts and terminology introduced in earlier chapters may be unfamiliar when encountered in later chapters. For this reason, we have re-presented critical concepts and terminology that may have been initially introduced in earlier chapters. We hope that for those who read the chapters in the order in which they are presented the subsequent repetitiveness will be perceived as "reader friendly" rather than annoying or unnecessary!

The Glossary

Discussions of early literacy development are often replete with terms that may be relatively (or totally) unfamiliar to many of our readers. Therefore, we have provided a comprehensive Glossary at the end of this book. While most of the terms that may be unfamiliar to our readers are defined when they are first used in the text, many of them come up repeatedly as the text unfolds. Readers, therefore, may benefit from a quick reminder of the meanings of relevant terms that can be accessed by referencing the Glossary. Use of the Glossary, as needed, is likely to enhance one's overall comprehension of and learning from this text.

Theoretical and Practical Understandings of Early Literacy Learning and Instruction

Introduction to Part I

Part I provides some of the theoretical background that attempts to explain the process of literacy development, provides an overview of the type of comprehensive and responsive instruction that we advocate, and addresses the critical roles that motivation and engagement play in literacy learning.

In Chapter 1, we briefly review some of the most widely cited theories used to explain literacy development and offer a graphic illustration we developed to illustrate the interacting factors and elements that enable learners to achieve the end goal of literacy learning—the ability to comprehend and learn from the texts they read (and listen to). We also provide an overview of the Interactive Strategies Approach (ISA), which is the main focus of this text. We briefly review the research that has demonstrated the effectiveness of instruction based on the ISA in reducing the number of young children who experience difficulty with literacy learning in the primary grades. It is important to note that virtually all aspects of the ISA draw on the extensive research on ways to support early literacy development that we and several other research groups have pursued. The ISA offers a coordinated integration of instructional practices that have been shown to positively impact early literacy development. It places great emphasis on providing instruction that is both responsive to the knowledge and skills of individual children and comprehensive with respect to addressing the variety of factors that can influence the development of literacy learners.

A major theme of Chapter 2 is that literacy and language instruction should be responsive to the broad spectrum of students in a typical primary-grade classroom. To this end, we suggest that language arts instruction include a combination of whole-class, small-group, and one-to-one instruction. Whereas small groups should comprise children who are at similar points in development relative to their literacy skills, we argue that the diversity of learners in a given classroom must be considered in all aspects of language arts instruction (and instruction more generally). We illustrate the many contributors to early literacy development that can be addressed in whole-class instructional contexts such as interactive read-alouds, shared reading, and shared writing. (Check the Glossary at the end of this book if these terms are unfamiliar to you.) For children whose literacy skills are limited in relation to grade-level expectations, we contend that, in these whole-class contexts, teachers can vary the focus during a single instructional episode so that all children in the class have an opportunity to expand their understanding of important aspects of reading and writing processes. We also make a case for the critical role of small-group instruction in advancing literacy skills. We take the position that children with the most limited literacy skills will benefit most from small-group instruction that focuses on aspects of reading and writing, and on the foundational skills that support reading and writing, that are just a bit beyond what they are currently able to handle without assistance. Further, we argue that children with the most limited skills need instruction in smaller groups, for longer periods of time, and/or more frequently in order to experience the accelerated growth in literacy that is needed for them to meet or exceed grade-level expectations.

Chapter 3 addresses motivation, the first of the ISA's instructional goals. In our work with teachers relative to the ISA, we have always identified motivation to read and write as the first and most important goal of early literacy instruction, particularly for children who begin their schooling with comparatively limited literacy skills. We discuss the need to be attentive to motivational factors that impact reading development because these factors have a powerful influence on success (or lack thereof). Attention to motivational issues, particularly the development of intrinsic motivation and a sense of competence relative to literacy, should pervade interactions with all early literacy learners but particularly those with the most limited skills.

CHAPTER 1

Early Literacy Learning and the Interactive Strategies Approach

Reading is a complicated process. Theorists and researchers have been offering models intended to explain the process for decades. For example, in 1986 Gough and Tunmer offered their simple view of reading (SVR), which explains reading comprehension as being dependent on a combination of one's ability to read printed words and one's language comprehension. They argued that the relationship was multiplicative—reading comprehension (RC) is the product of word identification/recognition ability (WR) and language comprehension (LC). The formula they offer is RC= WR × LC. The implications for this model are clear. If an individual could not identify printed words at all, their reading comprehension would be 0. Similarly, if one had no ability to comprehend spoken language but somehow could decode the words (a highly unlikely possibility), one's reading comprehension would be 0. A more likely scenario, and one that characterizes learners who struggle with identifying printed words, is that reading comprehension would be impaired but likely not totally lacking. For example, limited ability with word reading, say 25% of what's needed relative to word identification for a given text coupled with 100% of the needed linguistic (spoken language) comprehension would result in limited reading comprehension (.25 × 1.00 = .25).

A widely recognized elaboration of the SVR is Scarborough's (2001) effort to "unpack" the two major factors in the SVR model, which she illustrates using what has come to be called the "reading rope." This model is presented in Figure 1.1. It carries over the two major contributing factors in the SVR and unpacks each factor—with the word recognition factor including phonological awareness (the ability to analyze spoken words into component sounds), decoding (the ability to "sound out" unfamiliar printed words), and sight recognition (the ability

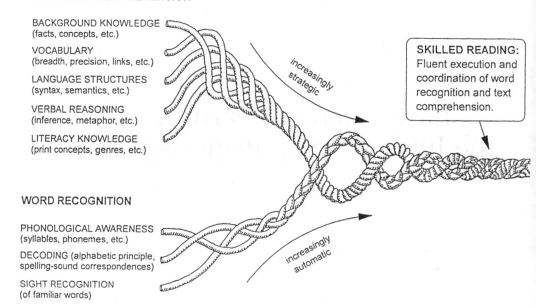

LANGUAGE COMPREHENSION

BACKGROUND KNOWLEDGE
(facts, concepts, etc.)

VOCABULARY
(breadth, precision, links, etc.)

LANGUAGE STRUCTURES
(syntax, semantics, etc.)

VERBAL REASONING
(inference, metaphor, etc.)

LITERACY KNOWLEDGE
(print concepts, genres, etc.)

increasingly strategic

SKILLED READING:
Fluent execution and
coordination of word
recognition and text
comprehension.

WORD RECOGNITION

PHONOLOGICAL AWARENESS
(syllables, phonemes, etc.)

DECODING (alphabetic principle,
spelling-sound correspondences)

SIGHT RECOGNITION
(of familiar words)

increasingly automatic

FIGURE 1.1. Scarborough's (2001) reading rope elaboration of the simple view of reading (SVR). Copyright © 2001 The Guilford Press. Reprinted by permission.

to effortlessly identify printed words)—each illustrated as separate strands that become intertwined over time. The language comprehension factor includes strands for background knowledge, vocabulary, language structures, verbal reasoning, and literacy knowledge. These strands too are illustrated as becoming intertwined over time. Ultimately, the two major factors are intertwined to result in skilled reading in which word recognition and language comprehension are coordinated in an effective manner—thus enabling reading comprehension.

Both the SVR and the reading rope have much to offer in terms of helping us to understand reading comprehension through naming what skilled readers do; yet neither model is sufficient for addressing the complexity of the process of becoming literate. Importantly, neither addresses the instruction that facilitates this process. In contrast to the theoretical explanations of reading development embodied by the SVR and Scarborough's reading rope, the Interactive Strategies Approach (ISA) is an approach to literacy instruction and intervention that we've been researching and refining since the early 1990s. While certainly influenced by these and other theoretical explanations of how literacy develops, it is also influenced by years of observing teachers working with young children in classroom and intervention settings and by our own teaching of young children as well as teaching teachers (and future teachers). In the ISA, we address all the elements Scarborough identifies, and we also take explicit account of contextual and motivational impacts on literacy development. Even more importantly, we view the processes involved in literacy development as being much more interactive and reciprocal than the theoretical models discussed above convey. In our view, development in one area influences and is influenced by development in other areas. The ISA addresses how individuals become literate, acknowledging unique contributions from within and beyond the learner, with an emphasis on instruction to facilitate the development of these processes.

Reading and Writing Are Complex Processes That Require Comprehensive and Responsive Literacy Instruction

We argue that reading is a complex process that requires the analysis, coordination, and interpretation of a variety of sources of information. In order to effectively meet the needs of literacy learners, especially those who experience difficulty, instruction needs to take account of this complexity. Consider, for example, what is involved in reading and understanding the simple text below:

> Amira is going to Emilia's party. She likes kites. Amira can bring her a kite.

To understand this text, the reader needs to be able to (1) read the words, (2) retrieve the words' meanings, (3) put the words together to form meaningful ideas, and (4) assemble a larger model of what the text is about (Kintsch, 1998). Because difficulties with any of these processes can result in reading difficulties, all of these important processes need to be considered when designing instruction to help children learn to read.

Because teachers are proficient readers and perform many, if not all, of these processes effortlessly, they are sometimes surprised by, and insensitive to, the complexity of the processes. By becoming more attuned to these complexities, teachers can become better able to provide instruction and guidance to students who are learning to read. To help teachers gain these insights, we begin with an (incomplete) analysis of what a reader might do while reading the text about Emilia's party.

Read the Words

All of the words in this text are known to proficient readers (with the possible exception of the proper names). They can identify them automatically with little or no conscious thought. As a result, readers can devote most, if not all, of their thinking to making sense of the text. For beginning readers and/or those who have difficulty with identifying printed words, however, some of the words will be somewhat or very unfamiliar, and they *will* have to devote thought to figuring out the words. Their success in doing so will depend on several things, including what they understand about how the writing system works (i.e., how the printed letters represent the sounds in spoken words) and their ability to make use of other sources of information, such as the context in which the words occur. For example, if students attempted to "sound out" the word *is,* it would rhyme with *miss* rather than with *fizz*! Using the information provided by the letters in the words in combination with the context of the sentence, readers at an early point in development would be more likely to figure out the word.

Retrieve the Words' Meaning(s)

The meanings of words are usually accessed quite automatically while reading *if* the words are in the readers' spoken vocabulary and are accurately identified. So, for example, readers who know what a kite is will activate that knowledge when reading the word *kites.* In fact, having knowledge of kites is likely to allow readers to confirm that the printed word is, in fact, pronounced as *kites* rather than as *kit-es* or *kite-es.* For a word such as *can,* which has more than one common meaning (the container vs. the ability to do something), readers who can read the words in the text with relative ease generally become aware of only the meaning of the word that is signaled by the context.

The meanings of pronouns (*she* and *her* in the current example) often require the reader to infer to whom they refer. In the current example, it is not clear whether *she* in the second sentence refers to Amira or Emilia—a problem that might well slow engaged readers down as proficient readers generally infer the referent for pronouns quite automatically and effortlessly. Proficient readers would likely quickly resolve their uncertainty about the referent of *she* upon reading the third sentence. However, readers who are struggling to read some of the words in the passage may well have difficulty making the needed inferences because their cognitive resources are divided between attempting to identify the words and attempting to understand the meaning of the text.

Assemble Words to Form Idea Units

As noted, the context in which a word occurs helps readers identify (or confirm the identity of) individual words that are initially unfamiliar and, for words with more than one meaning, helps readers to identify the intended meaning of the word. One of the ways that context operates is through readers' knowledge of spoken language and the implicit rules regarding which words can follow one another (an aspect of syntactic awareness). For example, the verb meaning of *can* is selected in the sentence *Amira can bring her a kite* partly because, within a sentence in English, a noun is more often followed by a verb than by another noun (i.e., a container). Moreover, if in this sentence the proper noun *Amira* was followed by another proper noun (such as *Melissa*), there would be a comma between the two proper nouns—another signal to which proficient readers attend—mostly without conscious thought. Even when none of the words has multiple meanings, a hallmark of proficient reading (and listening) is that readers/listeners process the words in meaningful units or phrases. A meaningful unit might be a sentence, if it is short enough, or it might be only part of a sentence—but the part would comprise a unit of meaning. For example, the sentence *She likes kites* might be processed as one meaningful unit because it is only three words long and presents a fairly simple idea (barring, of course, the complication regarding the referent of *she* in this example). However, the longer sentence *Amira was going to Emilia's party* might be processed as two meaningful units (e.g.,[1] *Amira was going [somewhere]* and *to Emilia's party*). Exactly how a sentence would be processed would depend on a variety of factors, including how familiar readers/listeners are with the general topic, how easily they can access the meanings of the individual words, how easily they can identify the individual words, and so on.

Assemble a Larger Model of the Text

By this point, readers of this chapter are likely growing weary of thinking about all the things that proficient readers do while reading just three fairly simple sentences. However, so far, the discussion has hardly touched on the major purpose of reading and what is, perhaps, the most complicated part of the process: to understand, interpret, and/or react to what is stated in the text. In order to fulfill this purpose, readers must relate the idea units to one another to form a conceptual and coherent understanding of the text that spans the sentences and taps readers' knowledge in ways that facilitate comprehension (Kintsch, 1998; Perfetti, Landi, & Oakhill, 2005). That is, while reading a text, readers "read" more than what is actually on the page, and how they understand the text depends on what they already know about the topic. So, for example, *if* they know something about birthday parties, readers may infer that Emilia's party is a birthday party because that is the kind of party to which one might bring a present. Conversely, readers not familiar with birthday parties might be somewhat confused. Readers are also likely to make some inference about Emilia's age because it is less likely that one would bring a kite to an infant or to an elderly adult. A discussion of the extent of thinking and inferencing that might go on relative to this little bit of text could be quite extensive. Some readers, for example, might construct a visual image of the two characters, including what they are wearing, what color hair they have, and so forth. The printed words stimulate readers to think and visualize. For fully engaged and proficient readers, the thinking generally goes far beyond what is literally stated.

The previous discussion is not intended to make anyone feel overwhelmed by what needs to be taught. Rather, the purpose is to help teachers more fully appreciate the complexity of the processes involved in reading and to develop insights into aspects of the process that may need explicit instructional attention and/or differentiation.

---

[1] Many people do not know the difference in meaning between the abbreviations e.g. and i.e., but the distinction between them is important for understanding the information provided. E.g., stands for "exempli gratia" and means "for example." I.e. stands for "id est" and means "that is."

A Conceptual Model of the Complexity
of the Reading Process

While the example above introduces the notion of complexity of the reading process, we will next go into greater detail, relying on a graphic representation presented in Figure 1.2. We have found this graphic to be useful for talking about the complexity of reading in our work with teachers. It is important to note that as readers become increasingly proficient, all these processes are being attended to simultaneously, to a certain degree. Mastery of one process is not a prerequisite for developing another process, but rather development of one process frequently leads to development in another and vice versa.

Attend to the Graphic!

As you read through the description of the graphic, we strongly encourage you to refer back frequently to the graphic as it will help you to better comprehend the interactive and inter-related nature of the processes involved in development.

Comprehension and Knowledge are located at the center of Figure 1.2, as comprehension and knowledge development are the central reason for reading and

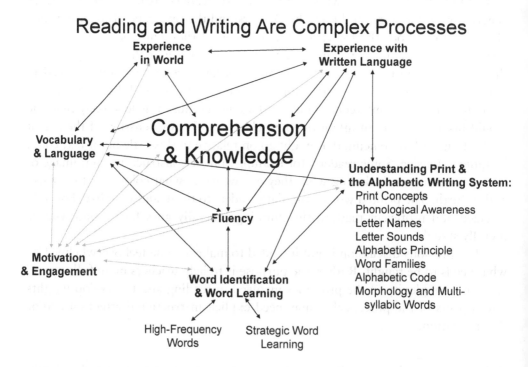

FIGURE 1.2. Conceptual model of reading and writing processes.

the two are inextricably linked. Comprehending a text allows the reader to build knowledge, and the readers' knowledge influences their ability to comprehend text. The more one knows about something, the more readily they can learn more about that subject through reading and/or listening to text. Comprehension and knowledge are influenced by and influence all the factors to which they are connected in the model, and most of the factors are reciprocally related to one another, as illustrated by the double-headed arrows. Here we discuss prominent interconnections but leave the reader to ponder the full complexity of the model and the processes. We discuss each aspect of the model in turn, beginning with **Vocabulary and Language** and moving around the model in a clockwise direction. However, it is important to keep in mind that the order in which we discuss the elements of the model *should not* be taken to suggest that there is an order in which the elements should be addressed instructionally. Rather, to a great extent, as we intend to illustrate with the double-headed arrows, virtually all the elements are developed more or less simultaneously—and in mutually supporting ways.

Obviously, in order to understand a text, a reader needs to understand the meaning of the vast majority of the words in the text and have sufficient skill with syntax (language structure) to be able to interpret the meanings of the sentences encountered. Knowledge of more diverse words and language structures may lead to stronger comprehension of texts. Thus, Vocabulary and Language skills influence Comprehension and Knowledge development. And the relationship is reciprocal. A reader's existing knowledge base and success in comprehending a text have the potential to build the reader's vocabulary and general language skills, as, generally, one encounters more sophisticated vocabulary and more sophisticated syntactic structures in text than in everyday spoken language. Further, research suggests that, once children are literate, most new words that become part of their spoken vocabularies are learned through engagement with written texts.

Experience in the World, obviously, builds knowledge. The experiences one has had will influence how one comprehends a text. For example, a child who has visited an aquarium and seen penguins will comprehend a text about penguins differently than a child who has never seen penguins. Reciprocally, a child who has read or listened to books about penguins prior to first seeing them in the flesh will have a different experience than a child who has no relevant prior knowledge. Further, as illustrated by the double-headed arrow connecting to Vocabulary and Language, Experience in the World influences and is influenced by one's vocabulary and language skills. To continue with the penguin example, a child who has read about and/or visited an aquarium with penguins has the potential to acquire vocabulary (and knowledge) related to penguins (e.g., flippers, insulation, icebergs, camouflage, Antarctica), and a child who has more advanced language skills is likely to be able to more effectively formulate questions (to be asked of adults accompanying them on a visit to an aquarium) that will elicit the desired information. They are also more likely to be able to comprehend the oral explanations that an aquarium guide might offer and the explanatory texts that may be read to them by the accompanying adult. Indeed, vocabulary is often viewed as a proxy for measuring conceptual knowledge, such that a larger vocabulary related to a particular topic is associated with a larger fund of knowledge of that topic.

There are many, many interconnections and reciprocal relationships related to **Experience with Written Language.** We have already touched on the role of experience with written language as it relates to comprehension and knowledge, experience in the world, and vocabulary and language skills. Such experience also influences and is influenced by skill with **Understanding Print and the Alphabetic Writing System.** In Figure 1.2, we list multiple aspects involved in coming to understand print and the writing system (each of which will be discussed in detail in Part II of this book). For now, it is useful to reflect on the fact that when young children engage with written language through reading and writing, their understanding of the workings of the writing system expands. Reciprocally, readers and writers who have greater understanding of the workings of the writing system will have different experiences with written language than will those with more limited understanding. For example, children who are at an early point in development may represent only the beginning sound of a word with a letter when writing, whereas children with greater knowledge of the alphabetic code and greater phonological awareness are likely to more fully represent the sounds in words they attempt to write. Children at these different points in development are apt to have different senses of the utility of print as a result of the reactions of their readers, who will either mostly understand what the writer has written or be fairly clueless about the message.

Unlike the other elements illustrated in the conceptual model (Figure 1.2), we do not view having an Understanding of Print and the Alphabetic Writing System as having a direct and reciprocal relationship with Comprehension and Knowledge. Rather, while it is clearly critical for readers and writers to develop skill with the writing system, the impact on comprehension and knowledge is indirect—through the process of **Word Identification and Word Learning.** Thus, for example, knowledge of the workings of the writing system enables the reader to more effectively solve unfamiliar words encountered while reading, and this more effective word solving enables development of Comprehension and Knowledge. Reciprocally, **Strategic Word Solving,** which for beginning readers often requires use of both alphabetic and contextual information to confirm the identity of unfamiliar words (Share, 2008), has the potential to help the student learn more about the alphabetic code. For example, upon having effectively puzzled through words such as pizza and piano, and across a variety of contexts, the child might learn, at least implicitly, that the letter *i* is sometimes pronounced like a long-*e*.

Knowledge of **High-Frequency Words** is also reciprocally related to Word Identification and Word Learning. Knowing some of the most frequently occurring words (e.g., the, to, and, in, is) enables the reader to more effectively draw on context to help identify unfamiliar words, and some high-frequency words may be added to a reader's sight vocabulary through effective word solving while reading.

The relationship between **Fluency** and Comprehension and Knowledge is also reciprocal in nature. In a reading context, fluency refers to the rate with which words are identified, as well as the reader's phrasing and intonation. In order to impose the proper intonation and phrasing during oral reading, the reader must comprehend what is being read—at least at the level of the sentence. At the same time, being able to quickly and accurately identify words, the skill that contributes to the rate aspect of fluency, enables comprehension by freeing up thinking skills (cognitive resources) to devote to the process of understanding the meaning of the text rather than to figuring out the identities of unfamiliar words.

It is also important to note that increases in learners' Understanding of Print and the Alphabetic Writing System as well as their Word Identification and Word Learning have the potential to enable them to communicate through writing for both social (interpersonal) reasons and documentation of their learning in the content areas.

The last factor in the model, **Motivation and Engagement**, has a pervasive and reciprocal relationship with all the other factors; note that there are arrows depicting reciprocal relationships with all the other elements of the complex model. Indeed, we view Motivation and Engagement as so important that we devote an entire chapter to developing motivation and engagement early in this book and revisit the topic often throughout the remainder of this text—reminding readers frequently of the power teachers have over children's attitudes toward reading and writing and their beliefs about themselves as literate individuals. Learners who believe that reading and writing are enjoyable, informative, and "doable" are more likely to be motivated by and engaged in learning opportunities and are more likely to profit from them. For example, they are more likely to ask questions and seek answers, and they are more likely to persist productively in the face of learning challenges, regulating their emotions in ways that enable them to engage in the word solving and/or comprehension challenges they encounter rather than becoming frustrated and/or avoidant.

Self-Regulation

Another element that has fairly pervasive influence on literacy learning and dispositions is *self-regulation,* which involves such things as maintaining attention and monitoring errors (Hanno, Jones, & McCoy, 2020). To an extent, it could be considered to be an element of the Motivation and Engagement component—which is also related to virtually all aspects of the complex model. The research suggests that there are both cognitive and behavioral aspects of self-regulation. The cognitive aspect of self-regulation includes processes that support goal-directed behavior, including:

• **Inhibitory control**, which is the ability to inhibit a dominant response in favor of a nondominant response. For example, in the primary grades, when reading a beginner-level book, a child trying to identify the printed word *dog* might be inclined to say *puppy* based on the picture but would need to inhibit that initial inclination and attend to the letters in the printed word instead.

• **Working memory**, which involves the ability to store information and revise or update one's understanding as new information becomes available. In the primary grades, that might, for example, involve revising one's understanding of a text as new information in the text unfolds.

• **Attention/task shifting** (also referred to as *cognitive flexibility*), which involves the ability to shift one's attention and respond to different aspects of a process. For example, while writing a text, authors in the primary grades may need to shift attention between meaning construction and how individual words might be spelled.

These cognitive processes are often referred to as *executive functions* and are thought to contribute to children's ability to successfully engage in literacy-learning activities.

The behavioral aspect of self-regulation involves effortful control, which Hanno et al. (2020) define as "behavioral regulation in the context of emotional arousal, marked by the ability to forego a dominant thought, emotion, or response (i.e., an impulse) in favor of the subdominant (i.e., intentional response)" (p. 280). In the primary grades, this might, for example, involve thinking about how to solve a dispute with a classmate over possession of a desired object rather than simply grabbing the object. Behavioral self-regulation is thought to contribute to children's ability to form positive relations with peers and teachers, thereby enhancing the quality of the learning environment.

There is evidence that, for children who demonstrate weaknesses in self-regulation in the preschool and primary grades, the development of early literacy skills and later reading comprehension can be negatively impacted. Examples of how to promote the development of self-regulation skills related to the components of the complex model will be offered in several of the upcoming chapters that address various aspects of literacy development.

Children Who Experience Difficulty with Literacy Development

Children vary considerably in the ease with which they learn to read. Some learn with comparatively little instructional guidance, whereas others find it to be a nearly impossible undertaking given the instruction typically offered in schools. In this book, we focus particularly on children who experience difficulty. We have known for many years that children who lag behind their peers in early literacy development are at high risk of experiencing prolonged reading difficulties (Francis, Shaywitz, & Steubing, 1996; Hernandez, 2011; Juel, 1988; Phillips, Norris, Osmond, & Maynard, 2002; Prochnow, Tunmer, & Chaptman, 2013; Rayner, Foorman, Perfetti, Pesetsky, & Seidenberg, 2002) and, potentially, of being identified as learning (or reading) disabled or dyslexic. Research comparing children who find literacy learning challenging and those who become literate with comparative ease has identified critical areas that differentiate the groups. Much of that research was comprehensively summarized in the book *Preventing Reading Difficulties in Young Children* (Snow, Burns, & Griffin, 1998), in an article by Vellutino, Fletcher, Snowling, and Scanlon (2004), and more recently in an article by Castles, Rastle, and Nation (2018). Similar findings emerged in two major reviews published by the National Reading Panel (2000) and the National Early Literacy Panel (2008).

Based on this body of research, there is a fairly strong consensus about the most common areas of difficulty that affect learners who have problems developing literacy skills and about the role of instruction in preventing long-term difficulties. Reading and writing are language skills, and, by far, the most consistent findings in the research on literacy learning point to difficulties with aspects of language processing. Difficulties with the phonological aspects of the language system are the most common reason why learners are identified as experiencing difficulties with early literacy development. These children have difficulty in developing the ability to notice and manipulate the sounds in spoken words and in connecting individual sounds in spoken words with their printed representations. At early points in literacy development, learners use these phonological skills when they are attempting to identify unfamiliar written words or spell words for which they haven't yet learned the conventional spelling. The good news is that there is strong evidence indicating that difficulties with phonological processing, especially when identified in the early primary grades, can often be remediated instructionally, thereby reducing the chances that learners will experience long-term difficulties. A focus on the primary grades is important for multiple reasons including the potential motivational impact of experiencing difficulties and the lost opportunities to engage in the extensive amounts of reading (and writing) progressively more challenging text that ultimately enables learners to become proficient readers and writers. When children do too little reading, they have too few opportunities to learn to connect printed words with their spoken representations (a process referred to as *orthographic mapping*; see Chapter 2). As a result, even when their phonological processing skills are remediated, they may not achieve the level of reading fluency needed to enable them to focus fairly exclusively on comprehending text.[2] Approaches to addressing phonological processing difficulties and ensuring that children have ample opportunity to apply phonological skills while reading, and thereby have the needed opportunities to engage in orthographic mapping, are major foci of this text.

---

[2] There is an ongoing debate among literacy researchers about whether fluency difficulties are due to limited early reading experience or to a distinct problem with orthographic mapping (OM)/naming speed (as measured by rapid automatized naming [RAN] tests; Fletcher, Lyon, Reid, Fuchs, & Barnes, 2019). There is no evidence that efforts to improve RAN have any impact on reading development. However, there is evidence that helping learners develop proficiency with orthographic mapping and engaging them in lots of reading of meaningful text can improve fluency. Therefore, we do not treat the OM/RAN hypothesis as a distinct problem.

In addition to phonological processing difficulties, multiple additional factors can and do impact literacy learning such as:

- Deep and rich knowledge of the meanings of spoken words,
- The ability to understand the meaning of syntactic structures[3] that tend to be more complex in written as compared to spoken language,
- The background/world knowledge that enables interpretation of information encountered in school settings, and
- The similarities and differences between one's spoken language and the language used in school and in books . . . just to name a few.

Instruction to prevent and remediate literacy learning difficulties would, ideally, take account of all these potential sources of difficulty. The latter skills tend to have their greatest impact on reading comprehension skill (e.g., Lyster, Snowling, Hulme, & Lervåg, 2021; Perfetti & Stafura, 2014). For example, when measured at the preschool and/or primary level, vocabulary is one of the best predictors of reading comprehension in late elementary grades and throughout schooling (e.g., Lyster et al., 2021; Scarborough, 2001; Storch & Whitehurst, 2002). That is, in general, children who have poorly developed vocabulary knowledge when they are young are apt to have greater difficulty comprehending the things they read when they are older (Cain & Oakhill, 2011; Cunningham & Stanovich, 1997; Quinn, Wagner, Petscher, & Lopez, 2015b). Here again, early efforts to intervene can be effective in reducing the risk of long-term reading difficulties.

The Contribution of Classroom Instruction

Characteristics of instruction have a substantial influence on the development of literacy skills. That is, essentially, the reason for this book. For example, Dickinson (2001) reports that, in preschool settings, the amount and quality of the language used by teachers, the kinds of verbal interactions that occur in the classroom, and, more specifically, the types of interchanges that occur during read-alouds influence the development of spoken language skills, including spoken vocabulary knowledge (see Barnes, Grifenhagen, & Dickinson, 2021, for guidance on the development of young children's language skills).

As another example, Connor et al. (2011) found that, in first grade, classroom teachers who differentiated instruction based on the skills of their students were more successful in moving all of their students forward than were teachers who did not differentiate instruction based on student skills. Further, our own research has documented a relationship between classroom practice and student outcomes in

---

[3]Syntactic structures have to do with the ordering of words in sentences. *The black-haired boy won* and *The boy with black hair won* are two different syntactical structures. The two sentences mean the same thing, but the latter is more syntactically complex.

observational studies (Scanlon & Vellutino, 1996, 1997) as well as in contexts in which we provided professional development for classroom teachers with the intent to influence instructional practices in efforts to reduce the incidence of reading difficulties (Scanlon et al., 2008; see also Scanlon & Anderson, 2020). The Scanlon et al., 2008 study, which was conducted in several different school districts, with each district using different reading/literacy curricula, was successful in reducing the number of children who experienced reading difficulties. The content of the professional development provided to classroom and/or intervention teachers is the foundation of this book, although we have updated topics/chapters based on the research that has been published in the intervening years.

Alert!

Years of working with learners at various levels of development have helped us (and those who research how individuals learn from written material) to understand that when some individuals read informational texts such as textbooks they miss important and clarifying information that is presented, clarified, and/or emphasized in text boxes (like this one), captions, graphs, inserts, and/or photos. As teachers of literacy learners, we encourage you to do what you want your students to (learn to) do—make full use of the information provided.

Throughout this book, we will make use of text boxes, graphics, and tables to emphasize, clarify, and, at times entertain via anecdotes. Ignoring such text features will likely significantly limit the knowledge gained from reading this or any text. As current and/or future teachers, we hope you will attend to these features in your own reading and remember to emphasize the importance of these resources in your instructional interactions.

The general point is that the nature and quality of classroom instruction can play a substantial role in preventing literacy learning difficulties. Further, summaries of research compiled by multiple research groups over the years (e.g., Chall, 1967; Snow et al., 1998; Tivnan & Hemphill, 2005) have generally concluded that teacher knowledge and practice, rather than the programs teachers use, are among the most (or *are* the most) important in-school factors in determining students' literacy outcomes.

The Role of Intervention/Prevention

A substantial body of research has established that primary-grade children who demonstrate literacy learning difficulties can be helped to catch up to their grade mates when they are provided with additional instructional supports (intervention) (e.g., Brown, Denton, Kelly, Outhred, & McNaught, 1999; Center, Wheldall, Freeman, Outhred, & McNaught, 1995; Coyne, McCoach, Loftus, Zipoli, & Kapp, 2013; Gomez-Bellenge, Rogers, & Fullerton, 2003; Mathes et al., 2005;

O'Connor, 2000; O'Connor, Harty, & Fulmer, 2005; Scanlon et al., 2005, 2008; Torgesen et al., 2001; Vaughn, Linan-Thompson, & Hickman, 2003; Vellutino et al., 1996, 2008; Wanzek & Vaughn, 2008; Wanzek et al., 2018). Such efforts often involve the implementation of appropriately targeted and intensified instructional interventions.

Recently, the types, intensity, and responsiveness of interventions have drawn researchers' attention as efforts are made to optimize instruction to reduce the incidence of literacy difficulties. This more recent research suggests that, especially for the children who experience the greatest difficulties learning to read, responsive instruction is critical (Coyne et al., 2013; Simmons, 2015; Wanzek et al., 2018). By responsive, we mean instruction that takes into account what the children currently know and what they are ready to learn next, as opposed to instruction that is the same for all students in a particular grade or setting, regardless of their skills or their progress.

Multilingual Learners and the ISA

In the past few decades, there has been a dramatic increase in the number of students in U.S. schools who are identified as *multilingual learners* (MLs).[4] As of 2019, the U.S. Department of Education estimated that MLs constituted approximately 10.4% of the public school population and, by all estimates, that number is growing. Goldenberg (2020) recently summarized the research on what is known about instruction for children who need to rely on school to help them learn to speak and read the English language. He concluded that "[w]hat is known about effective literacy instruction for non-ELs is the foundation of effective literacy instruction for ELs" (p. S139) and that "learning to read in a language with an alphabetic orthography such as English is very similar for English speakers and for ELs" (p. S139). In addition, he concluded that schooling should place emphasis on helping ELs (MLs) to develop their oral English—especially the vocabulary they are learning to read and, as they progress, academic language in general.

In our research on the ISA, because of the locale and the time at which the research was done and the populations served by the schools that agreed to participate, we did not have the opportunity to explicitly evaluate the effects of the ISA on MLs' (English) literacy development. However, our reading of the research on how to help MLs develop oral as well as written language skill in English suggests that the instructional practices that we advocate are aligned with what the research suggests, albeit sometimes with some modifications that are responsive to the children's first language. We briefly discuss these modifications in the relevant chapters.

---

[4]A variety of terms are used to refer to individuals who are learning English as an additional language, including English learners (ELs), English language learners (ELLs), multilingual learners (MLs), and emergent bilinguals (EBs). In this text, we will use the term MLs except when providing direct quotes, in which case we will use the term utilized by the authors of the piece being quoted.

The Interactive Strategies Approach to Instruction and Intervention

We began our efforts to prevent and remediate reading difficulties in the 1990s, when we developed the first iteration of what came to be called the Interactive Strategies Approach (ISA). We have revised and updated the approach through a series of four studies in the primary grades and two intervention studies in the intermediate grades. These studies were recently summarized in an article by Scanlon and Anderson (2020).

We refer to our approach as the Interactive Strategies Approach (Vellutino & Scanlon, 2002) to reflect the fact that, to comprehend a written text, the learner needs to draw upon multiple types of knowledge in *interactive* and confirmatory ways in order to accurately identify written words, compile the words into meaningful sentences, and ultimately, integrate information across sentences and with the learners' existing knowledge base. For the beginning reader and for older readers who struggle with the word-identification process, many of the words they encounter while reading are likely to be unfamiliar in their written form. Thus, they need to develop ways, which we refer to as strategies, to figure out those words. Clearly, they need to think about the sounds that the letters and letter patterns represent and blend them together to try to form a meaningful word. They also need to check whether the word they come up with makes sense in the context in which it is encountered. If it doesn't, they would, ideally, try different pronunciations for the word using the written form in combination with the context in an interactive way. While the letters and letter patterns allow the reader to hypothesize about the likely pronunciation/identity of unknown words, the reader's knowledge of spoken words as well as the context in which the unknown word is encountered can help to determine whether the word has been accurately identified. Thus, we view literacy development as being an interactive and strategic process—hence the name.

Research-Based versus Research-Tested Instruction

As schools are called upon to implement research-based instruction, it is important to consider the distinction between "research-based" approaches and "research-tested" approaches. Many instructional approaches that are identified as *research-based* (and as being aligned with the science of reading [SOR]) are simply that—based on research. No authority controls the use of that label. The label can be attached to products or programs if the developers have familiarized themselves with (some of) the research related to particular instructional goal(s) and then based their program on what was learned in that research. Therefore, just because an approach or program is *based* on research *does not,* in any way, ensure that it will work to improve literacy outcomes in a given context or at all.

The approach to instruction we detail in this book has been research-tested. In our 2005 and 2008 studies, which were conducted in middle-income and high-needs school districts, we compared literacy performances among primary-grade children who were randomly assigned to receive instruction from teachers who had participated in the ISA professional development offerings with that of children who received the instruction normally available to them in their schools. We consistently found that, as a group, the children in the ISA conditions outperformed children in the comparison groups. Further, our earliest intervention study (Vellutino et al., 1996) has been identified as a "game changer" with respect to how educators might fruitfully address the needs of early literacy learners who struggle (Kilpatrick, 2020). As Kilpatrick noted, our 1996 study demonstrated that students who experience reading difficulties in the early grades can develop average, or near average (and sometimes better than average), performance if provided with appropriate instruction/intervention as first graders. The Scanlon et al. (2005) study that followed extended those findings by beginning ISA-based instruction in kindergarten. This latter study is cited heavily in the U.S. Department of Education Practice Guide, *Foundational Skills to Support Reading for Understanding in Kindergarten through 3rd Grade* (Foorman et al., 2016).

Characteristics of the ISA

The ISA is an *approach* to early literacy instruction, not a program. It is not tied to particular instructional materials, nor does it provide highly scripted instructional interactions. Rather, the ISA offers a way to conceptualize (early) literacy development and to support children as they learn to read and write as well as use spoken language in increasingly sophisticated ways. We view teachers as professionals who use their knowledge of their students' skills and abilities, in combination with knowledge of their curricula and the processes involved in literacy development more generally, to plan and deliver effective and responsive literacy instruction. Although we do make some suggestions for instructional materials that are illustrative of the types of materials we have found to be useful, and we do offer some of these in a freely downloadable form on the book's companion website (see the box at the end of the table of contents), we also offer ideas for how teachers might evaluate and utilize the materials they have available to more effectively meet the needs of their students—particularly those who find it challenging to learn to read and write. Our primary goal in this book is to help teachers more thoroughly understand early literacy development and, thereby, to effectively respond to, plan for, and teach primary grade learners.

The ISA places particular emphasis on meeting the needs of children at the early stages of learning to read and write, especially those who experience difficulty, through careful analysis of children's literacy skills and provision of instruction that is responsive to their current capabilities. In order to provide such responsive instruction, teachers need to become highly knowledgeable about early literacy, how it develops, and how to respond to literacy learning difficulties. Therefore, the development of teacher knowledge related to early literacy development is a major focus of the ISA and thus a major focus of this book.

The name of the approach conveys the importance placed on helping children become strategic in their reading and writing endeavors. From our perspective, the goal of instruction should be to teach foundational skills (i.e., phonemic awareness, phonics, and high-frequency words) and strategies that children will learn to use independently, flexibly, and interactively while reading and writing. Through this active and thoughtful engagement, children will grow as readers and writers. An important goal of instruction is to help children develop a *self-teaching mechanism* (Share 1995, 2008) that will enable them to learn more about written language through engagement in the processes of reading and writing. To facilitate self-teaching, instruction needs to help learners develop the foundational skills needed to enable them to solve unfamiliar words encountered while reading and to at least approximate the spellings of words they want to use in their writing. Drawing on these phonological skills, children need to be provided with guided practice in reading and writing in contexts that are motivating and using materials that are interesting, personally meaningful, and manageable (meaning not too difficult).

The logic behind the ISA stems from what we know about the development of certain reading-related skills and the young child's ability to comprehend written text—which is, after all, the reason for reading. For children in the primary grades, the ability to comprehend written material is heavily dependent on their ability to accurately and quickly identify the words in the text. This is true partly because many of the materials that primary-grade children read are not very challenging conceptually. Of course, when children do encounter reading materials that are conceptually challenging, fast and accurate identification of most of the words in the text is still an important determinant of comprehension. However, the child's general world knowledge, language skills, and active thinking about the meaning of the text are also important determinants of comprehension.

In discussing the ISA, we are often asked to indicate how it differs from other approaches to early literacy instruction and intervention. If teachers experienced in using the ISA were asked this question, they would most likely talk about the approach to helping young children learn how to effectively puzzle through and identify unfamiliar words encountered while reading. We advocate explicitly teaching children a small set of word-solving strategies and coaching them in their use. The goal is for the children to become so effective and independent in word solving that, over multiple encounters with the same printed word they learn to read the word effortlessly. Becoming effective word solvers, over time, enables children to learn to read the huge number of words that proficient readers ultimately know.

If we were asked the same question, we would agree that the approach to teaching word-solving strategies is the most obvious difference between the ISA and other comprehensive approaches. However, we would add that while the approach to teaching about phonological analysis and phonics skills for the purpose of enabling word solving and spelling is explicit and thorough, we are much more attentive to the need for children to learn to be flexible in their decoding attempts due to the variable nature of many English spellings (e.g., the long-*a* sound can be represented in print in multiple ways: *cake, play, break, train,* and *ballet,* to name a few). We would also argue that the attention given to enhancing children's language skills and world knowledge and to the impact of these knowledge sources on both oral reading and comprehension distinguishes the ISA from many other approaches to early literacy instruction, which, in our opinion, tend to pay too little attention to these important contributors to comprehension. Finally, we would add that, unlike some approaches, the foundational principles upon which the ISA is built are applicable across both classroom and intervention settings.

The ISA, Response to Intervention, and Multi-Tiered Systems of Support

As a result of the extensive research on the effectiveness of instructional enhancements in preventing long-term literacy difficulties that might otherwise lead to a child being identified as learning/reading disabled, in the past few decades there has been a major conceptual shift in thinking about how schools and teachers should respond to children who demonstrate such difficulties. In the past, children who were judged to be otherwise "normal" (to use the terminology of that era) but who lagged seriously behind their peers in the development of reading and other literacy skills were often identified as being (learning/reading) disabled. However, it is now widely recognized that children's ability to become literate is the result of a complex interaction between the underlying characteristics of the learner and the learner's prior experiences and the amount, type, and quality of the instruction provided (Fletcher, Lyon, Fuchs, & Barnes, 2019). Although it is certainly recognized that some children need more instructional guidance to learn to read and write and that some, in fact, need very intensive and individualized support, we now recognize that nearly all children who are not hampered by severe intellectual, perceptual, or emotional difficulties can develop reading and writing skill. As a result of this shift in thinking, the United States' 2004 Individuals with Disabilities Education Improvement Act (IDEIA) encourages schools to identify children who appear to be at risk of experiencing learning difficulties early in their schooling and to begin intervention in efforts to ameliorate those difficulties. Further, information about children's response to instruction/intervention is used in determining whether they should ultimately be identified as learning/reading disabled (or dyslexic in some settings). This process is widely referred to as *response to intervention* (RTI; National Association of State Directors of Special Education, 2005). An important advantage of an RTI process is that it has the potential to prevent children from experiencing long-term learning difficulties because efforts to intervene are instituted before learning gaps have a chance to grow and become disabling. As a result, the process has the potential to reduce the number of children who may be inaccurately identified as learning/reading disabled due to inadequate instructional experiences.

Multi-tiered systems of support (MTSS) is a more recent development with regard to responding to the needs of learners who struggle. It incorporates RTI's focus on instructional concerns but takes a broader approach by attending to a greater range of factors (especially behavioral factors) that may be impacting children's ability to learn. To us, this is very much a welcome shift but one we will not discuss in detail since our focus is on the instructional components in an RTI process, particularly regarding how they pertain to literacy.

The most widely recognized model of RTI utilizes a tiered approach to implementation. This approach (as described by Fuchs & Fuchs, 2006) entails (1) universal screening of all children, (2) identification of children who appear to be at risk of not meeting grade-level expectations and closely monitoring their progress, and (3) gradually increasing or decreasing the amount and/or intensity of instructional support offered based on student progress.

The National Joint Committee on Learning Disabilities (NJCLD, 2020) describes RTI as a "response-based problem solving process" (p. 196). While many different models of RTI implementation exist (Scanlon, 2011), most models involve three or four tiers of intervention, with Tier 1 encompassing instruction provided by the classroom teacher, Tier 2 involving more intensive and, often, more expert instruction provided beyond the classroom (and preferably *in addition* to Tier 1 instruction), and Tier 3 (and perhaps Tier 4) providing even more intensive intervention.

Since passage of the IDEIA legislation in 2004 and the issuance of the accompanying regulations (Yell, Shriner, & Katsiyannis, 2006), much has been written about the RTI process (e.g., Balu et al., 2015; Fuchs & Vaughn, 2012; Gersten et al., 2008; Hendricks & Fuchs, 2020). Much of the practitioner-oriented literature has focused on the broad frameworks for RTI approaches and on the demands of the record keeping needed to document interventions and progress. In fact, especially in the early years of RTI implementation, instructional recommendations were often limited to advice to adopt research-based programs and to implement them with fidelity (e.g., Brown-Chidsey & Steege, 2005; Mellard & Johnson, 2008). In many instances, teachers were expected to provide more or less scripted programs without adjusting to what the children were learning (or not learning). However, research on instructional effectiveness suggests that it is what teachers do rather than the programs they use that is the most important determinant of children's achievement (Duffy & Hoffman, 1999; Konstantopolous & Sun, 2012; Nye, Konstantopolous, & Hedges, 2004; Scanlon et al., 2008; Tivnan & Hemphill, 2005), and there is a developing consensus in this regard as articulated by the National Joint Committee on Learning Disabilities (2020): "A data-based problem-solving approach in schooling is at the heart of all good instruction and intervention. Educators should continually monitor student performance and behavior and adapt instruction and support to meet individualized student needs" (p. 199). Consistent with this approach, some recent studies of the effectiveness of RTI indicate that child outcomes are improved when the intervention they receive is more responsive to what they know and are able to do (Al Otaiba et al., 2014; Coyne et al., 2013; Simmons, 2015) rather than being highly scripted and delivered with strong adherence to a script (fidelity). Further, a practice guide focused on intensive interventions issued by the Center on Instruction (Vaughn, Wanzek, Murray, & Roberts, 2012) drew on existing research in providing guidance related to intensifying interventions through (1) the use of strategies that promote cognitive processes, (2) delivering more explicit and systematic instruction in addition to increased opportunities for feedback, (3) providing additional instructional time, and (4) decreasing group size (Vaughn et al., 2012).

From early on, in work on the development of the ISA, as noted earlier, we focused on the development of teacher knowledge related to early literacy development and instruction so as to enable teachers to provide responsive early literacy instruction across instructional contexts and curricula. We take the position that the nature and quality of instruction, along with the amount of time the child spends engaged in reading and writing continuous (meaningful) text are among the most important determinants of a child's response to instruction and intervention. Further, we argue that, to be optimally effective, the instruction offered across instructional settings and contexts (i.e., the different tiers of instruction/ intervention) should be responsive to children's needs and be coherent and mutually reinforcing. This position is based on both empirical and logical grounds. Empirically, it has been found, in at least a few studies, that a greater degree of curricular congruence across instructional settings is associated with stronger reading outcomes in the primary grades (Borman, Wong, Hedges, & D'Agostino, 2001; Wonder-McDowell, Reutzel, & Smith, 2011).[5] On logical grounds, if our goal is to enable children who qualify for intervention to benefit from and succeed in the classroom language arts program, it seems that alignment of instruction across classroom and intervention settings would be the most prudent approach—a position we took in all of the studies of the ISA. Of course, if the classroom language arts program is weak and/or inappropriate for the children who qualify for intervention, modifications to the classroom program would be an important (first) step in enhancing the quality of instruction that is offered.

Instructional Goals of the ISA

In this text, we present information on how to support children's development as they are learning to read and write. Early in literacy development, learning to read and spell words is a major hurdle, so we focus a good deal of the discussion on these critical aspects. However, as the preceding analysis emphasizes, reading and writing words is only a part of the process. Early literacy instruction needs to attend to the full complexity of the processes. Teachers need to provide instruction that helps children develop language skills and background knowledge that will enable them to do the kind of inferencing and reading between the lines that proficient readers do quite effortlessly. Teachers of beginning readers also need to ensure that children understand that the purpose of print is to communicate,

---

[5]This is not an entirely consistent finding. For example, Foorman, Herrera, and Dombek (2018) did not find a clear advantage for coherence. The relationship between classroom instruction and instructional support provided beyond the classroom is clearly an area in need of additional research.

because only when readers understand that there is a message in the print will they engage in thinking beyond the initially challenging step of figuring out the words.

Considering the multiple factors that influence an individual's ability to comprehend written texts, the ISA is organized around a set of instructional goals. We encourage teachers to view instruction as a goal-oriented activity wherein they strive to help children achieve identified goals, using a variety of instructional formats and materials. The goals range from the relatively simple and straightforward (e.g., developing letter-name knowledge) to those that are quite complex and involved (e.g., helping children become strategic and active readers). Chapters 3 through 16 of this book are devoted to discussing each of the goals in detail. As we discuss each goal, we highlight the importance of being able to view literacy and literacy-related skills from the perspective of a young child who is a relative novice when it comes to understanding the intricacies of written language and how it relates to spoken language. Often, in our formal and informal observations of teachers working with young children and in our own work with young children who experience difficulty in learning about written language, we are struck by how difficult it is for highly literate people to take a step back and understand the complexity of reading and writing processes from the perspective of a child who is just beginning to experience print. We return to this perspective-taking theme frequently in discussing the ISA goals, because one of our major purposes in this book is to help teachers develop greater expertise in identifying and responding to difficulties experienced by literacy learners. Understanding the source of a child's confusion is an important step in responding effectively to that confusion.

In the instructional goals chapters, we review the relevant research for each goal and discuss how the goal relates to reading and writing processes more generally. We also discuss and provide sample instructional activities (often including sample instructional dialogues) that can be used to help children achieve the goal. Where relevant, we discuss more and less challenging aspects of particular activities—often presenting a sequence of objectives within given goals. We discuss assessment tools for many of the goals and the need to use observation and informal assessment to guide grouping decisions and instructional planning.

While for purposes of clarity, we address the goals in individual chapters, it is important to point out that, for the most part, the goals would *not* be addressed independently of one another. Indeed, in Chapter 2 we take up the topic of *responsive instruction* with the purpose of illustrating how goal-driven instruction can occur across the school day, with teachers adjusting their focus based on the current capabilities of the students they are teaching.

The first goal chapter focuses on "motivation to read and write" and closes out the first part of the book. In Part II, *Understanding Print and the English (Alphabetic) Writing System*, we describe instruction designed to help children learn about a variety of aspects of language and the relations between its spoken and written forms. The focus is on helping children learn about how printed language works—especially how the sounds in spoken language are represented in written language. In Part III, *Word Learning*, we discuss, more specifically, how children learn to read individual words and how they become automatic in their ability to do so. In Part IV, *Meaning Construction,* we focus on the end goal of literacy instruction—the ability to understand texts that are read and, to a lesser extent, the ability to write meaningful texts. In the final section of the book (Part V) we discuss how the instructional goals might be addressed and integrated in the context of small-group lessons for children at different points in their literacy development (Chapter 17). In Chapter 18, we review some of the major principles discussed throughout the book and encourage teachers to strive to become reflective practitioners in relation to these goals and the early literacy instruction they provide. To this end, we remind teachers of several of the resources provided throughout the book that can support their understanding of and response to children's performance.

To an extent, the forgoing description of the organization of the goals addressed in this book could suggest that the content addressed in Part IV is the last or the least of our concerns. But nothing could be further from the truth. As discussed earlier in this chapter and depicted in Figure 1.2, in our view, comprehension (meaning making) and knowledge development are the reasons we learn to read and write and, of course, the reason we teach children to read and write. The purpose of Parts II and III of the book is to get students to the point where they can focus all or nearly all of their cognitive resources on the meaning-making purposes of reading and writing. That said, it is certainly not our intent to suggest that the goals be addressed in the sequence in which they are discussed. Rather, many of the goals can and should be addressed within a single school day—often within a single instructional context—as we illustrate in Chapter 2 (see pp. 46–49) and throughout the book.

Each of the goals is briefly described below.

Part I: Theoretical and Practical Understandings of Early Literacy Learning and Instruction

Motivation to Read and Write (Chapter 3)

> Children will develop the belief that reading and writing are enjoyable and informative activities that are not beyond their capabilities.

In discussing this goal, we focus on a variety of factors that contribute to motivation, such as ensuring that children face an appropriate level of challenge in literacy activities, expressing enthusiasm for reading and writing, actively engaging children in thinking about and responding to texts, making read-alouds an important and interactive part of the day, and construing reading and writing as privileges rather than as jobs (e.g., "You *get* to finish your book before recess" rather than "You *have* to finish your book before recess"). An important part of supporting motivation is to convey that the aspects of the process that are initially a bit challenging will become less so with practice/experience.

Part II: Understanding Print and the English (Alphabetic) Writing System

Children will understand the relationships between printed and spoken language and will learn these relationships well enough to be able to use them in reading and spelling previously unfamiliar written words. This is a process of connecting the letters in written words with the sounds in spoken words—a process referred to as *orthographic mapping.*

This overarching goal includes several subgoals related to the development of skill in using the alphabetic and orthographic code. Each of the goals addressed in Part II is identified and described briefly here.

Purposes, Concepts, and Conventions of Print (Chapter 4)

Children will understand that the purpose of print is to communicate. Children will also understand the basic concepts and conventions of print, such as the concepts of letter and word, the left-to-right and top-to-bottom sequencing of print, where to begin reading, punctuation, and so forth.

Children who have had little exposure to written language are apt to be unaware that print is actually a form of language and that it is possible to translate print into spoken language and spoken language into print. In addressing this goal, we discuss the need to be explicit about the relationship between spoken and written language and the multiple ways in which print is used to communicate.

Understanding these foundational concepts is critical if children are going to make progress with literacy development. For children who do not yet have these concepts established, instruction needs to be explicit and should introduce one new concept at a time. Previously taught concepts should be revisited until they are well understood.

Phonemic Awareness (Chapter 5)

Children will have a conceptual grasp of the fact that words are made up of somewhat separable sound segments. Further, they will be able to say individual sounds in words spoken by the teacher and blend separate sounds to form whole words.

In addressing this goal, we begin by working to attune teachers to the phonemes (sounds) in spoken language. Many highly literate adults are confused about how to segment words in which there are more letters than sounds (e.g., *mouse* has three sounds) or more sounds than letters (e.g., *box* has four sounds: /b/ /ŏ/ /k/ /s/). We discuss various approaches to developing phonemic awareness, with a particular emphasis on blending (listening to individual sounds/phonemes spoken by the teacher and combining them to produce a word) and segmenting (separating the sounds in a spoken word). We also discuss the features of phonemes that make them more and less challenging for children to attend to and/or manipulate. To help in determining whether and how to approach phonemic awareness instruction, we provide suggestions for ways to assess students' phonemic analysis skills.

Letter Naming (Chapter 6)

> Children will be able to name, rapidly and accurately, all 26 letters of the alphabet, both upper- and lower-case versions.

In discussing this goal, we begin to address fluency with foundational skills as an important contributor to reading comprehension. We stress that automaticity (speed) with letter naming/identification is important in order to free up cognitive resources for higher-level (more advanced) skills. To promote fluency with letter identification, we highlight the importance of having children say the letter names frequently during the course of the various instructional activities used to promote letter-name knowledge.

We also discuss the tendency of young children to rely on the names of the letters as an aid to remembering their sounds. For example, the sound for the letter *b* is the first phoneme in its name (/b/).[6] Thus, for many letters, if children know the name of the letter, it will be easier for them to learn the sound for the letter.

Letter–Sound Correspondence (and Grapheme–Phoneme Correspondence) (Chapter 7)

> Children will be able to associate the most common sounds of individual letters/graph-emes with their printed representations. (*Note:* A grapheme is a letter or combination of letters that represent a single sound; *m, s, ch*, and *th* are all examples of graphemes.)

For this goal, we continue to focus on the relationship between letter names and letter sounds, how to take advantage of that relationship, and how to address the confusions that arise with letters for which the relationship does not hold (i.e., *h, w*, and *y*). We also discuss the introduction of common consonant digraphs (two letters that represent a single sound/phoneme (e.g., *ch*). Further, we discuss the utility of using key words to help children remember grapheme–phoneme correspondences, of using the same key words across instructional settings and grade levels, and of explicitly teaching children how to use the key words, when needed, to support reading and writing.

The Alphabetic Principle and the Alphabetic Code: Early Development (Chapter 8)

> Children will understand that the letters/graphemes in printed words represent the sounds/phonemes in spoken words, and they will also understand how to use the letters/graphemes in single syllable words to read and spell words.

In the chapter devoted to this goal, we describe instruction designed to help children acquire a conceptual understanding of the alphabetic principle; that is, the

---

[6]To denote the sound of a letter/grapheme, we follow the convention of enclosing the grapheme in slashes.

fact that the letters in printed words represent the sounds in spoken words. At this early point in development, to make the concept as clear as possible, we limit the words used to those for which there is a one-to-one correspondence between individual graphemes and their associated sounds. For example, the word *hop* is characterized by one-to-one correspondence—one letter for each sound. In contrast, the word *hope* is not, as two letters are used to spell the vowel sound (*o–e*).

Rimes and Word Families (Chapter 9)

> Children will develop the ability to use frequently occurring rimes (e.g., *ay, ell, old*) to read and spell words.

A *rime* comprises the vowel and what comes after it in a syllable. For example, *ap, ell, ike, og,* and *ut* are all rimes. Orthographic word families are built around rimes. For example, from the *ay* rime, the words *day, may, say, way, play, stay, tray,* and several others can be formed. Rimes are also part of words with more than one syllable (*today, hearsay, replay*), so knowledge of rimes has utility beyond the early stages of literacy development. One purpose of teaching common rimes is to help children learn to use them to effectively puzzle through printed words that contain those rimes and to support conventional spelling of those words as well. Teaching about rimes is also intended to attune children to the fact that there are recurrent orthographic patterns in the English writing system which, once learned, can enable them to more readily identify unfamiliar words and spell words they have not yet committed to memory.

The Alphabetic Principle and the Alphabetic Code: Later Development (Chapter 10)

> Children will understand how to use all the letters/graphemes in printed words in determining the likely pronunciation of unfamiliar printed words. Similarly, children will learn to represent each of the sounds in a spoken word with a logical grapheme when writing.

In discussing this goal, we address ways to increase skill with decoding (reading) and encoding (spelling) by teaching children how to analyze consonant clusters (e.g., *cl, sn, st*) and how short- and long-vowel sounds are commonly (and variably) represented in print. Instruction around vowel teams (e.g., *aw, ea, or*) is also discussed. We stress the benefits of guiding children to be strategic as they apply their developing knowledge of the alphabetic code in authentic reading and writing situations, using both their knowledge of the alphabetic code and the context in which unfamiliar words are encountered. We also introduce the need to be flexible in determining the pronunciation of some of the graphemes in printed words—for example, the two different pronunciations of the *ow* vowel team (as in *snow* and *how*).

Morphological Units and Multisyllabic Words (Chapter 11)

> Children will understand that some words are composed of more than one unit of meaning (e.g., base words plus prefixes and/or suffixes) and will learn how to break longer words into meaningful units and/or syllables as an assist to understanding, reading, and spelling them.

It is important for children to attend to all the letters in written words when attempting to identify unfamiliar words as, over time, this will help them to store the words in memory so that they can identify them more readily on future encounters and spell them more accurately. Ultimately, however, children need to learn to process larger orthographic units rather than only puzzling through words in a letter-by-letter fashion, as this will help them develop fluency in word solving/ word identification as well as spelling. Explicit instruction in how to make use of larger orthographic units can help learners make progress toward proficient word reading and spelling and can support their understanding of words with more than one morphological unit. In this same chapter, we also discuss ways to help children learn about clues to syllable boundaries and how to apply this knowledge when attempting to read unfamiliar words composed of more than one syllable.

Part III: Word Learning

> Children will learn to effortlessly identify a large number of written words.

This major goal is addressed via two subgoals, each of which focuses on a different vehicle for word learning. Although the term *sight vocabulary* is sometimes used to refer to high-frequency words or irregular words, we use the term to refer to all words that can be identified effortlessly "at sight."

Strategic Word Learning (Chapter 12)

> Children will develop flexibility and independence in using a combination of code-based (phonics) and meaning-based (context) strategies in interactive and confirmatory ways to identify and learn unfamiliar words encountered while reading. Learning to accurately identify words will also assist children in developing conventional spelling skills.

Strategic word learning is a central goal of the ISA. Having the ability to puzzle through and accurately identify unfamiliar words provides children with a powerful mechanism for expanding their sight vocabulary and, thereby, their ability to read (and spell). Because, in English (as opposed to several other alphabetic languages), there is a relatively large number of words that cannot be accurately identified using phonics knowledge alone, we emphasize the need for children to use both code-based (phonics) *and* meaning-based (context) strategies in interactive and confirmatory ways. We describe how, for children who are at a very early point in developing their phonics skills, contextual information (pictures and other contextual information) will likely play a larger role in word solving, with phonics knowledge becoming the prominent means by which unfamiliar words are identified as phonics skills mature.

High-Frequency Words (Chapter 13)

Children will be able to read and spell the most frequently occurring words accurately and quickly.

Although many of the words that become part of a child's sight vocabulary are learned during the course of strategic reading, some words warrant special instructional attention. These are words that occur frequently in print. Some are somewhat more difficult to learn due to their "irregular" spellings and/or abstract nature (e.g., *was, have, they*), while others have regular spellings but are often encountered in texts before children have the phonics knowledge needed to decode them (e.g., *like, she, for*). We encourage teachers to explicitly teach and provide practice with such words. We discuss game-like activities that motivate children to practice high-frequency words and texts that provide additional practice.

Part IV: Meaning Construction

Children will develop the automaticity with word identification and facility with language skills needed to enable them to derive and construct meaning from texts that are read and to accurately express their intended meaning when writing.

Comprehension is the goal of reading. Because many children who experience difficulty learning to read in the early primary grades do so because of their difficulties with the alphabetic coding and word-reading aspects of reading, the importance of attending to meaning construction is sometimes overlooked—but it should not be. Instruction specifically focused on enhancing comprehension is addressed through discussion of three goals: oral reading fluency, language development, and comprehension and knowledge.

Fluency (Chapter 14)

Children will be able to read grade-appropriate text accurately, with appropriate speed, and with phrasing and intonation that convey the intended meaning of the text.

We have included fluency under the overarching goal of meaning construction because, in order to construct meaning while reading, readers need to devote the majority of their cognitive resources (thinking) to meaning construction rather than to word solving. Fluent reading is also a signal that the reader is comprehending—at least at the sentence level—because, without comprehending the sentence being read, it would be difficult for the reader to apply the appropriate intonation.

Being able to read fluently does not, of course, guarantee comprehension of the larger text, but it increases the likelihood that the reader will comprehend.

Vocabulary and Oral Language Development (Chapter 15)

> Children will learn the meanings of new words encountered in instructional interactions and will be able to use the words conversationally. Further, children's ability to understand and use complex grammatical structures will improve.

Reading is a language skill. Children need to develop the vocabulary and other language skills essential for reading comprehension and communicative writing. We encourage teachers to be alert to vocabulary and syntactic challenges as well as variations in the structure of texts related to genre, throughout their instructional interactions. The opportunities for the development of language skills provided by interactive read-alouds are a major focus relative to this goal. However, we also encourage teachers to be attentive to the fact that children frequently encounter words for which they do not know the meaning and/or syntactic constructions in their own reading and that word-identification difficulties are sometimes caused by not knowing the meaning of printed words or understanding the context in which they are encountered. When this happens, the reader cannot decide (or confirm) whether a word has been accurately identified/decoded, and, therefore, meaning construction will be disrupted. Language skills also impact communicative writing. Here again, engaging in interactive read-alouds provides learners with the opportunity to encounter more sophisticated vocabulary and language structures that can later be reflected in their own writing.

Comprehension and General Knowledge (Chapter 16)

> Children will develop the foundational knowledge and comprehension skills and strategies that will enhance their ability to construct the meaning of, learn from, and ideally enjoy, texts heard, read, and/or written.

For children in the early primary grades, the development of active engagement in meaning construction is discussed in the context of read-alouds, shared reading, and supported reading (reading with teacher engagement). We encourage teachers to model comprehension strategies and to engage children in conversations that require the use of those strategies (e.g., "I think he's going to get a puppy for his birthday. What do you think he's going to get? Why?"). To help build the critical knowledge base upon which comprehension depends, we encourage teachers to read informational books to children as often as possible and to engage them in the thinking that such books invite ("Wow! Amazing to think about how a little critter that looks like a fish changes into a frog!"). As children begin to read texts on their own, we urge teachers to engage children in discussions of what they are reading to avoid allowing children to develop the belief that reading is about saying the words right (and quickly) and not about meaning construction. Providing children with the opportunity to write about what they are reading and to create their own texts will help to make clear that reading and writing are primarily about meaning construction.

KEY POINTS OF THIS CHAPTER

✓ Reading and writing are complex processes that require skill with accurate word identification, language skills, background knowledge, and the intention/motivation to construct meaning.

✓ Children who experience difficulty with literacy learning are at risk of experiencing long-term difficulties. Therefore, efforts to intervene need to begin early.

✓ Most early literacy difficulties are related to phonological processing difficulties—the development of phonemic awareness and phonics skills.

✓ Broader language skills, especially knowledge of word meanings, measured in the primary grades, are related to reading comprehension throughout schooling.

✓ Instruction and intervention play a prominent role in children's literacy learning and in preventing long-term reading difficulties.

✓ The ISA is a comprehensive and responsive approach to literacy instruction that focuses on the role of teacher knowledge in enabling effective instruction.

  • It revolves around instructional goals—instruction should be goal oriented rather than activity oriented.
  • Instruction should be responsive to students' current points in development.
  • It places heavy emphasis on the development of phonological skills and word-solving strategies.
  • The ultimate goal of literacy instruction is to enable comprehension and knowledge development.

CHAPTER 2

Responsive Instruction

Effective and differentiated classroom instruction is a crucial component in early literacy instruction. This is especially so in efforts to support the development of children who appear to be experiencing literacy learning difficulties. In the response-to-intervention (RTI) model that we advocate, classroom instruction takes account of the diversity of student skills and knowledge sources during the course of whole-class, small-group, and one-to-one (or two) instruction. Further, to accelerate the literacy growth of children who are experiencing difficulties, classroom teachers plan small-group instruction. This approach allows them to teach the children who are in greatest need of support more intensively than the children not experiencing difficulty. Intensification can be accomplished in several ways. For example, teachers might arrange their weekly schedules so that they can meet with those who have more limited skills daily, while working with children who demonstrate age/grade-appropriate skills somewhat less frequently. In addition, ideally group size would be smaller for those needing more teacher support. Children with the most extreme needs—that is, those who make limited progress when provided with intensified classroom instruction—would receive *additional* instruction beyond the classroom either in the context of small-group (Tier 2) or one-to-one (Tier 3) instruction. These more intensive forms of intervention are discussed later in the chapter. We first focus on instruction provided by the classroom teacher for the full spectrum of students.

Classroom Instruction in an RTI Context

In a typical primary-grade classroom, children will have a variety of skills and will be at different performance levels with regard to reading, writing, and language more generally. In fact, it is estimated that in a typical classroom, the reading levels of the children can range across three grade levels or more (Chorzempa & Graham, 2006). Instructional plans need to consider the current literacy status of all children in the class. Once this information is established, a teacher with a clear understanding of the instructional goals will be better able to address students' literacy development via instructional formats that include whole-class, small-group, and (ideally) one-to-one (or side-by-side) instruction. Although it is not possible to specify the ideal mix of formats, it is clear that a mix is ideal. Several research groups have provided evidence that children, particularly those who experience difficulty, make better progress in classroom programs and intervention settings in which they are grouped with students who have similar literacy skills for supported reading lessons and are given the opportunity to read texts that provide some, but not too much, challenge (e.g., Ehri, Dreyer, Flugman, & Gross, 2007; National Early Literacy Panel, 2008; Scanlon et al., 2008; Taylor, Pearson, Clark, & Walpole, 2000; Wanzek, Roberts, Al Otaiba, & Kent, 2014; see also Pressley, Allington, & Pressley, 2023). However, there is also some evidence that instructional grouping based on literacy skills in the primary grades is associated with poorer long-term literacy outcomes (Buttaro & Catsambis, 2019). This, we hypothesize, may be due to the failure of instruction in the earliest grades to actually accelerate children's development—as noted, some children need more support to become literate. Being grouped for instruction with children at similar points in their literacy development, with no attempt to accelerate their development through more responsive and intensive instruction, is not likely to accelerate literacy development. Children who begin the school year with more limited literacy skills need to learn more in a school year than their peers if they are to attain grade-level performance standards.

Whole-Class Instruction

Instruction offered to the entire class is appropriate for many components of language arts instruction, including read-alouds, shared reading, shared writing, and oral language activities. Whole-class instruction provides the opportunity to involve all children in activities that (1) foster active engagement with the meanings of texts, (2) illustrate the use of word-identification strategies, (3) build foundational skills such as knowledge of how the alphabet works, and (4) build the oral language skills and general (world) knowledge that are so crucial in enabling learners to comprehend the kinds of texts they will encounter as they move through the grades. However, even during whole-class instruction, teachers need to be mindful of, and plan for, the variety of skill levels in the class. For example, during a shared writing activity, in which the teacher writes in collaboration with the students, a first-grade teacher might:

- Engage all the children in developing/composing the message.
- Model and engage the children in stretching and segmenting some of the

words to meet the needs of children who are not yet fully phonemically aware.

- Encourage the children to refer to the class high-frequency word list for the spellings of words that have been explicitly taught.
- Explicitly discuss and model the formation of a few of the letters as the teacher writes them, especially those letters that are more challenging for children.
- Discuss spelling and print conventions for children who are at different points along the developmental continuum (e.g., perhaps directing attention to the key-word chart for the spelling of the short-*a* sound for the children at an earlier point of development and discussing the -*tion* spelling pattern for children who are further along).

Thus, in whole-class instruction, the teacher should plan to provide multilevel instruction that keeps all children engaged and moving forward.

Small-Group Instruction

Small-group configurations generally involve grouping children by the need for instruction on particular skills or strategies and/or by interest (e.g., a group interested in a particular topic or book). All these approaches to grouping may occur in any given classroom. For purposes of primary reading instruction, however, it is important that the children receive their supported reading lessons in small groups formed on the basis of their current reading and writing skills.

Supported Reading

Utilization of the ISA involves placing heavy emphasis on explicit and systematic instruction related to the alphabetic code. In most lessons, new decoding elements (e.g., graphemes [letters or letter combinations such as *sh*]) and associated phonemes (the sounds represented by graphemes) are taught and practiced in preparation for reading a book in which words that include those elements will be encountered. Further, recently taught elements of the code are revisited until they are mastered. In addition, children are taught a small number of specific word-solving strategies (as described in detail in Chapter 12) and are explicitly taught how to utilize them in interactive and confirmatory ways upon encountering unfamiliar words in context. Knowing how to solve unfamiliar printed words and how to use context to check the accuracy of decoding attempts increases the likelihood that a previously unknown word will become a "known" word. This, in turn, enables children to read (and understand) progressively more challenging texts. Thus, independence in the use of the strategies is an important instructional objective.

Small-group formats are more effective in accelerating children's progress because they allow the teacher to differentiate instruction: the texts that the children read provide an appropriate degree of challenge, and the focus of skill and strategy instruction is targeted so as to bring the children just a bit further along relative to what they are currently able to do. Further, small-group instruction allows the teacher to more effectively monitor what the children understand about reading and writing and to determine what they are ready to learn next. The group snapshots provided in Chapters 3–16 are intended to help teachers keep abreast of the skills, strategies, and dispositions of the children who have been grouped together and to allow teachers to consider whether children are appropriately placed in a given group by examining similarities and differences in profiles within and across groups.

One-to-One Instruction

Virtually every classroom teacher in the primary grades offers some one-to-one instruction (sometimes referred to as *side-by-side* instruction). Such instruction is provided in contexts in which the teacher confers with individual children about their reading, writing, and other academic work. In the context of both whole-class and small-group instruction, teachers often provide children with the opportunity to work independently for periods of time. For example, children might be asked to discuss with a partner how they think a particular book will end or to write a journal entry relating to the same question. Younger children can play phonics games with a friend or two or listen to a recorded book. During such activities, the teacher can be attentive to individual children to make sure that they are engaged in productive ways. The teacher can also be alert for opportunities to guide their thinking relative to the instructional activity in which they are involved. The problem-solving skills and strategies that teachers address in these one-to-one interactions will vary considerably from child to child.

Developing a Language Arts Program for Readers at Multiple Levels

Literacy instruction at the primary level typically comprises several fairly distinct components that together address the instructional goals discussed in Chapters 3–16. Table 2.1 lists the goals and the components of instruction during which the goals might be addressed. The checkmarks in the table indicate which goals might be addressed within the various components of language arts instruction. The purpose of this table is to demonstrate that multiple goals can and should be addressed in each component of language arts instruction.

In a typical classroom, a substantial proportion of literacy instruction is delivered to the whole class at once. To plan for the full spectrum of students who will participate and to engage all of them productively, teachers need to be knowledgeable about the skills, understandings, and dispositions of all the children and to rely on this information as they interact instructionally with individual students within the larger context. For example, at the beginning of first grade, students are likely to be at very different places in terms of their literacy development. For purposes of discussion, we describe four different "types" of students that might be in a single early primary class. However, before doing so, it is important to emphasize that literacy development is a fluid and multidimensional process and that children do not necessarily fit neatly into a given "type." Of the many different dimensions along which a literacy learner might be described and considered, for current purposes we focus primarily on the dimensions related to *the development of the ability to read and spell the words needed to engage effectively with meaningful text.* In doing so, we do not wish to diminish the importance of general language and vocabulary knowledge, nor do we want to minimize the importance of background knowledge in contributing to children's ability to comprehend and create texts. However, because in the primary grades, the latter characteristics are often unrelated to the child's abilities to read the words in the text (see Paris & Paris, 2007) and because most of the research on reading difficulties suggests that most early reading difficulties are due to difficulties with figuring out how to read (decode) and write (encode) words, we develop our characterization around those early, foundational skills.

TABLE 2.1. Intersection of the Goals of Instruction and the Components of Language Arts Instruction

Language arts components	Instructional groupings	Motivation	Alphabetics			Word learning		Fluency	Meaning construction	
			Print concepts	Phonological analysis	Alphabetic coding skills (letter names, sounds, alphabetic principle, etc.)	Strategic word identification	High-frequency sight words		Language and vocabulary development	Knowledge and comprehension
Read-aloud	WC, SG, and I	✓		✓	✓	✓		✓	✓	✓
Shared reading	WC, SG, and I	✓	✓	✓	✓	✓	✓	✓	✓	✓
Independent and buddy reading	WC, SG, and I	✓	✓	✓	✓	✓	✓	✓	✓	✓
Writing/composition	WC, SG, and I	✓	✓	✓	✓	✓	✓		✓	✓
Oral language	WC, SG, and I	✓		✓	✓	✓		✓	✓	✓
Foundational skills	WC, SG, and I	✓	✓	✓	✓	✓	✓	✓	✓	✓
Supported reading group	SG and I		✓	✓	✓	✓	✓	✓	✓	✓

Note. WC, whole class; SG, small group; I, individual. Adapted from Scanlon and Anderson (2010). Copyright © 2010 The International Literacy Association. Adapted by permission.

Beginning Readers

Beginning readers (sometimes referred to as emergent readers) have very limited understanding of the role played by print in the reading process. Beginning readers may know the names of few, if any, letters and have limited understanding of the most basic print conventions. When they attempt to read books intended for beginning readers, they rely primarily on the pictures and their memory of the text—if it has been read to them previously. They may or may not understand many other aspects of reading, such as that books tell stories and/or are sources of useful and interesting information.

Developing Readers

Developing readers have begun to learn something about the alphabet and the alphabetic principle (the idea that graphemes represent the sounds in spoken words). They may know the names of most of the graphemes and the sounds of many of them. When attempting to identify printed words, developing readers tend to rely on a combination of the alphabetic code and the context in which the word occurs, with the relative weight placed on one source of information changing gradually from heavy reliance on context to greater reliance on the code. Developing readers may be able to identify many of the most frequently occurring words with relatively little effort.

Maturing Readers

Maturing readers are effective word solvers who use both code-based and meaning-based strategies fairly efficiently to puzzle through unfamiliar words. However, their need to word-solve is still apparent, as evidenced by either multiple attempts at the pronunciation of the occasional word (during oral reading) or by hesitation over a word followed by accurate identification. Because maturing readers are effective word solvers, their sight vocabulary (words they can identify effortlessly) grows rapidly (when they engage in reading, of course). Further, when reading texts that do not contain too many unfamiliar words, they tend to sound quite fluent as they read.

Proficient Readers

Proficient readers are able to quickly analyze and identify unfamiliar words, even those that are composed of multiple syllables. Their efficiency is due in part to their strong *orthographic processing* skills which have enabled them to store many larger orthographic units (e.g., *-tion, re-, -ly, -ing*) in memory. Thus, although they do not necessarily know all of the words, they figure them out so quickly that they sound fluent. Proficient readers are able to devote virtually all of their thinking to interpreting and responding to the texts as they read.

In the primary grades, a classroom might be composed of all four types of readers—as well as readers at all the intermediate points between the types described. However, at each grade level and at different points in the year, the mix of children is likely to be different. Thus, early in kindergarten most children are likely to be beginning or developing readers, whereas at the beginning of first grade most are likely to be developing readers, a few might be described as maturing, and a very few as either beginning or proficient. By the beginning of second grade, the balance will likely shift again, with a few being described as developing readers, most looking like maturing readers, several likely to be proficient, and hopefully few, if any, described as beginning. Regardless of the distribution of students along the continuum, the classroom teacher is responsible for providing instruction that moves all students forward.

Although small-group instruction is one of the most effective ways of addressing the diversity of skill levels found in typical primary-grade classrooms, many instructional needs of the children in a class can be addressed through whole-class instruction. Because whole-class instruction influences the development of all children, it could be argued that, for some goals, it is a more efficient form of instruction.

A Weekly and a Daily Schedule in First Grade

In this section, we discuss the balancing act that teachers face in planning and delivering language arts instruction for a classroom full of students who differ substantially in their foundational literacy skills. We illustrate how small-group instruction might fit into the context of the broader language arts program and the instructional day. As an example, we provide a possible first-grade weekly schedule and discuss each component of the day. The schedule itself is outlined in Figure 2.1. All of the components on the schedule involve literacy skills—broadly defined as reading, writing, listening, speaking, and representing/illustrating.

Next we provide a brief overview of each item listed on the schedule. In subsequent chapters, we detail what might occur during each instructional period that is explicitly devoted to the development of literacy and language skills.

Attendance, Lunch Count, Book Browsing, and Writing

The day begins with a 10- to 15-minute period during which the children have time to put their belongings away, socialize a bit, sign in for attendance and lunch purposes, and do a little reading or writing if time permits. They may read one or more books that were read previously, browse through a book previously read by the teacher, explore the classroom library, and so forth. Many teachers also offer the children the opportunity to do some writing during this segment of the day. They might write notes or letters to friends, write in their journals, or document observations related to an ongoing science project, for example. During this

	Monday	**Tuesday**	**Wednesday**	**Thursday**	**Friday**
8:15–8:30	Attendance, lunch count, book browsing, and writing	Attendance, lunch count, book browsing, and writing	Attendance, lunch count, book browsing, and writing	Attendance, lunch count, book browsing, and writing	Attendance, lunch count, book browsing, and writing
8:30–8:40	Morning meeting	Morning meeting	Morning meeting	Morning meeting	Morning meeting
8:40–8:55	Shared reading	Shared reading	Shared reading	Shared reading	Shared reading
8:55–9:10	Introduction of center activities	Introduction of center activities	Introduction of center activities	Introduction of center activities	Introduction of center activities
9:10–9:35	Group 1	Group 4	Group 3	Group 1	Group 2
9:40–10:05	Group 2	Group 1	Group 4	Group 2	Group 1
10:10–10:35	Group 3	Group 2	Group 1	Group 3	Group 4
10:35–10:50	Snack and conversation	Snack and conversation	Snack and conversation	Snack and conversation	Snack and conversation
10:50–11:20	Read-aloud	Read-aloud	Read-aloud	Read-aloud	Read-aloud
11:20–11:50	Writing and composition	Writing and composition	Writing and composition	Writing and composition	Writing and composition
11:50–12:35	Lunch and recess	Lunch and recess	Lunch and recess	Lunch and recess	Lunch and recess
12:35–1:15	Special	Special	Special	Special	Special
1:20–2:05	Math	Math	Math	Math	Math
2:05–2:20	Wrap-up and reflection	Wrap-up and reflection	Wrap-up and reflection	Wrap-up and reflection	Wrap-up and reflection

FIGURE 2.1. A day and a week in first grade.

period, the teacher has time to attend to necessary record keeping, including notes/texts from parents, and to greet individual children and make them feel welcome.

Morning Meeting

Many teachers have a brief morning meeting in which they bring the whole class together and outline the day. Teachers use this period to address literacy and other academic goals in many different ways. For example, some teachers focus the children's attention on a large calendar to help the children learn to read numbers, or the names of the days of the week, or the letters in the name of the month. They might also use it to teach and reinforce certain science concepts by, for example, engaging the children in observing and recording characteristics of the weather and placing symbols for rainy, sunny, snowy, or cloudy on the calendar each day.

Shared Reading

During shared reading, the teacher and the class read a text in which the print is large enough for all the children to see comfortably, and the teacher explicitly directs their attention to the print by pointing to the words as they're read. Shared reading often occurs immediately after the morning meeting and may, in fact, blend in with the morning meeting. For example, one of the texts used for shared reading may be a teacher-prepared passage that describes the schedule for the day (e.g., what the special [art, music, library] is, whose birthday it is, plans for a field trip) for the class to read together. Alternatively, the teacher may use a big book or poem for shared reading. Often teachers use such texts to introduce, review, and/or practice high-frequency words and/or specific decoding elements.

Many big books (or digital texts) used for shared reading are at a level of challenge that would make them accessible to most children following a few experiences with shared reading of the text. Thus, shared reading can provide an opportunity to expose all children to texts that may be too challenging for most of them to read on their own. Some publishers provide instructional materials that include a big book and accompanying child-size versions of the text.

Teachers implementing the ISA use shared reading as an opportunity to model and engage children in the use of word-solving strategies. Periodically, while sharing the reading, the teacher stops at a word that lends itself to being identified by using particular strategies. Modeling and discussing with the class how to puzzle through the word, the teacher notes the usefulness of the strategies once the word is identified. Teachers often post a large-print version of the strategies chart (see Chapter 12 and Figure 12.1, p. 303) so that it can be seen by all the children. Many teachers leave the materials used during shared reading out for the children to use during center time or as a free-choice activity. Young children often delight in playing teacher and will enthusiastically gather some friends to serve as students as they take on the role.

As teachers plan and deliver a whole-class shared reading lesson, they need to think about the full spectrum of students who will participate in the lesson, so they can attempt to engage all students productively. This, of course, requires that the teacher does different things for different students in the class. In Table 2.2, we describe how a shared reading lesson might vary for children at different points along the developmental continuum. The table presents each of the instructional goals (introduced in Chapter 1 and discussed in detail in Chapters 3–16) that teachers might address in the lesson and provides a brief glimpse of what teachers might do (or plan to do) for children at different points along the continuum. Typically, of course, the students in a given class will not be distributed evenly along the continuum. Therefore, teachers would distribute their time and focus in accord with the composition of their class. That is, if most of the children are at an early point in learning to read, the instructional interaction would focus on basic print concepts and the identity of individual letters that the children are learning, as well as the meaning of the text being read. If, on the other hand, most of the children are developing readers, most of the instructional interaction related to alphabetics would focus on engaging the children in puzzling through single-syllable words. As noted in Table 2.2, instructional interactions during *shared reading* can and should attend to multiple aspects of the reading process.

Introduction of Center Activities

Centers provide the opportunity for children to work productively toward academic goals when the teacher is working with other children in a small-group context. While it may not be necessary to set aside time to introduce center activities every day, it is important to leave enough time in the schedule to do so if necessary. Several suggestions for literacy-focused center activities are described later in this book. In addition, centers focused on math, science, social studies, and art—all of which involve literacy to some degree—should be included. In considering the daily schedule, notice that there is a permeable (dashed) line between the "shared reading" segment and the "introduction of center activities" segment in Figure 2.1. As it is often necessary to allocate more time to introduce more complicated centers and projects, this permeable line suggests this need for flexibility. For example, in preparing children to learn in a center that is cross-curricular (e.g., involves science and/or math and reading and writing), such as studying the life cycle of a plant, the teacher might utilize the entire 30-minute block to familiarize the children with center activities and expectations.

Small Literacy Groups

Small-group literacy instruction provides the classroom teacher with the greatest opportunity to differentiate instruction and to better meet the needs of children who are at different points in development (Lou, Abrami, & Spence, 2000; McCoach, O'Connell, & Levitt, 2006; Valiandes, 2015). This format is a critical component of language arts instruction and requires careful planning and organization to realize its full potential. In order to discuss small-group instruction in detail while not "breaking the flow" of our description of the daily schedule, we have postponed a full discussion to a later segment of this chapter.

Snack and Conversation

Snack time can be used to support the development of children's language skills by encouraging children to engage in conversations—with multiple, multi-word turns with small groups of their classmates and with periodic modeling of how to engage in conversations if need be. Conversations might center around books read, ongoing class projects, experiences outside of school, and so on. For some children it may be important for the teacher to model *how* to have a conversation, and, particularly in such situations, it is important to avoid leading a conversation that calls for only one- or two-word responses, as discussed in Chapter 15. Thus, this

(text resumes on p. 50)

TABLE 2.2. Teacher Thinking before and during Shared Reading, Related to the Goals and to Children at Various Points in Development

Goal	Beginning	Developing	Maturing	Proficient
Motivation (Chapter 3)	Encourage enjoyment and engagement with text.			
Alphabetics				
Purposes and conventions of print (Chapter 4)	Model and discuss print conventions, such as the left-to-right and top-to-bottom directionality of print.	Model and discuss print conventions such as the use of spaces to separate words and some of the most frequent punctuation (e.g., capitalization of the first word, use of periods and question marks).	Model and discuss more advanced print conventions, such as print size, exclamation points, and quotation marks.	Goal accomplished.
Phonemic awareness (Chapter 5)	Occasionally select texts characterized by rhyme and alliteration to help heighten children's sensitivity to sounds.	Occasionally select texts characterized by rhyme and alliteration to help heighten children's sensitivity to sounds.	Goal accomplished.	Goal accomplished.
Letter names (Chapter 6)	Draw children's attention to the letters for which they are learning the names. Name letters that have recently been introduced and ask children to find them in the text. Or, point to letters children are expected to know and ask them to name them.	Build fluency with letter identification by occasionally inviting children to name all the letters in particular words.	Goal accomplished.	Goal accomplished.
Letter/grapheme sounds (Chapter 7)	Not a focus at this point.	Emphasize the sounds of some letters or graphemes as words are articulated or ask children to provide the sound for a particular grapheme encountered in the text (e.g., "This word starts with the letter	Encourage children to participate in puzzling through words to enhance fluency with letter sounds.	Goal accomplished.

	Not a focus at this point.	s; what sound will this word start with?"). Occasionally model use of the key-word chart when discussing letter sounds.		
Early development of skill with the alphabetic code (Chapter 8)	Not a focus at this point.	Occasionally draw children's attention to the beginning letters in words as they are reading. As readers' skills grow, draw attention to ending letters and short vowel sounds in the middle of one-syllable words as well. Introduce consonant digraphs when children know many of the most frequently occurring letter sounds.	Goal accomplished.	Goal accomplished.
Rimes and word families (Chapter 9)	Not a focus at this point.	Draw children's attention to examples of words that include rimes that have been taught. Model use of the rimes chart if one has been established.	Provide opportunities for children to attempt to solve words in word families that have been taught.	Goal accomplished.
Later development of skill with the alphabetic code (Chapter 10)	Not a focus at this point.	Not a focus at this point.	Draw attention to complex vowel spellings (for example, the silent-e generalization and vowel teams such as aw, oi, and ea).	Goal accomplished.
Morphological units and multisyllabic words (Chapter 11)	Draw attention to common prefixes and suffixes encountered in texts. Explain the meaning if needed.	Draw attention to common prefixes and suffixes encountered in texts. Explain the meaning if needed. Discuss pronunciation and meaning changes with inflectional endings.	Draw attention to common prefixes and suffixes encountered in texts. Explain the meaning if needed. Model and engage students in approaches to puzzling through words with multiple syllables, including words with prefixes and suffixes.	Draw attention to common prefixes and suffixes encountered in texts. Explain the meaning if needed. Engage students in solving words with a variety of derivational and inflectional prefixes and suffixes and/or multiple syllables.

(continued)

TABLE 2.2. (*continued*)

Goal	Beginning	Developing	Maturing	Proficient
Word learning				
Strategic word learning (Chapter 12)	When reading highly predictable text demonstrate and encourage the use of pictures in combination with any grapheme–phoneme relationships that have already been taught/learned.	Guide word solving by occasionally modeling the use of context in combination with partial alphabetic information—beginning letters and, later, final letters. Remind children of strategies they could try while puzzling over a word. After reading and discussing the entire text, revisit some of the word-learning strategies that were used while reading.	Occasionally draw children's attention to more detailed alphabetic information and to larger orthographic units and illustrate how to use that information to derive a likely pronunciation of unfamiliar words and then to use contextual information to determine whether the word has been accurately identified because sometimes one's decoding attempt doesn't result in a real word that makes sense in the context.	Occasionally draw children's attention to larger orthographic units (word families, prefixes, suffixes, and other recurrent spelling patterns) and illustrate how these units can be used in combination with context to facilitate accurate identification of and deduce the meanings of unfamiliar words.
High-frequency words (Chapter 13)	Occasionally point out any high-frequency words that are being taught and provide the opportunity to do a word hunt (finding and naming the word)	Occasionally point out the high-frequency words that the children have been learning. After the entire text has been read and discussed, occasionally give	Occasionally fade voice while leading a shared reading so that children have the opportunity to retrieve recently learned high-frequency words from memory.	Goal accomplished.

	after the text has been read and discussed.	children the opportunity to do a word hunt for words they know or are learning.	Goal accomplished.

Meaning construction

Fluency (Chapter 14)	Read the text multiple times to enable the children to chime in on second and subsequent readings.	Read the text multiple times. Encourage the children to chime in on second and subsequent readings. On occasion draw attention to the voice changes signaled by common sentence-ending punctuation marks and how those changes influence interpretation of the meaning of the text.	Model fluent and disfluent reading of the text and engage the students in discussion of the characteristics of fluent reading. On occasion, draw attention to the role of punctuation marks such as quotation marks and commas and their influence on phrasing and intonation.
Vocabulary and oral language (Chapter 15)	Explain the meanings of unfamiliar words and syntactic structures as they come up in the text. Encourage the children to ask about the meanings of words or phrases they do not understand. Teach or revisit meanings of a few words in follow-up activities.		
Comprehension and world knowledge (Chapter 16)	Engage children in actively thinking about the meaning of the text before, during, and after reading it with them. Facilitate the process of making connections between what the children already know and what they encounter in the text. Encourage the children to ask questions when they do not understand what is happening in the text. Across the year, include a balance of information-rich and literary texts and texts that are representative of a variety of cultures and genres.		

is a time for the teacher to model and encourage social but unstructured conversations among children. If the teacher explicitly models conversations by joining different groups of children, over time the children are likely to begin to emulate the conversational conventions that the teacher demonstrates.

Read-Aloud

A read-aloud involves the teacher reading a book or other text without the expectation that the children will attend to the print. Reading aloud to children and engaging them in discussion of the text before, during, and after it is read provides a powerful vehicle for:

- Expanding their vocabulary and syntactic skills.
- Developing knowledge and vocabulary related to the science and social studies content, particularly if several books on the same or related topics/themes are read.
- Modeling and engaging the children in active processing of the text such as questioning the author's craft or the characters' motivations and choices.
- Helping children learn about the characteristics of different types of literary and informational texts.
- Increasing motivation for and interest in reading.

Further, in the early primary grades, books used for read-aloud can help to promote the development of phonological awareness if they contain rhyme or alliteration. And alphabet books help develop knowledge of letter names and letter sounds because, in most such books, the letter that is the focus of each page is large enough for children to see even when the rest of the words are not.

Many times, the books teachers select for reading aloud are related to a classroom topic or theme (e.g., seasons, oceans, early settlers). Reading several books related to a topic helps children to develop more thorough knowledge and vocabulary related to that topic and enables the teacher to integrate science and social studies content into the language arts curriculum.

Teachers might also organize book selection around author or genre studies. Reading and discussing several books by the same author helps children learn about the authors' craft and contributes to their writing development by highlighting the characteristics and tactics of different authors. Genre studies (biography, fairy tales, memoirs, etc.) help children develop schemas for the different genres. When children understand the characteristics of a particular genre, they are likely to use that knowledge to guide their interpretation of texts. For example, knowledge that a folk tale generally is intended to teach a lesson puts the reader on the alert to look for the lesson the tale is intended to teach. Thus, the genre itself can give the reader a purpose for reading. Moreover, engaging children in noticing the characteristics of various genres and writing styles provides them with models that they may want to emulate in their own writing.

As for other components of instruction offered in a whole-class format, it is important to try to engage the entire class and to give some forethought to how a particular text might be used to support progress toward the various instructional goals. Moreover, particularly for children whose literacy skills are at an earlier point in development, for example, those who have limited experience with being read to, and/or those who find it difficult to attend to text in the context of whole-class instruction, it is also productive to read aloud in small-group or one-to-one situations. Classroom volunteers can be particularly helpful in providing additional opportunities for children to listen to and respond to books. Of course, volunteers may need guidance in how to effectively engage children in read-alouds, as some well-intentioned adults believe that children should be silent while being read to—which is the opposite of what we are advocating.

Writing and Composition

Different formats for writing activities should routinely be part of the instructional day for primary-level readers, including beginning and developing readers. In one format, the teacher does the writing with assistance from the child(ren). In another, the children do the writing with guidance from the teacher. In addition, children should explore writing independently in the context of open-ended writing opportunities in the classroom (e.g., journal writing, observation logs).

In the sample schedule provided in Figure 2.1, writing and composition immediately follows read-aloud largely because teachers sometimes want their students to incorporate, in their own writing, elements of what was discussed during the read-aloud. So, for example, early in first grade, the teacher might ask the children to draw a picture of the portion of a text that interested them the most (or that surprised or bothered them the most) and to write a caption for the picture. As children progress as readers and writers, they might engage in a variety of writing types. For example, the children might be asked to:

- Collaborate in developing a class book that tells further adventures of a character they learned about during a read-aloud.
- Write a letter to an author inquiring about reasons for certain decisions that the author made in writing the text.
- Write a new ending for a story that was read.
- Keep a journal telling what they have learned related to a particular theme they have been pursuing through read-alouds.
- Model their writing after a particular genre or author's style.
- Write a note to a friend explaining why the friend would probably like a particular book.

Whether the writing is focused on reacting to specific texts or is of a more creative nature, the writing/composition portion of the day often begins with a brief lesson in which the teacher models and discusses certain aspects of the writing process. In the early primary grades, teachers often focus on both the mechanics of writing (letter formation, spacing between words, punctuation, sound spelling, conventional spelling, etc.) and the construction of meaning (formulating the intended message, considering wording, revising for clarity, etc.). Mini-lessons often take the form of shared writing, during which the children have the opportunity to observe as the teacher writes, modeling her thinking and engaging the children in as much of the problem solving as they are able to do (e.g., thinking about how to word a statement, stretching the words to analyze the sounds, thinking of the letters needed to represent the sounds).

Once the children begin to write, the teacher circulates for a period of time, providing guidance and encouragement in the form of mini-conferences. Alternatively, teachers sometimes choose to create temporary groups to teach specific writing conventions and strategies during writing time. Thus, the teacher might meet with one group of children one day and a different group of children the next. While the teacher is meeting with groups, the remaining children continue to work on their own compositions and/or engage in conferences with their peers. Some time is set aside at least a couple of times each week for individual children to share their writing with classmates. This activity is often referred to as *authors' chair*.

In planning and delivering writing instruction, teachers engage in the same sort of thinking about the instructional goals and the competencies of their students as was detailed in Table 2.2.

Where Do Science and Social Studies Fit in the Daily Schedule?

Although the packed daily schedule presented in Figure 2.1 could suggest that no time is allocated to science and social studies, this is not the case. When the class is focusing on particular themes or topics in science or social studies, books related to those themes should be selected for shared reading and/or read aloud; those themes could also be carried forward in the writing/composition block. Further, as noted previously, one or more of the centers offered during small-group time could be devoted to providing children with additional opportunities to engage with that content.

Small-Group Literacy Instruction

In order to work productively with children at various points in developing language arts skills, teachers need to plan and organize instruction carefully. As noted above, providing small-group instruction is particularly important for primary reading instruction and, therefore, should be a daily occurrence once the school year gets under way. Initially, however, in preparation for small-group instruction, teachers need to (1) identify which children will be grouped for instruction and (2) prepare children to work productively when they are not directly engaged with the teacher.

Grouping for Supported Small-Group Literacy Instruction

The process by which teachers might form groups for small-group supported instruction varies considerably depending on the children's grade level, the instructional program in use, and the point in the school year. For example, early in the school year in kindergarten, groups may be formed on the basis of the children's phonological skills and understanding of the (alphabetic) writing system. Children who demonstrate similar levels of skill would be grouped together. As the school year progresses, however, the teacher might regroup children based on ongoing observations of what the children know and are able to do, perhaps using checklists such as the snapshots described in each of the instructional goals chapters (Chapters 3–16).

As the children advance, their ability to read texts at increasing levels of challenge or their ability to read texts in the core reading series may serve as the basis for forming instructional groups. Young children who are learning to read in a particular curriculum are likely to learn the things that are emphasized in that curriculum, so assessment should certainly evaluate the extent to which children have learned what has been taught (e.g., specific decoding principles, high-frequency words, specific strategies for word solving). As children progress as readers and as they read more and more texts, their abilities will broaden and likely be progressively less dependent on the particular curriculum. At this point, assessment for the purpose of forming instructional groups (and informing instruction) can use more general (less curriculum-specific) measures of reading.

KEEP IN MIND Regardless of the approach used to form instructional groups, it is important to consider the groups to be temporary and flexible. Children's reading progress typically does not proceed at a fixed rate, particularly when efforts to intervene are in place.

As an alternative, instructional groups might be formed on the basis of periodic administrations of more formal assessments that can be used for the purpose of documenting progress. However, depending on the assessment used, multiple administrations can be time-consuming and may add little to inform grouping decisions or instructional planning. It is the child's performance on a day-to-day basis that is particularly relevant rather than the child's performance at a single point in time. This last point should not, of course, be taken as a rationale for doing away altogether with systematic data collection; such data are needed for the purpose of documenting growth. Rather, the point is that teachers who are well informed about early literacy development, who are working closely and thoughtfully with children in small-group settings, and who are systematically documenting children's performance during ongoing instructional interactions will likely know more about their students' abilities than can be learned from more formal, periodic assessments.

Preparing Children to Work without the Teacher during Small-Group Time

Ideally, the children in a supported small-group literacy context should receive the teacher's undivided attention. However, because teachers are generally responsible for the entire class, they need to prepare the children to work effectively and independently when they are involved with their small groups. To accomplish this preparation, many teachers, particularly in the primary grades, report that during the initial couple of weeks of school, they do not actually work with small groups but rather invest time in teaching children the routines and procedures that will eventually govern their independent work once the teacher begins to meet with groups. Teachers typically develop a number of centers or stations in the classroom where individuals or groups of children engage in practice and reinforcement activities for particular academic skills and/or in activities that provide the opportunity for new learning/knowledge building. For example, a teacher might develop a listening center where the children listen to recordings of informational books or a computer center where the children watch videos relating to the science or social studies content about which the class is learning.

Planning, Planning, Planning

The activities in which the children engage should be so well planned and so well described to them that little or no teacher support is required once the children have learned what to do at each center. All the necessary materials should be readily available and accessible to the children. For centers that focus on the development of early literacy skills, such as knowledge of high-frequency words or the development of skill with the alphabetic code, the activities should lend themselves to some degree of differentiation. Thus, each child might have a folder at the center that contains items that are matched to their current skill level.

Another aspect of planning is deciding which children will be placed together at each center. In our opinion, centers work best when children at various points of development interact. This way the children who are a bit further along can assist children who are less so, and both are likely to benefit from the interaction. Explaining a process or concept to a friend can serve to broaden and deepen the understanding of one who is more knowledgeable.

Setting Reasonable Expectations

It is unlikely that young children will be able to sustain productive engagement with the same activity for prolonged periods of time. Therefore, the activities designed for each center should generally require no more than 20 or so minutes to complete, and at least some of the centers should encourage the children to talk with their friends as they engage in learning activities. This conversational aspect will help to promote language development and to deepen the children's learning by providing them with the opportunity to gain other children's perspectives.

To ensure quiet, productive activity as transition times approach, it is important to have appealing but simple activities for the children to engage in once they have completed the major center activity. For example, there might be options such as playing games with high-frequency words or decoding elements or book browsing and independent or buddy reading.

Promoting the Development of Self-Regulation

In order to provide the teacher with the focused time needed to provide instruction in small-group contexts and to ensure that learners who are not directly involved with the teacher can work productively, children need to learn to work with some independence. Learning to do so is aided by helping children learn to focus their attention, remember instructions, and effectively juggle multiple tasks (for example, when reading, think about the sounds of the letters in an unknown word and the meaning of the context in which the word is encountered). In an effort to promote the development of these focusing, remembering, and juggling skills (discussed in Chapter 1), the teacher might spend the first couple of weeks of school demonstrating what to do in the centers, discussing what to do if problems arise (including asking children to recall what to do under various circumstances), monitoring and guiding the children's problem-solving skills while engaged in the centers, and noticing and explicitly acknowledging evidence of self-regulation (e.g., "Juan already found his folder and got busy with writing and checking his spelling words right away"; "I see that Xavier and Olivia are already working on their writing!").

As noted, self-regulation skills influence children's behavior and learning far beyond managing to engage productively and with relative independence during center time. Efforts to promote the development of self-regulation skills as the school year proceeds should continue.

"Eyes in the Front of Their Head"

Although effective primary-grade teachers are often described as "having eyes in the backs of their heads" because they seem to know what's going on in all parts of their classrooms at all times, it is more likely that their "with-it-ness" is due to careful planning and positioning: They anticipate potential difficulties in the classroom and try to prevent them. Moreover, when they organize for small-group instruction, they position themselves so that they can see the entire classroom and monitor the children who are not in the group with which they are working.

Assistants in the Classroom

So far, our discussion has assumed that the classroom teacher is the lone adult in the room. However, if additional adult resources are available, instruction may be even more productive. For example, if a classroom aide is available while the teacher is providing small-group instruction, the aide can monitor and support the children engaged in center activities. If more than one additional adult is available, those adults can be pressed into service in providing guided practice opportunities for the children. For example, they might listen to individual children reread and discuss books that were previously read with the teacher, or they might do small-group interactive read-alouds. To be optimally effective in either of these roles, the assistants/volunteers will typically benefit from some orientation and guidance concerning the goals of these activities and how they might support children in achieving those goals. It is our observation that many adults have a tendency to jump in too quickly when a child encounters a bit of challenge in an academic endeavor, thereby robbing children of the thinking time that may be needed to figure things out on their own. Teaching assistants and volunteers may need encouragement to provide young children the "think time" they need to negotiate the learning challenges they encounter.

Teaching Small Groups

In the schedule presented in Figure 2.1 (p. 43), it is assumed that the teachers have four different groups of children with whom they work during the course of a week. Group 1 is at the earliest point in development and would consist largely or exclusively of children who have not yet achieved the level of literacy skill expected at their grade level. The schedule allows the teacher to meet with these children 5 days a week. Group 2 comprises children who are somewhat more advanced in terms of their early literacy skills but are not yet at the expected level of performance. They may not need the level of intensity provided for the children in Group 1. The schedule allows the teacher to meet with students in Group 2 on 4 days of the week. Group 3 consists of children who are meeting grade-level expectations, and Group 4 consists of children who are somewhat above grade level. Because these children are predicted to readily meet or exceed grade-level expectations by the end of the year, the teacher can meet with them less frequently and/or less intensively to support their development. The schedule allows time for the teacher to meet with each of these groups three times per week. An alternative for Groups 3 and 4 might be to meet with them 5 days per week but for abbreviated lessons on 2 of the days. Thus, in the schedule depicted in Figure 2.1, the teacher might opt to meet with Group 3 and Group 4 students on both Thursday and Friday, with the time set aside for that block divided between the two groups.

As depicted in the sample schedule, the teacher meets with different groups in different time slots each day. The rationale for this arrangement is twofold. First, because children are likely to move back and forth between and among groups as their literacy skills develop, having the groups meet in a different order on each day may help to avoid having the children develop a strong sense of which group is the "top" and "bottom" reading group. Given that identifying oneself as being in the bottom reading group can have a serious negative impact on one's sense of efficacy, it is clearly desirable for the children to perceive the groups as fluid (and for the groups to *be* fluid, of course). Second, having the groups meet at a different time each day will help to ensure that the students in each group have the opportunity to receive some of their small-group literacy instruction when they are relatively fresh.

The instruction provided during small-group time should be guided by the skills and performance levels of the children in the group. Children who are performing at levels substantially below grade expectations (Group 1 in the current scenario) are obviously ready to learn very different things than children who are performing substantially above grade level. For example, the children in Group 1 may have limited phonemic awareness, knowledge of the alphabet, and understanding of print conventions. Therefore, these skills will need to be explicitly addressed in the small-group context, at least early in the year (and these children would, ideally, be provided with additional support services in an RTI context from the beginning of the school year). Children in Groups 3 and 4, on the other hand, probably have these skills fairly well established, and, as a result, most of their small-group time can focus on engaging them in learning more advanced skills and strategies and in reading and responding to books and other texts.

In the ISA, the typical components of a small-group lesson include the following:

- Rereading one or more books from previous lesson(s).
- Phonemic analysis practice—for children who do not yet know much about the alphabet and who are not yet able to attend to/manipulate the sounds in one-syllable spoken words.
- Decoding (reading) and encoding (writing) individual words (phonics) instruction—new phonics elements taught should be those which the children will have the opportunity to apply in the day's new book. Practice with the new skills would incorporate previously taught skills that are not yet mastered/automatic. Practice with *both* decoding and encoding skills will help children decipher unfamiliar words encountered while reading.
- Reading a new book or books.
- Writing.
- Practice with previously taught high-frequency words.

Table 2.3 provides an outline of what small-group lessons might look like toward the beginning of first grade for children in the four groups described above. For purposes of illustration, Group 1 is assumed to be at a beginning level, and Groups 2, 3, and 4 are considered to be at various points along the continuum that might be considered "developing." If there are maturing or proficient readers in the class, the teacher might need to consider adding a group and/or arranging for these children to join a second-grade group taught by another teacher. (Please note that the group designations in Table 2.3 are different from the *beginning, developing,*

(text resumes on p. 60)

TABLE 2.3. Small-Group Lesson: Four Different Groups in One Classroom at the Beginning of First Grade

Lesson components		Group 1 (earliest)	Group 2	Group 3	Group 4
Rereading	All Groups	Each child individually reads one or two books from a prior small-group session. Children are allowed to choose their books from a selection provided by the teacher. The teacher listens in and provides guidance to individual children.			
	Separate Groups	Teacher attends to print concepts and conventions.	Teacher attends to children's ability to accurately point to the words as they are read. Guidance may focus on use of letters and context.	Teacher attends to confirmatory use of print (including single letters and larger orthographic units) and the use of context to confirm the accuracy of decoding attempts.	
Phonemic analysis	Separate groups	Teacher engages children in sorting pictures by similarity in ending (or middle) sounds in picture labels.	Teacher engages children in phoneme segmentation using sound boxes.	Not needed.	
Phonics and Spelling (decoding and encoding)	All groups	Teacher plans to teach a specific phonics skill that can be applied in the new book(s) that the children will read.			
	Separate groups	Sing whole alphabet song a few times while pointing to letters. Then focus on learning the names of one or two letters that occur frequently in the new book for the day.	Focus on grapheme–phoneme correspondences for graphemes that have recently been introduced and that occur frequently in the new book for the day and/or on a new rime that will appear multiple times in the book. For rimes/word families, practice incorporates one or more previously taught (or known) rimes.	Depending on the characteristics of the book to be read, the teacher may teach and/or review rimes or other decoding elements (e.g., morphemes or multi-letter spelling patterns) that will enable children to successfully puzzle through unfamiliar words that will appear in the day's new book(s).	
Reading new books	All groups	Teacher prepares the children to successfully read the book selected for the group. Part of the preparation occurs in the phonics and spelling segment of the lesson (see above). Additional preparation may include: (1) teaching a new word-identification strategy that can be applied in the new book and/or reviewing strategies that have already been taught; (2) teaching one or more high-frequency words that will occur in the text and that the children are unlikely to be able to identify, given their current decoding/phonics skills and the contextual support for word identification provided by the text; and/or (3) providing a book introduction that is sufficiently detailed as to allow the children to be successful in the text but not so detailed as to limit the children's opportunities to be strategic in word solving. Each child will have the opportunity to read the entire book at least once during the small-group session. The teacher provides sufficient support to allow the children to be successful but not so much support that the children do not have the opportunity to apply their word-solving and comprehension skills and strategies. There should be a focus on the meaning of the text before, during, and after reading the new book. If time allows, two books may be read during this segment of the lesson.			
	Separate groups	Text selection: Use texts in which there is a reliable and repetitive language pattern and a close correspondence between the	Text selection: Use texts that make some use of repetitive language and provide the opportunity for the children to effectively	Text selection: Dependent on the instructional materials in use.	

58

		use the development decoding/phonics skills in combination with context to puzzle through unfamiliar words. Texts specifically designed to promote the development of high-frequency sight vocabulary might also be used.		
Writing	All groups	Shared writing conducted in whole-class contexts provides the teacher with the opportunity to demonstrate various aspects of the writing process. In small groups, children should be involved in both shared and supported writing, with the teacher specifically focusing on what the children are ready to learn. In small-group and intervention lessons, writing may occur following the reading of a book, and typically (but not always) it involves writing a response to the book that was read. To maximize the use of the time available to write, the teacher often provides a fairly specific writing prompt in small-group settings.		
	Separate groups	Teachers need to focus on print concepts and the formation of individual letters. They may serve as scribes in the composition process. Teachers frequently model, and engage children in analyzing, the phonemic components of words to be written.	Teachers model and engage children in composing messages and analyzing the phonemes in individual words. Particular emphasis is placed on analyzing and spelling the beginning sounds in words. Children are encouraged to use the key-word chart to remind them of letter–sound relationships and to refer to the "Words I Know" chart (see Chapter 13) for the spellings of previously taught high-frequency words.	Teachers model and engage children in more thorough sound analysis and spelling of words. Children are encouraged to refer to available resources to support their spelling, including, where appropriate, the book they are responding to and the key word (see Chapter 7), "Words I Know" (see Chapter 13), and Word Family (see Chapter 9) charts.
High-frequency words	All groups	High-frequency words serve as an important anchor for children in puzzling through texts. Helping children to become automatic in identifying words they have encountered in text will allow them to be more effectively strategic in puzzling through less familiar words. A variety of game-like activities, such as sticky-note bingo (see Chapter 13), can be used to support the development of fluency with high-frequency words.		
	Separate groups	Children rely on nonalphabetic features for word learning until they learn about the alphabet. Word learning is very idiosyncratic. Only words in which the children can identify all the letters should be taught, as this promotes orthographic mapping. Words should be initially taught in preparation for a book that the children will read and should be practiced in subsequent lessons until they can be identified effortlessly.	To begin to learn high-frequency words, children need to attend to the letters in the words. Texts in which the high-frequency words occur in slightly different contexts will facilitate this learning; so too will having opportunities to write and name the words in word-learning games (see Chapter 13) and in the writing portion of the lesson.	The introduction of high-frequency words before reading a text should become more selective. Teachers should explicitly introduce high-frequency words from upcoming texts only if it is expected that the children do not have the skills and strategies to successfully identify them on their own. (The ability to do so for words for which the children have not yet learned the needed phonic skills may depend on the contextual support for word solving.)

maturing, and *proficient* designations illustrated in Table 2.2.) At the beginning of first grade, it is unlikely that many children would have the skills of a maturing or proficient reader. However, the range of skills within the "developing" designation is likely to be broad enough to warrant separating children into groups for reading instruction.

Prior to meeting with the groups, the teacher selects the new book(s) for each group to read. Because the groups are at different points in development, each group will read different books—books that provide them with some challenge but not so much challenge as to create frustration. The teacher plans the phonics portion of the lesson with an eye toward helping the children to meet the challenge(s) that the day's book(s) will present.

In reviewing Table 2.3, note that, when specific instructional activities are named (e.g., segmenting a one-syllable word into component phonemes, singing the alphabet), these are meant as examples only. Different activities (e.g., sorting pictures by ending sound, filling in missing letters on an alphabet strip), based on students' developing skills, would be selected on different days. These other instructional activities will be described in the relevant goals chapters (Chapters 3–16).

Interventions beyond the Classroom

Where Does Time for Intervention Fit In?

For children who appear to be in need of additional support services, it can be more than a bit of a challenge to find time in the day to provide *additional* intervention services. However, if it is determined that a child needs more support than what can be provided within the classroom program, that support needs to be provided *in addition* to the supported small-group reading instruction provided in the classroom. Only then can the delivery of the needed instructional experiences be achieved. In the sample schedule provided in Figure 2.1 (p. 43), the ideal time for additional intervention would be during the times when the classroom teacher is engaged in providing small-group instruction to children in groups other than the one to which the child belongs. Because children would probably benefit from a bit of a break between their small-group classroom instruction and their intervention lesson, it may be ideal to allow them 15–25 minutes of center time between the two lessons. If the intervention teachers cannot accommodate to the rotating schedule suggested, of course, the time slots for individual groups would need to be stabilized.

What Do/Should Intervention Lessons Look Like?

Early research on the ISA focused solely on providing interventions beyond the classroom (Vellutino et al., 1996; Scanlon et al., 2005). The classroom application of the approach (Scanlon et al., 2008) was based on the success of the interventions and the belief that classroom teachers would benefit from having the knowledge and insights into literacy development that we had been developing with the intervention teachers with whom we worked. Therefore, from our perspective, Tier 2 and Tier 3 interventions should look very much like high-quality, supported, small-group literacy lessons that would be provided in the classroom. Ideally, however, the group size in intervention settings beyond the classroom would be smaller than the group sizes that are possible or necessary at the classroom level. This smaller size would allow the intervention teacher to individualize instruction a bit more than the classroom teacher is typically able to do. As we stress at several points throughout this book, to maximize the effectiveness of literacy instruction for children in intervention, it is important to ensure that the instruction offered in the classroom and the instruction offered in intervention settings are mutually supportive. We address this topic in several ways in upcoming chapters that focus on the instructional goals. We feel that when classroom and intervention teachers share a common set of instructional goals and continually reflect on ways to address those goals, the instruction they offer is more likely to be effective in supporting children's literacy development.

General Principles for Early Literacy Instruction and Preventing Reading Difficulties

One of the main purposes of comprehensive and responsive early literacy instruction and intervention is to prevent early differences in literacy skills from growing and becoming disabling. Although the specific content of what is taught is important, there are equally important general principles of instruction that can help maximize the impact of the instruction and intervention efforts.

Teach Children to Be Effective and Independent Problem Solvers

Vygotsky (1978) was a developmental theorist who believed that much of what children learn as they grow and develop is the result of extended interactions with adults or more expert "others." Vygotsky argued that the skills that children acquire reflect the internalization of problem solving that they have initially done in collaboration with adults, who have provided *careful verbal guidance to direct and guide children's thinking.* The theory is that children internalize the verbal guidance initially provided by their teachers (including all significant others) in such a way that it becomes a form of inner speech that influences their thinking when they encounter "problems" that are similar to those that were previously solved with teacher guidance.

If we assume that adults' speech (and, through it, adults' thinking) are, on some level, internalized by children, then it becomes important to carefully consider our instructional language and to try to take the perspective of children relative to our language. Do we use terms or expressions that may not hold the same meaning for children? It is all too easy to inadvertently use terminology that carries no meaning or a different meaning for children who struggle with literacy acquisition. For example, for some early literacy learners, a *short a* may be thought of as an *a* that is literally shorter (visually) than other *a*'s. It is remarkably easy to wrongly assume that children know or understand things as we do; as a result, an instructional episode may be quite confusing to them. Virtually every teacher has had this experience.

It is also important to give children the opportunity to see how to use the problem-solving processes we teach. Because problem solving is a thinking process, the only way the children can "see" the process is if we think out loud so that they can vicariously experience the process. The instructional jargon for this approach to instruction is *think-aloud*, and it is an important component of instruction designed to develop strategic thinking. When we think out loud for children, we are, essentially, guiding the development of their thinking.

Vygotsky (1978) also argued that the most effective instruction focuses on skills and abilities that are somewhat challenging for a child to handle independently but that are easy enough for the child to handle when assistance is offered at key points. The disparity between what children are able to do with and without assistance is referred to as the *zone of proximal development* (often referred to as the ZPD). From a Vygotskian perspective, the role of a teacher is that of a skilled collaborator. In this role, teachers must be:

- Adept at evaluating children's current level of competence and deciding what they are ready to learn next.
- Facile at modifying the demands of the task so that it suits the needs of each child.

Relatedly, Wood, Bruner, and Ross (1976) developed the concept of *scaffolding* as an analogy for the role that skilled collaborators play in supporting a child's learning. Scaffolding involves the provision of various types of support that allow children to successfully accomplish a task that is too challenging for them to accomplish on their own. Scaffolding also involves the gradual *reduction* of support as students demonstrate the ability to regulate their own thinking and problem solving. In order to carry out the types of assessment, modification, and scaffolding suggested here, it is necessary for teachers to have a firm grasp of the developmental progression of the skills they are helping students develop. In the upcoming chapters, our intent is to help teachers establish strong understandings of these developmental progressions.

Ensure That Students Are Actively Engaged in Learning

The more reading and writing children do and the more they practice the underlying skills that are foundational for reading and writing, the more quickly they become proficient. This is true when children actively engage in the cognitive processes required to read and write. Unfortunately, young children sometimes find ways to avoid the thinking parts of instructional activities. For example, in a choral reading situation, when the entire class or group is engaged in reading the same text aloud, some of the children may not be looking at the words and thinking about them. Rather, they may be simply gazing in the right direction and saying the words just slightly after their friends say them. These children may look engaged, but they are not. They need the opportunity to read text to the teacher or to a friend in order to fully engage in the necessary thinking processes.

Similar types of disengagement can arise when a teacher calls on one child *before* asking a question. For example, if the teacher is engaging children in a shared writing activity and wants to know what letter to use at the beginning of the word *dog*, she might call on one child, saying, "Jem, what letter do I need at the beginning of the word *dog*?" As soon as the teacher says Jem's name, some of the children in the group may disengage, knowing that they will not be expected to answer. If, on the other hand, the teacher asks the question without immediately calling on an individual, more of the children are likely to engage in the thinking. Better still, if all the children have dry-erase boards on which to write, they could all engage in the task. The teacher might say, "Write down the letter you think I need at the beginning of the word *dog*." This allows every student to respond; as a result, they are *all* likely to benefit from the instructional interaction. We strongly encourage teachers to incorporate opportunities for every student to respond during instruction and to try to take account of the learning potential of all the children in the instructional group.

KEEP IN MIND In developing instructional activities, an important question to ask is "What are the children likely to be thinking about/focusing on during the activity?" If the conclusion is that they are unlikely to be focused on the skill or concept (the goal) that the activity was designed to support, the activity should be redesigned. For example, at early points in learning, a motor focus (letter formation) may be appropriate as long as it is accompanied by a verbal focus (naming the letter as it is formed).

Who's Doing the Thinking?

Most of us go into teaching because we enjoy helping others learn. However, it is possible to be too helpful and/or too quick to step in when children are engaged in a cognitively demanding activity. We need to be mindful of giving children the time they need to puzzle through the challenges they encounter, and we have to keep reminding ourselves that our intention should be to help children develop the thinking skills they need to grow as learners. We've sometimes observed teachers who appear to be more concerned about eliciting the correct response than about helping children understand how to solve a challenge.

Another consideration relative to the relationship between engagement and learning is the fact that children sometimes become overly involved in the hands-on (e.g., cutting, gluing, coloring) aspects of instructional activities and are not really thinking about the skill or concept that the task was designed to support. It is important to make clear to children *why* they are doing specific things and *what* they can do during the hands-on aspects of the activity to support their learning. For example, children learning the sound of the letter *m* might be engaged in gluing macaroni onto a cut-out of an *M*. While they are doing this, they can be encouraged to think of other words that have the /mmm/ sound that is heard at the beginning of the word *mmmmacaroni* and to share their ideas with other children at the table. If children are not provided with guidance in how to think about the instructional activity, at least some are apt to devote most of their thinking to the gluing and fine-motor activity or, in this instance, to thinking about the food they are manipulating (perhaps *noodles?*). Similarly, if children are practicing their spelling words by writing them several times, it would be helpful for them to say each letter as they write it and then say the word each time it is completed. It would also help if they tried to write the word from memory each time and then checked it against a model. Otherwise, the spelling practice may become nothing more than an unengaged, and therefore unproductive, copying task.

The general point about engagement is that teachers need to guide how children *think* about instructional activities so that the activities actually move the children forward in literacy acquisition.

Strive to Ensure Culturally Responsive and Sustaining Instruction

We live in a multicultural and multilingual society—a fact that, in many settings, has been underappreciated. This diversity can contribute greatly to the classroom culture. Students arrive in school with varying funds of linguistic knowledge, some of which aligns more closely with the language of the classroom than others. Appreciating and leveraging linguistic strengths allows students to draw from their funds of knowledge as they become conventionally literate in English.

In their efforts to address the priority of providing culturally responsive and sustaining instruction, researchers encourage teachers to value home customs, beliefs, and language, for example by inviting families in to share their traditions, languages, foods, and art, by offering books that represent diversity (and when possible have family members do read-alouds), and by allowing children to use their first language(s) in conversation and in writing.

Regarding linguistic diversity, Barnes et al. (2021) encourage teachers to "consider this linguistic diversity in your academic language instruction to simultaneously apprentice students into the academic register and affirm the linguistic assets that all of your students bring" (p. 23). Citing Lobeck (2019), they indicate that the "diversity signals that you need to explicitly make teaching the academic register and building all students' awareness about linguistic diversity the rule rather than the exception" (Barnes et al., 2021, p. 23). This approach is inclusive because all young children are learning the language of schooling during the PreK through third-grade years.

As we will discuss as the book unfolds, children profit when multilingualism (which includes variations of English) is viewed as a strength for literacy learning. For example, it has the potential to promote metalinguistic awareness—the ability to reflect upon and manipulate the structure of speech (Gottardo, Chen, & Huo, 2021). Such awareness can positively impact many of the components of the complex model discussed earlier.

Set High Expectations for All Children

At various points in the history of education, people have believed that some children were simply destined to have great difficulty learning to read and/or write and that there was little to be done to help them overcome their difficulties. Research has demonstrated that students tend to live up to the expectations we have for them (Smith, Jussim, & Eccles, 1999). Thus, a belief that a child is unlikely to make progress has the clear potential to slow the progress made by that child. Conversely, the expectation that a child will succeed academically increases the likelihood that they will do so. In fact, research conducted in "beat-the-odds" schools, in which children succeed at much higher levels than might be expected given their socioeconomic circumstances, indicates that a common characteristic of such schools is that school staff held high expectations for all the children (Taylor et al., 2000).

What Does "Ready to Learn" Mean?

For many years it was commonly believed that children needed to be developmentally *ready* to learn to read. Exactly what people meant by "being ready" varied, but it was certainly tied to the child's age and, in some cases, physical development. For example, some thought that children should not be taught to read until they had lost their first tooth!

When we use the phrase *ready to learn*, we mean that the children have the prerequisite conceptual understandings and skills to allow them to benefit from instruction in a certain area. Every child is ready to learn something. Our job as educators is to figure out *what* the child is ready to learn, not *whether* the child is ready to learn.

Research on the success of early literacy interventions makes it easier to hold high expectations for children who initially demonstrate limited literacy skills. Every child is expected to do well in reading and writing development, and, if the child is not progressing, we are more inclined to examine the instruction than to examine the child to determine what has gone wrong. In other words, instruction is now considered to be a much more powerful influence on a child's reading and writing development than it once was. Children do learn what we teach them, as long as we teach them what they are *ready to learn*. The challenge, of course, is that generally not all the children in a given classroom are ready to learn the same things. Nevertheless, they are all expected to attain the same grade-level standards. This is why different amounts and intensities of instruction and intervention are so important to promoting literacy success. In a classroom setting, working with small, flexible, skills-based groups for a substantial portion of the language arts block offers the greatest opportunity for the teacher to meet this challenge. Similarly focused small-group and one-to-one instructional contexts enable intervention teachers to respond to the needs of the children who require more expert instruction and/or instructional intensification to make progress.

What Is the Role of "Learning Styles" in (Literacy) Learning?

The suggestion that individuals have preferred learning styles has been part of educational lore for many decades. Those who subscribe to the idea of learning styles believe that individuals have preferred modes or styles of learning that are either visual, auditory, or kinesthetic (having to do with movement). According to Willingham (2018), there is some evidence that individuals do have preferred learning styles and tend to act on those preferences when engaging in learning and problem solving. However, there is no evidence that teaching in ways that accommodate to individuals' preferred learning styles results in improved learning. Therefore, while the focus of this chapter is on providing responsive instruction, we would not include accommodating preferred learning styles as an important component of responsive instruction. According to Willingham "People believe they have learning styles, and they try to think in their preferred style, but doing so does not help them think" (p. 29). Further, he states that "using learning-styles theories in the classroom does not bring advantage to students" (p. 28).

Integrate Support Services with the Classroom Program

For children who are receiving intervention services beyond the classroom, it is important that the instruction in all settings works toward mutually supportive ends (Allington & Johnston, 1989; Mosenthal, Lipson, Torncello, Russ, & Mekkelsen, 2004; Wonder-McDowell et al., 2011). To the greatest extent possible, intervention teachers should support and reinforce the content of the classroom program. For example, at the kindergarten level, if instruction about the alphabet is ordered in a particular way, it makes sense to sequence alphabet instruction in intervention settings to parallel the classroom sequence. Similarly, if key words are used in the classroom to support the learning of letter sounds, supplementary instruction should use the same key words. Likewise, it is helpful to determine which high-frequency words children are expected to know by the end of a given grade level and to make these words a priority for instruction. Additionally, some of the reading materials used in intervention settings would ideally come from the classroom program. Such a purposeful selection gives the children the opportunity to interact with these materials in a way that they may not experience in the larger classroom context. Many more opportunities to build congruence could be suggested. By increasing the congruence between classroom and supplementary instruction, we hope to increase the impact of both the classroom instruction and the intervention support. Children who experience difficulty in the classroom program will be better prepared for subsequent instruction in the classroom if they have reviewed some of the material in the intervention context.

Plan for Success

In all instructional interactions, we encourage teachers to make every effort to structure the activities so that children experience success and the rewarding feelings that go along with success. Further, teachers can help students recognize that their successes are due to their efforts. When challenges arise, teachers should avoid making negative and discouraging comments. For example, although a teacher may sometimes feel frustrated by not having found a way to help a particular child accomplish a particular objective, communicating this frustration will only serve to make the child feel that the situation may be hopeless. If the child is not progressing in a certain area, it is important to try to determine the source of the problem. Perhaps the level of difficulty needs to be reduced. Perhaps the child is misconstruing the task. Perhaps the teacher is using terminology for certain concepts that is different from the terminology to which the child is accustomed. It is particularly important for teachers who are providing supplementary instruction (intervention services) to be aware of the terminology used in the children's classrooms. For example, whereas adults and most older children readily recognize the equivalence of terms such as *upper-case* and *capital*, young children often do not. Attending to potential stumbling blocks such as task difficulty or confusion regarding terminology before they occur will help to ensure that children experience success and continually move forward in their literacy development.

Document Student Progress

Because knowing what children are already able to do is so essential to knowing what they are ready to learn next, it is important for teachers to keep records of their students' skills and strategies. To this end, for most aspects of literacy development discussed in this book, we provide skill and strategy checklists to facilitate record keeping and, most importantly, to support teachers as they reflect on their students' current abilities and plan instruction.

Because teachers usually use such record-keeping devices in the context of working with small groups of children, each checklist provides space for teachers to record information on up to five children. We refer to these checklists as "snapshots" because they allow teachers to get a quick look at the skills, strategies, and attitudes/beliefs of children in a particular group to inform their instructional planning. Each snapshot is discussed in some detail in the relevant chapters of this book. The group snapshots are most effectively used once instructional groups have been formed. Individual versions of the snapshots—available on the book's companion website (see the box at the end of the table of contents)—might be used during the first few weeks of school as teachers are getting to know their students (with an eye toward forming instructional groups). The individual snapshot can also be updated periodically across the school year to track progress and may be shared between classroom and specialist/intervention teachers to support coordination of instructional targets. The group version of the snapshot can be used in the context of small-group instruction to identify common instructional needs for group members as well as to periodically inform decision making about whether the composition of the group is appropriate. To the greatest extent possible, children grouped together for instruction should be similar in their understandings and grasp of concepts and, for the most part, should all be ready to learn the same kinds of things.

Many of the snapshots call for the teacher to document children's skills and strategies using a 3-point scale: *beginning, developing,* and *proficient*. Such documentation is appropriate for what Paris (2005) refers to as *constrained skills*— skills that are learned over a relatively short time span and that are mastered by most students. These records are also appropriate for documenting word-solving strategy usage. As we will illustrate, to make the record keeping as efficient as possible, we suggest that, when using the group snapshot, teachers use slashes to denote their judgment of individual children's standing relative to particular skills and strategies.

> *Beginning* (designated by a single slash in the box provided ◹) indicates that instruction has addressed the objective but that the child has only a preliminary understanding or capability with regard to that particular objective.
> *Developing* (designated by adding a slash to the box—forming an ◲) indicates that the child has some understanding of the objective but does not reliably demonstrate that understanding or capability or is not yet automatic (fluent) with the skill and therefore needs continued instruction and/or practice.
> *Proficient* (designated by adding a third slash in the box—forming an asterisk ⊠) indicates that the child, across time, reliably and automatically demonstrates the understanding or capability and that, in the teacher's view, instruction no longer needs to address the particular skill or process. Proficiency should be determined based on multiple observations in most cases, as the skill should be demonstrated with fluency and consistently over time.

We suggest the use of slashes, rather than the letter designations, to enable teachers to update the snapshots during the course of instruction. Thus, if through observation, the teacher recognizes that a child has moved from a *beginning* to a *developing* point of development, or from *developing* to *proficient*, there is no need to erase previous designations or to create a new snapshot—simply adding a slash will suffice. In fact, some teachers report using a half slash when they perceive that a student is on the verge of moving to the next level of development with a particular skill or strategy.

For the individual snapshot, for efficiency sake, many teachers opt to use the designations of B (beginning), D (developing), and P (proficient)—to save having to make all those slashes and asterisks.

Some of the snapshots call for teachers to indicate whether they perceive that individual children's capabilities in given areas are *well developed*, *appropriately developed*, or *needs development*. Essentially, these designations reflect the teachers' judgment as to whether this is an aspect of literacy development that requires greater instructional emphasis.

KEY POINTS OF THIS CHAPTER

✓ Early literacy instruction needs to be responsive to what children know and are able to do. All primary-grade children are ready to learn something, but they are not all ready to learn the same things.

✓ Children who have the most limited skills relative to their grade placement need more instructional support in classroom and intervention settings.

✓ Instructional services across classroom and intervention settings need to be mutually supportive.

✓ While decoding and encoding skills are a common focus for primary grade children, reading and writing are largely language skills and depend on world/background knowledge.

✓ Effective classroom management and guidance to support the development of self-regulation skills will enable the teacher to provide focused instruction during small-group time and will likely enable learners to grow their academic skills more effectively.

CHAPTER 3

Motivation to Read and Write

MOTIVATION GOAL

Children will develop the belief that reading and writing are enjoyable and informative activities that are not beyond their capabilities.

Motivation is what gets one going, keeps one engaged, and moves one forward in any task that requires effort. Learning to read and write requires effort for (nearly) all children—although the amount of effort required varies considerably across children. Attention to children's motivation for and engagement in reading and writing is especially important for those who encounter literacy learning difficulties in the primary grades because, as we have pointed out, early difficulties can lead children to avoid engaging in the very activities that will help them develop their reading and writing skills. Indeed, a substantial body of research indicates that initial difficulties in learning to read can have a negative impact on students' reading motivation in both the short and the long term (e.g., Cunningham & Stanovich, 1997; Morgan & Fuchs, 2007). More recently, Soemer and Schiefele (2018) reported that reading motivation and reading comprehension in the middle elementary grades are both related to early success in learning to read. This is, of course, an important reason to make every effort to improve young children's success in developing literacy skills. This is why we include a chapter on motivation in a text on early literacy development.

Children who, prior to kindergarten, have had lots of opportunity to engage in literate activities (e.g., listening to and talking about books, engaging in conversations about past, current, and future experiences, having access to tools for writing and drawing) are likely to approach literacy learning with a positive attitude and an expectation of successful literacy learning—which is important but doesn't necessarily guarantee success in becoming literate. The primary grades are an extremely important period during which children begin to develop their literate identities, that is, their beliefs about themselves as readers and writers. Their experiences at home and at school play prominent roles.

Children who experience early difficulties with literacy learning (those who are apt to be involved in an RTI process related to literacy) are apt to view literacy learning as difficult or overwhelming. However, we can do many things to increase young learners' motivation to learn to read and write. This chapter reviews some of the research that provides guidance on how to support and enhance young learners' literacy-related motivation.

Most young children begin school eager to learn to read and write and fully expecting that they will successfully learn to do so (McKenna, Kear, & Ellsworth, 1995). Unfortunately, this initial motivation begins to wane by as early as second grade (Marinak, Malloy, Gambrell, & Mazzoni, 2015). When children encounter difficulties with learning, their enthusiasm is likely to dissipate, their beliefs about themselves as learners are apt to change, and they may come to view literate activities as work rather than as the enjoyable and informative undertakings that we would like them to be (Afflerbach, 2022). Unfortunately, children who experience difficulty with becoming literate often try to avoid reading and writing; as a result, they do less of it and make less progress. The challenge for teachers, then, is to try to avoid this downward spiral.

Documenting (Perceived) Literacy Motivation

To help teachers be mindful of their students' motivational status, we provide a list of characteristics that can be used to periodically document students' standing on a variety of dimensions of motivation (see Figure 3.1). This tool, like the snapshots provided in most of the subsequent chapters, is intended to allow teachers to document the characteristics of children who are assigned to the same small group for literacy instruction. The teacher would list the names of children in the group at the top of each column and then indicate, for each child, to what extent each item is characteristic of the child—based on informal observations made during instruction. As depicted in the key for Figure 3.1, we suggest using a 3-point scale ranging from a "Not at all" characteristic of the child to "Absolutely" for this particular snapshot. The purpose of this documentation is *not* to provide an overall "score" for motivation but to record insight into the motivational status of individual children in an instructional group. The purpose is to enable the teacher to reflect on what may need to be done instructionally when students are observed to lack motivation and/or to hold beliefs associated with limitations in motivation.

The companion website for this book (see the box at the end of the table of contents) provides similar snapshots that can be used to document the status of individual students across time as a means of documenting growth and change.

Group Snapshot—Motivation					
Student names					
Interest and engagement in read-alouds					
Child is enthusiastic about fictional read-alouds.					
Child is enthusiastic about informational read-alouds.					
Child demonstrates active engagement when being read to.					
Enthusiasm for reading and writing					
Child is enthusiastic about reading.					
Child is enthusiastic about writing.					
Self-perceptions					
Child perceives self as a capable reader.					
Child perceives self as a capable writer.					
When encountering difficulty while reading, child appears to have a sense of having the strategies needed to be successful.					
Interests					
Child has developed interests in particular genre/series of books.					
Understanding of the connection between practice and progress					
Child believes that one's status as a reader is dependent on one's effort.					
Child understands that reading practice will lead to reading growth.					

Key:
N = Not at all   S = Somewhat   A = Absolutely

FIGURE 3.1. Group snapshot for motivation.

Motivation and Linguistically Diverse Learners

Depending on their degree of proficiency with the variant of English used in school and in most books used in American schools, young children who are simultaneously learning the spoken and written forms of school English are apt to experience substantial challenges. Numerous aspects of varying linguistic backgrounds have the potential to be confusing and challenging to learners with regard to sentence structure, the way intonation is used to signal meaning, the phonemes that are used (or not used), and, for speakers of entirely different languages, words for common objects, concepts, and actions. Learning the written form of the variant of English used in school adds more challenges and potential points of confusion for children who have begun to learn to read and write in an entirely different language. For example, in comparison with the home language, the language encountered in school settings may differ in the level of information provided by the symbols that make up the printed language (e.g., phonemes in English, entire words in Chinese); by the reliability of the correspondences between the visual symbols and the phonemes they represent (e.g., in English there can be several different spellings for some of the phonemes while in some languages—such as Spanish and Italian—the spellings of individual phonemes are much more consistent); and by how the print is oriented (e.g., words are read from left to right in English, from right to left in Arabic, and from top to bottom in Chinese).

All these challenges have the potential to overwhelm young children whose home language differs from the language of schooling. To help these children build and maintain enthusiasm for learning to speak, read, and write the language encountered in school settings, teachers need to be sensitive to the types of challenges these children face, helping them to meet those challenges and have a sense of pride in their heritage. In subsequent chapters, as we discuss specific aspects of the reading and writing processes, we offer some examples of how teachers can be responsive to various types of language differences. In this chapter on motivation, we simply highlight the need for sensitivity to these differences. Virtually everything we discuss in this chapter related to motivation applies to all young children—those who are learning English as an additional language, those who speak variants of English in- and/or out-of-school that differ from the version of English most often encountered in the books they listen to and read, and those for whom the version of English encountered in books is consistent with their spoken language.

Teaching to Promote Motivation to Learn

In this chapter, we discuss the ways in which teachers can maintain and enhance children's initial enthusiasm for learning to read and write and help them to adopt beliefs that promote active and joyful engagement in literate activities. We discuss the following topics:

- Engaging children in reading and listening to interesting texts and discussing/reacting to them.
- Providing children with some choice in what they read and write.
- Developing intrinsic rather than extrinsic motivation for reading and writing. We want children to value literacy for its own sake rather than to view it as "work" for which they should be rewarded.
- Helping children develop a sense of competence and confidence in their literacy skills by:
  - Ensuring that the texts they encounter, particularly those they read and write, are not too challenging.
  - Helping them to develop effective approaches to solving problems they encounter with both word reading and comprehension.
  - Scaffolding their reading—providing just enough support to allow them to succeed but not so much support that they do not learn how to engage independently.
- Helping children to recognize their successes and attribute them to things that are under their control—such as the amount of effort they expend and the strategic problem solving they do—rather than to factors that are beyond their control.

Promoting Interest in Books

Teachers often identify "developing a love of reading" as one of their major instructional goals (Nolen, 2001). By this they likely mean that they want the children to love to read by themselves. Clearly, children are more likely to love reading if they love the texts that they read and hear and if they enjoy the interactions that occur around these texts. In the early primary grades (and before), reading aloud to children provides an important context for developing this love. Children who have had a lot of positive experiences with being read to prior to kindergarten are likely to already love being read to and will continue to enjoy and profit from it during the primary-grade years (and beyond). However, many children who experience difficulty with literacy learning in the primary grades have not had the hundreds (or thousands) of hours of book experience we would like them to have prior to kindergarten. Therefore, they may not yet know about the pleasure that books can provide. It will be especially helpful to engage these children in listening and reacting to books that are of particular interest to them. For example, teachers might make a point of choosing to read books on certain cultural traditions, certain animals, certain family dynamics, and so forth, because they know that those topics will be of particular interest to one or more of their students. Letting children know that a book was selected for them because of their particular interests will help them to understand that books can be special to them as individuals—a very motivating thought!

Web Resources

Several websites can assist teachers (and parents) as they endeavor to identify books that may appeal to the varied interests of young children. *Titlewave.com*, for example, allows searches based on major topics (e.g., animals, holidays, science, people) and subtopics (e.g., polar bears, Cinco de Mayo, habitats, U.S. presidents). Further, particular interest levels can be designated (e.g., kindergarten through third, fourth through sixth), as can reading levels as indicated by grade and month in school (e.g., a book at level 1.8 would be a book that an average child in the 8th month of first grade should be able to read fairly independently).[1] Other useful websites for searching for books by interest level include *Amazon.com, GlobalStorybooks.net, Readingrockets.org,* and *Scholastic.com*.

Interactive Read-Alouds

We discuss the value of interactive read-alouds in several of the upcoming chapters because they are valuable in many ways. In this chapter, we focus on the role of interactive read-alouds in promoting motivation to read and write. Books read during interactive read-alouds are often more challenging than books children would be able to read on their own, and the reader generally does not direct the children's attention to the print very much, if at all. When reading books with pictures, the reader does, of course, encourage the children to attend to the pictures to enhance both their understanding of the text and their aesthetic experience. What makes an interactive read-aloud *interactive* is that the children and the reader engage in conversation about the text and that the conversation is not entirely controlled or initiated by the proficient reader (generally the teacher—but members of the broader school community such as specialist teachers, administrators, and parents as well as the broader community are often happy to read as well). Ideally, in an interactive read-aloud, the children are free to offer their observations, ask and answer questions, make predictions, and generally react to the text. Readers also share their thinking and draw children's attention to various aspects of the text, depending on the purposes of reading a particular text.

   At the most obvious level, reading aloud to children helps to build motivation to read because listening to books that capture their imagination or offer information that interests them is just plain enjoyable for them. They get "hooked" and are apt to want to listen to more books on the same or similar topics, by the same author, or of the same genre. Reading aloud to children can also promote children's interest in composing their own texts, particularly when children are helped to notice and appreciate what authors and illustrators do in creating books. For example, while children often readily become involved in the storyline of a

---

[1]There are a number of ways in which books are "leveled" for readability, and the leveling systems generally do not totally agree with one another. We are not necessarily endorsing the leveling system utilized by any of the websites we cite.

fictional book, they are often surprised when, on occasion, the reader steps back a bit to help them think about the author's and illustrator's craft. For instance, the reader might point out how authors make the audience feel particular ways by the words that are used or by how illustrators convey information that is not made explicit by authors.

While teachers may, and typically should, have multiple reasons for selecting a particular book for an interactive read-aloud, developing a love of books and other texts should *always* be an important purpose. Thus, *the first encounter with a text in a read-aloud context should always be focused on stimulating enjoyment and comprehension of the text.* In the box entitled "Interactive Read-Alouds from a Motivational Perspective," we provide some suggestions for making interactive read-alouds fun and motivating experiences.

Interactive Read-Alouds from a Motivational Perspective

Be enthusiastic. The teacher should show enthusiasm for and interest in the reading materials in use.

Collaborate—don't test. Interactions concerning a text should have a collaborative tone. Teachers should avoid asking questions to which they clearly know the answer. There is no reason to ask such questions other than to "test" the children's understanding. (And, in some cultures, children will not answer questions when they know the adult already knows the answer.) Rather, teachers should offer their own thinking about the text and invite children to share theirs. Both the teacher and the children should ask genuine questions, and analyze, interpret, and react to the text. Teachers should avoid the use of evaluative language. For example, rather than asking whether a prediction about what would happen in the text was right or wrong, the teacher might ask how the children arrived at their prediction and then read to find out what the author decided to do.

Discuss the illustrations. The teacher should routinely provide opportunities for the children to enjoy and discuss the illustrations and to use the illustrations to inform their understanding of the text. For example, children might use an illustration to determine how a character was feeling (by considering the character's facial expression) or to infer what time of year the story takes place (by noticing what the characters are wearing or what the environment looks like). In an informational text, the children can be encouraged to attend to the illustrations to better understand the sequence of steps in a process or to assist in comparing characteristics.

Encourage personal reactions to the text. Encourage the children to discuss how they might have reacted and/or felt in a situation similar to that depicted in the text and/or what they found surprising or interesting about the information in the text. Teachers should also share their personal reactions (but should not dominate the conversation).

Edit or modify the text. Occasionally, rewrite a portion of the text in a way that the children suggest. For example, in the book *Alexander and the Horrible,*

Terrible, No Good Very Bad Day (Viorst, 1972), the students might add another incident that might occur on a bad day. Or, in an informational text about the life cycle of butterflies, the children might be assisted in finding additional illustrations or explanations of points in the metamorphosis.

Act out portions of the story. It is often fun for children to act out some or all aspects of a story they have heard. Such activities engage children in (sometimes passionate) discussions of the sequence of story events, which has many benefits for their language development and has the potential to support their ability to monitor their comprehension (did they miss something?). Reenactment may also encourage children to be more active in their meaning-making efforts by asking for the text to be reread and/or by being more attentive to monitoring their comprehension while listening to texts in the future. Providing a few props (e.g., items of clothing befitting the main characters) can be particularly motivating. Also, providing a copy of the text for children to reference as they plan their reenactment will help them to view books as valuable resources (Welsch, 2008). Acting out (dramatizing) also improves listening comprehension (Berenhaus, Oakhill, & Rusted, 2015).

Supported, Buddy, and/or Independent Reading

When children are doing the reading themselves, either with teacher guidance (supported reading), with a friend (buddy reading), or independently, attention to the motivational features of the experience is extremely important, as it is during these experiences that children develop their sense of themselves as readers. Regarding promoting interest in books, children, especially those with limited early exposure to books, need to be introduced to the wide variety of texts currently available to be read by beginning readers, and, once introduced, they need to be encouraged to notice which topics/authors/genres they find appealing. Owing to the emergence of various state learning standards, there has been much greater emphasis on including informational texts in young children's reading diet in recent years. With that emphasis has come an increase in the number of nonfiction texts that can be read by children who are learning to read. Motivationally, this shift may prove to be particularly beneficial for young boys who often demonstrate a stronger preference for reading informational texts than fictional offerings (McGeown, Osborne, Warhurst, Norgate, & Duncan, 2016).

Providing Choice in What Is Read

Providing children with choices about which books they read has been shown to have a large benefit in improving reading comprehension (Guthrie & Humenick, 2004; McBreen & Savage, 2021). As children become more familiar with various topics/authors/genres, they are likely to develop individual preferences, which, essentially, is part of developing an identity as a reader (Johnston, 2004). It is certainly not possible to offer children complete choice, especially in the context of small-group reading instruction, for which the teacher needs to plan book introductions and skill instruction that will prepare the children to read the books to be used during lessons. Nonetheless, there can be many opportunities for children to choose their reading materials at other points in the day.

Developing a Sense of Confidence and Competence

Several factors can influence the development of confidence and a sense of competence in young readers and in those who experience difficulty in gaining skill with written language. We discuss three particularly important factors in this section: keeping the challenge at a moderate level; helping children develop effective approaches to problem solving; and providing just enough support in problem-solving situations.

Moderate Degree of Challenge

As Schultheiss and Brunstein (2005) report, successful experiences lead to hopefulness and an inclination to seek further opportunities to solve similar problems, whereas repeated experiences with failure lead to expectations of further failure and therefore lead one away from engagement. This is one reason that RTI has the potential to be so powerful: In comparison to pre-RTI days, it encourages schools to organize instruction to meet students' needs sooner and in smaller instructional groupings. This, in turn, allows for greater individualization of instruction, and such individualization is likely to lead to greater gains by the children.

When children are frequently asked to read texts that are too difficult for them, they are likely to try to find ways to avoid the whole enterprise. They might, for example, try to engage the teacher and/or peers in conversation, or they might find multiple excuses to move around the classroom (to use the restroom, to sharpen a pencil, to get a drink of water, etc.) or indicate that they are tired and put their heads down on the table.

When the teacher sees behaviors such as these, an important question to consider is: "Am I asking this child to do something that, from the child's perspective, is too challenging?" If the answer is yes, or possibly yes, the teacher should consider ways to reduce the level of challenge, at least temporarily, in order to begin to build the child's confidence. In the context of reading, this might mean offering easier texts or making the texts more accessible by offering more support in preparing children to read a new text (see Preparing Children to Read a Specific Book, Chapter 12, pp. 333–335) and/or as the child encounters word identification challenges while reading (see Strategy Instruction during Reading, Chapter 12, pp. 337–340). In upcoming chapters, we revisit the issue of literacy-related challenges in various ways. For now, the "take-away message" is that the level of challenge that children encounter in literacy activities affects their sense of competence and their literacy motivation more generally.

Easy Reading

In my (JMS) reading room, in addition to books that are at an appropriate level for supported reading groups and that allow students the right amount of successful problem solving, I also have books available for my first graders that they can read independently. They enjoy going back to these books and reading them again and again. (This activity does not have to eat up a lot of time.) I think it's important for students to have these experiences with books in which they feel complete competence. They beam as they read these books. Video recording them and showing them the videos also provide feedback, which builds their confidence further and helps them to see themselves as readers. I think one of the benefits of this practice is that children in my reading room see peers in their classrooms who are reading without consciously employing strategies, and they recognize them as "good" readers. When the children experience reading texts without the need for conscious word solving, they, too, feel like "good" readers.

Developing Effective Approaches to Problem Solving

Instruction that focuses on developing word-identification strategies (as discussed in Chapter 12) can contribute to children's sense of competence[2] as readers because it gives them the tools to use in figuring out the unfamiliar words they encounter in text—which for many beginning and developing readers is one of the most challenging parts of the reading process. Here we address aspects of instructional and interpersonal interactions around word solving that can influence the child's willingness to engage in the process. This willingness (or motivation) is important because, if readers believe they can figure out the unfamiliar words they encounter, they are much more likely to expend the effort that it might take to do so.

For most individuals, a sense of competence develops through successful experiences with a particular activity and recognition of that success. As noted in Chapter 1 regarding word solving, we have found it useful to explicitly teach a small set of word-identification strategies (as discussed in detail in Chapter 12) and to provide the children with guidance and practice in using those strategies in interactive and confirmatory ways. This ultimately helps them become spontaneous and independent in the use of their problem-solving skills and to recognize their own ability. For example, the teacher might say to a beginning reader: "I saw you make that first sound and then read past that puzzling word to get a better idea of what word would make sense there. Then you went back and were able to figure out the

---

[2]A sense of competence is sometimes referred to as *self-efficacy*, which Bandura (1997) defines as learners' perceived capabilities for learning or performing actions at designated levels.

word. You are really thinking like a reader!" or "I see you checking your key-word chart to help you remember the sound of that letter! That's what readers do when they need to!" Both of these comments focus on the problem-solving process, provide readers with a vote of confidence in their word-solving skills, and, therefore, help them build a sense of competence.

In addition to explicit discussion of word-solving strategies, the way in which teachers and peers talk about and react to successes and difficulties with word solving can be very influential in shaping how learners think about the process and their own ability to engage in that process. For example, when a child encounters an unknown word in text and the teacher says, "Oh, that's a hard [tricky, challenging] word," it might lead some children to give up on solving the word. As an alternative, the teacher might use the term *puzzling* to describe the unknown word because it more clearly conveys the need to think about what the word might be and to use multiple sources of information to solve it.

The reactions of peers (and others, such as family members and other caregivers) to children's word-solving efforts can also influence their motivation and sense of competence. For example, when someone loses patience with a child's attempts at puzzling and does something that reflects that impatience, it is likely to diminish the child's sense of competence. Reactions that might undermine a child's confidence include providing the word (with an impatient tone of voice) or saying things like "You know that word!" or "You just read that word on the other page!" So too are comments such as "Who can help Alex?", which conveys the idea that, although Alex can't figure out a particular word, the teacher fully expects that other children can.

We encourage teachers to put word solving in a positive light by talking about how figuring out a word is a bit like doing a puzzle: You may need to think about several different things (e.g., the shape of the piece, the color of the piece, the larger picture into which the piece must fit) in order to figure out which piece fits just right. By emphasizing the pleasure of figuring something out, we can put word solving in an entirely different light. For example, when beginning and developing readers are reading in a small-group context in which they take turns reading different portions of a text, the "puzzling" analogy can help children who may become impatient while waiting for a peer to figure things out and those who may need a bit more time to puzzle through a word. We do not, of course, wish to suggest that word-solving assistance should never be provided. Indeed, providing thoughtful in-the-moment assistance with word solving is an important aspect of literacy instruction. However, the assistance offered should enhance children's word-solving strategies and their sense that they have the ability to puzzle through unfamiliar words successfully. For example, the teacher might ask: "What strategies have you tried already?" And/or "What could you try next?"

Providing Just Enough Support (Scaffolding Children's Reading)

Building a sense of competence for carrying out a complex process such as reading occurs over a protracted period of time and, for some children, requires a substantial amount of teacher guidance. The way in which the teacher provides guidance and the kind of guidance provided can make a difference. A teacher who is too directive may prevent children from engaging in the kind of problem-solving efforts that will build their ability to problem-solve independently and thereby may interfere with the children's ability to develop a sense of competence. On the other hand, a teacher who offers too little guidance may overwhelm children and frustrate their attempts to read; this too will interfere with their ability to develop a sense of competence. Thus, an early literacy teacher needs to do a bit of a balancing act to ensure that the support they offer is "just right."

To do so, teachers need insight into how children approach a task so that they can recognize the children's sources of confusion and help to effectively clear them up. For example, when a child misidentifies a word encountered while reading, the teacher is likely to recognize the error immediately—because the teacher already knows the word. The child, on the other hand, obviously does not already know the word and, therefore, may not realize that an error has occurred until reading further along in the sentence or paragraph. The teacher's response to individual children in such situations will influence the children's sense of competence and hence their motivation to persist. If the teacher jumps right in to correct the error before the context has clued the child in to the problem, the child's sense of competence can be undermined. If, however, the teacher provides the child with the time to notice and potentially correct the error, the child's sense of competence is likely to be enhanced. Tables 3.1 and 3.2 provide some examples to illustrate this point. We discuss the issue of trying to offer just the right amount of support in several places throughout this book. The point here is that appropriate scaffolding makes an important contribution to children's sense of competence.

TABLE 3.1. Sample Interactions Following a Word-Identification Error That _Will_ Promote a Sense of Competence in Reading

Teacher response	Child's possible interpretation
Waits until the child has read far enough along to realize that an error has occurred.	"I'm not sure about that word— but maybe I'll figure it out if I read a little further."
Notices when the child notices a word-identification error (e.g., "I hear you slowing down there—are you thinking that something is not quite right?").	"It's OK to slow down and think a bit when something doesn't seem right."
Notices when the child spontaneously corrects a word identification error and encourages the child to reflect on this success (e.g., "I noticed that you went back and changed that word. How did you know that that word was . . . ?").	"I know how to figure out words."
Subtly looks at the word-identification strategy chart (see Chapter 12) after the child has realized that a word-identification error has occurred.	"Oh right, I can use my strategies to figure that out!"

TABLE 3.2. Sample Interactions Following a Word Identification Error That *Will Not* Promote a Sense of Competence in Reading

Teacher response	Child's possible interpretation
Too much support: Identifies the error *before* the child has read far enough to realize that an error has occurred.	"I can't do this on my own" or "I need someone to tell me the words I don't know."
Too little support: Allows the child to keep reading, despite error(s).	"Guessing at the words seems to be OK with my teacher" or "All I have to do is say something and keep going—I'm not sure what I'm supposed to be doing here!"

Attributions for Success—and Mindsets

Early research focused on children's motivation to read indicated that children in the early primary grades tended to think of their abilities as changeable and under their control. They tended to believe that, if they put in enough effort, they could do just about anything (Chapman & Tunmer, 1995; Nicholls, 1978, 1990)—although children certainly wouldn't have put those beliefs in those terms. More recent research has focused on the influence of family members and teachers in the development of children's beliefs about themselves as learners. The work of Carol Dweck and colleagues (see Dweck, 2017) has been especially influential in this regard. They have identified two general types of beliefs that individuals may hold about their academic/intellectual abilities. These are referred to as *mindsets*. Some individuals tend to have a *fixed* mindset—they believe that their abilities are fixed or unchangeable. If such learners experience difficulty with literacy development, they may, for example, believe: "I'm not good at reading and I will never be." Students who hold a fixed belief may see little reason to expend the effort it might take to improve. Therefore, they are more apt to shy away from (avoid) learning challenges. Individuals characterized by a *growth* mindset, on the other hand, believe their abilities will grow and change—that their abilities are malleable. They believe that their current status, whatever it may be, is temporary. Those who hold this belief are more likely to maintain motivation in the face of difficulty (Niiya, Crocker, & Bartmess, 2004). They are, therefore, more likely to embrace learning challenges—and they tend to experience greater growth.

In researching the evolution of these two mindsets, Haimovitz and Dweck (2017) report that children's mindsets strongly influence their motivation and achievement. While most of the mindset research involving young children has focused on learning activities that can be more quickly completed (i.e., learning to solve a particular puzzle), there is a recent, very promising study focused on reading development among second-grade students. The children's parents (who were from a broad range of socioeconomic and language backgrounds) were taught how to promote a growth mindset among their children relative to reading (Andersen & Nielsen, 2016). Among other things, instruction for parents in the intervention condition involved helping them to understand that reading skills are malleable, that practice matters, and that greater growth is likely when the parent praises effort and process (e.g., what the child does to figure things out) rather than performance (e.g., reading accurately and quickly). In general, this and other studies contributed to Haimovitz and Dweck's (2017) conclusion that parents and teachers can influence the mindsets children adopt.

Encouraging Productive Beliefs about Students' Abilities

An important goal of early instruction and intervention for learners is to keep children from adopting beliefs about their abilities that are counterproductive. One way of doing so is to help children become stronger readers—which is the focus of much of this book. However, there are other ways to try to keep children from adopting a fixed view of their abilities. To this end, we encourage teachers to explain the roles of practice and effort and to help children reflect on their successes.

The Role of Practice and Effort

In general, the more reading a child does, the easier reading becomes. Although teachers clearly understand this principle, some children do not. Children who experience difficulty, particularly those who are frequently asked to read texts that are too challenging for them, can come to believe that reading will always be difficult for them—because it always has been. This is a very logical but unfortunate conclusion.

Several of the teachers with whom we have worked have found it useful to explain the practice–progress relationship through the use of analogies that illustrate how effort can make a task that seems very challenging eventually manageable and, ultimately, nearly effortless. For example, for a child who already knows how to ride a bike, a teacher might talk about how hard and frustrating it was to learn and how easy it is now. Alternatively, for children who have younger siblings, the teacher might talk about how difficult it is initially to learn to walk and/or talk and how easy it is for (most) children in kindergarten and first grade to do those things.

Attending to and Reflecting on Success

Although we certainly want children to be willing to expend the effort it will take to grow as readers, simply telling them to try harder is not likely to accomplish this goal. It has long been recognized that one of the most effective ways to elicit desired behaviors from children is to attend to desired behaviors. For example, when a group of kindergartners becomes too noisy during a read-aloud, one of the most effective ways to quiet them down is to notice the children who are engaged in the story in appropriate ways: "Odin and Fre'Asia are listening and thinking. . . ."

A similar tactic can be used in supporting individuals concerning word solving or comprehension monitoring: "You went back and reread that when it wasn't making sense to you. That worked, didn't it?" Particularly when children are first learning to be strategic readers, noticing and naming their productive attempts at problem solving reinforces those strategies. Further, children can be encouraged to attend to and reflect on their own successes initially by asking them to explain how they solved particular problems ("How did you know that word was . . . ?") and later by asking them to identify and reflect on instances when they were effective problem solvers. Engaging in discussions of their problem-solving attempts and successes contributes to their growth as self-regulated learners.

Goal Orientation: Intrinsic versus Extrinsic Motivation

Children who are intrinsically motivated want to do/learn/participate in something because it is interesting and valuable to them. On the other hand, children who are extrinsically motivated engage in activities for the sake of earning social rewards, such as praise or recognition, or physical rewards, such as stickers or some form of token that can be traded for a desired commodity (free time, reduction in homework, etc.). In a very simplified form, a summary of the research on extrinsic versus intrinsic motivation suggests that children who are intrinsically motivated to learn are more likely to succeed at challenging academic tasks (see Schunk, Pintrich, & Meece, 2008), whereas students who need to be extrinsically motivated to engage in academically challenging tasks tend to have poorer academic outcomes.

Although students can be both intrinsically and extrinsically motivated, schools tend to be organized around extrinsic motivation systems—grades, rewards, and praise—so many students tend to focus on the external reward. Because research suggests that intrinsic motivation leads to greater long-term learning, the motivational systems that characterize schools need to be carefully considered. McKenna et al. (1995) documented a general decline in motivation for reading among children as they progressed through the elementary years. This decline could well be related to the extrinsic motivational systems that characterize many schools.

Many of the suggestions made earlier in this chapter will help to promote the development of intrinsic motivation among early learners. In addition, we encourage teachers to:

• *Treat reading and writing as a privilege (not as work).* When teachers treat reading and writing as jobs that must be accomplished or completed in order to gain access to other activities (e.g., recess or free-choice time in the classroom), children, especially those who have difficulty with literacy acquisition, are likely to view reading and writing as work. If, on the other hand, teachers convey the idea that reading and writing are pleasurable activities that are valuable in their own right, children are more apt to adopt such a perspective. Think, for a moment, about what we convey to children when we say, "Let's get our (reading or writing) work done so that we can have free time." One translation of this is, "Let's get this unpleasant (reading or writing) work done so that we can have the reward of not having to read or write anymore!" Such a message is clearly not intended. Minor changes in wording can dramatically alter the interpretation of a statement or request. Table 3.3 provides some suggestions for rephrasing that will send very different motivational messages.

• *Avoid social comparisons and encourage personal comparisons.* Because children begin their school careers at very different points in literacy development, progress and achievement for each child need to be evaluated using different metrics. For example, a child who begins kindergarten knowing the names of all the letters of the alphabet is not necessarily a better student than one who knows few letters at the beginning of the school year but learns several during the first few weeks or months of school. Children who begin school with very limited early literacy skills are apt to begin to view themselves as inadequate early on. This self-perception of inadequacy can ultimately lead children to adopt fixed mindsets in which they perceive themselves as being unable to perform at a level commensurate with their peers. As noted above, such a perception is likely to limit the children's willingness to exert the effort needed to grow and develop in literacy. On the other hand, if the same children are given the opportunity to evaluate their performance relative to their previous levels, there is a greater likelihood that they will experience the motivating feelings that come with advancing skills and accomplishments. Furthermore, children who receive effective and responsive intervention are likely to experience rapid gains.

• *Use feedback judiciously to encourage intrinsic motivation and a mastery orientation.* What teachers say to children matters tremendously and can have a

TABLE 3.3. Unmotivating and Motivating Messages Teachers Might Send

Unmotivating messages	Motivating messages
"We need to read this book today before recess."	"We *get* to read this book today before recess."
"You need to practice these letters you don't know."	"You need to practice these letters you don't know *yet*."
"I want to see what you are going to write next. You need to finish your journal entry before you go to the block area."	"I can't wait to see what you are going to write next. I hope you *get* to finish your journal entry before it's time to change stations."
"Let's see how many of these letters you know."	"Let's see how many of these letters you *already* know."
"Each of you will do a report on dinosaurs."	"You will *get* to do a report on a dinosaur that you are especially interested in."
"That's a hard word."	"That's a *puzzling* word."

significant impact on how children view themselves as learners. Teachers can convey the notion that academic engagement and performance are primarily for the purpose of pleasing the teacher ("What a good job" or "I like the way you . . .") or gaining social recognition ("You're so smart!")—both of which are, essentially, forms of extrinsic motivation. On the other hand, teachers can convey the idea that learning and performance are rewarding in their own right ("What an interesting thought!" or "I bet it felt great to figure that out!"). Such responses to student thinking help to promote the development of intrinsic motivation.

Changes in Teachers' Language

In our work with both beginning and experienced teachers, we have sometimes been surprised by how challenging it is for some to change their language in the ways suggested above (including in Table 3.3), but we certainly understand why such a change is challenging. We are essentially encouraging people to change highly practiced ways of interacting. That said, most teachers who make the suggested changes report that they do see the impact on children's motivation. For example, the simple addition of the word *already* when a teacher sits with a child to do an assessment (e.g., "I want to see how many of these words you *already* know") changes the situation from one in which children may feel that the focus is on what they can't do, particularly those who may not *yet* be meeting grade-level expectations, to one in which they get to show off what they *already* know. As another example, the inclusion of the word *yet* (e.g., "We haven't learned how to do this *yet*") contributes to motivation and growth mindsets by conveying the teacher's belief that the children *will* learn and communicates that children's abilities are malleable. Teachers report that recording themselves teaching and listening to those recordings helps them to attend to their language choices and work toward making the suggested changes.

Family Members and Caregivers and Motivation

As noted above, family members and caregivers play important roles in children's literacy development, and their role regarding motivation can be especially prominent. Although a thorough discussion of their roles in children's literacy development is beyond the scope of this book, we developed a free resource to inform family members'/caregivers' efforts to support children's literacy learning and academic development more generally. The resource is a booklet entitled *Helping Your Child Become a Reader* (Scanlon, Anderson, Barnes, Morse, & Yurkewecz, 2024). It comprises 22 questions that are frequently asked by those who are attempting to support the literacy development of beginning readers and developing readers, along with answers to those questions. The answers are research-based and are intended to be accessible to family members and caregivers.

The booklet can be printed in its entirety or by individual question. The latter option was recommended by teachers who felt that family members and/or caregivers might not read the entire booklet but would read individual questions, particularly if they were responsive to the individual's questions or a teacher's concern about a child's literacy experiences at home. The booklet can be accessed at *eltep. org/isa-parent-booklet.*

KEY POINTS OF THIS CHAPTER

✓ Early difficulties with reading can have long-term impacts on reading motivation and comprehension—early intervention is key.

✓ The primary grades are an important time when children begin to develop beliefs about themselves as readers and writers.

✓ Children's interest in specific book and writing topics is an important motivator.

✓ A sense of competence and confidence is motivating. This can be promoted by:
  - Controlling the degree of challenge children encounter.
  - Helping children develop effective approaches and utilize strategies to puzzle through reading and writing challenges.
  - Scaffolding learning—providing enough support to allow success but not so much that children don't learn how to engage independently.

✓ Helping children develop a growth mindset can lead to greater long-term academic success.

✓ Intrinsic rather than extrinsic motivation should be promoted.

✓ Helping children understand the benefits of practice and effort in relation to progress is important.

✓ Making subtle changes in teacher language can influence children's thinking about themselves as learners.

PART II

Understanding Print and the English (Alphabetic) Writing System

Introduction to Part II

The ability to accurately and automatically read the words in printed text enables readers to devote most of their cognitive resources to the process of meaning construction. Proficient readers of English can read tens of thousands of different words effortlessly. The vast majority of these words are not explicitly taught but, instead, are learned by effectively puzzling through and identifying unfamiliar words encountered while reading. For beginning readers and those who experience reading difficulties, multiple accurate identifications of previously unfamiliar words may be required for a word to become part of the reader's *sight vocabulary* (words that can be identified automatically and effortlessly on sight). Skill with the writing system is an important, but certainly not the only, contributor to the ability to puzzle through and identify unfamiliar written words. But it is an aspect of literacy development that frequently lags behind for students who experience literacy learning difficulties (Castles et al., 2018; National Reading Panel, 2000; Snow et al., 1998; Vellutino et al., 2004) and therefore needs to be a strong and coherent focus of early literacy instruction.

The process of learning to read words at sight has been termed *orthographic mapping* (OM). According to Ehri (2014), OM "involves the formation of letter–sound connections to bond the spellings, pronunciations, and meanings of specific words in memory. It explains how children learn to read words by sight, to spell words from memory, and to acquire vocabulary words from print" (p. 5). In Part

II we focus on how to help children develop the knowledge and skills that enable them to engage in orthographic mapping.

Much of the literacy field's current understanding about the process of sight word learning has been influenced by more than 40 years of research conducted by Ehri and colleagues, and her *phase theory* of word learning which evolved during that work. The theory describes five phases that characterize the development of approaches to word identification and word learning:

• *Prealphabetic:* In the first phase of development, readers use cues rather than letters or words to "read." Often called emergent or pretend reading, this phase involves the use of visual cues such as illustrations as well as familiarity with the text derived from having previously heard the text read aloud to formulate the story. Learners may also identify individual written words by relying on the overall visual form of the words, but they do not focus on individual letters or their associated sounds. For example, they may rely on the overall shape of words—features that would not help them to distinguish many words from one another. They might, for instance, rely on the two l's in the middle of *yellow* to identify the word. This approach to word identification is also referred to as *selective cue* use.

• *Partial (early) alphabetic:* Readers in this phase use partial or incomplete knowledge of letters and their sounds to puzzle through and attempt to identify printed words. Readers may attempt a word after identifying prominent letters (first and/or last, typically). Readers in this phase are not yet using all available alphabetic information to identify unknown words. The context in which a word appears, in this and the prior phase, can enable accurate word identification despite only partial (or almost no) alphabetically based analysis.

• *Full (later) alphabetic:* Readers in this phase have relatively complete alphabetic knowledge and are able to use grapheme–phoneme relationships in conjunction with contextual information to identify and confirm the identity of printed words that are initially unfamiliar to them. Reading in this phase is typically slow and requires substantial effort as readers tend to have relatively small numbers of words that they can identify automatically and are not yet fluent with using grapheme–phoneme relationships for the purpose of word identification.

• *Consolidated alphabetic:* This is the last phase before a reader is considered to be in the automatic (fluent) phase. Readers in this phase tend to rely less on individual grapheme–phoneme relations and instead rely on larger orthographic "chunks" of print (syllables, prefixes and suffixes, rimes, and whole words). Readers may use analogy to recognize common patterns in words (e.g., using knowledge of the word *little* to identify the word *brittle)*. They use these various orthographic patterns to read words they have not seen before. The size of readers' sight word vocabularies grows substantially during this phase.

• *Automatic phase:* The reader is largely fluent with identifying words and becomes more automatic with increased practice and exposure to diverse texts. Readers are considered "conventional."

> ### Rime
>
> A *rime* is a part of a syllable—it includes the vowel and any consonants that follow it in the syllable. The word *hop* has one rime (*op*), *turning* has two rimes (*urn* and *ing*), and entertain has three rimes (*en, er,* and *ain*).

Ehri's use of the term *phase* (rather than stage) is important here as the theory is that changes in the ways learners attempt to identify and/or spell unfamiliar words tend to be gradual and their attempts at unknown words may reflect characteristics of different phases at a given point in time.

Ehri's depiction of how learners' control over alphabetic and orthographic processing changes over time is a useful guide for how our expectations of children's word solving, reading, and spelling efforts would change as a result of instruction and with regard to the focus of instruction for children whose reading and spelling attempts suggest that they are, primarily, functioning at a particular phase. In the ISA's description of the developmental process, we emphasize the use of alphabetic and orthographic information as described in Ehri's theory. As in Ehri's model, the ISA emphasizes the importance of alphabetic and orthographic information in the development of sight vocabulary. Additionally, we emphasize a more complex array of influences. (Consider all the elements in the Conceptual Model as depicted in Figure 1.2 [p. 12]—reflect on all the double-headed arrows connected to the word solving/word learning node in the model.)

Our position is that, when reading continuous (meaningful) text, OM requires that the learner attend to multiple sources of information (the graphemes, their sounds, phonemic information, word meanings, the context in which a word occurs, etc.) and that learners at earlier phases of development are apt to be more reliant on word meanings and context to support partial OM because they are not *yet* able to fully decode unknown words.

> ### Terminology
>
> **Alphabetic processing**—the use of individual graphemes to arrive at the pronunciation of an unfamiliar printed word.
>
> **Orthographic processing**—the use of familiar letter patterns to arrive at the pronunciation and spelling of initially unfamiliar words.
>
> These terms are sometimes used together, as deciphering an unfamiliar word may involve both types of processing. For example, in attempting to identify the unfamiliar word *bring,* a reader might rely on the familiar *ing* rime but may need to process the individual sounds for the letters *b* and *r* if *br* was not yet a familiar orthographic pattern.

In Part II of this book, we discuss some of the critical understandings and skills that readers need to develop in order to learn to read and write in English. In

Figure II.1, we provide a schematic representation of the progression from earlier to later development of skill with the English writing system. In this representation, we focus primarily on the written form of words (related to the ability to name and spell written words for which at least a basic understanding of their meaning is assumed).[1] The model also includes the chapter numbers in which we address the different components of the model.

All components of the model are supported by and facilitate engagement in reading and writing. That engagement is supported by, and helps to promote, foundational understandings of how the English writing system works—as depicted by the banner running across the bottom of Figure II.1. On the far left of the figure, phonemic awareness and letter identification (letter–name knowledge) are identified as starting points for the developmental sequence. Instructionally, these two skill areas serve mutually supportive roles as students develop some familiarity with each. As depicted by the arrows connecting the boxes, engagement in reading and writing (at this early point, shared reading and writing activities) can help children become phonemically aware, learn the names of printed letters, and simultaneously learn that the purpose of print is to communicate and that there are conventional ways that print is used and organized (e.g., it is written from left to right; words are separated by spaces). The processes are mutually supportive and iterative—so much so that it is hard to depict graphically. Descriptively, as an example, consider what happens when a child learns the names of some letters. Knowing those letter names influences how children will experience (shared) reading of a simple text. They will recognize symbols (letters) for which they know the names, and knowing the names of a few symbols may lead them to attend differently to other symbols in the text that look similar to (or different from) those they know. This may, in turn, prepare them to learn the names of the as yet unknown letters. At another level, knowing the names of a few letters may enable learners to analyze the phonemes in the letters' names, which, for many letters, will provide preliminary information about the letters' sounds. (For example, the name of the letter f [/ef/] includes the sound associated with the letter.) This, in turn, might influence their writing attempts. The basic idea is that learning about individual aspects of the writing system influences learning about multiple other aspects in reciprocal and mutually reinforcing (and facilitating) ways.

---

[1] Nonsense words/pseudowords (e.g., *kip, bem*) have become an all-too-common and time-consuming focus of instruction in some settings in recent years. This focus is, in our opinion, unfortunate as it has the potential to interfere with efforts to build students' sight vocabularies—because they are not seeing words that they will actually encounter when reading meaningful text. We suspect that this practice has emerged because children are often assessed on their ability to read nonsense words. To our knowledge, the developers of such assessments did not intend for children to be explicitly taught to read nonsense words. Rather, the intent of the assessments was to determine what a child would likely be able to do when encountering an unfamiliar *real* word. We do see utility in using nonsense words for assessing skill with the alphabetic code—which, in turn, provides insight into children's likely ability to use that skill in the process of attempting to identify unfamiliar words encountered while reading meaningful text.

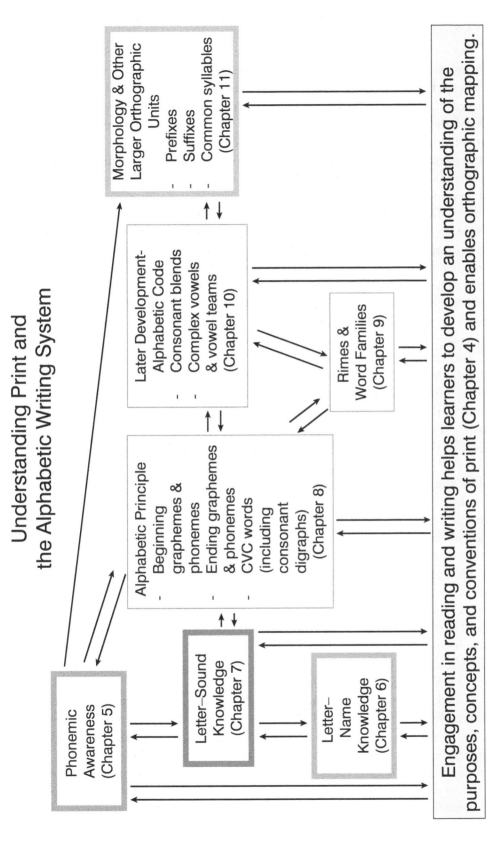

FIGURE II.1. Developmental progression in learning about print and the alphabetic code.

Once children know the names of some letters and are somewhat phonemically aware (e.g., they can at least isolate the beginning sounds in spoken words), they begin to learn about the relations between printed letters and the sounds they represent. Learning about letters' sounds extends children's phonemic awareness and enhances their learning as they engage in reading and writing, particularly shared reading and writing at early points in development. Reading and writing, in turn, extend children's knowledge of letter–sound relationships. Thus, the multiple experiences that children have with printed language become mutually supportive and reciprocal in nature.

Over time, skill with phonemic analysis and the development of letter–sound knowledge help children understand the *alphabetic principle*—the idea that the letters (graphemes) in printed words represent the sounds (phonemes) in spoken words. Understanding this principle allows children to learn about the workings of the alphabetic code. Early on, instruction typically focuses children's attention on the beginning letters and sounds in one-syllable words. In some programs, early focus is on words consisting of a beginning consonant, a vowel letter representing a short-vowel sound, and an ending consonant. These are often described as CVC (i.e., consonant–vowel–consonant) words. Some instructional approaches employ orthographic word families instead. Word families involve *rimes*.

Once children understand how to attend to and manipulate the letters and sounds at the beginnings of words, typically they next learn to attend to and use letters and their sounds at the ends of word. While going from the beginning to the middle to the end might seem logical, graphemes and phonemes at the beginning and end of words are easier to attend to than those in the middle, partly because middle vowel sounds can be influenced by the sounds that come before and/or after them. Ultimately, in order to have a useful understanding of the alphabetic principle, children need to be able to decode (read) and encode (spell) words composed of three phonemes (CVC words). This ability represents an early point in Ehri's full alphabetic phase.

To apply this developing knowledge in the process of reading meaningful text, readers also need to be able to identify at least a few frequently occurring printed words that cannot be identified solely by thinking about/analyzing their letters and sounds (e.g., *the* and *is*). While learning such words is not addressed in Figure II.1, which focuses on skill with the alphabetic code, such learning is important and is discussed in Part III of this text.

With knowledge of a few high-frequency words and early code-based skills established, engagement in appropriately challenging reading and writing opportunities helps to further extend children's understanding of, and skill with, the writing system. Eventually, children come to recognize and make productive use of rimes (e.g., *op, ight, oat*), which are at the center of word families (*hop, drop, stop; light, night, bright; coat, boat, float*). Depending in part on the instruction they receive, children may learn about rimes and word families through explicit instruction, or they may learn about them via their reading experience (during the consolidated alphabetic phase). In the depictions of the two possible pathways to the ability to learn to use orthographic word families (which are not mutually exclusive), we have positioned the rime/word family "box" in an intermediate position in Figure II.1.

Appropriately Challenging Text

Our definition of *appropriately challenging text:* text that is at or slightly beyond what readers can handle independently—that is, text that, with a bit of preparation (pre-teaching), children would likely be able to read fairly comfortably/confidently.

As children progress, they learn more details about the workings of the writing system, including how to decode and encode words with vowel teams (two or more letters that represent one phoneme) and consonant digraphs and trigraphs and consonant clusters. This additional knowledge enables learners to more effectively read and spell previously unfamiliar words. At this point, children would be functioning within Ehri's full alphabetic phase. Again, all of these relationships as depicted in the figure are reciprocal in nature; growth in one area stimulates growth in other areas (reflect back on all of the bidirectional arrows in Figure II.1, p. 93). To a great extent, what is learned in relation to these more advanced aspects of the code is dependent on the instructional materials in use, including the reading materials that learners encounter and, especially for readers who experience difficulty, on the instruction they receive.

Terminology

Consonant cluster—two or three consonant graphemes together in which the sound of each component grapheme is at least somewhat distinguishable (e.g., *bl, fr, str, thr*). These letter strings are sometimes referred to as blends. In this text we use the term *cluster* for the written form and *blend* for the spoken form.

Digraph—two letters that together represent one phoneme (e.g., *ch, ff, ck*)

Trigraph—three letters that together represent one phoneme (e.g., *sch* [when pronounced as /sh/], *tch*)

Readers in the full alphabetic phase learn more of the complexities of the English writing system. The complexities here revolve mostly around vowels—particularly vowel teams (e.g., *ea, oi, ew, igh*). These tend to present some of the greatest challenges for learners because the pronunciations of many vowel teams are not entirely consistent across words. Consider, for example, the pronunciation of the *ey* team in *they* and *key* or the *ai* in *rain, said,* and *mountain*. This is also true of the spelling for many vowel phonemes—for example, the spelling of the short-*e* sound in *bed, head,* and *said*. Engagement in extensive amounts of reading of a variety of texts, coupled with explicit instruction related to the more consistent spelling–sound patterns as needed, enables learners to build their repertoire of word reading skills through a process that Seidenberg (2017) refers to as *statistical learning*. The basic idea is that engagement in reading provides the learner with the opportunity to encounter a wide variety of spelling patterns. The more frequently given patterns are encountered and decoded accurately, the more fluent the learner becomes with those patterns. This, in turn, enables the reader to more readily identify unfamiliar printed words that include familiar patterns.

Statistical Learning

Statistics involve probabilities. Spoken and written languages are governed by probabilities. For example, it is much more probable that the words *to, want, I* will occur in the sequence *I want to* than *want I to* or *to want I*. As learners develop their spoken language, acceptable sequences for all of the words that are acquired are not explicitly taught but, rather, are learned implicitly through engagement in hearing (and using) language.

Statistical learning accounts for many aspects of cognitive development. While learners are certainly not consciously aware of the statistics per se, they govern most types of learning—including spoken and written language development. Proficient readers of English, for example, will readily recognize that doubled consonants are not permissible at the beginning of words (with the exception of *llama*) but do occur at the ends of words—for some consonants. This information is generally not specifically taught but is acquired via experience with thousands of written words. A major implication here is that the more one reads, the more one learns about written language.

With continued experience, learners begin to recognize and use larger orthographic patterns such as syllables, prefixes, and suffixes. Ehri refers to this phase as the consolidated phase. Children in this phase benefit from learning about other aspects of written language, such as English morphology, which helps learners understand that words are often composed of more than one meaningful part (e.g., prefixes and suffixes that modify the meaning of the base word). While learning about morphology is, to a great extent, related to understanding word meanings, recognizing the orthographic representation of these meaning components will enable readers to more readily identify unfamiliar written words. With continued engagement in reading and writing (and the additional guidance needed by some) learners will also come to recognize other larger orthographic units such as frequently occurring syllables (e.g., *ple, tion*). Recognizing these larger "chunks" helps children identify unfamiliar words more effectively and efficiently. As a result, children are likely to read and write more and build their sight vocabularies more quickly. This larger sight vocabulary, in turn, allows learners to read even more effectively and efficiently, which leads to gains in language skills and world knowledge, and, again, to more improvements in overall reading ability and the ability to devote more attention to comprehending the texts read rather than having to spend a lot of cognitive energy on identifying individual words. The ultimate goal, of course, is to give learners the ability to read nearly all of the words they encounter automatically and effortlessly (Ehri's automatic phase). While many children will not likely attain this phase during the primary grades, instruction and reading experience during this period will lay the foundation for long-term success.

The overarching purpose of Part II of this book is to help teachers understand the developmental progression in learning about the English writing system and to learn how to teach responsively to support children's progress. We focus only minimally on the meaning construction/comprehension aspect of literacy development in Part II, which we will take up in later portions of the book. However, it is important to emphasize that, if children do not have sufficient opportunity to apply what they are learning about how to use graphemes and their associated phonemes (the writing system) in the context of reading and writing meaningful text, they are not likely to accrue the benefits of learning about the workings of the writing system. Ideally, as we discuss throughout this text, from early on, children should be involved in reading and writing meaningful text multiple times and across multiple contexts in a given school day. We encourage explicitly teaching skills that children need for reading and writing, but they need to engage in reading and writing to grow their literate abilities.

The Alphabetic Writing System and Response to Intervention

Most young children who qualify for a response to intervention (RTI) process in relation to written language demonstrate limitations in the skills that are the focus of this section of the book. Many will need greater guidance in developing these skills than will children who learn to read and write with relative ease. In fact, research consistently demonstrates that the development of phonemic analysis and phonics skills is a major stumbling block for children who make limited progress in early literacy development. These findings were summarized by Adams in 1990 and more recently by Snow et al. (1998), the National Reading Panel (2000), Pressley et al. (2023) and Fletcher, Savage, and Vaughn (2021). Further, there is substantial evidence, including findings from our own studies (Scanlon et al., 2005, 2008; Vellutino et al., 1996), that children who qualify for intervention services benefit from expert and responsive instruction that helps them to build these foundational skills.

However, as implementation of RTI procedures has become a common practice, particularly in the primary grades, we have become aware that schools sometimes adopt highly manualized and scripted intervention programs to address children's needs related to the writing system (Scanlon, Anderson, & Goatley, 2015) and that teachers are often directed to deliver these programs *with fidelity* (which essentially means sticking to the script). While published programs can certainly provide useful structure, we caution against implementation of instruction that is not responsive to what students know and are able to do.

Concerns

While there is no question that proficient readers ultimately come to recognize a variety of orthographic patterns, there is reason to question how many/which patterns need to be/should be explicitly taught. Remarkably, little research speaks to this issue. We are inclined to agree with Seidenberg's (2017) statistical learning perspective that literacy learners come to recognize/identify most orthographic patterns based on extensive reading experience. From this perspective, as Figure II.1 illustrates, engagement in reading and writing is the primary driver of literacy development.

Yet another trend, in some settings, is for instruction in foundational reading skills to consist exclusively of whole-class instruction—including instruction for students who qualify for and/or are receiving intervention. We view this trend as highly problematic as most primary-grade classrooms are composed of students who are at a variety of points along the literacy development continuum. Whole-class implementation of published phonemic awareness and phonics programs can result in valuable instructional time being lost by teaching some children things they already know while attempting to teach other children things they are not yet ready to learn (McKay & Teale, 2015).

As we noted previously, in our view, instruction focused on teaching foundational skills, such as phonemic analysis and phonics, and on engaging children in reading meaningful text is more effective in moving all children forward when it is provided in small-group contexts and is responsive to children's current reading and phonics skills. Other aspects of literacy instruction (such as interactive read-alouds, writing, and language development activities) can certainly be provided in whole-class settings.

If supplemental programs are adopted for children who are at any tier in an RTI process, as noted in Chapter 2, one important principle of the approach we advocate is that the instruction offered be closely congruent with the instruction they experience in the general classroom. Thus, if schools are considering the adoption of supplementary phonemic awareness and/or phonics programs, we encourage them to examine the alignment with their core instruction to ensure that implementation of multiple programs does not require learners to learn conflicting information in the two contexts. For example, the key words used to help learners remember letter–sound relationships should be the same across settings, and the terminology used to refer to important concepts should be the same. We have long known that coherent instruction is likely to improve literacy learning outcomes (e.g., Allington & Johnston, 1989; Mosenthal et al., 2004; Wonder-McDowell et al., 2011). Moreover, as noted, it is important to ensure that supplemental instruction is responsive to what the children know and are able to do and that the children understand the utility and application of what they are learning to authentic reading and writing.

Part II of this book focuses on helping teachers to become highly knowledgeable about the developmental course of phonemic awareness and phonics skills, as well as other elements of the writing system. This knowledge will enable them to effectively identify what their students are ready to learn and how the various component skills might be most effectively taught in isolation and, ultimately, applied in context.

How Much Is Enough/Too Much?

Greater consensus has developed around the need to provide explicit instruction in phonemic analysis and phonics skills for beginning readers and older readers who have yet to attain expected levels with foundational skills. As a result, many school districts have turned to highly detailed and scripted programs to address these instructional needs. However, present research (e.g., Clemens et al., 2021; Fletcher et al., 2021) does not support the level of detail children are expected to learn about phonology and the writing system, and about the time allocated to relatively isolated and scripted phonological and phonics activities in some of these programs.

Whether phonemic awareness and/or phonics approaches are used in the regular classroom or in intervention settings, they should:

- Allow for differentiated, small-group instruction that is targeted and responsive to the specific needs of students in the group. Because some sort of arrangement for grouping students for instruction is typically needed in order to provide responsive instruction, it is important that the groups be considered flexible and be rearranged when it appears that not all children within given groups are ready for the same instructional foci.
- Teach to promote skill with the most important and useful aspects of the sound system (i.e., phonemic analysis) and the writing system (i.e., phonics), while avoiding details that even the most highly literate adults don't know.
- Take up a limited amount of instructional time, allowing for application of the skills being taught through the reading and writing of meaningful text.

We encourage teachers to provide direct and explicit instruction on foundational phonemic analysis and phonics skills—for the children who need such instruction. With regard to learning about the workings of the written language system, they also need to acknowledge that some children need much more explicit, intentional, and sustained instruction than do others. A given primary-grade classroom is likely to reflect wide variation in what the children know and are able to do as well as how quickly they learn about the things they don't yet know.

Support for Decision Making around Instructional Foci

To assist in the decision-making process involved in planning instruction related to understanding print and the English writing system for individuals and/or groups of children, Figure II.2 provides a decision tree with page references that point to relevant portions of this text. The goal is that, as teachers plan instruction for

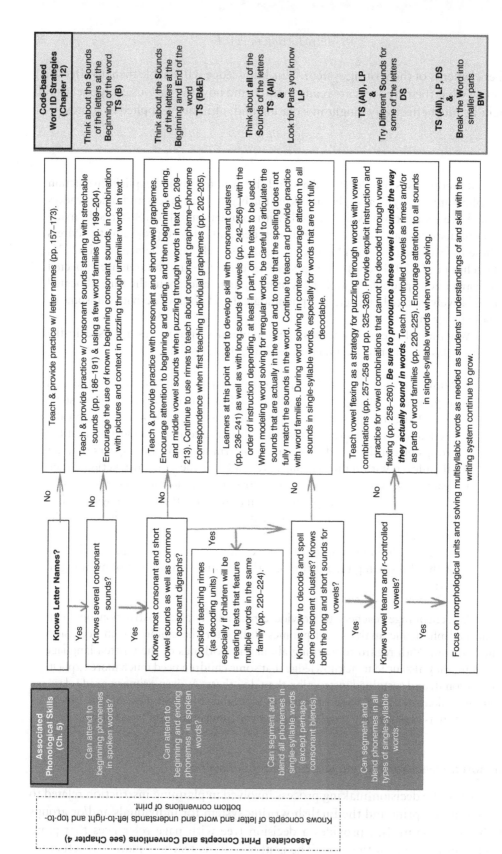

FIGURE II.2. Decision tree providing guidance for the focus of instruction on alphabetic skills.

children at various points along the developmental continuum, they can quickly reference applicable segments of this text.

This decision tree represents our effort to connect several aspects of the word-solving/word-identification process and, especially, to provide some detail/guidance about how skill with the alphabetic code progresses. The figure illustrates the development of skill with the writing system while also clarifying that such development occurs in conjunction with, and is enabled and reinforced by, the development of print concepts and conventions, skill with phonemic analysis, and use of code-based word-identification strategies.[2] We do not explicitly include meaning-based aspects of the word-solving process in the decision tree because our primary focus, for the moment, is on development of skill with the alphabetic and orthographic aspects of the writing system.

When first encountered, Figure II.2 likely looks a bit overwhelming. This is understandable. Reading and writing truly are complex processes, and we have tried to capture that complexity. We strongly encourage readers to return to this figure throughout their reading of Parts II and III. Our hope is that, after reading the chapters referenced in the figure, reflecting on this figure will feel much less overwhelming and will be helpful in the process of decision making regarding grouping and instructional planning for young learners.

We have organized our discussion of the decision tree around the central (unshaded) portion of the figure. This part is intended to support decision making in relation to which aspects of the writing system to focus on in instruction, based on students' current abilities. (We provide suggestions for assessing/evaluating students' skills in the chapters that follow.) The question at the top of the tree—"Knows Letter Names?"—deals with a fairly limited/constrained skill that has clear instructional implications, depending on whether the answer is "yes" or "no." This is also true for the other questions in the tree, although, of course, often the answer is not an unequivocal "yes" or "no." For example, students could know some, most, or nearly all the letters' names, in which case instruction would need to continue to focus on the names of letters yet to be learned. But instruction would also begin to address skills at the next point in the decision tree for the letters whose names are already known. Thus, to a certain extent, particularly at early points in literacy development, the decision-making process might be considered to be item-based. For example, when students know the names for a few letters at a fairly automatic level, teachers might begin to focus on the sounds associated with those letters while continuing to teach the names of letters that are not yet known.

To the right of the decision tree, we provide guidance with regard to expectations for students' use of code-based word-identification strategies while puzzling through unfamiliar words encountered while reading meaningful text. Our purpose is to illustrate how those expectations would change as students' skills

---

[2] Guidance related to instruction on both code- and meaning-based strategies is provided in Chapter 12.

with the alphabetic code increase (progressing down the tree). In our experience, students don't necessarily automatically apply, or know how to apply, the phonics skills that are taught in isolation. Explicit instruction in how these skills support word identification in context is important for many students. (Word-identification strategies are discussed in detail in Chapter 12.)

To the left of the decision tree, we present foundational skills and understandings (phonemic awareness and knowledge of print concepts and conventions) that are critical to the development of skill with the writing system but are not necessarily specifically related to the "steps" addressed in the decision tree itself. For example, some children become fairly phonemically aware while having only limited knowledge of printed language. However, for those who need explicit instruction to assist them in becoming phonemically aware, it is important to address the development of the skills listed in the phonological skills column before or while addressing specific alphabetic skills. Other than learning letter names, all other aspects of learning about the code require specific types of phonemic analysis skill.

With regard to print concepts and conventions (the far-left box in Figure II.2), again development occurs over a protracted period. There are both discrete skills that typically develop fully and early (e.g., knowing that print is processed from left to right) and skills related to print conventions that develop over a much longer period (e.g., details about punctuation). In this text, we do not focus explicitly on the development of more advanced knowledge of print conventions such as the use of colons and semicolons. But for children in the primary grades, particularly the early primary grades, foundational print concepts such as that print is organized from left to right and concepts such as what letters and words are must be established in order for functional use of the alphabetic code to develop.

In the chapters that follow, we discuss the progression through each step depicted in Figure II.2 in some detail. However, as we become immersed in the details of each process, it is important to keep in mind how all the processes fit together. They are intricately related and mutually supportive, and they are important only to the extent that they support the development of meaningful reading and writing. It is very easy for teachers, whether they teach beginning readers and writers or older children who are experiencing difficulty, to focus primarily or almost exclusively on these foundational processes, possibly losing sight of the goal—to help children understand the texts they read and to be able to write meaningful texts themselves. We cannot sufficiently underscore the need to focus on two pivotal goals: (1) reading and writing for developing and conveying meaning, and (2) the development of a love of literacy as a life-long endeavor. Because this book necessarily devotes considerable attention to foundational processes, we implore our readers to not lose sight of the desired outcome: children who read and write for understanding, learning, and enjoyment.

CHAPTER 4

Purposes, Concepts, and Conventions of Print

WRITING SYSTEM FOUNDATIONS GOAL 1

Children will understand that the purpose of print is to communicate. They will also understand basic print conventions, such as the left-to-right and top-to-bottom sequencing of print, where to begin reading, concepts of letter and word, and so forth.

Children's understanding of the purposes, concepts, and conventions of print at kindergarten entry can be quite variable. Some will have a strong grasp of the concepts addressed in this chapter, while others may need explicit and perhaps repeated instruction and guidance. To support instructional planning and decision making, it is useful to gather data about what the children know and are able to do. Often, formal assessments (tests) are used for these purposes, but a great deal can be learned about what children know and are able to do through careful observation of how children approach particular activities.

Documenting Children's Progress

Figure 4.1 presents the group snapshot that can be used to document children's understanding of the purposes and conventions of print as they change across time. (The individual snapshot that allows documenting individual children's skills across time is available on the book's companion website; see the box at the end of the table of contents.)

Group Snapshot—Purposes and Conventions of Print						
Student names						
Print as communication	Reading					
	Writing					
Left-to-right organization	Reading					
	Writing					
Top-to-bottom organization	Reading					
	Writing					
Concept of word	Reading					
	Writing					
Concept of letter	Reading					
	Writing					
One-to-one match	Reading					
Purpose/use of sentence-ending punctuation	Reading					
	Writing					
Quotation marks	Reading					
	Writing					
Capitalization	Writing					

Key:

◻ *B—Beginning* indicates that instruction has addressed the objective but that the child has only a preliminary understanding or capability regarding that particular objective.

⊠ *D—Developing* indicates that the child has some understanding of the objective but does not reliably demonstrate that understanding or capability or is not yet automatic (fluent) with the skill.

⊠ *P—Proficient* indicates that the child reliably and automatically demonstrates the understanding or capability.

FIGURE 4.1. Group snapshot for purposes and conventions of print.

Understanding of the various concepts listed on the snapshot can be demonstrated during shared reading and writing activities as well as in more informal contexts as, for example, when children choose to label a picture they have drawn. It is not necessary for children to be able to read and write independently/conventionally in order to be credited with at least early understandings of the purposes and conventions of print—as we'll explain below. In what follows, we describe each item on the snapshot and offer examples of the kinds of evidence that might be used in determining a child's standing (*beginning, developing, proficient*) relative to the concepts and conventions.

• *Print as communication.* Children's understanding of the fact that print is a form of communication can be demonstrated in a variety of ways, such as when they choose to write to someone for the purpose of conveying information or ask to have printed language read to them ("What does that say?"). When children first begin to write, it is common for their attempts to be quite different from conventional writing. Their attempts might look more like scribbling or an assortment of letter-like forms. But if they believe they have written something and maybe they even "read" what it says, that tells us that they are developing an understanding that print carries meaning.

• *Left-to-right and top-to-bottom directionality.* In English, print is followed from left to right and from top to bottom on a page. Close observation of what beginning readers do while engaged in reading beginner-level memorized texts will allow the teacher to note their understanding of these conventions. Short poems are particularly useful in this regard as there will typically be multiple lines of text on the page. Regarding writing, children's responses to questions during shared writing can demonstrate their current understanding. For example, the teacher might ask, "I've run out of room on this line, where should I write the next word?"

• *The concepts of letter and word.* Partly because some of the earliest words they learn are also letters (*I* and *a*), it can take children a while to fully understand the differences between words and letters. This understanding is usually evaluated through direct questioning. For example, individual children might be asked to count the number of letters in individual words or the number of words on the page of a beginner-level book. The ability to engage in finger-point reading of a memorized beginner-level text, pointing and saying the correct word, also provides evidence that children have developed a concept of what a word is. (See the next bullet point.)

• *One-to-one match.* Children who are just beginning to learn to read often start by learning to read *patterned/predictable books*. These books usually have one to four words on a page. At early points, such books are often read to children, after which they have the opportunity to "read" the book themselves. Once children have learned the pattern of the book (e.g., "I see a . . ."), they are able to read the book by repeating the patterned phrase and labeling the accompanying picture.

A child who can accurately point to each word as it is read and does so accurately when the text includes words with more than one syllable can be credited with having developed the ability to do one-to-one print-to-speech matching, They would, therefore, be considered proficient in relation to this concept. However, if children are successful only if the text is composed exclusively of single-syllable words, the children would be considered to be still developing the understanding.

• *Purpose/use of sentence-ending punctuation.* Punctuation is used to convey meaning within and across sentences. In evaluating young children's understanding of the purposes and uses of punctuation, we focus on the most basic, earliest forms of ending punctuation encountered. To be considered proficient in this context, young children should demonstrate the understanding that, in reading, the reader's voice reflects the ending punctuation (rising with a question mark, adding emphasis with an exclamation point, etc.) and that, in writing, sentences end with a punctuation mark, with different punctuation marks used for different kinds of sentences.

• *Quotation marks.* Quotation marks are used to convey the idea that a character is speaking. When students read or write texts that include dialogue, awareness of the role of quotation marks is important because such awareness impacts comprehension of texts that are read and comprehensibility of texts that are written.

• *Capitalization.* Capitalization has reference only to writing on the snapshot. Children are considered proficient if they reliably capitalize the first letter (and only the first letter) in the first words in sentences and in proper names. They are considered to be developing if capitalization is intermittently but appropriately applied.

The Purposes of Print

Some children arrive in kindergarten having had very limited prior experience with printed language and, as a result, may have little or no understanding of the purposes of print. For these children, it is important to frequently discuss and model how print is used for communication. The following presents some examples of things that teachers might do to help children develop an understanding of the communication value of print.[1]

Teacher Writing

While texting or writing a note to a parent or to another teacher, the teacher might explain that writing is a way to tell someone something without needing to talk to them.

---

[1] Note that in this section the discussion is limited to the Purposes and Conventions of Print goal. Many other goals can be addressed in (shared) reading and writing activities.

Writing Names on Papers and Belongings

When asking children to write their names on papers or other belongings, the teacher should explain the purpose of doing so (so that everyone knows to whom the item belongs).

Reading to Children

- When reading aloud to children, the teacher might periodically explain that, since the author couldn't be there to tell the story, they wrote it down instead.
- The teacher might start by looking at the pictures in the text with the children and explaining that the written words on the page(s) tell what's happening in the text.
- For texts that are read more than once, the teacher might stop at different points and ask the children to say what the author has told them and to try to remember what comes next.
- When questions come up in conversation, the teacher—using either print and/ or digital resources—might explain and model how answers can be found via reading.

Shared Writing

Children should have multiple opportunities to express their thoughts in print.

- Early on, the teacher might do the writing and record the children's thoughts while the children look on. After reading aloud what a particular child has dictated, the teacher might ask, "Is that what you want it to say?" (If necessary, the teacher and the child[ren] might need to collaborate to make the child's intended message clear.)
- The teacher might introduce a wordless book (e.g., *Good Dog, Carl* [Day, 1997]) and suggest that they all (the teacher and the children together) compose a story that goes with the pictures. The teacher would then guide the students through the process (e.g., "What do we want to say first? OK, I'll write that down so we can remember it. . . . So far, our story says . . . [while pointing to the words]"). If the teacher is engaging a group of children who are at varying points in their development of early literacy skills and understandings, this shared writing activity would typically include reference to other aspects of literacy development beyond the purpose of print (e.g., concepts of letter and word, the identities of individual letters). In such processes, the teacher should demonstrate and explain how and why the writer goes back and reads portions of the text that have already been written so that the writer remembers what they want to say next.
- Some teachers engage their students in writing a class letter to parents at the

end of each week to tell them about the class's experiences. Once the letter is completed, the teacher leads the class in shared reading of the letter a few times, and a copy of the letter is then sent home with the children or is posted on the class's webpage. The children are encouraged to share the writing piece at home so that family members will know what is happening in school. (The multiple shared readings may enable the children to "read" the letter to family members if the letter is short enough and practiced enough.)

Using Print for Record-Keeping Purposes

Even at early points in the development of print knowledge, children can either write or use a name card to sign up for activities or express preferences. For example, children can:

- Sign their names on an attendance list or place their name cards in the "present" box. If attendance is kept digitally, children can drag and drop their names in the appropriate column of a digital record.[2]
- Sign up for a turn at a specific center.
- Enter their lunch preferences next to their name on a lunch count list. (*Note:* Early on, it is helpful to have models to which the children can refer. For example, if pizza is on the lunch menu, a labeled picture of a slice of pizza would be provided.)

Conventions of Print

Different writing systems have different conventions regarding how print is organized and displayed. Children who are just beginning to learn about the writing system for their particular language sometimes need explicit guidance regarding the conventions of that language. Conventions in the English writing system include the following:

- There are special kinds of marks on paper (and other media) that are called letters. The letters represent sounds in spoken words. Except for the single-letter words *a* and *I*, words are made up of multiple letters that, when placed next to each other in specific sequences, form words.
- The word *word* refers to a unit of meaning.
- Printed words are separated by spaces.
- Words are organized into larger units of meaning called *sentences*.

---

[2]Some teachers put children's pictures on the name cards early on, but this can defeat the purpose of helping children learn that print is a form of communication. So, we would advise removing the pictures as soon as possible.

- Sentences are strung together to convey larger messages.
- Print is organized (written and read) from left to right on a line and from top to bottom on a page, and from the left-hand page to the right-hand page in books.
- In texts with multiple lines of print, the reader returns to the left to read the next line of print.
- There are other markings in written language (punctuation marks and the use of print size, italics, etc.) that signal intonation and phrasing.

Adults who are proficient readers are often so familiar with the conventions just described that they don't even think about them, and so they may neglect to explain them to early literacy learners. Whereas children who have been read to frequently and who have had the opportunity to experiment with writing often begin to understand some of these conventions before they start kindergarten, children who have had limited print experience are sometimes baffled by these rather arbitrary conventions. For these children, it is important to teach these conventions explicitly. Such explicit teaching about print conventions is also important for children whose primary language has different conventions (e.g., Chinese, Arabic, Korean, Hebrew), especially if the children have begun to learn to read and write in those languages.

Print Conventions and ELs

Many alphabetic languages share several of the English print conventions, including the conventions that there are letters that represent sounds, that together letters form words that are separated by spaces, and that words are strung together to form sentences. European languages also share the directionality conventions of English. Thus, children who are learning to read and write English after having learned or begun to learn to read and write in a European language will have knowledge that will facilitate their learning of English. However, some non-European alphabetic languages, such as Arabic and Hebrew, are written and read from right to left rather than from left to right. Children coming from those language backgrounds may find the competing conventions challenging to negotiate. Conventions pertaining to punctuation also vary across languages. For example, in Spanish, a question is signaled by an inverted question mark at the beginning of a sentence and by a "regular" question mark at the end of the sentence.

Logographic (nonalphabetic) languages such as Mandarin and Cantonese have print conventions that differ from English in many ways. An extensive discussion of differences in print conventions across the world's languages is beyond the scope of this book. They are mentioned here mainly to help teachers to understand that languages do differ, sometimes substantially, with regard to print conventions. Teachers are encouraged to try to learn about the conventions of multilingual learners' (MLs') first languages so that they can understand, plan for, and respond more effectively to students' potential sources of confusion. A text entitled *Learner English: A Teacher's Guide to Interference and Other Problems,* edited by Swan and Smith (2001), is an excellent resource in this regard.

Developing an Understanding of English Print Concepts and Conventions

Shared Reading

When reading to children, the primary focus should always be on the meaning of the text. In the early primary grades, it is useful to frequently read large-print texts (e.g., big books, language experience charts, morning messages) that allow the children to see the printed words. It is also useful to read the same large-print text multiple times on the same day the first time the text is introduced and across a couple of days. Multiple readings provide children with the opportunity to revisit concepts addressed, thereby increasing their opportunities to grow toward proficiency.

Shared reading[3] can have many purposes. When used to teach print concepts and conventions, it is important for the teacher to do the following:

• Point to the words while reading. The reading should be done with natural intonation and phrasing but at a somewhat slower pace than might be used when reading for other purposes. Slowed reading, coupled with pointing, will give children the opportunity to observe the left-to-right and top-to-bottom sequencing of print. On occasion, it is helpful to mention the "return sweep" one does while reading. That is, when readers get to the right-hand end of a line of print, they return to the left-hand side of the page—but one line down. To promote attention to this convention, it is useful, on occasion, to ask the children where to move next after finishing a line of text.

• Explicitly teach important print concepts. For example, the teacher might engage the children in discussions focused on the number of words in the title of a book, the number of letters in a character's name, and so forth, and provide opportunities for children to engage in this counting themselves. This will help children learn about the concepts of word and letter.

• Occasionally explain and demonstrate the directionality of print explicitly (e.g., "When we read, we always start on this side.").

• Occasionally explain the purpose of punctuation marks. For example, "This little dot is called a period. Authors put periods in to tell us when they are done with one idea. When we are reading and we see a period, it tells us to stop for a second and think about what we just read."

---

[3]As we use the term, *shared reading* refers to the teacher and the children reading a single text together—both the children's and the teacher's voices are heard.

• Share the reading with the children by encouraging them to chime in while the adult reads. Repeated readings of the same text will help the children realize that the same passage sounds essentially the same each time it is read.

• Encourage children to point to the words during shared reading either by having them take turns in doing the pointing on the large-print version of the text or by providing each child (or pair of children) with a smaller version of the text. Once the text is somewhat familiar to children, giving them the opportunity to point to the words while the group reads the text chorally will help them attend to the sequencing of print. This approach will also contribute to the development of the all-important *concept of word* (see the following box, "Development of the Concept of Word").

• If children know the sounds of several letters, encouraging them to think about the sounds of beginning letters in words can help them become more accurate in their pointing.

• Activities such as these should not supplant the focus on the meaning of the text. Too much discussion of print concepts and conventions during shared reading has the obvious potential to interfere with understanding the text.

Development of the Concept of Word

Perhaps the most central concept beginning readers need to grasp to begin to build their reading and writing skills is an understanding of what a word is. Clay (1991) indicated that the concept of word is a pivotal insight needed to move forward in literacy learning. And, as Adams (1990) pointed out, it is in considering words that alphabetic and phonological skills become useful. Words are the basic units of meaning from which larger messages are constructed. During shared reading activities, it is the words to which the teacher points. (*Note:* While pointing, it is important to point under the words rather than on the word. We want the children to see the words!)

Research suggests that children develop an understanding of what a word is through engagement with memorized printed texts (typically predictable/patterned texts) and an awareness of beginning consonant letters and sounds (Flannigan, 2007; Morris, Bloodgood, Lomax, & Perney, 2003). As opposed to being an all-or-nothing accomplishment, the concept of word is thought to develop in stages (Mesmer & Williams, 2015). At the earliest stage (Stage 1), children demonstrate an emerging awareness that print, rather than pictures, carries the meaning, but they do not yet understand how print is organized into words, and they do not yet point to individual words as they recite a memorized text. Children in the second stage understand that letters are grouped together in meaningful ways and that these groupings are separated by spaces. When operating on a memorized text with only single-syllable words, children at Stage 2 can accurately point to each word in the text[4] as it is read and can use beginning sound information in conjunction with rehearsal to locate specific words within a line

---

[4] This is often referred to as "finger-point reading."

of text. They cannot maintain accuracy, however, if the text contains multisyllabic words as well. For example, after a shared reading of a highly patterned text, *One Bee Got on the Bus* (Dowd, 1996), we observed a child accurately finger-point read (saying each word as he pointed to it) on four of the six pages.

> Six bears got on the bus.
> Five bunnies got on the bus.
> Four butterflies got on the bus.
> Three bats got on the bus.
> Two bugs got on the bus.
> One bee got on the bus.

Which pages were read accurately? Those that had only one-syllable words. Children in Stage 2 do not yet distinguish between spoken syllables and words, and they assume that each is represented by a bound set of letters on the page. It is not until Stage 3 that the concept of word is fully consolidated. At this stage, as they are reading a memorized text, children can accurately point to the words—including those that have more than one syllable (such as the text above)—and they can reliably use knowledge of beginning letter sounds to locate words within the text. Children at this point have come to understand that each grouping of letters represents an individual word, regardless of the number of syllables contained in the word (Mesmer & Williams, 2015).

Shared Writing

In shared writing, the teacher and students collaborate in constructing the message and capturing it in print. Generally, the teacher does the writing while the students look on. In order to promote an understanding of print concepts while writing, the teacher could do the following:

- Explicitly demonstrate and explain where on the page one starts to write and about the direction one follows when continuing to write.
- Demonstrate appropriate spacing between letters and words and discuss how the spacing helps the reader/writer know where one word ends and the next one begins.
- Demonstrate and explain when upper-case and lower-case letters are used.
- Model and explain the use and purpose of punctuation marks.

KEEP IN MIND   Sometimes teachers attempt to make some of these print concepts more memorable by using terms the children will find engaging. This can inadvertently confuse children—especially if they are shaky on the concepts and if they are receiving instruction in multiple settings (as children in an RTI process often do). This is especially problematic if the classroom and intervention teachers use different terms for the same concepts. For example, we've encountered teachers who refer to the spaces between letters in a word as "spaghetti spaces" and the spaces between words as "meatball spaces." Other teachers use pom-poms and pipe cleaners to reference the different-sized spaces. These are cute ideas, but if children receive instruction from both teachers and have yet to really grasp the purpose of spaces and their relative sizes, they are likely to become more rather than less confused by the experience! Teachers who share responsibility for teaching the same children should also share critical terminology.

KEY POINTS OF THIS CHAPTER

✓ Learners who have had limited experience with printed language often need explicit and repeated instruction related to the purposes and conventions of print.

✓ Children can be helped to learn about the purposes of print
- As the teacher writes (for various purposes),
- When the teacher discusses the communicative intentions of the authors of books, poems, and other texts,
- And when the children are encouraged to write their names for various purposes such as to identify ownership or preferences.

✓ Children can be helped to learn important print concepts when teachers talk explicitly about the concepts and engage the children in practicing them until the concepts are established.

✓ Efforts to address print concepts and conventions can also occur in the context of shared reading and writing activities that primarily have a meaning focus. Examples might include:
- The teacher saying "This is the **word** *can*; *can* has three **letters**: *c-a-n*."
- The teacher asking "Who would like to count the **letters** in the **word** *the*?"
- The teacher pointing to the title of a book and saying, "Our book today is called *The Big Apple*. How many **words** are in the title of our book—*The Big Apple*? What is the first **letter** in the **word** *the*?"

✓ Primary-grade children vary tremendously in terms of their experience with print and their understanding of print concepts and conventions. Small-group instruction allows teachers to more specifically address print concepts and conventions for children who are at different points in development.

CHAPTER 5

Phonemic Awareness

WRITING SYSTEM FOUNDATIONS GOAL 2

Children will have a conceptual grasp of the fact that words are made up of *somewhat* separable sound segments. Further, they will be able to say the individual sounds in words spoken by the teacher and blend separate sounds to form whole words.

The development of reading and writing skills requires that one develop important understandings about *oral* (spoken) language. Learners need to be able to notice/attend to the sounds in spoken words that are represented by the letters in printed words. These sounds are called *phonemes*. A phoneme is the smallest unit of sound that distinguishes between words. For example, the spoken forms of the words *sip* and *ship* are each composed of three phonemes; it is the initial (beginning) phonemes that differentiate the two words. (Note that the /sh/ grapheme/digraph represents a single phoneme even though it is composed of two letters.)

How Many Phonemes Are There in English?

There are approximately 44 phonemes in the English language—we say *approximately* because, due to accents and dialects, some speakers use somewhat more or fewer in their spoken language. If we stick with the 44-phoneme estimate, there are 25 consonant phonemes and 19 vowel phonemes.

Becoming aware of the fact that spoken words are made up of *somewhat* separable sounds (that is, becoming phonemically aware) enables learners to connect the sounds in spoken words to the letters/graphemes used to represent those sounds in written words. When a learner can segment (separate) the sounds in

spoken words and blend separate sounds to form whole words, they are considered
to be phonemically aware or to have achieved phonemic awareness. A learner who
is phonemically aware:

- Understands that spoken words are composed of somewhat separable sounds.
- Is able to analyze (sort) spoken words according to sound similarities. For example, when shown a small group of pictures (e.g., *soup, ball, sun, house*), and asked to select the pictures/words that have the same beginning sound, the learner can make a correct choice.
- Can name individual sounds in spoken words (e.g., What is the first sound in the word *cat*?).
- Can *blend* individual sounds to form a complete word (e.g., when hearing /k/-/ă/-/t/[1] can say the word *cat*).
- Can *segment* all the sounds in a one-syllable spoken word (e.g., hearing *cat* can say the individual sounds /k/- ă/-/t/).

For children in the early primary grades, the process of learning about printed language and the development of phonemic awareness generally occur fairly simultaneously with instruction in one skill supporting the development of the other skill (Brady, 2020; Clayton, West, Sears, Hulme, & Lervåg, 2020). The processes are reciprocal (learning one supports development of the other) as depicted in Figure II.1 (p. 93). In this chapter, we focus on how to help children become aware of the sounds in spoken words, and, for teachers, we focus on the characteristics of phonemes that may make the process of developing phonemic awareness challenging for some children. In subsequent chapters we describe instruction designed to help children make connections between the sounds in spoken words and the letters in written words. For now, it is important to note the widespread consensus that the ability to manipulate the sounds in spoken words at the level of the phoneme, particularly the ability to blend and segment phonemes, is key to the development of reading and spelling (e.g., Brady 2021; Brady, Shankweiler, & Mann, 1983; Bryant, MacLean, Bradley, & Crossland, 1990; Fletcher et al., 1994; Vellutino et al., 1996; Wagner, Torgesen, & Rashotte, 1994). Understanding this relationship between sounds (phonemes) and letters (graphemes) is one of the most fundamental tasks facing the beginning reader and writer (Adams, 1990).

Phonemic awareness enables learners to develop reading and spelling skills. For some children, the realization that spoken words can be segmented into individual phonemes takes a good deal of time to develop. Other children appear to develop this insight quite easily and without explicit instruction (Scarborough & Dobrich, 1994; Torgesen, Wagner, & Rashotte, 1994). Children who find it difficult to notice/

---

[1]In print, to distinguish between the long and the short sounds of vowel letters, we use breves (pronounced brevs) and macrons above the letter. A breve is a curved line above the vowel letter and is used to signal the short sound of the vowel letter (e.g., [ă] as in *apple*). A macron (a straight line above a vowel letter [e.g., ā]) is used to signal the long sound of a vowel (as in *make*).

attend to the individual phonemes in spoken words are likely to experience difficulty learning to read and spell. Therefore, assessment of children's ability to notice/isolate the sounds in spoken words can help to identify children who may need extra support in developing literacy skills (Clemens et al., 2021). Children who develop insight into the phonemic nature of spoken language with relatively little guidance will not need the type of explicit instruction described in this chapter. Instruction for them should focus on helping them learn about the connections between the sounds in spoken words and the letters in printed words. And for children who do need help in becoming phonemically aware, it is important to transition them into applying their developing phonemic analysis skills to the processes of reading and writing as soon as possible (Brady, 2021). Phonemic awareness is basically an insight that, once developed, should be put to work in the service of learning to read and spell.

In this chapter, we discuss several instructional activities that have been found to be useful in promoting the development of phonemic awareness. These include *phoneme sorting/matching* in which children sort pictures by commonalities in sounds in the names of the pictures; *phoneme blending* in which the teacher articulates/says individual sounds in words and children blend the sounds together and say the whole word; and *phoneme segmentation* in which the teacher says a word and the children say the individual sounds in the word. These activities, particularly blending and segmenting, are most closely associated with growth in reading and spelling. That is, to read an unfamiliar word, the reader needs to think about the sounds that the letters represent and then *blend* those sounds to identify the word. Similarly, in order to spell a word that has not been committed to memory, the writer needs to analyze/*segment* the sounds in the spoken word and connect those sounds to the letters that commonly represent those sounds.

Advanced Phoneme Awareness

Increased recognition of the value of developing phonemic awareness (which began in the early 2000s) has, in some cases, led to a significant increase in instructional time devoted to promoting phonemic analysis skill. In addition to teaching the sorting, blending, and segmenting skills described above, some programs/approaches have added more challenging phoneme manipulation activities. These activities include phoneme addition (e.g., "Say *all*. Now say *all* again but put a /t/ at the beginning"), phoneme deletion (e.g., "Say *tall*. Now say *tall* again but don't say /t/"), and phoneme substitution (e.g., "Say *tall*. Now say *tall* again but instead of the /t/, say '/f/' ").

We do not address these higher-level phonemic awareness tasks (which are sometimes referred to as advanced phonemic awareness) in this chapter, as there is no convincing evidence to support their use, when done without reference to print (see Clemens et al., 2021, for a review). We will, however, address these higher-level letter–sound manipulation tasks within the context of phonics instruction in Chapters 8, 9, and 10, as there is "long-standing evidence that reading outcomes are stronger when phonemic awareness is integrated with print" (Clemens et al., 2021, p. 16).

Phonemic Awareness versus Phonics

People sometimes confuse the concepts of *phonemic awareness* and *phonics*. Therefore, a more thorough discussion of the distinction and relationship between them is warranted.

In its purest form, phonemic awareness involves the ability to analyze and manipulate the sounds in *spoken* words and does not involve print. Phonics, on the other hand, involves learning the relationships between graphemes (letters) and their associated phonemes (sounds). Learning and using those relationships in reading and spelling words requires phonemic awareness. To develop phonics skills, a child must be at least somewhat phonemically aware.

One oft-quoted characterization of phonemic awareness is that it is something you can demonstrate with your eyes closed. A more useful characterization is that it is a skill you could demonstrate even if you were not given the opportunity to learn about printed language but were instead instructed in how to become attuned to the sounds in spoken language. But what would be the point? The value in becoming phonemically aware is that it assists in the development of reading and spelling skills in alphabetic languages.

Phonemic Awareness and Reading Difficulties

Children who experience significant difficulty in learning to read tend to have difficulty in developing the ability to segment and blend the phonemes in spoken words. Many researchers believe that this slower development of phonemic awareness is an important *cause* of reading difficulties. It has been known for decades that measures of phonemic awareness, administered in kindergarten, are strong predictors of reading success in first grade and beyond (e.g., Scanlon & Vellutino, 1996; Torgesen & Burgess, 1998; Yopp, 1988). As noted earlier, however, learning to read helps children become more sensitive to the phonemes in spoken words. Thus, phonemic awareness helps children learn to read and spell, and learning to read and spell helps children to become more phonemically aware (Quinn, Spencer, & Wagner, 2015a).

Instructional Influences and the Development of Phonemic Awareness and Phonics

Many studies (e.g., Ball & Blachman, 1991; Blachman, Ball, Black, & Tangel, 1994; Bradley & Bryant, 1991; Schneider, Roth, & Ennemoser, 2000) have demonstrated that explicit instruction designed to promote phonemic awareness has a positive effect on the reading and spelling performance of children who receive such instruction, in both the short term (immediately after instruction) and the long term (up to 10 years after instruction; Blachman et al., 2014). Further, positive effects have been noted in a variety of instructional groupings (one-to-one, small group, and whole class). While there is clear evidence for the importance of helping children to become phonemically aware, there is also consensus that instruction in phonemic awareness alone is less effective in promoting reading and spelling abilities than is instruction in phonemic awareness coupled with explicit instruction in both letter–sound correspondences and application of the alphabetic code (Brady, 2020; National Reading Panel, 2000).

Research Commentary/Update

According to Brady (2020), for most children, awareness of larger units of sound (syllables and onsets[2] and rimes) is more readily acquired than awareness of the individual phonemes in spoken words. For a long time, it was widely believed that it was important for children to learn to manipulate (segment and blend) these larger elements of sound and that children needed to have these skills *before* they could learn to manipulate individual phonemes. More recent analyses have found, however, that children do not need to be able to manipulate these larger phonological components in order to develop analysis skills at the level of the individual phonemes (Brady, 2020).

Why Is It Difficult for Some Children to Notice/Attend to/Manipulate Phonemes?

Readers and writers who are proficient in an alphabetic language often find it difficult to imagine how anyone would have difficulty noticing the phonemes in spoken language. It just seems obvious to them. However, people who are proficient readers and writers in languages that do not use an alphabetic writing system, as well as those who have never learned to read in an alphabetic language, are generally not very phonemically aware. They simply don't notice the phonemes because there is really no need to; the phonemes are not represented in their language's writing system (Kolinsky et al., 2021; Read, Zhang, Nie, & Ding, 1986). Thus, it is not surprising that many children with limited print-based literacy experience will not be phonemically aware. Many children may begin to become sensitized to the larger phonological structures through involvement in learning songs and poems that emphasize sound similarities (e.g., alliteration and rhyme). They will begin to develop more sophisticated insight when their attention is drawn to the sounds in words through their engagement in reading and writing activities. However, for a variety of reasons, some children need much more explicit and focused instruction in order to become aware of the component phonemes in spoken words.

---

[2] An onset is the part of a syllable that comes before the vowel. The onset in the word *ball* is /b/. In the word *sled*, the onset is /sl/. Some words do not have onsets (e.g., *up*, *ant*).

In what follows, we describe factors that may contribute to children's difficulty with learning to manipulate the phonemic aspects of spoken language.

A Natural Inclination to Focus on the Meaning of Words Rather Than Their Sounds

There is a natural inclination to attend to the meanings of words rather than to the component sounds. After all, the concept of a *dog* is much more interesting than the sounds that comprise the word. If you ask young children how many sounds are in *dog,* they are apt to say "woof, woof" rather than "three." Up to the point at which children are beginning to learn about printed language, words have primarily been units of meaning—not combinations of phonemes.

The Fleeting Nature of Speech Sounds

The phonemes in words are rather fleeting. It takes substantially less than a second to articulate the first sound in *ball* or the first sound in *sun.* As a result, it can be hard to draw children's attention to the individual sounds. When attempts are made to do so, they are differentially effective depending on the characteristics of the sound. For example, some consonant phonemes can be stretched or elongated—without distortion. Examples of stretchable consonant phonemes include /ssss/, /rrrrr/, /fffff/. (All vowel phonemes in English are also stretchable.) However, many consonant phonemes cannot be "stretched" without distortion. These phonemes, including those associated with the letters *b, d, g,* and *t,* are referred to as *stop-consonant sounds* because their production requires that the airflow be briefly stopped during articulation. As a result of this stoppage of the airflow, it is impossible to elongate the pronunciation without distorting the sound. For instance, when teachers attempt to draw children's attention to the initial sound in the word *boy,* they are likely to say /buh/ with an emphasis on the /uh/ portion. Children who are not yet attuned to the phonemic qualities of spoken language might well attend more to the /uh/, which takes longer to articulate than the /b/, which is fleeting. Figure 5.1 presents a list of the graphemes representing stretchable- (also called continuous or continuant) and stop-consonant sounds. Note that the letters *w, x,* and *y* do not appear on the list. The letter *x* is not on the list because it represents two phonemes, /k/ and /s/, and as such is a blend of two consonant phonemes (notice that the phonemes at the end of *box* and *blocks* are the same in spite of the different orthographic representations). For the letters *w* and *y,* most teachers are accustomed to pronouncing these phonemes in isolation as (*wuh*) and (*yuh*), respectively. The addition of the schwa sound (*uh*) makes these phonemes seem more like stop consonants. In fact, however, both phonemes are more similar to vowel phonemes and can be stretched without distortion. The sound for the letter *w* when articulated at the beginning of a word sounds like the /oo/ sound in *too* (e.g., consider the pronunciation of the word *wet* [/oo/-/ĕt/] or *win* [/oo/-/ĭn/]), and the sound for the letter *y* is like the long-*e* sound (consider the pronunciation of the word *yes* [/ē/-/ĕs/] or *young* [/ē/-/ŭng/]).

Stretchable	Stop
All vowel graphemes /c/ (when pronounced as /s/), /f/, /l/, /m/, /n/, /r/, /s/, /v/, /w/, /y/, /z/, /sh/, /th/	/c/ (when pronounced as /k/), /d/, /g/ (when pronounced as /guh/ or /juh/), /j/, /k/, /p/, /q/, /t/, /ch/, /tch/

FIGURE 5.1. Graphemes commonly representing stretchable and stop-consonant phonemes. *Note:* The sound associated with the letter *h* is not clearly "stretchable" because elongating the sound associated with it would, essentially, involve an elongated breath. However, it is clearly not a "stop" consonant.

The Problem of Coarticulation

Another reason phonemes are not particularly obvious is that the phonemes in words are hard to separate from one another. For the sake of efficiency, the articulators (the parts of the mouth that move while producing the intended phonemes) are preparing to say the next sound in a word while they are still articulating the previous sound. As a result, there is no clear point of demarcation between one phoneme and the next. The phonemes are literally blended together. This blending is referred to as *coarticulation*.

The Phoneme as a Convenient Fiction

"Separate" sounds don't actually exist in spoken words. That is why the goal statement for this chapter refers to sounds as "somewhat" separable. In spoken language, there is no point of demarcation between one phoneme and the next in a spoken word. The perception of phonemes/speech sounds as separate elements is, as Seidenberg (2023) suggests, a "convenient fiction" that enables learners to connect these "somewhat" separable sounds to the elements of print that represent them.

Examples of Coarticulation

To get a better sense of coarticulation, try this exercise:

Say the words *see* and *so* out loud a few times. Are the sounds you hear at the beginnings of those two words the same? Your answer is, of course, yes. Now, say the same words again (*see*, *so*) but notice the position of your lips as you make the /s/ sound in each word. Is your mouth position the same? No. When pronouncing the /s/ in *see*, your lips are stretched back a bit in preparation for pronouncing the /ē/ (long-e) sound. When pronouncing the /s/ in *so*, your lips are more rounded in preparation for pronouncing the /ō/ (long-o) sound. In this case, the change in mouth position doesn't result in a noticeable change in the /s/ sound. Our purpose with this example is to illustrate how the articulators adjust depending on the sequence of sounds.

For some changes in mouth position, and for some phonemes and phoneme combinations, the change in the movement of the articulators does affect sound—as illustrated next.

Say the words *at* and *ant* out loud. Listen to the vowel sound in each word. Pretend you don't know how the words are spelled. Do the vowels sound the same? Probably not. For most people the two sounds are actually quite different. The /ă/ in *ant* is sort of "twangy" as a result of the articulators preparing to produce the /n/ sound. In producing the /n/ sound, air is pushed through the nose (it is referred to as a *nasal* sound). Therefore, while producing the sound of *a* in *ant*, some of the air is pushed through the nose as well, resulting in a nasalized version of the vowel sound. On the other hand, in pronouncing the sound of *a* in *at*, all the air is pushed through the mouth. The path of air in the two words, which is changed by the position of the articulators, changes the sound—with the result that, to a learner who doesn't yet know the spellings of the two words, these two sounds of the "short-*a*" are not the same.

For instructional purposes, this distinction is important. For example, if a child who has not yet learned the spelling of the short-*a* sound was asked to decide whether the middle sounds in *lamp* and *lap* are the same, the child is likely to say no—appropriately so. The subtle difference between the pronunciations of the vowel in the two words is likely to escape notice by highly literate individuals whose perception of phonemes is influenced by their knowledge of spellings. Additionally, certain dialects and accents may impact pronunciation, such that the vowel sounds are essentially the same. Having a degree of awareness for how children pronounce words is important when analyzing phoneme perception.

Short- versus Long-Vowel Sounds

The terms *short* and *long* used in reference to vowel sounds can be confusing, as they suggest that the vowel sounds differ in duration. This is not the case in modern English (Venezky, 1999). However, because these terms are in common usage in classroom instruction, we use them in this book because they *are* in such common usage and they do provide a way to distinguish between the two sounds most commonly associated with each of the vowel letters.

As the terms long and short may prove confusing to young learners, when possible, we avoid their use with children. Instead, we talk about the two sounds for each vowel letter—one of which is the same as the letter's name as discussed in Chapter 7 and the other of which is the sound associated with the key word used to teach the "short" sound of the vowel.

Similarity of Many Phonemes

Because children tend to rely on what their mouths are doing as they articulate sounds, it is sometimes difficult for them to distinguish between two phonemes that are articulated in almost the same way. In many cases, the only difference in the articulation of two phonemes lies in whether the vocal cords vibrate when the phoneme is produced. Such phonemes are said to differ in *voicing*. For example, the phonemes /f/ and /v/ are articulated in the same way *except* that the /v/ sound is voiced (the vocal cords vibrate), whereas the /f/ sound is not voiced.

As illustrated in Figure 5.2, several pairs of phonemes in English differ only in voicing. Children often confuse these phonemes—particularly in their writing. Children who make these types of substitutions are more phonemically aware than teachers sometimes realize. For example, spelling *van* as *fan* may be due to the child engaging in sound spelling without vocalizing (if you don't vibrate your vocal cords in attempting to sound spell, the words *van* and *fan* could be perceived as identical for spelling purposes).

There are some clear instructional implications related to these potentially confusable sound pairs, including:

• In planning instruction to promote phonemic awareness, it is important to initially avoid asking children to discriminate between phonemes that are potentially confusable, because this makes the task more difficult. For example, if children were asked to sort groups of pictures by similarities in their beginning sounds, it would be much more challenging to sort a set consisting of *van, fork, fox,* and *vase* than to sort a set consisting of *mat, fork, fox,* and *mop*.

• In children's writing, particularly in early writing, substitutions within these minimally contrasted pairs (e.g., substituting *d* for *t,* or *b* for *p or vice versa*) are common. Teachers who understand the origin of these substitutions and who recognize that they are close approximations will provide children with more effective feedback—including, perhaps, encouraging children to say the words they are attempting to spell out loud. Noticing that attempted spellings are close approximations—rather than completely off-base—will encourage progress. For example, a teacher responding to *lidl* as a spelling for *little* could encourage the

Sound pairs that differ only in voicing		Other confusable pairs	
Voiced	Unvoiced	/l/	/r/
/b/	/p/	/m/	/n/
/d/	/t/		
/v/	/f/		
/g/	/k/		
/j/	/ch/		
/z/	/s/		

(*Note:* Both phonemes in these two pairs are voiced. They are confusable because there is only a slight change in mouth position when articulating one or the other member of the pair.)

FIGURE 5.2. Potentially confusable sound pairs.

writer by noting that the writer noticed and represented all the sounds in the attempted word. It would be helpful for the teacher to also acknowledge that the word *little* does sound like there's a /d/ in the middle but that in "book spelling"[3] the letter used is *t*. (Of course, depending on the learner's point in development, reference to the conventional [book] spelling might also be appropriate.)

Focusing on Phonemes

Proficient readers (including some teachers) sometimes have difficulty accurately analyzing words at the level of the phoneme when words have more letters than sounds (e.g., *though*—has two sounds) and when words have more sounds than letters (e.g., *box*—has four sounds—/b/-/ŏ/-/k/-/s/). To become attuned to the sounds in spoken words and sensitive to the variability in English spelling–sound relationships, it is helpful to consider the examples in Figure 5.3. For each picture, count and articulate the individual phonemes contained in the name of the pictured item. Also, consider what makes the words more or less difficult to segment into individual phonemes.

Teachers need to be sensitive to the phonemes that actually occur in spoken words in order to be effective in guiding children to attend to those sounds. Sometimes, highly literate people are taken in by the spellings in words (e.g., thinking that the middle sound in the word *can* is the same as the middle sound in the word *cat* when the phonemes are, in fact, not identical or that there are only three sounds in the word *box*). Teachers lacking this sensitivity may provide children with guidance and feedback that can confuse them. This will, of course, be especially problematic for children who find it difficult to develop foundational literacy skills.

Documenting and Assessing Phonemic Awareness

Figure 5.4 presents the group snapshot for phonemic awareness. (The individual snapshot can be found on this book's companion website—see the box at the end of the table of contents.) This snapshot can be used on an ongoing basis to track students' developing phonemic analysis skills in the context of instructional interactions, which, ideally, would occur in small-group settings with group members who are at similar points in their development of phonemic analysis skill. The major categories of skills listed on the snapshot (sorting, blending, and segmenting) tend to develop in roughly the order listed and involve analysis of single-syllable words. *Sorting* involves grouping items that share sound similarities in particular parts of spoken words—for example, grouping pictures of items that start with /s/ vs. /m/. Generally, children can notice/attend to similarities in the beginning sounds of words first, then they can notice/attend to the ending sounds

---

[3]The topic of how to refer to unconventional spellings provided by young writers will be taken up in subsequent chapters.

Words and the phonemes that compose them

Explanation and elaboration

/s/ /ŭ/ /n/

It is relatively easy to articulate the individual sounds in the word *sun* because each of the consonant sounds can be articulated without the addition of a vowel sound (i.e., /ssss/ and /nnnn/). However, some teachers have a habit of adding an unnecessary *schwa* (short-*u*) sound when articulating these sounds (they say "*suh*" rather than /sss/ or "*nuh*" rather than /nnn/). We encourage teachers who are "*schwa*-sayers" to own up to their habit and to try to eliminate the *schwa* sound whenever possible.

/f/ /ĭ/ /sh/

The word *fish* has three sounds but four letters. Sometimes teachers think that a word like *fish* should not be used in early phonemic analysis activities because it has a digraph (*sh*). However, the sound /sh/ is a common sound in spoken language, and it is stretchable. Since we are not focusing on the written word, there is nothing wrong with using a word with a digraph in phonemic analysis activities. Words with digraphs that have stretchable sounds (i.e., *sh, th, ph*) are more appropriate for early instruction.

/n/ /ō/ /z/

The last sound in the word *nose* is /z/, but it is represented by the letter *s*. Because it is often difficult for literate people to ignore the spellings of words, teachers illustrating how to say the individual sounds in words will sometimes incorrectly articulate the sounds in accord with the way the word is spelled (/n/-/ō/-/s/) rather than the way it sounds (/n/-/ō/-/z/). Since maintaining a focus on the sounds is critical when working on phonemic analysis skills, it is important to try to avoid letting the spellings of words interfere with one's perception of the sounds that compose the word. One mantra that might help: "Let the letters go!"

/f/ /ŏ/ /k/ /s/

Fox is another example that illustrates a discrepancy between the number of letters and the number of sounds. There are four sounds in *fox* but only three letters. The last sounds in fox are /k/ /s/. If in doubt, consider whether *fox* and *socks* rhyme. They do.

FIGURE 5.3. Becoming attuned to the characteristics of phonemes in spoken words.

in words, and finally they can notice/attend to the middle sounds in words. In a *blending* activity, the teacher would articulate the individual sounds in a word, and the children would blend (combine) them to form the whole word. In general, it will be easier for children to blend words in which the consonant sounds are stretchable. *Segmenting* (separating) the sounds in a spoken word tends to be the most challenging phonemic analysis task for learners.

Although the skills on the snapshot are presented in list form by necessity, it is important to note, as we'll discuss in detail going forward, that the various instructional techniques are mutually reinforcing. Teachers are encouraged to draw upon different techniques as needed. Within each set of instructional activities (e.g., sorting, blending), the tasks are sequenced to represent a developmental progression. In general, children should demonstrate success on the easier task within a

Group Snapshot—Phonemic Analysis Skills						
Student names						
Sound sorting						
Beginning sound						
Ending sound						
Medial vowel sound						
Phoneme blending						
With pictures						
Without pictures (three phonemes)						
Without pictures (four phonemes)						
Phoneme segmentation						
Two phonemes, stretchable consonants						
Two phonemes, stop consonants						
Three phonemes, stretchable consonants						
Three phonemes, stop consonants						
Words with consonant blends (four phonemes).						

Key:

▱ *B—Beginning* indicates that instruction has addressed the objective, but the child has only a preliminary understanding or capability with regard to that particular objective.

⊠ *D—Developing* indicates that the child has some understanding of the objective but does not reliably demonstrate that understanding or capability or is not yet automatic (fluent) with the skill.

⊠ *P—Proficient* indicates that the child reliably and automatically demonstrates the understanding or capability and no further instruction or practice with the skill is needed.

FIGURE 5.4. Group snapshot for phonemic analysis skills.

sequence (e.g., blending with picture choices) before moving on to the next most challenging task (e.g., blending without pictures). Children would be considered proficient when they can reliably and quickly demonstrate a particular skill.

While the snapshot is intended to be used once instructional groups have been formed, the items on the snapshot provide a rough guide to the developmental progression of phonemic analysis skills. Formal or informal assessment of phonemic analysis skills is an important way to guide grouping decisions.

Assessing via Analyses of Spoken Words

For children who know little or nothing about the alphabetic writing system, assessment of phonemic awareness involves engaging them in analyses of the sounds in spoken words. As noted, the most critical skills are blending and segmenting. Blending involves the child in listening to individual sounds spoken by the teacher and then blending them together to form a whole word. For example, the teacher might say the sounds /m/- /ă/ -/t/, with a brief pause between sounds, and ask the child to say the word that they form (*mat*). Segmenting involves the child in attempting to separate and say the sounds in a word spoken by the teacher.

Of course, in order for blending and segmenting skills to be functional for reading and spelling development, the child needs to know the sounds represented by individual graphemes. But, as noted in the Introduction to Part II, it is possible to begin to address phonemic analysis skills before learners have learned much, if anything, about how those sounds are represented in print. Think again about the interrelationships depicted in Figure II.1 (p. 93). Many interconnected/interacting processes are involved in reading and spelling.

Analyses of Written Spelling

Although *phonemic awareness* refers to the ability to analyze and manipulate the sounds in *spoken* words, written spelling can be used as an indicator of a child's phonemic analysis skill *if* the child has already learned something about the alphabetic writing system. Beginning readers and writers attempting to spell words they have not committed to memory need to analyze the sounds (phonemes) that make up the word and then represent those phonemes with letters. Because measures of written spelling can be administered fairly quickly and to several children at once, they can be an appropriate first step in analysis of phonemic awareness if there is reason to believe that children know something about written language. A child's spellings can provide a wealth of information about their phonemic analysis skills but, to get the full benefit, teachers need to think like a beginning reader/writer. For example, a child who accurately spells the word *jet* when asked to do so is likely to be fairly phonemically aware. So, too, is the child who spells *jet* with a *g* (*get*) or *jet* with an *a* (*jat*), or *jet* with both a *g* and an *a* (*gat*). Obviously, the latter spellings are at odds with the conventional spelling for *jet*. However, they all show that the child has noticed all of the phonemes in the word—choosing *g* rather than *j* because they notice the /j/ sound at the beginning of the name of the letter *g* and choosing *a* rather than *e* because the sound of short-*e* can be heard in the name of the letter *A*.[4] A child who produces this type of spelling is sufficiently phonemically aware and *does not* need explicit instruction in phonemic analysis to make continued progress with reading and spelling three-phoneme words. (Of course, the child still needs to learn about conventional spelling.)

Table 5.1 provides samples of written spellings that can be analyzed for the purpose of evaluating the writer's phonemic analysis skill. For purposes of attuning teachers to what can be learned by engaging in analyses of children's sound spellings, we present samples from children at different points in development and provide only one word for each child. Certainly, it would be inappropriate to rely on a single spelling attempt to make any confident evaluation of a child's phonemic analysis skills (or skill with the alphabetic code for that matter). Our purpose here is only to illustrate what can be learned about a learner's phonemic analysis skills by examination of their spelling attempts.

Guarding against Giving Confusing Feedback

It is sometimes mistakenly thought that children who make substitutions such as using *w* to represent /d/ and *h* to represent /ch/ as illustrated in Table 5.1 are not very phonemically aware. As a result, instruction may therefore focus on development of that skill rather than letter–sound relationships and other phonics skills that would clearly be valuable for such children.

For teachers, it is important to understand the origins of these types of errors—to avoid providing confusing feedback. For example, a teacher who does not realize the reason for these spellings might try to promote phonemic analysis by encouraging the child to listen as the teacher repeats the words with emphasis on the misspelled sound. The teacher might say *dog* several times, emphasizing the beginning sound (e.g., /d/-/d/-/d/ *dog*), while the child may be thinking, "That is why I chose /d/ /d/ double u." A similar issue arises with *church*. While the *hrh* spelling initially might seem bizarre, it represents an accurate analysis of the phonemes in the spoken word *church*. Similar to the example with *dog*, the teacher might have tried to address the misspelling of *church* by emphasizing the /ch/ sounds in the word. In both of these instances, if the teacher didn't understand what the child was thinking, it would be easy to provide feedback that might have confused the child and undermined the child's confidence.

A child who cannot sound-spell one syllable words may or may not be phonemically aware. Problems with sound spelling may be due to limited or lack of knowledge of the alphabetic code *or* to limited phonemic awareness *or* both. Thus, poor performance on a measure of sound spelling signals a need for further assessment of the child's phonemic analysis skills. Good performance on such a measure signals that the child may not need explicit instruction in phonemic analysis that doesn't include the use of graphemes to represent phonemes.

(text resumes on p. 131)

---

[4]This is explained in detail in Chapter 7.

TABLE 5.1. What Children's Spellings Can Reveal about Their Phonemic Awareness

Attempted word	Child's spelling	What the child's spelling reveals about the child's ability to analyze the phonemes in one-syllable words	What the child's spelling leaves open to question (more evidence is needed) and/or what instructional foci are appropriate for the child
dog	W	This spelling demonstrates limited phonemic analysis. However, the selection of the letter *W* may not be arbitrary. The child may have chosen the letter *W* because the first phoneme in the name of the letter *W* is /d/—the same phoneme as the first sound in *dog*. It is sometimes mistakenly thought that children who make these kinds of substitutions are not phonemically aware. Instruction is therefore focused on development of that skill rather than letter–sound relationships and other phonics skills which would clearly be valuable for this child.	For this type of response, more examples of the child's spellings would be needed to understand the child's ability to analyze words phonemically. However, given that this spelling attempt provides little, if any, information about the speller's level of phonemic awareness, likely more would be learned via the administration of an oral/verbal phonemic awareness assessment.
bed	bd	This spelling suggests that this child: • Is sensitive to beginning and ending phonemes—including stop consonants—at least in one-syllable words. In relation to the Phonemic Analysis Skills Snapshot (see Figure 5.4, p. 125), it might be reasonable to hypothesize that, at the least, the child: • Can sort pictures based on similarities in beginning and ending sounds. • May be able to segment one-syllable words which include stop consonants—at least those composed of two phonemes.	The absence of a medial vowel may be due to the child being unable to notice/attend to the middle phoneme or to being able to notice but not represent the middle sound. Instructional activities focused on sorting items by similarities in medial vowel sounds and/or instruction focused on helping the child to learn the short sounds of vowel letters may be useful. Analyses of additional instances of sound spelling would help clarify these decisions. An alphabet knowledge assessment (see Chapter 6) might be needed as well.
pet	bt	The sounds associated with the letters *p* and *b* are very similar. They differ only in voicing. In their early writing, children often interchange letters that differ only in terms of whether they are "voiced." Therefore, this substitution, coupled with the accurate representation of the final phoneme /t/, clearly suggests some degree of skill with segmenting words into their component sounds. It is also possible that the substitution of *b* for *p* is due to the child's uncertainty about the proper orientation of the letter *p*—which, if flipped top to bottom, would be identical to the letter *b*.	Assuming that this spelling is characteristic of the child, the spelling suggests that the child may not yet be attending to the medial sounds in single-syllable words and/or that the child does not know how to represent those sounds in print. Further spelling samples would be needed. However, it is unlikely that the child needs phonemic analysis instruction focused on beginning and ending consonant sounds. Note that children who are heavily reliant on letter names as a clue to letters' sounds and who are attempting to spell the short-*e* sound might choose letters whose

(continued)

TABLE 5.1. *(continued)*

Attempted word	Child's spelling	What the child's spelling reveals about the child's ability to analyze the phonemes in one-syllable words	What the child's spelling leaves open to question (more evidence is needed) and/or what instructional foci are appropriate for the child
		In either case, it is clear that the child is relatively good at isolating beginning and ending stop-consonant sounds.	names include the short-e sound to represent the middle sound (i.e., *f* [*ef*], *l* [*el*], *m* [*em*], *n* [*en*], *s* [*es*]). For example, children might spell *pet* as *bst* or *pmt* or *bft*. All these spellings would suggest that the child is fairly phonemically aware but does not yet know the conventional spellings for some of the phonemes. So, too, would spellings in which the final phoneme is represented by the letter *d* which contrasts only in voicing with the sound of the letter *t* (see Figure 5.2, p. 122). Thus, though rare, a learner might spell the word *pet* as *bsd* or *pmt*.
wait	*yat*	The child isolated and represented all three phonemes in the word, although use of the letter *y* rather than *w* for the initial phoneme is not conventional. The substitution of *y* for the sound typically spelled with a *w* is likely because the beginning phoneme in the word *wait* is the same as the beginning phoneme in the name of the letter *y*. Before children are fluent with the conventional relationships between graphemes and phonemes, they will often use the letter names to get to the letter sounds. For this child, it is likely that all the skills listed on the Phonemic Awareness Snapshot (p. 125), except perhaps for the last, are probably well established and, therefore, do not need to be addressed in instruction. When a child spells the word *wait* as *yat*, it indicates that the child is quite phonemically aware. It also appears that the child has not yet learned (or is not yet automatic with) all the letter–sound associations needed to spell words conventionally. It is very common for children to neglect to "mark" the long vowel sound by adding a final *e* or by using a vowel team (e.g., *ai*, *ay*, *ea*) at early points in reading and writing development. They are essentially using letter names to represent the sounds they hear. The child who provided this spelling needs to learn more about English writing system (orthography).	The child *may* be able to accurately segment the sounds in words that include consonant clusters/blends (e.g., *flip*, *stop*, *must*, *cry*). Attempted spellings of such words would need to be analyzed. However, it is important to understand that attempted spellings of such words do not need to be conventional in order to conclude that the child has the needed phonemic analysis skill. Our focus, at the moment, is on the child's ability to attend to the *phonemes* in spoken words. Thus, spelling the word *cry* as *kri* would demonstrate strong phonemic analysis skills because all three phonemes in the word are represented with a letter that does represent the phoneme in some contexts. Learners who produce these types of spellings do not need additional phonemic analysis instruction. They need instruction focused on grapheme–phoneme relationships that are not yet well established. In the current example, the learner needs to learn the phonemes represented by the letters *w* and *y*.

(continued)

TABLE 5.1. *(continued)*

Attempted word	Child's spelling	What the child's spelling reveals about the child's ability to analyze the phonemes in one-syllable words	What the child's spelling leaves open to question (more evidence is needed) and/or what instructional foci are appropriate for the child
church	*hrh*	This learner likely used the letter *h* to spell the /ch/ phoneme because the child didn't yet know the *ch* grapheme but noticed the /ch/ phoneme in the name of the letter *h* (*aich*). For children who are using letter names to decide on how to represent phonemes, *h* would be the logical choice for the /ch/ sound, since it is the only letter name that includes that sound. Regarding the spelling of the middle phoneme in *church*, the sound associated with the letter *r* is similar to the sound associated with the conventional *ur* spelling of the sound in the word *church*. Clearly, this child's phonemic analysis skills are fairly well developed.	Assuming that this spelling is characteristic of the child's approach to sound spelling, the child does not need isolated instruction of the sort described in most of the current chapter. However, this single spelling does not provide information about the child's ability to analyze the phonemes in consonant blends (e.g., /bl/, /st/). The teacher would look for evidence of that skill in the child's future sound spellings or might ask the child to write some words that include consonant blends/clusters.[a] The child's spelling of *church* makes clear that the child needs further instruction focused on the English writing system, which will help to move the child to more conventional spellings—including the understanding that every word must contain at least one vowel letter.
sled	*slad*	This sound spelling suggests that the child can segment all the sounds in a one-syllable word—including words that have consonant clusters/blends. The *a* for *e* substitution is likely due to the fact that the short-*e* (the sound heard at the beginning of the name *Ed*) can be heard at the beginning of the name of the letter *a*. Therefore, the child chose the letter *a* to spell the short-*e* sound. The name of the letter *e* does not include the short-*e* sound (more on this in Chapters 6 and 7). Thus, the inaccurate spelling of the vowel sound in the word *sled* is not due to difficulty with isolating the vowel phoneme. Rather, the difficulty is due to not knowing the conventional spelling for that phoneme.	Assuming that this spelling is characteristic of the child's approach to sound spelling, the child may not need instruction of the sort described in the current chapter. This child appears to be quite phonemically aware—at least to the extent that phonemic awareness would be addressed in isolated activities that do not include print. Rather, the child needs further instruction focused on the English writing system, which will help to move the child to more conventional spellings. And the child may need focused instruction on representing consonant clusters that occur at the end of words as these are more challenging and are not assessed in this example.

[a]As we use the terms, *blend* refers to combinations of consonant sounds in spoken language and *cluster* refers to combinations of consonants in written language.

Many teachers find developmental spelling assessments useful for gaining initial insights into children's phonemic analysis and phonics skills. The Primary Spelling Inventory from *Words Their Way* (Bear, Invernizzi, Templeton, & Johnston, 2019, or any recent edition—of which there are several) is widely used for this purpose. This assessment is administered much like a traditional spelling test. However, children are asked to spell words that have not been "studied," and the teacher analyzes the elements represented in the children's spelling attempts, not just whether the words are spelled conventionally. Teachers can use their analyses to make initial judgments about what an individual child already understands about phonemic analysis. For example, if a child represents most or all the beginning sounds for the dictated words but little else, the teacher can probably conclude that the child does not need phonemic analysis instruction focused on attending to beginning sounds. Further, the child is probably ready for instruction that focuses on the ending sounds in words. Such an assessment would, of course, also provide evidence of the child's understanding of letter–sound correspondences.

Blending and Segmenting Syllables Is an Unnecessary Instructional Focus for Early Literacy Learners

Typically, the earliest emerging phonological analysis skill is the ability to blend and segment the syllables in multisyllabic words. This skill emerges early (for most children by the age of 4 or 5) largely because, unlike phonemes, which are coarticulated, syllables are more distinctive and are more physically apparent via the movement of the mouth. This is so because every syllable contains a vowel sound, and vowel sounds are open-mouth sounds. As a result, there is slight movement of the jaw for each syllable. Because the abilities to blend and segment syllables are early and easily acquired skills, we do not address that skill in this chapter. Further, as noted previously, at this point the scientific evidence does not support focus on this type of skill for children who have already entered kindergarten. As Brady (2020) notes, the ability to blend and segment syllables is not a prerequisite for developing phonemic analysis skills.[5] Instead, we focus on the phonological skills proven to be challenging for children who experience difficulty with literacy acquisition.

Instruction to Promote Phonemic Awareness

Instructional activities that help children develop their phonemic analysis skills are sequenced in accord with what research indicates are typical developmental progressions and can be used to differentiate instruction for individual children or

---

[5]However, as students gain skill with the writing system, analyzing multisyllabic words at the level of the syllable may well help them to provide more literate-looking spellings, especially if they are attentive to the fact that every syllable needs to include at least one vowel letter.

groups of children. The phonemic awareness snapshot discussed earlier (see Figure 5.4, p. 125) is designed to help teachers keep these progressions in mind.

At early points in development, instruction to develop phonemic analysis skills is generally restricted to the use of single-syllable words and words that do not include consonant blends—at least in the part of the word that students are learning to focus on/analyze. That generally means that the words used would be composed of three phonemes, with the first and last phonemes being single-consonant phonemes. Stretchable consonants can be easily elongated without distortion, thereby making it easier to draw children's attention to those phonemes. Therefore, in early instruction it is useful to restrict the items used to those that have stretchable sounds in the focal part of the word. Figure 5.1 (p. 120) provides lists of stretchable and stop-consonant phonemes.

Children become able to attend to and manipulate phonemes in words in a predictable sequence. The first phonemic element that children learn to attend to, and therefore the first focus of instruction for those who need it, is the beginning sound in a word. Next, would be the final sound, and then the medial vowel. As children progress, they need to learn to notice, manipulate, and ultimately represent, the phonemic elements in words that include consonant blends—with the internal elements of those blends/clusters, the elements closest to the vowel, typically being the most challenging for the children to attend to.

Sound Sorting: Sorting Pictures or Objects by Sound Similarity

Sorting activities in which children arrange pictures or objects into groups based on similarities in the sounds of the pictures' labels (names) are frequently used to help learners become attuned to the sounds in spoken words. In what follows, we describe the typical progression of learners' ability to sort based on sound similarities.

Three different sorting principles are used for sound sorting: beginning sounds, ending sounds, and medial (middle) sounds. As children are provided with instruction and practice in sorting based on each of these principles, the teacher should note the child's level of proficiency (beginning, developing, proficient) on the snapshot (p. 125). However, it is important to attend to the children's alphabetic skills as well when determining the proper focus for phonemic awareness instruction. The point of phonemic analysis instruction is to enable children to attend to the sounds in spoken words. If it becomes evident in the children's attempted spellings that they can fairly reliably represent the sounds in particular parts of one-syllable words, engaging children in sound-sorting activities focused on that part of the words is not likely to be a useful focus of instructional time.

The general technique for sorting entails providing children with a group of objects or pictures of objects that can be sorted by sound similarity in a specified part of the words. For example, initially, children might be given pictures of a *mat*, a *moon*, a bar of *soap*, and a *mouth* and might be asked to put together the three that have the same sound at the beginning and/or to move the one with a different beginning sound away from the others. A bit later, children might be given larger sets of pictures to sort.

Materials

Developing materials for sound-sorting exercises takes some thought. Therefore, we have developed sets of pictures for use in sound sorting and have made them available on the book's companion website (see the box at the end of the table of contents). These picture sets follow the guidance we provide below related to the various sorting principles. For example, some picture sets are useful for sound sorting focused on stretchable beginning sounds. These picture sets can be printed on card stock, cut apart, and used repeatedly. Alternatively, the picture sets for a given day can be copied onto plain paper, and each child can be given a sheet containing the pictures. The children can then cut up the sheets into individual pictures in preparation for the day's sorting activities.

Other potentially useful materials are available as well. For example, pictures for use in sorting activities can be found in *Words Their Way* (Bear et al., 2019). In addition, numerous sets of materials for promoting phonemic awareness can be purchased, some of which use miniature objects rather than pictures.[6] When using purchased materials, it is important to analyze the materials carefully before using them as, all too frequently, pictures or objects are included in a set to which they do not belong (e.g., an object starting with the /sh/ sound included among objects beginning with the /s/ sound). The following guidelines can assist in that analysis.

When developing (or selecting) materials to use for sound sorting activities:

- Choose pictures/objects that are relatively unambiguous in terms of the labels that might be applied to them.
- Choose pictures/objects that have one-syllable names.
- Always apply the same name to an item. If you initially label an item *rug*, it will confuse children if you later decide to call it *mat*.

Especially for introductory purposes:

- Choose objects with names that contain a relatively simple phonemic structure in the part of the word that is the focus of the activity. For example, for a beginning sound sort, the words *fork, fox, rope, rake, fish,* and *rock* would be a good group to use because the beginning sounds are single consonants that can be elongated (stretched) without distortion. Words with stop consonants at the beginning (e.g., *ball, box, bike, cat, kite, cup*) would be more challenging to analyze, but they certainly can be used once the children have

---

[6]We advise against using miniature objects for phonological awareness activities, as they have too much play value and therefore may keep the children from focusing on the task at hand: thinking about the sounds.

demonstrated skill with the items that have stretchable sounds. Words with consonant clusters/blends would be more challenging still.

- Use contrasts that are very distinct so that the differences in the sounds are easier to notice. For example, the sounds /s/ and /r/ are quite different from one another, whereas the sounds /f/ and /v/ are quite similar (they differ only in voicing). Thus, it would be easier for children to notice that *rope* has a different beginning sound in the set *fork, fox, rope, fish* than to notice that *van* has a different beginning sound in the set *fork, fox, van, fish*.

As children begin to demonstrate the ability to detect similarities and differences in the sounds in words, the restrictions on word selection can be relaxed, and picture sorts can include items with stop consonants (i.e., *ball, top, box,* and *bike*).

Think Sounds, Not Letters

In working to attune children to the sounds in spoken words, it is important for teachers to think about the sounds in the words that are being analyzed, not just the letters. For example, the word *shoe* has four letters but just two sounds, and there is nothing particularly challenging about attending to the sound represented by the *sh* digraph—it can be stretched without distortion. Therefore, words beginning with /sh/, since it is a stretchable phoneme, can be included in early phonemic analysis activities such as sorting by beginning sounds (e.g., *shoe, shirt, shell, man, mop, mouse*).

As detailed in the next sections, children can engage in sound sorting in a variety of ways.

Odd-One-Out Sorting Activity

For an initial introduction to sorting by sound commonalities, the *odd-one-out* activity is useful because it allows children to focus on just a few words at a time. In this activity, children are presented with groups of pictures, one group at a time. In each group, all of the pictures except one have the same sound in a specified part of the word. The children are asked to figure out which word doesn't have the same sound (does not belong).

A fairly detailed description of the odd-one-out activity, using beginning sounds as the sorting principle, follows. The same format can be used to introduce and practice the other sorting principles. In general, children should work on a given sorting principle until they are both fast and accurate before moving on.

KEEP IN MIND   Children are most likely to attach the intended label to a picture if the teacher labels it immediately as it is presented. Sometimes teachers hold back and wait to see if the children can label the pictures. Sometimes the children will suggest a different label than the one intended. Once they've decided that the picture shows a shark, for example, it may be hard for them to remember that the teacher called it a fish.

FIGURE 5.5. Example of pictures for an odd-one-out sort.

BEGINNING-SOUND ODD-ONE-OUT SORT

For this activity, collect several groups of pictures. Each group should contain two or three pictures that begin with the same sound and one picture that begins with a different sound (see Figure 5.5). For initial demonstration and practice purposes, it is best to choose items for which the beginning sound can be easily elongated (stretched) when it is pronounced (i.e., words starting with the sounds for *f, l, m, n, r, s, sh, v, z*). Using stretchable sounds makes it easier to demonstrate the sorting principle of interest. Also, keep in mind that it is important for children to assign the correct labels to the pictures (the labels you intend). This can be ensured by saying the names of the pictures frequently, at least when the pictures are first introduced, and having the children repeat the names. In the following sample instructional dialogue, when letters appear between slash marks (e.g., /fffff/), it signals that the teacher is to articulate and elongate the sound of the letter—and not necessarily name it. But, if the printed version of the letter has already been introduced in other contexts, it is fine to make the connection for the students.

Sample Instructional Dialogue for Odd-One-Out Sort		
Materials needed: Groups of pictures—three or four per group constructed following the guideline described above.		
Teacher	**What the teacher says**	**Comments on the activity**
Sets a purpose.	"When we read and write, one of the things we need to think about is the sounds in the words we want to read or write. So, we are going to practice thinking about sounds in words. We will use pictures to help us remember what words we are thinking about."	
Shows first set of pictures.	"I have three pictures here. One of them doesn't belong in the group because it has a different sound at the **beginning**. This is a *sssseal;* you say it. This is a *sssssun;* you say it. And this is a *mmmmmop;* you say it." (*Points to each picture while labeling it.*)	Naming each picture while stretching the beginning sound helps the children notice the sounds that are the focus of the activity. Having the children repeat the name of the picture helps them to remember the name, and because they are repeating

| | | the name immediately after the teacher, they are apt to stretch the beginning sounds, which may help them to better attend to those sounds.

Note: if children repeat the article ("a") guide them to just say the label for the picture. |
|---|---|---|
| Illustrates the sound-sorting process. | "When I say *sssssun* and *sssseal*, do you hear that they both have /sssss/ at the beginning? *Sssssun, sssseal*

"Now when I say *mmmmop*, do I make that /sssss/ sound? *mmmmmop*." | Naming the two pictures that have the same beginning sound and then naming the sound emphasizes the similarity.
Naming the one that has a different beginning sound (mop) and asking if it has the /ssss/ emphasizes what the children need to do. |
| Provides feedback and illustrates the sorting process. | "That's right, *mmmmmop* doesn't have the /sssss/ sound, so I'm going to move the *mmmmmop* away from *sssssun* and *sssseal* because the beginning sound in *mmmmmop* is different from the beginning sounds in *sssssun* and *sssseal*. *Mmmmmop* doesn't have /sssss/ at the beginning. We hear /sssss/ in *sssssun* and in *sssseal*. (*Points to each picture while naming it*.) So, I'm going to put them together because they have the same sound at the beginning." | |
| Lays out three new pictures and points to each while naming each and having the children repeat the name. | "Now you try one. Here is *fffffan*, you say it. *Rrrrrake*, you say it. *Fffffox*, you say it. Two of these sound the same at the beginning, and one of them has a different sound at the beginning. Let's see if we can figure out which one has a different sound at the beginning. *Fffffan, rrrrrake, fffffox*." | Stretching the beginning sounds helps the children attend to them. |
| | "Let's think about this one togwether. First, we'll say each word. *Fffffan, rrrrrake, fffffox*. (*Encourages the children to join in labeling the pictures and stretching the beginning sounds*.) When we say *fffffan*, what is the first sound we make? Let's all make the first sound in *fffffan*. /fffff/. So *fffffan* has /fffff/ at the beginning. Now let's try *rrrrrake* and think about what sound we | If the children provide an incorrect answer (fan or fox), the teacher provides immediate feedback in the form of leading the children through the process again:
• Encouraging them to name the pictures again while stretching the beginning sounds. |

make first when we say *rrrrrake*. /*rrrrr*/. Do *fffffan* and *rrrrake* both have /*rrrr*/ at the beginning?" (CHILDREN: No!) "So, *ffffan* and *rrrrake* have different sounds at the beginning—and I am going to move them apart. "Now, let's try *ffffox*. Do you hear the same beginning sound as in *fffan*? Or do you hear the same sound you hear at the beginning of *rrrrake*?"	• Isolating the beginning sound. • Comparing the beginning sounds.

The teacher would continue to engage the group in collaborative sorting until the children seem to understand the process and then would provide each child with their own sets of pictures (one set at a time) and provide feedback as needed. Gradually, as children demonstrate their understanding of the task, the teacher should begin, on subsequent items, to reduce the elongation of the beginning sounds when saying the names of the pictures. When children can readily and accurately sort without the teacher elongating the sounds, the items used can be expanded to include words that begin with stop consonants (e.g., *b*, *d*, *g*, *h*, *c/k*). Although adding a *schwa* sound (e.g., the /uh/ in pronouncing the sound of *t*) is unavoidable when producing stop sounds in isolation, care should be taken to minimize it as much as possible as it may dominate the sound of the consonant, thereby making it harder to focus on the consonant sound.

KEEP IN MIND When stretching sounds in words for children, particular emphasis should be placed on stretching the part of the word to which the children are to attend. So, for the example in Figure 5.5, it is helpful to say *sssssun*, not *sssssuuuunnnnn*. The latter rendition of *sun* would be appropriate later, when children are attempting to analyze all the sounds in a word—as, for example, when they are writing.

Sorting Boards

Once children understand the general principle of separating pictures by whether they have the same sound in a particular part of the word, sorting boards can be used to provide additional practice. The same sorting principles would be used. The sorting boards contain two or three columns, each headed by a picture that begins (ends, etc.) with a different sound. The children are then given a packet of pictures that have the same beginning (ending, etc.) sound as one of the pictures heading a column. One by one, children then place the pictures with the same sounds in the appropriate column.

In using the sorting boards, children should be encouraged to say the name of each picture as they consider its placement. If they have difficulty deciding in which column to place a picture, they should be encouraged to name the pictures already in the column under consideration—especially the column header. Once the children have learned how to do this type of sorting, they can use these sorting boards fairly independently, perhaps as a center activity during which they glue the pictures in the correct columns.

An example of a sorting board for a beginning-sound sort is presented in Figure 5.6. The two pictures at the top serve as column headers and are posted on the board when the child begins to work with it. The pictures at the bottom of the figure are given to the child as a set. Each child is given their own set of pictures in a small pile—in mixed-up order—and is encouraged to place each picture in the proper column based on beginning sounds. Clearly, it is important to make sure children have the correct label for each picture before they are asked to do the sort. For that reason, it is useful to use the same pictures in a variety of phonemic analysis activities. For instance, a picture of (a bar of) soap can be used when the sorting principle is initial stretchable sounds, final stop sounds, or medial vowel sounds. If a child places a picture in the wrong column, the teacher might wait a bit and then tell the child there is one picture that doesn't belong in the column and encourage the child to try to figure out which one needs to be moved. Addressing the misplaced item in this way encourages the child to really think about the sounds in the words. It can help to ask the child to name all the pictures in the column, as that generally enables the child to self-correct. If the teacher simply identified which item was misplaced, the child wouldn't need to do much, if any, thinking about the process.

Phoneme Blending and Segmentation

Phoneme Blending and Reading

Learning to *blend* phonemes is generally easier than learning to *segment* the phonemes in a word. Practice with phoneme blending is helpful because, when beginning readers attempt to identify a word that they have not yet learned to read, one strategy they may use is to:

(1) identify the individual letters,
(2) think of the sound each letter represents (or could represent),
(3) hold the individual sounds in memory while other sounds are retrieved, and finally
(4) blend the individual sounds together.

Difficulty with the blending process (or any of the other processes involved) may interfere with the reader's ability to identify the printed word. This difficulty, in turn, will impact the process of adding the word to the reader's sight vocabulary and, ultimately, decrease comprehension of the written text. The reader needs to

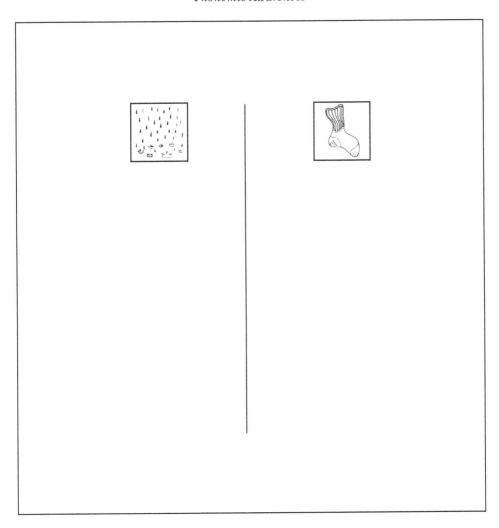

FIGURE 5.6. Beginning-sound sorting board. *Note:* Column headers are *rain* and *sock*; pictures to sort are *saw*, *soup*, *rug*, *ring*, *roof*, *sun*, and *rope*.

be able to read the words in order to comprehend the message. Providing children with practice in blending individual (spoken) sounds into words may make it easier for them to handle the blending process while reading. In addition, having children blend individual sounds into words will help attune them to the fact that words are composed of somewhat separable sounds. In turn, this should help children develop the ability to segment words at the level of the phoneme (which then assists with sound spelling).

Phoneme Segmentation and Writing

In order to write effectively, a beginning reader/writer who does not yet know the conventional spellings of words must be able to segment words into their component phonemes. For example, when children first begin to truly use the alphabet to communicate in writing, they often print the letter representing the first, or the most salient, sound in each word they want to write. To do so, the child must be able to focus on the beginning (or most salient) sound in a word and think of it as being somewhat distinct from the other sounds. Then the child might articulate the sound, try to think of which letter represents that particular sound, and, finally, write the letter. The activities described in this section help children learn to both attend to and isolate the individual sounds in words. When children have learned a bit about letters and their sounds, they are ready to coordinate these understandings and to begin to apply their phoneme analysis and letter–sound knowledge in writing.

KEEP IN MIND Throughout instruction to promote phonemic analysis skills, it is important to simultaneously consider what the children's reading and spelling indicates about their ability to analyze and manipulate the sounds in spoken words. Children who can represent all the sounds in single-syllable spoken words in their attempted spellings (even if their spellings are not conventional) likely do not need to continue with isolated phonemic analysis skills instruction and practice of the sort described in this chapter. The instructional activities discussed in Chapters 7–10 all involve phonemic analysis—but in a context that engages children in connecting phonemes with their associated graphemes—which is, after all, the main reason for helping students to become phonemically aware.

Phoneme Blending

A puppet or a picture of a character (like a robot or a space alien) is typically used in blending activities. The children are told that the characters have a strange way of talking: that is, they spread out the sounds in their words too much. The children are asked to help figure out what the character is trying to say, using the sounds as clues. Three or four pictures are then put in front of the children. The character (through the teacher) then names one of the pictures using the funny (segmented) speech. The children attempt to figure out which of the pictures the character named. Children typically love these blending activities. The characters are very popular and usually have names and personalities. These activities can have a playful tone but clearly need to stay focused on the instructional purpose: developing awareness of the phonemes in spoken words. The sample instructional dialogue that follows uses the pictures shown in Figure 5.7.

FIGURE 5.7. Pictures for the dialogue below.

Sample Instructional Dialogue for Phoneme Blending		
Materials needed:	Pictures with names that are one syllable in length with single phonemes at the beginning and end of the word. (In early blending activities, the consonants in the words should be stretchable [e.g., sun, rose, fan]).	
Teacher	**What the teacher says**	**Comment on the activity**
Sets the purpose.	"When we don't know a word we are trying to read, it helps us to think about the sounds in the words, by thinking about the sounds of the letters. You get to blend the sounds; that means put them together, to try to figure out the word. We are going to play a game to help us learn to do that blending part."	
Explains the activity.	"In this game, we'll use this puppet, named Stretch, who will pretend to talk in a funny way— by saying parts of the word he wants you to figure out. To help you figure out Stretch's words, I'll put some pictures out on the table. You'll listen to the sounds and then choose the picture Stretch names."	It is useful to name the puppet (we use Stretch in this example) and give it a back story as it makes the activity feel more engaging. But it is important to make sure that the playful part is only a small element in the activity.
Demonstrates with an example.	"Let's try one. First, I'll tell you what the pictures are, you say the names after I say them: *fish, mouse, fan, moon.* "If Stretch was trying to name this *mouse* picture, he would say /mmm/-/ou/-/sss/."	It is important to point to each picture while naming it, and if the children are not familiar with the pictured items, to have them practice naming the pictures a few times. When demonstrating how Stretch would name *mouse*, the teacher would elongate each of the phonemes, pausing slightly between phonemes.

Engages the children in doing the blending.	"Now you get to try to figure out what Stretch is saying. Remember, he's going to say the name of one of these pictures. "Let's remind ourselves of what each picture is called . . . say each of them with me. . . . "Now, listen to Stretch, and think about what picture he is naming—but don't call it out when you think you know—just raise your hand and I'll call on someone."	Name the pictures again if needed. When engaging the children in naming them, the teacher can hang back a bit and listen to determine whether the children can easily name the pictures. If so, it is not necessary to remind the children of what the pictures are called in future activities. It is important to give all the children time to think. If one child calls out before the others have figured out the word, the others will not have the opportunity to do the needed thinking.
Says the sounds—stretching each.	"Here we go . . . /ffff/ /aaaa/ /nnn/. Think about what picture he's naming:"	Stretch pauses briefly between phonemes.
Repeats the sounds.	"/ffff/ /aaaa/ /nnn/."	The teacher articulates the phonemes twice to give children more time to think about how to blend the phonemes.
Waits for all children in the group to indicate they have an answer. And calls on one—who says "man."	"You remembered some of the sounds. Listen again to all the sounds and blend them together. "/ffff/ /aaaa/ /nnnn/."	On an incorrect response, it is always useful to notice and name what the student(s) did right—as this builds confidence and motivation. If children have difficulty blending the sounds, it may help for them to quietly repeat the sounds that the character articulated before deciding on which picture was named.
Again tries to wait for all children to indicate they have a response and then calls on one who provides the correct response (fan).	"Fan! Yes, when you blend /ffff/ /aaaa/ /nnnn/ together, it makes the word *fan*."	If only one of the pictures displayed for this activity started with an *f* sound or had ended with an *n*, the children would not have to blend the parts in order to produce the correct response. All they would need to do is decide which of the pictured items started with *f* or ended with *n*. Therefore, the collection of pictures offered needs careful consideration.

As each of the puppet's words is correctly identified, the teacher would remove the picture from the display on the table (perhaps letting a child give it to the puppet) and place another picture in the display area. Pictures that are added can have a different beginning, middle, or ending sounds than those remaining on display. But the puppet's next word should be one that shares at least one phoneme with other items on display. When the children can readily blend words with stretchable beginning and ending sounds, it's time to include words that have stop consonants.

The initial use of pictures in sound-blending instruction and practice, as well as the use of words that are composed of stretchable phonemes, are both intended to make the blending process easier for children to learn to do. However, because the purpose of helping children learn to blend individual phonemes is, ultimately, to prepare them to use this skill during the process of decoding unfamiliar words while reading (by blending the sounds of the graphemes in the words), these scaffolds should be removed as the children's blending skills increase.

When children can easily blend sounds with picture choices (i.e., they are rated as proficient on "Phoneme blending, With pictures" on the snapshot [Figure 5.4, p. 125]), they would be asked to do the blending without the pictures being visible. Note that, in moving from instruction using picture choices to no picture choices, it is important to try to use words that are in the children's spoken vocabularies because this will allow children to determine whether the result of their blending attempt is a real word. When children can easily blend phonemes in one-syllable words without relying on pictures to support their thinking, there is no need to continue the blending activity. The skill, however, will be utilized in the word-reading activities described in Chapters 8–10 and, of course, as children engage in reading meaningful texts.

MLs, Vocabulary, and Blending

Children who may not know the words used in these activities—whether because of their ML status or for other reasons—should be provided with extra practice in naming the words and learning something about the objects if necessary, prior to engaging in the blending activities. For example, many children may be unfamiliar with ceiling fans.

Phoneme Segmentation

Phoneme segmentation is, for most children, the most challenging of the phonemic analysis tasks. For that reason, it is generally introduced once children have begun to demonstrate skill with sorting and blending.

Moving from Blending to Segmenting

Some children find it quite easy to learn to segment words into phonemes, whereas others find it much more challenging. Participating in the phoneme-blending activities described above is likely to make learning to segment easier because the blending tasks provide a lot of modeling of how words can be segmented. Practice with blending activities also makes phoneme segmentation seem like fun for many children, as they generally enjoy interacting with the puppet or whatever character is used. As the children begin to become facile at blending sounds to make words, they will usually be eager to take a turn at controlling the puppet and talking the way the puppet does. This sort of playful practice is useful and should be encouraged. Making the puppet that is used during blending activities available for the children to use during their free-choice periods or in a center can encourage this playful practice and can be useful even if their segmentation of the words is not entirely accurate—as they are still thinking about the phonemes in words.

Phoneme Segmentation

Phoneme segmentation involves segmenting a word into its individual phonemes and using counters to track the number of sounds.

TYPES OF WORDS

Initial instruction and practice for phoneme segmentation/counting should use words with only two sounds, both of which are stretchable (e.g., *me, say*). The rime portion should consist of a single vowel because it is generally more challenging to segment the individual sounds in the rime portion (e.g., the *ish* in *fish*) than it is to segment the onset from the rime. Segmenting the word *me* into individual phonemes requires the child to separate the onset (/m/) from the rime (/ē/). This type of segmentation is comparatively easy. Segmenting a word like *in*, on the other hand, requires breaking up the rime portion (there is no onset in the word *in*). Once children can successfully segment two-phoneme words with stretchable consonants, they should begin to focus on words with stop consonants. The general sequence for lessons focused on different types of words is presented in Table 5.2. Sample lists for each type of word used in sound-counting activities are provided in Figure 5.8.

TABLE 5.2. Progression of Difficulty for Sound-Counting/Segmenting Activities

Degree of challenge	Types of words to use
Easiest	Two-phoneme words with onsets and rimes and stretchable consonants (e.g., *me*)
	Two-phoneme words with stop consonants (e.g., *go*)
	Three-phoneme words with stretchable consonants (e.g., *sun*)
	Three-phoneme words with stop consonants (e.g., *bat*)
Most challenging	Three- or four-phoneme words that include consonant blends (e.g., *fly, stop, gift*)

Two Phonemes		Three Phonemes		Consonant Clusters/ Blends
Stretchable	Stop consonants	Stretchable	Stop consonants	
me	bow	safe	bat	fly
so	by	foam	bite	stop
new	Boo	face	bike	smile
my	do	fame	cap	frog
shoe	day	man	cake	snow
say	guy	mane	dot	plane
lie	go	mice	good	sweep
low	cow	moss	gate	grape
lay	hay	fan	hike	prize
moo	high	noon	kite	fry
mow	tie	news	keep	glue
may	who	nice	pot	stick
knee	he	mall	pack	bread
she	key	name	tape	block
ray	pay	knife	tight	ski
row	pie	some	tap	jump
sew	toe	zoom	top	help
zoo	tie	feel	take	fast

Note. Within a column, words need not be used in order. However, for words that include consonant clusters/blends, words with clusters at the beginning of word should be used first.

FIGURE 5.8. Words for phoneme counting.

MATERIALS

Phoneme-counting activities were originally described by Elkonin (1973). He used "sound boxes" to provide children with a concrete representation of the process of segmenting words. As children articulate each phoneme in a word, they are taught to move a counter into the box that represents that sound. Because Elkonin was the first to introduce this procedure for sound counting, many now refer to this method as *Elkonin*[7] *boxes.* Because the technique has proven so successful in helping children learn to segment words at the level of the phoneme, and because the sound boxes provide for an easy transition between sound counting and sound spelling, Elkonin boxes have been incorporated into many early literacy routines.

Typically, a sound-counting activity begins with providing each child with a piece of (laminated) paper or a dry-erase board on which connected squares have been drawn. Initially, the number of squares corresponds to the number of phonemes in the words that will be used for sound counting. Often, a small symbol is drawn in or under the leftmost box to indicate that it is the "beginning box." We use a star to signal "start." (Although no letters are used initially, sequencing the sounds in words from left to right will reinforce the convention that print is organized from left to right.) The teacher provides each child with the number of counters needed for the activity (counting chips or cubes, etc.). To start with, the teacher has the same materials as the children, perhaps in a bigger version depending on the number of children in the group. Figure 5.9 provides an example of Elkonin boxes.

Introduction to Phoneme Segmentation/Counting

The sample instructional dialogue that follows can be used when first introducing phoneme segmentation. In working with children, teachers typically refer to the process as sound counting to make the activity more understandable to young children.

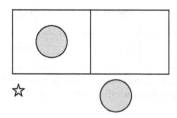

FIGURE 5.9. Illustration of Elkonin boxes.

---

[7] Many people incorrectly pronounce Elkonin's name as Elkonian.

Sample Instructional Dialogue for *Introducing* Phoneme Segmentation		
Materials needed (for the teacher and each child in the group):	• Set of boxes—with the needed number of boxes for the lesson • Needed number of counters for each participant • List of words to be used	
Teacher	**What the teacher says**	**Comment on the activity**
Sets the purpose.	Before, we were practicing listening to the sounds in words with Stretch. Now we are going to learn how to talk like Stretch. While we are doing that, we can figure out how many sounds there are in some words that we use all the time. If we know how many sounds there are in a word, it will help us decide how many letters we might need to use when we write that word.	
Explains the process.	Let's think about the word *me*. When I say the word *mmmmeeee*, I start with the /mmmm/ sound and then I make the /ēēēē/ sound. So *mmmmeeee* has two sounds: /mmmm/ and /ēēēē/.	Initially focusing on segmentation without using the counters makes it easier for the children to understand the process.
Introduces counting boxes.	I can use these boxes to help me count the sounds. The first box has a star under it to help me remember it is the box for the first sound in the word. The star will help us remember that this is where we *start* when we are using the counters.	Again, this separate explanation of how to use the boxes and the start indicator eases the learners into the process.
Demonstrates.	I'll show you how to use the boxes to count the sounds in *mmmmeeee*. When I say *mmmeee*, I start by saying /mmmm/, so I put a counter in the start box. Then, when I say /ēēēē/, I put a counter in the next box.	Explicit explanation and modeling is important when new skills are introduced.
Engages children in repeating the previous demonstration.	Now, let's all say the sounds in the word *mmmeee* and move our counters into our boxes. [Everybody] pick up a counter and get ready to put it in the start box. We are going to count the sounds in the word *mmmmeeeee*.	The teacher models while listening to and watching what the children do and provides any needed guidance.

	Let's all say *mmmmeeee*. First, we hear *mmmm* so we put a counter in the start box.	
Continues engaging the children in the demonstration.	So, we have our counter for the first sound in *mmmmeeee* in the start box. Get another counter ready for the next sound. Let's all say *meee* again and then say the last sound *eeee* and put the marker in the next box.	The teacher reduces the stretching for the first sound as the current focus is on the last sound. As above, the teacher listens and watches and provides any needed guidance.
Stops modeling the use of counters.	Take your counters out of your boxes and we'll do it again. Now I'll just say the sounds in *mmmeee*, and you move the counters into your boxes. /mmm/ /ēēēē/.	The teacher is beginning to release responsibility for the process and continues to observe and provide feedback.
Invites a child to do the segmenting.	Now, take your counters out of your boxes again. Who would like to say the sounds in *me* for us while the rest of us move our counters? First, you'll say the word *me* and then stretch the sounds out so we can count them.	More release of responsibility.
Moves counters along with other children as the volunteer child says the word and the sounds.	Nice job!	The teacher would provide corrective feedback as needed, which may require greater stretching of the sounds in the word and/or redirecting the placement of the counters.
	Now, let's all say the sounds in *mmmeee* and move the counters into the boxes as we say each sound.	Children now have responsibility for the entire process.

"How Would Stretch Say It?"

One of the teachers with whom we've worked (A. Daley) used a puppet named Stretch when she worked with her kindergarten groups. During blending activities, Stretch articulated the individual sounds, and the children would identify the word that Stretch was attempting to say. Stretch's memorable way of talking was very helpful to the children when, at a later point, they were attempting to write. If they demonstrated difficulty with segmenting the sounds of the words they wanted to write, the teacher would simply ask "How would Stretch say it?" This simple prompt reminded the children of the process and engaged them in doing the sound analysis more independently (and lightheartedly) than they otherwise might have done.

Practice with Phoneme Counting

Following the introduction to phoneme counting, the teacher would choose additional words from the first column of Figure 5.8 (p. 145) to provide additional practice with words with stretchable sounds that have both onsets and single phoneme rimes. It may well be necessary to provide more modeling of the process. As the children become more adept at sound counting, the teacher would gradually reduce and ultimately eliminate the stretching done when naming words for sound counting. The goal is for the children to be able to count the sounds in two-sound words (articulate the sounds and move the counters) independently. The teacher should continue to use words with stretchable sounds until the children can segment them easily and are, therefore, ready for more challenging words. Some children will be ready for the more challenging words sooner than others. In this case, individual children can be asked to segment and count the sounds in different words.

When the children are facile with counting the sounds in two-sound words that have stretchable consonants, they should be asked to count sounds in two-sound words with stop consonants. Later, they would work with words that have three sounds with stretchable consonants, then three-sound words with stop consonants, and so on.

When it is clear that the children understand the process, it is time to remove the scaffold of having the same number of boxes as there are sounds in the words. In order to apply their segmentation skills to authentic writing, children need to be able to determine the number of sounds in the words they want to write. At this point the children can have a standard set of boxes (four or five boxes) and use as many boxes as they need to represent all the sounds in the words—realizing that there will often be boxes left over.

Fiddling with Phonemes, Playing with Language at Odd Times

The activities described below can be squeezed into odd moments of the day. These activities typically should not be attempted unless the skills on which they build have already been introduced explicitly and practiced. For teachers who are working with children in an intervention setting, the "talking like the puppet" activity could be used to practice phonemic analysis skills while traveling through the hallway to the intervention setting.

Line Up by Sound

Have children line up for PE, recess, and so on in accordance with whether a certain sound (not letter) occurs in their names. For example, the teacher might ask children whose names begin with the /sss/ sound to line up first. *Sandeep* and *Sahra* would line up but not *Sean* (which is pronounced as *Shawn)* because the name starts with the /sh/ sound. For children with more advanced skills, the teacher might line children up by whether they have a particular phoneme anywhere in their name. The teacher might say, "if you have an /mmm/ in your name, line up," in which case *Jamal, Amy,* and *Miguel* would all line up.

Talking Like the Puppet

Occasionally, the teacher or other children can pretend to be the character used in sound-blending activities (in our case, Stretch). The teacher might use a segmented version of the child's name (e.g., for Sahra it would be "/S/ /ah/ /r/ /ah/, please bring me a pen") or object (e.g., "Miguel, please bring me a /p/ /ĕ/ /n/"). Such language play may encourage children to engage in similar play when the teacher is not interacting with them.

KEY POINTS OF THIS CHAPTER

✓ The ability to analyze and manipulate the sounds in spoken words is an important foundation for learning to read and spell. This ability can be developed through the following instructional activities:
  - Sound/phoneme sorting
  - Phoneme blending
  - Phoneme segmentation

✓ Children's sound spellings can provide important information about their degree of phonemic awareness.

✓ It is easier for children to learn to attend to phonemes that are stretchable (easily elongated without distortion). Therefore, early instruction on particular skills should use words with stretchable phonemes.

✓ It is important for teachers to understand the characteristics of phonemes that make them easier/harder and more/less confusing for children to attend to. For example, several pairs of sounds differ from one another only in voicing (d/t, b/p, f/v).

CHAPTER 6

Letter Naming
and Letter Formation

WRITING SYSTEM FOUNDATIONS GOAL 3

Children will be able to name and print all 26 letters of the alphabet, both upper- and lower-case versions, accurately and rapidly.

Among the earliest steps in learning to read and write is learning the names and forms of the individual letters that are the foundation of the English writing system. Virtually all recommendations for literacy learning call for children to know the names of all the letters of the alphabet and to be able to print many, if not all, of them by the end of kindergarten. Recent research suggests that it would be ideal for children to be able to name most of the letters (18 upper-case and 15 lower-case) by the end of preschool to ensure successful literacy development (Piasta, Petscher, & Justice, 2012). However, this does not mean that if we could simply get preschool teachers to drill their students on letter names we could avert reading difficulties! Rather, young children learn the names of printed letters in a variety of ways and through a variety of activities. And knowledge of letter names is a simple-to-measure indicator of a lot of things that lead to the development of letter–name knowledge, including:

- Having spent time in an environment (at home or at school or both) that values literacy and provides opportunity to interact with literacy materials (books, paper and writing/drawing tools, puzzles, magnetic letters, electronic devices, etc.).
- Being interested in learning and motivated to learn about print.
- Having access to adults who are responsive to and supportive of the child's emerging literacy skills.

Although explicit instruction focused on helping children learn the names of printed letters will assuredly help preschoolers and kindergartners learn letter names, if the approach makes learning about letters seem like work rather than play, and if it is done in such a way that children feel overwhelmed and/or frustrated, efforts to improve this knowledge base are apt to backfire with at least some children concluding that print-related activities are to be avoided.

Children who enter kindergarten lacking in letter–name knowledge are more likely to experience reading difficulties. Their future success with written language depends, at least in part, on their experiences with print and the effectiveness of those experiences in attuning them not only to the elements of print but also to the interrelationships between spoken and written language. Research demonstrating that instructional experiences in kindergarten make a big difference for children who arrive with comparatively little early literacy experience provides a strong argument for initiating intervention efforts in kindergarten (O'Connor et al., 2005; Scanlon & Vellutino, 1996, 1997; Scanlon et al., 2005, 2008). More recent research (Roberts, Vadasy, & Sanders, 2018) suggests that approaches that might be used to help preschool children learn about letters and their sounds may be differentially effective. Their study found that, rather than simultaneously teaching letter names and letter sounds, an approach that has been fairly typical in the early grades, teaching just the names *or* the sounds of the letters to begin with may accelerate learning. While we await replication of this research, it is important to note that, in our intervention research with young children, we have always advocated for teaching letter names first. Our logic is that teaching a letter's name and sound simultaneously, possibly along with a key word to help children remember the sound, could be overwhelming for young learners, especially if they know very little about the alphabet to begin with. We're not suggesting that children need to learn all the letter names before learning letter sounds. Rather, once children have begun to learn letter names and have some letters they can identify reliably, they may begin to learn the sounds associated with those letters while they continue to learn other letters' names.

Other research has indicated that the speed with which children can name the letters in kindergarten is also a strong predictor of their growth as readers (as measured by oral reading fluency measured in first grade; Stage, Sheppard, Davison, & Browning, 2001). This relationship may suggest that slow letter naming is an indication of some uncertainty about the names of the letters. This uncertainty requires children to expend more of their cognitive energy on this lower-level skill, and, as a result, children would have fewer cognitive resources to devote to word solving (i.e., figuring out unfamiliar written words) and fewer successful experiences with word solving. Over time, this would slow the growth of their sight vocabulary (i.e., words that can be identified effortlessly). For these reasons, we argue that it is important to help children at the preschool and kindergarten levels become fluent with letter names as soon as possible.

The goal identified for this chapter involves both the learning of letter names and letter formation (printing), but substantially less research has focused on the teaching and learning of letter formation early in the process of literacy acquisition. Nevertheless, we maintain that engaging children in learning to print letters has the clear potential to help them learn the critical features of the letters they are learning to name and to determine what features distinguish one letter from another (e.g., what makes a *B* a *B*?).

Documenting Letter Knowledge

Small-group and individual intervention settings provide the teacher with more opportunity to individualize instruction, making it possible to develop a more optimal instructional plan for teaching children about letters. A summary of the research on teaching the alphabet revealed that alphabet instruction was more effective when done in small-group rather than whole-class settings (Piasta et al., 2012). One likely reason for this finding is that instruction can be more responsive to the knowledge and skills of the children in the group. To make instruction more responsive, it is important to first determine which letters children can already recognize, name, and/or produce (print) and for which letters, if any, they know the corresponding sound(s). For children who know little about the alphabet, it is also important to take into consideration which letters may hold significance for them (e.g., because the letters are in their names or in the names of friends, pets, siblings). As the school year progresses, it is important to document growth in letter-level skills.

Although complete individualization is not possible for the classroom teacher, initial assessment of letter-level skills nevertheless provides important information that contributes to grouping decisions. In the early primary grades, periodic assessment of letter-level skills during the school year provides important information concerning whether children are in appropriate groups, whether they are making progress or need more intensive instructional support, and whether the class, as a whole, is making sufficient progress.

Initial Evaluation of Letter-Level Knowledge

As noted above, instruction to promote the development of letter-level skills is generally more effective when provided in small-group rather than whole-class contexts. Grouping children with similar skill levels is likely to enable more efficient use of instructional time. Table 6.1 provides an overview of how assessment of letter-level skills might be approached for the purpose of determining children's status and, thereby, informing instructional grouping decisions and appropriate foci for instruction.

To make the evaluation as efficient as possible, we recommend that teachers:

- Assess letter identification (naming) first.
- Assess recognition for any letters the child *cannot* name.

TABLE 6.1. Assessment of Letter-Level Skills

Letter-level skill	How the skill is measured	Example
Letter recognition	The child is shown a small group of letters and is asked to point to the one named by the teacher.	The teacher displays *B S M T O* and says, "Point to the *T*." (*Note:* If a correct response seems like a guess, the letter can be subsequently included in another set, and the child would be asked about that letter again.)
Letter identification	The child is shown a letter and asked to name it. The teacher notes whether the response is correct and, if so, whether it is fast (no hesitation).	The teacher shows the letter *B* and asks, "What is this letter called?"
Letter production	The child is asked to print individual letters.	The teacher provides the child with pencil and paper and says, "Make the letter *B* for me." (*Note:* In an assessment context, be sure that models of the letters are not in sight.)
Letter–sound association	The child is asked to say the sound represented by a printed letter.	The teacher displays or points to a single letter and asks, "What is the sound for this letter?" (*Note:* Do not name the letter when asking for its sound because the letter name often provides a good clue to the letter's sound.)
Use in decoding	The child is asked to decode words comprising the letter being evaluated and other known elements or orthographic units that are identified for the child.	For consonants, the child is shown a rime, such as *at* or *op*, and is told, "This is *at*." Then the teacher puts a *b* (or whatever letter is being evaluated) in front of the *at* and asks, "If I put this letter in front of *at*, what will the word be?" (*Note:* The words formed should be real words. Therefore, a variety of rimes would need to be used.)
		For vowel sounds, short vowels would be evaluated. The teacher would show and name a word with a short vowel sound, name the word, and then change the vowel letter. For example, the teacher might show and name the word *hat*, then change the vowel to *o* and ask "If I take away the *a* and put in an *o*, what word would I have?"

- Assess production (printing) for any letters the child *can* name.
- Assess letter–sound association for any letters for which the child was able to name the lower-case version.
- Assess use in decoding for any letter for which the child knows the sound.

This approach to assessment assumes that children will be able to recognize any letters they can identify; therefore, it is not necessary to evaluate their ability to recognize those letters. Similarly, it is assumed that children will not be able to print letters that they cannot identify; therefore, only letters that children can identify are evaluated for production (printing). Letter–sound knowledge is typically acquired either after children can identify (name) the letter or at approximately the same time. Thus, letter–sound knowledge should usually be assessed only for letters the child can already identify.[1] Use in decoding would be assessed only for letters for which the child knows the sounds. The child's ability to use letter sounds in decoding words can, of course, also be evaluated informally by noting the child's success while reading.

Our goal in conducting assessment in the way described is to make it as efficient as possible and, at the same time, avoid asking children to do many things that they are not yet ready to do—thereby potentially undermining their confidence and motivation.

Alphabet Knowledge and Decoding Assessment

On the companion website for this book (see the box at the end of the table of contents), we provide an assessment tool that follows the guidelines listed above and provides the materials, protocols, and instructions for administration.

Documenting Children's Progress during Instruction

Ongoing documentation of young children's skill with the alphabetic code is important both for identifying instructional priorities and for determining whether instructional groups should be reconfigured. During the course of instruction and practice activities, teachers can observe and record children's letter-level knowledge to help guide instructional decision making and planning. For example, if the teacher is not certain whether particular children know the names or sounds of particular letters, asking them to name or provide the sounds for just those letters can be readily done during the course of instructional interactions. Checking on children's ability to print particular letters can be addressed in this way too. Some of the instructional games described later in this chapter can be used to gather these kinds of information (as well as to provide practice to promote automaticity with letter-level skills). Also, by observing children as they attempt to read unfamiliar words, teachers can note what individual children know about letter sounds and how they apply their knowledge in the context of decoding. Similarly, as children write (for a variety of purposes), letter formation skill can be documented.

Figure 6.1 presents the group snapshot for alphabet knowledge. With reference to this chapter, this snapshot can be used to document the progress of children within a group in letter recognition, identification, and production. It can also be used to document the development of knowledge of letter sounds as discussed in Chapter 7.

---

[1]Some programs teach letter sounds before teaching letter names. In these instances, this pattern will likely be reversed.

	Group Snapshot—Alphabet Knowledge														
Student Names	REC/ID	Print	Sound	REC/ID	Print	Sound	REC/ID	Print	Sound	REC/ID	Print	Sound	REC/ID	Print	Sound
A															
a															
B															
b															
C (as in *cat*)															
C (as in *city*)															
D															
d															
E															
e															
F															
f															
G															
g (as in *goat*)															
g (as in *gym*)															
H															
h															
I															
i															
J															
j															
K															
k															
L															
l															
M															
m															
N															
n															
O															
P															
Q															
q															
R															
r															
S															
T															
t															
U															
V															
W															
X															
Y															
Z															

Notes: Often the upper- and lower-case versions of a letter are essentially identical in appearance. Therefore, it is not necessary to evaluate the two versions separately. Thus, the snapshot does not provide space to do so.

The REC/ID (recognition/identification) column is used to document children's knowledge of the names of individual letters, both their ability to recognize (REC) and identify (ID) individual letters. Children who can recognize but not name (identify) a letter would be considered to be at a beginning point in development (B designated by a single slash in the box ◻). Children who can name the letter but are not automatic or reliable across several days would be rated as developing (D designated by an additional slash to form an X ⊠). Children who are reliably fast and accurate in naming a letter would be considered proficient (P designated by another slash to form an asterisk ⊠).

Key:

◻ *B—Beginning* indicates that instruction focused on the letter has begun.

⊠ *D—Developing* indicates that the child demonstrates the skill but is slow/hesitant and/or sometimes inaccurate.

⊠ *P—Proficient* indicates that the child reliably and automatically demonstrates the skill and that no additional instructional focus needs to be placed on the skill.

FIGURE 6.1. Group snapshot for alphabet knowledge.

Letter Names in Different Languages

Children who are learning English as an additional language may encounter different challenges in learning the names of letters in English, depending on their levels of literacy in other languages. For example, if a child had already learned letter names in Spanish, the child would need to learn new names for many of the alphabetic symbols shared with English. The name of letter *j*, for example, is *hota* in Spanish and represents the phoneme /h/. On the other hand, many letter names in Spanish are similar to their English counterparts, but several of them have an extra syllable added to the letter's name in English (e.g., the Spanish names for the letters *l*, *m*, *n*, and *s* are *ellay*, *emmay*, *ennay*, and *essay*, respectively). Ideally, teachers would be alert for and responsive to letters for which the printed form is identical across languages that children are learning or have learned but that are called by different names in the two languages. For example, when Spanish-speaking children are asked to provide the name for the letter *s* and they say *"essay,"* an appropriate teacher response would be something like "Yes, in Spanish, that letter is called 'essay.' In English, it is called 'es.' "

While teachers certainly can't be expected to know about all of their ML students' different languages, teachers who are providing instruction for high concentrations of children from given language backgrounds will likely meet with more instructional success if they learn some foundations for that language.

Instruction to Promote Letter-Naming and Letter-Formation Skills

Choosing Letters for Instruction

While intervention teachers often have the luxury of being able to plan instruction that is more closely tied to the knowledge and skills of the children with whom they work, it is useful for both classroom and intervention teachers to give careful consideration to the order in which letters are taught to beginning readers.

Recommendations for Working with Children Who Know Little about the Alphabet

- *Avoid similar letters.* It is important to choose letters to teach that are as different as possible from one another in terms of their appearance and their sounds. For example, it would make sense to avoid teaching the letters *b* and *d* at the same time or in close proximity to one another because they look alike and the names of the letters rhyme (bee, dee). Also, teachers might want to avoid teaching *j* and *k* together because their names rhyme. When teaching letter sounds, teachers might want to avoid teaching sounds for letters such as *d* and *t* at the same time because of the similarity in their sounds (they only differ in voicing).

- *Begin with upper-case letters.* Upper-case letters are preferable because their features are more salient and they are less visually confusable. In addition, it is potentially very confusing for a child to have to learn the upper- and lower-case versions of letters simultaneously when the two versions are very dissimilar in appearance (more than half of the letters of the alphabet have different-looking upper- and lower-case versions). Research indicates that children are 16 times more likely to know the name of a lower-case letter if they know the name of the upper-case letter (Turnbull, Bowles, Skibbe, Justice, & Wiggins, 2010). This suggests that knowing the name of the upper-case version of a letter may facilitate learning the name of the lower-case version.

Terminology

Upper case/capital/big—These three terms are synonyms when used in reference to letters. However, for children who are learning about printed letters for the first time, using these terms interchangeably can be confusing. Teachers should be alert for this potential confusion. To avoid this problem, children would ideally encounter a single term across instructional contexts, *or* teachers should be careful to explain (repeatedly as needed) that all three terms mean the same thing.

Lower case/little/small—These terms are also synonymous and may also lead to confusion for beginning readers and writers.

• *Teach letters that are important to children.* Children are typically very interested in learning the letters in their names, and they tend to learn those letters first, especially the first letter in their first name (McKay & Teale, 2015). They are also interested in learning the letters in the names they use to refer to people who are important to them, including family members (e.g., Mom[my], Nana, Dad[dy]), and other caregivers.

• *Teach more frequently occurring letters first.* Some letters, such as *a, s, t,* and *m*, occur more frequently than others, such as *j, x,* and *z*.

Optimal Order of Instruction for Teaching the Alphabet

We have frequently been asked to provide guidance on the optimal order in which to teach the alphabet and have declined to do so because there is no evidence that any particular order is necessarily better than another. Further, we feel that the order of letter instruction should be tied to the instructional materials in use, as children will, ideally, see the letters they are learning in books and other texts soon after the letter has been introduced. The logic we provide for how to select letters for instruction for children who know little about the alphabet is, we think, more important than providing a specific, prescribed order. Further, virtually all of the research with which we are familiar indicates that what we *should not* be doing in the process of teaching the alphabet is teaching a letter of the week in a whole-class context. In their book *No More Teaching a Letter a Week,* McKay and Teale

(2015) make a very cogent argument, based on a substantial amount of research, for retiring that practice.

Reasons Not to Use a Letter-of-the-Week Approach

Use of this approach, which at one time was very common, means, obviously, that it would take 26 weeks to cover the entire alphabet; each letter would get the same amount of attention even though letters like *x* and *z* are not frequently used, whereas the vowels and letters such as *s*, *m*, and *t* are frequently used. Further, in some letter-of-the-week approaches there was/is far too little review of previously taught letters, and far too little attention is given to the use of letters in the contexts of reading and writing.

Sequence of Objectives for Learning about Letters

As noted above, children generally demonstrate letter-related skills in the following sequence:

1. Recognition
2. Identification (Naming)
3. Letter–sound association
4. Use in decoding

If a child has no knowledge of a given letter, initial instruction should focus on recognition of the letter. Once children can reliably and quickly recognize a letter, they are ready to move on to learning to reliably and quickly identify (name) the letter. Activities that engage children in printing the letter (production) can help

---

Recognition versus Identification

The term *letter recognition* is sometimes used synonymously with *letter identification*. As we use the term, *recognition* refers to the ability to pick out a specific item that has been named by someone else.

Here's an example that parallels what children are asked to do when they are engaged in a recognition activity versus an identification activity. Imagine going into a meeting and having someone ask you to point out a particular individual you sort of know (e.g., "Which one is Juanita?"). That would require you to *recognize* which individual is Juanita. The name has been provided to you, and you need to connect that name with, in this case, the person who goes by that name. This is likely an easier task than being asked to provide the name for a particular individual ("What's that person's name?"). This *identification* task is likely to be more challenging because it requires you to retrieve the name from memory and connect it to the individual.

them learn to recognize and identify the letter. However, their ability to print the letter on request, without referring to a visual model ("Print/write the letter *T* for me"), will typically occur after the children can both recognize and identify the letter. Once children know the name of a letter, they are ready to learn the letter's sound and ultimately to use that letter in reading and writing.

Rationale for the Sequence

Many teachers are initially uncomfortable with the idea of teaching about letter names and letter sounds separately and/or with the idea of teaching upper-case letters before lower-case letters. These recommendations apply primarily to children who begin with very little letter knowledge. In a whole-class context, teaching about both upper- and lower-case printed letters and their names and sounds simultaneously has the advantage of providing new information for all or most of the children in the class. Thus, the children who already know the names of many letters probably learn about letter sounds in this instructional context. Those who know some capital letters may learn something about the lower-case versions of those letters. However, those who know little, if anything, about the alphabet are faced with a huge amount of information and, potentially, little guidance concerning what they are to accomplish in these instructional episodes. (This is one reason that small-group instruction is preferred for children who know little about the alphabet.)

For example, programs/approaches to early phonics instruction sometimes recommend teaching the upper- and lower-case printed versions of the letters. For the letter *B*, for example, children are told that both of those letters are called *bee* and that both forms of the letter represent the /b/ sound that we hear at the beginning of *ball*, which serves as the key word for the sound of the letter *b* (see Figure 6.2). That is a lot of information for a child who may not yet even know what a letter is, let alone that individual letters have agreed-upon names and represent agreed-upon sounds. Moreover, it is important to note that children need to be somewhat phonemically aware in order to attend to the onset in a key word such as *ball* to help them remember the sound represented by the letter *b*. Also, it is likely that children who know little about the alphabet will be insensitive to the importance of orientation with regard to letters. For example, the letters *b*, *d*, *p*, and possibly *q* might often be confused with one another.

FIGURE 6.2. *B/ball* illustration.

Add to these potential points of confusion the various ways in which an individual letter might be presented (in different fonts and by different hands). Clearly, the child who comes to instruction knowing little about the alphabet could be overwhelmed if the upper- and lower-case versions of a letter are simultaneously introduced along with the associated sound and a key word meant to help them remember that sound. Children in this situation are being asked to learn much more than those who already know quite a bit about the alphabet. Instruction will be much more effective and efficient when it is guided by knowledge of what children already know and what they are ready to learn next. Further, in alignment with the philosophy that drives the implementation of RTI, children who are lagging behind classroom expectations need more instructional support than do their classroom peers (instruction in smaller groups and/or for more time).

Children Do Not See Letters Backward

Children often confuse certain pairs or groups of letters (e.g., *b/d, u/n, p/q, b/p*). Such confusion was once thought to indicate that the child somehow *saw* things differently or that the image was rotated or reversed as it traveled from the eye to the brain, or vice versa. Over 40 years ago, however, Vellutino and his colleagues demonstrated that such confusions arise from difficulties in remembering what visually similar letters are called. In other words, children who make errors such as calling *b d* are not having difficulty with the visual aspects of the process; it is the *verbal memory* aspect of the process that is problematic for them (Vellutino, 1987).

Letter Recognition

Whole-Alphabet Activities

A variety of useful methods are available to familiarize children with the entire alphabet and to attune them to the fact that specific forms are associated with particular names. Whole-alphabet activities help with the goal of enabling children to recognize individual letters.

• *Singing the alphabet song.* While singing, the teacher and/or the children point to the printed letters. In a small group, each child might use an alphabet strip while singing the song. Such an activity requires careful teacher monitoring to ensure that each child is, in fact, pointing to the letter that is being named in the song. It is also important to slow the song down enough so that the children who most need the practice actually hear the names of the individual letters. We have all met children who believe that one of the letters in the middle of the alphabet is called *"elemeno"* (L-M-N-O). For children who know very little about the alphabet, most of the song initially sounds like a string of meaningless syllables (*ay-bee-cee-dee-eee-ef-gee*)—which it is for them. Early on, particularly for children in intervention settings and for those with limited alphabetic knowledge, it is helpful to use letter strips that include just the upper-case letters. Later, letter strips that include just lower-case letters can be used.

Note

It is not necessary to focus on identifying all letters before moving on to teaching about the sounds for some of them. In general, the intention is to work forward from the child's current knowledge base. However, it is reasonable to work toward the ability to name both the upper- and lower-case versions of a given letter (when they are distinctly different) before beginning to teach the sound of that letter.

• *Singing to a specific letter.* Once children have learned the alphabet song, specific letters can be highlighted by singing the song up to a specific letter and then stopping at that letter. For example, the teacher might decide to sing to the letter *K*. The group would then sing the song and point to the letters, as usual, but stop at the *K*. The teacher might then discuss the letters that come before and after *K*. The purpose of this activity is to draw attention to individual letters. The song can, of course, be sung a number of times, and children can be invited to choose which letter to sing to.

• *Singing to the missing letter(s) and filling it (them) in.* In this activity, the children are provided with alphabet strips with a few letters missing (see Figure 6.3). The group sings to the first missing letter and then fills it in by selecting from a small group of letters provided, as illustrated in the figure, or by writing the letter in if they have begun to learn to form that letter. Then the song is begun again, continues to the next missing letter, and so forth.

• *Reading and discussing alphabet books.* Children, especially those who have had little print exposure prior to school, will enjoy listening and reacting to alphabet books almost as much as younger children do. Because such books typically devote an entire page (or more) to each letter, they are a great resource for focusing the child's attention on individual letters. They are also helpful for

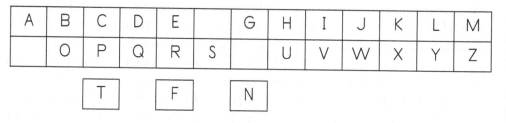

FIGURE 6.3. Missing letter illustration.

T T T T I T T

FIGURE 6.4. Font illustration.

teaching about letter–sound correspondences. Further, it has been demonstrated that reading alphabet books to children leads to more print-specific discussion than does reading other types of books (Justice & Piasta, 2011; Smolkin, Yaden, Brown, & Hofius, 1992). In addition, alphabet books have the potential to contribute to vocabulary development both for native speakers of English and for children who are learning English as an additional language, as many alphabet books include pictures of several objects on the page for each letter. Pointing to and naming those objects and the printed word associated with each of them, and perhaps discussing some of the objects a bit (their use, where they might be found, etc.), can help to expand the children's vocabularies.

A Note about Font

To reliably recognize a letter, a child needs to learn which features of the letter are characteristic of the letter per se and which features are simply embellishments. For example, the *T*'s presented in Figure 6.4 appear in different fonts, and some contain features that are not critical to the *T*'s identity.

Hand-printed letters and highly embellished fonts in books add even more variations that a child must sort through to determine which features define a letter. Children who learn to identify the letters of the alphabet without explicit and focused instruction generally extract the essential elements or critical features of letters either through their supported attempts to write or through exposure to multiple examples (Gibson & Levin, 1975). In other words, they learn what gives *T* its "*T*-ness." However, it is important to accelerate the pace of letter learning for children who begin kindergarten with limited letter–name knowledge. Therefore, the letters used in the earliest phases of explicit instruction should, ideally, consist only of the features that define the letter, and those features should be sufficiently prominent. All but the last example among the letters in Figure 6.4 would be poor choices for introducing the letter *T* because they include unnecessary features or features that are necessary but not sufficiently salient. The last example, comprising salient and critical features of the *T*, is clear and therefore more useful for instruction.

In considering instructional materials for beginning readers, teachers should look critically at the font used in the books that children are asked to read. Ideally, the font would be crisp and unembellished. Teachers should also note whether the "sticks" on the letters (the ascenders and descenders) sufficiently distinguish between similar-looking letters (such as n and h) and should avoid fonts that feature the "typewriter" a and *g* (as printed here). Following is an example of the type of primary font that is often found in books intended for beginning readers:

a b d p n h

Compare the font above to the example below, which is a very good primary font that was found for free on the Internet using the search term *primary font*.

a   b   d   p   n   h

Clearly, it will be easier for children to learn the letters that are presented in the second example because the length of the ascenders and descenders makes it easy to distinguish *a* from *d, n* from *h,* and so on.

Teaching about Specific Letters

Materials Needed

- A short text with large print (e.g., a book, song, poem, or teacher-created text) that contains several instances of the letter to be taught should be selected/prepared. In an intervention setting, it would be ideal to use materials that are routinely available in the children's classroom.

- A letter card containing the individual letter. The letter should be large enough for all the children in the group to see, and the font should be unembellished, containing only the critical features.

Introducing the Letter

Present the letter to be taught on a card (the letter *M* is used in the first example). Provide all the children in the group with a card that has the selected letter on it. Tell the children what the letter is and have them repeat the letter's name a couple of times.

- While leaving the letter in view, introduce the text.
- Tell the children that the words in the text contain many *M*'s and that, after the text is read, they are going to look for all the *M*'s. (Note that for letters with differing upper- and lower-case versions, only the upper-case version should be the focus of the hunt [assuming the lower-case version has not yet been addressed]).
- Explain that knowing the letters helps us to read and write; as always, it is important to set a purpose for the things that children are learning.
- Engage the children in a discussion of the text before beginning to read. For example, say something about what the text is about and encourage anticipation (prediction) and/or personal reactions to the text (depending on the content of the text).
- Read the text to the children, pointing to the words while reading. Read with natural phrasing and intonation (not word-by-word) but slowly enough that the children can follow the pointing.

- While reading, engage the children in discussing and reacting to the text.
- After reading, briefly discuss various (meaningful) aspects of the text.
- Then, focus in on the letter by saying something like: "Let's look for all the *M*'s in this book/poem/story/message. There were a lot of *M*'s in this book/poem/story/message[2]!"
- Do a letter hunt, encouraging the children to *name* the letter each time they find it. Or, if children simply point to the letter but do not name it, the teacher might do so (i.e., "There's an *M*" and "You found another *M*!") and remind the children of the need to name the letter each time they find it. Unless the name of the letter is used frequently, some children will treat this activity as a visual matching task rather than as a letter-naming activity. (Once several instances of the focal letter have been located, ask children to find a few instances of some letters that were taught previously—if any have been taught and are included in the text.)

Figure 6.5 provides a description of a book, *Monster Mop* (Mark, 1997), which would be useful for teaching about the letter *M*. In addition to teaching the

Page/text	Page description	Commentary
My mat.	Cute "monster" putting a placemat on a table.	Graphics are engaging and provide an opportunity for learners to identify the upper-case version of the letter *M* (as well as the lower-case version depending on the instructional objective).
My mug.	Monster places a mug on the mat.	Text develops a sequence—and another opportunity to identify the focal letter.
My milk.	Monster pours milk into the mug—which spills on the adjoining page.	The sequence continues. The milk/mug spills, but the spill is not named (as the focus in on the letter *M*). The text provides the opportunity to engage learners in meaning construction (e.g., "What do you think will happen after the spill?") The text provides an additional opportunity to identify the focal letter.
My mop.	Monster is shown using a mop to clean up the spill.	There are additional opportunities to develop comprehension skills including: • Using pictures to support meaning construction. • Relating text to life: "Who cleans up spills when they happen where you live?" Plus . . . text provides an additional opportunity to identify the focal letter.

FIGURE 6.5. Description of *Monster Mop* (Mark, 1997), listed page by page.

---

[2]Use the appropriate term based on the type of text in use.

name of the letter *M*, this text helps learners understand that books/written texts are informative, meaningful, and interesting—thereby helping children understand the communication value of print. The text presents a story about a "monster" who spills some milk.

The next example is a teacher-created text (a "Morning Message") that provides an opportunity to review a previously taught letter (*M* in this case) but is primarily focused on helping children learn the name and shape of the letter *S*. Because both upper- and lower-case versions of *S* are identical except for their size, a focus on both can be included. The teacher would follow the same procedure as when introducing the letter *M*, as described above (showing a large-print version and having the children name it several times, giving each child a card with the focal letter, and having them name the letter on their cards).

Then the teacher would introduce the text "Today's Morning Message" (see Figure 6.6) and explain that "Our message today is about Sara's birthday. There are some letters missing and we are going to put them in. We'll get to use the letter *M* that we talked about the other day, too, but mostly we get to put in *S*'s. So, let's get reading!"

The teacher would then proceed to read the message—one line at a time—stopping at each blank and engaging the children in thinking about the name and shape of the letter that needs to be added. (If children have already begun to learn about the sound of a previously taught letter [*M* in this example], that might be addressed as well.) The teacher would fill in the missing letter on each line as the text is read—narrating as the text is read. For example, "This word is Sara's name—Sara's name begins with *S*. So, I am going to write it in. To make an *S*, I start up here and then curve around and go back the other way and then curve around again." Once all the letters are filled in, the text would be read again. And then, the teacher would engage the group in finding and naming all the *S*'s. Afterward, one at a time, a few children would be invited to use a pointer to find and name all the *S*'s (and *M*'s). This might be followed by a discussion of the content of the text again (Sara's birthday in this example). Later, the text would be left available for the children to "read" and engage in a letter hunt.

Good ___orning Kindergartners,

    Today is ___onday. It is
Sara's birthday. ___ara brought us
___ome cupcake___.

    Please ___ake Sara a card
that ___ays happy birthday.

    Have a _uper day!

    Love,

    Mrs. Geary

FIGURE 6.6. Teaching about the letter *S*.

KEEP IN MIND The purpose of the letter hunt activity is to give children many opportunities to connect the printed letter to the letter's name. Do not have children count the letters as they find them because counting would likely keep them from thinking about the letter's name.

Practicing Letter Recognition

When the children can reliably find instances of the letter with the letter card in view, practice letter recognition without the letter card in view. If children have difficulty recognizing a letter without the letter card present, the letter card should be provided again.

Look for opportunities to have the children find the letter(s) they are learning in other contexts (for example, on a bulletin board or calendar, on display while walking through the hallway). Direct children's attention to these displays and encourage them to try to find the target letter. Our purpose in having children look around their environment for letters they can recognize is to encourage them to become attuned to the fact that they are often surrounded by print and that they are beginning to develop the skills to make some sense of it. Further, the children will, hopefully, think about the letters more frequently if they are attuned to their presence in a variety of contexts.

Games for Promoting Letter Recognition

Once some letters have been introduced for recognition, simple games can be constructed to reinforce recognition. Blank versions of the game boards and directions are available on this book's companion website (see the box at the end of the table of contents). These resources can be shared with parents and caregivers to encourage playful ways for families to support their children's skill development.

• *Letter bingo.* Customized bingo games can be created using only the letters that are the current focus of instruction (plus some previously taught letters to make the game interesting). For each bingo card, make three or four columns, each with three or four boxes. Print one letter in each box (letters can be used more than once, if necessary, to provide enough letters to fill the card). The teacher can call the letters while the children place markers (or using a dot marker) on the letters as they are called. The teacher should monitor the children's performance to ensure accuracy. Also, to promote children's ability to name the letters, they should be encouraged to name each letter as they cover it. (There needn't be any winners or losers with this game—the children are generally delighted to simply mark/cover up all their letters.)

• *Parking lot game.* In this game, a parking lot is drawn on a piece of paper that includes two rows of parking spaces with four or five spaces in each row. One of the letters that the children are learning is printed in each of the parking spaces

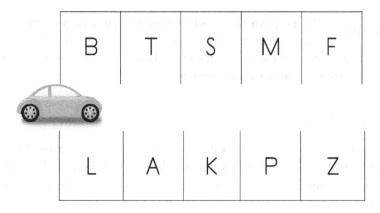

FIGURE 6.7. Example of a parking lot game board.

in such a way that, when the paper is placed in front of the child, all the letters will be right side up. Several different parking lots are made, all with the same letters but with the letters in different locations on each lot. To play the game, each child in the group is provided with a different parking lot sheet and a toy car that fits in the parking spaces. Then, the children are directed to park their cars in different spaces according to the letter named by the teacher (e.g., "Everyone park your car on the letter *T*"). To encourage letter–name retrieval, as children park their cars they might be asked, "What parking space is your car in?" Figure 6.7 provides an example of a parking lot game board.

Letter Identification

When the teacher notices that children quickly and accurately recognize given letters, the focus should shift to letter naming. For many children, once they can reliably recognize a letter, they are also able to identify (name) it. However, for some children, it takes a good deal of additional practice to be able to retrieve/ recall the names of given letters. An additional goal for letter identification is for children to be able to name letters quite quickly so that, as their reading becomes more demanding, slow letter identification skills will not interfere with the other processes involved. Thus, the goal of the letter-naming activities is not only accurate identification but fluent (fast) identification.

Focusing on Letter Identification

In preparing to teach in a small-group setting, the teacher should choose four or five letters that the children can recognize but not yet name reliably or quickly. During instruction, the teacher would show each letter, name it, and ask the children to repeat the name. If a child makes a mistake, the teacher would provide the correct letter name, point out the salient features of the letter, and ask the child to name the letter again. If appropriate, the teacher would point out how the misidentified letter differs visually from the letter the child named, perhaps by providing an example of the letter the child named. Before moving on, the child should be asked to repeat the name of the letter originally presented again. The same group of letters would be presented several times, in a different order each time, to provide children with lots of opportunities to practice the letters' names.

Letter–Name Review

Children who are just beginning to learn about the letters often forget letters that they learned previously. As new letters are presented, it is important to frequently review previously taught/learned letters. Below are some suggested activities for providing additional practice with letter identification:

- Provide individual children with a collection of the letters they know (perhaps in an envelope). Once every couple of days invite the children to go through their letter cards and name all the letters they *already* know. This activity can be used as an opportunity to evaluate letter identification skill, but the most important purpose is to promote fluency (speed) with letter identification.

- Occasionally choose a word in the text that is being read and ask the children to name all the letters in the word. For example, while pointing to the word *cat,* the teacher might say, "Here is the word *cat.* Tell me the names of the letters you see in the word *cat.*" Or the teacher might say: "What is the first [middle, last] letter you see in *cat?*" or "Spell the word *cat* for me by telling me all the letters in *cat* starting with the first one." (Until the children have print directionality firmly established, the teacher should always point to the letters when using words such as *first* and *last* in reference to print.)

KEEP IN MIND Classroom teachers generally work with multiple children at once, even in a small-group setting. In such situations, it is sometimes hard to ensure that all the visual materials (in this case, letters) are oriented properly (right side up) for every child in the instructional group. Proper orientation of letters is especially important in letter study because some letters are easily confused (e.g., *b/d, u/n, p/q, b/p*).

Matching Games for Promoting Letter Identification

Use letters that the children are currently learning for identification and fluency (and additional letters they can already identify reliably and fluently, if necessary, to make the game fun). As children begin to be able to identify a fairly large number of letters, it will sometimes be useful to include both upper- and lower-case versions of the same letter in these games. In this case *T* and *t* would be a match, as would *T* and *T.*

Use letter cards to play games of Go Fish or Concentration (Memory). In playing such games, make sure the letter cards are always properly oriented relative to the children. For example, if two children will be involved in a game of Concentration, make sure they are both on the same side of the playing surface. Further, make sure the cards are always being viewed right side up. A small dot at the top of both the front and the back of each card will help—particularly if the children are frequently reminded that they need to keep the cards turned so that the dot is on the top. Also, in all games, make sure the children name each letter as it is encountered. The purpose of playing the games is, after all, to help the children connect printed letters to their names and to become fluent in doing so.

A Common Parental Concern

Perhaps one of the most common parental concerns that primary-grade teachers encounter relative to literacy development has to do with young children's inclination to confuse visually similar letters (e.g., *b* and *d*, *p* and *b*, *u* and *n*). Many parents believe that such confusion is a sign of serious reading difficulty, often referred to as dyslexia.

Some children experience difficulty remembering what name to apply to two things that look a lot alike partly because, until they are learning about print, most objects they learn to label are called by the same name regardless of how the object is oriented in space. A pen is a pen regardless of whether its writing end is pointed to the top, bottom, left, or right. With letters, it is necessary to remember the symbol's orientation, as well as its other critical features, in order to recall the proper label. One of the questions in the parent booklet mentioned in Chapter 3 (p. 86) addresses this common concern.

To help children overcome difficulties with commonly confused letters, teachers can provide a model of the upper- and lower-case versions of the two confusable letters and encourage children to refer to the model whenever they are uncertain about a letter's identity or how to form a letter. Here is an example of such a model:

To encourage its use, teachers might encourage students to "Check your b-d chart." Many primary-grade teachers have found it useful to post such a model on all four walls of their classroom so that children can refer to it easily from wherever they are seated. A copy can also be sent home to serve as an assist in any letter or word work—or writing or reading children do at home.

Letter Production

Helping children learn to print letters will help them learn to recognize and identify them because printing draws children's attention to the critical features of individual letters. Thus, instruction designed to help children learn to print letters, although it comes *after* our discussion of helping children learn letter names, is something that would occur *while* children are learning letter names. In addition to helping children learn letter names, providing instruction and practice in printing individual letters efficiently and legibly will, going forward, enable children to focus on spelling and meaning construction when they write rather than having to expend a lot of cognitive energy on letter formation. Indeed, a recent study by Skar et al. (2022) found that first graders whose handwriting was more fluent produced higher-quality writing.

Introducing the Letter

KEEP IN MIND To support efforts to provide congruent instruction, if children in intervention settings do not have an established method for printing a letter, it is reasonable for the teacher to teach the method employed in the children's classroom.

To help children learn to print a given letter, the teacher might:

- Provide children with a large-print version of the letter.
- Explain that they will be learning to write the letter.
- Trace the letter with their finger as the children watch, explicitly describing the process while tracing. For example, in describing how to print the letter *T*, the teacher might say, "This is how we make an upper-case *T*. We make a straight line down. Then a *T* needs a straight line across the top. So, we make two lines when we make a *T*, a straight line down and then a line across the top of the *T*."
- Invite the children to trace the letter several times while again providing a verbal description of the process for printing the letter. As illustrated in the example above, the teacher should be sure to use the name of the letter many times while guiding the children through letter formation.
- The teacher can model the printing of the letter on a dry-erase board while the children watch. Once again, it is essential to provide a verbal description and to say the name of the letter several times.
- Have the children print the letter on paper, or a dry-erase board, guiding their initial printing attempts with the same verbal descriptions. The children should name the letter each time they write it.
- If a child has difficulty producing a recognizable letter, the teacher can assist, guiding the child's hand (while the child holds the writing implement)

to form the letter. Allowing children to write large versions of letters early on may make it easier for them to attend to and produce the critical features.

Note

Dry-erase boards are especially appealing to children for these kinds of activities. They enjoy both the opportunity to write and the opportunity to erase. Teachers can capitalize on this appeal by having erasure time serve instructional purposes. For example, if several letters were printed on the dry-erase board, the children could be directed to erase one letter at a time (e.g., "Erase the *T*, erase the *M*," and so on).

In letter production, the focus should be on general form. The goal is clearly recognizable letters, not necessarily beautiful ones. It is also important that the child ultimately be able to print letters fairly quickly. If children have already learned to form some letters fluently (as is often true of the letters in their names), it may be difficult for them to alter the letter formation while remaining fluent. A decision about whether to attempt to change their approach to forming particular letters should rest on a determination of whether their current approach will reduce their writing fluency in the future. The purpose of handwriting instruction (especially in an age where most things are done on computers) is to ensure that letter formation does not interfere with the process of communication (Graham, Harris, & Fink, 2000). In an intervention setting, perfect handwriting should not be a focus. (This does not, however, mean that neat and legible handwriting shouldn't be encouraged or that handwriting practice cannot be included at other times.)

KEEP IN MIND   Until children can form letters effortlessly and automatically, they should have ready access to an alphabet strip to use as a model. And they should be taught how to use the alphabet sequence, if need be, as an assist in finding the letter they want to use in their writing.

Games and Other Activities for Practicing Letter Formation and Letter Names

Children should be encouraged to print given letters many times, across multiple instructional sessions, until it is apparent that they do not need to refer to a model of the letter when they print it and that they can form the letter fairly quickly. Children should print the letters that are being focused upon several times during a given lesson, and they should name the letter each time it is printed. Below we describe several engaging ways to provide practice with letter formation.

- *Tic-tac-toe* is a particularly motivating way to engage children in practicing letter formation (and several other foundational literacy skills, as will be discussed in subsequent chapters). For purposes of learning the names of letters and how to print them, the game can be played in a couple of different ways.

- *One letter.* To focus on just one letter, each player in the game would use a different colored marker. On their turn, players would print and name the targeted letter in one of the boxes. The winner of the game would be determined by having three letters of the same color in a row.
- *Two letters.* Each player would have a different letter, which each would print and name on their turn. The winner of the game would be determined by having three of the same letters in a row (as in tic-tac-toe with *X*'s and *O*'s).
- *Multiple letters.* In this version, each player uses a different colored marker. On their turn, players each choose from a set of letter cards and name and write the letter they pick. The winner is the one who has three (different) letters of the same color in a row.

In order for tic-tac-toe to support letter–name learning, children need to name the letter as or after they write it. Teachers have found it useful to have dry-erase boards dedicated to tic tac toe. They make the game grid on the board using masking tape so that all that the children need to do when they play is write in the letters. Having dedicated boards allows the teacher to ensure that the boxes are large enough to easily contain the children's writing and that instructional time is not lost to erasing and redrawing the grid. If dry-erase boards are not available, a grid can also be made on white paper, which is placed in a plastic page protector.

- *Sticky-note bingo.* Bingo game cards are created using the letters children are learning. Each card has a different arrangement of letters. As letters are called, the children cover the letter with a sticky note (Post-it) and then write the letter on the sticky note. If need be, they can be encouraged to check letter formation by peeking under the sticky note.

- *Print in a variety of media.* A variety of media can be used to promote interest in letter naming and letter formation. For example, children might be given the opportunity to print:
  - Using different colors or kinds of markers on paper
  - In whipped cream or shaving cream on the table or desk
  - With chalk on the pavement outside
  - Using markers on dry-erase boards
  - In sand or salt on a cookie sheet
  - Using drawing toys such as Magna Doodle or Ghost Writer or a paint program on a computer or tablet.

Remember to have children say the letter names as often as possible during these activities.

KEY POINTS OF THIS CHAPTER

✓ Unembellished fonts should be used for instruction on letter names for children who have limited letter knowledge.

✓ Whole-alphabet activities can help to familiarize children with the entire alphabet (singing and pointing to letters on an alphabet strip—slowly).

✓ Recognition of letters is easier than identification and, therefore, is a reasonable first step in instruction.

✓ Learning to print letters while simultaneously naming them promotes letter–name learning.

✓ Letters that are potentially confusable because of similarities in their forms or names should not be taught in close succession.

✓ Letters should be taught in preparation for "reading" a text in which the letter will be encountered several times.

✓ Helping children become fluent with letter writing can help improve the quality of the meaning-focused writing they ultimately produce because they will not need to devote cognitive resources to the letter formation process.

CHAPTER 7

Letter–Sound (Grapheme–Phoneme) Relationships

WRITING SYSTEM FOUNDATIONS GOAL 4

Children will be able to associate the most common sounds of individual letters and common consonant digraphs with their printed representations.

To decode unfamiliar words, children need to know about the relationships between printed letters (graphemes) and the sounds (phonemes) they represent. This chapter focuses on helping teachers to (1) understand grapheme–phoneme relationships from the perspective of beginning and developing readers, and (2) teach children the conventional grapheme–phoneme relationships for consonants and short-vowel sounds/phonemes.

In this chapter, we describe a process for explicitly teaching the relationships between individual graphemes (including some of the common consonant digraphs) and their most common sounds. We also describe practice activities for reinforcing these relationships including activities that help children begin to apply what they are learning about these relationships in the context of reading meaningful text (e.g., books, charts, and poems). The easiest place to begin to apply knowledge of grapheme–phoneme relationships is at the beginnings of words. (Remember that as children begin to develop phonemic awareness, the first sound in a word is the one they are most likely to be able to attend to and manipulate. Thus, connecting that sound with the first letter in a printed word is correspondingly easy.) Therefore, we include application activities that focus on the letters and sounds at the beginnings of words in demonstrating and practicing early application. For vowel letters, we discuss explicit instruction of the short-vowel sounds but reserve discussion of application in attempting to read and spell words for later chapters in which our focus turns to helping learners more fully understand and apply the alphabetic principle. For now, it is important to reiterate that children learn about letters and their sounds in an incremental fashion. Once they know the name of a letter, in general, it is easier for them to learn the sound. Once they know the sound, they can begin to learn to apply their letter knowledge in reading and spelling words in isolated word work (addressed in Chapters 8 and 9) and when reading meaningful text (addressed primarily in Chapter 12).

Letter Names versus Letter Sounds

For children who are just beginning to learn about written language, the distinction between letter names and letter sounds can be unclear. This is complicated by the fact that, for most letters, the name of the letter includes the letter's sound. Instructionally, it is important to clarify the distinction as some letters do not consistently represent their most common sound. For example, the letter *S* generally represents the /sss/ sound but does not represent that sound either in the *sh* digraph or when it occurs at the end of some words wherein it represents the /z/ phoneme as in *has*, *gives*, and *balls*. Therefore, it is important that during the course of instruction the teacher emphasize that there is a difference between the name of the letter—which is consistent—and the sound(s) that it can represent.

Consonant Digraphs

When two consonant letters together represent a single sound, the letter combination is called a *digraph*. The English writing system includes multiple consonant digraphs (e.g., *sh* as in *shoe*, *ch* as in *inch*, *th* as in *the*, *ss* as in *class*, *ff* as in *sniff*, the *ck* as in *back*). The pronunciation of some digraphs is quite transparent—for example, the *ff* in *sniff* in which the two letters, together, represent a single phoneme /f/. (Note that many programs teach double consonants [e.g., *ff*, *ll*, *ss*] as a category separate from digraphs.) Another fairly transparent digraph is the *ck*, which, like the doubled consonants, only occurs at the end of short vowel words or syllables. However, some frequently occurring digraphs are not at all transparent in that neither of the letters in the digraph, by itself, represents the sound of the digraph. The most frequent of these digraphs are *th*, *sh*, and *ch*.

Double-letter digraphs (such as *ff*) generally do not need to be explicitly taught—except with regard to spelling—which we discuss in Chapter 10. However, the most frequently occurring digraphs that are not doubled letters *(th, sh, ch, ck)* may need to be explicitly taught and practiced as decoding and spelling elements. Only one digraph would be introduced on a given day/lesson.

Initial Assessment of Letter–Sound Knowledge

In Chapter 6 we introduced the Alphabet Knowledge and Decoding Assessment (which is available on the book's companion website—see the box at the end of the table of contents). The assessment can be used to identify children's status relative to the alphabetic code. It includes assessment of knowledge of letter names, sounds, printing/formation, and the learners' ability to apply letter–sound knowledge in decoding attempts. Initial assessment of these early print-related skills can help to inform decision making for forming instructional groups of children who are at similar points in their development.

Documenting Children's Progress during Instruction

In Chapter 6, we also presented the group snapshot for alphabet knowledge (see Figure 6.1, p. 156). That snapshot gives teachers the opportunity to document the progress of children in a group on particular skills across time. This information is intended to support instructional planning for individual groups and, over time, for decisions about whether children are appropriately grouped for small-group instruction.

For ongoing documentation of children's status regarding letter–sound knowledge, teachers can observe and record children's proficiency with letter sounds informally through instructional interactions. Teachers would rate a child as *Beginning* for a particular grapheme's sound if the sound had been introduced in an instructional context. A rating of *Developing* would be used when a child can often provide a grapheme's sound but is slow to respond and/or sometimes inaccurate. A rating of *Proficient* would be assigned, for a given grapheme, when a child is reliably fast and accurate in providing the sound either when specifically asked about the sound or when engaged in instructional and practice activities that require the child to use the sound in reading or writing.

The Link between Letter Names and Letter Sounds

Before focusing on instruction for young learners, we begin with a discussion of the relationships between the names of letters and the sounds they most commonly represent. These relationships sometimes lead children to make reading and spelling errors that can be challenging for proficient readers (including teachers) to understand.

Decades ago, Charles Read (1971) demonstrated that when young children write, they often use letter names as a source of information about letter sounds. Because the names of many letters include the most common sound represented by the letter, children's spellings are often at least somewhat interpretable. For example, the sound represented by the letter *b* is the first phoneme in the letter's name (/b/- /ē/). For *m*, the letter's sound is the second phoneme in its name (/ĕ/-/m/). However, children sometimes choose the wrong phoneme from a letter's name, especially when they are writing, and may produce odd-looking spellings—such as spelling the word *said* as *smd* (with the *m* representing the short-*e* sound—because the first sound in the name of the letter *m* is the short-*e* sound).[1] (Recall the analysis of written spelling discussed in Chapter 5, pp. 126–131.) When teachers understand children's inclination to do this, the feedback and guidance they offer to them can be more effective in moving them forward (as we discuss later in this chapter).

Consonants

For the letters *b, d, j, k, p, t, v,* and *z,* the initial phoneme in the letter's name is the sound represented by that letter. This is also true of the soft sounds of *g* (as in *gym*) and *c* (as in *city*). For the letters *f, l, m, n, r,* and *s,* the final phoneme in the letter's name is the sound represented by the letter. For all these letters, knowing the letter's name provides useful information about the letter's sound. This is one reason why we stress the utility of helping children learn the names of individual letters before expecting them to learn their sounds. However, for some letters, the sound is not contained in the letter's name. This is true of the hard sounds for the letters *g* (as in *get*) and *c* (as in *cat*). Additionally, for the consonants *h, w,* and *y,* the letters' names do not include the letters' sounds—except for the long-*i* sound for *y* as in *my* and *fly* (in this case the letter *y* is representing a vowel sound). The letter–sound associations for these letters, *h, w,* and *y,* are notoriously difficult for young children to learn. It is often in their attempts to use them in spelling that we see the strongest evidence of their inclination to use letter names as a resource. Thus, a child might spell the word *was* as *yz* (illustrated in Figure 7.1).

In this example, the *y* is used to represent the /w/ sound, consistent with the first sound in the letter's name (*why*). The *z* represents the /z/ sound heard at the end of the word *was*—but, of course, this spelling is not conventional. Table 7.1 illustrates the link between letter names and letter sounds by writing out the name for each letter.[2]

Thus, if children want to write the word *cat* and do not already know how to spell it, they are likely to start the word with a *k* because the first phoneme heard in the word *cat* is also the first phoneme in the name of the letter *k*. Obviously, in order for children to be able to do this type of analysis, they need to know the

---

[1] Note that such spellings are rare and generally only occur when children are just beginning to learn about letter-sound relationships.

[2] Note that we are not proposing that children learn the names of all of the letters before they begin to learn the sounds of some of the letters. Rather, as we discuss below, once they know a letter's name the instructional focus can turn to teaching about the sound for that letter.

FIGURE 7.1. Sound spelling of *was*.

name of the letter and to be somewhat phonemically aware (i.e., able to notice the similarity in the onsets [the first phoneme] in the word *cat* and in the name of the letter *k*).

It is also interesting to note (and very predictable, given what is known about the development of phonemic awareness) that, in general, children tend to learn the sounds of letters in which the letter's sound is in the onset of the letter name (e.g., *b, k, t*) more readily than the sounds of letters in which the letter sound is embedded in the rime (e.g., *s, m, f*; Treiman, Sotak, & Bowman, 2001). This is at least partially because children tend to be able to separate syllables into onsets and rimes (/b/-/e/) before they can segment the rime portion of a word into its component phonemes (/e/-/m/; there is no onset in the name of the letter *m*).

Vowels

The sounds for vowel letters are more complicated than those for consonants. Long-vowel sounds are, of course, very transparent. The sound is the same as the name of the letter. However, spellings for long-vowel sounds are more complex and variable. For example, there are many ways to spell the long-*a* sound (e.g.,

TABLE 7.1. The Link between Letter Names and Letter Sounds

Letter sound at the beginning of letter name	Letter sound at the end of letter name	Letter sound not in letter name
B (*bee*)	F (*ef*)	C (as in *cat*)
C (*see* as in *city*)	L (*el*)	G (as in *give*)
D (*dee*)	M (*em*)	H (*aich*)
G (*jee* as in *gym*)	N (*en*)	W (*double you*)
J (*jay*)	R (*ar*)	Y (*why*)
K (*kay*)	S (*es*)	
P (*pea*)	X (*ex*)	
T (*tea*)		
V (*vee*)		
Z (*zee*)		
Q (*kyou*)		

cake, way, maid, prey, weigh, buffet). Short vowel sounds, however, present children with challenges because there is little relationship between the name of the vowel letter and the short sound associated with it. For example, for the letter *e*, the short sound is not heard in the name of the letter. Rather, the sound teachers refer to as short-*e* sounds like the beginning of the name of the letter *a*!

In fact, for the vowels *e, i, o,* and *u,* the short vowel sound associated with the letter is discernible in the name of the vowel letter that immediately precedes it in the alphabet.

Note

The discussion of vowels in this section represents some of the most challenging text in this book. Try as we might, we were not able to make it simpler. Therefore, a few suggestions are in order:

- Do the exercise described below *out loud*. You really need to *hear* the letter sounds and the letter names in order to understand the points being made.
- If you do not engage in these exercises in a professional development or class setting, do them with a friend or colleague. Sometimes what confuses one person will be clear to someone else.
- Realize that expending the effort to understand these relationships will help you to better understand aspects of children's literacy development and serve to improve the feedback you provide.

These letter–name, letter–sound relationships are typically very difficult for literate people (such as teachers) to notice because they have been so accustomed to the conventional letter–sound relationships that they seem natural. Some insight into these relationships can be gained using Table 7.2 and following the directions provided below.

Directions: Say the sound of the vowel in the middle column of the table (don't say the word—just the vowel sound it contains). As you are saying the vowel sound, begin to say the name of the letter in the right-hand column. Do not stop—glide right from the vowel sound into saying the name of the letter. *Do this out loud and*

TABLE 7.2. Links between Vowel Letter Names and Short Vowel Sounds

Letter used in conventional spelling	Short vowel sound as heard in . . .	Vowel letter name containing that sound
E	Short *e*, as in pet	*A*
I	Short *i*, as in pit	*E*
O	Short *o*, as in pot	*I*
U	Short *u*, as in putt	*O*

pay attention to how your mouth moves. Most people notice that the sound of the vowel in the center column occurs at the beginning of the name of the letter in the right-hand column.

The left-hand column in Table 7.2 has the letter that is most often used to spell the short vowel sound (that is, the short-*e* sound is spelled with an *e*). If you try to glide from the sound of the vowel in the middle column into the name of the letter in the left-hand column, you'll find that you can't really glide easily into the name of the letter. Again, pay attention to how your mouth moves. You'll probably notice much more movement. That's because the *short sound of the vowel is not contained in the name of the vowel letter.*

What does all this mean for children? It means that children who are beginning to include vowels in their writing and who do not yet know the conventional spelling for the short-*e* sound are likely to spell it with an *a*. They would write *pat* when writing about their *pet*. A teacher who does not understand the reason for the use of the letter *a* in this context might well provide feedback focused on helping children to isolate the middle phoneme in the word *pet*. In other words, the teacher is apt to operate on the assumption that the difficulty in spelling this word is due to inaccurate phonemic analysis rather than to not knowing the conventional spelling of the short-*e* sound. Children are likely to be confused by this feedback because they actually did isolate the /ĕĕĕĕ/ (short-*e* sound), which the teacher so helpfully articulates by way of feedback. The problem is they don't yet know how the short-*e* sound is spelled.

Feedback for Learners

The tendency for beginning literacy learners to produce unconventional spellings by using letter names (or parts of letter names) to represent sounds has been widely documented in the research arena and across multiple languages (Ellefson, Treiman, & Kessler, 2009), but, in our experience, surprisingly few primary-grade teachers are aware of what the children are doing when they produce spellings such as *yz* for *was* or *wk* for *duck* (the beginning sound in the name of the letter *w* is /d/). Understanding the origins of these spellings, and doing so quickly, will allow teachers to provide more productive feedback for children. For example, for the *wk* spelling of *duck*, the teacher might say "You noticed that /d/ sound at the beginning of *duck*. The letter that we use for that sound is the letter *d*." Or, if the sound and the key word for *d* have already been taught, the teacher might say, "You noticed that /d/ sound at the beginning of *duck*. Let's look at our key words and find the one that has the same beginning sound that we hear at the beginning as *duck*."[3]

---

[3]In providing this example, we do not mean to suggest that every unconventional spelling that a child produces should be corrected. Whether or not an unconventional spelling should be addressed in this way depends on a variety of factors—especially what the child has already learned about the writing system and the child's purpose for writing.

Selecting and Using Key Words (Mnemonics)

Key words are often used to help children learn and remember letter–sound relationships—and they can be especially useful for the harder-to-remember relationships discussed above. However, for key words to be helpful, they need to be "good" key words. That is, they need to provide clear and representative examples of the sounds on which we want the children to focus. A revision of the key-word chart used in ISA research studies appears in Figure 7.2. Our purpose in presenting this chart is not to suggest that ours is necessarily better than others that might be available—but it is certainly better than some. It is just an example of what a well-planned and constructed key-word chart might look like.[4]

Classroom Resource

An 8½″ × 11″ version of each key word is available on the book's companion website (see the box at the end of the table of contents). Also available is a copy of the chart provided on p. 183, which can be used in small-group and one-to-one instructional settings or sent home as a resource.

In developing these key words, several considerations played a role. Below we share these considerations as they may be useful to teachers as they consider the utility and appropriateness of the key words they currently use or are thinking about using.

- Key words will be most helpful to children if they are familiar with the word and its referent. For example, *house* and *cat* are familiar, but *hut* and *leopard* are less so for most children. Obviously, if the picture for the key word does not help learners remember the spoken word, it will not help them remember the sound associated with the letter/grapheme. If children are familiar with the concepts that the key words represent, they will be better able to use the key word as it is intended to be used: to help them remember the grapheme–phoneme correspondence. A related consideration is that it is easier to analyze the phonemes in a known word than in an unfamiliar word (Metsala, 2011).

- Do not include key words for the long-vowel sounds because the long sound and the letter name are one and the same. Therefore, a key word is unnecessary. Children just need to learn that one of the sounds that a vowel letter can represent is the same as its name.

- For the short-*a* sound:
  - Avoid words in which the *a* is followed by an *n* (*ant*), an *r* (*arm*), or an *l* (*alligator*) because, as a result of coarticulation, these letters tend to

---

[4] Teachers refer to such charts by various names (letter chart, alphabet chart, key words, etc.). Consistent terminology should be used across instructional settings.

A a apple	B b ball	C c	D d dog	E e	F f fish
gas	G g giraffe	circle	J j jar	Ed the elephant	K k kite
					L l leaf
M m monkey	H h house	I i itch	Q q queen	R r rain	S s sun
T t tent	O o octopus	P p pencil	X x box	Y y yarn	Z z zipper
umbrella	V v vacuum	W w window			

ch chair	sh shoe	th thumb	wh whale	-ck sock

FIGURE 7.2. Key-word chart for single-letter and digraph graphemes.

change the sound of the *a*, such that it is not a good example of the short-*a* sound.

- For the short-*e* sound:
  - Avoid words like *elephant* and *envelope* because, for children who are just learning about letter sounds, the first syllables in those words are the same as the names of the letters *l* and *n*, respectively. Thus, a beginning writer might use the letter *l* to represent the entire first syllable in *elephant*. To avoid this problem, we named the elephant on our key-word chart *Ed the Elephant*.[5]
  - Avoid the word *egg*. Many people pronounce the word *egg* such that it sounds very much like a (non)word spelled with a long-*a* spelling pattern (*aig*). (For doubters, note that *Craig* and *Greg* rhyme for many speakers of General American English—although there are certainly regional variations.) Teachers already using the key word *egg* for *e* have found it useful to draw a smiley face on the egg and name it *Ed* to address this problem.

- For the short-*i* sound:
  - Avoid words in which the *i* sounds more like a long-*e*. For example, some people pronounce the word *igloo* such that it sounds like *ee-gloo* and *iguana* such that it sounds like *ee-guana*. Our key word for short-*i* is *itchy*.

- For the short-*o* sound:
  - Avoid words in which the *o* sounds more like an *au*. For example, some people pronounce the word *ostrich* in such a way that it sounds like *aus-trich*.
  - Do not use the word *orange* because *o* combined with *r* produces an *r*-controlled vowel (*or*)—not a short-*o* sound.

- For all consonants (including consonant digraphs):
  - Avoid words in which the focal grapheme is included in a consonant cluster (e.g., *br, fl, st, thr*) because it is harder for young children to break apart those combinations into their component phonemes. Clusters that include *r* are especially problematic for the letters *t* and *d* at the beginnings of words because, in the resulting clusters, the sound of the focal letter (*t* or *d*) cannot be isolated. (For example, the word *train* and the nonword *chrain* sound the same when pronounced. Neither of them includes a recognizable /t/ sound. A similar problem arises for the *dr* cluster—the pronunciations of *drum* and *jrum* are the same, and there is no recognizable /d/ sound.)

---

[5] We elected to use an elephant as our key word for *E* because, although young children may think that it begins with an *L*, it does begin with a true short-*e* sound and there are no other picturable, familiar objects that begin with a true short-*e* sound. As noted, we refer to the picture as Ed the Elephant.

The *th* digraph represents two different phonemes—the unvoiced sound (as in *thumb)* and the voiced sound (as in *these*). The voiced /th/ phoneme generally occurs only at the beginning of abstract words such as *the, this, though,* and *these.* So, while we do not provide a separate key word for the voiced *th,* some teachers have opted to use "the thumb" to refer to *the thumb* key word and explicitly explain the two sounds for *th.*

Another characteristic of key words that may make them more useful in helping children learn letter–sound correspondences is the integration of the grapheme and the picture representing the key word. Ehri, Deffner, and Wilce (1984) found that when letters and key words are integrated (as ours are), children seem to learn the letter–sound correspondences more readily. Similar results were found by Roberts and Sadler (2019) and Schmidman and Ehri (2010).

Grapheme–Phoneme Relationships and Key Words and Linguistic Diversity

The issue of using "familiar" words as key words may seem simple on the surface, but when it comes to having labels for common objects, the learners' world experiences and language background obviously play an important role. Therefore, it may be helpful to imbue at least some of the less common key words with meaning beyond the context of the key-word chart. For example, if *octopus* is used as the key word for short-*o,* it may be helpful to show a video clip of an octopus or to read a book such as *An Octopus Is Amazing* (Lauber, 1990). If *yarn* is used for *y,* using yarn in a measuring project in math or demonstrating knitting or crocheting would imbue it with meaning and thus help to make it more memorable. For a word to become part of a child's spoken vocabulary, it generally helps if the child encounters the word several times and across contexts (as is discussed in Chapter 15).

KEEP IN MIND If a child is receiving reading instruction in more than one setting, the key words used in the different settings should be the same. The purpose of key words is to assist memory of letters' sounds. If children are taught more than one set of key words (because they are receiving instruction in more than one setting), then they are, essentially, being asked to learn more than children who are receiving instruction in only one setting. This is also a concern as children move from one grade to the next. Children who have already learned the letter–sound correspondences well will no longer need to rely on key words. However, those who have yet to learn all the correspondences will benefit from not having to learn a whole new set when they move from one grade to the next. Asking that they do so is neither useful nor fair to the children! Note that, in grade 2 and beyond, teachers often opt to display only the key words for the short vowels and for the vowel teams (discussed in Chapter 10).

Teaching and Practicing
Consonant Grapheme–Phoneme Correspondences

In general, children are ready to learn a letter's sound as soon as they can reliably identify the upper- and lower-case versions of the letter. Teaching about grapheme–phoneme correspondences generally begins with some of the more frequently occurring single-letter consonant sounds (e.g., *m*, *s*, *t*) and then introduces short vowel sounds—typically, one at a time (e.g., /ă/, /ĭ/). Additional consonant sounds, including common consonant digraphs (*ch, sh, th*) and the remaining short vowel sounds follow. There is no universally agreed upon order for teaching grapheme–phoneme correspondences. We strongly recommend that the order of introduction be linked to the texts that are available for students to read.

To begin instruction on letter sounds, teachers should demonstrate that the sound for the letter tends to be the same in the different contexts in which it occurs. If a set of key words is to be used, the key word should be included when the sound for the letter is initially introduced. A sample dialogue for teaching the sound for the letter *s*, using *sun* as the key word (see Figure 7.3), is provided below. Note that, for the first few letter sounds taught, it makes sense to begin with stretchable sounds as this makes it easier to draw the children's attention to the sound.

Ways to Describe a Letter–Sound Relationship

Note that teachers and published curricula vary in the language used to explain letter–sound relationships. For example, some might say:

- "The letter s makes the /sss/ sound."
- "S says /sss/."
- "S spells /sss/."
- "S stands for /sss/."
- "S represents the /sss/ sound."

Ideally, for children who are first learning letter–sound relationships, the language used to explain them should be consistent across instructional settings. Probably the clearest way to explain these relationships is "The sound for (letter name) is (letter sound)."

FIGURE 7.3. Key word for teaching the sound for the letter *s*.

Sample Instructional Dialogue: Letter–Sound Correspondence for *S*		
Materials needed: Large-print letter *S* on a card, word cards with words beginning with the letter *S* and the /s/ sound (e.g., *sun, soup, sock, seat, some, said*), card with key word for *S*. For children who are a bit more advanced in understanding the alphabetic code, words with the *s* at the end of the word might also be used—these should all be words in which the *s* represents the /s/ sound (e.g., *bus, rips, mitts*).		
Teacher	**What the teacher says**	**Comments on the activity**
Says:	"We are going to learn about one of the sounds for the letter *s*—the sound is /sssss/. When we see an s in a word, often, its sound is /ssss/."	Notice the explicit language in this example.
Shows letter *s* and says:	"/sssss/."	Note the utility of beginning with a stretchable sound.
Shows the word *sun* and says:	"Here is the word *sun*. It has the letters s, u, n. The sound for s in this word is /ssss/. /ssssun/. Lots of times, when we see an s in a word, we make the /ssss/ sound."	*S* sometimes represents the /zzz/ sound as in *was, has, bags,* and *teams*. It also appears as part of the *sh* digraph. This variation would not be addressed at this early point. However, we don't want to mislead children by implying that a given letter *always* represents a particular sound.
Shows a picture of a *sun* with the letter *s* next to it (or in it, depending on the key words in use) and says:	"Here's a picture of a *sun*. We are going to use this picture to help us remember the sound for the letter *s*. So, when we see the letter *s*, thinking of a sun can help us remember the sound for *s*. The word *ssssun* has an *s* at the beginning, and the sound for *s* in the word *ssssun* word is /ssss/."	Repetition of key points is useful when new information is being provided.
Shows several other printed words that start with *s* and for which the children know the meaning, and says:	"Here are some more words that start with *s* and the /ssss/ sound at the beginning: *ssssoup, ssssock, sssseat, ssssome, sssssaid*."	Elongating the beginning sound makes it easier for the children to attend to it.
Points to the *s* in each word and says:	"These words all have an *s* at the beginning."	

Points to each word while saying it.	"The sound for the letter *s* is the same in all of these words: *sssoup, sssock, ssseat, sssome,* and *sssaid.* "Do you hear the /sss/ at the beginning of each of these words? *Sssoup, sssssock, sssseat, sssssome, sssssaid.*"	
Draws children's attention to the key word and reminds learners of its utility.	"So, remember, when we see the letter *s*, if we can't remember the sound that goes with it, we can look here at [wherever key words are posted], find the *s*, and then use the picture to help us remember the /sssss/ sound for *s*."	At least for the first few letter sounds taught, it is important to be very explicit about how to use the key words.
Notes that the *s* sometimes occurs at the ends of words as well.	"We will also see the letter *s* in other parts of words. For example, sometimes when the letter *s* is at the end of a word, the sound for s is /ssss/."	
Shows a few printed words with the letter *s* at the end—only words in which the *s* represents the /ssss/ sound would be used.	"Here are some words in which an *s* comes at the end of the word."	
Points to each word, names the word, and stretches the *s* sound.	"The words are *hatsss, bussss, ripssss, yessss.*"	The words displayed would have only a single *s* and the sound for the s should be /ssss/ rather that /zzz/ (as in *bibs, gives, bags*).

After this introduction, the children should be invited to think of words that have the /sss/ sound. The teacher might write each word the children suggest on a chart large enough for the children to see and draw their attention to the *s* in the word. The words should be grouped by the position of the *s* in the words (beginning or end of the word). If a child suggests a word that has the /s/ sound but no *s* (e.g., *city, celery*), the teacher should acknowledge that the words do begin with the /ssss/ sound but explain that the word does not have an *s* at the beginning. To honor the children's contributions, words that start with the target sound but not with the target letter could be put on a separate list for later consideration. The teacher might briefly note that *c* sometimes represents the /ssss/ sound.

The sequence in which consonant grapheme–phoneme correspondences are taught would, ideally, be coordinated with the texts that children will be reading soon. In our work with early literacy learners, we tried to ensure that children had the opportunity to apply newly taught grapheme–phoneme associations in meaningful text shortly after they learned about them (typically in the same small-group lesson).

Practicing Grapheme–Phoneme Associations for Consonants

Activities designed to reinforce grapheme–phoneme associations should typically focus on the sounds of letters that occur at the beginning of words until the children are very facile with these associations. Later, the focus can be shifted to the sounds in other parts of words. In small-group instructional settings, different skill levels among children may be accommodated by asking different children to focus on different parts of the word.

Following are several activities that can be used to provide practice in applying developing letter–sound knowledge.

Sorting by Beginning Letter Sound

This activity is very similar to the sound-sorting activity described in Chapter 5 (p. 139). In order to sort pictures of objects by the beginning letter sound, children must be able to notice/attend to the beginning sounds in spoken words. For this activity, the teacher would do the following:

• Select several pictures of objects that either do or do not start with the sound of the grapheme that is the focus of instruction. Avoid objects that start with the target phoneme but not with the letter. Also avoid objects that start with the letter but not the sound that is being targeted (e.g., *sugar* starts with *s* but not with the /sss/ sound) and avoid words with consonant clusters at the beginning— because it is harder to isolate the beginning phoneme in a cluster. (Note that the picture-sorting resources described in Chapter 5 can be used as resources for this type of activity as well.)

• Name each object, have the children repeat the name, and then decide whether it starts with the sound of the target grapheme.

• Have the children place all pictures that start with the target grapheme under a printed version of the grapheme.

• Later, when the children have learned about several grapheme–phoneme correspondences, have them sort groups of pictures according to the initial sound in the word. They would use a sorting board such as the one illustrated in Figure 5.6 (p. 139), with letters heading the columns rather than pictures.

As described in Chapter 5, after the initial modeling, children in a small-group context would each have their own sorting boards so that they would have the opportunity to do their own thinking. As for the sound-sorting activity described in Chapter 5, when a teacher notices that a child has placed a picture in the wrong column, the teacher would encourage the child to name all the pictures in the column and decide which one doesn't really fit—and move it. The goal is to encourage the child to do the thinking required. Simply telling the child which item is misplaced will not accomplish this goal.

"How Would I Spell the Beginning Sound?"

This activity helps prepare children to effectively apply their grapheme–phoneme knowledge in writing. Rather than thinking about multiple aspects of the writing process, they can concentrate on thinking about how to spell the first sound in a word. In this activity, the teacher would do the following:

• Give each child three or four graphemes for which they are learning the sounds. (For consonant digraphs, the two letters that spell the phoneme would be taped together if letter tiles are being used or printed on a single card if cards are used.)

• Hold up a picture, name it, and ask the children to find the letter(s) that spell the first sound in the word. Each child should be allowed enough time to make a choice before the other children give their responses. (The teacher would ask the children to keep their choices private until everyone has decided.)

• Remind children who need the key words to use them by saying something like "Think of the sound that you hear at the beginning of the word I say and look at the pictures of our key words [*pointing to an available display*] and think about which one starts with the same sound as the word I say. Then look at the letter(s) that go with the key word, and you'll know which letter(s) to choose."

As the children become more proficient with this activity, the teacher might ask them to write the beginning letter(s) for the word on paper or on a dry-erase

---

Consonant Digraphs

The digraphs *ch* and *sh* can be taught in much the same way as single-consonant graphemes. The new bit of information that needs to be included is that sometimes two letters go together to represent one sound. Instruction for these would typically occur after children had learned about many of the single-consonant graphemes and at least some of the graphemes for short vowel sounds.

The unvoiced sound for *th* occurs most frequently at the ends of words or syllables (e.g., *bath, with, both, birthday*). Therefore, while the key word for the unvoiced *th* digraph (e.g., *thumb*) would be used to remind children of the sound, practice with the sound would occur primarily in the context of word building, word reading, and written spelling activities described in Chapter 8 when the focus is not limited to the beginnings of words.

board instead of picking the letter from a set of alternatives (e.g., "If I wanted to write the word *tub,* what letter would I write first?"). Having the children write the letters is more challenging and translates more directly into writing.

KEEP IN MIND If we want children to make good use of key words, we need to show them how to use them (by modeling and thinking aloud) on several occasions. It is also important to:

- Provide them with guided practice in using the key words.
- Encourage them to use the key words during both reading and writing.
- Notice when they use the key words spontaneously and help them reflect on the utility of doing so (e.g., "I saw Fre'asia look up at our key words when she wasn't sure what sound that *W* made. That helped, didn't it, Fre'asia?").

To provide all children in an instructional group with the opportunity to do their own thinking, teachers have found it useful to provide the children with "offices" in which to work. The office is constructed from two manila folders stapled together in such a way that, when opened and set on the table, they form a three-sided enclosure in which each child can determine their responses independently.

Strategic Reading: Early Partial Alphabetic Phase

To help children understand how letters can help them identify unfamiliar words, they need instruction and guided practice in applying their letter–sound knowledge while puzzling through words encountered in text. To address this need, the teacher might do the following:

- Explain to the children that they are learning about the sounds of letters because the letters will help them figure out words when they are reading.

- Engage the children in *shared reading* of beginner-level texts that highlight the grapheme(s) they are learning about.

- While reading, explicitly model how to use the letters in combination with any available contextual information for word identification. For example, if the text says *I saw a mouse* and is accompanied by a picture of a mouse-like critter, the teacher might say something like: "Hmm, that's a puzzling word. I know it's going to start with /mmm/ because I see that letter *m* at the beginning of the word. In the picture I see a rat or a squirrel or something. But I know it must be something that starts with /mmm/. So that helps me decide that the word is probably *mouse.*"

As the children engage in either shared or supported reading, encourage them to use the letter sounds they know to try to determine the beginning sound in unknown words. Descriptions of shared reading and supported reading are provided in Chapter 2 (see pp. 38 and 44).

Repetitive/Patterned Beginner-Level Texts

Repetitive beginner-level texts are designed to enable children to get a sense of the reading process before they can read in a conventional way. Such texts usually include repetitive, predictable language and pictures that closely parallel the print. Some beginner-level texts provide opportunities to focus on particular letters (see for example, *Monster Mop* in Figure 6.5, p. 165). Such books can be very useful for helping children learn about the utility of the letters they are learning about. (As discussed in Chapter 4, they are also useful for helping children to develop foundational print concepts.)

Consonant Grapheme–Phoneme Correspondence Frequency and Instructional Emphasis

The word *the* is one of the most frequently occurring words in spoken and written English. Therefore, the voiced *th* digraph is typically encountered early in children's reading experience. When introducing the printed form of the word *the*, it is appropriate to explain that sometimes two letters go together to represent one sound. However, because the word's spelling is not consistent with the grapheme–phoneme correspondences that are taught early on, helping children learn to identify the word would typically involve showing a printed version of the word, pronouncing the word and naming the letters: "This word is *the, t-h-e* spells *the*. Let's practice saying and spelling the word *the*." We discuss instruction focused on high-frequency words (like *the*) in Chapter 13.

Some consonant graphemes occur quite infrequently (i.e., *qu, x,* and *z*). Therefore, instruction for these graphemes would occur toward the end of the process of teaching about letter–sound correspondences and would typically involve fewer practice activities, as these graphemes (especially *qu* and *x*) do not lend themselves to many of the activities described in this chapter.

The *y* grapheme represents three different phonemes (as in *yellow, my* [long-*i* phoneme], and *happy* [long-*e* phoneme]). The phoneme associated with *y* at the

---

Why Is the Grapheme S Sometimes Pronounced /z/?

The s grapheme sometimes represents the /z/ phoneme as in *lids* and *digs*. S takes the z-sound when it follows a voiced phoneme. Remember from Chapter 5 that the phonemes /s/ and /z/ are articulated the same way except that one is voiced and the other isn't. Consider the pronunciation of the *s* in the words *cabs* versus *caps*. The graphemes b and p are articulated in the same way, except one is voiced (the /b/) and the other isn't. The *s* is pronounced as /z/ following the /b/ due to coarticulation. When a phoneme is "voiced," the vocal cords vibrate. That vibration continues as the next phoneme is pronounced, causing the final phoneme in *cabs* to sound like /z/. Try pronouncing *cab* followed by /s/. The articulation is not as smooth. It is necessary to briefly interrupt the pronunciation of the end of the word *cab* (to stop the vibration of the vocal cords) in order to pronounce the final phoneme as /s/.

beginning of words (e.g., *yellow, yes, yet*) would be explicitly taught using the key-word approach. The long-*i* and long-*e* phonemes associated with *y* would be taught in the context of learning words that contain those phonemes. For example, in teaching the high-frequency word *my*, the teacher would explain that the *y* represents the /ī/ sound at the end of short words like *my* and *by* and *try*. At a different point, when children are further along in their understanding of the writing system, the teacher would point out that the letter y sometimes represents the /ē/ sound at the end of longer words such as *happy, baby,* and *candy*.

Using Elkonin (Sound) Boxes
to Reinforce Grapheme–Phoneme Correspondences

In Chapter 5 we discussed the use of Elkonin boxes to help children analyze the sounds in spoken words (see p. 146). Sound boxes can also be used to teach and reinforce the sounds of consonant graphemes. For example, if the children are learning the sound of the letter *m*, the teacher might display three sound boxes and provide a letter tile with the letter *m* on it. The teacher would say a series of words, each of which has the sound of *m* either at the beginning or end of the word, and then model and explain the process of stretching the word, thinking about where the /mmm/ sound is heard, and then moving the *m* tile into the box that represents the position of the /mmm/ sound in the word.

After modeling the process with a few words (making sure that the /mmm/ sound occurs sometimes at the beginning and sometimes at the end), the teacher would invite the children to participate in the sound analysis and decision making concerning the location of the /mmm/ sound. By initially representing only one sound in the word, the process will be more manageable for children who are at an early point in learning about print. Once consonant digraphs have been introduced, the letter card or letter tile would include both letters in the digraph.

KEEP IN MIND Sound boxes are used to represent sounds, not letters. If a sound is represented in print by digraph (e.g., *ch, sh, th*), both letters would go in the box for the sound.

Short-Vowel Sounds

When children have learned the grapheme–phoneme correspondences for some of the consonants and can use the consonant graphemes they know to represent sounds at the beginnings and ends of words, instruction can begin to focus on some vowel sounds. When vowels are first introduced, instruction typically focuses on the short sound for the vowel because the spelling for short sounds is simpler than it is for long-vowel sounds—which typically involve at least two letters (e.g., *make, maid, may*). However, instruction focused on short-vowel sounds needs to be approached somewhat differently than instruction focused on consonant sounds because short-vowel sounds only occur at the beginning or in the middle of single-syllable words. As a result, instruction and practice using Elkonin boxes (as described above for consonant graphemes) wouldn't work very well. The other instruction and practice activities described for consonant graphemes can be utilized once at least two short-vowel grapheme–phoneme correspondences have been taught. The two activities are:

- "Sorting by Beginning Sound," which would be modified to "Sorting by Middle Sound," and
- "How Would I Spell the Beginning Sound," which would be modified as "How Would I Spell the Middle Sound?"

Sorting by Middle Sound

If the short sounds for the vowels *a* and *i* have been taught using the key words and example words as described above for consonant graphemes/phonemes, a sorting activity can be used to reinforce knowledge of the short-vowel sounds. For this sorting activity, children might be given pictures of *cap, bag, cat, gas, mat, pig, ship, gift,* and *crib* in mixed-up order and asked to sort them under the letters *a* and *i*. (Note that these pictures are listed as Vowel Sounds for Picture Sorts on the book's companion website—see the box at the end of the table of contents.) As always, it would be important to ensure that the children know the labels for the pictures before being asked to sort them.

"How Would I Spell the Middle Sound?"

The children would be given two or three of the vowel letters for which they had been taught the short-vowel sounds. The teacher would dictate words and the children would select the letter that would be used to represent the middle sound in the dictated words. Early on, the teacher might need to elongate/stretch the vowel sound, but as the children gain proficiency, the emphasis on the vowel sound should be eliminated.

Reinforcing Grapheme–Phoneme Correspondence for All Taught Graphemes

Writing Helper

During shared writing activities, as teachers write, they should invite children to help by saying which letter should be written for the beginning, middle, or end (depending on children's skills) of particular words. For example, if the teacher is writing a caption for a picture a child has drawn, the teacher might ask the child to say what the first letter would be for words that start with letter sounds that the child has learned. Again, it is important to remind children to use the key words they have learned for a particular letter sound if they cannot immediately recall the letter that represents the sound. The child would be encouraged to look at the pictures associated with the key words and find the one that has the same beginning sound as the word they want to write.

Personal Dictionaries

In our kindergarten intervention groups, each of the children developed their own personal dictionary that contained a page for each letter of the alphabet and the associated key words that were used in the classroom. Blank personal dictionaries with the ISA key words are available on the companion website for this book (see the box at the end of the table of contents).

As the children learned the sound for each of the letters/graphemes, they put pictures of things that start with that letter on the appropriate page in the dictionary. To save time, the children were given several pictures that had been cut from the phonemic awareness resources provided on the book's website or from newspapers, magazines, old phonics books, and so forth, and were told to select a few to paste into their picture dictionaries based on the letter sound they were learning about. (Note that in intervention settings, time for drawing and coloring should be strictly limited so as to fully capitalize on the intensity of the small instructional grouping.)

As children progressed in learning about the writing system (as described in subsequent chapters), they were encouraged to label some of the pictures that they put in the dictionaries. Because the dictionary is a long-term project and because it is in book form (and, therefore, may be considered "published"), the spelling that appears in the book should be conventional. To accomplish this in a small-group setting, individual children, supported by the teacher, might work out the spelling of the word on a piece of scrap paper, and then each child would copy the conventionally spelled picture label into their dictionary. Some children also enjoy copying words that start with a given letter onto the appropriate page of their dictionary by referring to a published children's dictionary. As the children's literacy skills progressed, the captions for the pictures often became longer and included some of the high-frequency words that the children were learning.

The personal dictionaries in our projects represented an ongoing project for the children. The goal was *not* to fill up the entire page on the day that page was begun. Rather, the children were encouraged to add entries over time. These dictionaries were sent home with the children at the end of the school year, with the invitation to continue to add pictures over the summer and to share the booklet with family members and friends. This was intended to encourage the children to continue to think about the relationships between the sounds in spoken words and the letters in printed words as well as other skills (such as high-frequency words and punctuation) that were incorporated over time.

Games for Reinforcing Letter Sounds

A variety of simple games can be redesigned to help reinforce letter–sound associations. Most of them will only work with beginning sounds:

- *Letter bingo*. Each playing card has letters on it. The caller says sounds for both consonants and vowels. Alternatively, the caller might say words, and the children might isolate the first sound and mark the associated letter.

- *Beginning sound picture bingo*. Each playing card has pictures beginning with particular sounds. The caller says letter names.

- *Beginning sound picture post office*. A "post office" is set up with three or four "mail slots," each identified with a letter. The children have cards to mail. Each card has a picture of an item with a name that begins with one of the letters on the post office slots. The children can check their own accuracy if the correct pictures are pasted into the box under each slot.

- *Parking lot*. The parking lot director (teacher) names objects, and the children park their cars on the letter that comes at the beginning of the word named. Within a group, the children's game boards can have the same letters, but the letters should be in different locations; each child therefore needs to find the beginning letter for the word named rather than simply checking on the location where a neighbor parked.

- "*I spy* (with my little eye something that begins with the letter __)." The children are given the first letter in a word and perhaps some meaning-based clue. They are encouraged to guess the word. When they offer guesses that are wide of the mark, there should be discussion about why their guesses don't fit the clues.

Useful Resource

Words Their Way by Bear et al. (2019) contains an abundance of appealing games and activities that provide practice with letter sounds.

KEY POINTS OF THIS CHAPTER

✓ Reading and writing require the use of letters/graphemes and their associated sounds.

✓ Developing automaticity with the sounds of graphemes contributes heavily to learners' ability to decode and spell accurately.

✓ The names of many consonant letters include the letters' sounds. Children's sound spellings reveal that they rely on these relationships early on (recall the use of the letter *h* to represent the /ch/ phoneme). This is especially evident when they choose the wrong part of a letter's name in their sound spellings (e.g., using the letter *s* [es] to spell the short-*e* sound in words like *bell* [bsl]).

✓ Teachers who understand how children use letter names in their sound spellings provide more effective feedback that focuses on letter–sound relationships rather than phonemic analysis.

CHAPTER 8

The Alphabetic Principle and the Alphabetic Code

Early Development

WRITING SYSTEM FOUNDATIONS GOAL 5

Children will understand that the letters in printed words represent the sounds in spoken words and will understand how to use consonant and short-vowel graphemes to build, read, and spell one-syllable words.

In order to progress as readers and writers, children need to understand how to use the alphabetic writing system to both decipher and write printed words. In the previous chapter we discussed teaching grapheme–phoneme relationships. In this chapter we focus on ways to help children who are at early points in development learn how to apply that knowledge in the contexts of reading and writing. Children develop proficiency with alphabetic decoding and encoding at different rates, and, depending on the materials they read and the instruction they receive, they learn about different aspects of the code in different sequences. The ISA is not tied to a particular curriculum. Therefore, although in what follows we suggest a sequence for teaching about aspects of the code and provide a rationale for that sequence, we recognize that the curricula in place will play a large role in determining the order in which various aspects of the code are addressed. In this and the next chapter, which focuses on teaching rimes and word families, we offer approaches to helping children develop various decoding and spelling skills but stress that the order in which particular skills are taught and practiced should, to a great extent, be determined by what the children already know and by the materials they will be reading in the near future. In other words, *the sequence in which we present the skills is not necessarily the sequence in which the skills must be taught.*

In this chapter we describe instruction designed to

- help children develop a conceptual understanding that the graphemes (including individual letters and consonant digraphs) in printed words represent the sounds in spoken words, and
- understand how to apply this understanding at early points in reading and writing development.

Early Development of Skill in Using the Alphabetic Code

The instruction described in this chapter is appropriate for children who, at the outset, know the sounds associated with at least a few letters, including the short sounds for at least one or two vowel letters. These skills are expected to develop in kindergarten or before. Older children who do not yet demonstrate these skills will benefit from instruction designed to promote phonemic awareness (Chapter 5) and knowledge of letter names and their sounds (Chapters 6 and 7). In this chapter, we discuss instruction that is intended to help children learn to use all the graphemes in single-syllable words composed of a beginning consonant, a short vowel sound, and an ending consonant (i.e., CVC words) to read and spell words.

In teaching children about the alphabetic principle, we begin by engaging them in a standard sequence of instructional and practice activities: making (building) words with movable letters, reading words formed by the teacher using movable letters, and writing words dictated by the teacher. These three activities—building, reading, and writing words—would typically all occur in the same lesson. Therefore, each involves only a few words, and the same words might be used in all three activities.

We begin with instruction focused on the beginning letters and sounds in one-syllable short-vowel words (e.g., changing *mat* to *fat* to *sat*). These activities are useful both for introducing the alphabetic principle and for giving children practice with the letter sounds they are learning. We would expect that children would be well prepared for this instruction based on their experience with the "How Would I Spell . . . ?" procedure described in Chapter 7. Once children appear to be proficient with beginning letters and sounds, we move on to ending sounds in written words—while also continuing to practice with beginning letters and sounds. Once again, we use word-building, word-reading, and written-spelling activities. When children are proficient with reading and spelling single-syllable words that involve changes at just the beginning and end (e.g., changing *mat* to *map, map* to *tap, tap* to *tag, tag* to *bag, bag* to *bat*), they are prepared to attend to the middle vowel letters/sounds in words as well (e.g., changing *hot* to *hit, hit* to *hat, hat* to *mat, mat* to *map, map* to *mop*).

The approach described in this chapter differs from some other approaches to instruction in the alphabetic code. For example, some call for explicitly teaching word families prior to focusing on individual vowel sounds. We address teaching about word families in Chapter 9. It also differs from approaches that call for working with letters and sounds in all positions in consonant–vowel–consonant (CVC) words as soon as children know some consonant and short-vowel sounds. While some children involved in such an approach may find it easy to learn about the workings of the alphabetic code, for children who find learning about the code difficult, this approach may require too much too soon. And, as a result, it could frustrate them and have a negative impact on their motivation and engagement (see the discussion of challenge in Chapter 3). We anticipate that the more gradual approach would be more successful for more children and would not expect it to hold children back, as our approach calls for moving children on to the next level of challenge as soon as they demonstrate proficiency with earlier skills in the sequence. Also, we should clarify that instruction of the sort described in this chapter and in Chapter 9 may occur more or less simultaneously, and the specific focus for a given lesson should be influenced by the texts that the children will be reading in the same lesson or, if need be, in the very next lesson.

Assessing and Documenting Children's Progress

Figure 8.1 presents the snapshot for the skills discussed in this chapter. Application of the skills discussed is considered in terms of children's performance both in isolated word work and their application of their developing skills in the context of reading and writing meaningful text. Children would be considered *proficient* with given skills when they are reliable and automatic (fluent) in demonstrating the skill. For reading and writing isolated words, children would not be considered to be proficient until they are able to make changes to the words without needing the scaffold of teacher emphasis on the part of the word that needs to be changed and without needing to refer to the key-word chart (see the discussion of these points later in this chapter).

When children are fairly proficient with the earlier skills listed in each section of the snapshot, they are ready to focus on vowel sounds. In Chapter 7, we discussed explicitly teaching the short sound for each vowel letter. Therefore, in isolated word work, a rating of proficient would require use of the correct vowel letter. However, in the context of writing words in meaningful text, children will often represent long-vowel sounds with the vowel letter whose name is the same as the sound. For example, the child might spell *cape* as *cap*. On the Early Development snapshot, children would be rated as proficient if they simply include the correct vowel letter without using conventional spellings of the long-vowel sound.

Teaching the Concept of the Alphabetic Principle: Focusing on Initial Graphemes (Letters and Digraphs) and Consonant Phonemes

The first instructional activities involve having the child make (build) words using movable letters (e.g., letter tiles, letters printed on squares of cardstock or paper).

Group Snapshot—Alphabetic Code, Early Development					
Student names					
Building isolated words (dictated by the teacher)					
Initial consonant substitution					
Final consonant substitution					
Medial (short) vowel substitution					
Reading isolated words (presented by the teacher)					
Changes in initial consonant					
Changes in final consonant					
Changes in medial (short) vowel					
Writing isolated words (dictated by the teacher)					
Initial consonant substitution					
Final consonant substitution					
Medial (short) vowel substitution					
Reading single-syllable words in text					
Uses accurate or a "justifiable" initial consonant sound					
Uses accurate or a "justifiable" final consonant sound					
Uses accurate or a "justifiable" medial vowel sound					
Writing words in continuous text					
Represents beginning sound in word with an accurate or a "justifiable" letter					
Represents ending sound in word with an accurate or a "justifiable" letter					
Represents short vowel sounds with an accurate or a "justifiable" letter.					

Key:

☐ *B—Beginning* indicates that the instruction has addressed the objective but that the child has only a preliminary understanding or capability with regard to that particular objective.

☒ *D—Developing* indicates that the child has some understanding of the objective but does not reliably demonstrate that understanding or capability or is not yet automatic (fluent) with the skill.

☒ *P—Proficient* indicates that the child reliably and automatically demonstrates the understanding or capability.

Note. We use the term *justifiable* in this snapshot to take account of the fact that, until a word has become part of a child's automatic sight vocabulary, the variability in the English orthography will lead to reasonable (justifiable) but inaccurate substitutions. For example, a child might spell the word *was* as *wuz*—the last two letters are "justifiable" because they do in fact represent the last two sounds in the word *was*. As another example, a child might spell *cup* as *kup*—because the sound at the beginning of the word can justifiably be represented by the letter *k*. Teachers should take careful note of these substitutions, as they provide valuable information that informs future instruction.

FIGURE 8.1. Group snapshot for early development of skill with the alphabetic code.

Note that to enable learners to better focus on the letters, all letters and digraphs should be presented on the same background color, and the consonants and consonant digraphs should be printed in the same color. The vowel letters can be in a color that contrasts with the color of the consonants.

Sample Introductory Dialogue for Introducing the Alphabetic Principle—Focusing on Beginning Letters/Graphemes and Sounds/Phonemes		
Materials needed:	Three or four letters for which the children know the sounds and a rime that, when combined with the individual letters, will produce three or four words. The rime should be printed on a single card. (On the first few times this activity is used, it is useful to begin with beginning graphemes that have stretchable sounds.) In this example, we use the rime *it* and the letters *f, l, s*. (Note that the rime is used here as a foundation for making changes to the beginning graphemes/phonemes. The purpose is not to explicitly teach the rime.)	
Teacher	**What the teacher says**	**Comments on the activity**
Says:	"When we read, we use the letters to figure out the sounds in the words. They help us figure out what each word is."	It is important to provide an explicit description of the role of individual letters.
Displays the word *it* and says:	"This little word is *it*. I can put a letter in front of the word *it*, and I will have a new word."	Helping learners understand how changing just one letter changes the sound and meaning of the word is important in helping them to understand the alphabetic principle more generally.
Puts an *s* in front of *it* and says:	"When I put an *s* here, *it* becomes *sssssit*. We already learned about the sound for *s* . . . the sound is /sssss/. When I put /sssss/ and /it/ together, it makes the word *sssit*."	Using a consonant with a stretchable sound enables the teacher to more easily draw attention to the role of the beginning letter.
Explains:	"I can change *sssit* to *ffffit* by changing just one letter. *Sssssit* and *fffffit* have different sounds at the beginning of the word, so I need to change the beginning letter. So, I'll take the *s* away. Now the word is *it* again. I need to put another letter in front of *it* to make the word *ffffit*."	Multiple illustrations of the same concept help children to better understand the concept. Again, using a letter with a stretchable sound enables the teacher to more readily draw attention to changes at the beginning of the word.
Separates the onset (*s*) and the rime (*it*) and says:	If I take the *s* away, I just have *it* again.	Reminding the children of the pronunciation of the rime portion supports their ability to build additional words.

Displays the letters *f*, *s*, and *l* and rime *it* and says:	"What letter is used for the /fffff/ sound that you hear at the beginning of *fffft*?"	Engaging the children in thinking about the sounds of the small number of displayed letters makes the new concept manageable.
Reinforces or scaffolds or, if necessary, models by saying:	[Reinforces.] "Yes, the letter "f" is used for the /fff/ sound. Or: [Scaffolds.] "If you are not sure about the sound for each of these letters, you can look at your key words. Which letter has a key word that starts like *fffit*?" Or: [Models, if necessary.] "If I am not sure what letter to use to make *fffit*, I can look at my key words to find one that starts like *fffit*. I've only got three letters here, so that makes it easy. I'll start with the letter *l*. I look up at the key-word chart and I find the *l*. The key word for *l* is *leaf*. /llll/ is the sound at the beginning of *llleaf*. That is not the same as the beginning sound in *fffit*, so *l* is not the letter I need. Next, I'll try *f*. I go to my key words and find the *f*, and I see that the key word for f is *fish*. Fffffish and *fit* have the same sound at the beginning. So, *f* is the letter I need to use to change *sit* to *fit*."	Teacher feedback is responsive to the children who seem to find the task most challenging. If any of the children in the group seem to need scaffolding or modeling, it should be provided even if some children respond automatically and effortlessly. If children in a group routinely demonstrate that they differ in their ability to engage in this type of activity, consideration should be given to regrouping.
Provides additional practice	"How would we change *fffit* to *lllit* (*lit* to *sit* again, *sit* to *fit* . . .)?"	Particularly for children who were not automatic in the response on multiple changes of the beginning letter, using the same three or four beginning letters will promote automaticity and, ideally, reduce the need to reference the key words.

Guided Practice: Changing Beginning Letters to Build, Read, and Spell Words

Once the concept of the alphabetic principle has been introduced, children should be provided with guided practice in applying it. Three practice activities are used: word building, word reading, and written spelling. The teacher should explicitly demonstrate the task before asking the children to do it.

Word Building

This is the easiest of the practice activities and should be used first. Children are given a single rime (such as *it*, *an*, or *op*) that can be used to form several different words. The teacher names the rime and then asks the children to make words by changing just the beginning letter. For example, the teacher might use letter tiles to show the word *mat* (see Figure 8.2) and say, "This is the word *mat*. If I take the *m* away, all I have left is *at*. If I add one of these other letters, I can make a new word. If I put an *r* in front of *at*, I have the word *rat*."

Once the process has been demonstrated, children can be asked to form the words the teacher dictates using the same rime. As needed, they should be encouraged to refer to the key words that have been taught to help them recall the sounds for individual letters or digraphs (once they have been taught as described in Chapter 7). Word building in this context is relatively easy for children because the number of graphemes that might be used to form the new word is limited, and the key words are readily available for reference.

Word Reading

In this activity, the teacher changes the beginning letter in the word, while the children watch, and asks the children to read the new word. This task is somewhat more challenging than word building because the children need to recall both the sound of the beginning letter and the sound of the rime and then blend the sounds together. Until the children learn the routine for this activity, the teacher would guide their attention by saying something like, "This word is *mat*. If I take the *m* away, and put an *f* at the beginning instead, what will my new word be?"

Written Spelling

In this activity, children are asked to spell the words they have been building and reading. For children at this point in development, the rime would be left in view, and they would be expected to refer to it in order to properly spell the word dictated

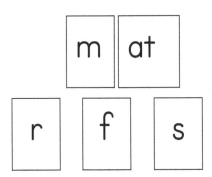

FIGURE 8.2. Word building: Initial consonant substitution.

by the teacher. Their major task is to analyze the word spoken by the teacher and then decide which letter to use to represent the beginning sound in the word.

The Role of Rimes and Word Families in Early Decoding and Encoding Activities

In the activities described above, we use rimes to form multiple words in a word family by changing just the beginning letter. In these early activities, it is unlikely that the children will actually learn the rime that is the central component of the word family because most of their attention is drawn to the beginning of the word, which is the only part that changes. The goal in the activities that focus on beginning letters is for the children to become facile with using the beginning letters as cues when they are attempting to read and spell words.[1]

Ultimately, however, it is important that children learn that words containing the same sound pattern often share the same orthographic (letter) pattern. Once children learn a number of frequently occurring rimes and understand how the rimes can be generalized, they will be better able to efficiently analyze and identify unfamiliar words. A more thorough discussion of teaching to promote the effective use of rimes for reading and writing words in a family is provided in Chapter 9.

Independent Practice: Real Word or Not?

Once children have learned to build and read words by changing the beginning letter, additional independent practice can be provided by giving children a rime and several individual letters and asking them to make two lists of words using that rime: real words and words that are not real. Teachers sometimes use a letter slide for this activity to encourage the children to be a bit more systematic (see Figure 8.3). Teachers have also found the letter slide useful when working with children who fidget a lot with letter tiles or letter cards.[2]

Note that we are not recommending that children be simply asked to read nonsense words; to do so would undermine a child's ability to develop understanding of how to construct meaning while reading. By asking the child to determine whether a word is a real word, we are, in fact, helping to establish the understanding that the words we read should make sense. Asking the question "Is the word I just said a real word?" is an important step in self-monitoring, cross-checking, and, ultimately, self-correction while reading meaningful text. Because young children vary considerably in their knowledge of vocabulary, letter slides can be usefully employed by groups of two or three children; this would allow the children

---

[1] Note that when children are reading words in the context of a book or other text, they will have additional sources of information to support their word-solving efforts.

[2] Letter slides can be used to for changing beginning, ending, and medial graphemes/sounds as well as consonant clusters. Once children are learning to focus on the beginning, middle, and end of one-syllable short-vowel words, a letter strip could be used in all three positions simultaneously.

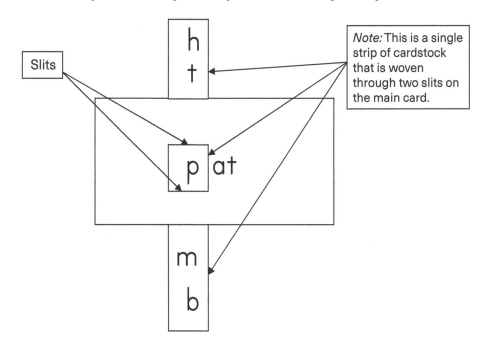

FIGURE 8.3. Example of a letter slide.

to discuss which words are real or not as the lists are constructed. When the group disagrees about a word, those who believe it is a real word should explain what it means. This approach has the potential added value of enhancing the vocabulary of children with less well-developed language skills—including multilingual learners. To enhance the reading and writing benefits of this activity, each child in the group should construct their own lists and compare them by reading them to one another.

Phonemes That Are Easily Confused

In Chapter 5 we noted that multiple pairs of phonemes differ only in voicing (e.g., /b/-/p/, /d/-/t/; see Figure 5.2, p. 122). For children who are just beginning to learn how the alphabetic code works, it is best to avoid asking them to make changes that require them to distinguish between easily confused phonemes. Thus, in word building, for example, changing *bat* to *pat* or *mad* to *mat* requires much more precise analysis of the beginning and ending sounds, respectively, than would changing *bat* to *fat* or *mad* to *map*, as the beginning and ending sounds in the latter word pairs are more readily distinguished.

Strategic Beginning Reading and Writing

It is easy to assume that children understand the connections between phonics activities and authentic reading and writing—because they are so obvious to us!

However, such assumptions should not be made. It is important to intentionally help children understand the relationship between decoding and constructing the meaning of printed language. Some suggestions for helping children make these connections, while reading to and with them are provided next.

To promote word solving during shared reading, the teacher might:

- Periodically point to individual words in the text and draw the children's attention to the beginning letter. Ask them to use the first letter to decide what the first sound in the word will be.
- Identify a character or object in the picture and ask the children to try to find the printed word for it. ("Can you find the word *bear* on this page? What letter do you think it will start with?") In order to find the word, the children must first attend to the initial sound in the spoken word, think of what letter represents that sound, and, finally, examine the printed words to find one that starts with that letter. Of course, for children at this point in development, we would only ask them to find a specific word on a page when there was only one word with that beginning sound.

To promote effective sound spelling during shared writing, the teacher might:

- Encourage children to participate in isolating the beginning sound in the word that is about to be written and in deciding what letter should be used to represent that sound.
- Write the first letter of the upcoming word and ask the children to figure out what the word will probably be, based on information provided by the context and by the first letter.

Throughout the activities discussed above, children would be frequently reminded to refer to the key-word chart as needed until reference to the chart becomes habitual and/or the children no longer need to rely on key words to remind them of the letter–sound correspondences.

Teaching the Concept of the Alphabetic Principle: Focusing on Ending Letters

Teachers using the ISA continue working on single-consonant sounds using initial consonant substitution with rimes until children are quite facile with the sounds for consonant graphemes that have been taught. When children know these sounds well, and when they are able to attend to the ending sounds in spoken words (i.e., sort pictures by ending sound), they are ready to learn to build, read, and spell words by making changes to both the beginnings and ends of words.

Sample Introductory Dialogue for Teaching Children to Attend to Ending Sounds as Well as Beginning Sounds in Word Building		
Materials needed: Six or seven consonants (see Figure 8.4) for which the children know the sounds and a single vowel which, in combination, can be used to form several three-phoneme words.		
Teacher	**What the teacher says**	**Comments on the activity**
Says:	"When we read, the letters help us figure out what the word will sound like. We have already practiced making and reading words with different beginning sounds. Now we are going to learn to pay attention to the letters at the ends of words, too. Paying attention to *both* the beginning and ending sounds will help us figure out even more words when we read."	Reminding students of what they have *already* learned supports motivation and promotes the expectation that they will learn more.
Displays the letters *s, a,* and *d* next to each other to form the word *sad* and the remaining letters below, as illustrated below. The teacher says and models:	"This is the word *sad*. We can change one letter and make the word *mad*, just like we were doing before. "Watch. I take the *s* away and put an *m* at the beginning, and that makes the word *mad*. "Now I will change *mad* to *man*. I need to think about the sounds in *mmmmaaaannnn* and decide which letter I need to change. *Mmmmaaannnnn* has an /mmmm/ sound at the beginning, so the *m* needs to stay. So, I'm going to think about the end of the word *mannnn*. I hear the /nnnn/ sound at the end	Changing just one letter at a time makes the task easier. The teacher articulates the kind of thinking that the students will need to do to successfully build the words named. After stretching the whole word, the teacher switches to stretching just the part of the word to which the children need to attend. If needed, the teacher might draw the children's attention to the key word for the /nnnnn/ sound.

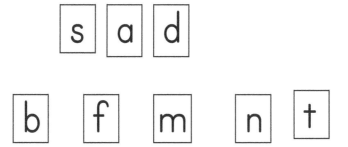

FIGURE 8.4. Consonants and a vowel for forming three-phoneme words.

	of the word *mannnnnn*—so I'll need to change that ending letter to the letter that makes the /nnnn/ sound—that's the letter *n*." [The teacher might elongate the pronunciation of the name of the letter *n* to emphasize the /nnnn/.]	
Displays a few additional letters that will be needed for making the planned changes to the word and says:	"Let's practice making more changes. We've got more letters we can use here. We have . . . [names the additional consonants displayed]."	All letters used should be those for which the letter's sound has already been introduced and practiced— although some children may still need to refer to the key words to recall the letters' sounds. Varying the part of the word that needs to change (either beginning or end) encourages children to think carefully about the sounds in the words and the parts of the printed word that need to be modified.
Says:	"Which letter do I need to change to change *man* to *fan*—the first letter or the last letter?"	Locating the part of the word that needs to be changed is the first step. If children have difficulty with this step, the teacher can elongate the beginning sounds in the two words. Or if the sound is not stretchable, emphasize the sound by vocalizing it a bit more loudly than the other sounds in the word.
Provides feedback:	"Right, the words *man* and *fan* are different at the beginning of the words—so we need to change the first letter." Or, if the response is incorrect: "Listen to those two words again— *mmmman, fffffan*. Is the different sound at the beginning or end of those words?	The teacher provides responsive feedback—elongating or emphasizing the part of the word that needs to be changed if need be.
Prompts for letter change:	"So, we decided we need to change the first letter. So, let's take the *m* away. Now this says *an*. What letter do we need to add to change *an* to *fan*?"	Depending on children's responses, the teacher may need to emphasize the initial sound in *fan* or may need to refer the children to the key-word chart to find a key word that begins with the same sound as *fan*.

Continued practice. Following this initial introduction, the teacher would engage the children in word-building activities that focus on beginning and ending sounds using letters for which the children have already at least begun to learn the sounds.

Guided Practice: Changing Beginning and Ending Letters to Build and Read Words

Following this initial introduction, the teacher would engage the children in collaboratively making (building) several additional words by changing just one letter at a time. For example, the teacher might ask the children to change *fan* to *fat*, *fat* to *bat*, *bat* to *bad*, *bad* to *sad*, *sad* to *mad*, *mad* to *man*. For children who find the activity challenging, use of consonants with stretchable sounds should be given priority.

In subsequent lessons, the children would be engaged in word building, word reading, and written spelling of words in which changes are made at either the beginning or end of each word to form a new word. In word-building and written-spelling activities in early lessons, the teacher should emphasize the part of the word that needs to change by stretching the sound if possible and/or by saying it somewhat louder. As the children's skills increase, this type of teacher scaffolding should be reduced and ultimately eliminated.

Independent Practice: Making Words

Once children have learned to build and read words by changing the beginning and ending letters, additional independent practice can be provided by giving children a single vowel for which the sound has been taught and several consonant letters. The children would be asked to make a list of as many real words as they can make, keeping the same vowel in the middle.

Strategic Emergent Reading and Writing

Children who can build words by making requested changes to both the beginning and ending sounds/letters are ready to apply that knowledge while reading and writing. Thus, in addition to drawing the children's attention to the beginning letters as they puzzle over unfamiliar words, they should be encouraged to attend to the ending letters as well to confirm their attempt to identify the word. Note that some beginner-level texts provide so much support for word identification through a combination of the context, the pictures, and the beginning letters that children are often able to effectively word-solve without needing to attend to the ending letters. However, once a word is accurately identified, the children should be encouraged to check the ending letter to confirm that the word has, indeed, been accurately identified (e.g., "Did you check the ending letter/sound to make sure it matches the word you said?").

In writing, children who are beginning to attend to ending sounds in isolated word-study activities should be encouraged to engage in analyzing and spelling the final sounds in words both during shared writing and in their own independent writing. Teacher modeling of this more complete analysis of the printed word is, of course, important.

KEEP IN MIND   When children hesitate over reading or spelling a word, it is appropriate to scaffold their attempts by referring to the key words that are being used to support letter–sound learning. For example, the teacher might:

- In the context of reading say: "If you can't remember what sound that letter makes, check your key words. Look for the letter and then think about the first sound in the name of the picture that goes with that letter.
- In the context of writing say: "If you are not sure what letter will make the sound you hear in that part (beginning, middle, end) of that word, check your key words. Look for a picture that has the same beginning sound as the sound you want to write."

The purpose of this type of scaffolding is to build independence in reading and spelling unfamiliar words. The prompts can be abbreviated to something as simple as "Check your key words" once children understand how to make effective use of the key words.

Strategic Reading: An Example

We once observed a kindergartner reading a beginner-level text with a picture of a log laying on the ground. The text read "Look at the log." The child read it as "Look at the land." Because the teacher had just begun to draw the children's attention to the ending sounds in words, she was able to reinforce what the child had done right ("I see you are thinking like a reader. We do see land in that picture and the word does begin with *l*") and to extend the child's thinking about how to use print. ("Remember, we've been talking about how we need to look all the way through to the end of the word to make sure that our word has the right sound at the end.")

Teaching the Concept of the Alphabetic Principle:
Focusing on Medial (Short) Vowels

When children are fairly proficient in building, reading, and spelling words that involve changes in beginning and ending letters/sounds, the focus should shift to medial short-vowel sounds. Approaches to teaching the correspondences between vowel letters and their short-vowel sounds were addressed in Chapter 7. In teaching the application of this knowledge, we recommend beginning with the short-vowel sounds that are most distinct from one another—that is the short sounds for *a* and *i*—as this degree of distinction will be easiest for children to notice.

Sample Instructional Dialogue for Teaching Children to Attend to Medial Short-Vowel Sounds in Word Building		
Materials needed:	Sample words to build: *bat, hat, hit, hid, had, bad, sad, sat, sit.*	
	Letters needed: *h, t, s, d, b, f, a, i*	
	(Eight or nine letters for which the children know the sounds—six or seven consonants and two vowels which, in combination, can be used to form several three-phoneme words with the short-vowel sounds in the middle of the words.)	

Teacher	What the teacher says	Comments on the activity
Says:	"We know that the letters in words help us know what the sounds in the word will be. We have already practiced making and reading words with different beginning and ending sounds. Now we are going to learn to pay attention to the letters in the middle of words, too. So, we will be paying attention to all the letters in words that have three letters—the beginning and ending sounds, which we already know how to do, and now the letters in the middle. Paying attention to *all* the letters and their sounds will help us figure out even more words when we read."	Reminding students of what they have *already* learned supports motivation and promotes the expectation that they will learn more.
Displays the letters *f, a,* and *t* next to each other to form the word *fat* and the remaining letters below. Says and models:	"This is the word *fat*. As we've been doing, we can change just one letter to make a new word. Since we are thinking about the middle of words now, let's change the word *faaaat (pointing to the word)* to *fiiit*. To change the word *fat* to *fit*, I take away the letter in the middle—the /ăăăă/—and put an i there because one of the sounds for *i* is /ĭĭĭĭ/. So, now this word is *fiiit*."	Changing just one letter at a time makes the task easier. The teacher articulates the kind of thinking the students will need to do in order to successfully build the words named. Stretching the middle sound in the word helps the children focus on the part that needs to be changed.
Motions to the additional letters that will be needed for making the planned changes to the words and says:	"Let's practice making more changes. We have more letters we can use here. We have . . . [names the additional consonants displayed and asks the children to provide the sounds for each]."	All letters used should be those for which the letter's sound has already been introduced and practiced—although some children may still need to refer to the key words to recall the letters' sounds. Varying the part of the word that needs to change (either beginning, middle, or end) encourages children to think carefully about

		the sounds in the words and the parts of the written word that need to be modified.
Says:	"Which letter do I need to change to change *fit* to *bit*? The first, middle, or last letter?"	Locating the part of the word that needs to be changed is the first step. If children have difficulty with this step, the teacher can elongate or emphasize the sound that changes in the new word (change *fffit* to **b**it). Note that the bolded b is intended indicate that the /b/ in the *bit* word should be pronounced with more emphasis (i.e., louder than the rest of the word). Drawing attention to any of the stop consonants in a word can be accomplished by saying the phoneme more loudly. Recall that stop consonants cannot be stretched/elongated without distortion.
Provides feedback:	"Right, the words *fit* and *bit* have different beginning sounds, so we need to change the beginning/first letter." Or, if the response is incorrect . . . "Listen to those two words again: *fffit*, **b**it. Is the different sound at the beginning, middle, or end of those words?"	The teacher provides responsive feedback—elongating or emphasizing the part of the word that needs to be changed if need be.
Prompts for letter change:	"So, we decided we need to change the first letter. Let's take the *f* away. Now we have the little word *it*. What letter do we need to add to change *it* to *bit*?"	Depending on children's responses, the teacher may need to emphasize the initial sound in *bit* or to refer the children to the key-word chart to find a key word that begins with the same sound as *bit*.

Continued practice. Following this initial introduction, the teacher would engage the children in word-building activities that focus on beginning, middle, and ending sounds using letters for which the children have already at least begun to learn the sounds. Following word building, the children would be engaged in word reading and written spelling that involves changes in beginning, middle, and ending letters and sounds. Early on, only one letter/sound should be changed on each move. As children gain skill, they can be asked to change more than one letter/sound from one dictated word to the next.

Figure 8.5 presents examples of words that might be used in word building, word reading, and written spelling in a single small-group lesson when the children

Letters needed: *f, a, n, t, i, s, m, p*

Words for building: *fan, fat, pat, pit, sit, sat, mat*

Words for reading: *fan, fin, pin, pan, tan, tin, sin*

Words for written spelling: *fit, fat, pat, pit, pin, tin, tan*

FIGURE 8.5. Example of letters and words used in a word-building, word-reading, and written-spelling activity.

are at a point where they are practicing changes in the beginning, middle, and end of single-syllable words with short vowels in the medial position.

KEY POINTS OF THIS CHAPTER

✓ Children learn about the alphabetic principle and the role of letters/graphemes and their associated sounds/phonemes in a predictable sequence:
  - Beginning letters and sounds
  - Ending letters and sounds
  - Medial letters and sounds

✓ In early instruction, it is useful to focus on consonants with stretchable sounds.

✓ Word building, reading, and writing all contribute to the development of fluency with the alphabetic code and should be included in each lesson that focuses on the various elements.

✓ Children at similar points in development should be grouped together for instruction focused on the code.

✓ Ideally, the specific elements of the code that are the focus of instruction would be encountered in books or other texts read in the same lesson or the very next lesson after which they are addressed.

CHAPTER 9

Rimes and Word Families

In the English writing system, certain spelling–sound patterns involving multiple letters and sounds tend to occur with some frequency. In this chapter, we focus on rimes (the vowel and what comes after it in a syllable)[1] and how to use them productively in reading and spelling single-syllable words. For example, the letter string *ing* occurs in several different words, such as *ring, sing, thing,* and *wing.* Proficient readers process such spelling patterns as orthographic units rather than as individual graphemes. In addition, English is more regular at the level of the rime than it is when vowel letters are considered individually (Kessler & Treiman, 2003). For example, the letter *i* is pronounced the same way whenever it appears in the *ing* rime. However, it can be pronounced as a long-*i* as in *kind,* a short-*i* as in *hid,* a long-*e* as in *pizza,* or as a short-*u* as in *pencil.*[2] In relation to vowel sounds, Johnston (1999) explains that "the exact sound varies depending upon environments. This may be true of geographical or regional environments as well as the environment created by the letters that come before or after the vowel" (p. 66).

---

[1] Rimes are frequently referred to as phonograms (e.g., Adams, 1990; Fry, 1999–2000), a term we used in previous editions of this book. We made the switch because the term *phonogram* is used in some approaches and programs to refer to graphemes. In this edition, we use the term *rime* because it is less ambiguous.

[2] The variability in English spellings can be an advantage when reading for meaning as the spellings are often related to meaningful relations across words. For example, the word *signature* includes the word *sign.* This overlap in spelling may help readers understand that the words are meaningfully related.

She goes on to explain that "while the pronunciation of vowel sounds may not be stable across word families it tends to be stable within" (p. 66). Thus, for a variety of reasons, it appears that processing these larger orthographic units allows the reader to read and spell more efficiently and fluently.

In Chapter 8, rimes and word families were used to teach and provide practice with consonant graphemes at the beginnings of words (the same rime was used repeatedly as the beginning letter was changed). In this chapter, the focus is on teaching the rimes and how to use them to decode and spell the multiple words that include individual rimes. We refer to groups of words that share a rime as word families. Note that if children do not yet have fairly good skills with using a single rime and making new words by changing the beginning letter (sometimes referred to as initial consonant substitution) as discussed in Chapter 7, it will be more productive for them to continue focusing on those skills than to engage in the instructional activities discussed in this chapter.

Rimes and Word Families

The written representation of words varies across alphabetic languages with regard to the variety of the spelling–sound correspondences. The English orthography is one of the most variable, whereas Spanish, Italian, and German, for example, are quite consistent in terms of the spelling–sound relationships. In fact, studies suggest that most children learning to read in these more regular/consistent orthographies can learn to decode just about any word by the end of first grade (see Reinking & Reinking, 2022, for a more complete discussion).

Individuals who have learned to read and write in these more consistent orthographies will likely find learning to read and write English a bit confusing initially because they are so accustomed to the one-to-one grapheme–phoneme correspondence that characterizes their first language. It may well be helpful to explicitly point out to these learners that they need to think differently about how to decode words. For example, in working with a student who has reasonable command of oral English, the teacher might explain: "I know when you read Spanish, the sound for a letter is almost always the same. In English, sometimes the letters and sounds don't match up the same way." For children with less skill in oral language English, it would be useful for someone who speaks the child's language to translate this idea. The fact that the English writing system has so many inconsistencies in single grapheme–phoneme correspondence can also serve as a rationale for MLs, as well as all beginning readers, for learning and using larger orthographic units, such as rimes, to read and spell words.

Rimes as Decoding and Encoding Units

As children learn more and more words, they begin to become attuned to (and are often explicitly taught) recurring spelling patterns (e.g., *ing*, *ook*). Over time, they come to use these patterns in attempting to read and spell words. For example, children who can easily read the words *look* and *took* are likely to find it easier to identify the word *cook* than children who only know the sounds for each of the graphemes that make up the word *cook*. The children might have learned -*ook* as a rime, or they might have learned to use an analogy strategy that allows them to apply what they know about the pronunciation of *look* and *took* in their attempts to read the word *cook*. Either way, they are learning to use these larger ortho-graphic units in attempting to figure out words, and this makes their attempts more efficient. As students engage in more and more reading and writing, these units become consolidated in their memories (Ehri, 2005), and they become able to use these units when attempting to identify words with more than one syllable. For example, children who can readily read the words *thing*, *ring*, and *sing*, and who can read *look* and *took*, might be able to effectively puzzle out the pronunciation of the word *cooking* as well as its conventional spelling.

Word Families

The term *word family* can have multiple meanings. As used in this chapter, it refers to a group of words that share the same rime (e.g., *hat, cat, mat, sat*). It is sometimes used in reference to semantically related groups of words. For example, the words *believe, believer, believable,* and *unbelievable* constitute a semantically related word family for *believe*, as they are all related in meaning (see Kearns & Whaley, 2019).

Teachers often use the term *word family* to refer to both the (rime) spell-ing patterns and the groups of words that can be formed using the rime. As it is unclear whether children will benefit from understanding the distinction between a rime and the family of words that can be generated from the rime, we think it is appropriate to use the general term *word family* for instructional purposes. Other terms, such as *chunk, decoding key,* or *spelling pattern* are also used for these ele-ments. For instructional purposes, it is important that, at least for beginning read-ers, one term is used rather than multiple. Further, the same term should be used in all settings for children who receive reading instruction in more than one setting.

Research by Ehri (1998) suggested that children need to be fairly familiar with individual letter–sound correspondences and how they are used in encoding and decoding before they can learn to effectively use larger orthographic units such as rimes. However, more recent research suggests that in languages such as English, which is characterized by a good deal of variability in spelling–sound correspon-dences, it may be beneficial for children to learn larger orthographic units, such as rimes, from early on (Ziegler & Goswami, 2005). Research has yet to settle this particular debate. For this reason, we are not recommending a rime-based approach instead of single-unit decoding. Rather, each has a place in develop-ing word-reading skills, especially in inconsistent orthographies such as English (Rayner, Foorman, Perfetti, Pesetsky, & Seidenberg, 2001). And, as we noted in the introduction to Part 2, depending in part on the instruction they receive, children may learn about rimes and word families through explicit instruction, or they may learn about them via their reading experience (during the consolidated alphabetic phase).

Ultimately, it is important for children to learn that words containing the same sound pattern often share the same spelling pattern, and vice versa. When children learn a number of common spelling patterns and know how spelling patterns can be generalized, they will be better prepared to efficiently analyze and identify words they do not immediately recognize. They will also be more strategic in their attempts to spell words.

Rimes are more efficient decoding and spelling units both because they allow the reader to avoid potentially tedious letter-by-letter processing and because, as noted, the pronunciation of the vowels in words that contain common rimes is often more reliable than the pronunciation of individual vowels, as determined by letter-by-letter decoding and spelling "rules."

Figure 9.1 provides a list of rimes from which more than 500 primary-grade words can be derived. The list includes 37 rimes identified by Durrell (1963). We have added a few others that teachers felt should be included for primary-level learners.

Note that some of the rimes listed in Figure 9.1 (e.g., the *r*-controlled vowels [*ar, er*, etc.] and *aw*) will also be discussed as vowel teams in the next chapter. If a vowel team can be used to generate multiple words without adding letters, it can be treated as a rime. Thus, *ay* is treated as a rime because it comes at the end of several common words—for example, *say, may, day, play*, and *tray*. However, *au* is not treated as a rime because additional letters would generally need to be added to the end to form words.

Documenting Children's Knowledge and Progress with Rimes and Word Families

Figure 9.2 presents the group snapshot for rimes and word families. The snapshot allows teachers to document proficiency relative to both isolated practice activities, which is the context in which rimes and word families are explicitly taught, and the application/use of word families in the context of reading and writing

Beginning Letters of Rimes

A		E	I		O	U
ack	ap	eat	ice	ine	ock	uck
ail	ar	ell	ick	ing	oke	ug
ain	ash	er	ide	ink	op	ump
ale	ash	est	ight	ip	or	unk
ame	at		ill	ir	ore	ur
an	ate		in	it		
ank	aw					
	ay					

FIGURE 9.1. Rimes that can be used to form over 500 primary-grade words.

Group Snapshot—Rimes and Word Families								
Student names								
Practice in isolation	Word building							
	Word reading							
	Written spelling							
Application	Reading							
	Writing							

Key:

☐ B—*Beginning* indicates that instruction has addressed the objective but that the child has only a preliminary understanding or capability with regard to that particular objective.

☒ D—*Developing* indicates that the child has some understanding of the objective but does not reliably demonstrate that understanding or capability or is not yet automatic (fluent) with the skill.

☒ P—*Proficient* indicates that the child reliably and automatically demonstrates the understanding or capability.

FIGURE 9.2. Group snapshot for rimes and word families.

meaningful text. Skill with rimes and word families will be variable as, for many learners, it will be dependent upon the instructional emphasis placed on these orthographic elements. Therefore, the key provided for rating children's status needs to be considered in light of the instruction the children have received. If no emphasis is placed on rimes and word families, this snapshot may not be useful for documenting children's status. However, in contexts where heavy emphasis is placed on these orthographic elements, this snapshot may prove useful. In this case, for children to be considered proficient with respect to the isolated practice activities, they need to be able to quickly and accurately build, read, and spell words composed of taught word families and easily learn new rimes as they are introduced. Regarding application, to be considered proficient in reading, children need to readily decode words that are members of taught word families when they are encountered in context. For writing, children would be considered proficient if they reliably spell words using appropriate word families that have been taught. Of course, children would not be considered proficient in any of these skills if only a few word families have been taught and learned. Rather, children should know quite a few word families and should be readily expanding their repertoires.

Selecting Rimes for Instruction

The rimes selected for instruction should be composed of letters for which the child already knows the names: knowing the names of the component letters will help the learner recall the pattern. Further, the rimes should be drawn from books the children will read in the near future, ideally shortly after instruction and practice with the rime. To help children see the utility of learning rimes and to provide sufficient practice, it is useful to use books in which the instructed rime occurs several times, ideally in different words (e.g., *fan, can, tan, man, ran*). In our intervention studies, we recommended that the earliest rimes taught be as distinct from one another as possible so that children would be more apt to treat the rime as an orthographic unit rather than to analyze it letter by letter. For example, if the first few rimes taught were *an, ap,* and *at,* the child would need to attend very carefully to the final letter in order to distinguish them from one another. On the other hand, if the first few rimes taught were *an, op,* and *it,* the child could more readily process them as units because they look so different from one another. Thus, use of distinctly different rimes early on is recommended to help children develop an understanding that not all words need to be read letter-by-letter.

At the same time, we are acquainted with reading programs that take a different approach to the early teaching of rimes. For example, some programs introduce several rimes with the same short vowel (e.g., *at, ap, an*) consecutively and then move on to a second vowel (e.g., *on, op, ot*). A program that takes such an approach would presumably provide books in which the most recently taught rimes appear with some frequency. We see the opportunity to apply the orthographic units that are being taught in isolation as the most crucial issue in supporting the development of skill through use of these units in word solving. Decisions about which rimes to teach should be driven, at least in part, by the texts that the children will read.[3]

Teaching Children to Read and Write Words Using Rimes and Word Families

The teaching of rimes is fairly common in the primary grades. The approach to instruction that we have frequently seen is one in which the teacher introduces a new rime and then engages the children in generating and writing a list of words that can be built with the rime. The list is commonly created on charts, which are displayed for future reference. Although this approach certainly has value, it presents a risk: this activity won't really help children who are slower to acquire these skills because most of the attention during construction of the list is on the letter or letters that precede the rime (i.e., the onsets) as that is what changes from one word to the next. To help children learn rimes so well that they can use them productively in their reading and writing, we advise that, once a new rime has been introduced and used to build some words, further work with it should include one or two rimes that were previously taught. The rimes would initially be taught and practiced in a word-building activity. Thereafter the teacher would engage the children in reading words that the teacher builds with the rimes, and, later still, the children would write the words. In classrooms where reading programs that introduce multiple rimes with the same short vowel successively are in use, teachers are encouraged to incorporate previously taught rimes as soon as possible. So, for example, children who have already learned *at*, *ap*, and *an* and are now learning *op* might be engaged in working with *at* and *op* together.

KEEP IN MIND When teaching new decoding elements, the sequence of word building (with movable letters or letter patterns), word reading, and written spelling helps to reinforce the skills being taught. To optimize learning, previously taught decoding elements should be incorporated into the practice activities. For example, if the *ing* rime is the focus of the lesson, a previously taught rime (e.g., *at*) should be incorporated in the practice activity. In this case, the children might be asked to build, read, and write the words *ring, rat, sat, sing, thing, ping, pat, rat, ring*.

Sample Instructional Dialogue for Word Building with Rimes

Materials needed (for each child in the group):	• The new rime to be taught (*ot* in this example) plus one or two previously taught rimes (if available). We'll use *ap* in this example. The rimes should be on cards (or, if letter tiles are being used, the letters making up the rime should be taped together).

---

[3]To our knowledge, there is no research that has evaluated the relative utility of teaching multiple rimes that all share the same vowel (e.g., *ag, am, an, ap, at*) versus teaching rimes that do not share a vowel in (e.g, *ed, ig, op, at, un*).

- Several individual graphemes that will allow several different words to be built with each rime (the letters *l, n, m, t, c, ch*, and *h* in this example).

Teacher	What the teacher says	Comment on the activity
Shows new rime and says:	"We are going to practice reading a group of words that all have the same spelling pattern. Words with the same spelling pattern are called a *word family*. The family we are learning about today is the /ŏt/ family. Words in this family all have the letters *o* and *t* at the end. Those letters together sound like /ŏt/."	The teacher names the word family and the letters that comprise it several times to help the children store it in memory.
Says:	"Tell me what the letters *o-t* sound like when they are together . . ."	The teacher has the children practice the pronunciation of the rime. It is useful to have the children name the letters in the rime and then say the rime itself. This can be repeated a couple of times.
Says:	"We'll see lots of words in the /ŏt/ family in our reading, and you'll use /ŏt/ words in your writing, too. Learning this and other word families will help us with our reading and writing."	The teacher gives the children a purpose for learning word families.
Shows several consonant graphemes for which the children have been taught the sounds and says:	"We are going to use these letters to make some words in the /ŏt/ family. You may remember the sounds for these letters, but if you don't, you can check our key words to help you remember the sounds."	The activity at this point is similar to the initial consonant substitution activity described in Chapter 8 and so shouldn't require much teaching or practice.
Says:	"Let's make the word *pot*. Sometimes people cook in a *pot*. How would I make the word *pot*?"	In working with children with limited vocabulary, if the teacher thinks the children might not know the meanings of the words used, it may help to show pictures for the words that are imageable and/or provide a quick definition.
Provides feedback.	"Right. I put a *p* in front of *ot* and it makes the word *pot*."	
Says:	"How would I make the word *not*? I am *not* standing up."	

| Says: | "How would I change *not* to *tot*? Sometimes a little child is called a *tot*." | The teacher would provide feedback with each change. |
| Shows *ap* phonogram and says: | "Now let's make a word from our /ăp/ word family that we learned before. How would I change *tot* to *tap*? I *tap* the table with my finger. *Tap*." | The *ap* word family doesn't share any letters with the *ot* word family. Using distinctly different word families early on is intended to encourage the children to process the rimes as units. |

After a few more examples—for example, changing *tap* to *nap*, *nap* to *not*, *not* to *lot*, *lot* to *lap*—the teacher would give each child the rimes and individual letters and would engage them in building words that the teacher dictates. It is important, when working with only two word families, not to ask the children to make changes in a highly predictable sequence, such as changing the beginning letter, then the rime, then the beginning letter, and so forth, as this may diminish the children's attention to the word families. A reasonable sequence for this pair of rimes would be *tot* to *tap*, *tap* to *nap*, *nap* to *not*, *not* to *lot*, *lot* to *lap*, *lap* to *map*, *map* to *cap*, *cap* to *cot*, *cot* to *hot*. With such a sequence, the child must consider both the beginning sound (the onset) and the rime and decide which part of the word needs to change each time.

After the children have engaged in word building and seem fairly confident with it, the teacher would use one set of the instructional materials to make words one at a time, as the children watch, and for each word the teacher would ask different children to read the word. At a later point, the children write words dictated by the teacher. For this written spelling activity, it is often helpful to start by creating a column for each rime that will be used. Then the teacher dictates words, and the children decide in which column each word belongs and write the dictated word in the correct column. Teachers sometimes use a graphic of a house and talk about these charts as two- or three-family houses; the children need to decide in which family each dictated word belongs (see Figure 9.3).

KEEP IN MIND   Before calling on a child to read a word in this activity, as well as all of the other activities that call for children to read words in isolation, the teacher should provide enough time for all of the children to think of the word. If the teacher too quickly calls on the first child to raise a hand, which is a fairly common practice, those children who need more time to process will lose the opportunity to do the necessary thinking. Similarly, if the teacher directs a child to read the word before displaying it (e.g., "The next one is for Michael"), the other children in the group may pay less attention to the word.

Further Practice with Rimes and Word Families

Once a rime has been introduced and practiced, children can be asked to generate as many real words as they can using the rime and make a list of them. Alternatively,

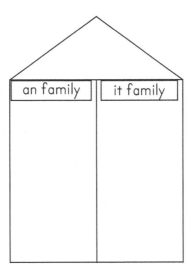

FIGURE 9.3. A two-family house used for word family practice.

they could be asked to systematically use a set of single consonants and digraphs to try to form words with the rime and to read each resulting combination, making a list of all the real words and nonwords that are formed. When using the word family houses described above, some have used the idea of a "garage" for the nonwords. In this case, as children generate words, the real words go into the house, and the nonwords go into the garage. As noted in Chapter 8, having children work together to generate lists may be more engaging and can support the language skills of children who are less fluent in English.

Note

Making decisions about which combinations yield real words and which result in nonwords is, potentially, a helpful activity in promoting self-regulation when children read meaningful text. If a decoding attempt results in a nonword, they are more likely to notice it and rethink the pronunciation of the word. While this can be an appropriate independent or buddy practice activity for students, some MLs will need teacher support to discern real words from nonwords and to learn the meaning of words not already known.

Maintaining a Focus on Rimes

After each rime has been introduced and practiced, the goal is for children to use it in decoding words they do not immediately recognize while reading and in spelling words for which they have not memorized the conventional spellings. The activities described next are designed to promote the use of rimes for these purposes.

The Rime Display

Rimes that have been introduced and practiced should be prominently displayed for children to refer to during reading and writing. For this display, we recommend that the rimes be organized by the vowel they contain. Long- and short-vowel rimes should be grouped separately. Rimes that have neither a long- nor a short-vowel sound (e.g., the *a* in *all*) would also be grouped separately. An example of a rime display (which we refer to as Word Families We Know) is provided in Figure 9.4. Note that the key words for the short-vowel sounds are included in the display as an extra scaffold. (We provide guidance on the teaching of long vowels and vowel teams in Chapter 10.) The display is built across time as children learn new rimes.

Note that by grouping the rimes by vowel sound, the chart provides children with an additional support/scaffold about how the rime will be pronounced, so it is important for the teacher to explain the organization of the display. Rimes in the upper section have short-vowel sounds, while those in the middle section have long-vowel sounds, and those in the lowest section have vowel sounds that are neither long nor short. In addition, for rimes with which children have particular difficulty, it is helpful to provide a familiar high-frequency word to facilitate their recall of the sound of the rime (see Figure 9.4). This is especially helpful for rimes that are contained in high-frequency words that the children can readily identify.

Word Families We Know

A a	E e	I i	O o	U u
at	en	it	ot	up
an	ess		op	ug
ame	eet	ite	oat	ute
ay (play)	ean	ight(night)	ope	
ain			old	
all	er	ir	or	
ar		ing	oy	
			ook (look)	

FIGURE 9.4. Word family display.

Reading Meaningful Text

While reading, when children encounter a word they do not immediately recognize, they can be encouraged to refer to the word family chart to determine whether any familiar rimes are contained in the word. The vowel or vowels in the word should serve as a point of reference for looking for known rimes. Ideally, children would remember the rimes that they have learned. However, if they don't, the word family display will facilitate their attempts to make use of the rimes. Children would be guided to find the first vowel in the word they are attempting to identify and then check the rimes in the column for that vowel. If the word in question contains more than one syllable, with more than one rime that has been taught, it may help the children to identify the word. For example, if the rimes displayed in Figure 9.4 had been taught and the children encountered the word *entering*, they could make progress toward identifying the word by recognizing the three rimes contained in the word (*en, er,* and *ing*). Children should always, of course, be encouraged to determine whether their decoding attempts make sense in the context of the text they are reading.

Spelling

Children should be encouraged to use rimes when they are attempting to spell words for which they do not know the conventional spelling. To do so, the children would first determine the number of syllables contained in the word they wish to spell (by counting the number of "beats"[4] in the word). Often, it is helpful to have children draw a line for each syllable in the word. Over time, and with teacher guidance and support, for each syllable children would learn to:

- Determine what the initial sound(s) is (are) and how it (they) should be represented in print.
- Think about whether they know any rimes that sound like the remainder of the syllable. If so, that rime should be used to complete the spelling for that syllable.

Subsequent syllables in the word would be analyzed in a similar fashion.

Children will become more efficient in using rimes in their spelling if they periodically have "spelling tests" in which they use a rime-based spelling strategy. For example, by referring to the "Word Families We Know" display illustrated in Figure 9.4, children might be asked to spell *mess, feet, shop, coat, raining,* and *daylight*. While the use of rimes as one spelling strategy will certainly, on occasion, lead to unconventional spellings (e.g., some children will provide *daylite* as the spelling for *daylight*), the use of rimes will considerably improve the initial spelling attempts of many children.

---

[4] Every syllable contains a vowel sound. Vowels are open-mouth sounds—so the speaker's jaw moves a bit for each syllable. Attending to this movement helps learners count the beats/syllables.

Games for Promoting Fluent Use of Rimes

The games described next can be used in centers and/or for practice at home.

- *Rime guessing game.* The clue giver thinks of a word containing one or more of the rimes on the chart and provides a clue concerning the meaning of that word (e.g., "I'm thinking of something kids usually don't like to have to clean up"). The children try to think of a word that fits the clue and contains one of the rimes. If they cannot think of the word with only the meaning clue, the clue giver would provide another clue that focuses attention on a smaller group of rimes (e.g., "The word I'm thinking of has one of the word families that start with *e*."). If the children are still unable to think of the word, the clue giver might point to the rime contained in the word, tell the children that the word belongs to that word family, and then remind the children of the meaning clue initially provided.

- *Go Fish.* Go Fish games can be created using words derived from rimes that have been taught. In this game, the children ask for words containing a specific rime. For example, a child might ask for a word in the *ake* family (pronouncing the rime rather than naming the letters). A match is created by having two words with the same rime.

- *Tic-tac-toe.* For this game the children are provided with two or more rimes that have been taught. On each turn, the player has to think of a word using one of the rimes and write it in the square of choice. Repetitions of words are not allowed. All words need to be real when pronounced (although if the children are playing without an adult, there may be unconventional spellings of real words). Children use different-colored markers to write the words, and the winner is determined by the colored entries on the game board.

- *Rime hunt.* Children are given a text in which they are to go on a "word family hunt." That is, they are invited to see how many taught rimes they can find in the text. The text may be covered with a transparency or plastic sheet protector, and children can underline or circle the words belonging to the families they have learned. Alternatively, they might use a dry-erase board to keep a running list of all the words with known rimes that they find. This game helps to increase children's awareness of rimes and their ability to use them productively for reading and spelling.

- *Great big words.* Children are encouraged to find words that contain many rimes. A cumulative list of words containing several rimes might be maintained with an eye toward finding a really big word by the end of the school year. Children can be on the lookout for such words in their classroom as well as at home.

KEY POINTS OF THIS CHAPTER

✓ Teaching about rimes helps attune children to the value of attending to larger orthographic patterns, as this enables them to identify more words more easily.

✓ The sounds of vowels in rimes tend to be more consistent than the sounds of vowels that are not included in these larger orthographic patterns.

✓ In early instruction related to rimes and word families, we argue that it is helpful to use rimes that are distinctly different from one another (i.e., that do not contain any of the same letters). This can encourage children to think of the rimes as orthographic units rather than as a series of individual letters.

✓ A display of word families that have been taught and practiced can serve as a useful resource to support children's reading and spelling of words containing instructed rimes.

CHAPTER 10

The Alphabetic Principle and the Alphabetic Code
Later Development

> **WRITING SYSTEM FOUNDATIONS GOAL 7**
>
> Children will understand how to use all the letters/graphemes in printed one-syllable words to determine their likely pronunciation. Similarly, when writing, children will learn to represent all the sounds in spoken words with accurate or "justifiable" letters.

The instructional focus in this chapter is on helping children learn to process some of the more complex aspects of the writing system—consonant clusters and various types of complex vowels. As noted in Chapter 9, there are differing points of view with regard to the emphasis that should be placed on explicitly teaching learners multi-letter patterns (e.g., rimes) versus teaching them to puzzle through printed words by relying on individual graphemes. However, there is agreement that, to become proficient readers, students need to be skilled at *using* both approaches to word identification to make their decoding efforts more efficient. There is also wide agreement that many of the orthographic patterns (e.g., words, rimes, syllables) that readers come to recognize automatically are learned through extensive amounts of reading and repeated, successful, engagement in word solving (which we discuss in Chapter 12). The additional phonics skills addressed in this chapter, once learned, will further enable successful word solving.

In this chapter, we discuss ways to further the development of children's skill with decoding (reading) and encoding (writing) by teaching them about consonant clusters and long-vowel and other complex vowel spelling patterns. For children who experience difficulty with learning the elements of the English writing system, it is typically these more advanced aspects of the writing system that present

---

Ehri's Phase Theory: Full Alphabetic to Consolidated Phase

In this chapter, we discuss instruction that enables learners to gain greater skill in using the alphabetic code to puzzle through, identify, and ultimately learn the many thousands of words that proficient readers can identify effortlessly. These skills are characteristic of learners who are in Ehri's full alphabetic phase of word learning. With sufficient engagement in reading, learners move on to the consolidated phase in which they are able to learn and use larger orthographic patterns (e.g., *tion, ly*) to solve words more efficiently.

---

the biggest challenge. Developing the ability to effectively puzzle through words that include these elements will enable learners to more effectively and efficiently identify, and ultimately learn, previously unfamiliar printed words. We focus on:

- Consonant clusters (e.g., *cl, str, ft, lt*)
- Long-vowel sounds spelled with the VC*e* (vowel–consonant–e) pattern (e.g., *ate, ime, ope*)
- Vowel teams that generally consist of two letters (at least one of which is a vowel) that appear together in words and together represent one vowel phoneme (e.g., *ai, er, ew, oy*).

Later Development of Skill in Using the Alphabetic Code

Grouping and Pacing

The activities described in this chapter are intended for children who:

- Know the names of most, if not all, of the letters, the sounds of most of the consonant graphemes and the short sounds for the vowels.
- Can segment single-syllable words into their individual phonemes— although consonant clusters may present a challenge.
- Can build, read, and spell words with the consonant–vowel–consonant (CVC) pattern.
- When writing,
  - Can represent the prominent consonants with an accurate or "justifiable"[1] letter
  - Are fairly secure with writing one-syllable words with short-vowel sounds, although they may occasionally represent short-vowel sounds with a letter that is unconventional (e.g., PAT for *pet*)
  - Include "justifiable" letters for long vowels (i.e., they frequently represent long vowels with the correct vowel letter but do not mark it in a way that designates the long sound (e.g., CAK for *cake*)

---

[1] See the explanation of "justifiable" in the note for the group snapshot provided in Chapter 8 (p. 200).

While some children will move very quickly through the content discussed in this chapter, others will move more slowly and will need many more repetitions and reinforcements. It is important to remember that *education is about teaching children, not about teaching the curriculum regardless of what the children are learning.*

Assessment for Grouping

As noted in earlier chapters, one of the most efficient ways of evaluating children's skills with the alphabetic code is through an evaluation of their written spelling. One useful tool for that purpose is the Decoding Elements Assessment by Gelzheiser, Scanlon, Hallgren Flynn, and Connors (2019). The assessment includes two short spelling assessments. The first assesses spellings of words with consonants, short vowels, and common digraphs. The second assesses spelling of short and long vowels and consonant clusters (which the assessment refers to as blends). The assessment is available on the companion website for this book (see the box at the end of the table of contents). The assessment also includes word-reading subtests that assess similar skills but also more advanced skills such as the ability to read words with vowel teams (referred to as vowel parts on the assessment). The assessment can also be used to evaluate learners' ability to decode words with multiple syllables and inflected endings (the topic of Chapter 11). Performance on such an assessment can help teachers identify groups of children who have similar understandings about the workings of the writing system and are, therefore, ready for similarly focused instruction.

Once instructional groups have been identified, the snapshot presented in Figure 10.1 can be used to document children's progress over time in relation to the aspects of the alphabetic and orthographic code discussed in this chapter.

The order in which aspects of the code are listed on the snapshot is not intended to indicate a specific order for instruction. Rather, the instructional materials in use should provide guidance with regard to which aspects of the alphabetic code are addressed when—assuming, of course, the materials available introduce decoding skills in a sequence that moves learners gradually from simpler to more complex phonics skills and integrate practice with previously taught skills. Whenever possible, children should have the opportunity to read (and reread) texts in which newly introduced skills can be applied. As we have indicated elsewhere, decisions about what to teach when should be driven to a large extent by when the elements come up in the texts that students will be reading. When children are taught about an aspect of the alphabetic/orthographic code in isolation, they should have the opportunity to apply that knowledge in text shortly thereafter— even if it is a teacher-created text written for that purpose.

Below we describe how the snapshot might be used.

• *Consonant digraphs.* Because there is a limited set of common digraphs, students would be considered proficient when they are fast and accurate in reading

Group Snapshot—Alphabetic Code, Later Development											
Student names											
		Isolated	In text	Isolated	In text	Isolated	In text	Isolated	In text	Isolated	In text
Consonant digraphs (*sh, ch, th, . . .*)	Reading										
	Writing										
Consonant clusters (*fl, st, br, ft, str . . .*)	Reading										
	Writing										
Short-vowel sounds in CVC words	Reading										
	Writing										
Long vowel– silent-*e* pattern (VC*e*)	Reading										
	Writing										
Other vowel patterns via vowel flexing	Reading										
Other vowel patterns (*aw, igh, or, ar, . . .*)	Reading										
	Writing										

Key:

⬁ *B—Beginning* indicates that instruction has addressed the objective but that the child has only a preliminary understanding or capability with regard to that particular objective.

⊠ *D—Developing* indicates that the child has some understanding of the objective but does not reliably demonstrate that understanding or capability or is not yet automatic (fluent) with the skill.

⊠ *P—Proficient* indicates that the child reliably and automatically demonstrates the understanding or capability.

FIGURE 10.1. Group snapshot for alphabetic code, later development.

and writing words with the digraphs *ch, th, sh, wh, ck*. The digraph *ph* is comparatively rare, especially in texts for younger students, and may only need to be taught incidentally when it comes up in text. Digraphs that are doubled consonants (*ff, ll, ss, zz*) generally do not need to be explicitly taught for purposes of decoding.

- *Consonant clusters/blends*. There are many consonant clusters (two or three consonant letters that occur adjacent to one another in a syllable, with each of the letters' sounds being at least somewhat discernible). We do not advocate teaching all of them explicitly. Rather, students should be taught a process for working with consonant clusters and would be considered proficient when they can read and spell words containing clusters that have not been explicitly addressed in instruction, as this would indicate that they have learned the process for decoding and spelling clusters.

- *Short and long vowels*. Children would be considered proficient when they readily apply the generalization that in words with the CVC pattern the short-vowel sounds will most often occur, while in words with the vowel-consonant-*e* (VC*e*) spelling pattern, the long-vowel sound will more often occur. In writing, proficiency would be demonstrated by reliably including the silent-*e* when the word contains a long-vowel sound (even if the long vowel is conventionally spelled with a different spelling pattern). The point here is that learners understand the conventions of the CVC and VC*e* patterns even though their spelling of long-vowel sounds is not entirely conventional.

- *Other vowel patterns via vowel flexing*. Some vowel combinations/patterns are pronounced differently in different words (e.g., the *ea* in *head, bead, break*). Vowel flexing involves trying alternative pronunciations for the vowel when the readers' first attempt at identifying a word doesn't produce a real word that makes sense in the context in which it is encountered. This is a skill we can only observe during reading, and it will be most useful to the child while reading meaningful text. Proficiency would be recorded when the learner is reliably able to identify words in which vowel flexing can be usefully applied.

- *Other vowel patterns*. Some vowel patterns cannot be decoded via vowel flexing and therefore need to be explicitly taught/learned—for example, *r*-controlled vowels (*ar, er, ir, or,* and *ur*), *oy* as in *boy*, and so on. Proficiency would be recorded when the learner knows and uses many taught (or independently learned) patterns reliably.

Instruction to Develop Skills with the Alphabetic Code

Consonant Combinations

Printed words often include adjacent consonants. When two adjacent consonants represent a single phoneme (e.g., *sh, th, ch*) they are referred to as *digraphs*. When two adjacent consonants occur *within* a syllable and each represents their

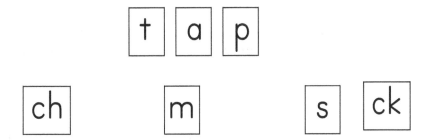

FIGURE 10.2. Setup for a word-building/word-reading lesson that includes consonant digraphs.

individual phonemes, their written form is referred to as a *cluster* and their spoken form is referred to as a *blend*. Here's a useful way of remembering the terminology: the word *digraph* includes a digraph —the ph; the words *cluster* and *blend* do not—in fact, they both begin with a cluster/blend.

Consonant Digraphs

Consonant digraphs were discussed in Chapter 7 (pp. 176, 190, 199) and are revisited here because there will be children who have made progress in many areas but who still need instruction/review on the digraphs. For these children, the consonant digraphs will need to be explicitly taught and practiced as decoding elements. Only one digraph would be introduced in any given lesson, but previously taught/ learned digraphs may be included in the practice activities. It is also important to revisit consonant digraphs so that students understand the difference between them and consonant clusters. Figure 10.2 illustrates the setup for a word-building, word-reading lesson that includes consonant digraphs.

Consonant Clusters

In a consonant cluster, the sounds of two or three consonants are blended together, but the individual sounds of each consonant is discernible (*cl, cr, sm, lt, nd, str,* etc.). In the ISA, we teach blending as a process rather than teaching every possible cluster as a unit because there are far too many of them.

WHEN ARE CHILDREN READY TO LEARN ABOUT CONSONANT CLUSTERS/BLENDS?

The concept of blending consonants can be introduced when children know the sounds of most, if not all, of the single consonants and can use those consonant sounds in decoding and spelling single-syllable words. To learn to decode and spell words with consonant clusters, at the very least, children need to know the sounds of the individual consonants in the clusters. All the clusters *do not* need to be explicitly taught. The goal is to help the children learn a process for decoding and spelling clusters/blends. This requires learners to draw on their knowledge of individual letters and their sounds to puzzle through unfamiliar words that include consonant clusters.

ORDER OF DIFFICULTY FOR CONSONANT CLUSTERS

Some clusters/blends are easier for children to analyze (segment, read, and spell) than others. As with all instruction, it is helpful to begin with the clearest, easiest examples and to move to more challenging items once the children are facile with the easier ones.

Terminology

Consonant cluster—two- or three-consonant *graphemes* that occur together within a syllable in which the sound of each grapheme is at least somewhat discernible. Examples include *sm, bl, str, spr, ft, nd,* and *lt.*

Consonant blend—two- or three-consonant *phonemes* that occur together within a word or syllable in which each phoneme is at least somewhat discernible.

Note that in some settings the term *consonant blend* is used exclusively, while others use *consonant blend* and *consonant cluster* interchangeably.

• *Easiest clusters.* Because it is easier to draw children's attention to consonant sounds that can be elongated (stretched) without distortion (e.g., *s, m, n, f, r, l*) than to stop consonants (e.g., *p, b, d,* hard *c* [as in *cat*], and hard *g* [as in *goat*]), it makes sense to start teaching the decoding process with clusters in which both consonants are stretchable (*sm, fr, sl, fl, sn,* etc.). The specific clusters selected for instruction would ideally be determined by the reading the children will do the same day or soon thereafter. Work with a variety of clusters composed of stretchable consonants should continue until the children are fairly proficient with reading and spelling them.

• *More difficult clusters.* Consonant clusters that have a combination of stretchable and stop consonants (*pr, br, bl, cl, sc, str, ft, nd,* etc.) are somewhat more challenging because it can be difficult to draw children's attention to the stop consonant portion of the cluster.

• *Most difficult clusters.* Some of the most challenging consonant clusters in the initial position are *dr* and *tr.* These are challenging because the sounds of the stop consonants *d* and *t* are not easily detected due to coarticulation. That is, because of the way that the mouth positions itself to make the /r/ sound as it is articulating the /d/ or /t/ sound, the sounds of the *d* and *t* are distorted. (This explains why a child might spell the word *drip* with the letters *jrip* or *jip* or spell *truck* with the letters *chrk*.)

How Coarticulation Can Influence Reading

We once observed a kindergarten child reading a beginner-level book about a toy bear. The story unfolded something like this. "My bear can sit. My bear can swing. My bear can swim. My bear can dry." The child read the book quite comfortably until the very last page, which showed the bear hanging on a clothesline. The child puzzled over the last word for a bit and then said, "It's not *dry* because it doesn't start with a *j*." In this case, the child's inclination was to say the word *dry*, but in checking the letters carefully she decided they did not match her pronunciation of the word.

Some of the most challenging consonant clusters in the final position are those in which a nasal consonant (i.e., *m* or *n*) precedes a stop consonant (e.g., *t, p*). These are difficult because children use changes in mouth position as clues to the sounds in words. The subtle changes in mouth position when the nasal consonant is present or absent are hard to detect. This can be experienced by saying the words *wet* and *went* or *rap* and *ramp* and carefully attending to the various parts of the mouth that are involved in the pronunciation. Most would agree that the mouth movements for each pair of words are very similar. Difficulties with nasal + stop consonant clusters will be most apparent in the children's writing where, until they have learned the conventional spellings of words, they will typically fail to include the nasal consonant. Thus, *jump* may be spelled *jup*, and *hand* may be spelled *had*. Children's attention can be drawn to nasal consonants by asking them to say, for example, *jump* but don't say the /p/.

Note

In pronouncing a "nasal consonant," air flows through the nose (the nasal passage) instead of through the mouth. The sounds for *m*, *n*, and *ng* (which is a single phoneme) are the only nasal consonants in the English language.

CONSONANT CLUSTERS AND MULTILINGUAL LEARNERS

Consonant blends are relatively uncommon in the first language of many multilingual students (e.g., Arabic, Farsi, Spanish, Turkish, and many South Asian languages; see Swan and Smith, 2001). The relative lack of these structures in the MLs' first language can make it difficult for them to perceive and produce the blends that occur in English. These difficulties result in mispronunciations in spoken words. Thus, students might pronounce *breakfast* as *breffess* or *hand* as *han*. Or they may add short-vowel sounds to the consonant sounds in the cluster.

For example, *stop* might be pronounced *estop,* and *spring* might be pronounced *espering.*

TEACHING CHILDREN TO READ AND SPELL WORDS WITH CONSONANT CLUSTERS

Word building, word reading, and written spelling can be used to teach and practice decoding and encoding consonant clusters/blends. The first step in helping children learn to read and spell consonant clusters is to make sure they can blend spoken consonant sounds to form words (see Chapter 5). The next step would be to teach and provide practice with printed representations of consonant clusters at the beginnings of words, starting with word building. For this initial instruction, it is helpful to use groups of words that can be formed with one or the other of the single stretchable consonants in the blend, as well as a combination of the two consonants (see examples in Figure 10.3). Often during initial instruction, we use a family of words in which the rime remains constant, and the focus is on changing and modifying the elements of the initial cluster.

It is generally more challenging for learners to attend to the interior consonants in consonant clusters (those closest to the vowels). Therefore, it is useful in initial instruction to emphasize/highlight the interior consonants. Figure 10.3 provides groups of words that can be used to that end. As noted previously, instruction should be initiated with the easiest clusters—those with two stretchable sounds. The figure provides a suggested sequence that can be used in word building and word reading. The intent of the sequence is to highlight the interior consonants— especially in early instruction. Thus, in early demonstrations, as the sequence progresses, it leads to the exterior consonant being added to the interior consonant to make the final word. For example, the teacher might begin by demonstration— first building the word *sip* as the children observe, then changing *sip* to *lip,* then adding the *s* to make *slip,* then removing the *l* to go back to *sip,* changing *sip* to *lip,* and finally putting the *s* back on. Thereafter, the children would be given the opportunity to go through the same sequence as the teacher guides their thinking— engaging the group in discussing how, when there are two consonants together in a word, often it is necessary to think about the sound of each letter and then blend them together. It might help to start by thinking about the consonant that is closest to the vowel and how that will sound with the vowel and what comes after it and then add the other consonant(s) back on and read the whole word.

When the children can build, read, and spell words with clusters in which both consonants are stretchable, the focus of instruction can shift to clusters in which only one of the consonants is stretchable and, over time, to the more challenging clusters. Here it is important to note that the goal is NOT to teach all possible clusters, but rather to teach a process for reading and spelling words with clusters/ blends. Once the process is understood, with practice the children will gradually learn to handle the more challenging clusters/blends. Also, aside from early lessons where the focus is on learning the process for decoding clusters and blending their sounds, other aspects of the alphabetic code can be addressed in the decoding/

	Initial word	Change to	Change to	Change to	Change to	Change to
Easiest clusters (both initial consonants are stretchable)	sip	lip	slip	sip	lip	slip
	fake	lake	flake	fake	lake	flake
	sock	mock	smock	sock	mock	smock
	sag	nag	snag	sag	nag	snag
More difficult clusters (one stretchable and one stop)	boom	loom	bloom	boom	loom	bloom
	camp	ramp	cramp	camp	ramp	cramp
	gain	rain	grain	gain	rain	grain
	pay	lay	play	pay	lay	play
	sill	pill	spill	sill	pill	spill
	sick	tick	stick	sick	tick	stick
DR and TR clusters	dip	rip	drip	dip	rip	drip
	dug	rug	drug	dug	rug	drug
	tack	rack	track	tack	rack	track
	tail	rail	trail	tail	rail	trail
	tap	rap	trap	tap	rap	trap
	tip	rip	trip	tip	rip	trip
Three-letter clusters	rip	trip	strip	trip	rip	strip
	rap	trap	strap	trap	tap	rap
	tuck	stuck	struck	truck	tuck	stuck
	sit	slit	split	spit	sit	slit

FIGURE 10.3. Word sets for practicing consonant clusters/blends.

encoding segment of a lesson. For example, children may be asked to build, read, and/or spell words that involve all the elements of the code that have already been taught, especially those that, in the teacher's opinion, need more practice.

Sample Instructional Dialogue for Teaching Children to Read and Spell Words with Consonant Clusters		
Step 1: Phoneme Blending		
Teacher	What the teacher says	Comments on the activity
Says:	"Many of the words that we read have two consonant letters together, and each letter makes its own sound. When we see these words, we need to think of the sound for each letter and then blend them together. We'll start by practicing blending with Stretch [or whatever character is used in phoneme analysis activities]. Stretch is going to say some words one sound at a time, and you need to figure out what Stretch is saying. We are going to use words that have two consonant letters together."	After this introduction, the teacher articulates the sounds in several words that contain (stretchable) consonant blends. After the sounds for each word are articulated, the children attempt to blend them to form a whole word. Ideally, the children should be able to do this type of blending before they are asked to do the more challenging task of looking at the letters, thinking about the sounds they represent, and then blending them to form words. By the time children are learning about consonant clusters, they shouldn't need the picture choices (as described in Chapter 5) to successfully complete phoneme blending. However, if they struggle, continued work on phoneme blending with words containing consonant blends is warranted, perhaps with picture choices if necessary to support the development of this skill.
Examples of words with two stretchable consonants for phoneme blending: *flake, snow, smile, frog, fly, slide, smoke, sleep, flat, free*		
Step 2: Demonstration—Decoding a Consonant Cluster (Using the ip Rime)		
Teacher	What the teacher says	Comments on the activity
Displays and says:	"Some of the words we are going to make today have consonant clusters in them. That's when there are two consonants, like *s* and *l*, next to each other. When you read words like that, you make the sound for each letter and then blend them together."	The letters to be used in word-building activities are displayed. All the consonants to be used in the initial consonant blends are stretchable.

Displays phonogram and says:	"All of the words we are going to make now have these two letters: *i* and *p*. When they are together in a word, they sound like this—/ip/. There are a lot of words in the /ip/ word family. Let's make some words with /ip/."	The *ip* phonogram can be printed on a single card rather than on two separate letter cards.
Says:	"If I put an *s* in front of *ip*, what word would it make?"	The teacher places an *s* in front of *ip* for all children in the group to see.
Provides feedback.	"Right, the word would be *sip*."	If the children cannot respond accurately at this step, they are not ready to work on consonant clusters/blends. They need continued work with single consonants.
Reminds children of what they have already learned.	"Watch, now I am going to change *sip* to *lip*—we've done this kind of thing a lot before. I take away the *s* and put an *l* there instead."	The teacher should move through these steps slowly so that the children can focus on how the display changes.
Replaces the *s* with the *l* and says:	"Now, we have *lip*."	
Adds the *s* again and says:	"If I put the *s* in front of *lip*, the word would be . . . *sssllllip*. "	The teacher would pause briefly before saying the word *slip* so that the children have the opportunity to think of it on their own.
Removes the *l* and says:	"Now, what will happen to the word *slip* if I take the *l* away?"	The teacher should, again, give the children enough "think time" before answering the question.
Responds.	"Right, we are back to *sip*. Now let's change *sip* to *lip*."	
Comments and demonstrates.	"Now, all I need to do if I want to make the word *slip* again is put the *s* at the beginning."	
Explains.	"So, when we see a word with two consonants together, often we will need to make the sound of each consonant and then blend them together to try to figure out what the word is. "Often, if we can't figure out the word right away, it helps to think about the sound of each letter and then blend them together. Some people think it helps to cover up	

| | the first letter, think about what the word would sound like without that letter and then add that first letter back on." | |
| Reminds children of exceptions. | "Sometimes, this doesn't work. You already know, for example, that when *c* and *h* are together, the sound is usually /ch/." | The teacher might remind the children of any other consonant digraphs that have already been taught. |

Step 3: Word Building

Teacher	What the teacher says	Comments on the activity
Presents letter and rime cards and says:	"We are going to make some more words in the /ip/ word family. You need to listen carefully to the words I say and put letters at the beginning of the word so that you make the word I say. Sometimes you'll need one letter at the beginning and sometimes you'll need two letters."	The teacher would provide the children with the rime and the letters needed to make all the words in the family.
Dictates words in the set.	"Make the word *sip*." "Change *sip* to *lip*." (Refer to the sample word set in Figure 10.3, p. 237)	The teacher watches as children attempt to build the words and provides needed scaffolding, which may include elongating sounds, reminding the children to use the key words, and so forth.
Provides feedback and reinforcement.	Sample comments: • "You stretched that word when you were trying to figure out what letter[s] you needed, and it worked!" • "I noticed you looking at the key words when you weren't sure what letter to use. That helped, didn't it?"	The teacher would continue to work with the children on sets of words that include consonant clusters composed of stretchable consonants until the children appear to be fairly proficient. With slight modifications, the sample comments provided to the left could be used as scaffolds (e.g., "Stretch that word to figure out what letter you need").

Step 4: Word Reading

The teacher forms words with one or both elements of the consonant clusters and asks the children to read them. Assistance is provided as needed.

Step 5: Written Spelling

The teacher presents the rime used for word formation, tells the children that all words will be in that word family, and then dictates words with one or both elements of the consonant cluster that is the focus of the activity. The children write the words on paper or on a dry-erase board.

The *Floss* Rule

Some advocate teaching the "*floss* rule" to help children remember to double the final consonant in one-syllable short-vowel words ending in *f*, *l*, or *s*. (It's called the "*floss* rule" because the word *floss* includes the letters *f*, *l*, and *s*.) As with many of the "rules" that apply to English orthography, there are exceptions, such as the words *bus* and *gas*, in which the final consonant is not doubled, and the words in the "all" word family, which do not have a short-vowel sound. However, for learners who are refining their spelling skills, knowing the "rule" may increase the accuracy of the spellings more than it would interfere.

Research on the Role of Written Spelling in Orthographic Word Learning

In the last several years, a number of studies indicating that children learn to identify written words more quickly when instruction engages them in spelling words in writing have been published; spelling them orally did not have the same impact (e.g., Colenbrander et al., 2022; Ouellette, 2010; Ouellette, Martin-Chang, & Rossi, 2017; Shahar-Yames & Share, 2008). In teaching students new phonic/orthographic elements in the context of word study, the ISA emphasizes the value of having students build, read, and spell (in writing) words containing the decoding elements that are under study. We can't stress enough the value in having early literacy learners engage in word building (with movable letters or letter tiles), word reading, and written spelling. Having children spell the words they are learning to read draws their attention to all the orthographic elements in the words. Both word building and written spelling play that role.

Vowels

Learning to decode and encode vowel sounds is significantly more complicated than learning to decode and encode consonant sounds. This is true for several reasons, including the following:

- Within a word or syllable, the sound of the vowel tends to be influenced by (coarticulated with) the surrounding consonants (as discussed in Chapter 5).
- There are no clear-cut acoustic boundaries between vowels (for example, there is very little difference between the sounds for short-*e* and short-*i* sounds).
- Vowels are pronounced differently by people from different locales. For example, when people are perceived to have accents, it is usually because of the way they pronounce vowel sounds.
- Many of the "rules" for representing vowel sounds in print are rather unreliable. For example, the "silent-*e* rule" only works (meaning it signals that the vowel sound should be long) about 50 or 60% of the time (Clymer, 1963).

- The printed representations of many vowel sounds, other than the short vowels, are complex.
- It generally takes more than one letter to represent long-vowel sounds.
- Sometimes the two letters that represent a vowel sound are separated by one or more consonants, as in *smoke* and *bathe.*
- Sometimes the two letters represent more than one vowel sound. For example, the *ea* combination is used to represent the long-*e* in *bead,* the short-*e* in *bread,* and the long-*a* in *break.*
- Sometimes the same vowel sound is spelled in many different ways. For example, all these words have the long-*a* sound: *cake, great, weigh, play, rain, prey,* and *ballet.*

Because of this complexity, in the ISA we encourage teachers to teach children to be *flexible* in decoding vowels and to explain to them that, when they are reading and they come to a word they don't already know, they should be prepared to try different pronunciations for the vowel if their first attempt does not result in a real word that makes sense in the context. These attempts should *not* be random but, rather, be based on the most likely pronunciation. For example, students are taught to first try the long sound for the first vowel letter when encountering a vowel team such as *ai, ea,* or *oa.* If that attempt doesn't result in a real word that fits the context, children would be encouraged to try either the short sound for the first vowel or the long sound for the second vowel. We'll address this notion of flexibility in greater detail in Chapter 12.

Vowels and MLs

English has a greater variety of vowel sounds than do many other languages. So, here again, MLs may find it challenging to perceive and produce the sounds of the English language. Further, for MLs who have learned to read in a language that uses the same letters used in English, the pronunciations associated with the vowel letters may well be different from what they learned in their first language. Therefore, to become proficient in reading and writing English, they will need to learn new associations to those letters. Yet another challenge for MLs is the lack of regularity in the sound–spelling system of English that is especially prominent with vowels.

Instruction for Long Vowels with the VCe Spelling Pattern

To help children develop flexibility with decoding vowels, we practice the most common spellings for the two most common sounds of each vowel letter when we begin to teach about long vowels. That is, we explain that vowel letters can represent two different sounds—one of which they already know. (The short-vowel sound and the associated key word for each vowel letter would have been previously introduced and practiced as discussed in Chapter 8.) Since children already know the name of the letter (which is the same as its long-vowel sound) and have previously been taught the short sound of the vowel, what they need to learn is the conventional spellings of the two sounds. Further, at the point where we would begin work on teaching the spellings of the two sounds for a given vowel, many children may have already been using the vowel letter to represent the long-vowel sound in their writing. For example, a child at an early point in development might use the letters *A* and *T* to spell the word *ate,* or the letters *B* and *I* to spell the word *buy.* Thus, children generally have a sense that the letter *A* can be used to represent the long-*a* sound before we begin to teach the conventional spelling of that sound. Moreover, over the many years that we have recommended teaching and practicing long- and short-vowel sounds together, teachers have consistently reported success.[2]

A suggested order for instruction on the spellings of vowel sounds is provided below. This order is based on the similarities between and among the vowel sounds. The vowels whose short sounds are most different from one another are the first focus, as it is easier to discriminate one from the other. Teachers who are using a core program or phonics series will, of course, follow the progression recommended by that series for teaching short- (and long-) vowel sounds.

The suggested order is as follows:

- Long and short sounds for *a,* using long-*a* words spelled with the silent-*e* (VC*e*) pattern (as in *make* and *late*) and short-vowel words spelled with the CVC pattern. These spelling patterns characterize many one-syllable words.
- Long and short sounds for *i,* using long-*i* words spelled with the VC*e* pattern.
- Review of long and short sounds for both *a* and *i.*
- Long and short sounds for *o,* using long-*o* words spelled with the VC*e* pattern.
- Review of long- and short-*a, i,* and *o* sounds.
- Long and short sounds for *e,* using long-*e* words spelled with the double-*e* pattern (because very few long-*e* words are spelled with the VC*e* pattern).
- Review long- and short-vowel sounds and spellings for *a, i, o,* and *e.*
- Long- and short-*u* sounds, with the long-*u* spelled with the VC*e* pattern. Note that it is important to initially introduce long-*u* words that have a "true" long-*u* (*mute* and *cube*) rather than words with an /oo/ sound, as in *toot* (and *tube, rude, dude, blue,* etc.). Of course, the latter type of long-*u* words is quite common and should ultimately be included in practice activities.
- Review vowel sounds and spellings taught thus far.

---

[2]In our earlier work, we advocated for explicitly teaching the spelling for the two sounds of each vowel when vowel spellings were first addressed instructionally. But, because it was difficult to find texts in which readers at early points in development would encounter sufficient opportunities to read words with the long-vowel spellings, we have shifted our perspective and (recommended) practice.

Ideally, as each vowel is taught, children would be provided with enough practice to allow them to really learn the sounds and common spellings for the vowels. Ideally, children would not be rushed on to the next vowels in the sequence before they are fairly secure with those that have already been taught.

Lists of words that can be used for teaching and practicing each of the vowel sounds are provided in Figure 10.4. The first page of Figure 10.4 provides lists for teaching about individual vowels. The second page provides lists for reviewing vowels once more than one vowel has been taught and practiced. The words on each list are intended to be used in the order in which they are listed for word building, as doing so requires a change in just one letter/phoneme as the children move from one word to the next. This serves to reduce the level of challenge a bit and, therefore, increases the likelihood that the children will be able to focus on the new skill they are learning. However, as children's skills develop, it is not necessary, and probably better not to strictly adhere to the ordering on these lists. Below we describe procedures for teaching about the vowels.

Note

We try to avoid referring to the silent-*e* rule because the silent-*e* is far from entirely reliable in relation to signaling the long-vowel sound. Therefore, it does not really constitute a "rule." Many one-syllable words that end in *e* do not have the long-vowel sound (e.g., *have, come, give, one, some, live*). Some teachers refer to the *e* at the end as a clue that the other vowel in the word might make the sound that is the same as its name.

Also note that teachers use different terms for the silent-*e* (e.g., silent, bossy, magic). Children who are first learning about the concept will be confused if they are receiving instruction from more than one teacher and the teachers use different terms—to a young child, the terms *silent*, *bossy*, and *magic* may not mean the same thing.

Teaching Children to Decode and Encode Long- and Short-Vowel Sounds

Below we illustrate the process for teaching and practicing the long and short sounds and spellings of a vowel simultaneously. We begin with a brief overview of the process and then provide a more detailed explanation in the form of a sample script for each step. The instructional routine is abbreviated once the first couple of vowels have been taught.

Terminology

Note that it is not necessary for children to use the terms *long* and *short* in reference to the two sounds of a vowel. Indeed, some children are confused by these terms because they suggest that the pronunciations differ in duration, which they don't. What children most need to know is that each of the vowel letters

Long and short *a*	Long and short *i*	Long and short *o*	Long and short *e*	Long and short *u*
mat	bit	mom	seed	cube
mate	bite	mop	feed	cub
fate	kite	mope	fed	cut
fat	kit	mode	wed	cute
fad	hit	mod	weed	jute
fade	him	rod	week	jut
made	dim	rode	seek	but
mad	dime	robe	seen	cut
sad	time	rob	teen	cute
Sam	tide	sob	ten	mute
same	hide	sop	men	muse
tame	hid	top	met	fuse
tape	rid	tone	meet	use
tap	ride	cone	beet	us
cap	wide	con	bet	bug
cape	wine	cop	bed	hug
came	win	cope	fed	hub
cane	pin	hope	feed	cub
can	pine	hop	feet	cube
man	dine	pop	meet	tube*
mane	line	pope	met	tub
make	fine	rope	net	
take	fin	rode	nee'd	
tame	sin	rod	seed	
game	sit	cod	weed	
gate	site	code	wed	
hate	side	cob	red	
hat	ride	lob	reel	
rat	ripe	lobe	peel	
rate	rip	lone	pen	

Tube does not have a true long-*u* sound. Rather it is pronounced with the double-*o* sound as in *toot*. However, since the children ultimately need to learn to decode words with this spelling–sound relationship, it is fine to include it once the children are fairly secure with the more rule-based spelling–sound correspondence for long *u*.

FIGURE 10.4. Word lists for practicing on long- and short-vowel sounds.

Review of *a* and *i*	Review of *a*, *i*, and *o*	Review of *a*, *i*, *o*, and *e*	Review of *a*, *e*, *i*, *o*, and *u*
bit	cot	feed	cute
bat	cat	fed	cut
fat	fat	fad	cat
fate	fit	fade	cop
fame	fin	made	cope
tame	fine	mad	cape
time	pine	bad	cap
dime	pane	bid	tap
dim	pan	bide	tip
Tim	pad	ride	dip
tin	pod	rode	did
tan	cod	rod	deed
fan	code	nod	deep
fin	rode	need	keep
fine	rod	weed	beep
mine	rid	wed	bop
mane	ride	wet	top
man	ripe	get	tap
can	rope	got	tab
cane	robe	lot	cab
cape	rob	let	cub
cap	rib	net	cube
tap	rig	not	tube
tip	rag	rot	tub
sip	tag	rob	sub
sap	bag	robe	sun
sat	big	rope	sin
sit	bin	hope	tin
site	win	hop	tan
kite	wine	top	teen
kit	line	tap	ten
hit	like	tape	men
hat	lake	take	met
hate	rake	tame	meet
		time	mat
		Tim	mate
		Tom	fate
			fit

FIGURE 10.4. *(page 2 of 2)*

commonly represents two sounds and how each of those sounds is commonly represented in print. However, if children receiving instruction in an intervention setting are hearing these terms in their classroom (or vice versa), making this connection explicit should help to support the application of skills across settings.

- *Locating vowel sounds.* This activity involves having the children listen for the vowel sounds to be taught and deciding whether the sound occurs at the beginning, in the middle, or at the end of given words. The purpose is to ensure that the children can notice and isolate the vowel sounds.

- *Comparing and contrasting vowel sounds.* In this sound-sorting activity, children listen to spoken words and sort them into long- and short-vowel groups. Some teachers use pictures as an initial step in the sorting process. The comparing and contrasting step is, again, intended to attune children to the sounds of the vowels before they begin to attend to the written representations of those sounds.

- *Explaining the silent-*e *generalization.* This activity involves providing an explicit explanation of how the silent-*e* works. Because the silent-*e* is one of the most common ways of representing the long-vowel sound, it is important that children understand the generalization well.

- *Reviewing the key word for the short-vowel sound.* The short-vowel sounds are among the hardest letter sounds for children to remember. Therefore, encouraging children to actively use the key words when needed is important. Early on, children benefit from explicit guidance in how the key words can support their reading and writing efforts.

- *Word building.* This activity involves making words the teacher dictates, using movable letters.

- *Word reading.* This exercise involves reading words the teacher either writes or makes using movable letters. At least early on, we recommend using movable letters, as this makes the changes from one word to the next more evident.

- *Written spelling.* This activity involves the children in writing words dictated by the teacher.

Each of these instructional steps is elaborated more fully in the following.

Step 1: Sample Instructional Dialogue for Locating Vowel Sounds	
Rationale:	It is important that children be able to notice the targeted vowel sounds in words. By asking them to decide whether the targeted sound comes at the beginning, middle, or end of the word, we can determine whether they are ready for the more challenging task of using letters to represent those sounds.
Materials needed:	A large-print letter *a* and the picture for the key word to be used for the short sound of *A*.

Teacher	What the teacher says	Comments on the activity
Says:	"We are going to start learning more about the sounds of vowels. Vowels are special letters. One of the things that makes them special is that every word must have a vowel in it. Another thing that makes vowels special is that every vowel letter can be used to spell more than one sound. The vowel letter that we are going to start with is the letter *a*."	
Displays letter *a* and says:	"Sometimes when there is an *a* in a word, the sound for it is the same as its name, /ā ā ā/. Listen for the /ā ā ā/ sound at the beginning of these words: *aaaage, aaaache, aaaate, aaaape*."	The teacher elongates the long-*a* sound in each word as it is pronounced. (*Note:* An *a* [or any vowel] with a straight line over it—/ā/—denotes the long sound. The line is called a macron.)
Says:	"Now listen for the /ā ā ā/ sound at the end of these words: *maaaay, plaaaay, saaaay*."	The teacher elongates the long-*a* sound as it is pronounced.
Says:	"Sometimes the /ā ā ā/ sound is in the middle of a word. Listen for the /ā ā ā/ sound in these words: *maaaake, gaaaame, taaaape*."	The teacher elongates the long-*a* sound in each word as it is pronounced.
Asks:	"Listen to this next word and tell me where the /ā ā ā/ sound is—at the beginning, in the middle, or at the end: *aaaape*."	The teacher might use Elkonin boxes as a support/scaffold to ensure that every child has an opportunity to respond. Each child would have three boxes and would place a marker in the first, middle, or last box—depending on the word.
Provides feedback:	"Yes, the /ā ā ā/ sound is at the beginning." Or: "Listen again—*aaaape*—we hear the /ā ā ā/ sound at the beginning of *aaape*. The /ā ā ā/ sound is the first sound I make when I say *aaape*."	Explicit and corrective feedback at early points in the learning process is always helpful.
Continues with activity, adding new words.	*make, play, aid, tape, ace, say, shake, fame, ape, safe, tray,* etc.	The teacher says each word and provides feedback. Practice continues with various one-syllable long-*a* words until the children don't need the teacher to elongate the sound and are fairly quick at locating the sound in words with two or three sounds.

Says:	"So far, we've learned that a lot of times when there is an *a* in a word, it means we are supposed to say its name. But sometimes when there is an *a* in a word we are supposed to make a different sound /ă ă ă/—like the sound we hear at the beginning of the word *aaaapple* [or whatever key word was used]."	The word used to introduce the short-vowel sound should be the key word that will be used to remind the children of the vowel's sound. The teacher should show the picture of the key word when articulating its first sound. (*Note:* An *a* with a curved line over it [ă] denotes the short-*a* sound. The curved line is called a *breve* [pronounced *brev*].)[3]
Says:	"Everyone say the sound of *a* that comes at the beginning of the word *aaaapple*."	The teacher provides corrective feedback as needed—perhaps stretching the sound of the short *a* even further.
Asks:	"Now listen to the word *aaaat*. Do you hear the /ă ă ă/ sound at the beginning or at the end of the word *aaaat*?"	The teacher elongates the short-*a* sound when presenting the first couple of items.
Provides feedback:	"Yes, the /ă ă ă/ is at the beginning of the word *aaaat*." Or: "Listen again to the word *aaaaaat*. The /ă ă ă/ sound is at the beginning."	The teacher elongates the short-*a* sound even more when providing corrective feedback.
Asks:	"How about the word *maaat*? Is the /ă ă ă/ sound at the beginning, in the middle, or at the end of the word *maaat*?"	If the response is incorrect, the teacher should say the word again, elongating the vowel sound even further.
Continues:	"Where is the /ă ă ă/ sound in the word *add*?"	The teacher should provide practice with locating the short-*a* sound in different words until the children are fast and accurate in locating the sound in words.
Reduces support and continues.	*cap, as, back, add, sat, mad, axe, tap, bat, sad, at, pack, act, had,* etc.	Ideally, the children should be able to identify the location of the vowel sound without the teacher elongating it. The teacher should reduce the amount of elongation as quickly as possible while still ensuring the children's success. The teacher may need to provide different amounts of elongation for different children.
Continues with activity, adding new words.	*cap, as, back, add, sat, mad, axe, tap, bat, sad, at, pack, act, had,* etc.	The teacher says each word and provides feedback. Practice continues with various one-

[3]Children do not need to know the terms macron and breve.

	syllable short-*a* words until the children no longer need the teacher to elongate the sound and are fairly quick at identifying the location of the sound in words with two or three sounds.

Step 2: Sample Instructional Dialogue for Comparing and Contrasting Vowel Sounds

Rationale:	In order to ultimately use letters to accurately represent vowel sounds, children need to be able to distinguish between the two sounds associated with the vowel.
Preparation:	Steps 2 and 3 should occur in the same instructional episode, so be sure to allow enough time for both.
Materials needed:	A T-chart, with one column headed by a word with the long-*a* sound in the middle and one headed by a word that has a short-*a* sound in the middle. We'll use *tap* and *tape* as column headers in this example. A highlighter is also used in this activity. (*Note:* Do not use words with an *n* or an *m* following the vowel for the headings of the columns because these letters distort the sound of the vowel a bit, and this may confuse the children. All the words used for the long-*a* column should be spelled using the silent-*e* pattern. Lists of words for these activities are provided in Figure 10.4 [p. 245].)

Teacher activity	What the teacher says	Comments on the activity
Points to each word that will be the header for the short-*a* or long-*a* column as it is said.	"We are going to make a chart with words that have the /ă ă ă/ sound and words that have the /ā ā ā/ sound. In the first column on the chart, I have written the word *tap* and in the second column I've written the word *tape*."	If this activity occurs on a different day from Step 1, it may be helpful to have the children locate the sound of the short and long *a* in the words at the top of each column.
Says:	"Now I'm going to say another word, and I want you to decide if the middle sound in the word I say sounds like the middle sound in *taaap* or if it sounds like the middle sound in *taaape*."	This is an auditory activity at this point. Therefore, the teacher would not have the printed word visible to the children.
Presents words.	"The first word is *maaaake*. Does the middle sound in *maaaake* sound like the middle sound in *taaaaap* or the middle sound in *taaape*?"	At least on the first couple of items, the teacher should emphasize the middle sounds in the words by elongating them. However, the goal should be to reduce or remove this scaffold as soon as the children are ready. (*Note:* If children struggle with determining in which column a word belongs,

		it may be necessary to revert to more focused phonemic analysis instruction before proceeding with the decoding instruction. Or, it may suffice to remind children of the pronunciation of each column header by pointing to the words as they are pronounced.)
Writes the word in the appropriate column as the children look on, engaging the children in the process of spelling the word as much as possible.	"What's the first sound we hear in *make*? And what letter do we need for that /mmm/ sound? And we know the middle sound is . . . ? And the last sound in *make*?"	The words on the list should be conventionally spelled. For long-vowel words, the teacher would add the *e* and say something like "In the book spelling for *make*, there's an *e* at the end—so we'll put that on."
Asks:	"Our next word is *cat*. Which column does *cat* go in? Does the middle sound in *cat* sound like the middle sound in *tap*? Or like the middle sound in *tape*?"	Again, if need be, the teacher should elongate the vowel sounds in the words to help children make their decisions.
Continues.	*face, cat, bake, gate, nap, dad*	The teacher says additional words, asking children to decide in which column to place each word and engaging the children in interactive writing of the words until four or five words have been added to each column. It is not necessary to have the same number of words in each column.
Says:	"Now let's read our lists and see what we notice about the letters in these words."	The teacher should read down the first column, pointing to each word as it is read.
Asks:	"What do you notice that's the same in all of these words?"	Generally, children quickly notice that all the words have an *a*. If they don't, the teacher should direct their attention ("What letter do you see in every word?").
Confirms:	"Yes, all of the words under *tap* have an *a*."	
Says:	"Now let's read the words in this next column. See if you can figure out what's the same in all these words."	The teacher reads down the column, pointing to each word as it is read.

Asks:	"What did you notice that's the same in all the words in this column?"	Sometimes a child will notice just the *e*'s or just the *a*'s. If the teacher is working with an individual, it may help to have the child highlight all the vowels in the word to make the pattern more apparent. In a group, with group effort, usually both the *e*'s and the *a*'s are noticed—but it may help, nevertheless, for the teacher to highlight all the vowels to emphasize the pattern.

Step 3: Sample Instructional Dialogue for the Explanation of Silent-*e*
Rationale: English orthography is quite complicated. It is helpful to provide children with clear explanations about some of the conventions of the orthography.
Preparation: Step 2 should immediately precede this step the first time the explanation is given. It may well be necessary to repeat this explanation, perhaps in abbreviated form, on several occasions— both when working with the sounds for *a* and for the other vowels.
Materials needed: The chart that was created during Step 2.

Teacher	What the teacher says	Comments on the activity
Explains:	"For all the words on this list that have that /ā ā ā/ sound, there's an *a* in the middle and an *e* at the end. All the words on this other list have an *a* in the middle but no *e* at the end. They all have the /ă ă ă/ sound because they don't have an *e* at the end."	The teacher points to the words in each list as the similarities and differences are explained.
Continues:	"The *e* doesn't represent a sound in these words. It is silent. When something is silent that means it is not making any sound. Even though the *e* is silent, it still has an important job. It is a clue we can use when we are thinking about how a word might sound. When the *e* comes at the end of words like these, it means we should probably say the name of the vowel that's in the middle of the word."	The teacher points to the words in the column under *tape*. Remember that if children are receiving instruction in more than one setting, it is important to use the same terminology for the silent-*e* generalization across settings so as not to confuse them.
Continues:	"When there's no *e* at the end, and there's only one vowel in the word, that usually means that we are supposed to say the vowel's other sound. For the letter *a*, that's the /ă ă ă/ sound."	The teacher points to the words in the column under *tap*. (If the classroom program in use expects children to understand and use CVC and VC*e* terminology, that connection would be made/reinforced here.)

Step 4: Sample Instructional Dialogue for the Discussion of the Key Word		
Rationale:	The short-vowel sounds are among the hardest letter–sound correspondences to remember. Key words, when used effectively, allow children to independently remind themselves of the short-vowel sounds.	
Materials needed:	The picture for the key word for the letter *A*.	

Teacher	What the teacher says	Comments on the activity
Shows vowel key word and says:	"We are learning that, when we are looking at the letters in a word and trying to figure out what the word will sound like, we need to think carefully, especially about the vowel letters. The sound for the letter *a* may be /ă ă ă/ or it may be the /ā ā ā/ sound. If there's an *e* at the end of the word, we try the /ā ā ā/ sound first. If there's no *e* at the end, we try the /ă ă ă/ sound. It's easy to remember that /ā ā ā/ sound because it is just the same as the letter's name. But the /ă ă ă/ sound is a little harder to remember. To help us remember the /ă ă ă/ sound, we have this picture of an aaaaapple [or of whatever key word is used]."	
Further explains the process of how to use key words to remember the short vowel sound.	"The word *aaapple* starts with that /ă ă ă/ sound. So, if you are looking at the letter *a* and you can't remember its other sound, then you could find the letter *a* on the key word chart and look at the picture that goes with it. The /ă ă ă/ sound at the beginning of *aaaaaapple* will remind you of the /ă ă ă/ sound of *a*."	This explanation is intended to help children develop self-regulation related to decoding. It helps them think about available resources and how to use them.

Step 5: Sample Instructional Dialogue for Word Building	
Rationale:	In word building, the children are given a fairly small set of letters with which to work. This simplifies the task of building the words. We are, in essence, providing the children with a scaffold by limiting the letter set from which they are to choose.
Preparation:	Word building can be done with a single large set of letter cards that all the children can see, or each child might be given a set of letters with which to work. Often teachers use both large cards and letters for individual children. That way each child can think about a given word independently, and then the children can check their attempts against what is displayed with the larger cards.
Materials needed:	Word list for long-*a* and short-*a* words and the movable letters needed to make the words that will be used in the lesson. Figure 10.4 (p. 245) provides lists of words that can be used. For any given lesson, teachers would choose only a segment of a given list.

Teacher	What the teacher says	Comments on the activity
Says:	"Now we are going to use these letters to make some words. Today, all the words we are going to make will have an *a* in them. Sometimes the words will need that silent-*e* to show that the sound of the *a* is just like its name. Sometimes, we won't need an *e* at the end because the sound of the *a* will be /ă ă ă/, as in *aaaapple*."	Explaining that all the words will have an *a* in them is a useful scaffold. The children are each provided with all the letters they will need to make the words that will be dictated. Having their own letters to manipulate increases their level of engagement and helps the teacher understand which children may need more guidance and support.
Makes the first word with the letter tiles and says:	"Let's have everyone use three letters to make the word *mat*. *Mmmaaat*. Now, change *mat* to *mate*. Change *mate* to *fate*. Change *fate* to *fat*. Change *fat* to *fad*. Change *fad* to *fade*," etc.	Early on, the teacher should provide as much support as the children need—stretching the sounds, isolating and articulating sounds individually, reminding them to use the key words, and so forth. The teacher should also monitor children's attempts at each word and provide corrective feedback as needed (commenting on what they did right and what needs further thought). However, the goal is for the children to ultimately be able to independently analyze and represent the sounds. Therefore, the teacher should always be thinking carefully about which aspects of the task the children need help with and which aspects they might be able to handle alone.

Step 6: Sample Instructional Dialogue for Word Reading	
Rationale:	After building the words during Step 5, the children are familiar with the words that they will be asked to read. They have been "primed," so to speak. As a result, it will be easier for them to identify these words than it would have been without the word-building step.
Preparation:	In this activity, the teacher uses movable letters to form the same words that the children were making during the word-building activity.
Materials needed:	Letters large enough for all the children in the group to see; the word list for long-*a* and short-*a* words (in Figure 10.4).

Teacher	What the teacher says	Comments on the activity
Says:	"Now I am going to make some words, and I want you to figure out what each word is. Remember to check for that silent-*e*. It tells us the *a* will probably sound like /ā ā ā/." "Also remember, if you are not sure about the sound of one of the letters, you can use your key words to figure it out."	Drawing from the words on the long-*a* and short-*a* word list (and other words the children may see in texts they will be reading soon), the teacher uses the movable letters to form words that the children attempt to read. The teacher again provides scaffolding on an as-needed basis by reminding the children to attend to the presence or absence of the silent-*e* and by guiding them to use the key words. The teacher would provide individuals with assistance as needed. For example, the teacher might elongate the pronunciation of the vowel sound, remind them of the role of the silent-*e*, and so on. It is important for the teacher to provide only as much support as seems needed. The goal is for the children to, ultimately, be able to puzzle through one-syllable words independently when reading meaningful text.

Step 7: Written Spelling	
Rationale:	Spelling out an entire word can be very challenging, as it requires being able to do both the phonemic analysis and the alphabetic coding component. Having children spell words that they have been working on in other ways helps to build their confidence and competence and to increase their proficiency with the types of analysis required for spelling.
Materials needed:	Word list for long *a* and short *a* (in Figure 10.4) and writing materials (paper and pencil, dry-erase boards and markers, etc.).

Teacher	What the teacher says	Comments on the activity
Says:	"Now we are going to write some words. All the words we write will have the letter *a* in them. You need to listen to the words I say carefully and decide whether the word has an /ā ā ā/ sound. If it does, you need to be sure that the word you write ends with a silent-*e*. If the word has an /ă ă ă/ sound, then you don't need to put an *e* at the end."	The teacher should monitor the children's spelling of each word and provide any needed scaffolding. The children should discuss their decisions (e.g., about whether or not to include a silent-*e*). Discussions of these decisions will help to make the reasoning more prominent to the children and therefore, hopefully, more generalizable. To help the children internalize the logic, and especially for children who either leave off or include the *e* inappropriately, the teacher can guide their thinking (and their ability to self-regulate) by asking questions such as: • "When do we use the silent-*e*?" • "Do you need the silent-*e* for that word? Why or why not?" • "Tell me which sound needs the silent-*e*."

Similar procedures might be followed as each new vowel is introduced and practiced. However, as children demonstrate that they understand the processes involved, it may not be necessary to spend as much time or do as much explaining as the example above suggests. Following instruction and practice with each new vowel, the review lists in Figure 10.4 should be used for reinforcement of the vowel sounds and spellings that have already been taught.

Learning the alphabetic code is challenging for some children, especially learning about vowel sounds, as the spelling–sound correspondences for vowels are more variable than the correspondences for consonant letters and digraphs. Therefore, helping children become very familiar with the spellings of the two most common sounds for the major vowels will enable them to develop the flexibility (to try alternate pronunciations for vowel letters) they ultimately need in puzzling through the unfamiliar words they encounter while reading, as there are many words in written English that do not "follow the rules" that are often taught.

Organizational Tip

Some teachers make a sheet with the letters needed for the words used for practice activities. Each child is given a sheet, which the child cuts apart in preparation for the word-building activities. After the letters are used, they can be stored in an envelope or snack bag to be used by the child on subsequent days. When they are fairly proficient with spelling and reading the words on the list, the children can take the words and the associated letters home for additional practice supported by a more proficient reader. A take-home template for these practice activities can be found on the book's companion website (see the box at the end of the table of contents).

Sound Boxes and Written Spelling

In Chapter 5, we discussed the use of sound boxes (Elkonin boxes) to support children's ability to attend to the individual phonemes in spoken words. These boxes can be used in a similar way to support children's ability to work out the spellings of one-syllable words. When children begin to use this skill while writing, we would encourage them to start by thinking about how many sounds they hear in a word, then draw a line for each sound (as drawing boxes would take too much time), and then write in the letters for the sounds on the lines. For example, if a child who has had some experience with using sound boxes wanted to write the word *plane,* the child would start by thinking about how many sounds there are (four in this example). Then the child would draw a line for each sound and then place the letter(s) that represent those sounds on the lines. If the child has learned that a long-vowel sound is (could be) marked by the silent-*e*, the child would (be guided to) add the silent-*e* at the end—but not on a line as the lines/boxes are placeholders for letters representing sounds (see Figure 10.5). Also, if the word to be spelled includes a digraph, the two letters in the digraph would go in a single box (or on a single line).

p l a n e sh e

FIGURE 10.5. Using sound boxes/lines to work out the spellings of one-syllable words.

Instruction for Vowel Teams

When two vowel letters occur next to each other in a word, they usually represent one vowel sound. Teachers sometimes teach students, "When two vowels go walking, the first one does the talking" (meaning the first vowel letter "says its name"). However, this "rule" does not work for many words, including some of the highest frequency words (e.g., *been, great*). Perhaps a better bit of guidance would be "When two vowels are together in a word, usually only one vowel sound is heard."

Flexibility with Decoding Unknown Words in Context

We have encouraged teachers, in both research and professional development contexts, to teach children to be flexible in decoding vowel and consonant sounds for many years. Many teachers are initially skeptical about children's ability to use this strategy, which is currently described in the research literature as having a "set for variability" (Savage et al., 2018; Steacy et al., 2019). However, every teacher who has reported back after teaching this strategy (described in more detail in Chapter 12) has indicated that the strategy is very useful. In fact, one experienced teacher who was working with fourth-grade children identified as learning disabled reported that she thought it was the most powerful decoding strategy she had ever taught her students.

Usually, when two vowels are together in a word, the sound of one of them is heard. Most often it is the long sound of the first vowel (e.g., *bean, rain, boat*). Sometimes it is the short sound of the first vowel (e.g., *head, plaid*). Occasionally, it is the long sound of the second vowel (e.g., *great, break*), and sometimes its neither (e.g., *again*).

Sometimes, of course, two vowels together signal a sound that is different from the sound represented by either letter individually (e.g., *oy, oi, au, ei*). Still other vowels are influenced by the letter that immediately follows. This is especially true of *r*-controlled vowels (*ar, er, ir, or,* and *ur*) in which neither the long nor the short sound of the vowels can be distinctly heard.

For purposes of instruction, the various kinds of vowels are handled differently in our approach.

VOWEL TEAMS THAT CAN USUALLY BE DECODED WITH VOWEL FLEXING

Figure 10.6 presents a listing of the vowel teams that can *usually* be accurately decoded by trying the long and short sounds for each of the vowels, including the /oo/ sound for long-*u* as in *blue*. These teams do not require explicit instruction

ai	ea	ie	oa	ue
ay	ee		oe	ui
	eu*			

*As in *pseudo.*

FIGURE 10.6. Vowel combinations that can be decoded with vowel flexing.

beyond teaching the two sounds of the vowel letters and the vowel flexing strategy, which is discussed in Chapter 12. *Practice with vowel flexing can occur in isolation IF only one real word would result.* For example, for a word like *plaid* a reader who was unfamiliar with the word could potentially come up with three real words via vowel flexing—*played, plaid,* and *plied.* For a word like *real,* vowel flexing would result in two real words—*real* and *rail.* A useful approach would be to teach the vowel-flexing strategy by pulling a word out of the context in which it was encountered. The teacher would demonstrate how trying both sounds for each of the vowels would yield multiple real words and how to settle on the correct word by checking which of the possible pronunciations fits the context in which it was encountered (Anderson, 2023).

VOWEL TEAMS THAT MAY NEED TO BE EXPLICITLY TAUGHT

Several teams represent vowel sounds that cannot be identified via vowel flexing. Some of these teams include two vowel letters (e.g., *au* and *oi*), and some include a vowel and a consonant (e.g., *or* and *ow*). The vowel teams that may need to be explicitly taught include:

- Teams with only one common pronunciation:

  au aw ew oi oy

- Teams with two common pronunciations:

oo	ou	ow
(as in *look* and *boot*)	(as in *out* and *soup*)	(as in *now* and *snow*)

- *r*-controlled vowels: When a single vowel is followed by the letter *r* in the same syllable, the sound of the vowel is altered (coarticulated) such that it is hard to distinguish the sound of the vowel from the sound of the *r*. Therefore, *r*-controlled vowels are generally taught as decoding units, because, linguistically, they represent single phonemes:

  ar er ir or ur

INSTRUCTION FOR VOWEL TEAMS THAT CANNOT BE DECODED USING VOWEL FLEXING

Children's knowledge of these various vowel teams and the ease with which they acquire new knowledge about the alphabetic code should determine how much emphasis is placed on teaching these decoding details. It may be, for example, that simply showing and discussing a word or two that includes the vowel team will suffice to allow children to successfully puzzle through words with that letter combination, especially when they are encountered in a meaningful context. However, some children may need the type of practice that is provided in the word-building, word-reading, and written spelling routines described previously.

Note that it would be difficult to use some of these vowel teams in word-building exercises because sometimes a given sound might be spelled several different ways (e.g., the sound at the end of the word *drew* could be spelled with an *ew*, a *ue* [as in *blue*], or an *oo* [as in *too*]). In this example, the *ue* spelling does not need to be explicitly taught because it can be solved through vowel flexing. However, the *ew* and the *oo* may need to be explicitly taught. In doing so, we advise starting out by teaching and providing practice with the different spellings in separate lessons, incorporating other vowel sounds in a given lesson so that the students get some practice in working with the vowel combination. Thus, for example, if the *ar* and *oi* vowel teams have already been taught, the teacher could introduce the *ew* combination, talk about the sound it typically represents, and introduce the key word (*chew*) and the picture mnemonic (see Figure 10.7). Then the teacher would engage the students in word building, word reading, and written spelling for words containing one of the three vowel teams. Words used for such exercises might include *new, coin, car, flew, far, point, part, stew, join,* and *brew*. (Note that for students who are at a point in their development at which they are ready to learn vowel teams, it is not necessary to change only one part of the word at a time, as is done in the lists provided in Figure 10.4.) Note also that it is useful to point out to students that the /oi/ sound is generally spelled with *oy* at the end of words.

In a subsequent lesson, the teacher might introduce the double-*o* spelling that represents the same sound as *ew*, talk about the fact that it represents another way that the /oo/ (as in *boot*) sound is spelled, introduce the key word (see Figure 10.7), and then engage in word building, word reading, and written spelling with the new spelling pattern while incorporating other previously taught spelling patterns. For example, the following words might be used: *food, corn, chart, tooth, moon, short, zoo, worn,* and *sharp*. Note that until children have committed to memory spellings of words with more than one potential spelling, it will not be possible for them to determine which spelling to use. Therefore, the alternative spellings should not be included in the same lessons.

For vowel teams that have two common pronunciations, students need to learn both pronunciations and to be encouraged to be flexible in decoding the combination—alternating the sound until a word is identified that fits the context in which the word is encountered. For the vowel teams that need to be explicitly taught, it can be helpful to introduce and teach the key words for vowel teams depicted in Figure 10.7. Note that for some of the phonemes that have two common

FIGURE 10.7. Key words for vowel teams that cannot be decoded via vowel flexing.

spellings, such as *oi* and *oy* for the /oi/ sound, the pictures in Figure 10.7 are described by a phrase that incorporates words with both spellings. Thus, for the /oi/ phoneme, we have a picture of a *noisy boy*. For the /au/ phoneme that can be spelled as *au* as in *sauce* or as *aw* as in *straw*, we have a picture of a child *drinking sauce with a straw*.

THE SCHWA SOUND

All vowel letters, in some contexts, represent the schwa sound, which most often sounds like a short-*u* and sometimes like a short-*i*. Schwa sounds occur in both one-syllable words (son, of, a, does, love) and in words with more than one syllable (about, camel, animal, brother, orange, upon, vinyl, important, paragraph).[4] In

---

[4]Bolded letters represent schwas in these words.

fact, the schwa sound is the most frequent vowel sound in English and, according to Venezky (1999), is the "largest source of problems not only for spelling to sound translation (reading) but also for translation in the other direction (spelling)" (p. 62). In words with more than one syllable, the schwa occurs in unaccented syllables (those that are pronounced a bit more softly). If, when puzzling over a word, a child has tried both the short and the long sounds for a particular vowel and hasn't identified the word, it may help to suggest that the child try the /uh/ sound. When combined with the other orthographic information in the word, along with the context in which the word occurs, trying the /uh/ sound for one or more of the vowels can help the child to identify a word that makes sense in context. Note that, in dictionaries, the symbol for the schwa sound is an upside-down e (ə).

Diphthongs

Where do diphthongs fit in our approach to teaching about vowel sounds? A *diphthong* (pronounced "**dif**-thong") is a vowel sound that changes quality due to changes in mouth position during pronunciation. For example, in pronouncing the diphthong /oi/, the mouth position is initially similar to the one used in pronouncing a long-*o* sound, but then it changes to the position similar to that used in pronouncing the long-*e* sound. The sound that is emitted changes accordingly. The English language has several diphthongs, including the /ou/ sound as in *shout*, the long-*a* (*ay-ee*), the long-*i* (*i-ee*) and the /oi/ (oh-ee) sound as in *toy*. In teaching vowel sounds to children, we do not make distinctions between diphthongs and monophthongs (vowels that don't change quality during pronunciation), for it seems likely that an attempt to do so would unnecessarily complicate decoding and encoding processes.

Vowel Flexing and Word Learning

In Chapter 12, we discuss the use of vowel flexing as an important tool for word solving. Children are taught that when they encounter an unfamiliar word in text and their first attempt doesn't result in a word that fits the context, one thing they can do to solve the word is to "try different sounds for some of the letters, especially the vowels." For example, if they are puzzling over the word *great*, they would be encouraged to try the long sound of the *e*, the short sound of the *e*, and then to move on to the long and the short sounds of the *a* until they identify a real word that makes sense in the context of what they are reading. To be able to approach vowel teams in this way, children need to be very familiar with the two common sounds of each vowel, understand that all vowel letters sometimes represent a schwa sound, and view vowels as "decision points" that often require them to do some thoughtful problem solving—trying different pronunciations for some of the vowels.

Decoding Skills and the Set for Variability

The elements of the alphabetic code discussed in this and the last few chapters are critical to children's growth as readers and writers. As we have detailed in this chapter, many aspects of the English writing system require flexibility with regard to which graphemes represent which sounds and vice versa. And, in some cases, readers need to rely on contextual information (while reading meaningful text) to settle on the accurate identification/pronunciation of a word. That is, they need to try different pronunciations for some of the letters/graphemes in order to settle on a real word that fits the context in which it is encountered. As we'll discuss in Chapter 12, teachers using the ISA are encouraged to explicitly teach and engage children in practicing that flexibility. This flexibility is now frequently referred to as a *set for variability* (SfV), a term introduced by Gibson and Levin in 1975. The SfV has become a focus of recent reading research—a development that delights us as we have found it to be so powerful with both primary and middle elementary students, especially those who experience difficulty. However, we have never separately tested the vowel-flexing aspect of the overall approach to instruction and intervention. To date, only limited research has been done on the effects of explicit instruction that promotes an SfV (e.g., Savage, Georgiou, Parrila, & Maiorino, 2018). However, we expect such research to be a focus in the future. So far, most of the research that has explored the effects of having an SfV has determined that students who demonstrate a stronger SfV (are more successful at identifying individual words out of context), especially those with spellings that are not consistent with the grapheme–phoneme relationships typically taught (e.g., Steacy et al., 2019, 2022), make better progress in reading development.

KEY POINTS OF THIS CHAPTER

✓ Skill with the alphabetic code and the orthography more generally is a critical element in developing reading and spelling/writing skills.

✓ Some learners gain this skill with relative ease, but others benefit from carefully planned and delivered instruction, with repeated practice in and out of context.

✓ Explicit instruction and practice, including word building, word reading, and written spelling, help learners become automatic with many elements of the writing system.

✓ Teaching learners to be flexible in their decoding attempts and to try different sounds for some of the letters, especially the vowels, increases the likelihood that they will be able to accurately identify unfamiliar printed words.

✓ Relatedly, the utility of having a set for variability (SfV), that is the ability to try alternative pronunciations for some of the letters/graphemes in a word in efforts to accurately identify it, is gaining recognition as a useful skill. We expect to see a greater emphasis on the importance of teaching students to be flexible in their decoding attempts in the coming years. We have found it to be very useful in the ISA.

✓ Owing to the variability in the relationships between letters and larger orthographic units and their sounds, it is often necessary for readers to use contextual information to determine whether their decoding of an unfamiliar printed word has yielded a real word that makes sense in context.

✓ The use of context to confirm the accuracy of decoding attempts builds independence in word solving and ultimately helps learners build their sight vocabularies.

CHAPTER 11

Morphological Units and Multisyllabic Words

WRITING SYSTEM FOUNDATIONS GOAL 8

Children will understand that some words are composed of more than one unit of meaning (e.g., base words plus prefixes and/or suffixes) and will learn how to break longer words into meaningful units and/or syllables as an assist to understanding, reading, and spelling them.

In Chapter 9, we discussed the utility of teaching children to notice and use rimes to read and spell words within *orthographic word families* (e.g., *cake, bake, take, make*) for the purpose of helping them to develop fluency with word identification and spelling. In this chapter, we again focus on fluency with word identification and spelling but now with an emphasis on helping children learn to read and spell words in *morphological word families*. A *morpheme* is a unit of meaning. The word *wanted* consists of two morphemes—the base word *want* and the past tense suffix (*ed*). Multimorphemic words can be formed with the addition of various prefixes and suffixes (e.g., *wanted, wants, wanting, unwanted*). These form morphological word families. We also discuss methods for teaching children how to read words that are composed of more than one syllable (e.g., *table, puppy)*—some of which are also composed of more than one morpheme (e.g., *unhappy*). Both types of words come up early in children's reading and writing experience. Knowing the meaning and function of the most common prefixes and suffixes will enable learners to identify (and understand) many of the novel words they encounter in texts. In this chapter, we examine ways to help young learners learn to read and spell both multisyllabic and multimorphemic words.

Words with Multiple Meaningful Parts

Morphology

The English language is morphophonemic in nature. That is, words are made up of units of meaning (morphemes) and units of sound (phonemes). In the terminology typically used by teachers and students, morphemes are referred to as *root words,*[1] *prefixes,* and *suffixes.* Levesque, Breadmore, and Deacon (2021), in summarizing earlier research, report that approximately 80% of English words are composed of more than one morpheme and that words that include more than one morpheme represent the majority of unfamiliar words that children encounter while reading. Further, Nunes and Bryant (2006) suggest that "[s]ome of the most important correspondences between spoken and written language are at the level of the morpheme. . . . The system of morphemes, therefore, is a powerful resource for those learning literacy" (p. 157). Some of the important correspondences that Nunes and Bryant refer to account for some of the apparent inconsistencies in the spelling–sound correspondences in the English writing system. These inconsistencies, however, have the advantage of conveying and/or preserving meaning. For example, the past tense (*-ed*) ending in *looked, wanted,* and *played* are all pronounced differently (/t/ in *looked,* /ĕd/ in *wanted,* and /d/ in *played*), but the *-ed* spelling carries the same meaning in all three words. The plural morpheme *-s* or *-es* presents a similar situation; sometimes it is pronounced as /ĕz/ as in *watches,* sometimes as /z/ as in *beds,* and sometimes as /s/ as in *tops.* But despite these variations in pronunciation and spelling, the meaning of the ending remains the same.

There are two basic types of morphemes: *free morphemes* (base words that can stand alone such as *house, walk,* and *happy*) and *bound morphemes* (prefixes and suffixes which, together, are referred to as *affixes,* and meaningful elements of words called roots that are not in themselves words). For example, *vis* is a meaningful element in the words *visual, vision,* and *visible* (Kearns & Whaley, 2019). Bound morphemes include *inflectional morphemes* and *derivational morphemes.* Inflectional morphemes occur as suffixes and serve to change the grammatical role of the base word so that it appropriately fits the context of the sentence. Inflectional morphemes do not change the word's part of speech or meaning. They include past tense and plural markers as well as indications of possession and comparison. These tend to be the most common bound morphemes encountered by young children in their reading. Examples of inflectional morphemes are bolded in the following words: *walked, friends, dog's, smaller.*

Derivational morphemes change the meaning and/or part of speech of the base word and occur as either prefixes or suffixes. Derivational morphemes include *un-, re-, -less, -ly,* and *-able.* For example, the verb *do* with the morpheme *able* added becomes the word *doable,* which is an adjective. While very young readers are

---

[1] Linguists make a distinction between roots and base words. A root is a meaningful part that is not itself a word. *Vis* in the words *visible, visual,* and *vision* is a root. A base word is a word, the meaning of which can be modified by the addition of prefixes and suffixes.

unlikely to encounter such morphemes in their reading (unless they are unusually advanced), they do encounter them in spoken language and in the context of read-alouds. Experiences with spoken language help children learn the meanings of the most common derivational morphemes and can prepare them to learn to read words composed of multiple morphemes in their future.

By the time they begin kindergarten, most English-speaking children already have at least an implicit understanding of the morphemic nature of spoken language (Berko, 1958). This understanding is evident in their tendency to overregularize nouns and verbs for which plural and past tense pronunciations are not formed in the "regular" way. For example, they may refer to multiple *deer* as *deers*, or form the past tense of *go* as *goed*, or form some novel words (e.g., "crackering" soup, as cited in Carlisle & Goodwin, 2014). Because young children know how these morphemes work in spoken language, they can use this knowledge to their advantage in written language—at least once they have enough command of the writing system to be able to focus on what are, essentially, orthographic and morphemic units.

Inflectional Morphemes

The first suffixes that children are likely to encounter in their reading and writing are the inflectional endings *-ing, -er, -s* (or *-es*), and *-ed*. The various endings present different levels of challenge. The *-ing* and *-er* endings are pronounced the same way in all contexts and so are fairly easy endings for children to use in spoken and written language. We refer to these endings as "regular" inflectional endings in the snapshot (see Figure 11.1, p. 269). The *-s* (or *-es*) and *-ed* suffixes, however, are termed "conditional" because their pronunciation differs based on the final phoneme in the base word.

The *-ed* used to mark past tense is spelled consistently, making it somewhat easier to teach and learn about than the plural morpheme, which is spelled in two different ways (as *-s* or *-es*). Table 11.1 provides details regarding the contexts in which the past tense and plural endings take on different pronunciations. (We provide this information because we have frequently observed children asking for an explanation of the variability in pronunciation. The basic explanation is that the pronunciation of past-tense and plural morphemes depends on the phonological characteristics of the ending sound of the uninflected form of the base word.)

In general, if in their spoken language, children pronounce plural and past-tense inflections as they are typically pronounced in General American English, and if they understand that, in print, *-ed* indicates that something already happened, they are likely to assign the correct pronunciation to the ending in their attempts to read regular past words—at least if they are making sense of the text as they read. Once children have some experience with noticing and using the *-ed* inflection in their reading, they may well begin to use it in their writing—particularly if the *ed* spelling is explicitly explained. For example, if a child spells the word *dropped* as *dropt* the teacher might say:

TABLE 11.1. Pronunciations of Inflectional Suffixes

Words ending in . . .	Pronunciation	Examples
Pronunciations of past-tense endings		
/d/ or /t/	/ĕd/ (or /ĭd/)	*needed, wanted*
Unvoiced consonants other than /t/: /f/, /k/, /s/, /ch/, /sh/, /p/, and /th/	/t/	*sniffed, looked, dressed, washed, dipped*
All other ending sounds	/d/	*rubbed, hugged, spilled, snowed, arrived, played*
Pronunciations of plural and third-person present-tense endings		
Some unvoiced consonants: /f/, /k/, /p/, /t/, and unvoiced /th/	/s/	*cuffs, kicks, cups, mitts, paths*
Voiced consonants (/b/, /d/, /g/, /l/, /m/, /n/, /ng/, /r/, /v/, and /th/) and all vowels	/z/	*bibs, beds, mugs, calls, dimes, buns, rings, cars, knives, bathes, bees*
/ch/, /s/, /z/, and /sh/	/ĕz/	*bunches, dresses, buzzes, dishes, foxes* (The final phoneme in fox is /s/.)

"You noticed that /t/ sound at the end of the word *dropped*[2]—but *dropped* means that the *dropping* has already happened. When we are writing about something that already happened, for a lot of words, we use the letters *-ed* at the end of the word to show that it already happened. Sometimes *ed* sounds like /ĕd/ or /ĭd/ as in *wanted*, sometimes it sounds like /d/ as in *played*, and sometimes like /t/ as in *dropped*."

This explanation would be too much for children at early points in their development but would be appropriate when their skills are further advanced.

The *-s* (or *-es*) used to mark plurals and third-person present tense of a verb (e.g., "She *likes* candy") is pronounced in different ways as well. The determination of which pronunciation is assigned is, once again, based on the sound of the final phoneme in the uninflected form of the base word (see Table 11.1). These inflectional endings are a bit more complicated than the *ed* ending because the same orthographic representations have two different roles to play (marking the plural and the third-person present tense) and because they are spelled in two different and seemingly arbitrary ways and take on three different pronunciations! Here again, however, we have found that it is useful to teach children that *s* and *es* are units of meaning (when they are actually serving as units of meaning).[3]

Instructionally, it is useful to explain that, in reading, both types of inflectional endings can be temporarily ignored and then added back on once the base

---

[2] Doubling the *p* in *dropped* is done to maintain the short-*o* sound in the base word. This might be explained to children whose spelling skills are relatively advanced.

[3] Of course, *s* and *es* can sometimes be part of the base word—as in *bus* and *yes*.

word is identified. This often allows learners to assign the expected pronunciation to the marker (if they use the appropriate inflection in their spoken language) because they know, implicitly, how the past tense, plural, and third-person present-tense forms of the base words sound. For children whose spoken language varies from the language used in school, it may not be possible to assign the expected pronunciation. Therefore, the teacher might read the sentence/phrase and slightly emphasize the pronunciation of the inflection.

Syllables

A syllable is a unit of pronunciation. Every syllable contains one and only one *vowel phoneme*—although that phoneme may be represented by more than one letter (e.g., *oy, igh, oa*). As discussed in the previous chapter, usually when two vowels are together in a word, they represent just one vowel phoneme (e.g., *friend, captain, approach*). Words with more than one syllable generally present a greater challenge for beginning and developing readers than do words with just one syllable. In attempting to read a longer unfamiliar word, it may help readers to look for the vowels in the word (recognizing, of course, that the silent *e* and vowel teams will sometimes cause problems with this approach). The reader may find it useful to group sounds around the vowels, thereby forming syllables. For example, for the word *recognizing,* looking for vowels allows the reader to accurately note that there are four syllables in the word. However, knowing that there are four syllables does not allow the reader to determine how those syllables will be pronounced—especially with regard to the sounds of the vowel letters, which could be long, short, or some reduced form that is often pronounced as a schwa (*uh*) sound (e.g., rē-cŭg-nīz-ing or rĕ-cōg-nĭz-ing or rĕc-ŭg-nīz-ing). In attempting to solve words with multiple syllables (and vowel sounds more generally), the reader truly needs to be flexible in the pronunciation of vowel sounds—discussed as the *set for variability (SfV)* in Chapters 10 and 12. They can also be aided by the guidance suggested by Kearns and Whaley (2019)—breaking words such that each syllable conforms to orthographically acceptable English spellings of words or syllables. When this criterion is used, the word *recognizing* would not be segmented/decoded as *re-co-gniz-ing* since *gn* is almost never found at the beginning of a word or syllable in English.

Documenting Children's Progress—Morphemes

Figure 11.1 presents the group snapshot for documenting children's status and progress in using bound morphological units in their reading and spelling. Although the group snapshot is presented in a list format, it is important to point out that instruction does not proceed from the top to the bottom of the list. Instruction related to multimorphemic (words with more than one morpheme) and multisyllabic written words is not likely to move in a linear fashion relative to the

Group Snapshot—Morphemes								
	Morpheme taught ↓	Student names →						
"Regular" inflectional suffixes (-ing, -er)		Reading						
		Spelling						
		Reading						
		Spelling						
"Conditional" inflectional suffixes (-ed, -s, -es)		Reading						
		Spelling						
		Reading						
		Spelling						
		Reading						
		Spelling						
Prefixes (re-, un-, . . .)		Reading						
		Spelling						
		Reading						
		Spelling						
		Reading						
		Spelling						
Derivational suffixes (-ly, -ness, -er, -ful, -ness . . .)		Reading						
		Spelling						
		Reading						
		Spelling						
		Reading						
		Spelling						

Key:

☐ *B—Beginning* indicates that instruction has addressed the objective but that the child has only a preliminary understanding or capability with regard to that particular objective.

☒ *D—Developing* indicates that the child has some understanding of the objective but does not reliably demonstrate that understanding or capability or is not yet automatic (fluent) with the skill.

☒ *P—Proficient* indicates that the child reliably and automatically demonstrates the understanding or capability.

FIGURE 11.1. Group snapshot for morphology and multisyllabic words.

listed skills. Rather, children's progress will be highly dependent on the instructional materials in use (i.e., the types of words that the children encounter in their reading) and/or on their inclination to include such words in their writing. Children should *not* be expected to demonstrate proficiency with all the inflectional endings, for example, and then the derivational prefixes and suffixes, and so on. Rather, young children should receive instruction and guidance in understanding how these various word parts can be used in reading and spelling—as well as in spoken language if needed, of course.

The snapshot provides space for teachers to identify the morphemes that are explicitly taught and to document children's skill with both reading and spelling words that include those morphemes. Learners would be considered to be proficient with reading and/or spelling taught morphemes when they demonstrate the ability to accurately and effortlessly read or spell words that include those morphemes in meaningful contexts. For inflectional morphemes, children would be considered to be *proficient* in reading when their word reading attempts consistently include the acceptable pronunciation of the inflectional morpheme. For example, when children read single-syllable words like *played* accurately rather than as a two-syllable word (i.e., *play-ed*), it suggests that they, at least implicitly, understand that the *ed* is acting as a past-tense marker and therefore they pronounced the word as it would be pronounced in spoken language. Similarly, when they spell a word like played as *playd* or *plad*, it suggests that they do not yet understand how the past tense is represented in print—as both of the latter spellings are phonologically acceptable (all the phonemes have been represented) but morphologically incorrect.

In the primary grades, most children will not likely reach a point where they might be considered to be "proficient" with morphology in written language contexts. However, because at least rudimentary skill with morphology is so important to the word-solving process, we include the snapshot items to remind teachers to be attentive, both instructionally and observationally, to children's ability to make use of morphemic elements in their reading and spelling.

Notice that, on the snapshot, we make a distinction between "regular" inflectional suffixes that are pronounced the same way regardless of the spelling of the word to which they are bound and "conditional" inflectional suffixes which are pronounced differently depending on the word to which they are bound. The remaining affixes listed on the snapshot are generally pronounced the same way regardless of the spelling of the word to which they are bound.

Instruction to Support Reading and Writing Words with More Than One Meaningful Part

In recent years, there has been a growing recognition of the role of morphology in the development of word reading, reading comprehension, and spelling skills (Levesque et al., 2021) and successful efforts have been made to enhance young children's morphological awareness. These efforts have been associated with improved reading comprehension, word-reading, and spelling skills (e.g., Apel, Brimo, Diehm, & Apel, 2013). In systematic reviews of the literature on interventions to promote morphological awareness skills, Bowers, Kirby, and Deacon (2010) and Carlisle and Goodwin (2014) suggest that morphological knowledge plays a greater role in children's spelling, word reading, and vocabulary knowledge in the upper elementary grades than in the primary grades. However, Berninger, Abbott, Nagy, and Carlisle (2010) studied first through sixth graders and found that the greatest growth in morphological awareness occurred in the first three grades. Although these findings do not directly address the optimal timeline for morphological interventions, there is no debate about the importance of helping learners become morphologically aware. In terms of word reading, Kearns and Whaley (2019) suggest that morphemes are helpful for two reasons. First, they are frequent word parts that are usually longer than graphemes. Therefore, when students divide words into known morphemes, there are fewer parts than with graphemes—thereby reducing the decoding/encoding challenge. Second, morphemes are meaning-bearing units and, therefore, support comprehension (Kearns & Whaley, 2019, p. 220). Research indicates that, at least for older children, teaching students to identify and manipulate morphemes can improve vocabulary and comprehension (Goodwin & Ahn, 2013). While our current focus is on helping learners accurately identify printed words, there is a clear value beyond accurate word identification.

Further, in a review of intervention studies, Bowers et al. (2010) reported that morphological interventions had a greater impact when offered in small-group contexts and with children who were experiencing literacy learning difficulties. In alignment with these findings, in the ISA, we have found it useful to explicitly teach how to read and spell some of the most frequently occurring bound morphemes during the segment of a lesson that focuses on the development of skill with the alphabetic and orthographic code (see Chapter 17). Then, when children encounter words with known prefixes and/or suffixes in their reading, we encourage them to notice the affixes and temporarily ignore them (possibly by covering them with their finger[s]) while attempting to identify the base word. Often, when children are at a point where they are reading materials that include affixes, they quickly recognize the base word when the affixes have been removed. Once the base word is identified, they can add the prefix and/or suffix back in and, ideally, confirm that the word makes sense in the context in which it is encountered.

Won't Taking Off the *-ed* or *-es* Cause Problems for Long-Vowel Words?

Teachers sometimes worry that by encouraging children to temporarily ignore inflectional endings, we might impede children's ability to accurately identify words with long-vowel sounds. For example, if you ignore the *ed* in the word *named,* you'll pronounce it as *nam.* This is certainly true, but, as we discuss in Chapter 12, thinking about the sounds represented by the letters in a word is only part of the process of identifying an unfamiliar word. Readers also need to think about whether the hypothesized pronunciation is a real word that makes sense in context. If not, the reader needs to do some additional thinking by, for example, trying a different pronunciation for some of the letters (i.e., employ the set for variability), especially the vowels.

Derivational Morphemes

While our focus in this chapter is mostly on helping children learn to read and write individual words that are composed of multiple morphemes and/or syllables, clearly children need to know the meanings of the words they are attempting to read and write. Therefore, in what follows we discuss the meaning of derivational morphemes, as these are likely to be less familiar to young children than are the inflectional morphemes.

COMMON PREFIXES

Table 11.2 lists the most common prefixes, which account for 97% of prefixed words in printed school English (Honig, Diamond, & Gutlohn, 2018). The table also provides the meanings and examples of the prefixes.

As the examples suggest, words that include these prefixes can be easily worked into many conversations across the instructional day in both casual conversation (e.g., "Let me *retie* your shoe.") and more instructionally focused situations—for example, in the context of a read-aloud (e.g., "Who *disagrees* with the decision the character made?"). On occasion, the teacher might be explicit about the meaning of the prefix if children do not seem to understand. Although these prefixes

TABLE 11.2. Common Prefixes, Their Meanings, and Examples

Prefix	Meaning	Examples
dis-	not, opposite of	*disappear, disagree, dislike*
in-, im-, il-, ir-	not	*inaccurate, impossible, illogical, irreplaceable*
re-	again	*retie, redo, replay*
un-	not	*unappealing, unlikely, unbelievable*

may not come up in the texts that young children read themselves, helping them understand the meanings of them in conversational contexts will prepare children to understand prefixed words when they do encounter them in print in the future.

COMMON DERIVATIONAL SUFFIXES

Derivational suffixes change a word's part of speech. For example, adding *-ly* changes an adjective to an adverb (*nice–nicely*), and adding *-ness* changes an adjective to a noun (*happy–happiness*). Although young children likely do not yet have a strong grasp of the terminology for parts of speech (nouns, verbs, adjectives, etc.), they do have an implicit understanding that how words are used in a sentence can change. Most children who are familiar with the variant of English typically encountered in school and in books have fairly decent syntactic awareness, or at least knowledge of most syntactic structures, by age 5. They can't explain it, but they do know how to properly use it. For purposes of word solving and vocabulary growth, this implicit understanding does help them to recognize these suffixes as orthographic "chunks" so that they can, again, temporarily ignore them while attempting to decode the base word. Table 11.3 lists common derivational suffixes.

While the derivational suffixes listed are fairly common, the four *most common* suffixes according to Honig et al. (2018) are three of the inflectional suffixes (*-ed, -s* or *-es*, and *-ing*) and the derivational suffix *-ly*. These four suffixes are reported to account for 97% of the suffixed words in printed school English.

Teaching Children to Use Meaningful Word Parts

As noted, the first suffixes children are likely to encounter in their reading are inflectional suffixes that mark plurals—for example, *blocks* (/s/), *dogs* (/z/), *dresses* (/ĕz/)—and past-tense verbs—for example, *wanted* (/ĕd/), *looked* (/t/), *played* (/d/). It is logical to explicitly introduce plural and past-tense morphemes when children have fairly strong control of the alphabetic code and in preparation for engaging them in reading a text in which one or more of these bound morphemes will be

TABLE 11.3. Common Derivational Suffixes and Their Meanings

Suffix	Meaning	Examples
-er	a person who does an action	*builder, teacher, performer*
-ful	full of	*careful, hopeful, beautiful*
-less	without	*careless, hopeless, speechless*
-ly	in what way or manner	*sadly, happily, carefully*
-ment	action or result	*argument, agreement, excitement*
-ness	state or quality	*happiness, kindness, sickness*

encountered. In the process of teaching about these morphemes, the teacher would explain that a single word sometimes has more than one meaningful part, using, as an example, a word with a prefix or a suffix that the children will soon encounter in their reading. The teacher would present the base word[4] on a card and the prefix and/or suffix on separate cards and demonstrate how adding or removing the prefix and/or suffix changes the pronunciation and meaning. The same prefix and/or suffix can be used to modify additional base words to further illustrate the process and further familiarize children with the pronunciation and meaning of the affix. The teacher should explain that noticing the parts will help readers to puzzle out words by letting them focus on one part at a time. Children should be encouraged to notice the affix, think of how it might/would sound, and then temporarily cover it while thinking about what the rest of the word will sound like and then put the two (or more) parts of the word together. (Of course, when puzzling over a word with multiple meaningful parts in context, the children would be encouraged to also consider whether the pronunciation and meaning of the word makes sense in the context in which the word is encountered, as discussed in more detail in Chapter 12.)

In any given lesson, only one new affix would be taught. However, as new affixes are taught, previously taught affixes can be integrated into instruction to help children become automatic in noticing and interpreting them and in using them to assist in their decoding and spelling of words with multiple syllables. Word-building activities using base words and the prefixes and suffixes that have been taught can be periodically revisited until the children are quite facile in using them. For example, if the prefixes *re-* and *un-* and the suffixes *-ly, -ful, -ness, -ed, -(e)s, -er,* and *-ing* have been taught, children might use several different base words to build and read multisyllabic words. For example:

> **build**: rebuild, building, rebuilding, builder, builders
> **watch**: watches, watched, watchful, unwatchful, watchfulness
> **forgive**: forgives, forgiving, forgiveness
> **event**: events, eventful, uneventful
> **swim**: swims, swimming, swimmer
> **bright**: brighter, brightly, brightness
> **happy**: happily, happiness, unhappy, unhappily

Early on, for instructional purposes, individual morphemes might be presented on cards and the children would be engaged in word building and word reading. For example, for the base word *build*, children might be asked to make the words *builder, building, rebuild, rebuilding.*

---

[4] When first beginning to teach about suffixes, it is best to avoid using words in which a spelling change in the base word would be required when adding the suffix (e.g., happy—happily), as this adds a layer of complexity. Later, of course, spelling changes to the base word will need to be explained and practiced.

build   er   ing   re

Note that, for some words that end in a vowel, such as happy, a change in the spelling of the base word (free morpheme) is often required. Such words would not be introduced until learners are familiar with adding suffixes that do not require a change in the final letter.

When children are at the point where they are reading words composed of more than one morpheme—which will happen fairly early for the past tense (*-ed*), plural (*-s* or *-es*), and progressive (*-ing*) morphemes—they should be periodically reminded of the utility of thinking about, and temporarily ignoring, suffixes while they puzzle through base words (see the "break the word into smaller parts" strategy in Chapter 12). When they write, they should also be periodically reminded to use the meaningful word parts they have learned.

Morphological Awareness and Linguistic Diversity

There are, of course, multiple ways in which differences in spoken language impact learners' ability to decode and understand inflected forms of English words. For teachers who do not have expertise related to multilanguage learning (ML) instruction, it is important to note that orthographic markers of meaningful distinctions such as number (e.g., singular and plural nouns) and verb tense (e.g., present, past, future) vary tremendously across languages and differ from English. For example, in Spanish, aspects of verb tense are typically marked within the word, whereas in English, certain aspects of tense are represented in unique words. For example, in English the present tense *I speak* would be translated as *hablo* in Spanish, and the future tense (*I shall/will speak*) would be translated as *hablaré*—no extra words, just a within-word modification.

Teachers who are teaching large concentrations of a given language group are encouraged to learn as much as they can about the home language of their students and to consider those language differences in planning and implementing instruction. For example, it would likely be useful to be explicit about the differences in the way nuances in meaning are expressed between the two languages. For example, in explaining the future tense example above, the teacher might say: "In Spanish, *hablo* and *hablaré* tell about speaking now (*hablo*) and speaking later (*hablaré*). So just the word is changed. In English, an extra word would be added instead (*I speak, I will speak*)." If teachers are not able to access information about how the morphological components of their students' home languages may differ from English, they should, nevertheless, attempt to note which constructions tend to be difficult for students and provide explicit instruction related to those constructions.

Breaking Words into Parts That Are Not Meaningful

Many multisyllabic words are made up of syllables that do not have individual meanings. Readers can often find these syllables and decode the word if they attempt one or more of the following:

- Attempt to determine the likely number of syllables by counting the vowels—excluding the final (silent) *e* as in *alone, inside, become* and counting vowel teams (e.g., *ai, ea, ie, oi, ue*) as single vowels.
- Be flexible with the vowel sounds and the sounds of *c, g,* and *s.* Try different pronunciations for the vowels—try the long and short sound of the vowels alternately until a word that fits the context emerges. It may be helpful to tell/remind children that all the vowels sometimes represent the /uh/ (schwa) sound, as in *about, effect, other* (as these words are pronounced in everyday conversation).
- Cover up and temporarily ignore prefixes and suffixes. Decode the base word and then add the affixes back on.
- For words with doubled consonants, break the word between the two consonants and decode each part (syllable).
- For words with two different consonants together in the middle of the word, try breaking the word between the consonants (e.g., *bas/ket, chim/ney, ser/vant*).
- For words with the *consonant + -le* syllable structure (e.g., *ma-ple, trou-ble, scram-ble*), go back one letter from the *-le* and decode that consonant plus the *-le* as a syllable pronounced with the preceding consonant plus /ul/. Decode the first syllable and then decode the *consonant + -le* syllable. For example, for the word *table* the reader would decode the second syllable as bul and then connect it with the first syllable.
- For words that include spelling elements that are not very decodable (e.g., *tion, sion, ture*), the teacher could provide the pronunciation (e.g., "That part says *shun*" or "That part says *chur*") and explain that it will be seen in lots of words and is, therefore, useful to remember.

Decoding Multisyllabic Words

To initially make the approaches described above explicit, challenging words that are encountered while reading text can be written out and analyzed briefly in isolation. It is useful to illustrate that multiple approaches can be applied together in attempting to decode a multisyllable word. It is also important to stress the need to think of words that would make sense in the context and to always confirm that the decoded word fits the context. For example, when reading a text about forest fires, early in the text the word *ignite* might be encountered. At that point, the meaning of the word would be explained. If the word *reignited* is encountered later in the text, the teacher could take advantage of this complex word to demonstrate for students how they might go about figuring out multisyllabic, multimorphemic words.

For instance, the teacher might start by writing the word on a dry-erase board and then explain a process for figuring out the meaning. For example, the teacher might say:

"There are a lot of things we can try when we come to a puzzling word like this. Let's start by looking for any prefixes or suffixes we know. I see *re,* which we know means *again.* I also see an *ed* ending, which probably means it is something that happened in the past. I am going to cover up those two word parts with my fingers while I look at the rest of the word. So, now I've got *i–g–n–i–t.* Hmmm. If I'm still not sure what the word is, I can try breaking it apart between the two consonants. And then I can think about what the two parts will sound like. The first part is probably *ig,* because there is just that one vowel there. The second part could be *nit* or *nite,* because sometimes when we take the *ed* ending off it is really just the *d* that needed to come off. First, I'll try *ignit, ignit.* . . . That doesn't sound like a word I've heard before. So, let's try *ignite.* Ah! That's a word I know! The author already used that word in this book when talking about how the fire got started. *Ignite* means to start a fire. Now, I need to put the other parts of the word back on. I'll start with the ending [uncovers the *-ed*]. So, now I've got *ignited.* That means it already happened. If I put the *re* back on, I have the word *reignited. Re* means again. The fire reignited—Oh! It started again!"

Tips for Breaking Apart Words

Figure 11.2 presents a "Tip Sheet" to assist learners in puzzling through multisyllabic words based on the guidance just discussed. We suggest introducing the tip sheet once learners have been taught about the multiple ways in which longer words might be broken down in attempts to arrive at their pronunciation. This tool would be appropriate for use by students who have fairly strong decoding skills and who are encountering many multisyllabic words in their reading. Teachers of middle elementary level readers who are still experiencing word-solving difficulties have also found it useful (Gelzheiser et al., 2019). At that level, the tip sheet is typically provided as a laminated bookmark that students use as needed when encountering word-solving challenges. A reproducible version of the tip sheet can be found on this book's companion website (see the box at the end of the table of contents).

Tips for Breaking Apart Words

Every syllable must have at least one vowel!	
Be **flexible** with the **sounds for a, e, i, o, u, c,** and **g**.	
Cover up **prefixes and suffixes**.	unwanted
Try breaking a word **between doubled consonants**.	stub/born
Try breaking a word between two different consonants.	en/ter/tain
Consonant + **le** syllable type.	ta-ble pud-dle

FIGURE 11.2. Tips for breaking words apart. From Gelzheiser et al. (2019). Copyright © 2019 The Guilford Press. Reprinted by permission.

Documenting Children's Progress— Breaking Words Apart

Once the *Tips for Breaking Words Apart* resource has been introduced, teachers may wish to document children's understanding of and skill with using the various *Tips*. Because children who are routinely encountering multisyllable words in their reading may not demonstrate their word-solving efforts in an explicit way, teachers may need to question children about their efforts both while they are puzzling over a word and once they have identified a word (accurately or not). For example, when a student hesitates over an unfamiliar multisyllabic word, the teacher might ask, "What can you do to figure out that word? What *Tips* could you try?" The teacher might simultaneously point to the *Tips* chart and, if need be, identify a specific *Tip* that might be productively applied in solving a particular word. When a student hesitates and then accurately identifies a multisyllable word, the teacher might ask the student to tell which tips were utilized during word solving. As discussed in Chapter 12, which focuses on the process of word solving more generally, conversations about the processes/approaches to word solving should only occur until the student is quite effective and independent in applying these skills and strategies.

Students' understanding of the *Tips* and how to use them can be documented using the snapshot provided in Figure 11.3. As noted above, the *Tip* sheet might not be introduced until after the various ways of breaking words apart have been introduced and practiced a bit. (Alternatively, teachers may wish to post each *Tip* once it has been introduced.) Learners would be considered to be at a *beginning* point with regard to a particular *Tip* when the *Tip* has been introduced and its application illustrated and practiced a bit. A learner who is successful in using a particular *Tip* when prompted to do so, or who spontaneously does so but only intermittently, would be considered to be *developing* relative to the *Tip*. Readers at beginning and developing points relative to the application of the *Tips* would benefit from periodic discussion of and guided practice in utilizing the *Tips* they do not yet use reliably. Students who routinely solve unfamiliar multisyllabic words without teacher guidance can probably be considered to be proficient relative to particular *Tips* that seem applicable. However, it is important to note that readers at this point in development, in all likelihood, draw on a variety of skills and strategies during the process of word solving (see Chapter 12) with breaking words into their component syllables being only one of the strategies employed.

Note that two of the *Tips* have application to spelling as well as word solving (*Every syllable must have at least one vowel* and the *Consonant +le syllable type*). Student writing samples can be reviewed to determine whether there is evidence of application of the *Tips* and, if so, whether application is intermittent (*developing*) or routine (*proficient*).

With regard to spelling, development/proficiency would be demonstrated if the child spells each syllable, including letters that could *reasonably* represent each of the phonemes and including a vowel letter in each syllable. For example, spelling the two-syllable word *trouble* as TRUBUL would be considered reasonably (or justifiably) spelled for current purposes because all the phonemes are represented and there is a vowel in each syllable. This snapshot is not intended to serve as an assessment of conventional spelling. Recall that a major purpose of group snapshots is to help teachers identify areas in which additional instructional emphasis appears to be needed. In the case of spelling multisyllabic words, a major objective is for the children to understand that every syllable needs to contain at least one vowel letter.

Group Snapshot—Breaking Words Apart (See Tips for Breaking Words Apart [Figure 11.2, p. 278])							
Student names							
Every syllable must have at least one vowel!	Reading						
	Spelling						
Be flexible with the sounds for a, e, i, o, u, c, and g.	Reading						
Cover up prefixes and suffixes.	Reading						
Try breaking words between doubled consonants.	Reading						
Try breaking a word between two different consonants.	Reading						
Consonant +le syllable type.	Reading						
	Spelling						

Key:

◻ *B—Beginning* indicates that instruction has addressed the objective but that the child has only a preliminary understanding or capability with regard to that particular objective.

⊠ *D—Developing* indicates that the child has some understanding of the objective but does not reliably demonstrate that understanding or capability or is not yet automatic (fluent) with the skill.

⊠ *P—Proficient* indicates that the child reliably and automatically demonstrates the understanding or capability.

FIGURE 11.3. Group snapshot for breaking words apart.

Is There Value in Teaching the Six Syllable Types?

In discussions about assisting children with decoding multisyllabic words, we are sometimes asked about the value of teaching children the six syllable types that characterize written English. The six types are:

1. Open: a syllable that ends in a vowel sound, such as in the words *say* and *me* or the first syllable in *robot*. They are referred to as *open syllables* because there is no consonant sound to "close" the syllable.
2. Closed: a syllable that ends with a consonant sound, as in the words *house* and *run* or the first syllable in *lemon*.
3. Vowel–consonant–*e* (VC*e*): a syllable with a long-vowel sound that is signaled by the presence of the silent-*e*, as in the words *time* and *race* and in the second syllable in *outside*.
4. *r*-controlled vowel: a syllable that includes an *r*-controlled vowel such as in the words *part* and *for* or in the first syllable of the word *person*.
5. Vowel team: a syllable in which two or more letters together represent a single vowel sound as in *friend, boat, sleigh,* and *bough*.
6. Consonant + -*le*: a syllable that involves the pronunciation of the consonant sound that precedes the *le* plus /ul/, as in the words *little* and *table*.

All six of these syllable types focus on the pronunciation of the vowel sound. While we encourage teachers to explicitly teach skills and strategies that support accurate pronunciation of the vowel sounds in words, we have not advised teachers to explicitly teach young children the six syllable types. It is not clear that thinking about syllable types will be as useful or as generalizable as the approaches to decoding vowels that we do teach. For example, for the words *robot* and *lemon,* knowing about open and closed syllables will not reliably assist the child in determining the proper pronunciation of the first vowel letter. The suggested guidance is to teach students to break a longer word between the first vowel and the consonant (*ro|bot*). With this breakdown, the first syllable would have the long-*o* sound, and the word is apt to be accurately decoded. However, for the word *lemon* (*le|mon*), this guidance would not result in accurate identification. Advocates of using syllable types would guide children to be flexible about where to break the word (before or after a single medial consonant). To us, this seems like an extra step that may serve to slow the process of word solving down.

   Children who have learned to be flexible with vowel sounds (as discussed in detail in Chapters 10 and 12) will know that if their first attempt at a word doesn't result in a real word that fits the context in which it was encountered, they should try the other common pronunciation(s) of the vowel(s). Similarly, flexibility with vowel sounds will assist children in negotiating vowel-team-type syllables. In this instance, it is important for children to know that when two vowels are together in a word, usually only one vowel sound is heard. Regarding *r*-controlled vowels, we do think it is useful to teach them (as indicated by our providing key words for them in Chapter 10; see Figure 10.7, p. 260). However, we see no additional utility in teaching children that there is a specific syllable type for them.

We do, of course, teach the VC*e* generalization (as discussed in Chapter 10), because lots of practice with the application of that generalization is one way we help children to become fluent and flexible with the vowel sounds. Finally, we do explicitly teach the consonant + -*le* syllable type, as that is the only way to explain to learners why the second syllables in words such as *little* and *table* end with a sound other than what might be expected.

Research on Teaching Students about Syllable Types

While some programs and approaches encourage teachers to explicitly teach the six syllable types, along with syllable division rules, Kearns (2020) states that "there has been no study to determine whether the recommended patterns work consistently" (p. S146). In addressing this concern, he used a large set of words with two or more syllables. Kearns investigated the frequency with which the pronunciation of the vowels in open and closed syllables "followed the rules" that are sometimes taught:

- The vowel will have its long sound in words with a vowel-consonant-vowel (VCV) pattern in which the syllable would be divided between the first vowel and the consonant (V|CV—as in *robot*).
- The vowel will have its short sound in words with a vowel-consonant-consonant-vowel (VCCV) pattern in which the syllable would be divided between the two consonants (VC|CV—as in *happy*).

Although the "rule" did work for some words in Kearns's analysis, there were many for which it did not. Consider, for example, *robin* (which has a VCV structure, but the syllable breaks after the consonant rather than before (*rob|in*), or the word *about* in which the letter *a* composed the first syllable but represents the schwa (uh) sound. In general, Kearns's findings did not support the utility of explicitly teaching syllable types and division rules for words with two or more syllables. He expressed concern that teaching such rules would slow readers down and distract them from the meaning of the text they are reading. Indeed, Kearns concluded, and we agree, that teaching syllable division rules is a time-consuming process that can turn the learner's attention away from a focus on making sense of the text being read.

In a review of several approaches to teaching students to break long words into smaller parts, Kearns et al. (2020) noted that all effective approaches have two key features. They teach students that vowels have multiple pronunciations, which requires a flexible approach to word identification. In addition, flexibility with vowel sounds is paired with attention to morphemes (the meaning units of words). Thus, instead of a syllable rules approach, Kearns (2020) advises attending to morphemes and teaching learners to be flexible in their decoding attempts—trying different pronunciations for some of the letters, especially the vowels, until a real word that fits the context is identified. This is our advice as well, and we detail instruction aligned with this approach in Chapter 12.

Spelling Multisyllabic Words

As noted in Chapter 5, it is fairly easy for even beginning readers to detect the number of syllables in a spoken word. This skill can be put to good use when children attempt to spell words with more than one syllable, especially when children learn that every syllable includes a vowel sound and, therefore, every syllable in a written word must have at least one vowel letter. Early in the process of teaching children to spell multisyllabic words, we would start by having the children count the number of syllables in the word they are attempting to write and draw a line for each syllable. They would then be encouraged to spell each syllable, being mindful that each syllable needs to have at least one vowel letter. They can also be encouraged to refer to their key word and/or word family charts if they need help in deciding which vowel letter(s) to use. Spellings constructed in this way will certainly not always be conventional. However, they will look more literate and will be more interpretable for the writer's audience. Thus, for example, a child who hasn't had this guidance might write BUTFL for *beautiful* (using the letter *t* to represent the syllable /tĭ/ and /tē/, respectively). A child who had been taught to count the syllables and to include a vowel letter in each syllable, on the other hand, might produce BUTIFUL, which, although still not the conventional spelling, is more likely to convey the child's meaning.

Decoding by Analogy to Known Words

When proficient readers encounter an unfamiliar word, they typically do not consciously engage in the types of analysis discussed in this and previous chapters in Part II. Rather, they are likely to identify the word by analogy to known words (e.g., the word *prattle* would be read effortlessly by analogy to words such as *battle* and *cattle*). Teachers should be alert for opportunities to move children toward this type of word-solving approach. For example, when a child encounters a word that is unfamiliar but very similar to one or more words that the child knows well, the teacher might comment, "You can figure out that word easily if you think about how similar it looks to. . . ." Initially, the teacher would name the similar word. Over time, the teacher would reduce the support by asking, rather than telling, "Can you think of another word you know that looks like that one?"

KEEP IN MIND   Multisyllabic words may present a word-identification challenge, and they also often present a vocabulary challenge. It is difficult for readers to ascertain that a word has been accurately identified if there is no word in their listening vocabulary that corresponds to it. For that reason, a critical element of instruction is anticipating unfamiliar vocabulary and using it in prereading discussions.

Since children differ widely in their knowledge of vocabulary, it is important that teachers be alert to terms that may be challenging for some children and be prepared to individualize the vocabulary terms addressed. As the texts that children read become more challenging, a significant part of planning would involve the teacher's prereading of the text selection and choosing multisyllabic words that are appropriate to focus on for the purposes of decoding and building children's knowledge of word meanings.

KEY POINTS OF THIS CHAPTER

✓ A high proportion of the words children encounter in their reading are composed of more than one syllable and/or more than one meaningful part (morpheme).

✓ A relatively small number of bound morphemes account for the large majority of bound morphemes present in the multimorphemic words children encounter in their reading.

✓ Learning the meanings of inflectional and derivational affixes and how to decode them enables learners to more effectively identify and understand multisyllabic/multimorphemic words.

✓ Explicit instruction and guided practice in puzzling through multisyllabic/multimorphemic words helps learners successfully solve and ultimately learn to read such words independently.

✓ At this point, there is no strong evidence to support explicit instruction on syllable types.

✓ Learning to be flexible in assigning pronunciations to vowel graphemes can support word solving in context.

✓ Spelling of multisyllabic/multimorphemic words can be enhanced if learners begin by counting the syllables in the intended word and remembering that each syllable needs to include at least one vowel letter.

PART III

Word Learning

Introduction to Part III

In Part II, we discussed the development of foundational knowledge in relation to the English writing system. The ultimate value in developing that knowledge is that it enables learners to quickly and accurately figure out the identities of printed words they have never read before. Accurate word identification enables the learner to begin to add those words to their sight vocabularies.

Written words that readers can identify quickly and accurately and in all contexts are said to be in the reader's *sight vocabulary* (that is, they are *sight words*). Fast and accurate word identification is critically important to comprehension for both beginning and more proficient readers because readers for whom most of the words in a text are sight words can devote most of their thinking to understanding the text rather than to figuring out the words. In this part of the book, we focus on ways to help children learn to become active and, ultimately, independent in their ability to learn to read unfamiliar printed words so well that they become part of their sight vocabularies.

Nagy and Anderson (1984) estimated that the print that students encounter in school consists of approximately 88,500 distinct word families.[1] Their definition of a word family is a group of words with clear and predictable relationships between form and meaning (e.g., *assume, assumed, assuming,* and *assumption* would all be in a single word family). Nagy and Herman (1987) estimated that the typical fifth-grade student encounters 10,000 new word families in a year. There is no way a teacher could possibly teach the huge numbers of words that students must ultimately be able to read effortlessly. The focus of this part of the book is on

---

[1]The reference here is to morphological word families, which were discussed in Chapter 11 (words that share semantic [meaning] relationships). In Chapter 9, we discussed orthographic word families—which are based on rimes (e.g., *boat, coat, float, throat*).

instructional practices that can enable learners to develop the massive sight vocabulary they need in order to become proficient readers—and, thereby, be able to devote most of their thinking to understanding/comprehending the texts they read.

Shifts in Approaches to Word Identification

It is generally agreed that there are three basic approaches individuals might use in attempting to identify a printed word: a selective cue approach, a strategic approach, and an automatic approach. Of these three, the automatic approach is the desired end goal. Words that are in a reader's sight vocabulary are identified via an automatic approach. When readers can identify most or all printed words in a text with automaticity, they are able to devote their cognitive resources to comprehending the things they read. One's automatic sight vocabulary is, for the most part, built through effective word solving while reading, with the words initially identified via a strategic approach. Helping readers develop a strategic approach to word solving is the focus of Chapter 12. A selective cue approach is the approach used by learners who are at a very beginning point in learning to read. It is an approach that we want to move them away from as quickly as possible. Below we describe each of the approaches in the order in which they appear developmentally.

A Selective Cue Approach

Before children understand how to apply phonics skills (and before they have learned much if anything about phonics) they often learn to identify a small number of printed words by attending to prominent visual cues. Often the sources of information they choose have little or nothing to do with the printed letters in the words. They may, for example, attend to the overall shape of the word, to a picture (or even a smudge) that appears on the same page as the word, to the color of the paper on which the word appears, to the location of the word on a word list, and so forth. Using these prominent cues, in many instances, will allow children to rapidly and accurately identify some words, but only if the words appear in the same context across time and/or if the children have encountered no other words with similar visual characteristics. For example, many years ago, we had a child in our clinic who, across several sessions, was able to reliably identify the word *not* when it appeared in isolation on a word card that his tutor was using for high-frequency word practice. But he was consistently unable to identify the word when it appeared in the context of a book. After much debate about what the problem might be, we finally thought to ask the child (a generally good plan when a teacher is confused by what a child does). He told us that the way he identified *not* on the word card was by the presence of a small pencil mark that appeared on that card and no other. In other words, he wasn't even looking at the word; the errant pencil mark was sufficient for him to do what he understood was expected of him—say the word *not* when that particular card was displayed. Gough, Juel, and Griffith (1992) found that attention to such selective cues was common among 4- and 5-year-olds. Most primary-grade teachers have encountered children who can identify a word in one context but not in others and have found it to be rather mysterious. Understanding children's inclinations to use selective cues helps to demystify the behavior and has implications for how words are displayed on word walls (see Chapter 13 and Glossary) and other instructional resources. For example, early primary teachers often post word-wall words on cards that highlight the shape of the word or on different colored cards or use different color markers for different words. Although these shape and color cues likely help children find particular words on the display (perhaps when they want to use the word in their writing), these cues may also lead the children to attend less thoroughly to the alphabetic and orthographic information and thus impede their ability to identify the word in other contexts. To promote literacy development, we want children to focus on the alphabetic and orthographic information, not the colors of cards or fonts.

The use of selective cues is quite natural because children who are just beginning to learn to read do not yet know what features of words are most relevant for reliable identification. In fact, the use of selective cues can be an effective way of identifying words early on if the words that are being learned are fairly distinct from one another. Further, in some cases, selective cues may completely suffice—particularly for words that are very distinctive (e.g., the word *Cheerios* on a cereal box) and that occur in limited contexts (e.g., the names of characters in Russian novels). However, as the number of written words children encounter grows, reliance on nonalphabetic cues such as the shape of the word or on very limited alphabetic information such as the first letter and the general context will lead to confusion and certainly will not lead to the ability to identify the word in other contexts going forward. Children who do not thoroughly analyze the orthographic information in the words they are learning are likely to confuse similar-looking words such as *was* and *saw*; *on* and *no*; *of, from,* and *for*; and so forth. Reliance on a selective cue approach is likely to result in stagnation in the growth of sight vocabulary and confusion about the reading process more generally. Teachers who are aware of beginning readers' inclination to rely on selective cues will, we hope, try to avoid developing or using instructional materials that provide irrelevant cues like the color, shape, and/or position of a word on a word list.

A Strategic Approach

Readers who use a strategic approach use deliberate (conscious) actions in their efforts to identify unfamiliar words. Once children have begun to learn about the alphabetic code, teachers should help them move beyond a selective cue approach to word identification. We have found it useful to explicitly teach children to use code-based and meaning-based word identification strategies and to use those strategies flexibly and interactively while engaging in word solving as they read. The ultimate goal is for initially unfamiliar words to be learned so well that they can be identified effortlessly and in all contexts in the future. That is, they become part of the reader's sight vocabulary. For this to occur, readers need to carefully analyze words in terms of both their phonological and orthographic characteristics and the way they are used in context. The instruction that children receive can play a critical role in the development of such a strategic approach (Anderson, 2009; Brown, 2003; Scanlon & Anderson, 2020). As we discuss in detail in Chapter 12, we encourage teachers in the primary grades to explicitly teach and model strategic word solving and to help children internalize the strategies that are taught so that the children, ultimately, become skilled word solvers.

An Automatic Approach

The goal of teaching children to be strategic in their attempts to identify unfamiliar words is to help them learn to read printed words so well that they become part of their sight vocabulary. Although a strategic approach to word solving may result in accurate word identification, a word would not be considered to have been learned until the child can identify the word effortlessly and in all contexts—without needing to be strategic. Being able to identify words automatically frees up the cognitive resources needed for meaning construction.

Reading Skill and Approaches to Word Identification

As children progress as readers, the proportion of words they identify using each of the three approaches described above shifts. Most children who have just begun to learn to read use a selective cue approach to identify a small number of words. As children begin to understand how the writing system works and how printed words are used to convey ideas, they develop, with appropriate instruction, guidance, and practice, the ability to be independently strategic in their word solving. At this point, most of the words they can identify while reading may be the result of using a strategic approach, although those that have been identified successfully on several previous occasions may be so familiar that they are automatically identified. Proficient readers identify nearly all the words they encounter quickly and accurately, both because many of them are part of their sight vocabularies and because, in the process of becoming proficient (which involves engaging in a great deal of reading), they have learned many of the commonly occurring spelling patterns in written English and, therefore, can decode many new words without needing to become consciously strategic. For example, many proficient readers may never have seen the word *blight*; however, none are likely to have difficulty determining how it is pronounced. Proficient readers will, on occasion, however, encounter words that require a strategic approach and perhaps even a few words (e.g., the names of certain medications) that they will identify via a selective cue approach.

The Development of Self-Teaching

Children use a strategic approach to learn nearly all the words that ultimately are added to their sight vocabularies. They effectively puzzle through and figure out the unfamiliar words they encounter while reading. Share (1995) suggests that the ability to figure out unfamiliar printed words serves as a *self-teaching mechanism* that allows readers to gradually increase their sight vocabularies through reading. This is not to suggest, of course, that correctly identifying a word just once will necessarily allow it to become part of a reader's sight vocabulary. Rather, for most words, it is through multiple encounters with and correct identifications of the words that students come to learn them to the point of automaticity. This occurs through the process of orthographic mapping as described by Ehri (2020). Orthographic mapping involves connecting the graphemes in a printed word with the phonemes in the spoken form of the word. For words that are in the learner's spoken or listening vocabulary, the process of orthographic mapping connects the printed word with its meaning. Thus, the first time readers encounter an unfamiliar printed word, they may need to devote quite a bit of effort to thinking about what the word is and how it is pronounced. On the next encounter, a little less thinking may be needed for correct identification. On each subsequent encounter, readers are likely to be able to identify the word more and more easily and fluently until, ultimately, it becomes part of their sight vocabulary and is identified effortlessly/automatically.

Exactly how a child comes to "know" a previously unfamiliar word has been the source of much debate over the years (Adams, 1990; Chall, 1967; Goodman, 1967; Pressley, 2006). While we are far from having reached scientific certainty as to how children accomplish this remarkable sight word-learning feat, there are a few points on which near unanimity exists:

- Learners need to have some degree of command of the alphabetic code—although the optimal level of detailed knowledge learners need has not been firmly established (Castles et al., 2018).
- Children need to read, read, read—as, among other things, this provides them with the opportunity to encounter (and learn to read) the many words they ultimately need to know.
- At least at early points in development, children need some guidance and feedback while they are reading to become effective word solvers. However, the amount needed varies substantially among children.
- The texts that children read need to be somewhat but not too challenging with regard to the number of unfamiliar/unknown words they encounter.

These points of agreement, however, still leave unanswered questions about what readers actually do when they encounter an unfamiliar word in context. One of the reasons this question is so difficult to answer is that what readers do depends on:

- Their knowledge and skills—both with regard to their knowledge of the workings of the writing system and their language and world/background knowledge.
- The text they are reading and the types of supports the text provides.
- The instruction they have received about how to identify unfamiliar words in text.

Characteristics of the Reader

Word solving is dependent on what readers know about the writing system and on what they know about the language and concepts presented in a particular text. Although beginning readers are often taught the most common correspondences between graphemes and their associated phonemes (as discussed in Part II), it is important to keep in mind that written English is characterized by a fair amount of variability with regard to how particular phonemes, especially vowel phonemes, are represented in print. Therefore, it is simply not possible for readers to rely exclusively on alphabetic and orthographic information for the purpose of identifying unfamiliar words because such an approach would lead to far too many inaccuracies in word solving—even for some of the most commonly occurring words, such as *have, was,* and *to* (which, if pronounced the way they are spelled, would result in words that rhyme with *brave, pass,* and *go*). Nevertheless, virtually all words consist of letters that at least partially signal their pronunciation. Therefore, knowing the most common correspondences between graphemes and phonemes and knowing how to apply that knowledge are critically important for building sight vocabulary.

Knowledge of the workings of the writing system develops gradually and, for many/most children, requires explicit instructional guidance and practice.

• Readers who are just beginning to learn about letters/graphemes and their sounds will, as noted above, make limited use of the alphabetic information in attempting to identify unfamiliar printed words encountered while reading (in context) because their alphabetic knowledge is limited and tenuous. Even if children know most or all of the common grapheme–phoneme/letter–sound correspondences, it is quite taxing to think about all the letters/graphemes in a word and the sound(s) they may represent, hold those sounds in memory, and then blend them together and say the resulting word. Moreover, the kinds of texts that beginning readers encounter may provide many other sources of information that assist them in identifying unfamiliar words. For example, in some contexts, students who are just beginning to learn to read are often given texts that are repetitive/predictable (see Figure III.1) and that have pictures that provide so much contextual support that they are able to "read" the text successfully by relying primarily on the pictures and the repetitive language. With such texts, children are typically prepared to read via shared reading (teacher-led reading) of either the entire text or the first few pages. Children reading such texts do not necessarily need to attend carefully to the letter- and word-level information provided in the text. However, such texts are very useful for helping learners understand basic print concepts and conventions (as discussed in Chapter 4). Such understanding is critical at early points in literacy development because, without such experiences, phonologically based word-solving instruction may not make sense. As of this writing, texts of this type are not used in instructional settings as commonly as they once were. There is reason to be concerned about this because, as noted,

I like to paint.   I like to slide.

FIGURE III.1. Sample pages from a beginner-level text.

they do have a role in helping novice readers learn important print concepts and conventions.

• Readers who are more familiar with the workings of an alphabetic writing system and more fluent at recalling the most common sounds associated with printed letters/graphemes will find it less taxing to look through the word for more alphabetic information about words' possible identities. Such readers do not need and likely will not profit from working with texts that make heavy use of repetitive language patterns and pictures because repetitive texts can, more or less, be read by remembering the pattern and naming the pictures. Readers who have done quite a bit of reading and who have learned to read many words automatically will begin to recognize larger units of print, such as *bl, ink,* and *er.* These larger orthographic units will allow readers to be more efficient in puzzling through unfamiliar words. Instead of having to think about each separate sound in the consonant cluster *bl,* these readers may process it as a unit or "chunk." Thus, identification of the word *blinker* might require readers at this point in development to think about only three orthographic elements (*bl, ink, er*) rather than the seven letters that make up the word.

• Regarding readers' familiarity with the language and concepts presented in the text: Readers must know the meaning of unfamiliar words encountered in text in order to know whether their attempt to identify a word is accurate. For instance, in reading a book about a farm that relies on repetitive language and pictures to make reading the text easier, children might read sentences such as

Look at the cow. Look at the horse.

quite easily because the pictures and the repetitive pattern are so helpful. However, if the text included the sentence

Look at the hen.

children might experience difficulty because the word *hen* is less likely to be in their spoken vocabulary than the word *chicken*. Even though the word *hen* is relatively easy to decode (if one knows the most common grapheme–phoneme correspondences), children will not be able to conclude that their decoding efforts are accurate if they do not know the meaning of the word.

• Readers' sensitivity to the syntactic or grammatical aspects of a text also influences their ability to successfully puzzle through unfamiliar words. For example, the sentence "I have a _____" leads grammatically sensitive readers to expect either an adjective (e.g., *big*) or a noun (e.g., *cow*). This sensitivity will limit the number of options readers might consider and/or may signal them that an initial attempt at a word is inaccurate because it doesn't fit the syntactic/grammatical constraints of the sentence.

• Readers' general knowledge (or schemas) for the circumstances or events portrayed in a text can also influence their ability to accurately identify unfamiliar words. For example, children who know a fair amount about farms are likely to more readily identify the last word in the sentence

Look at the goat.

because they know that goats are apt to be found on farms.

Characteristics of the Text

Multiple kinds of texts might be used to promote the development of early reading skill. The variety and types of texts children encounter may play a substantial role in their approach to word solving. Below we describe some of the types of texts that are often used in early reading instruction.

PREDICTABLE TEXTS

Highly predictable texts are often used in the earliest phases of reading development/instruction. These texts generally have one line of print per page, which may be only a phrase (e.g., "The cow") or a complete sentence (e.g., "Look at the cow"). Generally, only one word changes from one page to the next, and that word is frequently something that can be illustrated pictorially (see Figure III.1). The picture on each successive page highlights the word that changed. With this type of book, once children know the pattern (e.g., "I like to _____"), they can rely primarily on the pictures to "read" the entire text. One advantage of these texts for children who are just beginning to learn to read is that they help to build motivation for reading because children can generally experience the positive feeling of success when they correctly "read." Another advantage is that these texts can be used to help children learn about critical print concepts, such as the concepts of *letter* and *word* and the fact that print is processed from left to right. A significant potential disadvantage is that exclusive (and/or long-term) reliance on these kinds of texts can serve to confuse children about what it means to read because many of these texts can be "read" primarily by looking at the pictures once the reader knows the repetitive pattern. They do not require that children devote much attention to the print. Thus, extended use of such texts may well serve to slow readers' progress (Tunmer & Chapman, 1998).

DECODABLE TEXTS

Texts in which most of the words can be identified by applying knowledge of common and (previously taught) grapheme–phoneme correspondences are often referred to as *decodable texts*—because most of the words can be "sounded out." A decodable text might include a sentence like

Ben and Jen pet the cat.

In this sentence, all the words except *the* can be decoded (if one knows the commonly taught grapheme–phoneme correspondences for the individual letters). The text, supported by appropriate illustrations, might continue:

The cat sits. Ben sits. Jen sits. Jen pets the cat. Ben pets the cat.

The advantage of this kind of text is that it provides practice with using the alphabetic code to decipher words. Such texts will be most useful when there is a match between the grapheme–phoneme relationships previously taught and the decoding elements that are encountered in the text. A potential disadvantage is that the structure of the sentences in some such texts tends to be quite different from typical spoken and written language (e.g., "Ben sits. Jen sits."), which may make it difficult for children to confirm that they have read a sentence correctly. Currently, as compared to texts that are not so phonologically constrained, there is no evidence that such texts are more effective in promoting reading comprehension than texts that are less phonologically constrained (Price-Mohr & Price, 2017, 2018; Pugh, Kearns, & Hiebert, 2023). However, given the utility of providing learners the opportunity to apply phonics skills that have been explicitly taught, providing them with texts in which newly taught phonics skills will be useful makes sense, particularly at the early stages of reading development, when students are first learning to apply the alphabetic code (Castles at al., 2018). But this type of text should *not* be the only type that beginning readers have the opportunity to read and, ideally, the decodable texts that are offered would be comprehensible/meaningful—not all of them are.

Early Sight Word Readers

Many high-frequency words are not entirely decodable, and they often occupy roles in sentences that make them hard to identify using contextual information. Therefore, these words are often given special instructional attention—as they should be. Several publishers have developed "sight word readers" to help build automaticity with these words. These materials are intended to help make these frequently occurring words part of children's sight vocabularies. However, sight word readers are not all alike. Indeed, some series consist of books that look quite like the predictable texts described earlier. Thus, the book *The Farm*, described in that section, contains text that repeatedly uses the phrase "Look at the _____." *Look, at,* and *the* are all high-frequency words. As noted above, in reading this text, beginning readers may attend very little to the printed words once they know the pattern, and therefore reading this text may not help them learn these high-frequency words. Although many series devoted to the teaching of high-frequency words feature predictable patterns, we are aware of at least one series, published by The Short Books (1999; *www.myshortbooks.com*), that varies the language structure in a way that encourages more careful attention to the individual words. These texts use a few high-frequency words over and over in the context of a single book, but the words are used in slightly different syntactic structures. As a result, readers need to focus more carefully on the words in order to read the text; such books seem more likely to help children build high-frequency sight vocabulary. For example, the book *The Farm* could be rewritten as

Look at the cow. Look at the horse. Look! The pig. The cat. Look, look, look!

In this version, the reader would likely still rely on the pictures to name the animals. However, the lack of a pattern would require readers to attend more carefully to the high-frequency words. As a further illustration, Figure III.2 presents two versions of the book *See My Pets,* only one of which is likely to help children learn the high-frequency words that are utilized.

More Advanced Sight Word Readers

For children who are a bit more advanced in their reading skills but who are having difficulty learning high-frequency words, we have found that books that include many repetitions of very-high-frequency words help to facilitate the development of skill with these words. Books by Margaret Hillert, for example, are particularly helpful in this regard. Several of her books involve retellings of fairy tales such as Cinderella and Hansel and Gretel. Because these books emphasize the use of high-frequency words, the language patterns are far from natural. For example, the book entitled *Not I, Not I* (Hillert, 2017, p. 19), reads

Here I go. Away, away. Can you come? Can you help?

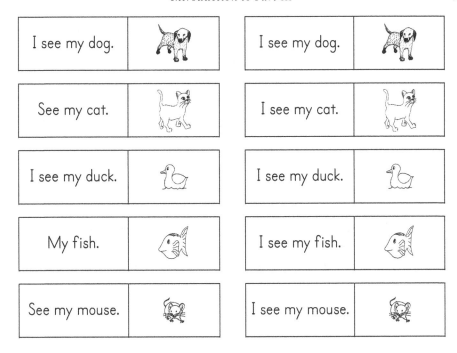

FIGURE III.2. Two renditions of a book called *See My Pets*. The version on the left is much more likely to help children learn the words *I, see,* and *my* than is the version on the right. From Scanlon and Anderson (2010). Copyright © 2010 The International Literacy Association. Reprinted by permission.

However, because these books tell stories, some of which are apt to be familiar to children (or that may be made familiar through read-alouds of the originals), and because they look like small chapter books, the books are more appealing and engaging for children than might be expected. We have observed that many children who are initially slow to develop high-frequency sight vocabulary show rapid gains in this regard when provided with the opportunity to read some of these books. This happens, we think, because of the frequent repetition of high-frequency words across many pages and in different types of sentence structures.

STRATEGY-PROMOTING TEXTS

For readers at an early point in development, *strategy-promoting texts*, as we use the term, are those that involve some ambiguity in terms of the pictures included in the text and therefore require children to pay more attention to the print than they otherwise might. For example, the text illustrated in Figure III.2 (above) has a few pictures that could not be accurately identified simply by relying on (naming) the picture (*dog/puppy, duck/bird, mouse/rat*). We don't include *cat/kitten* here because both words begin with the /k/ phoneme and therefore either label provided would offer at least suggestive evidence that children were attending to the beginning letter when identifying that word. (Children transitioning from the prealphabetic to the partial alphabetic phase, and who are learning important print concepts through reading books such as these, are likely to attend only to the beginning letter when attempting to identify an unknown word in context.)

We have found books with some ambiguous pictures to be useful in moving young learners toward greater reliance on alphabetic information in their reading. In the illustration provided in Figure III.2, children at an early point in reading development would need to attend to the print to determine the exact word for several of the pictures. For example, in the book depicted in the right side of the figure, to confidently read the word duck in "I see my duck" (as opposed to "I see my bird"), a reader would need to think about at least three different sources of information: the printed word *duck*, the repetitive pattern in the book, and the picture. Note that readers at this point of development would not have the phonics skills needed to process the entire word. We have found that books with the occasional ambiguous picture are particularly conducive to promoting the interactive use of a variety of information sources for word solving, while also providing opportunities for students to begin to apply the letter–sound associations they are learning in meaningful contexts.

In our work with beginning readers, we have found use for all the kinds of texts described above. The highly predictable and patterned books are particularly useful for children who know little about how the writing system works as they help them to learn about important print concepts and conventions. Decodable books are useful in helping children understand the application of the phonics skills they are learning. However, we would not advise using decodable texts exclusively for extended periods of time for fear that children will adopt an attitude toward reading that is exclusively code-focused. Because so many words in English are not entirely decodable and because beginning readers have limited command of the alphabetic code, it is important for children to learn to use other sources of information to check and confirm their initial decoding attempts. By doing so, beginning readers are better able to explore a variety of texts that are of interest to them and are not restricted to the decodable texts being used to align with phonics instruction. We have found that some children are slow to develop automaticity with high-frequency words. For these children, some series of sight word readers seems to be especially useful.

In our early intervention efforts, we have turned to strategy-promoting texts most frequently, and many kindergarten and first-grade classroom teachers have also found them helpful for the broad spectrum of children they teach. From our perspective, these texts capitalize on the advantages provided by many of the other kinds of texts we have described here, but do not suffer from their potential disadvantages. At present, many new series of books are being published for beginning readers; these new offerings are largely of the decodable variety. We encourage teachers and others responsible for purchasing reading materials to carefully evaluate the texts being purchased, with an eye toward texts that, like the strategy-promoting texts described previously, address multiple facets of reading instruction and development. Even within the category of decodable texts, there is a wide range in quality, with some much more engaging and supportive of meaning construction than others. We are glad to see the overall quality of decodable texts improving, and we expect the available options to continue to grow in the coming years.

Characteristics of Instruction

In addition to the characteristics of the child and the characteristics of the texts, the other major factor that influences children's ability to build their sight vocabulary is the instruction that guides their thinking about word solving. Whereas some children seem to learn to word-solve easily, without much instructional guidance, others need explicit guidance and extended opportunities for guided practice to become proficient word solvers. As Gerald Duffy (2003) puts it in his book *Explaining Reading*:

> Some students struggle with reading because they lack information about what they are trying to do and how to do it. They look around at their fellow students who are learning to read easily and say to themselves, "How are they doing that?" In short, they are mystified about how to do what other students seem to do with ease. (p. 9)

Because many children who experience difficulty with learning to read have particular difficulty with learning to use the alphabetic and orthographic code, schools and teachers often respond to these difficulties by emphasizing decoding strategies to the near exclusion of the other sources of word-solving information that texts provide. As a result, when these children encounter a word that is not fully decodable—a word such as *done,* for example, which, when decoded, would rhyme with *bone*—they have no other problem-solving strategies at their disposal. They are stuck. They have made no progress toward adding the word *done* to their sight vocabulary, and their ability to comprehend the remaining text may be limited as a result.

On the other hand, some instructional approaches encourage children to rely primarily on the meaningful context in which a word occurs when attempting to solve unfamiliar words. Children are directed to attend to the alphabetic information provided in the word primarily to confirm their prediction of what the word is. In fact, many children have been taught to think of a word that would make sense in the context in which the unfamiliar word is encountered, and then check the letters to see if they are consistent with their "guess." Teachers who subscribe to this approach might consider a match on the first letter to be satisfactory. Thus, for example, in reading the book *The Farm,* suppose a child reads the page that says "Look at the cow" as "Look at the calf" because the child knows a lot about cows, and the particular cow pictured looks like a young animal to the child. By some instructional philosophies, this error would be considered acceptable and would provide evidence that the reader was accessing the important sources of information for word identification. Further, because such an error did not substantially change the meaning of the text, teachers aligned with this instructional approach might decide that there was no value in redirecting the child's thinking on this particular word. However, children who make such an error have made little progress toward adding the word *cow* to the set of words they can identify easily. Thus, the next time the word *cow* is encountered, it will be no more familiar to them than the first time they encountered it.

Children who are reliably able to use the beginning letter in a word to guide their identification attempts are ready to learn how to use more of the available alphabetic information to word-solve. Directing such children to consider both the beginning and ending letters in the word *cow,* as well as the general context and pictorial information, would help to disconfirm *calf* and encourage children to think about other possible identities for the word. Most likely, this guidance would lead to accurate identification of the word in this particular example.

In the ISA, we explicitly teach word-solving strategies that are intended to help children negotiate such trouble spots by encouraging the use of as much of the alphabetic information as they are ready to handle, in combination with the contextual information that is available (including sentential context and pictures). Although there is little research that explicitly evaluates the specific effects of our approach to teaching word-solving strategies, because in most of our studies it has always been only one component of the larger instructional approach, testimonials from both classroom and intervention teachers suggest that it is an extremely important and powerful component and may be *the* most important contribution that the ISA makes to teachers' effectiveness with children who experience literacy learning difficulties. In a 2009 study, Anderson compared the effects of teaching intervention teachers about just the content of the material covered in Part II of this text (Understanding Print and the English [Alphabetic] Writing System) or just the content covered in Chapter 12 (Strategic Word Solving). Anderson found that first-grade readers whose intervention teachers learned about the strategic word-solving component outperformed students whose teachers learned the phonics content on measures of word identification and oral reading accuracy. (Scanlon & Anderson, 2020, provided a summary of the theory and evidence related to our approach to word-solving instruction.) In general, we conclude that while alphabetics/phonics knowledge is essential, it may not be sufficient for students to become accurate and fluent word solvers. Additional strategies that attend to the meaning in conjunction with the print are pivotal to reading achievement.

Although most of the words that children ultimately learn to identify will be learned through effective word solving while reading, we encourage teachers to explicitly teach and provide practice with some of the most frequently occurring words (e.g., *have, the, was*) because these words are often not entirely decodable and are difficult to identify strategically. Further, because they occur so frequently, being able to identify them allows children to be more strategic in identifying other unfamiliar words. In Chapter 12, we discuss ways to promote the development of strategic word solving, and in Chapter 13 we discuss approaches to teaching high-frequency words. The ordering of these two chapters is not intended to suggest that teaching children word-identification strategies precedes the teaching of high-frequency words. Rather, teachers would address the two types of word-learning instruction more or less simultaneously and would be guided by the texts the children will be reading.

CHAPTER 12

Strategic Word Solving, Word Identification, and Word Learning

How do a bunch of curves and lines go from being totally meaningless to becoming meaningful—interesting, informative, and moving? Think about it. . . . Did you have to think about *how* to identify any of the individual words as you read the previous sentence? Probably not. In all likelihood, the printed words "registered" in your mind much like spoken words do—requiring virtually no cognitive effort—at the word level. (Of course, comprehending the message, rather than accurately identifying the words, is variably challenging—and dependent on one's interest, motivation, background knowledge, and so on.) In Part II of this book we talked about the foundational skills that learners use to translate print into meaningful communication. In this chapter, we focus on how learners get to the point where they can effortlessly read the tens of thousands of words that are required for proficient reading—and on how to help them get there. Ultimately, words need to be read with a level of automaticity (effortlessness) that allows the reader to focus on the meaning of the text they are reading rather than having to labor over figuring out the identities of individual words.

Most words that become part of an individual's sight vocabulary are not explicitly taught—there is simply not enough time to explicitly teach them all.

Rather, the vast majority of words that become part of a reader's sight vocabulary are learned through effective word solving while reading. The previous sentence has two important implications: (1) to become a proficient reader, the learner needs to read a lot, and (2) the learner needs to have effective ways of figuring out the identities of unfamiliar words encountered while reading.

The focus of this chapter is on teaching learners how to solve the unfamiliar printed words they encounter while reading by applying the foundational skills (i.e., phonemic analysis and phonics) discussed in Part II in combination with the contextual information provided in the text and their own background knowledge. Learning to use the code-based (alphabetic and orthographic) information in combination with the meaning-based information to puzzle through unfamiliar words is important because, in English, a substantial number of words cannot be decoded by relying exclusively on the code-based skills typically taught. Further, for beginning readers, who do not yet have full command of the alphabetic and orthographic code, even more words are not fully decodable. Figure 12.1 provides a graphic illustration of how the word-solving/word-learning process might be conceptualized.

Upon encountering an unfamiliar written word while reading (box 1 in the figure), the reader would engage in an analysis of the alphabetic and orthographic information in the word and, perhaps the contextual information provided by the text (box 2).[1] The analysis of the alphabetic and orthographic information needs to be especially thorough in order for the unfamiliar word to ultimately be added to the reader's sight vocabulary. The initial analysis would lead to a likely/possible pronunciation (box 3), which the reader would first evaluate for "goodness of fit" by (implicitly) asking "Is it a word I've heard before?" (box 4). If the answer to this question is yes, the reader would go on to the next question: "Does the word make sense in the current context?" (box 5). If the answer, once again, is yes, the reader would confirm that the word had been accurately identified and the identity of the word *could* be on the way to becoming part of the reader's sight vocabulary (as symbolized by the cloud). We say *could* here because, in order for a word to ultimately become part of one's sight vocabulary, the reader needs to have engaged in a fairly thorough orthographic mapping process (having connected the graphemes in the printed word with their associated phonemes).

Of course, as illustrated in the figure, an initial attempt at identifying a word may not result in a real word (box 4) or in one that fits the context (box 5). When either of those things happen, a reader who understands that reading is supposed to make sense, would, ideally, rethink the initial attempt, perhaps trying different pronunciations for some of the parts and/or thinking more about the contextual information provided by preceding and/or succeeding text (box 7). Once the

---

[1]Children who are at a very early point in reading development, while mostly in the process of developing foundational reading skills (discussed in Chapters 4, 5, 6, and 7), may well rely on pictures to help them get the gist of the book they are reading—assuming, of course, that the book has pictures that are helpful.

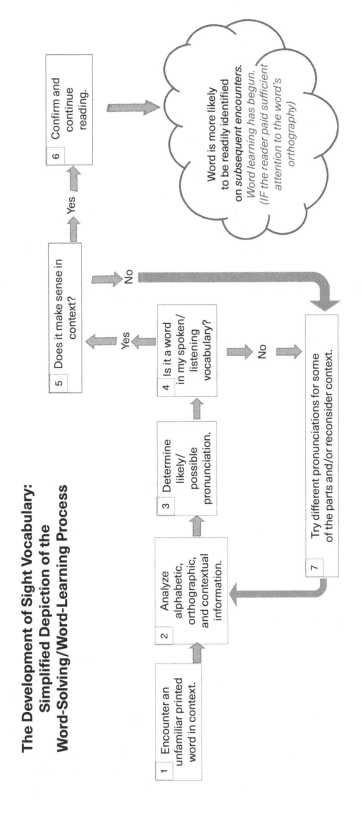

The Development of Sight Vocabulary: Simplified Depiction of the Word-Solving/Word-Learning Process

1 Encounter an unfamiliar printed word in context.

2 Analyze alphabetic, orthographic, and contextual information.

3 Determine likely/possible pronunciation.

4 Is it a word in my spoken/listening vocabulary?

Yes

No

5 Does it make sense in context?

Yes

No

6 Confirm and continue reading.

7 Try different pronunciations for some of the parts and/or reconsider context.

Word is more likely to be readily identified on *subsequent encounters*. *Word learning has begun.* *(IF the reader paid sufficient attention to the word's orthography)*

FIGURE 12.1. Simplified depiction of the process of learning to identify printed words.

reader comes up with a possible alternative pronunciation, the learner would, theoretically, go through the same series of questions in an effort to settle on (confirm) the word's identity. This process could go through multiple iterations depending on (1) the strength of the context in which the unknown word occurs (i.e., how easy it would be to predict what the word is based on context), and (2) how decodable the word is—in terms of both its orthographic regularity and the reader's skill with the orthography. The point is that word solving during the process of reading meaningful text and, ultimately, word learning, involves a lot of cross-referencing of code-based (alphabetic and orthographic) information and meaning-based (contextual) information.

It is important to note that because many printed words in English don't fully follow the "rules" typically taught, learners need to be flexible in using both the code-based information (the word's spelling) and the contextual information. The level of detail that readers attend to will vary depending both on their alphabetic and orthographic knowledge and the degree to which the unfamiliar word is "predictable" based on the context in which it is encountered. The more knowledge about the orthography the learner has, the more likely the learner is to store the identity of a correctly identified printed word in memory. The more heavily the reader relies on context to identify a word, the less likely the reader is to store the word in memory—because the reader hasn't attended sufficiently to the word's orthography.

Skill with the Alphabetic Code Develops

As learners learn about the workings of the writing system, their ability to "decode" changes. Early on, they know little about the code and therefore many words will not be decodable for them. As their knowledge increases, more words become decodable.

Instruction that helps children learn the code (as described in Part II) enables them to use the code in efforts to identify unfamiliar printed words. It is an essential part of the orthographic mapping process.

What Can/Do Proficient Word Readers Do?

Individuals who are proficient word readers are able to effortlessly read nearly every printed word they encounter—in or out of context. These words were either added to their sight vocabularies as the result of effective word solving while reading (as illustrated in Figure 12.1) or they figure them out "on the fly"—drawing on orthographic elements stored in their memory (for example, knowing the word *light* would allow a reader to readily identify the word *blight*). Of course, if readers encounter words in context that they haven't heard before (*blight*, for example), they would not be able to confirm that the word had been accurately identified.

However, if the context is supportive, that is, if it provides at least some indication of the word's meaning, readers may *begin* to add the unfamiliar word to the body of words for which they know the meaning. Thus, another benefit of readers attending to both the code and the context in the process of word solving is that it has the potential to expand the breadth and depth of their knowledge of word meanings and language more generally.

Knowledge of Word Meanings

As we discuss in Chapter 15, the development of knowledge of word meanings is an incremental process. The language user typically adds knowledge of word meanings across time and multiple encounters with a word in multiple contexts.

Strategies for Solving Unfamiliar Words Encountered in Context

The approach to word solving we encourage involves teaching children to use both code-based and meaning-based strategies in interactive and confirmatory ways to solve (i.e., identify) unfamiliar printed words encountered while reading. Figure 12.2 lists the eight word-solving strategies we teach learners. The left side of the figure lists the code-based strategies that are intended to help learners attend to the orthographic (code-based) information in unknown words. The reader must understand this information thoroughly enough to enable once unfamiliar words to be stored in memory with enough detail that the words will be more readily recognized on future encounters. The strategies listed on the right, the meaning-based strategies, are taught to focus learners on the goal of meaning construction *and* to enable learners to verify that their word-solving efforts have resulted in a real word that fits the context.

Using a combination of the two general types of strategies is intended, over time, to help readers learn initially unfamiliar words so well that they become part of their sight vocabulary. The idea is that effective word-solving skills and strategies allow readers to "teach" themselves to read the vast number of words they must ultimately be able to identify without effort—a process that Share (1995) referred to as *self-teaching*. According to Share, "the ability to translate printed words *independently* into their spoken equivalents assumes a central role in reading acquisition" (p. 155). He credits the use of letter–sound relationships (the code/orthographic information as we refer to it) to identify unfamiliar words as the primary path toward attaining reading proficiency. However, he argues that beginning readers need to develop a variety of word-identification strategies that can be used to build their sight vocabularies. Although he places primary importance on decoding, Share acknowledges the significance of context in the word-identification

Use the Letters *and* Use the Meaning

Use the Letters		Use the Meaning
fun	Think about the sounds of the letters in the word.	**??** Does the word make sense?
sat	Look for parts you know.	
aeiou	Try different sounds for some of the letters, especially the vowel(s). Be flexible.	Check the pictures.
Look/ing	Break the word into smaller parts.	↰ Read past the puzzling word.
		↳ Go back to the beginning of the sentence and start again.

FIGURE 12.2. Word-solving strategies taught in the ISA. Adapted from Scanlon and Anderson (2010). Copyright © the International Literacy Association. Adapted by permission.

From *Early Literacy Instruction and Intervention: The Interactive Strategies Approach, Third Edition*, by Donna M. Scanlon, Kimberly L. Anderson, Erica M. Barnes, and Joan M. Sweeney. Copyright © 2024 The Guilford Press. Permission to photocopy this material, or to download and print additional copies (*www.guilford.com/scanlon-materials*), is granted to purchasers of this book for personal use or use with their students (see copyright page for details).

process. Indeed, he asserts that it is the individual's sensitivity to the constraints of the text, used in combination with a "willingness to test multiple alternative pronunciations for 'goodness of fit'" (1995, p. 166), that allows even the partial decoding of unfamiliar words to take on a self-teaching value. This "set for variability," as Venezky (1999) and others have referred to it, helps to increase learners' repertoire of word-solving skills by sensitizing them to the multiple ways in which a given spelling pattern might be decoded (e.g., the *ow* in *cow* and *glow*). Moreover, experiences with successful decoding help children become familiar with new letter–sound correspondences and patterns, thus expanding the power of the self-teaching mechanism (Castles et al., 2018; Share, 1995). According to the self-teaching hypothesis, automatic word recognition depends on both the number of times a learner has been exposed to a particular printed word and the nature and success of the child's previous attempts to read the word. Thus, learning to read words is, essentially, an item-based process—at a given point in time, a developing reader may be reading some words in a slow and effortful way while identifying and understanding other words quickly and accurately and without the need to engage in word solving because the words have become part of their sight vocabulary (Castles & Nation, 2006; Share, 1995). When children independently apply skills and strategies to read unfamiliar words encountered in text, they learn more words, and more about words, each time they read.

To facilitate the development of effective self-teaching, we advocate explicitly teaching beginning readers and older children who demonstrate difficulties with word solving/word identification the small number of word-solving strategies listed in Figure 12.2. The intent of teaching a *small* number of strategies is to enable learners to internalize them—that is, to ultimately be able to independently call them to mind when encountering a word they don't initially recognize. As noted, two general types of strategies are taught: code-based strategies, which focus on the use of letters and larger orthographic units to arrive at a likely pronunciation of a word, and meaning-based strategies, which enable children to focus on whether attempted pronunciations produce words that fit the contexts in which they are encountered. When children have difficulty settling on what a word is, they are encouraged to utilize additional strategies. For example, readers might try alternative sounds for some of the letters, or they might read beyond the as yet unidentified word for additional contextual information that might inform their word-solving efforts. The goal is for children to learn to use both code-based and meaning-based strategies in interactive *and* confirmatory ways. As Adams (1990) noted, proficient readers have a multitude of strategies which they can draw upon when encountering an unfamiliar word. Strategies that privilege the alphabetic and orthographic information in words (code-based strategies) are more reliable than those that privilege contextual information (hence the level of detail in Chapters 4–11). Nonetheless, the assist provided by meaning is useful to all readers at varying points. It is particularly useful during the earliest phases of learning to read, when learners have not yet acquired the full repertoire of code-based approaches to word identification.

Documenting Word-Identification Strategy Use

Explicit teaching and guidance in the use of word-solving strategies is the focus of much of the rest of this chapter. However, we first provide some guidance on how teachers can notice and note the strategies that students do and do not use effectively while reading. Figure 12.3 provides the group snapshot for strategic word solving.

In a small-group context, the teacher might choose to focus on the strategy use of a different student each day. To document strategy use in a given lesson, the teacher would listen to the child read and note, using the two-letter codes on the snapshot, which strategies the child uses spontaneously (e.g., TS for Think about the Sounds; RP for Read Past the puzzling word) or only with prompting (e.g., TS-P)—noting all of the strategies the child appears to use when attempting to solve individual words. Although it is not always possible to determine which strategies children are using, especially for those children who do a lot of their word solving in their heads, careful attention to the types of errors they make and to where their eyes go as they puzzle over a word can provide insight. When listening to a child read, it is also appropriate to comment on and ask about their word-solving process as this can provide important insights into their approach to word solving. By reviewing observational notations made over several occasions, the teacher would be able to update the snapshot for the children in each instructional group. Looking across the children's application of strategies, the teacher might notice patterns of use and nonuse that would inform planning for upcoming strategy lessons and perhaps suggest the need to modify group membership. Such analysis can also inform ongoing instruction related to the code.

In using the snapshot to capture information about children's strategy use, the teacher would place a single slash (/) in the box for each strategy if the child(ren) have been introduced to the strategy; an additional slash, to make an X, when the teacher has observed that the child can use the strategy but generally needs

---

Noting One Child's Strategy Use

- Sentence reads: "I don't want to leave my friends," said Mike.
- First attempt: "I don't want to lev . . ."
- Second attempt: "I don't want to lave my friends . . ."
- Third attempt: "I don't want to leave my friends," said Mike.

All attempts were independent. The teacher's code recorded for this word-solving episode would be TS, MS, DP, RP, and IC. (See snapshot [Figure 12.3] for codes.)

If the reader routinely demonstrates spontaneous and independent use of these strategies, the snapshot would indicate proficiency (☒) in the use of those strategies for that child.

Group Snapshot—Strategic Word Solving, Use of Word-Identification Strategies						
Student names						
Code-based strategies						
TS—**T**hink about the **S**ounds of the letters in the word	First					
	Last					
	Medial					
LP—**L**ook for **P**arts you know						
DP—Try **D**ifferent **P**ronunciations for some of the letters, especially the vowels						
BW—**B**reak the **W**ord into smaller parts						
Meaning-based strategies						
MS—Think of words that might **M**ake **S**ense						
CP—**C**heck the **P**ictures						
RP—**R**ead **P**ast the puzzling word						
SA—Go back to the beginning of the sentence and **S**tart **A**gain						
IC—Use multiple strategies in an **I**nteractive and **C**onfirmatory way						

Key:

◻ *B—Beginning* indicates that instruction has addressed the strategy but that the child has only a preliminary understanding or capability with regard to its use.

⊠ *D—Developing* indicates that the child has some understanding of the strategy but does not reliably and/or spontaneously use the strategy.

⊠ *P—Proficient* indicates that the child reliably and spontaneously demonstrates use of the strategy.

FIGURE 12.3. Group snapshot for strategic word solving. Adapted from Scanlon and Anderson (2010). Copyright © 2010 The International Literacy Association. Adapted by permission.

prompting to do so; and an additional slash, to make an asterisk, when the teacher observes that the child uses the strategy effectively and reliably without prompting across several occasions. Essentially, an asterisk signals that, for that child, future instruction on that strategy is probably unnecessary. The snapshot also includes an item entitled *Interactive and Confirmatory* use, which is intended to remind teachers to consider whether readers use both general types of strategies (code- and meaning-based) in the process of word solving. For example, in the Noting One Child's Strategy Use box, it is evident that the child used both code- and meaning-based strategies and didn't need prompting to do so. Across multiple occasions of listening to a child read, the teacher would consider whether interactive and confirmatory use of both types of strategies is just beginning to occur (single slash), is used but inconsistently (X), or is routine (⊠).

Using the Individual Snapshot

The individual version of the snapshot, which is available on the book's companion website (see the box at the end of the table of contents), can be used to track children's progress across time. In this case, the letter codes would be more efficient—B for beginning, D for developing, and P for proficient.

The general goal is to notice which strategies individual children are using, or neglecting to use, to plan instruction that is responsive to those observations, and to offer assistance and guidance as opportunities arise. For children who are first learning to be strategic word solvers, teachers can note which strategies are used spontaneously and which are used only with prompting. Such notations allow teachers to plan instruction more effectively. For example, if children in a group are routinely and reliably using a particular strategy, that strategy probably does not need to be discussed at length or modeled in future lessons. If, on the other hand, children are using a particular strategy effectively but only when prompted to do so, the teacher needs to plan ways to promote independence in the use of that strategy—perhaps by reminding the children of the strategy before they begin reading (e.g., "Some of us are forgetting to use the _____ strategy when we are puzzled by a word. Let's try to remember that strategy today."). Also, when a child transitions from using a strategy only with prompting to using it spontaneously, the teacher can notice and name it to reinforce spontaneous strategy use both for that child and for others in the group. For strategies children do not utilize effectively, even when prompted, additional explanation and modeling before they begin to read and explicit prompting while they are reading is needed. The group snapshot is designed to help teachers notice whether one or more of the group members is tending to ignore code-based versus meaning-based strategies. It also allows the teacher to see what the group as a whole can do as word solvers, which may signal a need for side-by-side instruction for children who do not appear to be growing as strategic word solvers.

In addition to documenting strategy use, it is also useful to document the ease with which children build their sight vocabulary through strategic word solving. The snapshot in Figure 12.4 is intended for this purpose. As with several of the snapshots, the primary purpose of this form is to prompt teachers' thinking about which children might benefit from extra, more focused, instructional attention. To use this form, the teacher would record observations of the ease with which sight words are acquired (*readily, slowly,* or *very slowly*). Such observations should be made at several points in time across the school year. This snapshot allows for that. Thus, in the first column, the teacher would record the date on which notations are entered for the children in the group. For each child, the teacher would record the apparent rate at which the child's sight vocabulary is growing. Rate estimates can be recorded on up to 10 different dates. Children who appear to be building their sight vocabulary slowly or very slowly relative to peers may be in need of more explicit instruction and/or more guided practice in the use of word-identification strategies. Further, they clearly need more opportunities to read and reread texts that are not too challenging.

Prerequisites for Learning to Identify Printed Words

Early on, learning to identify individual printed words via a self-teaching approach, generally, requires that the reader knows the meaning of the unfamiliar printed word because that enables them to confirm that a real word has been identified (box 4 in Figure 12.1). Readers must also have the syntactic/grammatical knowledge needed to determine that their attempt at a word fits the syntactic/grammatical constraints of the sentence in which it occurs. And, of course, if the word is going to be added to their sight vocabulary, they must have sufficiently well-developed phonics skills to enable them to do the necessary orthographic mapping. Obviously, these conditions present unique challenges for teachers of children who are learning English as an additional language and those who speak a variant of English that differs from the version of English typically represented in books. Teachers need to be sensitive to these challenges and provide more support and guidance for children who are less familiar with the language typically used in the texts they are reading. For example, it would be helpful to explicitly introduce the spoken forms of words that may be new to the children's vocabulary by using the pictures and context in the books they are preparing the children to read.

The Importance of Phonics Skills for Word Learning

Summaries of the scientific research on literacy development have strongly concluded that it is critical for children to learn to use all of the graphic (letter) information in printed words as soon as possible (Castles et al., 2018) because *children who do not use all of the orthographic information (the graphemes) when attempting to read an unfamiliar word do not effectively store that word in memory* (Anderson & Scanlon, 2020; Ehri, 2005; Share, 1995). As a result,

Group Snapshot—Observations of Strategic Sight Word Learning					
	Student names				
Dates					
Builds sight vocabulary through strategic word identification while reading Code as: **R**eadily **S**lowly **V**ery slowly					

FIGURE 12.4. Group snapshot to document growth in strategic word learning.

when they encounter the word in the future, it may be no more familiar to them than it was the first time they figured it out. Children who attend to all of the orthographic information in printed words store more complete word information in memory and are more likely to successfully identify those words on subsequent encounters—and with less effort.

One of the biggest differences between children who experience difficulty with learning to read and spell and those who learn with relative ease is in their abilities to use alphabetic and orthographic information. Strong readers learn to use this information more quickly than do children who experience difficulty and who depend more on meaning-based strategies. This is likely because their alphabetic and orthographic skills are weaker and therefore are not as useful to them (Tunmer & Nicholson, 2011). Because children who struggle do not make adequate use of this type of information, they do not effectively store the identities of printed words in memory. As a result, their sight vocabulary develops more slowly, thus impeding their ability to read grade-appropriate texts.

Such a finding might lead some to conclude that code-based strategies and an emphasis on the orthography should be the primary and perhaps the exclusive focus of early reading instruction, at least for children who experience difficulty with literacy development. However, there is no evidence to support this position. In fact, in our own research, we have found that young children who participate in intervention that, in addition to teaching about the orthography, places emphasis on using meaning-based strategies in word solving, on average, show greater gains than do those in intervention contexts that place greater emphasis on the alphabetic code and orthography more generally (Anderson, 2009; Scanlon & Anderson, 2020; Scanlon et al., 2005). The bottom line is that to become proficient readers, children need to use additional strategies when they are puzzled by a word and their efforts at using code-based strategies have not yielded a real word that fits the context. This is essentially what Share's self-teaching hypothesis is about. Indeed, to quote Castles et al. (2019): "The self-teaching hypothesis provides a powerful paradigm for representing how children move from novice to expert" (p. 19).

Strategic Word Learning

What Is a Strategy, and What Are Word-Identification Strategies?

A strategy is a purposeful plan of action used to achieve a desired goal or outcome. A useful strategy is applicable across multiple contexts and allows for gradual reduction in the cognitive effort required to accomplish the goal. Word-identification strategies are purposeful plans of action with the goal of accurately identifying unfamiliar words encountered in context. Explicit teaching of word-identification strategies is intended to help learners become actively and cognitively engaged in puzzling through unfamiliar printed words encountered while reading. With extensive word-solving experience, it is expected that the need to be consciously strategic will lessen and that readers will engage in word solving more or less automatically.

While it is not a perfect analogy, an experience that many readers of this book have had is learning to drive. In the beginning, a novice driver has to be strategic about nearly every aspect of the driving process—how to get into the proper driving position, how to start the vehicle, how to back up, accelerate, brake, how and when to signal, and so on. All these things, initially, take conscious effort and, in some cases, strategies. However, with experience, most drivers learn to do these things effortlessly and can focus on things entirely unrelated to the driving process—unless a problem is encountered, of course. This is one way to construe the situation in going from being consciously strategic in word solving to being able to do it automatically for the most part and, as a result, being able to focus most of one's conscious thought on the end goals of reading (and writing)—meaning construction. So, this is the goal of teaching word-identification strategies—to get readers to the point where they are so effective in word solving—using code- and meaning-based strategies in interactive, confirmatory, and ultimately automatic ways, that they don't think about the word-solving process but, rather, can devote their attention to making sense of what they are reading.

Code-Based Word-Solving Strategies

Code-based strategies are taught because one major aspect of reading important to early literacy learners involves translating printed language into its spoken equivalent and translating speech/thought into print. Ehri (1998, 2005) theorizes that, for the printed version of a word to be thoroughly stored in memory so that it ultimately becomes part of the reader's sight vocabulary, the reader needs to have mapped the sounds in the (spoken) word onto the letters in the printed word. She refers to this process as orthographic mapping. That is, the reader needs to attempt to connect each phoneme in the spoken word to the graphemes in the written word.

In order to effectively use code-based strategies, a reader must:

• Understand that (spoken) words are composed of smaller units of sound (the *phonemes* we discussed in Chapter 5) and have the ability to attend to and manipulate those phonemes (i.e., blend and segment them). They can certainly be learning about phonemic analysis and the workings of the writing system more or less simultaneously.

• Be familiar with how the English alphabetic writing system works; readers need to understand that the phonemes in spoken words are represented by the letters/graphemes in printed words.

• Over time, recognize that the alphabetic code for English is not entirely consistent and that there are alternative ways of pronouncing the same grapheme, just as there are alternative ways of representing the same phoneme in writing (for example, the long-*e* sound can be represented in multiple ways, including: *ee*, *ea*, *ei*, *ey*, and *y*).

Meaning-Based Word-Solving Strategies

Meaning-based strategies serve to inform decoding attempts by allowing readers to anticipate what an unknown word might be and/or to test whether an initial decoding attempt fits the context in which the word is encountered. The use of meaning-based strategies also allows readers to evaluate, on an ongoing basis, whether the text is making sense; if not, such strategies lead readers to institute some sort of "fix-up" strategy (strategies) to recover meaning. In order to effectively use meaning-based strategies, readers must:

- Construe reading as a communicative, meaning-making process.
- Have sufficient background knowledge, vocabulary, and general language skill to notice when communication has broken down.
- Read materials that present some but not too much challenge; when a text is too challenging, readers are unable to build the context needed to recognize that a word-solving error has occurred.

Interactive and Confirmatory Strategy Use

In order to effectively puzzle through unfamiliar words encountered in context, students generally need to use both code-based and meaning-based strategies in interactive and confirmatory ways—checking one source of information against the

---

Children Tend to Learn What We Teach Them

Sometimes children who experience difficulty with literacy development come to believe that reading is about saying the words quickly and accurately and that writing is about neatly writing and accurately spelling the words. These beliefs may result from the emphasis the children's teachers place on accuracy. It is estimated that somewhere between 3 and 10% of upper elementary children can read fairly accurately and fluently but cannot adequately comprehend what they read (Spencer & Wagner, 2018). While a variety of reasons likely account for children's comprehension difficulties, one important contributing factor may be overemphasis on accuracy and fluency in instructional contexts. While we certainly fully support and encourage teachers' efforts to address the needs of their students with respect to word-reading accuracy and fluency skills, we also caution that this focus should not supersede a focus on understanding, enjoyment, and learning. If we want children to focus on meaning, teachers need to emphasize that reading and writing are about *meaning making*.

The approach we encourage focuses on ensuring that learners view reading as having a meaning-making purpose. This includes promoting active use of meaning-based strategies in word-solving efforts and through the interactions with children during read-alouds and in other contexts making a concerted effort to develop general world (background) knowledge, vocabulary and language skills, and promoting active engagement with the meaning of the texts that are read or heard.

other (as illustrated in Figure 12.1, p. 303). Because the English language includes variable spellings for individual phonemes (especially vowel spellings), decoding attempts often result in only an approximate pronunciation of the printed word. To settle on the actual pronunciation, the reader needs to think of a word that sounds like the result of the decoding attempt *and* that makes sense in the context. For example, if the reader encounters a text that includes the word *great* in the context "That is a great toy!", the reader might initially decode *great* as *greet* (with the *ea* pronounced as in *bead*). That decoding attempt would be rejected because it didn't make sense in context. The reader might then try a short-*e* sound for the *ea* digraph (as in *head*), which would again result in a rejection because *gret* is not a real word. A tenacious reader committed to making sense of the text might go on to try the long-*a* sound for the *ea* digraph—with the result that a real word that fits the context is identified.

Research on Word-Solving Strategies

Almost no research has been done specifically on the effects of explicit teaching of word-identification strategies. In fact, the only such study we are aware of is one of our own (Anderson, 2009). However, research has been done on the strategies primary-grade readers appear to use when they come to a word they don't yet know and on the response of teachers to children's word-solving errors. This research generally supports the idea that children make more progress as readers if they attend to the multiple sources of information available to support word solving in context (McGee, Kim, Nelson, & Fried, 2015). They are also helped when teachers respond to word-solving errors in a way that redirects students' attention to available sources of information they may have neglected—that is, code- versus meaning-based information (Rodgers, D'Agostino, Harmey, Kelly, & Brownfield, 2016). While these studies are relatively small scale and were conducted in a limited context (first graders in a Reading Recovery intervention), they do corroborate that teacher guidance around word solving and the use of both code- and meaning-based sources of information have an impact on young learners' reading growth.

Code-Based Strategies—Explained

Code-based strategies include using individual graphemes and larger orthographic elements (rimes, affixes, etc.) to figure out the likely pronunciation of unfamiliar printed words. The aspects of the code children are expected to attend to in utilizing the code-based strategies change as their skill with the alphabetic code develops. Teachers are cautioned to ensure that children demonstrate the needed code-based skills in isolation before expecting them to apply them in the context of reading meaningful text (see Part II). For example, if children do not know the sounds associated with some of the graphemes in a particular text, they would not be expected to fully decode words with those graphemes when attempting to identify a word in context. However, this *does not* mean that they would not be asked to read a book that contains as yet unknown decoding elements. With the use of other sources of information (including meaning), children may be able to accurately identify words with those elements and may in fact learn something about the as yet unknown decoding element in the process.

Below we explain/describe the code-based strategies:

- *Think about the sounds of the letters in the word.* At the earliest points in development, children are taught to attend to just the beginning letter and sound in unfamiliar words encountered while reading and to use that information in conjunction with pictorial or other contextual supports to identify unknown words. As children progress, the teacher focuses on encouraging them to use both beginning and ending sounds. Ultimately, children are expected to look all the way through one-syllable words, thinking about the sounds and blending them to make a word that fits the context. This expectation would "kick in" when the children's decoding/phonics skills have advanced to the point where they are able to decode single-syllable words in isolated word work.

- *Look for parts you know.* In using this strategy, readers look for word parts in the unfamiliar word that have either been taught explicitly or that they have learned through their reading of meaningful text (e.g., consonant digraphs and vowel teams, rimes, and spelling patterns such as *tion*). Depending on the element, children might be referred to a word family or to a key-word chart as an assist.

- *Try different sounds for some of the letters, especially the vowel(s). Be flexible.* In using this strategy, students retrieve from memory alternate sounds for graphemes to determine which sound produces a meaningful word that fits the context. This strategy is particularly useful for vowels, as they tend to be the most variable graphemes in terms of how they are pronounced. As illustrated previously, in regard to puzzling through the word *great*, the child might need to try the long and the short sounds for both of the vowel letters before coming up with the pronunciation of a real word that fits the context. The strategy of trying different sounds is also useful for vowel teams that have more than one common pronunciation (e.g., *oo* and *ow*), as well as for the hard and soft sounds of *c* (as in *cub* vs. *city*) and *g* (as in *girl* vs. *gentle*). This strategy can also be used to address silent letters in some consonant digraphs (e.g., *kn* as in *know*, *gh* as in *ghost*), and the schwa vowel sound in unstressed syllables in multisyllabic words (as discussed in Chapter 11).

- *Break the word into smaller parts.* This strategy is useful in identifying words with inflectional endings (e.g., *-ed*, *-ing*, *-s*), words with prefixes (e.g., *un-*, *re-*, *pre-*) and derivational suffixes (e.g.,*-er*, *-ful*, *-ly*) as well as words that have multiple syllables more generally. By breaking a word into smaller parts, the decoding of an unfamiliar word can be somewhat simplified. As with the other word-solving strategies, this strategy would generally be used in combination with other code- and meaning-based strategies in efforts to accurately identify unfamiliar words encountered in context.

Clearly, the code-based strategies that learners can use and how they use them depend on what the children know about the code. Figure 12.5 depicts the relationships between code-based word-identification strategies and the decoding elements and principles learners may draw upon when employing the strategies.

The Role of Flexibility in Decoding and in Word Solving/Word Learning

According to Share (1995), readers' sensitivity to contextual information, along with a willingness to try multiple pronunciations of a word, supports self-teaching of unfamiliar words even for words that are only partially decoded/decodable. Rudimentary self-teaching, he explained, depends on three factors: basic phonemic awareness, use of letter–sound knowledge, and the ability to use both partial decodings and contextual information to accurately determine the pronunciation of words. With regard to flexibility, Share noted that it would be highly counterproductive for readers to be wedded to singular letter–sound relations, particularly with vowels. Essentially what we are talking about here is the notion of *set for variability*, which was discussed in some detail in Part II of this book.

Meaning-Based Strategies—Explained

Meaning-based strategies utilize the context of the sentence and the larger text, including illustrations, photographs, diagrams, and charts. We teach the following meaning-based strategies:

- *Think of words that might make sense.* In applying this strategy, readers use the meaning and syntax to confirm the identity of an unknown word that has been attempted using code-based strategies. When the pronunciation is not confirmed, the meaning and syntax help generate additional hypotheses about what the unfamiliar word might be. Note that, although it is sometimes possible to accurately identify an unfamiliar word encountered in context by relying solely on this strategy, this practice should *not* be encouraged because such an approach would not draw students' attention to the printed form of the word and would, therefore, not help students add the word to their sight vocabularies. Additionally, such an approach can promote a habit of overreliance on context and hinder children's literacy growth over the long term.

- *Check the pictures.* In using this strategy, if needed, students check the picture to see if there is information that might be useful in identifying a puzzling word. This strategy is particularly helpful for students who are just beginning to learn about the reading process—those who do not yet have much ability to use code-based strategies to puzzle through unfamiliar words. However, we have also noted that some older children tend to disregard the illustrations, maps, and charts

Decoding Element/Principle	Word Identification Strategy
• Single consonants • Consonant digraphs • Short vowels • Long vowel sound/silent-*e* generalization • Blends	Think about the sounds of the letters in the word.
• Long vowel sound/silent-*e* generalization • Vowel combinations that can be decoded by trying different sounds for the vowel because they represent either the long or short sound of one of the vowels (*ai, ay, ea, ee, eu, ie, oa, oe, ue, ui*) • Vowel parts that have two sounds (*oo, ow*)	Try different sounds for some of the letters, especially the vowel(s). Be flexible!
• Consonant digraphs • Rimes/word families • Vowel combinations that cannot be decoded by trying different sounds for the vowel because they represent a sound that is different from the long or short sound of either vowel (*au, aw, ew, oi, oo, ou, ow, oy*) • *r*-controlled vowels (*ar, er, ir, or, ur*)	Look for parts you know.
• Inflected endings (*-ing, -es, -ed*) • Prefixes such as *un-, re-, in-* • Suffixes such as *-ly, -ment, -ness* • Compound words • Words with two consonants together—especially double consonants • Consonant + *le* syllables	Break the word into smaller parts.

Note. Blends referred to both clusters and blends in this text.

FIGURE 12.5. Strategies that use decoding elements knowledge. From Gelzheiser et al. (2019). Copyright © 2019 The Guilford Press. Reprinted by permission.

that are meant to elaborate and clarify some of the information provided in written texts. We have found this to be true among middle school students who have weak reading skills and even with some of our own college students. To encourage older students to use this type of information, we recommend substituting the word *illustrations* for *pictures.*

• *Read past the puzzling word and then come back to it.* In using this strategy, upon encountering an unfamiliar word and coming up with a pronunciation that isn't a word they have heard before or that doesn't initially make sense, students read on, often to the end of the sentence, to gain more insight into what the puzzling word might be. This strategy can be especially helpful when it is used early in a sentence or paragraph, when readers have not yet developed much sense of what the sentence or paragraph is about. This strategy is also useful if the puzzling word occurs later in the sentence; sometimes reading the next sentence will help to clarify the identity of an unfamiliar printed word.

• *Go back to the beginning of the sentence and start again.* Sometimes when readers encounter an unfamiliar word, taking the time to puzzle over its identity causes them to forget what has already been read. In using this strategy, readers go back to the beginning of the sentence and start again to regain the context that the earlier part of the sentence provides. This additional context sometimes provides the needed information to *confirm* and/or *adjust* a hypothesis about a word's identity.

Example of Interactive and Confirmatory Use of Both Code-Based and Meaning-Based Strategies

In initially teaching the *Break the word into smaller parts* strategy, as discussed in Chapter 11, the teacher would encourage students to cover known parts of unfamiliar words, try a pronunciation for the part that isn't covered, uncover any parts that were covered (perhaps one at a time), and then try to pronounce the entire word. Next, readers would, ideally, consider whether the result is a word they have heard before and, if so, consider whether the word fits the current context. This strategy becomes particularly useful for learners when they are frequently encountering multisyllabic words in their reading.

KEEP IN MIND Instruction in word-solving strategies has two major purposes: to enable children to identify particular words in particular texts at a given moment in time; and the larger purpose, to help children learn given words so well that they become part of their sight vocabularies. Thus, word solving leads to word identification in a particular context. Successful identification of a given word, generally across multiple contexts, leads to the ability to read the word automatically (word learning).

Teaching to Promote the Use of Word-Identification Strategies

In beginning to teach about word-identification strategies, it is important to explain what a strategy is and why it is useful and to explain and model the use of individual strategies. For young children, we might explain it this way:

> "You are all learning to read. You are going to get to learn how to read lots and lots of words. Being able to read lots and lots of words is exciting because then you will be able to read lots and lots of books and other things by yourselves. There are so many words I can't teach them all! So, I am going to teach you strategies you can use to figure out words you don't already know. A strategy is sort of a plan, a way to figure out how to do something."

The goal is for children to learn to use code-based and meaning-based strategies in interactive and confirmatory ways. We generally teach the first code-based strategy (*Think about the sounds of the letters in the word*) first, along with the top two meaning-based strategies: *Think of words that might make sense* and

Check the pictures. These two meaning-based strategies are things young children, hopefully, do quite naturally and implicitly. So, the new strategy we are adding is *Think about the sounds of the letters in the words.* This also makes sense at the point when children are first learning about the workings of the alphabetic code; if they are learning decoding skills, we obviously want them to understand how to use them. This group of three strategies allows children to "get started" with reading books from early on—which we think is important both because it helps them understand the purpose and utility of the decoding skills they are learning and because reading beginner-level books can be very motivating. Once children have a reasonable grasp of those first three strategies, additional strategies would be introduced one at a time, since learning to use a new strategy takes time and effort. Following initial teaching of each strategy, children would be provided with a good deal of guided practice with the application of the newly introduced strategy, in combination with any others they already know how to use or have learned about. However, it is not necessary to wait until children are proficient in the use of particular strategies before introducing another. Rather, children should be provided with focused practice with each new strategy and guidance in the interactive use of all the strategies that have been taught.

Resources That Support Strategy Use

Reading is a complicated process for beginning readers. Often, they are asked to access a great deal of information as they read. For example, they need to remember the sounds associated with each of the graphemes and perhaps some larger orthographic units (e.g., rimes) that have been taught, the high-frequency words they are learning, and the word-identification strategies they are expected to use. Meanwhile, they need to comprehend the text they are reading—considering what they have read and drawing on their prior knowledge.

Early in reading development, several of these knowledge sources are not automatically available. Therefore, it makes sense to provide resources to support children's processing. For the strategy component, as children are in the process of developing a repertoire of strategies they can use, they can be provided with a chart with those strategies and should be encouraged to refer to this chart, as needed, when trying to figure out a word. Figure 12.2 (p. 306) provides the chart of the strategies used in the ISA. A larger version that can be printed for use with groups of students is available on the book's companion website (see the box at the end of the table of contents). The icon to the left of each strategy listed in Figure 12.2 is intended to serve as a reminder of the strategy. The icons require a bit of explanation if they are to serve their intended function. For example, as further explanation of the *fun* icon, which is the icon for the *think about the sounds of the letters in the word* strategy, the teacher might say something like "We use fun to remind us of this strategy because you can figure out the word *fun* just by thinking of the sounds of the letters—and it is *fun* to figure out words by yourself." For the *check the picture strategy*, children might be told that the little picture is a reminder that the pictures in a book might help them figure out a word they can't identify right away.

KEEP IN MIND Strategies should generally be introduced one at a time. A strategy chart containing only those strategies that have been introduced can be posted and made available to the children while they read. As new strategies are taught, they can be added to the chart. Some teachers post the entire chart right from the beginning with the strategies that have yet to be taught covered. At the point where an additional (covered) strategy is to be introduced, it is uncovered and there is a bit of fanfare for the "big reveal," which may serve to create enthusiasm for using the newly introduced strategy.

In addition to the strategy chart, it makes sense to have other supports available, including the *key words* used to remind the children of the sounds of letters and other graphemes they have been taught, a list of *rimes* that have been taught (see, for example, Figure 9.4, p. 224), a *word wall* (perhaps personalized for individuals or groups) with the high-frequency words they have learned (see Chapter 13, p. 371), and the *Bb/Dd* chart (see Chapter 6, p. 170). We have observed that children who have been explicitly taught to use such resources are able to more effectively engage in word solving. These resources essentially serve as supports for self-regulation in the word-solving process and in reading more generally.

Note

Some teachers, when first told about providing a display of resources, have expressed concern that the display will become a crutch for the children and will *prevent* them from learning. We have not seen this happen. Moreover, once teachers gain experience with teaching with the resources as suggested, their concern about the resources being a crutch is alleviated. Also, having the strategy chart available means that the teacher has to do less coaching around word solving and having the BbDd chart handy reduces children's tendency to confuse *b*'s and *d*'s.

Example of Early Interactive Strategy Instruction

Teaching about the *Think about the sounds* strategy is typically introduced in preparation for engaging children in reading a book that has a fairly high number of words they can "decode" based on the graphemes for which they have been taught the sounds. In our intervention research, we used a series of books called Ready Readers (1996).[2] The first book in the series is called *Monster Mop*. It reads, on successive pages, *My mug, My milk, My mess* (the picture showed spilled milk). The last page reads *My mop*. A book like this gives beginning readers lots of opportunity to learn to apply the newly learned sound for the letter *m* in the

---

[2]Unfortunately, these books, for the most part, are no longer in print.

context of a meaningful book while giving them the opportunity to be actively strategic—for example, recognizing, or being guided to recognize, that the picture of the cup/mug can't be called a cup because that word doesn't start with an /m/. Books like this also provide an opportunity to teach/learn foundational understandings about print—such as that print is tracked from left to right, what a word is and how it is different from a letter, that you think and, hopefully talk, about what you are reading, and so on. Of course, this kind of book also provides the opportunity to begin teaching the *Check the picture* strategy. In explaining this strategy, the teacher might say: "When you are reading and you come to a word you don't know, and you've thought about the sounds of the letters and still can't come up with the word, sometimes it helps to also look at the picture. The picture might give you some ideas about what the word is. Then you need to go back to the word and think about the letters in the word again—that's what readers do. We can't just look at the pictures; we also need to think about the letters and their sounds. What could that word be that has the sounds made by those letters?" Explaining the strategy this way will help to make it clear that it is the *word* that needs to be identified and that the picture may provide an assist. The additional strategy *Think about a word that might make sense* can also be brought into the conversation "Yes, *my mug* makes sense there because we see the character putting a mug, which is like a cup, on the table."

As each new strategy is introduced, the teacher should *demonstrate* how the strategy would be applied and, when appropriate, show how its use can be combined with other strategies the children have been learning.

Eventually, the strategy prompts should evolve into a shorthand way of reminding children of how they might figure out an unfamiliar word. The children should be taught to use the icons to trigger their memory for the strategies. However, when a strategy is first introduced, it is important to try to ensure that the children really understand what the strategy entails.

The Components of Strategy Instruction

Research on strategy instruction in reading has largely focused on comprehension strategy instruction and has yielded a general consensus with regard to the critical components of strategy instruction (Duffy, 2003; Paris, Lipson, & Wixson, 1983; Pearson & Gallagher, 1983). We have used the same general approach in the context of teaching about word-solving strategies. In general, the components of strategy instruction involve (1) clear explanations of each strategy, (2) teacher think-alouds to model and illustrate the strategy's use, (3) guided practice in the use of the strategy, and (4) gradual release of responsibility (Pearson & Gallagher, 1983; Pearson, McVee, & Shanahan, 2019) to the student for strategy use, with the goal of promoting independent application. We also include a reflection component to encourage learners, after having successfully utilized one or more strategies, to talk about their strategy use and how successful they were. Each of these components of strategy instruction is described next.

Clear Explanations: Using Explicit Language to Communicate What the Strategy Is and When and How to Use It

Beginning readers and especially children who experience difficulty with the beginning phases of learning to read are often confused about how the process works. In explaining a strategy, it is important to consider what each child understands about the process. Word-identification strategies need to be explained from a child's perspective. This may be more difficult than it initially seems. It is often hard to explain how to do something that one does without conscious thought. Therefore, in preparing to teach a word-identification strategy, teachers are encouraged to think about how to explain the strategy *before* beginning instruction. To this end, we have provided suggested introductory language for each strategy in Tables 12.1 (code-based strategies) and 12.2 (meaning-based strategies). Teachers are encouraged to introduce new strategies in preparation for reading a book in which children will have the opportunity to apply the new strategy.

Introductory Strategy Language

When encountering an unknown word while reading, two main questions we ultimately want learners to ask themselves are "What will that word probably sound like?" and "Does my attempt make sense?" Each question potentially involves the application of four strategies. And from early on, learners should be encouraged to use a combination of code- and meaning-based strategies in interactive and confirmatory ways—modifying early attempts and drawing on both types of information, until they are able to confirm that a real word that fits the context has been identified. Exactly which strategies would be introduced and when would depend on both the decoding (phonics) skills the children are developing and the characteristics of the text they are being prepared to read. The numbers associated with each strategy in Tables 12.1 and 12.2 provide a rough guideline in relation to the order in which the strategies *might* be introduced. (Note that the numbering goes across the two tables.) When introducing a strategy, the icon associated with the strategy and the strategy itself would be presented. For example, in teaching about the *Think about the sounds* strategy, the icon for the strategy (the printed word *fun*) along with the wording of the strategy would be presented.

Think-Alouds: Modeling the Use of the Strategy

Teachers can use think-aloud techniques to help students understand the kind of thinking that strategies involve. Research on the use of think-alouds in the context of comprehension strategy instruction indicates that they are most effective when they are explicit, leaving students little to infer about how the strategy should be applied, and when they are flexibly adjusted to reflect the demands of the text (Duke & Pearson, 2002). In a think-aloud, teachers talk about their thinking as they demonstrate their approach to solving a cognitive problem.

(text resumes on p. 328)

TABLE 12.1. Suggested Introductory Language for Code-Based Strategies

Strategy	Suggested introductory language	Explanation/clarification
1. Think about the sounds of the letters in the word.	"When we read, the letters in the word help us figure out what the word is. We have been learning the sounds of [some of] the letters, and now you are ready to use those letter sounds to figure out words when you are reading. To start with, we are going to think about the first letter in our words, because the first letter will give us some ideas about what the word might be. Thinking about the sounds for the letters is a strategy that we will use a lot as we learn to read. "To remind us to use the *Think about the sounds of the letters in the word* strategy, we have the word *fun* here because it is *fun* to figure out words by thinking about the sounds of the letters. As we learn more about letters and their sounds, we'll learn to use all the letters in words to help us read new words."	As children's skills with decoding elements increase, the teacher would encourage attention, ultimately, to all parts of printed words. In addition, as new strategies are introduced, previously taught strategies should be reviewed and connected with the new strategy. When the "Think about the sounds" strategy is explicitly taught, from experience with being read to, children likely already know, at least implicitly, the second and third strategies that would be discussed at this point: *Think about words that might make sense* and *Check the pictures* (see strategies 2 and 3 in Table 12.2).
4. Look for parts you know.	"Now that we've learned about the pattern, it will help us read some of the words in our book today. So, when we come to words that we don't already know, we can check to see if the word has any parts that we *do* know. Using word families/patterns can help us to do that. To find a word family, we need to look at the vowel and what comes after it. Looking for parts we know, like word families, is a strategy we can try when we come to words we don't already know. "To help us remember to *Look for parts you know*, we have the word *sat* with part of it highlighted [point to the icon and draw attention to the highlighted part]. This picture of the word with the highlighted part will remind us to look for parts we know. When we look for parts we know, we can then use the other strategies we've been learning—especially thinking about whether the word we're trying makes sense in the sentence."	This strategy can be introduced after children have been taught and had some practice with their first word family or any other orthographic pattern that has been explicitly taught [and, if terminology other than word family is used (e.g., chunk, decoding key) that terminology should replace the word family terminology]. As appropriate, the teacher will want to encourage the use of this strategy in reference to other word parts that are familiar (e.g., consonant digraphs, vowel teams, inflectional endings, spelling patterns such as *tion*).

7. Try different sounds for some of the letters, especially the vowel(s). Be flexible.	"We have been talking about how the vowel letter *a* sometimes sounds like / ă ă ă ă / in words, like in *aaaapple*, and sometimes sounds like / ā ā ā ā / just like its name. Knowing the two sounds can help us figure out some words because sometimes we need to try different sounds for some of the letters, especially the vowels.
	    "Trying different sounds means try one sound of the letter and, if it doesn't make a word that makes sense in the sentence, then try the other sound for the letter. When we do this, we are being *flexible* with the vowels.
	    "People use the word *flexible* in different ways. We say that things that bend easily are *flexible*. When someone tries more than one
		It would be appropriate to introduce this strategy when children have been taught about both the long- and the short-sounds of a vowel—even if they need to rely on the key word to remind them of the short-vowel sound. We use the vowel *a* in this illustration.
		
		This strategy is also useful for some consonant sounds, especially the hard and soft sounds for *c* and *g*.

(continued)

TABLE 12.1. (continued)

Strategy	Suggested introductory language	Explanation/clarification
	way to solve a puzzle or a problem, we say they are being *flexible*. When you try different sounds for a letter, you are being *flexible* with the sounds. To help you remember to be flexible with the sounds of some of the letters, our picture here [point to the icon for the strategy] shows a line of letters that is flexible (or sort of bendy)."	
8. Break the word into smaller parts.	"Sometimes when we see a word that is sort of long and we don't know what the word is, we can try breaking it into smaller parts, figure out what each part sounds like, and then blend the parts back together. For example, if the word has two consonants in the middle, like this word [show *zipper*], we can try breaking it between the two consonants. To show you what I mean, I am going to draw a line between the two *p*'s. Then we can think about what the first part will sound like. [Give the children time to come up with *zip*.] OK, so we think the first part is *zip*. The next part is *p-e-r* [name the letters]. What do we think that part will sound like? [Give the children time to come up with *per*. Or provide it if need be—perhaps noting that *er* together makes the sound /er/.] So now we've got *zip* and *per*. Let's blend those parts together, saying the two parts quickly: /zip/-/per/. What will that sound like? Is it a word? "When we use this new strategy of breaking the word into smaller parts while we're reading, we will also need to think about whether the word we come up with makes sense in the sentence. "To remind us of this break the word into smaller parts strategy, we have the word *looking* (point to the icon). *Looking* has two parts that we already know . . . *look* and *ing*, and we have a line between the two parts to remind us that sometimes it helps to *Break the word into smaller parts*."	It would be appropriate to introduce this strategy in preparation for a book in which the children will encounter at least a couple of words that they do not yet know and that have more than one syllable. Start by showing the children how to break words into syllables in an isolated context (see Chapter 11). Use words that have syllable patterns that are similar to, but not the same as, the words they will encounter in the book. For example, if the word in the book has a doubled consonant (e.g., *butter*), illustrate with a word that has a doubled consonant (e.g., *hammer*). Or if the children will encounter words with affixes that may be challenging to decode, teach about the affix (again, see Chapter 11) in preparation for reading the book. *Note:* When children are at a point where they are routinely encountering multisyllabic words, the Tips for Breaking Words Apart should be introduced (see Chapter 11, p. 278). Keep in mind that multiple code-based strategies are often needed when solving multisyllabic words, and children may approach this word solving in different ways. For example, with the word *looking*, some children might use the Look for parts you know strategy, covering up the *ing*, reading the word *look*, then blending the two parts back together.

TABLE 12.2. Suggested Introductory Language for Meaning-Based Strategies

Strategy	Suggested introductory language
2. Think about words that might make sense.	"We read because we want to understand what the author is telling us. When we come to a word we don't already know, we start by thinking about the sounds of the letters in the word and what the word might sound like/be. But we also need to think about what the author is telling us because that will help us decide if we have figured out a word that makes sense. If not, we can think about the sounds again to try to come up with a word that does make sense. "To remind us to *Think about words that might make sense,* we have these two question marks [point to the icon]. The question marks remind us that we need to ask a question. If you already have an idea of what a word might be, you ask yourself the question 'Would that word make sense here?' Or, if after thinking about the sounds of the letters in the word you haven't come up with a word you've heard before you could ask yourself 'What word would have these letters and would make sense here?' "
3. Check the picture.	"When you are reading and you come to a word you don't already know, sometimes it helps to also look at the picture. The picture might give you some ideas about what the word is. "We have a picture here [point to the icon] to remind us that we could try checking the picture to help us figure out words." When you check the picture, you then get to go back to the letters in the word you're trying to figure out again and think about their sounds."[a]
5 or 6. Read past the puzzling word.	"Sometimes if you are having trouble figuring out what a word is, it helps to read past the puzzling word. That means to keep on reading to see if the words that come after the puzzling word will give you more ideas about what the puzzling word could be. Then you can go back to the puzzling word and use your other strategies, like thinking about the sounds and other parts you know, to try to come up with a word that makes sense. "We have this arrow [point to the icon] to remind us that when we are puzzling over a word and can't decide what it is, we can *Read past the puzzling word* to get some more ideas about what the word might be. The arrow is pointing in the direction we need to look to see the words that come *after* the puzzling word that might help us decide what that word is."
5 or 6. Go back to the beginning of the sentence and start again.	"Sometimes when you stop to puzzle over a word you might forget what you have already read in the sentence. Going back to the beginning of the sentence and starting again might help you figure out what the puzzling word is. After you've thought about the sounds of the letters and maybe some of the parts you know, going back to the beginning of the sentence and starting again may help you figure out a word that makes sense. "The arrow [point to the icon] is here to remind us that sometimes it helps to go back to what we've already read to see if it helps us decide what the puzzling word is. When we *Go back to the beginning of the sentence and start again*, it can help us figure out the puzzling word."

[a]Recall that "check the pictures" should be construed as "check the illustrations" for older students as well as for young readers who are reading informational texts that include charts and graphs.

In the context of word-identification strategy instruction, for instance, during a shared reading activity, as the teacher reads a text that is visible to all the children in the instructional group, the teacher might occasionally puzzle through a word that they pretend not to recognize. For example, in a think-aloud for teaching children to *Think about the sounds of the letters in the word* and *Check the picture*, teachers might use a beginner-level book about picking apples to illustrate the thinking process. To begin with, the teacher might say: "I have put some highlighting tape over some of the words in this book so that I can show you how using the strategies *Think about the sounds* and *Check the pictures* together can help us figure out words we don't already know." (The words selected for highlighting should be one-syllable CVC words for which the children know the sounds of the graphemes in the initial and final position—and possibly the middle position.) Then the teacher would read through the book, pointing to the words, until coming to the first highlighted word (e.g., *bag*). At that point the teacher might say:

> "This page says, 'Look at the. . . . Hmmm. I'm not sure what this word is. I know the first letter, *B*, has the /b/ sound, and the last letter, *G*, has the /g/ sound, but I'm not sure about the sound for the letter *A*. I am going to look at the picture to see if it gives me any ideas about what this word is. I see a lot of apples in a bag. *Look at the apples* would make sense, but when I say *aaaaples*, I hear /ăăă/ at the beginning, so I know this word (*pointing to the highlighted word*) can't be *apples*, because this word begins with the /b/ sound. Hmmm. The apples are in a bag, so maybe this word is *bag*. When I say *bag*, I do hear the /b/ sound at the beginning, and I hear the /g/ sound at the end, and I see a bag in the picture, so I think this word must be *bag*."

As noted above, the *Check the picture* strategy is combined with the *Think about the sounds* strategy in the same lesson. This reinforces the understanding that the pictures can be an assist for figuring out a word when the child does not yet have the decoding skills to rely more heavily on the sounds for the letters in the word. For children who can decode the word *bag*, the teacher would still, on occasion, direct their attention to the picture to help them confirm that the word they arrived at makes sense. (Depending on the current skills of the children in the group, the teacher might also use this particular opportunity to explicitly teach [or review] the sound for the letter *A*.)

When children have learned multiple strategies and are proficient in the use of several of them, the teacher might use multiple strategies during a think-aloud:

> "Hmmm, I'm going to pretend I don't know this word. I'm going to use my strategies to figure it out. I know lots of things I can try. I can look at the letters in the word and think about their sounds—that will help me think about what the word will sound like. Maybe I'll notice a word family or some other part I know. I can think about words that would make sense. Maybe the

picture will give me some ideas." (It would be useful for the teacher to point to the icon for each of the strategies as it is named.)

KEEP IN MIND The way we talk about the process of identifying unfamiliar words may influence children's willingness to engage in the process. Referring to words as *hard* or *tricky* may lead some children to feel defeated before they even try to identify a word. So too might talking about being *stuck* on a word. Referring to unfamiliar words as *puzzling* or as *detective words*, however, may be a bit more motivating. Use of the word *challenging* may also be appropriate in settings where children have learned to embrace challenges.

Guided Practice and Gradual Release of Responsibility

Upon first attempting to use a given strategy, children need to work collaboratively to develop the thinking processes involved. The first several opportunities for children to use a newly taught strategy may be contrived to ensure that the utility of the strategy is very clear to them. For example, for the strategy *Try different sounds for some of the letters, especially the vowels*, the first time the children are asked to use the strategy, the teacher might show a sentence containing the word *child*:

Maria is a child.

(The name of one of the children in the instructional group might be substituted for *Maria*.) For children who know a fair amount about the alphabetic code (which is when this strategy would be appropriate to teach), the most reasonable first attempt at the word *child* would be to pronounce it with a short-*i* sound.[3] After discussing that this decoding attempt did not result in a word that made sense in the sentence, the teacher might prompt the students to use the new strategy that had been taught (and perhaps reiterate the strategy). "Hmmm. Maria is a chilled? That doesn't make sense. So, let's try our new strategy: *Try different sounds for some of the letters, especially the vowels*. What is the other sound we know for the vowel *i*?" Once the word is successfully identified, the teacher would encourage the children to reread the sentence to determine if it makes sense. Having concluded that it does, the students and teacher would briefly reflect on the utility of the newly taught strategy and how useful it is to check to confirm that word identification attempts make sense in context.

Across many different reading episodes, teachers should provide children with practice in using newly taught strategies in contexts in which the particular strategy will work effectively (e.g., when children encounter a word they do not immediately recognize, and the new strategy, in combination with other known strategies, is likely to enable accurate word identification). The teacher might begin by noticing and naming what the child has done effectively in trying to solve the

---

[3] Assuming, of course, the *ild* rime/word family has not been taught/learned.

word (thought about the sounds, checked the picture, etc.) and would suggest that they try the new strategy—by naming the strategy—perhaps while simultaneously pointing to the strategy icon on the strategy chart. Once children have experienced some success in applying the strategy, they need experience with using the strategy when it doesn't work. This will help them to understand the need to be flexible in applying the various strategies and to use multiple sources of information in their word-solving efforts.

Guiding Strategy Use

During guided practice, the teacher should act as a coach, initially advising children to try a particular strategy only when the teacher is fairly certain that it will work and later encouraging children to try the strategy both when it will work and when it is not clear that it will work. Early on, when a strategy does not work, the teacher and children should reflect on the fact that the strategy did not work in that particular situation. For example, the teacher might say: "Hmm, sometimes checking the pictures doesn't help us to figure out the word. Later on, we will learn some other strategies that might have worked for this word." Or "What other strategies do we know that we could try?"

Helping Children Take Ownership of Strategy Use

The goal is for the children to internalize the word-solving strategies and to become independent in their use. One way to encourage internalization is to have them rehearse by reciting the strategies they have learned, initially by referring to the strategy chart (and attending to the icons to remind them of the strategies), but later by relying on memory. For example, before reading a book, children might be asked, "What are some of the things we can do if we come to a word we don't already know in this book?" In addition, when a child pauses on a word while reading, the teacher might say, "That word is puzzling you—what could you do to try to figure it out?" Engaging children in thinking aloud about the problem-solving strategies serves to enhance their awareness of the process (Prawat, 1989). When a teacher responds to difficulties in this way, on a consistent basis, the children are likely to ask themselves the same questions when they encounter an unfamiliar word. They might say to themselves: "I don't know what that word is. What can I do to figure it out?"

KEEP IN MIND   "Guided practice is something we too often skip. We teach, assume the teaching has paid off in learning, and then go straight to independent practice, the next step in the learning process" (Saunders-Smith, 2003, p. 50). Providing guidance as the children begin to use new strategies and use them in interactive and confirmatory ways will serve to move children toward independence in effective strategy use. In other words, it helps them to become self-regulated word solvers and, thereby, word learners.

Independent Practice

The ultimate goal of strategy teaching is for children to be able to independently employ the strategies that are taught. To ensure that the children do, in fact, use the strategies when they are not engaged with the teacher, it is helpful to engage them in reflecting on and discussing their strategy use when they have been reading independently: "Tell me/us what you did to figure out that word." Teachers have found it useful to encourage children who are learning word-identification strategies to use small sticky notes or flags to mark places in text where they have relied on strategies for word solving during independent reading. At a later point, the teacher confers with the students about the places they have marked.

Encouraging Interactive Strategy Use

Although teaching the individual strategies is important, it is critical that children learn to use strategies in combination and in mutually supportive and confirming ways. For example, a child who has learned to effectively use the strategy of *Try different sounds for some of the letters, especially the vowels,* might reasonably decode the word *read* such that it rhymes with *seed.* However, before settling on this pronunciation, the reader would evaluate whether that word fits the context in which it occurred and, if not, the reader would try a different pronunciation (such as pronouncing it with the short-*e* vowel sound and then check to see whether that word fits the context). Thus, as described at the beginning of this chapter, interactive and confirmatory strategy use often involves an iterative process in which different pronunciations of individual words are checked against the reader's evolving understanding of the text. This would be an example of making use of one's set for variability (described in Chapter 10).

Word-Identification Strategy-Focused Instruction

In this section, we describe how word-identification strategy instruction, and the teacher thinking that goes along with that instruction, might unfold before, during, and after children engage in reading a book.

Strategy Instruction before Reading

Preparing to Read a New Book

Until children are routinely and effectively strategic, it is important to provide them with guidance and instruction in the use of word-identification strategies prior to reading each new book. The characteristics of the books used to promote strategic reading are important to consider both because the level of challenge that the children encounter in each book will influence their ability to be strategic and because some books facilitate strategy instruction and practice more than others (see the "Characteristics of the Text" section in the introduction to Part III, pp. 292–297).

Selection of Texts That Will Be Somewhat Challenging

At one point, texts that children could read with 90–95% word-reading accuracy were considered to be appropriate for instructional purposes. However, current understanding of what makes texts more and less challenging for early-grade readers calls for consideration of additional text characteristics as well as the capabilities and characteristics of the students who will be reading those texts. These characteristics include the frequency of the words in the text (and/or the percentage of rare words [words that occur infrequently in spoken and written language]), the length of the sentences, the frequency of repetition of individual words, whether the texts have a predictable pattern and, of course, the children's decoding skills. Further, when comprehension is considered, as, ideally, it always would be, the learner's background knowledge and language skills relative to the content of the text play a major role.

As of this writing, the two most commonly used systems for rating books' readability (complexity) levels are Guided Reading Levels, with levels ranging from A (beginning of kindergarten) to Z (seventh/eighth grade) (Fountas & Pinnell, 2012), and Lexiles, which range from 0 (beginning of kindergarten) to 1100 (by eighth grade) (Stenner, Burdick, Sanford, & Burdick, 2007).[4] The use of Lexile levels has become increasingly popular since passage of the Common Core State Standards. While the two leveling systems tend to correlate with one another reasonably well, analyses by Hiebert and Tortorelli (2022) and others are raising questions about the utility of existing systems for text leveling and have suggested that the single letters or numbers assigned as level indicators for individual texts do not sufficiently acknowledge the changes that occur within and across texts. Teachers are encouraged to consider their readers' vocabulary, general language skills, and background knowledge when evaluating whether a particular text is a good match for their students and to consider what they may need to do in order to prepare learners to read a given text. In the early grades, Fitzgerald et al. (2016) suggest that "[i]n light of evidence that today's reading programs tend to have difficult vocabulary, teachers might particularly observe degrees of repetition and patterning because no patterning or relatively little patterning may couple with the difficult vocabulary to result in relatively high challenge to students' comprehension" (p. 63). The point is that, simply relying on a text's level or scanning a text to identify word-identification challenges that a reader might encounter—with an eye for preparing them for those challenges—will not necessarily enable teachers to prepare children for all the challenges a given text might present.

---

[4]Many systems for assessing the readability of children's books have been developed over the years. More examples and comparisons among the different systems can be found by Googling *text leveling*.

In addition, some schools use series of texts composed of decodable texts *rather* than leveled texts in the early grades. Comparisons of the two types of texts reveal that texts deemed appropriate for children at a given grade and point in a school year make very different demands on learners and often vary considerably within a level (Koons & Hiebert, 2019).

Another approach involves following the sequence in a structured series of texts. This may help to keep students in the appropriate range of challenge, as most such series attempt to systematically develop the decoding skills and high-frequency sight vocabulary that students need to negotiate upcoming texts. Under these conditions, children may be able to comfortably read a book within the series that is at a higher "level" (whatever leveling system is used) than they would another book at the same level that is not part of the series' sequence. This is because the needed foundations developed in the series will not necessarily serve them in a book that is not from the series. However, with such an approach, as with the others mentioned above, individual student characteristics will still impact the level of challenge an individual child encounters when attempting to read a particular text. Certainly, there are cultural and linguistic factors, but more specific experiential factors can impact the level of challenge a child encounters with a specific text on a particular day. As there are many important considerations in relation to texts for learners at early points in development, attention needs to be given to the level of challenge given texts present for individual learners. When there are many unknown words (in either spoken or written language) and/or when the content is too unfamiliar, it is extremely difficult, if not impossible, for children to be effectively strategic in working through a given text. The point is, a wide range of factors contributes to the level of challenge that a text provides for individual children (see Mesmer, 2008; Pearson & Hiebert, 2014; Walski, 2020). Teachers who work closely and thoughtfully with small groups of children will, ideally, come to know their students well enough that they are able to select books (and prepare children to read books) that provide sufficient challenge. Books with appropriate challenge provide teachers with the opportunity to observe and guide strategic processing but do not frustrate or overwhelm the children in the group.

KEEP IN MIND Children learn to read by reading. Some reading programs engage children in reading and rereading the same passages or texts for an entire week. If this is the only reading children do, their rate of progress *and* their motivation are likely to be more limited than if a greater variety of texts are read. Greater variety provides children with more opportunities to be strategic in their word-solving efforts and to engage with more diverse and interesting texts.

Preparing Children to Read a Specific Book

The supportiveness of the introduction of a new book should be based on the characteristics of the text and the skills, strategies, and past experiences[5] of the

───────────

[5] More about this in Chapter 16.

children. If we provide more support than the children need to read a book (for example, explicitly teaching all the unfamiliar words they are going to encounter in the book), their opportunities to grow as readers will be limited because they will not have the opportunity to use their developing word-identification strategies. If we provide too little support, they may become frustrated. Further, they will not be able to effectively apply their developing word-identification strategies because, when a text is too difficult, children will be unable to decide if what they are reading makes sense. In this instance, it will be difficult for children to determine whether word-identification errors have occurred.

Several different approaches to the provision of support prior to reading a new book are presented below. The procedures are listed in order of their supportiveness, with the most supportive approaches listed first.

More Support

↑

• *Read the text to the child(ren).* Children at the earliest points of reading development often benefit from having a book read to them before they attempt to read it. This approach allows them to focus more of their attention on the printed words when they ultimately read, since they have had the opportunity to enjoy and think about the meaning of the text when it was read to them. However, for children to become independent readers, they need to have the opportunity to engage in the strategic thinking and problem solving that reading a new book entails. If every text is read to them before they attempt it, which is sometimes the practice for early readers, it will limit their opportunities to become strategic thinkers.

• *Introduce the book.* Previewing a book by looking at and discussing the pictures (sometimes called a *picture walk*) can help children develop an overview of what the book is about and provide the teacher with the opportunity to introduce some of the language structures and concepts that will allow children to read the text more easily. Book introductions typically include several of the following components:

  o Introducing the title and author of the book.
  o Relating the book to something the children know about, care about, have read or heard previously, etc.
  o Collaborative wondering about what might happen or be learned in the book.
  o Flipping through the pages of the book and discussing what is happening and possibly refining expectations about what will happen or be learned.
  o For books that include challenging language or language patterns, incorporating the language from the text into the discussion.

• *Teach important unfamiliar words and/or decoding elements before children read the text.* For a given text, it is generally possible to anticipate which words and/or decoding elements (e.g., word families, affixes, vowel teams) will be challenging for a specific group of children. The important words or elements to teach ahead of time are those that both occur with some frequency in the text and that would be difficult for children to figure out, given their current level of decoding skill and the contextual supports in the book. Teaching these words and/or decoding elements prior to having the children read the text will allow them to read more fluently and comfortably on their first attempt.

• *Provide a brief book introduction and allow the children to independently preview the text before reading.* Children who have had extensive experience with book introductions can often gather a good deal of information about a text by looking through the book independently before reading. The teacher might provide an overall schema for the text by briefly telling the children the topic of the text. For example: "Today we are going to read this book about snakes; before you read, look through the book a bit to see what we might learn about snakes." And, if it appears the children have no knowledge about the topic, for example in response to a question like "What do you already know about snakes?" the teacher would provide them with some information about snakes that will help them make sense of the text they are about to read. The children would then be given time to preview the text on their own before reading.

Less
Support

KEEP IN MIND It is possible to do too much in preparing children to read a new book. For example, we have observed teachers who teach far too many words from the book before asking the children to read. Only words that are important for understanding the text and that the children are unlikely to be able to figure out, given their current word-solving strategies and the contextual/pictorial support, should be taught prior to reading. We have also observed teachers routinely having children locate and read the most challenging language in the text prior to having them read the book. As a result, when the children come to that portion of the text while reading, their opportunities for problem solving will be reduced because they have already looked at and read the language with teacher guidance. As an alternative, the teacher might use the challenging language during the book introduction but not directly draw the children's attention to the print. That way, the children will be primed for the unfamiliar language but will have the opportunity to puzzle through it when they encounter it in print.

Strategy Talk

The nature of strategy discussions that are provided before a new text is read will depend on the children's point in development with word-identification strategies. If new strategies have been taught recently, they might be reviewed fairly thoroughly, whereas strategies that the children understand and use well might only be briefly mentioned or not mentioned at all. Alternatively, if all the strategies have been taught but the children need more support in effectively using some more than others, a brief lesson concerning the use of one or two strategies might be offered. Sometimes a strategy talk before reading might involve having the children name the strategies they know. This approach will help them internalize the strategies so that they can call upon them when neither the teacher nor the chart is available. This might be supported by having children use the strategy icons to remind them of the strategies. Also, the teacher might construct a sentence or two that is unrelated to the new book but includes some of the decoding elements and challenges the children are working on mastering and that provide opportunities to apply word-solving strategies.

An Example of Multiple-Strategy Use in a Single Sentence

In preparing a first-grade child who had already learned about all the word-solving strategies to read a new book, the teacher constructed a sentence that would give the child the opportunity to apply all the strategies (except *Check the pictures,* as there were no pictures). Here's the sentence:

I like racing cars with my friends.

This sentence provided the child with the opportunity to:

- Think about the sounds of the letters—the word *racing* was novel to the child.
- Look for parts you know—the child covered the *ing* in the word *racing* with his finger as he attempted to figure out the first part of the word.
- Think about words that might make sense—the child initially identified the word *racing* as *raking.*
- Read past the puzzling word—*raking* didn't make sense when followed by *cars.*
- Try different sounds of some of the letters—the child needed to assign a different pronunciation to the letter *c* in the word *racing.*
- Go back to the beginning of the sentence and start again—the child read the entire sentence to confirm that all words had been identified correctly.

Strategy Instruction during Reading

Teachers should attempt to listen to individual children read as often as possible, particularly children who are making limited progress with reading. Observing children's approaches to word solving provides opportunities for the teacher to coach and guide students' strategic behaviors and will inform the teacher's planning of future strategy instruction. As noted earlier, in small-group contexts, teachers ideally listen to one child read during each reading opportunity. As a child reads, it is important for the teacher to attend to each component described below.

Allowing the Child Enough (Relaxed) Time to Puzzle through Difficult Sections of Text

It takes a good deal of time for young children to orchestrate the various strategies. If children are given assistance with puzzling through an unfamiliar word before they have had time to think things through, they may not develop the independence that is critical to becoming an effective word learner. Teachers need to think carefully about how much support/scaffolding will help to move the child forward in the independent application of word-solving strategies. As we've noted previously, children's development can be limited by providing either too little or too much assistance. The assistance given needs to take different forms for different students at different points in time (and in different contexts). Thus, the recommendation to "allow the child enough time" does not come with an explicit recommendation concerning how long one should wait.

In some contexts, it may be appropriate to provide assistance almost immediately. This is especially the case when a child encounters a word that the teacher knows the child cannot decode and the context is not helpful. In other situations, it may be appropriate to wait as much as 10 seconds or more if the child appears to be word solving productively.

When they are involved in partner reading or other group formats, children who need more time to puzzle through words may feel anxious about taking the time they need, and/or their partners may provide the word before they have had time to think it through. When children routinely have the words that they are puzzling over solved for them, their sense of efficacy with word solving may be undermined. As a result, they may come to view themselves as unable to word-solve.

Rather than allowing a partner to provide the word that another child is puzzling over, it is helpful to encourage children to view taking the time to figure out a word as something positive. ("It's fun to be able to figure out words yourself—it's like being a detective.") If a child is not able to make progress with solving a particular word, the partner(s) might be encouraged to make suggestions concerning different word-solving strategies to try. But it should be done only when the child who is reading indicates the need for some ideas. For example, the teacher might say, "Take the time you need to figure out the word and let your partner(s) know if you would like them to suggest strategies that might work." This approach not only provides the reader with a bit more relaxed time to think but engages the partner(s) in thinking about the strategies and can lead to productive conversations about how multiple strategies may be needed to figure out and confirm the identity of a word.

Noticing and Acknowledging
Children's Strategic Word Solving

Listening to children read and noting their strategic word solving focuses teachers' attention on what the children are doing to solve words—both when they are successful and when they are not. We have long known that guiding children's thinking and problem solving (and behavior) is more effective when we give more attention to what they have done well than to what they have not done well. This principle applies to word solving as well. Teachers should look for occasions when children use one or more of the word-solving strategies spontaneously and attend to their efforts even if they are not entirely successful in identifying unfamiliar words. Indicators that a child is being strategic include the following:

- The child spontaneously corrects a word-identification error.
- The child hesitates briefly over an unfamiliar word before identifying it accurately.
- The child refers to resources such as a strategy chart, key-word chart, or word wall for assistance in identifying a puzzling word.

When children begin to demonstrate the inclination to be strategic, it is important to notice and name it. Examples of noticing and naming include the following:

- "I noticed that you looked at the key-word chart when you puzzled through that word; that helped you remember the sounds of some of those letters and figure out what word would fit there."
- "I noticed you looking at your strategy chart when you came to that puzzling word—that is a very good way to help you remember some of the things you can try when you need to puzzle through a word."
- "Wow! Good thinking! When you got to the end of that sentence and realized that something didn't make sense, you went back and reread the sentence and tried some different sounds for the vowels in that word that was new to you, and it worked!"

Gradual Release of Responsibility

For strategy instruction to have the desired effect, children ultimately need to become independent in their strategy use. For some children, teachers will have to hand over responsibility for strategic word solving in a very planned and gradual way. Teachers should provide enough support for word solving to allow children to be successful but not so much support that they don't need to do much thinking. For example, in some cases it might be appropriate to suggest a specific strategy for a child to use; in other cases, patient waiting will be the most helpful thing to do. The following is an ordering of prompts teachers might provide or actions they might take that range from more to less supportive. In general, we want to provide children with the least support possible while still enabling success.

More
Support

- *Purpose:* Avoid having the child become frustrated and help the child experience success in the application of word-solving strategies.
  - o Suggest a specific strategy or combination of strategies that is likely to work well for the child in the given context and help the child apply the strategy(ies) if need be. For example: "Think about the sound of the first letter in that word and then look at the picture to see if it gives you some ideas." (This particular prompt would be appropriate for children at the very beginning of learning to read.)
- *Purpose:* Helping the child to learn to use available resources in the process of word solving, thereby helping the child to begin to appreciate their utility.
  - o Remind the child to look at the strategy chart for ideas on how to solve the word (e.g., "That word is puzzling you; look at your strategy chart for some ideas on how to figure it out").
- *Purpose:* Encourage the child to begin to internalize the strategies. The child may refer to the chart if desired, but if the teacher believes that the child is beginning to internalize the strategies, the teacher may not want to direct the child to the chart (e.g., "That word is puzzling you; what are some of the things you could try?").
- *Purpose:* Communicate to the child that they are becoming effectively strategic.
  - o Wait patiently while the child puzzles through the word and try to notice what the child does to figure it out and explicitly name it. For example: "You had to do some thinking on that word; I noticed you broke the word into smaller parts by covering up the ending while you were trying to figure it out—that worked, didn't it?"
- *Purpose:* Encourage independence in word solving.
  - o Wait patiently while a child puzzles through a word and then ask how they figured it out (e.g., "I noticed you had to think about that word a bit; what did you do to figure it out?"). Engagement in this type of reflection helps children internalize the strategies by engaging them in talking about how the strategies were used.
- *Purpose:* Move to even greater independence. Wait patiently while the child puzzles through words and then briefly acknowledge what they did and move on. For example: "I see you are really thinking like

a reader!" This is partly just a pat on the back, but it also helps to reinforce the notion that reading involves (is) thinking.

- *Purpose:* Remove the teacher from the word-solving process. The goal of word-solving strategy instruction is to develop the ability to independently word-solve, as that enables the reader to focus on comprehension. At this point, just let children keep reading. Do not interrupt for strategy talk once children seem to be secure in their use of (particular) strategies.

Less
Support

Promoting Self-Regulation, Not Dependence

In the context of reading, *self-regulation* refers to the ability to independently notice and at least attempt to solve problems that arise with either word identification or comprehension. Teachers have a fair amount of control over whether children become self-regulated learners. In our experience, particularly in intervention settings, teachers are often inclined to do too much of the thinking for students. As a result, the students come to depend on the teacher in ways that are counterproductive for their reading growth. When a child routinely looks at the teacher upon encountering difficulty with word identification, it is usually a good sign that the teacher has been too helpful to the child. It is important for teachers to reflect on what they do (or do not do) to promote self-regulation regarding word learning (as well as other instructional goals of course!). Many times, fairly small changes in how the teacher reacts to a student's difficulties will lead to big advances in the student's ability to problem-solve independently. Table 12.3 provides a listing of some common student reading behaviors, along with the teacher behaviors and responses that either promote dependence on the teacher or promote independence.

Strategy Instruction after Reading

When children who are still becoming proficient with strategy use have finished reading a text, it is helpful to focus on the strategies they used effectively. For example, teachers might prompt them in one or more of the following ways:

- "What strategies do you think you used well today?"
- "What strategies do you think you need more practice with?"
- "Are there any strategies you forget to use? If so, what can you do to remember to use that strategy?"
- "You puzzled through this word a bit and figured it out. Tell me how you did it."

It is also a good idea to name the things that the children did well—especially the things that are current objectives for the child(ren).

TABLE 12.3. Teacher Behaviors That Promote Dependence or Independence in Word Learning

Student reading behavior	Teacher response that promotes dependence	Teacher response that promotes self-regulation and independence
Child looks at the teacher upon encountering an unfamiliar word.	Teacher tells child the word. Or Teacher gives a partial response (e.g., articulates the first sound in the unfamiliar word).	Teacher continues to look at the word rather than making eye contact with the child. Or Teacher asks, "What could you try there?" Or Teacher prompts with a word-identification strategy that has recently been taught.
Child reads many unfamiliar words with a rising (questioning) intonation.	Teacher confirms or disconfirms for the child ("Uh-huh" or "Nooo . . .").	Teacher waits for the child to do the confirmation, saying nothing. The teacher's eyes remain on the text rather than looking at the child. Or, if need be: Teacher prompts the child to confirm/disconfirm (e.g., "Keep reading [or reread] to see if that makes sense").
Child produces words that don't fit the context.	Teacher asks, "Does that make sense?" before the child has read far enough along to realize that meaning has been lost. Or Teacher asks, "Does that make sense?" *only* when it doesn't make sense.	Teacher does not comment on word-identification errors until the child has read far enough along to notice that something doesn't make sense. Or Teacher asks, "Does that make sense?" both when the word *read* does make sense and when it doesn't. This makes the question a genuine one rather than a signal that a word-identification error has occurred.

- "I saw that you used the word family chart to help you figure out some words."
- "I heard a lot of people thinking like readers today. I notice that you are helping each other remember to use your strategies."
- "You all are really getting good at being flexible with those vowel sounds!"

KEEP IN MIND All the discussion in this chapter has been focused on word-identification strategy instruction. This is one major goal that is pursued in the context of engaging the children in reading text. The other major goal is for the children to become active, engaged comprehenders. For children who are at the early stages of learning to read and for those who are struggling with reading, it is easy for teachers to become so focused on facilitating the development of skill in word identification that the focus on meaning is lost—at least to the child. So, while in this chapter we discussed instruction that is intended to promote the development of skill in word identification that should occur before, during, and after children read a text, this instruction should not replace instruction intended to develop meaning-focused reading.

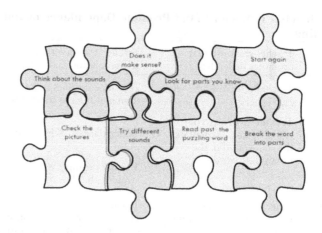

FIGURE 12.6. The eight word-identification strategies taught in the ISA.

Conceptualizing Word Solving/Word Learning

Word solving and word learning are complex processes. The puzzle depicted in Figure 12.6 illustrates the eight word-identification strategies that are explicitly taught in the ISA; they are depicted as separate pieces of a puzzle that fit together but form an incomplete puzzle. Effective word solvers draw on a lot of knowledge sources and experiences to support their word solving/word learning; not all of them can be captured by the eight strategies described.

KEY POINTS OF THIS CHAPTER

✓ Reading comprehension depends on accurate and fluent identification of all or nearly all of the words in a text.

✓ Most words that become part of a reader's sight vocabulary are not explicitly taught but are learned through effective word solving while reading. Share (1995, 2008) refers to this as self-teaching.

✓ Because accurate word solving is critical to word learning and because written English has many inconsistencies in how certain phonemes are represented in print, it is important that children learn to use the context in which unknown words occur to verify/confirm their decoding attempts.

✓ Children who rely too exclusively on decoding strategies will produce many word-identification errors when attempting to read unfamiliar words and will, therefore, not only fail to learn at least some of the words they are attempting but will also fail to make sense of some of the materials they read.

✓ Learners need to use a combination of code- and meaning-based strategies to solve and ultimately learn the huge number of words that a proficient reader can read effortlessly—because the English language is characterized by variability in the relationships between graphemes and their associated phonemes—especially the vowels.

✓ Word-solving strategies and the application of the alphabetic principle are thought, by many theorists, to be the primary way by which sight vocabulary is built.

✓ Independent use of the strategies discussed in this chapter serves as a "self-teaching mechanism," whereby readers learn to read previously unknown words in the process of reading meaningful texts.

✓ Strategic reading of manageable texts (i.e., texts that include a small proportion of words that are not already sight words) helps build sight vocabulary because learners are more likely to be able to identify the limited number of unfamiliar words they encounter while reading.

✓ Rereading texts is helpful for promoting fluency with words that were new to the reader on the first read.

✓ Children need to engage in extensive amounts of reading to build their sight vocabularies.

CHAPTER 13

High-Frequency Word Learning and Word Identification

WORD-LEARNING GOAL 2

Children will be able to read and spell the most frequently occurring words accurately and quickly.

Estimates indicate that approximately 50% of the words in any written text are among the 100 most frequently occurring words (e.g., *is, on, was*) and that approximately 70% of the words in any written text are among the 300 most frequently occurring words (which include words like *other, sound, something*).[1] Words that occur at a high rate of frequency in print (and in spoken language) are often referred to as high-frequency words. Because they are so frequent, it is important to help learners add them to their sight vocabularies as soon as possible. Knowing the most frequently occurring words will enable learners to more readily puzzle through and identify the many thousands of other words they will learn, for the most part, through effective word solving while reading (as discussed in Chapter 12). As we have indicated previously, the more words readers can identify automatically/effortlessly, the more cognitive resources they have to devote to making sense of the texts they read.

---

[1] Note that this estimate may not apply to the highly decodable texts that are sometimes used to teach phonics in early literacy settings. This is true because, in order to create a text with a high proportion of words that include the decoding elements that have already been taught, it is often necessary to include relatively rare words such as *jam, yam,* and *clam.*

Characteristics of High-Frequency Words

An important characteristic of most high-frequency words is that they refer to abstractions (that is, they do not refer to things that can be seen or envisioned), and the role they play in sentences is often hard to explain. For example, how would the meaning of the words *the* or *of* be explained? The abstract nature of many high-frequency words makes them comparatively difficult to learn even with explicit instruction (Rawlins & Invernizzi, 2018). Further, some are relatively difficult to solve owing to the fact that they may not be fully decodable, especially for children who are at early points in their development of decoding skills. For example, for children who are first learning about the most common letter–sound (grapheme–phoneme) correspondences, the words *is* (iz), *was* (wuz), *one* (wun), and *what* (wut) are not entirely decodable. Such words have traditionally been referred to as *irregular* words. However, the way to determine which words should be considered irregular has shifted a bit in recent years. For example, in some approaches, the fact that the grapheme *s* represents the phoneme /z/ is often explicitly taught. Thus, a word like *is* might be considered to be *temporarily* irregular for literacy learners—until the /z/ pronunciation for *s* has been taught/learned. The general point is that, for children who are first learning a decoding system, the variation in how the phonemes in some words are represented in print can make learning to identify those words challenging. For all of these reasons, it is useful to explicitly teach the most frequently occurring words and to provide sufficient practice to enable children to identify them effortlessly when reading and, ideally, eventually spell them conventionally from memory when writing.

The most recent compilation of high-frequency words is provided by Kearns (*www.devinkearns.org/reading-materials*). Note that, unlike most word lists which are arranged vertically, the Kearns list is arranged horizontally—the five most frequent words are across the top row). Figure 13.1 presents the 25 most frequent words on the Kearns list for purposes of illustration. (Note that other compilations of high-frequency words would include pretty much the same words—although not necessarily in the exact same order.)

The abstract nature of the words on this list is evident. Also evident is the fact that many of the words (those that appear in bold print) are not fully decodable—at least not for children at the very beginning of learning about the writing system.

Words 1–5	**the**	to	and	**of**	in
Words 6–10	**is**	I	**you**	it	for
Words 11–15	that	on	**was**	with	**are**
Words 16–20	this	be	not	**as**	at
Words 21–25	he	**have**	**from**	or	**they**

FIGURE 13.1. The 25 most frequently used words in written language according to Kearns.

Alert!

Teachers, like most literate adults, are often insensitive to or unaware of the fact that some words are not fully decodable. This is especially true in the case of high-frequency words. For example, many adults have difficulty identifying the one word in Figure 13.1 that is not at all decodable, given the letter–sound (grapheme–phoneme) correspondences typically taught to beginning readers.[2] Many teachers are surprised by the prevalence of words that are not entirely decodable for readers at early points in development. Perhaps the most prevalent "irregularity" is that every vowel letter sometimes represents the schwa ("uh") sound as in the words *the, of, was,* and *from.*

Figure 13.1 illustrates how common it is for some of the most frequently occurring words to be less than fully decodable for beginning readers and to raise teachers' awareness of when words are, and are not, fully decodable for young children. This is important as, hopefully, it will impact the guidance that teachers provide as children engage in word solving and the types of instruction and practice that occurs in relation to these very common words. In this chapter, we caution that instruction to help learners add these words to their sight vocabularies needs to be especially focused and planful.

Assessing and Tracking Growth in High-Frequency Sight-Word Knowledge

Assessment of the ability to identify high-frequency printed words can help to inform instructional grouping decisions as, in the early primary grades, children who are at similar points in their knowledge of high-frequency words often have similar instructional needs related to reading. Therefore, it is useful to have an efficient way to conduct an initial assessment and to track progress over time.

Multiple considerations need to go into teaching, assessing, and tracking growth in high-frequency word knowledge. From our perspective, the first criterion should be whether children are learning the words that have been explicitly taught and encountered in the texts they have had the opportunity to read. However, beginning literacy learners *may* experience a wide variety of beginner-level texts—beyond those that are used for instruction. Therefore, it is entirely possible that high frequently word knowledge will expand faster and beyond the words that are explicitly taught. Thus, while it is important to assess knowledge of words that have been taught, it is also useful to use word lists such as those provided by Kearns to evaluate children's progress—and, thereby, make grouping and planning decisions. To that end, we suggest that teachers use a high-frequency word list such as that provided by Kearns and break the first 100-word list into four or five lists

---

[2]Neither of the letters in the word *of* (pronounced "uv") represents their most common sounds.

of 20 to 25 words. A record sheet for recording the child's performance would also be kept. Figure 13.2 provides an example of a record sheet that can track a child's performance across multiple administrations.

On the first administration, at the beginning of the school year at least for kindergartners and first graders,[3] the assessment would begin with the first 20 or 25 words and continue until the child is unable to read more than half of the words on a given list (continuing past this point would be too frustrating for children). Words identified both accurately and automatically (about 2 seconds or less) would be marked with a checkmark (✓). Those identified accurately but more slowly would be identified with an X. When a child misidentifies a word, it is helpful to record what the child says, as this will provide insight into the child's approach to word solving. On subsequent administrations, it is not necessary to readminister lists on which the child read all or nearly all (19/20) of the words accurately and automatically. The words that a child reads accurately but slowly are words that should be selected for some of the practice activities described later in the chapter. Additional high-frequency words for instruction and practice should be selected from books or other texts the children will be reading—privileging the words from those books that are among the most frequent based on the Kearns (or other) high-frequency word list.

Figure 13.3 provides a vehicle for teachers to record their observations of children's acquisition of high-frequency word knowledge. The form allows space for teachers to record their observations of individual children multiple times over the course of a school year. For children in intervention settings, teachers will probably want to closely document their progress in learning high-frequency sight words. This can be done most easily by counting the number of words that appear on a child's individual "Words I Know" chart (described later). Alternatively, for students who are not in intervention beyond the classroom, the high-frequency word assessment using a list such as Kearns's (p. 345) can be periodically readministered and the highest numbered portions of the list that the child reads fluently with 90–95% or better accuracy can be recorded. Note, however, that children should not be considered to "know" a word unless they can identify that word both in isolation and when encountered in text. For that reason, children should not simply practice lists of high-frequency words that will be used for assessment, because a word's position on an assessment list, if practiced in list form, may help children identify individual words.

Rather, words should be learned in preparation for use in meaningful reading and writing contexts and, ideally, through children's exposure to print across the school day and in their lives beyond the school walls.

(text resumes on p. 350)

---

[3] For second graders, especially those who were considered to be average or better readers at the end of the previous school year, assessment might reasonably start with the highest list on which the reader was successful at the end of the previous school year.

Child's Name _____ Grade _____

First 20	Date	Date	Date	Second 20	Date	Date	Date
the				he			
to				have			
and				from			
of				or			
in				they			
is				all			
I				but			
you				by			
it				your			
for				one			
that				can			
on				we			
was				his			
with				if			
are				will			
this				what			
be				about			
not				my			
as				do			
at				there			
First 20 Total				**Second 20 Total**			

FIGURE 13.2. Record sheet for tracking skill in high-frequency word identification. (These lists are based on the high-frequency word list provided by Kearns [*www.devinkearns.org/reading-materials*]).

Group Snapshot—Observations of High-Frequency Word Learning						
Student names						
Number of known high-frequency words (that can be identified effortlessly/at sight).	Date					
	Date					
	Date					
	Date					
	Date					
	Date					
	Date					
	Date					
	Date					
	Date					
	Date					
	Date					

Record the number of words on the child's "Words I/We Know" chart or the number of the highest 20/25–word list (see p. 371), which the child reads with 95% or better accuracy. For example, if using the Kearns list as described on page 345, the teacher would record the number of the highest list on which the accuracy and fluency criterion is met.

FIGURE 13.3. Group snapshot for observation of high-frequency word learning.

Early Instruction of High-Frequency Words

The first words children learn to read need special instructional consideration because children may have little conceptual framework for understanding the reading process and the role of printed words. Therefore, in this section we focus on ways to help children learn to read and write a small set of very-high-frequency words.

To our knowledge, no research has been published that specifically guides teachers as to how many high-frequency words should be taught in the early stages of learning to read. In our kindergarten intervention work, in which we provided small-group instruction for half an hour twice a week to children who demonstrated limited early literacy skills at kindergarten entry, it was not unusual for the children to know 50 or more high-frequency words at the end of kindergarten. So, clearly, even children who begin kindergarten with limited literacy skills can learn quite a few high-frequency words by the end of the year. Because knowledge of high-frequency words provides children with so much access to reading materials and allows them to be strategic in learning other new words, setting higher expectations for high-frequency word knowledge is probably in the children's best interest. In fact, Rawlins and Invernizzi (2018) suggest that, currently, it is not unusual for kindergartners to be expected to know 100 or so high-frequency words by the end of the kindergarten year. Expectations for the development of literacy skills have clearly increased substantially in the last two decades.

It is important to note that, in our approach, teaching high-frequency words entails much more than the drill-type activities that are often associated with teaching high-frequency sight words. These include reading the words in meaningful text, engaging in word searches in text and in the classroom and school environment, and engaging in games that provide additional practice with the words.

KEEP IN MIND Although the term *sight words* is often used when discussing *high-frequency words*, the two terms are not synonymous. As defined in Chapter 12, sight words consist of all the words that a reader can identify automatically (at sight)—without cognitive effort. While proficient readers' sight vocabularies will include virtually all of the high-frequency words, they will also include many thousands of words that occur with less frequency. Since the goal of instruction in high-frequency words is for these words to become part of the individual's sight vocabulary, both terms are used in this chapter.

As we have noted previously, most words that eventually become part of a reader's sight vocabulary are learned over time through effective word solving while reading. Unfortunately for early literacy learners, initially, some of the words they encounter may appear to violate some of the guidance provided in early phonics instruction. For example, the silent-*e* "rule" generally indicates that the preceding vowel in a one-syllable word should have a long sound. Abiding by this guidance would result in a word such as *give* being pronounced such that it rhymes with *dive* and *have* would rhyme with *gave*. Readers who are reading with the intention of understanding what they read and who know how to apply word-solving strategies discussed in Chapter 12, would be able to adjust their pronunciation of the words so that they make sense in context. The seemingly "irregular" word[4] would potentially be on its way to becoming part of the reader's sight vocabulary.

KEEP IN MIND   *High-frequency words* are a subset of all the words that become part of a reader's *sight vocabulary.*

High-Frequency Words and Meaning Construction

In addition to providing opportunities for students to learn to identify/pronounce the printed versions of high-frequency words with automaticity, it is important to help children understand how these words function in spoken and written language. For example, before attempting to teach children to identify the written word *the,* it would be useful to illustrate for them how the word functions in spoken language. For example, the teacher might introduce the printed version of the word *the* and begin by being very explicit in the use of the word, providing several examples of its use and emphasizing its pronunciation. For example, while pointing to the word *the* (printed in a script large enough for all the children in the group to see), the teacher might say, "This is the word *the*. It has three letters—*t–h–e*. Those letters make the word *the*. We use the word *the* a lot. We say *the* car, *the* store, *the* hand, *the* paper. . . . We use *the* a lot when talking about things, we will see *the* a lot in our reading, and we will use it a lot when we write. Let's say the letters in the word *the* together: the word is *the . . . t –h –e . . . the*!" The children would be engaged in saying the word, naming the letters in order, and saying the word again several times while looking at a large-print version of the word. They might also be asked to use the word in their own sentences. For example, the teacher might say, "Tell me something using the word *the*—you could say 'I like *the* book,' or 'I like *the* picture,' or. . . . " Engaging the children in using the word in a grammatically accurate way will help them connect it to their spoken language. As noted previously, many of the high-frequency words have spellings that do not fully conform to their pronunciation. For example, many (most) people pronounce *the* as *thuh*. When the spelling of a word and the common pronunciation do not fully correspond, it can be helpful to point out this variation when first teaching a high-frequency word *if* learners already know the applicable spelling–sound correspondences.

This type of explicit instruction about word usage is likely useful for most, if not all, children but may be especially important for children who are multilingual.

---

[4]In English, by convention established hundreds of years ago, the letters *v* and *u* at the ends of words are followed by an *e* (e.g., *have, give, blue, sue*). According to Venezky (1999), this convention developed in part because the letters *v* and *u* at the end of words were hard to distinguish from one another in the script of the day.

Although there can be no doubt that MLs need to be able to automatically identify the most commonly occurring words in printed English, their ability to do so in a way that supports their ability to read and make sense of meaningful text requires that they know how these typically abstract words function in context.

The general point here is that it is easier to learn the identity of a printed word if the reader knows something about the meaning and use of the word and can connect that word to their spoken language.

Selecting Words for Instruction

Children who can identify few written words will generally be most interested in learning words that are important to them (e.g., the child's name, the names of family members or friends, words for feelings [e.g., *love, like, happy*], words for favorite toys, animals, etc.). Therefore, some of these words should be included when children are first learning to read and write words. The most frequently occurring words, on the other hand, are neither important nor interesting to children. They are, nevertheless, important for children to be able to identify.

Some of the earliest words taught should be drawn from the list of very-high-frequency words listed in Figure 13.1. Other considerations in selecting words for early instruction include the following:

• Choose words that are composed of letters for which the children already know the names. Otherwise, children are more apt to attempt to learn the word through use of selective cues. Knowing the names and forms of the individual letters that comprise the words they are learning will help children remember the word better—as will having children name the word, spell the word aloud while pointing to the letters, and name the word again. Game-like activities (described later) in which the children name the word, write it while naming the letters, and then name it again are also useful. These activities might well involve having the children name, write, and orally spell the same word several times.

• Select words from texts that will enable the children to read the words they are learning in meaningful contexts. We want children to be able to apply their growing knowledge of high-frequency words in meaningful ways.

• At least early on, words chosen for instruction should be fairly distinct from one another. Until children have some grasp of phonics, words such as *of, for*, and *from* are likely to be quite confusing, as are the words *the* and *they*.

• Consider which words the children are expected to know at the next grade level and try to provide opportunities to learn them.

• As children build their knowledge of the alphabetic code, help them make use of the letter–sound correspondences they know to remember the high-frequency words they are learning.

Teaching High-Frequency Words

For children who are able to identify few, if any, printed words, we would introduce only one new word at a time. In preparing to teach a new high-frequency word, it is important to have a text available that contains opportunities for children to read (see) the word in context. It is often possible for the teacher to construct a text (such as a morning message) that uses the target high-frequency word several times and also carries a lot of meaning for the children. Many book publishers have developed series of books for beginning readers that, in a single book, use specific high-frequency words frequently enough that the children have the opportunity to become very familiar with them. As noted in the introduction to Part III, the Short Books, Inc., publishes a very useful set of books for helping students learn some of the most frequently occurring words (see p. 294).

Initial Teaching of High-Frequency Words

The first several high-frequency words should be introduced explicitly, presented in isolation and in context, and children should be given a rationale for learning the word, as well as practice to support that learning. For example, the teacher might do the following:

• Choose a text in which the word appears several times. Read the text to the children, engaging them in a discussion of the meaning.

• Point to the targeted word in the text that was read and say something like "Here's a word that the author used a lot in this text/book. The word is _____. This word is used in a lot of things we will be reading, so we are going to learn this word. That way, when we see it in other places such as in books or on some of our charts, we'll already know it."

• Write the word in large print on a card or chart paper, naming each letter as it is written. Invite individual children to name the word and to spell it while everyone in the instructional group is looking at the word.

• Provide the children with the opportunity to make the word using movable letters and/or write the word several times—naming the word, naming the letters as they are arranged/written, and naming the word again.

• While leaving a printed version of the word in view, invite individual children to find the word in several different locations in the text that was originally read. As the children find the word and name it, as needed, the teacher may name the word and ask the child(ren) to repeat the word. The ultimate goal is for the children to be able to name the word independently each time the word is encountered. This may require more than one pass through the text.

• If a child chooses an incorrect match for the word, the teacher should discuss how the selected word is similar to, and differs from, the target word and talk about the letters in the word—for example: "The word you picked starts with *h,* just like the word *he.* I'm glad you noticed the *h*'s in those words. Now let's look at the end of those two words. *He* ends with an *e.* Do you see an *e* at the end of this word [*her*] (*pointing to the end of the word*)? This is the word *her*; it has an *r* at the end. So the word you picked looks a lot like the word *he*—it has an *h* and an *e.* To make sure we have the right match, though, we need to think about all the letters in the word. You can always check the word on the card (or wherever it is displayed) to make sure you've found a word that matches. As we learn more and more words, we will become real word detectives and look very carefully at all of the letters in the words as we learn them."

KEEP IN MIND   As illustrated in the previous example, when teachers are providing feedback following an incorrect response, they should always make note of what the child did correctly, as well as what aspect of the response needs more attention. If feedback only conveys inaccuracy, some children may lose their motivation to engage in the challenging activities being pursued.

When a child finds a correct match, the teacher might read aloud the sentence in which the matching word occurs, emphasizing the target word when it is read with both voice and pointing. Once children can find the word reliably with the model available, the model might be removed from view while the children continue to look for the target word in the text, as before. This approach encourages children to try to internalize the orthographic representation of the word and to connect it to the word's pronunciation.

Alert!

On occasion we have witnessed teachers ask children to *count* how many times the word occurs in a particular text. The counting process may lead children to attend too little to the letters in the word and potentially interfere with the children's word learning. It is much more productive to have children name the word each time they find it and point to it.

For children receiving intervention services beyond the classroom, communication between classroom and intervention teachers concerning the words that children are expected to know in the classroom is important. Intervention teachers should consider initially teaching and practicing the most frequent words that have been addressed in their students' classrooms but that the students do not yet know. Over the course of intervention, the goal is, of course, to ensure that each child knows the words they are expected to know at a given point in the school year. Therefore, intervention teachers should be helping children to add to their collection of known words, and the classroom word-learning expectations should be given high priority.

Practicing Early High-Frequency Words

Reading Little Books

Provide the children with the opportunity to read beginner-level books that include the high-frequency words they are learning. (Sometimes it may be possible to create an appropriate book by building on a classroom theme and/or modifying a book that has been read to the children.) Read these books several times with the children. Consider utilizing the types of "high-frequency word readers" that were described in the introduction to Part III (see the example on the left side of Figure III.2, p. 295). Books of the sort described can be readily made using apps such as Book Creator (bookcreator.com).

Repeated Reading

The more children read, the faster they grow as readers. Children should frequently have the opportunity to read and reread books that are at an appropriate level of challenge for them. Books that have been read with the teacher should be made available for the children to read independently or with a partner. Ideally, children would be able to take these books home to read to family members as well or, if possible, access them online. Children and families can be encouraged to accumulate such resources for use at home so that children always have a ready source of appropriately challenging reading material. It is important to help family members understand the value of children reading beginner-level books they (appear to) have memorized. Otherwise, with the best interest of the child at heart, family members sometimes engage children in interactions with books that are potentially counterproductive (e.g., some parents have reported that they cover the pictures or have children begin reading on the last page of the book and read the pages in reverse order!). Therefore, we suggest that teachers provide parents with insights into the purposes of having children read and reread beginner-level books and provide specific guidance on what family members can do while interacting with children in this context. For example, if a particular book was used to help children learn specific high-frequency words, those words should be identified for family members when the books go home. (See Figure 13.4 for suggestions to family members of children who are at beginning points in learning to read.) Additional information for family members can be found in our *Helping Your Child Become a Reader* resource (Scanlon et al., 2024), which can be accessed at *eltep. org/isa-parent-booklet*.

Writing

Be alert for opportunities to include the high-frequency words that have been taught in writing experiences. The high-frequency words that are in the children's sight vocabulary at very early points in development should be made available to

Dear Family,

Your child is beginning to learn to read. At this early point in development, children "read" books that provide them with the opportunity to develop familiarity with important skills but that do not require them to be able to read the words on the page in a conventional way. In fact, to a great extent, children "memorize" parts of the books (or the entire book) and "read" them by using the pictures to remind them of what changes from one page to the next.

Caregivers are encouraged to spend some time listening to children read these beginner-level books on a daily basis. While reading, encourage the child to point to the words because this will help the child to:

- Become familiar with the directionality of print (that it goes from left to right).
- Begin to learn some of the words that occur frequently in the book by focusing on each word as it is said.
- Begin to use the letters at the beginning of individual words to trigger their memory of what the word is.
- Understand that the pictures help to tell the story and may help to remind them of what a particular word is.

It is also important to discuss the information presented in the book with the child so they develop the understanding that we read for the purpose of understanding *what* we read. By discussing books with a child, even these beginner-level books, you can help to build the child's comprehension skills. Below are some examples of the kinds of conversation starters that you might use both when a child reads to you and when you read to a child.

Before reading,
   If the child has read or heard the book before, you might ask questions such as these:
- "What was this book about?"
- "Is it like any other books we've read?"

If the child has not read or heard the book before, then you might ask:
- "What do you think this book will be about?"

During reading, you might ask questions directly related to events and ideas presented in the book. Ideally, the questions would be open-ended:
- "Why do you think . . . ?"
- "What do you think would have happened if . . . ?"
- "What do you think is going to happen?"

During and after reading, you might share your reactions to the book and encourage the child to do so as well:
- "I liked the part where. . . ."
- "I thought it was funny when. . . ."
- "What a surprise. . . . I didn't know that . . ."

An important goal for family members and caregivers is to support children's interest in reading by making these early reading experiences enjoyable.

Sincerely,

FIGURE 13.4. Example of communication for family members in relation to engaging children in "reading" beginner-level books.

them in list form, and they should be "given permission" to spell these words conventionally in their writing by referring to the list (if need be).

When using word lists to facilitate conventional spelling, teachers should try to ensure that the list is readily accessible to all the children. We are all more likely to use resources if they are handy. Some teachers post the list prominently at the front of the room, in letters big enough for all children to see, regardless of where they are sitting. Other teachers post copies of the list at each table, often on all sides of a supply box if one is kept there.

Motivation and Conventional Spelling

Think for a moment about the message that is conveyed by a statement such as "If the word is on our list, you *must* spell it the right way whenever you use it in your writing" versus "Since the word is on our list, you *get to* spell it using book spelling whenever you use it in your writing." The subtle difference in wording in these two statements could make a substantial difference in how a child approaches a writing activity.

Sentence Building

Once children can readily identify several words, use the words to create simple sentences. Some additional, more meaningful, words would need to be added to the set to allow for the creation of these sentences. These additional words should be of interest to children and be very distinct from the other words in use for a particular sentence-building episode. These words might include the children's names or those of friends or family members, favorite animals, toys, and so forth.

Our first example of sentence building is appropriate for children who know very few words but do know some letters and their sounds. The sentence used is *The cat is fat.* The major goal for this particular example is to reinforce the recently taught high-frequency words *the* and *is*. The words *cat* and *fat* are included to make a meaningful sentence. While *cat* and *fat* receive as much attention in this activity as do *the* and *is, the* and *is* will be used more in other practice activities and so are more likely to be learned to the point where the children can identify them automatically.

For this activity, a sentence is written on a sentence strip (which could be just a piece of paper):

> The cat is fat.

The teacher would:

- Display the strip and read it with the children a few times, while pointing to the words.
- Have individual children read the sentence a few times, while pointing.

- Ask the children to count the words in the sentence.
- Discuss/ask what kind of letter comes at the beginning of a sentence and note that the sentence starts with a capital *T*.
- Notice that there is a period after the last word in the sentence.
- As the children watch, cut the sentence strip into words and display the words in order and read the sentence again. (Be sure the space before and after each word is approximately the same when the words are cut apart. Otherwise, children might use the larger blank space for the words at the beginning and end of the sentence strip as cues for building the sentence. Also, be sure that the cuts are not irregular in a way that would allow children to try to form a visual puzzle by matching irregular edges.)

The cat is fat.

- Explain that the children will get to use the words to make the sentence after they are mixed up.
- Mix up the words and engage the children in reading them (in the order in which they are displayed).

The teacher might then *think aloud* about how to reconstruct the sentence, as illustrated below:

Teacher	Interactive think-aloud
Says:	"Hmm. I know the sentence said *The cat is fat*. So, the first word I need is the word *the, the*. We just learned that word, so we probably remember that *t-h-e* spells *the*."
Finds the word *The* and observes:	"This word has the letters *t, h,* and *e* and the *t* is a capital *T*. We know that sentences start with a capital (upper-case) letter. So, I am going to put this word—*The*—first. "OK. Let's read the words we have left to find the one that comes next. The sentence said, *The cat is fat. The cat . . .*"
Leads the children in reading the remaining words and then.	"So, our sentence was *The cat is fat*. Which of these words do we need to put after the word *The*?"
Says:	"(Yes,) The next word I need is *cat*. /k/k/k/ *cat*. What letter makes that /k/k/k/ sound? Maybe my key words will help. I need to check to see if I know a key word that starts like /k/k/k/ *cat*."

Directs children's attention to the key-word chart and says:	"I see the key word *cat! Cat* is one of the key words for the letter *c.* —*Cat* starts with a *c*—/k/k/k/ *cat.* /k/k/k/ *cat.* So I need to find a word that starts with a *c.*"
Points to the word cards and says:	"Let's see which of the words I have left here starts with the letter *c.*"
Finds the word *cat* and says:	"I think this word probably says *cat* because it starts with a *c.* So now I've got *The cat.* (*Points to each word as it is said.*) *The cat is fat. The cat is.* . . . I need to find the word *is.*"
Points back and forth between the two remaining words and says:	"*Is* is one of the words we have just learned. Hmm. What letters are in the word *is*?"
Agrees with children.	"Right. The word *is* has the letters *i* and *s.* Let's find that word and put that word next in our sentence."
Says:	"So, we only have one word left. Before we cut it up, the sentence said *The cat is fat.* So, this last word must be *fat.* And, it starts with a /fffff/ sound just like our key word for *f—ffffish.*"
Reads the entire sentence pointing to each word as it is read.	"Let's see if this all works. The sentence says *The cat is fat.*"

Afterward, the teacher would mix up the words in the sentence again and invite the children to collaborate in reconstructing the sentence by arranging the words in the proper order. The teacher would provide prompts as needed. For example, the teacher might say:

- "What kind of letter will we need at the beginning of the sentence?"
- "What is the first sound you hear in *cat*?"
- "How could you figure out what letter will be at the beginning of the word *fat*?"

Note

The first several times that the children are engaged in these kinds of sentence-building activities, it may be helpful to leave an intact model of the sentence in view as the children do the reconstruction. When this is done, the children should be encouraged to name the words as they place them in the proper sequence. Otherwise, some children may be inclined to simply treat the activity as a visual matching task.

The teacher would gradually withdraw these supportive prompts as the children seem to be able to handle things on their own. As children collaborate with each other, the teacher should openly notice and encourage the problem-solving skills they demonstrate (e.g., "Jamal checked the key words when he was trying to figure out what letter would be at the beginning of cat.").

Variations for Children with Larger High-Frequency Sight Vocabularies

As children progress, the sentences can be longer; eventually, the initial sentence strip can be eliminated, and children can be challenged to form a meaningful sentence from a set of words. One teacher (D. Snyder) with whom we worked used sentence building as a center activity toward the end of the kindergarten year. (Recall that Centers provide opportunities for children to engage in learning/ practice activities while the teacher works with other children in a small-group context [see Chapter 2, p. 45]). She provided the words to build four or five different sentences. The words for each sentence were on different colored cards, so that it was easy to keep all the words for a given sentence together. During their time at the sentence-building center, children were to take all the cards of the same color and assemble a meaningful sentence. Different children could work on different sentences, or two children could collaborate. Once a meaningful sentence was assembled, the children wrote the sentence on their paper. When they finished with one sentence, they moved on to the next group of cards.

Below are the word cards for one of the sentences that the children might be asked to build. Clearly, children would need to read all the words multiple times before managing to build the meaningful sentence: *The cat likes to play with the hat.*

| with | cat | to | likes | play | hat. | The | the |

As should be evident from the preceding description, sentence-building activities provide practice with high-frequency words but also help to reinforce several print concepts (e.g., the first word in a sentence starts with a capital letter, the last word has a period or some other punctuation mark after it). They also provide children with opportunities to practice sound segmentation and letter–sound correspondences in a somewhat more meaningful way. Moreover, the process of reconstructing the sentence requires that children attend to the meaning and syntax of the sentence to ensure that it is properly ordered. Thus, sentence building gives children the opportunity to exercise many important literacy skills. The teacher should be alert for opportunities to reinforce these concepts and the problem-solving strategies associated with them.

Other Ways to Build Automaticity with Early High-Frequency Words

The words that children are learning can be used in a variety of games and activities that will help build their fluency in identifying them. Next, we describe several such activities, for which there are many possible variations.

MAKING A COLLECTION OF THE HIGH-FREQUENCY WORDS
THAT CHILDREN CAN IDENTIFY

When children are first learning some high-frequency words, they often enjoy having a collection of the words they have learned. Giving each child a special way to store their words is very motivating. Envelopes or small plastic pouches are often used for storage. Allowing children to decorate their collection device may encourage them to keep the words together and to practice them periodically. A variety of games can be played with word cards, so these collections can come in very handy.

Family members can also be kept informed of the words children are learning and be given suggestions for how they can help their children practice those words. For example, if a weekly newsletter is sent to family members, one section might be devoted to providing the families with a list of the newest high-frequency words that have been taught and practiced. Sending along some of the practice games described later in this chapter can be helpful too.

PRACTICE READING THE LIST

When the number of high-frequency words that have been taught is fairly small (e.g., 5 to 10), a list can be used in practicing them. For children who are just beginning to learn some high-frequency words, the words' positions on the list will likely support their ability to read the words and to find words they may want to use in their writing. However, children need to be able to identify given words both in isolation and in context in order for the words to be considered to be known by them. Words that children readily identify in isolation over several occasions need not be practiced as often, but they should be reviewed periodically—especially if children are not able to automatically identify them in context. Children who continue to be uncertain about some of the words should be provided with additional practice with the most frequent of these words. Having children form the words several times using letter tiles or writing them several times will help them to focus on the letters and the order of the letters that form a given word. Each time a child makes a word or writes it, it is very important that the child:

- name the word,
- name the letters in the word as they are placed or written,
- think about the sounds that the letters represent, and
- name the word again.

The goal is to build automaticity with these high-frequency words so that children can read and write more efficiently when they are encountered or used in meaningful contexts.

TIC-TAC-TOE

For this version of tic-tac-toe, each player uses a different colored marker to write high-frequency words (instead of using X and O) in the squares of the game board.

For children who know very few words, the children might write the same word on each turn. As they write the word, they would name the letters and then say the word. For children who know more words, the game would involve selecting a word card from a deck of cards containing words that have been taught. They would then read the word, write it in their selected square (naming the letters as they do so), and then name the word again. In both versions of the game, the winner is determined by having three words of the same color in a row.

PARKING LOT

The parking lot game described on pp. 167–168 can be used to reinforce high-frequency word knowledge when words are written in the parking spaces. The parking director then tells the players in which space to park. It is important that words be arranged differently on each player's parking lot so that they need to find the correct word rather than simply parking in the same relative position as their neighbor (see Figure 13.5).

CONCENTRATION (MEMORY)

Using a deck of cards that includes two copies of each of the high-frequency words under study, children can play a traditional game of Concentration (Memory). It is important that all players be on the same side of the playing surface so that all words are viewed in the proper orientation. The top or bottom of each word card should also be clearly marked so that when the cards are turned over the children are viewing them in the proper orientation. It is also important that each player,

| was | of | in | the | my | say |

| like | is | for | with | are | to |

FIGURE 13.5. High-frequency word parking lot game board.

on their turn, says each word as it is turned over; otherwise, some of the children will treat the game as a visual matching activity and come no closer to being able to identify the words automatically.

STICKY-NOTE BINGO

Bingo boards with 12–16 squares are set up. Each square contains a high-frequency word. The caller says the word, and players cover the word with a sticky note and try to write the covered word from memory (on the sticky note). In preparation for the game, each child can prepare their own playing board by writing in the words that the teacher dictates in the square of their choice. When preparing the game boards, the words that are dictated should be displayed to ensure proper spelling. While playing the game, children should be encouraged to peek under the sticky note to check the spelling, if need be. Children who misspell a word should be given a new sticky note and asked to write the word on it using a model and then use that sticky note to cover that word on their game board. As always, students who are not yet automatic in their ability to read and spell given words should name the letters in the word as they write it and then name the word again.

READING THE ROOM

Using a pointer or a flashlight, children are encouraged to search the print posted around the room for the high-frequency words they can read. (This assumes, of course, that the classroom has lots of poems, posters, language experience charts, and/or morning messages displayed.) As the children find words they can read, they can write them down and then read the list to the teacher or classmate at a later point.

Later Instruction of High-Frequency Words and Building Automaticity

The development of accuracy and automaticity in identifying and spelling high-frequency words should be a particular emphasis for all children until they have mastered the most frequently occurring words. Remember that approximately 50% of the words that one encounters in any text consist of a fairly small number of high-frequency words (about 100 of them). Therefore, the 100 or so most frequently occurring words are a particular priority: when children are able to identify and spell these high-frequency words effortlessly, they are able to devote more attention to the message of the text and, if necessary, to figuring out the less frequent (and often more meaning-bearing) words. Once children have begun to understand how the reading process works and have developed some phonological and orthographic skills, they begin to learn new words through reading (as discussed in Chapter 12) instead of needing to have the words taught to them directly.

Therefore, as children grow as readers, the high-frequency words that need the most explicit instructional attention are those that children are unlikely to be able to figure out, given their current word-solving skills and strategies.

Grouping and Pacing

The instructional procedures described in this section are appropriate for children who already know a small set of high-frequency words (10 to 20). In general, the more words a child knows, the more quickly the child will learn additional words. This is true for a variety of reasons but primarily because, as for virtually all learning situations, the more you know about something, the easier it is to learn more about that same thing. That said, it should be clear that, although we might start teaching high-frequency words by introducing only one new word at a time, as children progress, they can generally handle three to five new words in a given lesson. These words would, of course, need to be reviewed and practiced in subsequent lessons.

Teaching High-Frequency Words

Selecting Words for Instruction

As discussed above, the earliest words taught should be highly distinct from one another because children's primary approach to word learning at early points is likely to be through selective cue use (i.e., using salient visual features but often not relying much on the word's letters and associated sounds). Children do this because they do not yet understand the writing system. We, of course, want to move children away from this approach to word learning as soon as possible because it is counterproductive and will not enable them to learn to read and spell the huge number of words they ultimately need to have command of.

By working with high-frequency words in a variety of ways, children begin to attend to their letters and sounds in addition to their overall visual configuration. The potential confusability of words will remain an issue for a while as children's sight vocabularies grow. This issue, as well as other factors involved in selecting high-frequency words for instruction, are discussed in Table 13.1.

Teaching High-Frequency Words in Preparation for Reading a New Text

In our approach, the first time a high-frequency word is taught and practiced is often in the context of preparing children to read a new book (see Chapter 12, pp. 334–335). Teachers periodically remind children that learning these words is helpful because they are used a lot in reading and writing. When introducing a new word, it is presented on a card or sticky note. The teacher names the word, names and points to the letters in the word, and names the word again. Then the children do the same (name the word, name the letters, name the word), with

TABLE 13.1. Considerations for Selecting High-Frequency Words for Instruction

Things to consider	Advice
Is the word likely to be easily confused with another word(s) that has recently been taught?	Avoid teaching visually confusable words in close succession (e.g., *he* and *her*; *was* and *saw*). Children at the earlier points in development tend to use the overall configuration of the word as a prominent clue for word identification.
How frequently is the word used?	Words that appear very frequently in print should be among the earliest words taught.
Do children have the decoding skills to identify the word on their own?	Depending on the phonics/decoding skills that children have already learned, words will vary in their level of decodability. Words that follow spelling–sound correspondences that the children have already learned probably do not need to be taught explicitly. We want children to have opportunities to apply their decoding skills and to be strategic in their reading.
Will children encounter the word in meaningful text in the near future?	Explicitly teaching high-frequency words prior to having children read a text containing those words helps them to be more fluent on the first reading. The high-frequency words will serve as anchors that allow children to be more strategic in analyzing other unfamiliar words in the text and in constructing an understanding of the text.

teacher support as needed. The teacher should also point out known spelling–sound correspondences and/or spelling patterns to scaffold children's abilities to puzzle through such words independently.

Logistical Tip

Intervention teachers have found it helpful to write the new words that will be taught for a given book on sticky notes and to place the sticky notes inside the front cover of the book prior to the lesson. In preparing the children to read the book, the sticky notes are taken out and placed on the table. The words are named, and the children's attention is drawn to the letters and sounds in the word. They have the opportunity to name and spell each word at least a couple of times before they engage in reading the book. The sticky notes remain on the table during the reading. Children often find it useful to refer to these words while reading. After the book has been read, the new words are reviewed and then placed back in the book, ready for the next time the book is used.

Practicing High-Frequency Words

Once a high-frequency word has been taught, it is incorporated into a set of words that will be practiced until children are fairly automatic in identifying them. Many of the practice activities described for children at the early stages of learning high-frequency words are also appropriate for students who are a bit further along (see the section "Practicing Early High-Frequency Words," pp. 355–363). However, as children progress, the number of words with which they practice will be larger.

Practice activities include reading and rereading books, using a resource to spell high-frequency words conventionally while writing, and using various game-like word-reading and spelling practice activities.

For children who receive intensive intervention in very small groups or in one-to-one settings, we have found a word game we call Your Pile/My Pile to be helpful for practicing high-frequency words to the point of automaticity.

YOUR PILE/MY PILE: A GAME FOR PRACTICING HIGH-FREQUENCY WORDS

This quick game is designed to promote accuracy and automaticity in identifying high-frequency words that have already been taught. The game is played in a one-to-one context and can occur while other children in a small-group lesson engage in other activities—such as rereading books or playing a game that doesn't need to involve the teacher (such as tic-tac-toe or Memory). The game can also be suggested as a playful way to practice high-frequency words at home.

High priority should be placed on the highest-frequency words (see Figure 13.1). Depending on children's current competence, the number of words in an activity may vary from a small number (i.e., from 5 to 10 words with several copies of each word included) to 20 to 30 words. Words for any given game should generally consist of the following:

- Some that the child routinely identifies accurately *and* relatively quickly.
- Some that the child can usually identify accurately *but not* quickly.
- A few that have only recently been introduced to the child.

This combination of words serves to make the game manageable yet challenging enough to hold children's interest.

The selected words should be written on cards. The cards should all be the same color, and all the words should be printed in the same color so that children do not try to rely on color cues as a means of remembering the word on a given card (recall the discussion of selective cue use on p. 286).

Explain to children that the more words they can identify right away, the easier it will be to read books and other kinds of texts. It is also helpful to explain that the words that are being practiced are words they will see a lot and will want to use in their writing; therefore, learning to read and write those words quickly will help them read and write many different things.

Tell the child that you will present the words one at a time and that they are to tell what the word is as quickly as possible without making mistakes. Words that the child identifies quickly and accurately go into the child's pile for any given game. Explain that, if they do make a mistake, you will tell them what the word is, they will repeat the word (while looking at it), and then the word will go back in the teacher's pile for more practice. Further, explain that if the child can't identify a word, you might give them a hint to help them think about the sounds in the word, but that if you give a hint, the word needs to go back in the teacher's pile for more practice. Finally, if the child recognizes the word accurately, but it takes more than a second or two, the word will also go into the teacher's pile for more practice. The goal is for the child to get all the words into their pile. Often, in playing the game, teachers refer to the two different piles of words as *your pile* (the child's pile of words that were recognized quickly and accurately) and *my pile* (the teacher's pile of words that need more practice).

The teacher would show the words one at a time, placing words in the child's pile if the child is accurate and relatively fast (for that child) in identifying the word. Once the teacher has gone through all the words in the original deck, the cards in the teacher's pile are used again to continue with the game. This procedure provides more practice on the words that the child was unable to name quickly and accurately on the first attempt. The game continues until all the words are in the child's pile.

KEEP IN MIND The major purpose of these practice activities is to help children get to the point at which they are both *fast* and *accurate* in identifying high-frequency words. Being automatic in their identification of the most frequently occurring words will allow children to devote more of their cognitive resources to constructing the meaning of the texts they read and to puzzling through unfamiliar, less frequent, words encountered in those texts.

For subsequent games of Your Pile/My Pile, words that the child routinely identifies accurately and quickly (within 1 or 2 seconds) can be removed from the deck and replaced with others. One way of easily tracking a child's knowledge of

---

Note

Checkmarks are placed on the cards by the teacher *after* the lesson so as not to slow the game down. The matter of checkmarks should not be brought to the child's attention. We want the child to be thinking about the words, not the checkmarks! To do so, once the deck has been gone through entirely the first time, the teacher would set aside all of the words in the child's pile saying something like "You were able to name all of those words quickly and correctly the first time you saw them today. Great! They will all get a checkmark on the back. Let's see if we can get the rest of these words into your pile." The game would then continue. The last few words to make it into the child's pile for the day might be used in an additional practice activity—such as tic-tac-toe as described above. The teacher can also ask the child to record the words from their pile of words that will be getting checkmarks in a list. This will provide additional independent practice with writing them, as well as a record for the teacher to use in recording checkmarks. While creating the list, the children should name the words as they write them.

particular words is to mark the back of the word cards with a small checkmark if the child identifies the word quickly and accurately *the first time it is shown* on a given day. Generally, when words have three or four checkmarks, they can be removed from the deck. When words are removed from the deck, they can be added to the child's "Words I Know" chart (see below).

Using "Words I/We Know and Use a Lot" Charts and Word Walls to Encourage Automaticity (Being Automatic) with High-Frequency Words

Charts listing the high-frequency words that children have learned serve as important resources for them as they continue to practice accurate and rapid identification of these words and as they work toward internalizing the conventional spellings. At a classroom level, teachers often maintain word walls that list high-frequency words that have been explicitly taught and that the majority of the class is expected to know. These charts are intended to enable conventional spelling of the words on the chart. In small-group and one-to-one intervention settings, teachers can develop similar "Words We Know" or "Words I Know" charts that include only the words the children in the group or the individual child knows. These charts help support the needs of children who cannot yet easily read many of the words on the classroom word wall.

Invented/Inventive/Temporary/Kindergarten/Sound Spelling versus Conventional/Correct/Book Spelling

Teachers in the primary grades use a variety of terms for the unconventional spellings produced by young writers. We feel that *sound spelling* is the most useful term because it most effectively communicates to children what they are expected to do: think about the sounds in the words they want to write and then use letters to represent those sounds. Using terms such as *invented* or *temporary* conveys nothing about the expected process, nor does *kindergarten spelling*— and that latter term has the potential to come across as somewhat demeaning, especially for older children who have yet to develop strong conventional spelling skills. We also feel that parents will be more accepting of the term and the practice of *sound spelling,* especially if teachers are careful to explain the role of sound spelling in literacy development: it helps children learn to attend to the sounds in spoken words (thus promoting phonemic awareness), and it draws children's attention to letter–sound relationships (thus promoting the development of phonics skills).

   With regard to the terminology used to contrast with *sound spelling,* we encourage the use of *book spelling,* as it conveys the fact that words in books are spelled in standard ways. With teacher guidance, it may encourage children to use books as a reference when they are writing and using words encountered in a recently read text. The term *book spelling* also allows for "translation" from spoken to written language.

Children should be given permission to spell words on the word wall and/or from their "Words I/We Know" charts conventionally (using "book spelling") by referring to the wall or the charts. Children are expected to spell the "Words I/ We Know" words correctly in their writing because allowing sound spelling of these high-frequency words is likely to slow down the process of getting these words to the point where they can be read automatically. For example, children who spell words like *was* as YZ or *from* as FRUM (both of which are reasonable sound spellings) and who read these spellings while developing and sharing their writing pieces are likely to have difficulty recognizing the words *was* and *from* accurately and quickly when they are encountered in other texts. Although sound spelling is an important contributor to developing phonemic awareness and phonics knowledge, accepting sound spellings for "known" high-frequency words is not recommended—particularly when there are handy resources that the children can access.

The use of the "Words I/We Know" chart to promote conventional spelling of high-frequency words will highlight for children the fact that sound (invented) spelling is only a temporary means of facilitating communication.

Word Walls: An Important Classroom Resource

In recent years, some literacy professionals have been arguing against the use of word walls. Their argument seems to arise from a vision of word walls as a place to display any word children might want to use in their writing. We do not share that vision. Rather, in our view, word walls serve as displays of the conventional spellings of the high-frequency words children have learned to read. Because, as previously discussed, the spellings of high-frequency words can be difficult to remember, word walls help children commit those spellings to memory so that their potentially inaccurate attempts at spelling do not interfere with their ability to automatically identify those words when reading. In the ISA, we encourage the use of multiple resources including word walls, key-word displays, and word family charts (if word families are taught). Importantly, we emphasize the need for explicit instruction and practice in using these resources, so children come to use them independently as needed for reading and spelling.

CHARACTERISTICS OF USEFUL CLASSROOM WORD WALLS

In order for classroom word walls to be effective for children, the words should be listed alphabetically by the first grapheme (letter or digraph), so that it is reasonably easy for children to find the word they want to write. Further, the words should be printed in a font large enough for children to see no matter where they are in the classroom. Finally, it is important that most of the words on the word wall be printed on a standard background color with a standard color of ink so that children are not tempted to rely on something other than alphabetic/orthographic features when they attempt to find a word.

CHARACTERISTICS OF USEFUL "WORDS I/WE KNOW" CHARTS

A "Words I Know" chart is an important resource for children who have compara-tively limited skill with high-frequency words. The words placed on these charts are high-frequency words that have been taught explicitly and that the teacher believes the children can read accurately. In our intervention work, decisions about which words to add to a chart were often based on a student's performance in the Your Pile/My Pile game described above (see pp. 366–368). *Very* early on, a "Words I Know" chart could be ordered in accord with the order in which children learned the words. For example, words that a child learned to read first would appear at the beginning of the list, whereas words learned more recently would be at the end. This ordering is for a child who is at a very early point in development (perhaps being able to read only 10 or so high-frequency words). For the child who has yet to learn anything about alphabetization, it provides a positional cue for finding the words that can be used in writing.

As learners' knowledge of high-frequency words expands and children know enough about the alphabet to effectively use it for locating words, children's "known" high-frequency words should be moved to an alphabetized "Words I Know" chart. This chart would look much like a classroom word wall except that the chart is much smaller because the words need be visible only to the children in a small group or to the individual. Moreover, they would typically include fewer words than the classroom word wall. An example of a "Words I Know" chart appears in Figure 13.6, and a two-page version that can be printed for use with students is available on the book's companion website (see the box at the end of the table of contents). The online version can be stapled on opposing faces of a manila folder and used for tracking individual children's high-frequency word knowledge, for providing practice opportunities, and for serving as a resource for conventional (book) spelling.

Use of this chart should be clearly explained. Children can be told that all the letters of the alphabet as well as some letter combinations that go together to make one sound (like *th*) are on the chart. The teacher would explain that the words that they see and write most often will go on the chart once they are learned. A word that starts with a particular letter or letter combination (digraph) will be put on the chart under the letter or letter combination. High-frequency words that have already been learned can then be placed on the chart with an explicit discussion of where each word should be placed and why it belongs there. Teachers would also explain that when children want to find a word to use in their writing, they need to think of the sound at the beginning of the word and then think about what letter(s) might make that sound. If digraphs such as *th, sh,* and *ch* have been taught, it would be appropriate to remind children of the letters used to spell those sounds and that the letter combinations can be found in the same box with the first letter of the combination. Next, they need to find the word's first letter(s) on the chart and read the words under the letter to see if the word they are looking for is there. This process, of course, implicitly requires that children review some of the

Aa and are am	Bb big because	Cc can come Ch children		Dd did does down	Ee eat every	Ff for	Gg good	Hh has he her	Ii is it
Jj jump	Kk keep	Ll love like	Mm make	Nn nice	Oo of on	Pp put	Qq	Rr run	
Ss said says Sh she show		Tt to tell Th the there		Uu us	Vv very	Ww was want Wh what		Yy you yes your	Zz

FIGURE 13.6. Sample "Words I Know" chart. (Note that the letter *X* does not appear on the chart because no high-frequency words begin with the letter *X*.)

high-frequency words they have learned as they read through the list and either accept or reject each word listed in a given section of the chart. Note that a few words, such as *of* and *one,* are outliers in that their initial sounds are not spelled in a way that can be discerned based on knowledge of grapheme–phoneme correspondences. Therefore, it is helpful to periodically remind children of the location of such outlier words on the chart.

For children who seem to have difficulty reading and spelling the words on their "Words I/We Know" charts, it is helpful to make their personal charts of high-frequency words readily available. (These charts should only contain high-frequency words.) Some teachers tape a page protector to children's desks (workspaces) for their "Words I Know" charts. That way, the chart can be easily modified for updating. For children who have a larger sight vocabulary and for whom spelling is a major concern, teachers have found it useful to provide the words in a personal dictionary format. This is either kept in their desks (often in their writing folder) or attached to their desks with a string that allows it to hang off the desk out of the way but remain readily available when a child needs it.

To help children remember which words appear on their charts and to become more automatic in identifying those words, the children should read the words on their charts frequently.

"SPELLING TESTS" TO ENCOURAGE USE OF "WORDS I KNOW" CHARTS AND OTHER RESOURCES

Periodic administration of spelling tests is useful in encouraging children to learn to refer to their charts to improve conventional spelling. During a spelling "test," the teacher can walk children through the process of finding the needed word on their charts as often as necessary. All children have the opportunity to obtain perfect scores on these tests if they understand how to use the chart. For example, the teacher might ask children to write the word on the chart that means "not little" and that starts with a *b*. Such an activity supports both orthography/phonology and vocabulary development.

GUESSING GAMES

There are a variety of ways to encourage children to make efficient use of word walls and "Words I Know" charts. For example, it is helpful to periodically play guessing games using the displays. Guessing games might take the form of the teacher providing verbal clues and the children using displayed words to assist them in figuring out the correct response. For example, if the word *in* is on the word wall, the teacher might say something like "I'm thinking of a word that begins with *i* and is the opposite of *out*." Such activities can also contribute to vocabulary development (including helping children to learn the meaning of *opposite*!).

KEEP IN MIND Procedures to ensure that every student has the opportunity to respond are easily incorporated into word wall activities. For example, in the guessing game described above, rather than having individual students make guesses, children can be asked to write their guesses on a dry-erase board before anyone is asked to share their thinking.

KEY POINTS OF THIS CHAPTER

✓ The majority of any text (50–70%) is composed of the 100–300 most frequently occurring words.

✓ The words that occur most frequently in spoken and written language should be given high priority in terms of helping children learn to read and spell them with automaticity.

✓ Most high-frequency words are abstract—they do not refer to concrete or imageable referents. This makes them harder to learn to read and spell, thus calling for more explicit instruction and practice.

✓ Many high-frequency words have some irregularities about their spelling, which makes it harder for children to stabilize regular/conventional spellings in memory. Thus, having a handy reference will be useful.

✓ Repeated exposure to and practice with high-frequency words increase the likelihood that they will become part of the learner's sight vocabulary and spelling vocabulary as well.

✓ Once a child has learned to identify a printed high-frequency word, it is important for the learner to use conventional spelling when using the word in writing, thereby reinforcing the connection between the written word and its spoken form. Learning to access available resources (e.g., word wall, texts) to enable conventional spelling is important.

PART IV

Meaning Construction

Introduction to Part IV

Meaning construction is the goal of reading and reading instruction. As was high-lighted in Chapter 1, reading is a complicated process that requires readers to draw on a wide array of knowledge sources and strategic processes. In order to under-stand a printed text, readers must be able to do much more than simply read the printed words quickly and accurately, although this ability is extremely important. They must also know what the words mean, and they must understand the con-cepts to which they refer. Further, they must be able to access the context specific meanings of words that have multiple meanings (e.g., *run*, *claim*, *bank*) and shades of meaning (e.g., *take* a picture vs. *take* a cookie). Perfetti (2007) describes this as lexical quality—"the extent to which a stored mental representation of a word specifies its form and meaning in a way that is both precise and flexible" (Castles et al., 2018, p. 21). Learners must be able to assemble the individual words into idea units, which become the building blocks for a more comprehensive under-standing of the text. Ultimately, to interpret and construct the meaning of a text readers need to integrate the information gleaned from the text with their existing knowledge. Those who have limited English language skills, background knowl-edge, and/or ability to draw logical inferences may have limited ability to under-stand texts (depending on the characteristics of the texts). Further, those who do not actively think about the meaning of texts as they are listening to or reading them are likely to have little recollection of the text. In the case of reading, those who need to devote a lot of attention to word identification and/or who cannot identify a substantial number of the words in the text are likely to have difficulty comprehending the text even if they possess the needed background knowledge and language skills.

Multilinguals and Comprehension

Multilingual learners may have well-developed language skills in their first language as well as a wealth of background knowledge. However, until they have developed the ability to understand spoken English fairly well, their assets may not sufficiently enable their learning in English-speaking educational settings. Additionally, spoken English may differ from written English in the frequency of complex syntax and vocabulary, which may impact listening and reading comprehension as well. Even those multilinguals with relatively well-developed spoken English skills may have some difficulty with comprehending written English given these differences.

In previous parts of the book, we focused largely on the word-reading aspects of the reading process. Because this component is often a major stumbling block for children at the early stages of learning to read and for older readers who struggle, it clearly needs to be an important focus of instruction. However, the other processes need to be addressed as well because, once skill with the orthography/word identification is established, language, knowledge, and active engagement in meaning construction (including comprehension skills and strategies) are the major determinants of reading comprehension. Further, unlike decoding skills, which represent a rather finite set of abilities (Paris, 2005), knowledge and language skills are limitless. Therefore, whereas children who begin school with limited early literacy skills may be readily helped to catch up to their peers in learning the alphabetic and orthographic code (because their more able peers stop growing when mastery is achieved), it is much more difficult to address differences in funds of knowledge that arise from different environmental influences outside of the classroom setting (Hirsch, 2006; Neuman, 2006; Pearson, Palincsar, Biancarosa, & Berman, 2020). Those who are learning to read and write in a language they do not yet comprehend and speak competently also encounter challenges (Goldenberg, 2020). Those with knowledge of the focal topic tend to have stronger reading comprehension, and they also tend to gain more knowledge about the topic more rapidly than those with less knowledge of the topic (Neuman, 2011).

Language and knowledge differences develop as a *result* of reading difficulty because limited engagement in reading results in limited opportunities to acquire new vocabulary and language structures and to encounter and develop new knowledge. Stanovich (1986) described this phenomenon as the *Matthew effect*, which is a biblical reference to the notion that the "rich get richer and the poor get poorer." Although the research to date has not yielded definitive results regarding the actual existence of Matthew effects for children who experience reading difficulties (Pfost, Hattie, Dörfler, & Artelt, 2014), it is hard to deny that such an effect could accrue.

In Part IV, we focus on the knowledge, strategies, and dispositions that need to be developed and integrated for children to make sense of what they listen to and read, and we discuss approaches to instruction that will help them do so.

Three major goals are addressed in this part: the development of (1) fluent/expressive reading, (2) language skills, including knowledge of word meanings and syntactic skills, and (3) comprehension skills and strategies, as well as the general background knowledge that will enable children to construct meaning from/with the texts they encounter.

Fluency (Chapter 14) is addressed under the overarching goal of meaning construction because, to construct meaning while reading, readers need to be able to devote most of their cognitive resources to understanding the text. This is possible only when most of the words in a text can be identified effortlessly and automatically. The reader must be able to access the text-relevant meaning of most of the words.[1] Additionally, the reader must parse sentences into meaningful parts (phrases and clauses) that convey higher-level meaning than words alone. It should also be noted that fluent reading, which includes appropriate phrasing and intonation, is also a signal of comprehension—at least at the sentence level. Applying proper intonation and phrasing is impossible without understanding the meaning of the sentence being read. For example, fluent readers know to pause at a comma, and they include a slight upshift in intonation for a question mark.

The division between the Language chapter and the Comprehension and Knowledge chapter (Chapters 15 and 16, respectively) is somewhat arbitrary. Language and knowledge are, obviously, intricately interconnected, and comprehension is heavily dependent on both. Nevertheless, because language develops on a different time course than does reading and often develops without much, if any, explicit instruction, treating the two topics somewhat separately is reasonable.

Meaning Construction and Early Intervention

The existing research on RTI has placed heavy emphasis on aspects of fluency (as measured by reading speed—with a focus on fast and accurate word recognition). But it has generally not attended to the role that limitations in language skills and background knowledge may play in the evolution of long-term reading difficulties. This is unfortunate because we suspect that both persistent and "late-emerging" reading difficulties (difficulties that don't become apparent until the middle of elementary school and that are largely related to difficulties with comprehension) are often attributable to insufficiently developed language skills and background knowledge (Neuman, 2011). Further, we fear that, because of the common emphasis on oral reading speed and accuracy, children who need support in developing language skills, world knowledge, and active engagement in meaning construction may not get this support until they begin to encounter texts that make heavier demands on these skills (in the middle elementary grades and beyond). Therefore, we encourage attention to the development of language skills, general/world/conceptual knowledge, and active engagement in meaning construction (especially in

---

[1] The English language includes many words that have multiple meanings—for example, *bank*, *ball*, *left*, *rose*, and *saw*.

the context of listening to texts read aloud) for young learners, with the goal of preventing later difficulties with reading comprehension.

The Reading for Understanding Initiative

The Reading for Understanding initiative (RfU) was funded by the United States Institute for Education Sciences to address concerns about the high proportion of U.S. students in fourth grade (and beyond) who are not reaching grade-appropriate reading proficiency, as evidenced by performance on the National Assessment of Educational Progress (NAEP). This comprehension measure is administered every four years to students in fourth, eighth, and twelfth grades. Pearson et al. (2020) and Cervetti et al. (2020) summarized some of the initial findings and reported "promising" outcomes for the intervention approaches developed as part of this major initiative. We are hopeful that the findings and approaches to intervention developed in the course of the initiative will inform future instructional efforts on a broad scale. We discuss some of the RfU findings in Chapter 16, which focuses on comprehension and knowledge development.

As is discussed in some detail in Chapters 15 and 16, language and knowledge develop incrementally over extended periods of time. The goals of increasing language abilities and promoting knowledge development need to be at the forefront of teachers' thinking as they plan and deliver instruction for all children but especially for those who have had limited opportunity to develop in these areas. Teachers should be constantly asking themselves whether their students understand the language (both vocabulary and syntax) and the concepts that children encounter in instructional interactions. Teachers also need to be prepared to take steps to intervene for those who do not yet have the requisite knowledge. Knowledge and language development can be promoted by engaging children in reading and listening to informational texts, watching information-rich videos, providing experiential learning opportunities, and the like. All such instructional opportunities are more productive for children when they have extensive opportunities to discuss what they are learning with peers and teachers.

Of course, even children with well-developed knowledge and language skills sometimes have difficulty comprehending the texts that they "read" with relative ease. For at least some of these children, the comprehension difficulties may be attributable to failure to attend to the meaning of the text as it is being read. Virtually every reader has had the experience of reading something and then having no idea what was just read. When this happens on occasion, it is because the reader's mind was on something else while reading. When this happens routinely, it can be a signal that the reader does not fully understand that the purpose of reading is to make sense of the text and to integrate the information provided in the text with already existing knowledge. This lack of understanding can arise for a variety of reasons. For readers who experience difficulty with comprehension, it may be due to the type of guidance and feedback they receive while reading. For example, if the feedback they receive primarily focuses on word-reading accuracy and speed, the learner is likely to focus on accuracy and speed and attend too little to the meaning of the text. Over time, such an approach may become habitual and, once established, it will require explicit intervention to help children overcome this inclination and to actively attend to the meaning of the text. In the ISA, we strive to prevent children from ever adopting such an attitude toward reading by engaging them in active meaning construction in all interactions with texts.

CHAPTER 14

Text-Reading Fluency

> **MEANING CONSTRUCTION GOAL 1**
>
> Children will be able to read grade-appropriate text accurately, with appropriate speed, and with phrasing and intonation that convey the intended meaning.

In Parts II and III of this book, the major emphasis was placed on helping children develop skill with decoding and word identification. The purpose of developing those skills is to help children to, ultimately, become so proficient with decoding/word-identification that they will be able to apply those skills while reading meaningful text with automaticity. Being able to do so enables learners to quickly identify never-before-encountered printed words, thus helping them to both build their sight vocabularies while reading and stay focused on the meaning of the text they are reading.

To read fluently, the reader needs to be able to accurately and quickly identify the words in the text (Samuels, 2006) and, while doing so, group the words into meaningful phrases (demarcated by slight pauses) and impose appropriate intonation. Together these processes serve to convey the author's intended meaning. Meaningful phrasing and appropriate intonation are often referred to as *prosody* (Kuhn & Levy, 2015). Thus, reading fluency, as many researchers define it, involves accuracy, automaticity, and prosody. Recent research indicates that, at least in the primary grades, reading comprehension is strongly related to (predicted by) reading fluency (Kim, 2022; Kim, Quinn, & Petscher, 2021).

Because beginning readers do not have a large number of words they can identify accurately and automatically, they generally do not read fluently unless they are reading a highly predictable or well-practiced text. They lack fluency because most of their cognitive resources are devoted to the process of identifying individual words. They literally read word-by-word. In contrast, for advanced read-ers, word identification is so automatic that the readers' eyes are actually focused on a word or two that is beyond the word they are articulating during oral reading (Inhoff, Solomon, Radach, & Seymour, 2011). This span between the reader's eyes and voice helps the reader determine the intonation that should be applied to the word that is being articulated because, by having one's eyes ahead of the voice, the reader knows what's coming next. This *eye–voice* span is possible only when word identification is automatic.

Of course, proper intonation is also determined by the larger context in which a given sentence occurs. Consider the sentence *This is my toy.* The sentence could be read as a simple statement. Alternatively, it could be read in a way that stresses ownership: *This is my toy.* It could also be read in a way that stresses the owner-ship of a particular toy relative to a larger group of toys: *This is my toy.* In the latter two instances, the stress placed on the words *my* and *this* subtly changes the meaning of the sentence. The point is that the prosodic aspect of fluency is inex-tricably linked to comprehension of the text in that it both conveys comprehension and facilitates it. For example, readers will often only know which words require emphasis if they have an adequate understanding of what's happening in the larger text.

Assessing Fluency

Measures of Accuracy and Automaticity

Measures of oral reading fluency (ORF) are often used to identify readers who need additional instructional support in a response-to-intervention (RTI) con-text. Common approaches to evaluating ORF involve calculation of the number of words read correctly per minute (WCPM)[1] while reading a text at the student's grade level. The tool takes relatively little time to administer, and there is evidence of moderate-to-strong relationships between measures of WCPM and measures of reading comprehension, with these relationships being stronger in earlier than in later elementary grades (Kim, Petscher, Schatschneider, & Foorman, 2010; Silver-man, Speece, Harring, & Ritchey, 2013). Thus, especially in the primary grades, children who obtain higher scores on measures of WCPM tend to score higher on measures of reading comprehension (Kim & Wagner, 2015). Using a measure of WCPM has also become a popular tool for progress monitoring—that is, tracking students' changes in reading performance across the school year.

To measure WCPM, the teacher gives a child an unfamiliar, on-grade-level text to read and, using a timing device, listens to the child read for one minute while marking errors and omissions on a copy of the text. The teacher would mark the point in the text where the minute ends and then allow the child to read to a logical

---

[1] The term *correct words per minute* (CWPM) is sometimes used instead.

stopping point (rather than stopping the child midsentence). To compute WCPM, the teacher would count the total number of words up to the stopping point and then subtract the number of words on which an error or omission occurred. The result is the child's WCPM score. Table 14.1 provides norms for WCPM for grades 1 and 2 as compiled by Hasbrouck and Tindal (2017). The data in the table are drawn from widely referenced norms for grades 1 through 6 compiled on a broadly representative national sample. As the table indicates, there are no WCPM fluency norms for the beginning of first grade—as most first graders are not expected to be able to engage in a "cold read" of a new text early in the school year. Note that faster reading is not necessarily the goal when considering WCPM. Fluency scores at or near the 50th percentile should be sufficient for supporting comprehension.

Although WCPM is certainly a useful indicator of oral reading skill, as noted above, prosody (phrasing and intonation) is also an important aspect of oral reading, especially with regard to its relationship to reading comprehension. Appropriate prosody both conveys and enables comprehension. As Rasinski and colleagues (2020) explain, "a reader's use of prosody while reading orally provides evidence that the reader is monitoring and capturing the meaning of the written text" (p. 3). Schilling, Carlisle, Scott, and Zeng (2007), for example, found that the ORF scores based exclusively on WCPM used in their study misidentified 32% of second graders and 37% of third graders as being at low risk for reading comprehension difficulties. That is, their reading rate was fast enough that they were predicted to be able to comprehend grade-level texts, but they couldn't. We suspect that, had prosody been included as part of the evaluation, there would have been greater accuracy in identifying students at risk of experiencing comprehension difficulties.

On the other hand, anecdotally, we have encountered children who are strategic about word solving and committed to solving the puzzling words they encounter. This process makes them slower readers than their peers who are willing to skip unknown words and/or ignore mispronunciations and keep moving through

TABLE 14.1. Percentiles for Oral Reading Fluency Norms

Grade	Percentile	Fall WCPM	Winter WCPM	Spring WCPM
1	90		97	116
	75		59	91
	50		29	60
	25		16	34
	10		9	18
2	90	111	131	148
	75	84	109	124
	50	50	84	100
	25	36	59	72
	10	23	36	43

Note. Data from Hasbrouck and Tindal (2017). On an assessment, an individual's percentile indicates what percentage of individuals score below the percentile ranking. Thus, an individual scoring at the 75th percentile is scoring higher than approximately 75% of those assessed.

a text. Children who are willing to skip words and/or ignore mispronunciations would seem to have a different understanding of what reading is all about (i.e., reading quickly with little attention to meaning construction) as compared with those who are willing to slow down and puzzle over words so that they can both accurately identify the words and construct meaning. We suspect that in the long term, the latter group will become the stronger comprehenders.

Of course, the relationship between measures of rate and accuracy (such as WCPM) and reading comprehension will also be influenced by the instruction children receive. If WCPM is given undue emphasis, children may learn that what's valued is reading the words as fast as they can, not understanding the text as best they can.

Measures of Prosody

Prosodic reading (also known as expressive reading) "is characterized as reading texts with greater range and variation in pitch, grouping words into meaningful units or pausing at grammatically relevant junctures, and pausing for appropriate durations" (Kim et al., 2021, p. 719). Schwanenflugel and Kuhn (2016) argued that measures of WCPM are insufficient and that indices of prosody should also be included in assessing fluency. Their summary of the research related to using measures of fluency to predict reading comprehension performance indicates that adding a measure of prosody to fluency evaluations improves the accuracy of predicting reading comprehension performance by as much as 20%. They argued that including measures of prosody is especially important because there is evidence that "children who read at acceptable rates but with poor expression comprehend less well" (Schwanenflugel & Kuhn, 2016, p. 109). Therefore, we urge teachers who choose to formally assess ORF, or are required to do so, to assess both WCPM *and* prosody. Further, in contexts in which teachers are required to assess all students' fluency on on-grade-level passages, we encourage teachers to also assess their students who are reading below grade level on passages that are in the range of their instructional/independent reading levels, that is, passages in which the student can accurately identify approximately 95% or more of the words.

On-Grade-Level Text

Multiple approaches have been used to determine the level of challenge provided by any given text intended for use with beginning readers. Unfortunately, the level of agreement across leveling methods is moderate at best (Pearson & Hiebert, 2014).

Assessing prosody in contexts when children can accurately identify most of the words will show whether students are attempting to construct meaning as they read. (Of course, teachers who routinely make time to listen to individual children read and who are making note of their word-identification strategies, as discussed in Chapter 12, and who are engaging their students in conversations about texts, as discussed in Chapters 15 and 16, will have little need of a measure of prosody in order to know whether their students perceive reading as being about meaning making. That will be evident in interactions during instruction.)

Several qualitative scales for evaluating prosody during oral reading have been developed. For example, the scale published by Rasinski (2004) provides guidance for assessing four dimensions of prosody:

- Expression and volume
- Phrasing
- Smoothness
- Pace

Figure 14.1 presents Rasinski's Multidimensional Fluency Scale which can be used to rate children's performance on each dimension using a 4-point scale.

As an alternative, the Oral Reading Fluency Passage Reading Expression Scoring Rubric used by the National Center for Education Statistics in the National Assessment of Educational Progress (NAEP, 2018/2023; White et al., 2021) uses a single 5-point scale to evaluate prosody (see Figure 14.2). The scale essentially asks teachers to consider the multiple elements included in Rasinski's assessment of prosody but does not require separate ratings for each element. The latter scale strikes us as potentially easier and more efficient for teachers to employ while still drawing teachers' attention to some of the most important elements of prosody. Note that while NAEP's oral reading fluency scale was developed for use in scientific data collection, the elements considered in rating prosody/expression can guide teachers' informal assessment of children's prosody. Note also that readers need to have read at least 12 words in a passage in order for the scale to be applicable. Thus, the scale is not intended to be used for learners at very early points in reading development. In fact, the NAEP developed the scale for use at the fourth- and eighth-grade levels. However, with the exception of requiring that a minimum number of words be read for ratings of 4 or 5, the rubric could be used for any text on a first or subsequent reading. Our purpose here is to share some of the characteristics of fluent and expressive reading that should be considered as children gain skill with reading.

Evaluating and Documenting Children's Progress during Instruction

When teachers have the opportunity to listen to individual children read, they likely attend to many aspects of the process, including the children's approaches to and success with word solving and their understanding of the texts they are

Multidimensional Fluency Scale

Use the following scales to rate reader fluency on the dimensions of expression and volume, phrasing, smoothness, and pace. Scores range from 4 to 16. Generally, scores below 8 indicate that fluency may be a concern. Scores of 8 or above indicate that the student is making good progress in fluency.

Dimension	1	2	3	4
A. Expression and Volume	Reads with little expression or enthusiasm in voice. Reads words as if simply to get them out. Little sense of trying to make text sound like natural language. Tends to read in a quiet voice.	Some expression. Begins to use voice to make text sound like natural language in some areas of the text, but not others. Focus remains largely on saying the words. Still reads in a quiet voice.	Sounds like natural language throughout the better part of the passage. Occasionally slips into expressionless reading. Voice volume is generally appropriate throughout the text.	Reads with good expression and enthusiasm throughout the text. Sounds like natural language. The reader is able to vary expression and volume to match his/her interpretation of the passage.
B. Phrasing	Monotonic with little sense of phrase boundaries, frequent word-by-word reading.	Frequent two- and three-word phrases giving the impression of choppy reading; improper stress and intonation that fail to mark ends of sentences and clauses.	Mixture of run-ons, mid-sentence pauses for breath, and possibly some choppiness; reasonable stress/intonation.	Generally well phrased, mostly in clause and sentence units, with adequate attention to expression.
C. Smoothness	Frequent extended pauses, hesitations. false starts, sound-outs. repetitions, and/or multiple attempts.	Several "rough spots" in text where extended pauses, hesitations, etc., are more frequent and disruptive.	Occasional breaks in smoothness caused by difficulties with specific words and/or structures.	Generally smooth reading with some breaks, but word and structure difficulties are resolved quickly, usually through self-correction.
D. Pace (during sections of min-imal disruption)	Slow and laborious.	Moderately slow.	Uneven mixture of fast and slow reading.	Consistently conversational.

FIGURE 14.1. Rasinski's (2004) Multidimensional Fluency Scale. Copyright © 2004 ASCD. Reprinted by permission.

	Rating	Characteristics of the Reading
0	Insufficient Sample	• Insufficient sample for rating (fewer than 12 words read aloud correctly).
1	Word by word	• Less than a quarter of the words[a] read aloud with appropriate expression. • Reading focuses on individual words (not phrases, sentences, or the passage). • Reading is all or mostly monotone.
2	Local grouping[b]	• More than a ¼ and less than ½ of the words read aloud with appropriate expression. • Reading focuses on local word groups (with little or no focus on phrases, sentences, or the passage). • Reading may be mostly monotone.
3	Phrase & Clause	• More than ½ of the words read aloud with appropriate expression. • Reading expresses the structure or meaning of the words, phrases, clauses, and a few sentences (with little or no focus on the passage). • Intonation may sometimes reinforce rhythmic grouping, or reading may be monotone.
4	Sentence prosody	• More than ¾ of the words read aloud with appropriate expression. • Reading correctly expresses text and sentence structure and meaning (which may include nonlocal text connections). • Reading can be occasionally inconsistent, but not monotone. • Reading rate is at least 55 words per minute (at least 80 text-words-read to merit this level or above).
5	Passage expression	• Passage read as if for a listener—of the passage portion read aloud, all or nearly all (at least 90%) is read with appropriate expression. The reading consistently expresses the structure and meaning of sentences, paragraphs, and the passage as a whole (which may include nonlocal text connections). • Reading may include a few word stumbles or misreading, but it is expressive throughout. • Reading rate is at least 80 words per minute (at least 120 text-words-read to merit this level).

[a]We are not suggesting that teachers would need to carefully calculate the proportion of words read with appropriate expression. A rough estimate can suffice to help teachers gauge students' prosodic reading.
[b]Local grouping involves reading two or three words without hesitating between words but the words do not necessarily form a meaningful phrase.

FIGURE 14.2. NAEP (2018/2023) Oral Reading Fluency Passage Reading Expression Scoring Rubric. From White et al. (2021).

reading. It is also useful to attend to children's ORF—although not in the more formal way described above. Ongoing attention to children's ORF can and should inform instructional planning both in terms of whether children will benefit from having additional opportunities to read a given text and in terms of aspects of fluency that would be appropriate instructional targets. Teachers' lesson notes would record the name of the book and the fluency rating(s) assigned, along with information about whether it was a first read or a reread. When a child's reading is fairly accurate (at least 90% or so of the words identified correctly), it is reasonable to document fluency regarding the child's rate, phrasing, expression, attention to punctuation, and/or attention to the text's signals for expression (see Figure 14.3), for this will guide instructional decision making for subsequent readings of the book and future books.

Figure 14.3 provides a snapshot for use in capturing aspects of the students' ORF across time. Ratings should be done based on reflection across individual children's reading of at least a few texts believed to be at the student's instructional level (read with 90–95% accuracy), texts that are read across a few lessons, and should not be based on the reading of a single text. Also note that we are not suggesting that teachers routinely do a count of WCPM when evaluating whether a student is reading at an appropriate rate. Rather, the point is for the teacher to determine whether, for the types of texts students read, the rate was appropriate. Thus, for example, in reading an informational text about whales—which, for young children, would likely be packed with pictures and illustrations—it would not be appropriate for the child to read the text straight through without pausing to look at and learn from the illustrations. The snapshot is intended to help teachers focus on contributors to fluent reading that may need to be addressed in instruction.

Once children have moved beyond reading repetitive and predictable texts, we think it is important for teachers to attend to prosody whenever they listen to children read (which, at least for those who are experiencing difficulty with reading development, would ideally occur frequently).

In the ISA, we try to prepare children to read new books with a fairly high rate of accuracy, which we do by:

- Providing them with books we expect they will be able to read with at least 90% accuracy
- Teaching and practicing specific decoding elements the children are ready to learn and that they will be able to apply in the new text (see Chapters 8–11)
- Explicitly teaching a few words that will be encountered in the book but that the children are unlikely to be able to identify given their current decoding skills and word-solving strategies (see Chapters 12 and 13)
- As needed, reminding children of word-identification strategies they have learned and/or introducing and explaining new strategies that they are ready to learn and that will be useful in the new book (see Chapter 12).

Teachers are encouraged to assess fluency for an individual book in a qualitative rather than a quantitative way by attending to prosody as children read in the context of small-group or one-to-one lessons. For each book read, the teacher simply rates whether the child's reading was word-by-word (WBW), demonstrated some phrasing (PHR), or sounded fluent (FL). Our definition of fluent reading is that the child's reading is accurate, with appropriate phrasing and intonation, at a smooth and reasonable pace, and that the teacher has a general sense that the child understands the meaning of the text. This rating is used in part to determine whether the book being read still presents enough learning opportunities for the

Group Snapshot—Oral Reading Prosody						
Student names						
Reads instructional level text with . . .	Appropriate rate (speed)					
	Appropriate phrasing					
	Appropriate expression (intonation)					
Attends to punctuation						
Attends to texts' signals for expression (e.g., all capital letters, italics, larger print)						

Key:

◻ *B—Beginning* indicates that instruction has addressed the skill or objective but that the child has only a preliminary understanding or ability to demonstrate the skill or objective.

⊠ *D—Developing* indicates that the child has some understanding of the skill or objective but does not reliably demonstrate that understanding or skill or is not yet automatic (fluent) with the skill.

⊠ *P—Proficient* indicates that the child reliably and spontaneously demonstrates the understanding or capability and that it no longer needs to be a focus of instruction.

FIGURE 14.3. Group snapshot for oral reading prosody.

child to benefit from reading the book again. Such learning opportunities might include increasing familiarity with previously unfamiliar written words, increased attention to meaning construction, and greater awareness of the role of punctuation. If a book is not rated as having been read fluently and is not considered to be overly challenging, it would be a candidate for rereading in a subsequent lesson (and in some instances in the same lesson, time permitting). For beginning readers, we believe multiple readings of a book are useful, as they provide the opportunity for children to both add words to their automatic sight vocabularies and experience smooth, expressive reading. Of course, there is no reason why a rating scale such as the Oral Reading Fluency Scale described above couldn't be used instead of our 3-point scale.

Fluency and MLs

For students who are multilingual, the relationship between reading fluency (as measured by WCPM) and reading comprehension is still apparent but weaker than for learners for whom English is their first language (Crosson & Lesaux, 2010). Not surprisingly, the strength of the relationship is dependent on the MLs' proficiency with the English language. Measures of WCPM can overestimate text-comprehension ability for MLs. That is, for example, students who appear to be reading at or above grade level on a measure of ORF may perform more poorly on a measure of comprehension than would native English speakers with similar fluency scores. Further, an assessment of ORF is likely to be a better predictor of reading comprehension for MLs with comparatively strong English language proficiency than it is for students with weaker English language skills.

Quirk and Beem (2012) found that for many ML students there was a substantial gap between their status on a measure of reading fluency and their status on a measure of reading comprehension. Lems (2022) suggests that measures of ORF are apt to overestimate readers' reading comprehension skills if they are relatively strong decoders but do not know the meanings of many of the words they can decode. The potential result is that they may be placed in reading materials that are too challenging for them. Thus, measures of fluency need to be interpreted with caution when considering the status of MLs. Based on these findings, Schwanenflugel and Kuhn (2016) argue that the national norms for fluency that existed at the time were not valid for MLs. Interestingly, however, Burns et al. (2017) report that second- and third-grade MLs with the weakest English language skills showed larger gains in fluency, as measured by WCPM than MLs with comparatively high English language skills during the course of reading intervention. They suggest that this finding argues against the (once) common practice of delaying reading intervention services until children had gained some degree of English proficiency. Ludwig, Guo, and Georgiou (2019) reached a similar conclusion based on an analysis (meta-analysis) of multiple reading intervention studies focused on MLs.

Instruction to Promote Fluency

The development of ORF depends on:

- Being able to automatically identify the most frequently occurring words (as discussed in Chapter 13)
- Having and using the ability to effectively puzzle through unfamiliar words encountered in context (the word solving skills and strategies discussed in Chapter 12)
- Knowing the meanings of most of the words encountered in a text (discussed in Chapter 15)
- Being familiar with the syntax and grammar of both spoken and written language (also discussed in Chapter 15)
- Understanding that written language is supposed to make sense (discussed in Chapters 1, 12, and 16)

There are multiple and widely accepted ways to support the development of reading fluency. The approaches basically entail a combination of teacher modeling and student practice, typically repeated practice, with reading texts that present some but not too much challenge.

Modeling

Reading aloud to children has multiple important benefits, many of which are discussed in Chapters 15 and 16. In this chapter we focus specifically on the role of reading aloud in promoting fluency, particularly the prosodic aspects of fluency. In order to understand what fluent reading should sound like, children need to hear text being read fluently. During a read-aloud, it is useful, on occasion, to draw the children's attention to the fluency of the reading. For example, at various times and depending on the text that is being read, teachers might demonstrate how one notices and uses punctuation (beginning with ending punctuation) or the difference between reading the text word-by-word versus in multiword phrases that make it easier to pay attention to the author's meaning.

When students are at a point in their own reading development at which the focus is shifting from a heavy emphasis on word identification and word learning to an emphasis on smooth, expressive reading, the teacher might, on occasion, have the children evaluate the teacher's fluency as the teacher reads word-by-word or in multiword strings with pauses that are not aligned with the phrasal boundaries of the passage, or when paying no attention to punctuation. The point of engaging in this type of activity is to draw the children's attention to the characteristics of appropriately expressive reading. Children generally think it is pretty funny when they get to evaluate whether their teacher is reading expressively (or sounds like a storyteller depending on the text). The experience may help them reflect on their own reading prosody.

Choral and Repeated Reading

In choral reading, the children are provided with both modeling and practice. This technique is often used to support children in reading texts that are too challenging for them to read on their own. Often, the text is first read to the children by the teacher, sometimes more than once. Thereafter, the children are invited to read along *with* the teacher. Often, a single large-print version of a text is used. Examples of the kinds of texts frequently used include big books, poems, and language-experience charts that have been co-constructed by the class. When a single text is used, the print needs to be large enough for all students in the instructional group to see. Smaller versions of texts can be enlarged using a document camera or interactive white board. The teacher points to the words as the group reads in unison.

Choral reading is also used when all the students in the instructional group have their own copies of the text. Here, the teacher reads the text to the children one or more times before the children are invited to join in the reading. Then the children read the text, following along in their copies of it, generally pointing to the words as the group reads. The pointing is an important element here, especially for the students with more limited literacy skills. Without the pointing, children can appear to be fully participating, even if they are not attending to the printed words but are just looking at their texts and echoing what they hear the other readers saying. The teacher monitors as the group reads to make sure that the children are looking at the correct place in the text as they read and redirects those children who are not doing so. Choral reading led by the teacher is often followed by repeated reading in which the children read the same texts independently— initially with one or more partners. Reading texts multiple times helps to promote word-identification skills as well as motivation for reading, for with each reading the text will seem easier and thereby build the learners' confidence.

Studies have found that repeated readings lead to improved word recognition accuracy, reading rates, automaticity, expressive and meaningful reading, reading comprehension, and confidence in reading (LaBerge & Samuels, 1974; Samuels, 1979). These reading capabilities not only apply to the passages that students have practiced but also transfer to new, never-before-seen texts (Mraz et al., 2013).

Rasinski et al. (2020) reported on the effects of an exploratory study that involved beginning first graders in an urban setting. They engaged in daily repeated and assisted reading of short texts in the context of what the authors referred to as Fluency Development Lessons (FDLs; see box). The impact of this 10-week intervention study was rather impressive when the reading performance of the students in the treatment group was compared to that of children in the comparison group: children in the treatment group made three times the gains on a measure of reading accuracy and comprehension as the children in the comparison group.

Rasinski et al.'s FDLs

In this study, intervention teachers spent 20 minutes per day on the FDL as part of their literacy block. In each lesson, a brief new text, typically a poem, was introduced and read to the students. Children were provided with individual copies of the poem and a large-print version was put on display.

During the course of the lesson, students read the text used the previous day, and then the teacher introduced and read the new text aloud to the students two or three times. Following a brief discussion of the meaning of the text, the students read the text chorally (with the teacher) a couple of times. Afterward, the students worked in small groups continuing to practice the text as the teacher circulated, providing guidance and support.

Thereafter, the students engaged in a brief word study activity involving words from the text. Students then took a copy of the text home to practice with family members.

Repeated Reading versus Wide Reading

It was once believed that having children read texts repeatedly was the preferred way to build fluency, not only with the texts that were read repeatedly but with texts more generally (National Reading Panel, 2000). However, more recent reviews of the research literature suggest that it is the volume of reading that students do that is critical to fluency development, whether that volume is due to repeated readings of texts or to wide reading of multiple different texts. In our opinion, for beginning readers, there is value in engaging the children in some repeated reading, as noted previously.

While the Rasinski et al. results clearly illustrate the value of repeated reading, there is also substantial value in wide reading—especially as children develop their reading skills. Wide reading provides children with the opportunity to extend their ability to identify unfamiliar written words in order to learn the meanings (and shades of meaning) of words (see Chapter 15) and to increase their world knowledge. All these knowledge sources are critical to helping children understand and learn from the texts they will encounter as they move through school (and life).

Supported Reading

Children learn to read by reading. The more reading they do, the more quickly they will become proficient. Pressley et al. (2023) argue that the reading they do should consist primarily of texts in which their reading is highly accurate. However, to grow as readers, children must, of course, encounter texts in which they do not already know all the words. High-accuracy reading for these students is the result of knowing many of the words in the texts they read and having the skills and strategies needed to figure out the not-yet-known words. In Part II of this text, we talked a lot about helping readers develop skill with the alphabetic and orthographic aspects of written language. Those skills, in combination with the word-identification strategies discussed in Chapter 12, will serve to enable this high-accuracy reading and help extend children's sight vocabularies. Extending children's sight vocabularies, in turn, enables them to handle progressively more challenging texts.

Supported reading presents one of the main instructional contexts in which teachers have the opportunity to guide the application of developing skill with the code-based skills and to encourage the development of self-teaching skills (see Chapter 12). In Chapter 2, we suggested that in a classroom context, the children with more limited literacy skills should spend more time in supported reading than their more skilled peers (who would certainly be reading, but more independently). The purpose is to provide the less skilled readers with greater opportunity to practice and receive guidance and feedback on the application of these skills and strategies—for the purpose of building their fluency.

Partner Practice/Buddy Reading

Teachers have limited time to spend with individual students and small groups. Therefore, to provide additional practice, children can read aloud to one another in pairs or small groups. When children are in a context in which they need to read aloud, they are more likely to attempt unfamiliar words and apply fix-up strategies when an attempt at a word does not result in a real word that fits the context (see Figure 12.1, p. 303). Further, a reader's partner(s) may be able to provide assistance in the form of a suggested strategy that will lead to accurate word identification. In partner reading situations, children should be encouraged to first allow their partner time to figure out an initially puzzling word, next offer strategy support (i.e., suggest a strategy or strategies), and finally, if need be, provide the pronunciation of the unknown word. (In all oral reading contexts, readers should reread the entire sentence after encountering and identifying an initially unfamiliar word, as this assists the reader in the orthographic mapping process as well as understanding and learning from the text.)

In partner reading contexts, children, in addition to taking turns reading texts to one another, should also be encouraged to react to and discuss the text. We must always strive to ensure that children perceive reading as a meaning-making enterprise. For the specific goal of promoting fluency and prosody, children should be encouraged to read the same texts multiple times, as in the Fluency Development Lessons described above. Texts used in small-group reading lessons can routinely be used during partner/buddy reading.

Independent Practice

Beginning readers should have ready access to a collection of books and other texts (such as poems, brief articles from children's magazines, lyrics from songs, and the chart texts that have been created) that they can read successfully. These would be texts that they have already read, with guidance and support and/or books that are at or near their independent reading level. Reading should be a free-choice activity when the children have completed other assignments. Although some children may never opt for that choice, many will, especially if teachers are successful in portraying reading as an appealing activity rather than a job ("You *get* to read some of the books in our basket"; see Chapter 3, which discusses increasing motivation for reading).

Reading for an Audience

Many students enjoy reading and rereading entertaining poems, nursery rhymes, plays, lyrics to popular music, jump-rope rhymes and/or jokes for the purpose of performing for an audience. For example, for older readers who struggle and who are reluctant to read books that are easy enough for them to read fairly fluently, and for students for whom fluency is a focal issue, we have found that, for the right purpose and audience, they are often willing to do so. Many second graders, for example, are happy to read and reread texts appropriate for beginning readers if their purpose is to record those texts to be used in the listening center in kindergarten (or to go into a kindergarten classroom to read to a younger learner). Many students are willing to engage in rereading if they know their reading will ultimately be recorded for later playback.

Learning and reciting poetry, songs, jokes, and the like and engagement in readers' theater also provide motivating reasons to engage in reading and rereading in preparation for performances—both in school and beyond.

KEY POINTS OF THIS CHAPTER

✓ To become fluent readers, learners need to engage in a lot of reading—the more reading children do, the more quickly they become fluent.

✓ In the primary grades, oral reading fluency (ORF), as measured by words correct per minute (WCPM), is a reasonably strong predictor of children's ability to comprehend the texts they read. But there is a risk that for some children too much emphasis on speed will turn their attention away from the goal of reading—meaning construction.

✓ Appropriate reading prosody/expression is an indicator that readers are making sense of text as they read.

  • Automaticity in word identification contributes to the prosodic reading.

✓ Teacher modeling and discussion of fluent and disfluent reading can help learners understand the characteristics of prosodic reading.

✓ Practicing repeated reading of a text to be read to an audience can encourage children to strive for appropriate prosody/expression in their reading.

CHAPTER 15

Vocabulary and Oral Language Development

> **MEANING CONSTRUCTION GOAL 2**
>
> Children will learn the meanings of new words encountered in instructional interactions and will be able to use the words conversationally. Further, children's ability to understand and use complex grammatical structures will improve.

Reading is a language skill. Thus, to a great extent, this entire book is about language development. However, in this chapter we focus specifically on oral language development. We will discuss word-, sentence-, and discourse-level features and how these features may vary across different varieties of language. We discuss how these aspects of language develop and how they are related to reading development in the primary grades and beyond. Our major focus in this chapter is on helping teachers become attuned to features of language that children speak or encounter while reading, writing, or listening to text. Additionally, this chapter addresses methods of instruction that may help strengthen these critical language skills.

Language and Reading

There is a strong predictive relationship between language skills, especially vocabulary, measured in the pre-primary and early-primary grades and reading comprehension performance all the way through high school (Cunningham &

Stanovich, 1997; Dickinson & Tabors, 2001; Gallagher, McClain, & Uccelli, 2000; Sénéchal, Ouellette, & Rodney, 2006; for reviews, see Dickinson, McCabe, & Clark-Chiarelli, 2004, and Scarborough, 2001). That is, children who have relatively strong language skills when they are young are likely to have stronger understanding of the things they read when they are older. The association between language skills and later reading comprehension is generally considered to be causal in nature and has led to calls for instituting efforts to improve early language skills in order to improve reading comprehension and academic performance more generally (e.g., Biemiller, 2006; Dickinson, McCabe, & Essex, 2006; Neuman, 2011).

Reading and writing are reciprocal processes rooted in language. Reading is the decoding of printed text into oral language, while writing is the encoding of oral language into print. Both focus on conveying meaning. Language is the foundation for meaning making and conveying meaning (Nation, 2016). Multiple features of oral language lay the groundwork for reading and writing. Students must have a grasp of phonology, word meaning, syntax (grammar), and discourse (genre) to comprehend or compose text. At the smallest level, readers need phonemic sensitivity, or the ability to detect the differing sounds in spoken language. This sensitivity assists with matching the sounds in spoken language to the orthographic representations in print. It is important to note the variations in pronunciations of words across varieties of English; hence, explicit instruction may be helpful. For example, speakers of African American English may omit final consonant sounds (e.g., *running* is pronounced "runnin"), which may impact their ability to match spoken to printed language in texts (Washington & Seidenberg, 2021). Readers must understand that print represents spoken language. Word knowledge, here defined as knowledge of the meaning and pronunciation of words, allows for efficient and effective word-solving attempts when reading. The reader must match the attempted pronunciation of a word in print to a word in their oral vocabulary and use their knowledge of the word meaning to determine whether their hypothesized pronunciation of the word makes sense of the context (sentence) in which the printed word is encountered.

Similarly, readers use their knowledge of syntax to help them determine the meaning of unknown words. How a word is used in a sentence can give clues about its meaning. When encountering an unknown word in meaningful text (spoken or printed), the reader may intuitively use the syntax of the sentence to determine the part of speech or function of the unknown word. For example, in the sentence *The girl sat on the stoop,* the reader may use the syntax of the sentence to determine that a *stoop* is a noun (thing) given how it functions in the sentence. While this doesn't provide the full meaning of the term, it does allow for developing basic knowledge about the term. And, depending on additional information provided in the text and future encounters with the same word in other contexts, the reader gradually increases their knowledge of the concept represented by the word. Discourse-level features help the reader determine how the print functions (i.e., as narrative story, persuasive essay, informational text), and distinguish the purpose and audience of the text. Texts are written for different purposes with language that supports the purpose. Students must have implicit knowledge of word, syntactic, and discourse features of language in order to fully comprehend and produce written texts.

Language Development

Virtually all children are capable of learning to communicate, and each culture and community has different means for fostering language development. In this text, we focus on language development in Western culture, primarily the United States, as the research aligned with and was conducted in U.S. classrooms. Most children acquire language with relative ease throughout the first years of life and are largely proficient speakers of their home language prior to school entry. Language development is considered to be an innate process in that it occurs in nearly all children, but only under the right conditions where children hear rich models of language from mature speakers. Language learning is influenced by cognitive, environmental, and biological capacities, implying that both nature and nurture play pivotal roles (Werker & Hensch, 2015). There is evidence that specific regions of the brain are devoted to language and that these regions are activated under the right environmental conditions.

Initially, the learning of spoken words is a slow process, but as children mature, they become more efficient and strategic word learners (Bergelson, 2020). Children typically utter their first word around their first birthday, but they begin understanding words between 6 and 9 months of age (as reviewed in Bergelson, 2020). These early words typically represent people and events in their environment, with the word consistently mapping onto the appropriate object or event (e.g., mama always refers to a mother figure). Prior to this point, infants play with the sounds in language through babbling, shrieking, crying, cooing, and giggling. This language play helps developing infants gain control over their tongue, lips, and mouth, which will help them form words as they mature. With time and linguistic input, children develop their oral vocabularies (i.e., knowledge of word meanings) and begin to string words together into early phrases (such as "more cookie") that are intelligible, but not necessarily grammatically correct. Children's length of utterance in words typically corresponds to their age in years, such that a 2-year-old produces utterances containing two words on average. Early utterances may be ripe with grammatical inconsistencies (e.g., "I goed there") that tend to mature into acceptable forms through increased exposure to grammatically correct language (Tomasello, 2001). Children learn the language to which they are exposed (children exposed to Mandarin learn Mandarin) and may acquire multiple languages simultaneously when provided with sufficient input and opportunities to use the language in meaningful contexts.

Vocabulary

A great deal of research has focused on the development of children's word knowledge/vocabulary. That research provides useful guidance on how to support children's vocabulary development/acquisition. Below we share the six principles for word learning as compiled by Harris, Golinkoff, and Hirsch-Pasek's (2011).

Six Principles for Word Learning
(Harris, Golinkoff, & Hirsch-Pasek, 2011)

1. **Frequency matters:** Children tend to learn the words they hear most frequently. Consider the first words spoken by infants and how they relate to the people and the surrounding environments in which they typically engage (mama, dada, doggie, apple, cup). These are the words the child has heard repeatedly, which provides the child with multiple opportunities for learning and reinforcement.

2. **Make it interesting:** Children learn words for things and events that interest them. Discussing topics, events, or items that have drawn the child's attention may result in word learning. Adults in the child's life are encouraged to follow the child's lead and discuss what is of interest to them. Thematic play (e.g., playing house, grocery store, restaurant) can build vocabularies.

3. **Make it responsive:** Interactive and responsive contexts rather than passive contexts favor word learning. A child who is actively engaged in conversations and/or language-rich environments is more likely to learn more language than a child who passively listens. Engaging children in conversations, including asking and answering questions, promotes language development.

4. **Focus on meaning:** Children learn words best in meaningful contexts where relationships among words and concepts are discussed. It is useful to teach words that are conceptually related to a topic to build a web of knowledge rather than teach words in isolation. For example, a child is more likely to learn the names of farm animals when visiting a farm or playing with a farm-themed playset following the reading of a book about a farm.

5. **Be clear:** Children need clear information about word meanings that is presented in child-friendly speech. Being clear about the meanings of words and providing sufficient details to see how the word is similar to and different from other words promote word learning. Providing definitions about what can be done with an object (e.g., a ball can roll or bounce) also promotes word learning in young children.

6. **Beyond the word:** Vocabulary learning and grammatical development are reciprocal processes. Children can learn about the meaning of a word based on how it is used in a sentence. Learning words means learning how words are used in sentences (e.g., the grammatical function of the word such as noun or verb).

Syntax

In addition to word-level skills and knowledge, students need strong sentence-level or syntactic (grammar) skills and knowledge to become proficient readers. Syntax is the manner in which sentences and phrases are constructed from words. Just as morphology governs word structure (e.g., prefixes go before the base word), syntax governs sentence structure. The order of the words in a sentence matters, such that rearranging "The boy ate the sandwich," to "ate boy sandwich the the" makes it incomprehensible. Indeed, syntax is the 'workhorse' of meaning (Scott, 2009). A list of words does not provide the same meaning as connected (meaningful) text; hence, reading a string of words fluently does not guarantee comprehension will occur. Syntactic knowledge develops early in life, with most children demonstrating relative proficiency in common syntactic forms by their fifth birthday (Paul, 1981). More complex forms of syntax, such as *embedded clauses* and *passive voice*, may emerge later as children become immersed in environments, such as read-alouds, where such syntax is used. As with vocabulary, children may first be able to understand prior to being able to produce complex syntax.

Prominent theories of reading comprehension indicate that syntax plays a key role in understanding texts (Perfetti & Strafura, 2014). Awareness of sentence structure may provide a mechanism for deciphering a word that is difficult for a reader to decode (as discussed in Chapter 12), which may support text understanding. For example, a student who reads the sentence "The girl swam at the r . . ." and is unable to decode the final word may use syntactic knowledge to determine that the final word is a noun rather than a verb (*river* rather than *running*). This limits the possible options in a strategic manner, which is substantially different from "guessing" based on context (MacKay, Lynch, Duncan, & Deacon, 2021).

Developing strong syntactic knowledge and skills is critical in the early years of schooling as syntactic complexity in texts increases as children progress through school (Curran, 2020). Graesser, McNamara, and Kulikowich (2011) argue that syntax is the strongest factor influencing text difficulty; hence, instruction should place emphasis on meaning construction at the sentence and phrase levels, as well as the overall meaning of the text. Intervention studies in which children are provided instruction focused on syntax resulted in improvements in listening comprehension for children in prekindergarten through first grade (Phillips, 2014), and reading comprehension for students in upper elementary grades (Morris et al., 2012; Proctor, Silverman, Harring, Jones, & Hartranft, 2020).

The syntax in books is often quite different from, and typically more complex than, the syntax of everyday spoken language. Therefore, if children have had limited experience with being read to, they are likely to find book syntax challenging. For example, many storybooks are told in the passive voice (e.g., "The wall was decorated with bright pictures"), which is infrequently used in casual conversation, which favors active voice (e.g., "She decorated the wall with bright pictures"). Teachers and proficient readers are so familiar with book syntax that they may not recognize the challenge it poses for some children. Consider this excerpt from *Hibernation* (Kosara, 2012):

> Brown fat makes heat, which helps to protect a hibernating animal's organs, such as the brain, while it sleeps through the cold winter.

Children who have been read to widely and frequently and who have discussed such books with their reading partners will have encountered the types of syntactic structures (e.g., multiple embedded clauses and phrases) and gained experience in interpreting those structures. For children without such experience, the syntactic challenges provided by this portion of the text may be difficult or impossible to negotiate without assistance. For example, students may not immediately identify that the brain is an organ, which is noted through the clause "such as the brain," or that the heat made by brown fat is what protects the animal's organs. It can be helpful to pose questions to students to help them identify how or what the embedded clauses and phrases relate to. For example, asking students "Which organ is protected by the fat?" or "How does brown fat protect the animal who is hibernating?" can draw attention to the reference in the sentence. Similarly, in contexts in which students are reading or are viewing print, it can be helpful to point out the commas in the sentence that offset the clauses and phrases.

Even books written to be read by beginning and developing readers sometimes include challenging syntax that could interfere with word-solving attempts. For example, a book titled *Where Is the Queen?* (Minkoff, 1996) includes the following as part of the description of a queen's preparation for giving a ball: "First, she set the table for eating in the green room" (p. 4). The phrase *set the table for eating* is at odds with the more typical phrase *set the table for dinner* and may well confuse children and lead them to reject an accurate decoding of the word *eating*. The more unfamiliar children are with the types of syntax encountered in books, the more likely they are to experience difficulty with such structures, which has the potential to interfere with both word learning and comprehension while reading.

Linguistic Registers

Within each language are multiple registers, which refer to the setting-specific ways of using language. We all shift the way we talk, consciously or not, throughout our day. Our histories, relationships, and bonds with people impact the way language is used. Compare the register used when talking with a group of 2-year-olds on a playground who are arguing over a ball, and the register employed when pleading with a police officer to not issue a speeding ticket. The word choices, tone, syntax, and discourse style are likely quite different, indicating the use of different linguistic registers. No register is superior to others (Dawson & Phelan, 2016). A person may shift from one register to another, called style shifting, based on the purpose, place, or participants in which the communication takes place (Barnes & Hadley, 2022).

Academic language, which is more generally known as the language of the classroom or of schools, refers to the word-, sentence-, and discourse-level features commonly found in academic texts and discussions (Galloway, McClain, & Uccelli, 2020). Academic language is a register and is composed of multiple registers, such as the language of science and mathematical language. Each academic discipline has a unique way of communicating that involves differences at the word, sentence, and discourse levels. At the word level, an academic discipline may involve specific terminology to convey precision. This vocabulary is frequently termed academic vocabulary, which is typically found in content-area texts rather than in casual talk. Academic vocabulary may be discipline-specific or general. Discipline-specific terms are found in only one discipline and are rarely heard or used outside of academic discourse (*habitat, addend, lung*). In contrast, general terms may be found across academic disciplines (*explanation, argument, hypothesis*) but may have different meanings based on the content area. At the sentence level, academic language tends to contain more syntactically complex sentences than casual language in order to convey more precise content. Academic language may contain more passive structures (*the weeds were removed from the garden*), elaborative phrases and clauses (*the birds, whose feathers were bright red and green, ate the berries*), nominalizations where processes become nouns (*evaporate* becomes *evaporation*), and embedded questions (*Sergio wondered where the fins on the whale were located*). At the discourse level, academic language conveys a degree of expertise through an unquestionable tone that implies a statement of fact rather than opinion. Different genres, such as explanations, arguments, and narratives are used to convey different types of information to different audiences.

As noted, environmental differences play a role in children's language development. As the linguistic environments of homes and communities vary, so do children's funds of linguistic knowledge. Some homes and communities use language in ways that are similar to the language used in classrooms. Some children are raised in homes where multiple languages are used, and they are able to easily shift and merge their language use through a process called translanguaging, which is described below. These differences in language knowledge and use should be considered during classroom instruction because they may impact how students approach texts (Garcia & Kleifgen, 2020).

Vocabulary and Language Development and MLs

It is obviously beyond the scope of a single chapter in a text on early reading development to fully address the topic of vocabulary and language development for children who are learning English as an additional language. According to recent reports, the 10 most common languages other than English spoken in the United States are Spanish, Chinese, Tagalog (the language of the Philippines), Vietnamese, French, German, Korean, Arabic, Russian, and Italian (roughly in that order—depending on the report). Taken together, the spoken forms of these languages vary from English in ways that are too numerous to address in the space available (to say nothing of the fact that we do not have the expertise to take on such a massive task!). Thankfully, Swan and Smith (2001), in their edited volume, have gathered, in one place, information on each of these languages that should help to inform teachers about the potential sources of confusion that MLs with given language backgrounds may encounter. We encourage teachers, especially those who teach concentrations of a given language group, to avail themselves of this resource.

Lacking the space and the expertise to provide detailed advice on supporting MLs with varying language backgrounds, in this section we address what is known about how to support the development of English language proficiency among MLs more generally. Claude Goldenberg, one of the most widely recognized experts on the education of MLs, offers three important principles that can help to guide instruction for MLs (Goldenberg, 2013, p. 5):

- Generally effective practices are likely to be effective with MLs.
- MLs require additional instructional supports.
- The home language can be used to promote academic development.

Beyond these general principles, Goldenberg (2013) reports that there is very little evidence that we know how to close the achievement gap that is typical in comparisons of MLs and their English-only peers. Given that there is a clear relationship between MLs' English proficiency and their academic achievement (Halle, Hair, Wandner, McNamara, & Chien, 2012), it is critical to support young MLs' development of proficiency with spoken English. This is a point highlighted in August and Shanahan's (2006) summary of the research on MLs: "Instruction in the key components of reading is necessary—but not sufficient—for teaching language-minority students to read and write proficiently in English. Oral proficiency in English is critical as well—but student performance suggests that it is often overlooked in instruction" (p. 4).

For the purpose of highlighting the need to attend to oral language development and usage among ML students as well as English-only students, the snapshot at the end of this chapter (Figure 15.1) encourages teachers to consider multiple aspects of language development and usage. Further, in reflecting on students' language skills, teachers are encouraged to identify students who need opportunities to extend their language skills and to provide opportunities for them to do so. These opportunities would include teacher–child and peer-to-peer engagements in extended conversations in various contexts, as described later in this chapter.

Translanguaging

Multilingual students are able to draw from all of their linguistic resources when a *translanguaging* standpoint is in place. Translanguaging springs from the idea that language is a single construct that cannot be separated into different repertoires such as English, Spanish, or Haitian-Creole. Boundaries between languages are artificial, having been established external to the speaker. Translanguaging recognizes how speakers draw from all language experiences and blend home, school, and community ways with words (Garcia & Kleyn, 2016). Limiting students to speaking only English when they are able to draw from Turkish and Arabic as well, may limit the students' ability to demonstrate their full knowledge and understanding. Translanguaging goes beyond a single culture and embraces multiple methods for meaning making while not succumbing to pressure to blindly adopt white, middle-class language practices. Translanguaging may be viewed as a means for affirming culture and valuing differences. A translanguaging stance places emphasis on meaning and the purpose of language (Flynn, 2021). For example, students may be able to craft more complete and complex sentences through drawing on their repertoire of Spanish and English: "Hicimos un sand castle en la playa on Saturday con mi family" ("We made a sand castle at the beach on Saturday with my family").

Recently, there has been a shift in the children's storybook publishing industry to include translanguaging in their texts. This may come in multiple forms. Some texts are written in two separate languages (e.g., English and Spanish), where the print on the top of the page features one language (e.g., Spanish), which is followed by the same content provided in the second language (e.g., English). When reading such texts aloud, the adult may read in one or both of the languages, or may slide between the two, varying the language from page to page. Other texts meld multiple languages in print, such that multiple languages may appear in a single sentence. Reading stories that model diverse and complex forms of language may benefit a variety of students. Websites such as Reading Rockets (*www.readingrockets.org/books*), Colorín Colorado (*www.colorincolorado.org*), and CUNY NYSIEB[1] provide resources for promoting a translanguaging stance.

Instruction for Developing Language

While much of language development occurs naturally, there are means for facilitating more robust language learning, particularly for language that is not typically featured in children's home environments.

Vocabulary

Most of the words for which children know the meanings are learned in the context of conversations and/or through being read to and reading. Only a limited number of words are learned through intentional, explicit instruction. Hence, there is a need to promote language-rich environments from which students may learn words incidentally and develop a sense of word consciousness that fuels their desire to expand their vocabularies. Although words certainly can be learned through purposeful instruction, children need to learn so many words that it would be virtually impossible for teachers (or anyone else) to specifically teach all of them.

---

[1] See *www.cuny-nysieb.org/translanguaging-resources/culturally-relevant-books-and-resources*.

However, teachers can, and should, selectively teach and provide ongoing engagement with the meanings of some high-utility words that may require support for acquisition. Indeed, numerous studies demonstrate that direct and explicit teaching of word meanings has a positive impact on young children's vocabulary (e.g., Beck & McKeown, 2007; Coyne, McCoach, Loftus, Zipoli, & Kapp, 2009; Silverman, 2007a, 2007b). The basic premises of these instructional approaches are described later in this chapter.

Of course, knowing a word's meaning is not an "all-or-nothing" phenomenon. Gradations in knowledge of word meanings exist, with knowledge ranging from knowing nothing about a word to having elaborated knowledge of the word's meaning and how it relates to other words, being able to use it fluently and appropriately in conversation and in writing, and so forth. Ouellette (2006) suggests that deep knowledge of word meanings is the type of vocabulary knowledge that is most strongly related to reading comprehension. For most words, deep knowledge of meaning develops gradually through multiple encounters with the words in different contexts. Bloom (2000) suggests that children do not learn 10 words a day, as some estimates suggest (Nagy & Herman, 1987), but rather that they learn one-hundredth of the meaning of each of one thousand different words each day. If Bloom's characterization is accurate, it becomes clear that vocabulary development is largely incidental and occurs through children's efforts to infer and refine the meanings of words as they participate in various language contexts over time. Teachers can assist in this incremental learning process by providing supportive language contexts for vocabulary acquisition, by being alert for occasions when children encounter words that are unfamiliar to them, and by providing explanations of those words. Of course, one of the most supportive contexts for vocabulary acquisition is engagement in making meaning of the texts that students read and that are read to them. Active meaning construction (discussed in Chapter 16) facilitates comprehension of the text, which, in turn, supports vocabulary development. For example, Cain and Oakhill (2011) report that students found to be poor comprehenders at age 8 experienced less growth in vocabulary knowledge by ages 11 and 14 than did students who were good comprehenders at age 8. This was true even though there were no differences between the poor and good comprehender groups in growth in word identification. Students who are stronger comprehenders tend to read more frequently, which introduces them to a greater variety of words, many of which would not be encountered in oral language. In early childhood, children learn words by hearing them used in their daily lives. As children grow, they tend to learn new vocabulary words through reading printed text, as printed text tends to contain more diverse vocabulary than oral conversations. Therefore, students who comprehend what they read are more likely to acquire new vocabulary terms with greater ease than those who have difficulty with comprehending.

Which Words to Teach?

Every student has a unique and diverse lexicon (the words for which the student knows the meaning). Thus, it can be challenging to determine which words to explicitly teach, particularly given the limited instructional time. While much vocabulary may be learned implicitly through exposure, some terms will require explicit instruction where definitions, examples, synonyms, and the like are provided. Selecting terms for explicit instruction should follow the core principles identified through decades of research (e.g., Beck, McKeown, & Kucan, 2013). Teachers should consider:

- teaching words that are not yet known to students,
- the usefulness of the word, and
- teaching conceptually related words that build knowledge.

Considering how difficult a word is to learn should also factor into word selection. Generally, nouns tend to be the easiest words for students to learn, with those that are concrete (having an imageable referent) being easier to learn than those representing more abstract concepts (*justice, liberty*). Verbs tend to be more challenging to acquire as many represent motions that may be challenging to define verbally or may represent mental states (think, hypothesize). Words that appear more frequently in conversation and print tend to be easier to learn, as repeated exposure to terms tends to lead to quicker acquisition.

Unknown words are those that students have never or rarely heard and have little or no knowledge of the meaning or of how they are used in a sentence or meaningful text (grammatical function). When students have a general understanding of a term, but do not know the technical definition, the word is not considered unknown. For example, the spoken word *sun* would be a known term if students could name it on sight (point to the sun in the sky while saying "sun"), even if they do not know the sun is a star.

Useful words are those that are encountered frequently across the content areas or within a specific content area and that add precision and detail. These words are useful in that students read, write, hear, and speak them in academic contexts. Therefore, they are useful for conveying knowledge. Useful words are frequently verbs such as explain, consider, compare, contrast, and investigate, which may be found across the content areas and are particularly common on assessments in the middle elementary grades and beyond. Because the utility of a word may depend on the context, teachers are encouraged to consider when and where students will encounter them and how critical it is for students to have a deep understanding of the term.

Conceptually related terms are words that are related to a specific topic or concept. These terms are particularly useful in the content areas as they convey precision and accuracy, demarcate categories, and build knowledge. Conceptually related terms can be selected by first identifying the topic or concept. For example, a common topic in first-grade classrooms focuses on light and solar patterns. Conceptually related terms for this topic could include *illuminate, solar, shadow, transparent,* and *visible.* Not only are these terms related to light and solar patterns, but they are also useful for discussing the topic; they would be relatively unfamiliar to many first graders and thus worthy of explicit instruction. Note how the term *sun* is not included as a term to explicitly teach in spite of its relationship with solar. Most students are already familiar with the term *sun* and therefore do not require explicit instruction. Teaching a conceptually related term, *solar*, is a better use of precious instructional time and certainly would include use of the term *sun*.

General Guidelines for Vocabulary Instruction

1. Select terms students do not yet know or are unfamiliar with.
2. Teach words that are useful.
3. Teach words that are conceptually related.

Core Vocabulary

Hiebert, Goodwin, and Cervetti (2018) set out to identify a set of words, the core vocabulary, that account for approximately 90% of the words found in printed texts. Students who can decode and who know the meaning of these words are more likely to comprehend written texts. Hence there is a need to emphasize these words in instruction. The core vocabulary was developed by analyzing texts to determine which words make up 90% of the words in texts, as this aligns with the concept that students can understand a text when they are able to correctly read 90% of the words. The core vocabulary (Hiebert et al., 2018) are the 2,500 word families (here, word families refers to base words and their affixes) that comprise the majority of the words found in printed texts. These words were then sorted into morphological families based on base words (*friend*, *unfriendly*, *friendlier*) and were linked conceptually to form broad topics. A full list of the core vocabulary, along with conceptual maps representing semantic connections may be found at *www.textproject.org*. The core vocabulary includes words that may be well known to students and therefore do not require instruction. Instruction should focus on the words that students do not yet know and, as discussed in Chapter 11, on how the associated affixes influence the words' meanings. Words may be selected from the core vocabulary based on the topical content of a unit of study, with consideration given to students' present funds of vocabulary knowledge.

When selecting words for explicit instruction, we encourage teachers to consider how difficult it might be to learn the word. As noted, not all words need to be taught. It makes sense to direct instructional time to those words that present the greater challenge for learning. Words that are more difficult to learn likely need to receive more instructional time and energy. Thus, developing an understanding of difficulty may assist with selecting words for instruction. An important consideration is how easy a word is to imagine or to experience in the real world (Maguire, Hirsh-Pasek, & Golinkoff, 2006). For example, the word *justice* is not tangible in the physical world, and it may be difficult to imagine what justice looks like in one's mind. In contrast, the term *canopy* is easy to visualize and can be experienced or seen in the physical world. Words that are easy to imagine or can be experienced or observed in the physical world do not require extensive instruction, for they may be easily displayed as a physical object or through an image as a picture or physical representation of the word. In contrast, words that are not easy to imagine or are not tangible may require explicit instruction. Multiple examples of the term *justice,* provisions of antonyms and synonyms, and experiences with instances of justice (or lack thereof) may be required for students to develop a deep understanding of the term. In the context of reading or reading aloud, it is important to reserve explicit instruction for words whose meanings cannot easily be discerned through the text or surrounding illustrations, as students may learn the latter terms independently through incidental exposure.

Hadley and Mendez (2021) provide the examples of *gunwale* (rhymes with funnel) and *analyze* for contrasting word learning. *Gunwale* is rarely used in conversation or in print; hence, it would be quite challenging to learn from exposure. However, this term can easily be defined through a pictorial representation showing the upper edge of a boat. In contrast, *analyze* occurs more frequently in academic conversations and texts but is very difficult to portray through a visual representation. For acquisition to occur, this term would likely need to be encountered in meaningful contexts, such as science instruction. Importantly, these terms differ in their usefulness: *gunwale* has little value for those outside the boating community, while *analyze* appears regularly in academic texts and conversations that students may engage with. Explicit instruction of *analyze* is clearly a better use of instructional time.

Student-Friendly Definitions

When directly teaching vocabulary, it is critical that teachers provide students with definitions that make sense and are easy to understand in the context of the students' lives. Much research supports the use of child- or student-friendly definitions (Beck et al., 2013) that differ from dictionary definitions in that they are less complex and use words known to students rather than sophisticated vocabulary, as this is critical for establishing meaning. When an unfamiliar word is used in a definition, the student must then do double the work of determining the meaning of a second unfamiliar term. Describing the word *meander* as *to wander aimlessly* may be more puzzling than clarifying to younger students who may not be familiar with either *wander* or *aimlessly,* or both. A more student-friendly definition of *meander* would be to *walk around without purpose or direction*—and even that definition would likely require some elaboration.

Student-friendly definitions should also help students understand how the word is used (Barnes et al., 2021). It can be useful to describe words as emotion words, movement words, idea words, and so on. For example, the word *frustrated* might be described as an emotion or feeling word ("*Frustrated* is an emotion or feeling word that means . . ."), while *maneuvered* would be a movement word ("*Maneuvered* is a movement word that means . . ."). Providing such categorizations allows for more efficient word learning because a framework is provided into which the new word may be embedded (Snow, 1990). Student-friendly definitions should also be couched in somewhat simple syntax with relatively few, if any, elaborative clauses. While elaborative clauses (e.g., *The artist, who had a rather simple style, painted primarily landscapes*) may provide precision, they are likely of little use to a younger student with no knowledge of the term (*primarily* in this example). Helping students first build general knowledge of a term provides a foundation for more elaboration in the future. For example, an initial student-friendly definition for *frightened* might be "really scared," which can be extended to include more descriptive language: "feeling worried and afraid, or really scared." It is important to remember that word learning is a *gradual* process and that we increase our understanding of word meanings with repeated exposure over time and in diverse contexts. Simple student-friendly definitions provide a foundation for this gradual word-learning process, with additional experiences being used to fill in additional details and precision of the word's meaning.

Student-Friendly Definitions

Zucker, Cabell, and Pico (2021) developed a quick checklist to determine whether a definition is student-friendly. Is the definition:

Simple? A *simple* definition includes terms that are understandable and known to students with little or no sophisticated or academic vocabulary.

Accurate and complete? *Accurate and complete* means the definition provides a clear description of the word and covers the full meaning of the term. The definition should be a complete thought (not necessarily a complete sentence) and should include the target word at the beginning of the sentence (e.g., *Frustrated* means to feel unhappy when you don't get your way or can't do what you wanted to do). If the previous definition of *frustrated* said "to feel angry," the definition would not be accurate or complete, as *frustrated* is not a synonym for *angry,* and the crucial portion of the definition ("because you don't get your way") is omitted. While student-friendly definitions should be simple, they must also be complete such that students are developing accurate understanding of words.

Conversational? *Conversational* implies the definition is couched in casual language, such as one might experience in a conversation rather than within a dictionary.

When introducing a new vocabulary item, it can be tempting to ask students what they know about a word's meaning. However, this is *not* recommended. At times, students believe they know the meaning of a word when in fact, they do not. In a group setting, a student may provide an incorrect definition, which may lead to confusion for other students. Rather than ask the students to provide the definition, you may ask them if they think they know what the word means by gesturing with a thumbs up or thumbs down. The teacher can then provide the student-friendly definition, and ask students if what they were thinking matched the provided definition. This allows the teacher to check whether students think they know the meaning without risking the chance of a student providing an incorrect definition that may lead to confusion for other students in the group.

Sample Instructional Dialogue for Teaching the Meaning of the Word *Fierce*

Following is a sample instructional dialogue taken from a video of D. Rutnik, one of the teachers who participated in the Scanlon et al. (2008) study. Using the procedure described by Beck, McKeown, and Kucan (2002), she implemented explicit vocabulary instruction following a read-aloud of the book *Swimmy* (Lionni, 1963). The focus of this vignette is on the word *fierce*, which occurred in the context of the book. Note how the teacher (1) asks the students to say the word, (2) provides a student-friendly definition, (3) asks the students to act out the word and provide examples, (4) repeats the definition, and (5) asks students to repeat the word. This basic routine can be used for teaching many words and can be accomplished quickly, thus helping to maintain focus on building comprehension of the text in which the word was encountered.

> TEACHER: In the story it said, "One bad day, a tuna fish, swift, *fierce*, and very hungry, came darting through the waves." The word I want to talk about is *fierce*. Say the word with me—*fierce*.
>
> STUDENTS: (*Say the word.*)
>
> TEACHER: When something is *fierce*, it is very powerful and strong. We have had some really bad weather lately, with lots of very hard rain and very *fierce* winds. The winds were very, very strong. Show me how they were blowing.
>
> TEACHER AND STUDENTS: (*Move arms to demonstrate strong, powerful, indeed, fierce winds.*)
>
> TEACHER: Tell me something you know that might be *fierce*. Try to use the word *fierce* when you tell about it.
>
> STUDENT: A fierce shark!!!
>
> TEACHER: Yes, a fierce shark. *Fierce* means strong and powerful, in a mean kind of a way. (*Several children were given the opportunity to use the word, and the teacher commented on and clarified usage for each one.*) You might want to use the word *fierce* today when you are talking or writing.
>
> TEACHER: Let's say the word *fierce* again.
>
> STUDENTS: (*Say the word.*)

Additional Suggestions for Learning Word Meanings

WORD PARTS

As described in Chapter 11, many words consist of a base word and one or more affixes (prefixes and suffixes). In that chapter, the focus was on helping children to learn how to decode and infer the meaning of printed words composed of more than one meaningful part. But, of course, children encounter words with prefixes and suffixes in read-aloud contexts and in everyday spoken language. Therefore, teachers can begin to develop children's sensitivity to morphology even before they can read any words independently. For example, with all of the tying, untying, and retying of shoes that goes on in kindergarten, why not take the opportunity to focus on the prefixes *un* and *re* and help the children to become aware of their use in other contexts, such as buttoning, zipping, and doing?

DICTIONARIES

As children gain proficiency in reading, dictionaries can sometimes be useful to them in learning about the meanings of words they encounter while reading. Children should be encouraged to look up words and then consider the definitions they find in light of the contexts in which the words were first encountered. Children's dictionaries should be made available for this purpose, particularly online dictionaries that provide oral pronunciations and/or images of the words' referents. Examples include:

Kids' Wordsmyth—*http://kids.wordsmyth.net/we*
Britannica Kids *https://kids.britannica.com/kids/browse/dictionary*
Learners' Dictionary—*www.learnersdictionary.com*

GLOSSARIES AND OTHER TEXT CONVENTIONS

Nonfiction books often provide explicit definitions of important words introduced in their texts. The important words are often signaled by boldface font in the text. Children need to be alert to this convention for signaling importance and to look for the definitions that may be provided either in the same section of text where the word is first encountered, in a text box or illustration on the same page, or in a glossary at the end of a text.

Instruction to Enhance Syntactic and Grammatical Skills

While direct and explicit instruction of vocabulary is useful for young readers, a less formal approach to supporting syntax may be more beneficial. Young readers need not learn the names of grammatical structures (embedded clause), but rather should learn how to translate from simple to complex syntax and vice versa. As complex syntax is frequently found in texts, it may be helpful to talk about syntax as casual conversation (simple syntax) and book language (complex syntax). Discussion of complex syntax may reside naturally in a shared book reading event.

Clarification of potentially confusing syntactic structures generally takes the form of reading the segment of text, as stated by the author, and then restating that segment using a more familiar syntactic structure. For example, in the book *The Turkey Girl,* one of the pages starts with the following sentence: "The Turkey Girl caught the excitement, imagining herself dancing with the others" (Pollock, 1996, n.p.). Both phrases in this sentence use syntax that is different from the syntax that is likely to be used in everyday conversation, wherein we might say, "The Turkey Girl got excited too and started to think about dancing with the others." In this context, teachers might choose to simply restate the sentence, or they might read to the end of the page and then engage the children in a conversation about how the Turkey Girl was thinking and feeling and, at this point, explain the meaning of "caught the excitement." On a second or subsequent reading of this book, it probably would not be necessary to explain this particular syntactic structure again, but when the children hear it again, their syntactic competence will be slightly extended. When they hear other, similar structures such as "caught the spirit," they are more likely to understand them, too.

Be on the Lookout!

It can be helpful to be on the lookout for language that may be puzzling to young children during instruction. While teachers may be adept in selecting specific words that are unknown to students, it may be more challenging to identify other features of language that may require explicit instruction. Be on the lookout for:

• *Words that have multiple meanings* (a table in the dining room is not the same as a table on a math worksheet). Explain to your students how words can have different meanings and be used in different ways based on the setting or topic. Even a word as simple as *and* means something different in English language arts ("Sam and Ryan," where *and* is a conjunction) and mathematics ("four and seven is eleven," meaning the act of addition).

• *Figurative language or idioms* ("can't see the forest for the trees," "he put his foot in his mouth," etc.). Idioms cannot be understood at the word level. A student may understand each of the words in the above examples but likely would need to be told the meaning of the idiom ("*he put his foot in his mouth* means he said something he shouldn't have at the wrong time"). Giving clear examples ("I really put my foot in my mouth when I talked about the plans for a surprise party for my brother right in front of him!") and then asking students to provide examples where the idiom applies may be helpful.

• *Affixes, including prefixes and suffixes,* that may alter the meaning of a known word or change the pronunciation of the base word. For example, students may understand the term *willing* but may be puzzled by the word *unwilling* if they are not familiar with the prefix un. Explicitly discussing and teaching about common prefixes and suffixes may assist students with better comprehending texts and learning new words. Taking a moment to explain that the prefix *un* means "not" ("The *un* at the beginning of the word *unwilling* means 'not,' so *unwilling* means "not willing") and providing other examples of the affix in use can build vocabulary and greater comprehension. By a different token, the word *magician* may be challenging, as the pronunciation is changed by adding a suffix. The word *magician* is developed by adding a suffix (*-ian*—which means "one who does") to the base word *magic*. Doing so changes the pronunciation of the word magic as the *c* shifts from a hard to soft sound. Pointing out the base word, *magic*, may help students understand the meaning of magician, while also explicitly noting the change in pronunciation. (More discussion of affixes is provided in Chapter 11.)

Linguistically Rich Environments and Activities

Facilitating language development requires more than explicit instruction, it also includes providing rich input in linguistically rich environments. Language may be used in different ways based on the place where the interaction occurs (Barnes & Hadley, 2022). Thus, it is critical to consider how to leverage different classroom spaces and engagements for language development. Below, we describe different instructional and noninstructional settings and activities that provide unique means for facilitating language growth in children from preschool through second grade. Language development should be addressed throughout the school day.

Read-Alouds

An interactive read-aloud involves reading to children and engaging them in conversations about what is read. This is a powerful tool for promoting vocabulary and literacy development more generally (e.g., Lennox, 2013; McGee & Schickedanz, 2007; Morrow & Gambrell, 2000). The major difference between an *interactive* read-aloud and a read-aloud is the expectation that, while reading the book, there will be extensive interaction between and among the teacher and the students and that the interaction will not be directed and controlled by the teacher. Both the children and the teacher should have opportunities to ask and answer questions, to share their reactions and expectations, to revisit parts of the book, and so on. Typically, the text read-aloud is above students' reading levels to provide an emphasis on comprehension and language rather than decoding print.

It is not merely the frequency of a word's appearance in texts that matters for word learning and reading, but also the type of texts in which the word is encountered. Reading and hearing words in diverse contexts and texts leads to deeper knowledge and more efficient understanding of the word. Not only can the student learn more about the meaning of a word when it is encountered across a variety of texts, but they are also more likely to become more efficient readers of a word when it is encountered across a variety of texts (Nation, 2016). Repeating a word in isolation (either in printed text or oral language) will likely not produce the same effects as experiencing the word in rich and diverse contexts, with the latter leading to stronger understanding of word meaning and greater efficiency with word reading.

Developing Text Sets

Current research supports the use of text sets for developing vocabulary and conceptual knowledge (e.g., Neuman & Wright, 2013). Word knowledge may be viewed as a proxy for conceptual knowledge (Anderson & Freebody, 1981). Hence, students who have strong funds of conceptual knowledge are likely to also possess wide and deep vocabularies associated with these funds. For example, a student who is an expert on space travel is likely to know a wide variety of words about the topic and likely knows far more words about space travel than a student who knows little about it. Students tend to learn words that are conceptually clustered and appear frequently in print and oral language. A conceptually related text set develops topical knowledge, while repeating key vocabulary terms across the selected texts, which bolsters learning opportunities related to developing word meanings and word identification.

When developing a text set, a conceptual topic should be selected. Using grade-level standards, particularly those associated with science or social studies, may help to identify important content to address in a text set. Keep in mind that many of these standards involve oral language skills; well-developed text sets may therefore build topical knowledge and language skills. After selecting a standard, the teacher would consider the key aspects to address as learning goals. This will serve as a foundation for selecting vocabulary to directly teach, as it will be important to explicitly instruct the vocabulary that is needed for addressing the learning goals. For example, in a unit on the seasons, the students may be expected to be able to explain how the movement of the Earth around the sun is related to the seasons. Associated vocabulary terms might be *revolution, hemisphere,* and *tilt*. These terms are not concrete and represent scientific vocabulary, which makes them strong candidates for direct instruction. Two have more than one meaning (revolution and tilt), which makes them ideal for instruction as students may confuse the multiple meanings without support. Each target term (*revolution, hemisphere, tilt*) should appear in several of the texts (at least two texts, but more is better), thus exposing students to the words multiple times, allowing for more opportunities for direct instruction and word learning. Examples of conceptually related text sets may be found in Appendix A of Neuman and Wright (2013) along with information on how to go about developing text sets.

Selecting Books for Read-Alouds

A number of factors need to be considered in selecting books to read aloud to children in a classroom or small-group context. While sometimes a book might be read just for the pure enjoyment of it, virtually every book lends itself to helping teachers address some of the many curricular goals they have for their students. To most effectively address those goals, some planning is required. At the very least, the teacher needs to be thoroughly familiar with a book before reading it to students. Previewing a book in order to determine how it might enhance students' language development (only one of the goals that a teacher might have for a book), the teacher needs to consider the following:

- The students
  - Will the text be interesting and engaging for the children in the instructional group?
  - What do they already know?
  - What are they ready to learn?
  - What are their interests?
- The classroom curriculum
  - How does the book fit with the topics and themes that have been and will be covered in language arts, science, social studies, and/or math?
  - How does the vocabulary in the book fit with other vocabulary words that have already been taught?
- The book
  - What kinds of language challenges does the book present?
  - What words and/or syntactic structures will need explanation or clarification?
  - How will those words and structures be explained?
  - Is the language so advanced relative to students' current language skills that they will feel overwhelmed?

Interactive Read-Alouds

Building language can be accomplished before, during, and after reading a selected book through careful planning. As part of this planning, the teacher should think about engaging the students in discussions of the book before, during, and after reading in order to take full advantage of all instructional opportunities that a read-aloud provides. Reading the selected text prior to introducing it to students is essential, for this allows the teacher to identify complex language, topics, and/or plot points that merit discussion and instruction. Much of the discussion will revolve around the events and information presented in the book (see the section on interactive read-alouds in Chapter 16). During these discussions, however, teachers have the opportunity to address vocabulary encountered in the book and some of the more complex syntactic structures. They also have the opportunity to encourage children to use more complete and ultimately more complex sentence structures and more sophisticated vocabulary in their conversations.

Remember that the goal is for the read-aloud to be interactive and focused. Interaction provides opportunities for students to engage in conversations about the book and its language. Research shows that interactive read-alouds where students comment, respond to queries, and discuss content are more likely to promote language growth than straight through read-alouds with limited or no interaction (Mol, Bus, DeJong, & Smeets, 2008). Focused read-alouds do not diverge from the task at hand. Students should be encouraged to talk about the text and relevant features, but conversation should be limited to addressing the instructional goals. Sharing personal stories and personal connections to the text are better accomplished during informal opportunities to have conversations, for example during snack or lunch time, transitions, or recess.

BEFORE READING

- Discuss critical vocabulary before beginning to read the text (e.g., "This book is about volcanoes. A volcano is a kind of mountain that can explode. It is a mountain that grows!").

- Ensure that children can pronounce the new word acceptably (e.g., "Let's all say that word, *volcano*"). This will help them store a phonological representation of the word in memory.

- Depending on where they are in their curriculum, teachers might also engage the students in a discussion of the type of book (e.g., nonfiction, informational) and other books on similar topics.

DURING READING

- Encourage thoughtfulness about knowledge of word meanings. For example, the teacher might say, "Last year when I read this book to my first graders they didn't know what the word *extremely* meant in the sentence *It was extremely hot*. It helps me be a better teacher when children tell me about words that they don't yet know. I hope you will tell me when you hear a word and you are not sure what it means."

- Stop and briefly explain or discuss the meanings of words that are novel for children especially those that they are likely to encounter in other contexts.

- On occasion, reread the portion of the text that includes a novel vocabulary item, and include a close synonym whose meaning the children already know. For example, if the novel word in the text is *frightened*—"Ziya was frightened when the door slammed shut"—include the definition "really scared" immediately following as an aside: "Ziya was frightened [really scared] when the door slammed shut."

- When children comment on or ask a question about an aspect of the text to which the new word could reasonably be applied or incorporated, encourage them to use the newly introduced word (or the teacher can use it in responding to the inquiry). For example, when a student asks a question about the lava featured in an illustration, make sure to point out the *volcano* that the lava is flowing down, and ask the student to use the term.

- Notice when children use the new words and celebrate. ("Ah! You are already using that new word we learned! Great!")

AFTER READING

- Review the meanings of new words that were explicitly taught either before or during the reading of the text. Children need multiple exposures to words in order for them to become part of their usable vocabulary.

- If the text introduces enough new words that it is reasonable to compare and contrast them, it is useful to do so after reading the text.

- Have children think of other words they may know that mean the same thing, or almost the same thing, as the new words encountered in the text.

- In the days and weeks after words have been introduced, teachers can look for multiple opportunities both to use them in their own speech and to encourage children to use them in speaking and writing.

- Continue to notice and celebrate the use of newly acquired words.

Beck et al. (2002, 2013) provide specific recommendations for helping children establish new vocabulary after a text has been read. These recommendations follow.

- Present the word in the context in which it occurs in the book.
- Ask the children to repeat the word to help them establish a phonological representation of it.
- Explain the meaning of the word.
- Provide examples of the word's usage other than the one used in the text.
- Have the children interact with the examples or provide their own examples.
- Have the children say the word again to reinforce its phonological representation.

Extended Engagement

It is useful to include extension activities following the read-alouds of text sets that include student-friendly definitions because students are more likely to learn words that are heard frequently and across a variety of contexts. Similarly, students learn words when they can engage with the terms, either linguistically or through hands-on engagements. Linguistically engaging with the terms refers to discussing the definitions, talking about the parts of words that bear meaning (morphemes), manipulating the word through adding inflectional endings (-s or –es, -ing, -ed, -est), and using the word in speaking, reading, and writing. Presenting the word in print is also useful, as reading, writing, speaking, and listening all contribute to the development of word meanings.

Hands-on or physical engagements may involve opportunities through which students enact the word or explore the meaning through experimentation. Acting out a verb can be a wonderful way for students to embody the meaning. Consider how students may demonstrate gallop, ponder, grimace, or slumber through acting out or physically demonstrating the terms. Such words may lead to a game of charades, where a student acts out a target vocabulary term that the other students attempt to guess. A more complex version of charades includes saying the correct word and providing the definition when guessing. Similarly, students may enact vocabulary terms through experimentation. For example, when learning about forces and motion, students may explore friction, pushes, pulls, and gravity on a playground (pushing the swings, friction on a slide, etc.). Discussing how the action demonstrates or relates to the term may facilitate greater depth of understanding.

Mealtimes and Sharing Time

Nonacademic times, such as meals (snacks, breakfast, or lunch) or sharing time (show-and-tell), are also ripe with opportunities for building language skills (Barnes, Grifenhagen, & Dickinson, 2020). Both settings may encourage the use of decontextualized talk that focuses on events beyond the here-and-now and incorporates precise language. Both settings may allow students to talk about events or objects of interest and can involve extended conversations that promote language and knowledge development. For example, students may talk about recent events they engaged in outside of school during meals or sharing time, which encourages the use of ordinal (first, next, last) and descriptive language similar to what may be found in narrative storybooks. Students may also be asked to create an argument or explanation (discourse-level features of academic language) for a favorite meal, items, or event to convince their classmates of their selection. Classmates may respond to and ask questions or pose their opinions, which may result in extended discourse, that supports language development (Dickinson & Smith, 1994). Such linguistic opportunities are considered as "oral preparations for literacy" (Michaels, 1981).

Cooperative Projects

When children work together to accomplish a common goal, they generally need to do a good deal of conversing in order to clarify aspects of what needs to be done, to negotiate roles and responsibilities, to evaluate progress toward the intended goal, and so on. Cooperative projects might include conducting and documenting the results of science experiments, gathering information about the local community and preparing and sharing what was learned, writing a book on a topic of mutual interest, and so forth. Cooperative projects are especially useful for encouraging language development among children who are past the point of engaging in socio-dramatic play in the classroom.

Share Your Thinking

This is a form of "every student response." During whole-class and small-group instruction, only one child gets to talk at a time if the teacher leads every discussion. If teachers frequently ask children to turn to their neighbors or to partners at their tables and talk about whatever the topic is, all of the children will have more opportunity to engage in conversation. This approach is becoming more and more common in the context of interactive read-alouds and is often referred to as "think, pair, share" (Lyman, 1981). However, virtually any context that might lend itself to a classroom conversation can incorporate opportunities for children to share their thinking with one another.

Television, Video, and Digital Resources to Support Vocabulary Development

Much research has focused on the role of technology in supporting language development and its many potential benefits when used appropriately and as intended. Paivio's dual-coding theory (1986) notes the importance of visual and verbal cues for developing mental representations for vocabulary. Hence, multimedia, including moving images, background music, and sound effects, may enhance word learning as these features may act as a scaffolding device (Bus, Takacs, & Kegel, 2015; Takacs, Swart, & Bus, 2014). Visual representations and effects as well as sounds and music may draw and increase students' attention to novel words while providing cues toward their meanings (Neuman, Wong, Flynn, & Kaefer, 2019). A synthesis of 29 studies found students' interactions with digital stories/texts to be more beneficial than reading traditional stories without additional adult scaffolding (Takacs et al., 2014). This is not surprising because actually seeing the undulating movements of a sea creature as it moves through the water will make the meaning of the word much more memorable than would an attempt by a teacher to explain undulation with hand gestures.

There is substantial evidence that viewing educational television shows and videos can enhance vocabulary development, and this seems to be especially true for children who are learning English as an additional language (Silverman & Hines, 2009). Programs such as *Super Why!*, *Sesame Street*, *Martha Speaks*, and *Bubble Guppies* were designed in coordination with vocabulary researchers to promote word learning in young children (Danielson, Wong, & Neuman, 2019).

Many educational programs, such as *Sesame Street*, also include translanguaging, which may be beneficial for students who speak multiple languages.

Digital texts have also been associated with language growth in young children. Video storybooks have produced expressive vocabulary gains in low-income immigrant children learning a second language (Verhallen & Bus, 2010), with animated books having stronger effects than books with static images (Verhallen, Bus, & de Jong, 2006). The well-researched intervention, *Story Friends*, teaches vocabulary through digital texts, with children from low-income homes experiencing strong vocabulary growth (Kelley, Goldstein, Spencer, & Sherman, 2015). This intervention requires minimal teacher support, which makes it an excellent supplement for use during center time. Many digital texts provide scaffolds such as hotspots that define sophisticated vocabulary and links to websites that build conceptual knowledge related to the story.

We encourage teachers to view these resources as important components of a multifaceted approach to vocabulary and language instruction. These resources also include discussion of texts read and listened to, explicit instruction focused on specific words, and, as children develop as readers, encouragement of broad reading across genres. Digital materials and technology should be carefully evaluated and vetted prior to use. The App Map (Israelson, 2015) is a useful tool for evaluating digital material, as is the TPACK model for evaluating e-books (Brueck & Lenhart, 2015). While digital features can be enormously helpful, teachers should be on the lookout for resources that have too many "bells and whistles," which may distract from reading.

Assessment and Assessments

Assessing students' language growth allows for early intervention and progress monitoring, which may prevent later literacy-learning difficulties. Assessing language may be formal and standardized or informal, on-the-spot, and formative depending on student need. Keep in mind that assessments performed by classroom teachers should inform instruction primarily. Prior to selecting an assessment, it is critical to consider the purpose of the assessment. Assessment may be used to measure whether students have learned target vocabulary terms that were directly instructed, or whether they can produce complex syntax. Having individual conversations with students is one informal means of assessing language use that may be helpful for planning out instruction, while utilizing a standardized assessment of vocabulary may be more practical for determining need for specialized language services. Such standardized assessments may require specialized training to administer and likely will not be completed by classroom teachers. Matching the assessment to purpose is critical as assessments may be time intensive.

Many quick, informal assessments may be incorporated into your instructional routine. Some are particularly useful for determining whether children are acquiring and retaining content addressed in the classroom. Table 15.1 briefly

TABLE 15.1. Assessments of Vocabulary Depth and Breadth

Task	Description
Yes/no task	The student is asked various yes/no questions about target vocabulary ("Is a carrot a vegetable?"; "Is a carrot green?"; "Is a carrot something you can eat?"). Each correct response is given 1 point, with higher scores equating to greater knowledge of the term.
Screener task	Students assess their knowledge of a word by selecting one of the four descriptions for each target term: (1) explain it or use it (knows it well), (2) knows something about it or can relate it to a situation, (3) has seen or heard the word, (4) doesn't know or recognize the word.
Picture choices	The student is provided with a target word and is asked to match it to one of four pictures presented by the teacher.
Demonstrate/act out/draw	The student is provided with a target word and asked to act out the word or demonstrate the word in action (excellent for verbs) or provide an iconic gesture. The student may also draw an illustration of the term.

describes a few on-the-spot assessments that can be easily performed during typical instruction and can help identify whether additional instruction and/or assessment is needed. Keep in mind that assessments need not be formal and that observing a student appropriately using a term in context may serve as an assessment.

Checklists and observational protocols may also be excellent choices for monitoring students' language in use. You may create a checklist of specific vocabulary terms or syntactic structures, and you may observe a student to see if they use the target language spontaneously. Published observational protocols, such as those found in Barnes et al. (2021) on academic language and the TROLL from Dickinson, McCabe, and Sprague (2003), may also be excellent choices for monitoring progress.

The snapshot featured in Figure 15.1 provides a record form for documenting teachers' observations of children's status with regard to knowledge and acquisition of word meanings, children's interest in and use of language, and their status related to the sentence structure. It is designed to be used in the context of small-group instruction (with children having been grouped on the basis of similarities in their print-related skills [alphabetic and orthographic knowledge]). This context provides teachers with the opportunity to more closely observe the language skills of individual children. However, observations beyond the small-group setting can certainly be taken into consideration in documenting perceptions of children's status relative to the characteristics listed on the snapshot.

Note that children who rarely or only sometimes appear to demonstrate the language behaviors described will likely benefit from having increased opportunities to work in small-group and one-on-one situations. This experience will expose them to extended opportunities to engage in conversations focused on books read or heard and in planned and supported activities intended to promote the development of expressive and receptive language skills.

Group Snapshot—Observation of Vocabulary (Word Meaning) and Language Development					
Student names					
Seems to understand the meanings of words at an age-appropriate level.					
Uses newly taught/ learned words conversationally.					
Is eager to use spoken language to communicate.					
Asks to have word meanings explained.					
Asks for clarification when confused by a statement.					
Uses complete sentences.					
Uses standard sentence structures.					
Uses standard inflectional endings for plurals, first-person singular verbs, and past-tense verbs.					
Engages in sustained conversations.					

Key:

R = Rarely   S = Sometimes   F = Frequently   A = Always or almost always

FIGURE 15.1. Group snapshot for vocabulary and language development.

KEY POINTS OF THIS CHAPTER

✓ Oral language is the foundation for reading and writing.

✓ Reading to children helps to expand their oral language skills because, in comparison to spoken language, written texts tend to include more diverse vocabulary and sentence structures.

✓ Engaging learners in conversations promotes development of the language skills needed for reading. Conversations about texts that have been read to or with children are particularly helpful in this regard.

✓ Learning the meanings of most words occurs incidentally and incrementally through exposure across a variety of contexts.

✓ Explicit vocabulary instruction is an effective way to expand children's knowledge of word meanings. However, children need to learn far more words than the number that can be explicitly taught.

✓ Technical vocabulary (e.g., in science, social studies, and math) is most readily learned through explicit instruction and engagement in meaning-making tasks.

CHAPTER 16

Comprehension and General Knowledge

The Process of Comprehension

Comprehension occurs as the learner builds a mental representation of texts as they are read (or heard; Perfetti et al., 2005). It is thought to be "one of the most complex and important cognitive activities humans perform" (Butterfuss & Kendeou, 2018, p. 802). Given this complexity, a text devoted to early literacy development more generally cannot do justice to the vast amount of theory and research related to comprehension that currently informs the field. However, given its importance, it is critical to address key aspects of theory and research that can help to inform instruction intended to enable young children to actively make sense of (comprehend) the texts they hear and read. The ultimate goal, of course, is to put children on the path to understanding, enjoying, and learning from texts they encounter throughout their lifespan.

Comprehension is an active, constructive process in which the ultimate understanding of the text is determined by the integration of what is stated directly in the text and the reader's existing knowledge related to the topic of the text (Anderson & Pearson, 1984; Kintsch, 1998). That understanding is reflected in the wording of the meaning construction goal above. The instructional goal is to help children

> ### What Is Comprehension?
>
> "Reading comprehension is not a single entity that can be explained by a unified cognitive model. Instead, it is the orchestrated product of a set of linguistic and cognitive processes operating on text and interacting with background knowledge, features of the text, and the purpose and goals of the reading situation" (Castles et al., 2018, p. 28).

develop the knowledge upon which comprehension depends and to become self-regulated learners who are motivated to understand the texts they read and hear. These learners therefore notice when things are not making sense to them and take action to resolve confusion that may arise. Thus, instruction to foster comprehension goes beyond helping children comprehend a particular text at a particular point in time. Rather, instruction needs to emphasize helping learners to develop productive ways of thinking about the text(s) they are currently listening to or reading and that will enhance their comprehension of texts they encounter in the future.

Active Meaning Construction

The following example provides an opportunity for you to become conscious of the type of active meaning construction in which proficient readers engage. The example is three sentences long. After reading each sentence, we encourage you to stop and think about the main character a bit.

> **Sentence 1:** Max walked nervously toward the building.
> (Stop and think.)
>
> **Sentence 2:** He was worried about today's big math test.
> (Stop and think.)
>
> **Sentence 3:** He feared he wouldn't get tenure if too many of his students failed.

Readers who participate in this type of exercise find that their thinking changes quite radically from one sentence to the next (if they really follow the directions and stop and think after each sentence). After reading the first sentence, active readers will likely have questions about what the building is and may make attributions about why Max is nervous. They may infer that something unpleasant will happen when Max gets to the building. Perhaps the building is a clinic or a courthouse. Upon reading the next sentence, active readers conclude that the building is a school and that Max is a student. They may infer that Max is not a strong math student and that he is older than elementary age—because that is when concern about grades tends to emerge more strongly. Readers may develop

an image of Max—probably carrying a backpack—and an image of the school—
not as intimidating as a courthouse, more welcoming than a clinic. Upon reading
the third sentence, the reader's understanding of the situation changes again. Max
is now a teacher, probably an early-career math teacher, and one who feels he has
not been sufficiently effective in his teaching.

This illustration demonstrates that active and engaged readers integrate information directly stated in the text with their existing knowledge to "fill in the gaps"
left by the author and to go well beyond the information directly stated in the text.
Further, they shift their thinking about a text as they encounter new information
that doesn't fit with their unfolding interpretation of it. Essentially, effective readers expect the texts they encounter to be coherent (that is, to make sense or "hang
together" in a logical way), and they interact with those texts in an effort to make
them so. Thus, when things don't make sense, effective readers change their thinking or reread the text to seek clarification. Or, more commonly, they do both in
an iterative fashion until the confusion is resolved. Often, engaged readers take
these steps without being conscious of them. They are mostly just thinking about
the text, not their approach to comprehending it, unless, of course, the process has
been purposefully slowed (as we have done in the *Max* example).

Readers who demonstrate reading comprehension difficulties, even those who
have adequate or strong word reading skills, often do not engage in the type of
revision of their understanding that characterizes stronger comprehenders. Rather,
they are apt to treat each sentence in the *Max* passage as more or less unrelated to
one another and, therefore, do not develop a coherent understanding of the text.
In their thinking, there is a mysterious building that, for some reason, makes Max
nervous. There is some unnamed person (referred to as he) who is worried about
a math test. Readers who strive for a coherent understanding of the text would
infer that *he* refers to *Max*. (This is an example of anaphor—use of a grammatical substitute, such as a pronoun, to refer to a word used earlier in the passage.)
Poor comprehenders tend not to make such inferences. In the third sentence, weak
comprehenders may realize that *he* is a teacher because, within the sentence *his
students* are referenced. Weak comprehenders may not connect that individual to
the *he* in the second sentence nor to Max in the first sentence. Thus, for these readers, the passage would not hang together—they will not have developed a coherent
understanding of the text.

Constructing and Reconstructing Meaning

The active, fluent construction and revision of the meaning of the text that proficient readers experience when reading the *Max* example represent the kind of processing that we would ultimately like to see all learners achieve. Such an achievement requires that they (1) know something about the topic of the text, (2) access
(think about) that information, (3) recognize when things don't make sense, and
(4) are willing to exert the cognitive effort it takes to revise/shift their thinking as
the text unfolds.

Levels of Comprehension

In constructing the meaning of a text, readers may engage in different types or *levels* of comprehension. Three levels of comprehension are typically discussed: literal, inferential, and critical.

- *Literal comprehension* involves the understanding of information stated directly in the text. Examples of literal comprehension from the *Max* example include knowing that:
  - Max was nervous.
  - Max walked toward a building.
  - He (someone) was worried.
  - There is a math test today.
  - He (someone) was a teacher.
  - A lot of his students might fail—at something.
- *Inferential comprehension* involves making inferences that bridge the information directly stated in the text with information that the reader already possesses. Effective readers draw on their knowledge to make inferences that fill in the gaps left by the author; ineffective readers are less likely to do so (Yuill & Oakhill, 1991). Early in the *Max* example, the reader is left to make inferences about such things as:
  - Max's age.
  - Max's reasons for being nervous.
  - What sort of building Max is walking toward.
- *Critical comprehension* involves evaluating the information in the text relative to what it means to the reader and relative to the intentions, expertise, and/or perspective of the author. In the *Max* text, the reader may conclude that the author developed the text with the intention of misleading the reader and might read additional texts by the same author with this in mind.

Comprehension Difficulties

Research suggests that readers who experience difficulty with comprehension, but not with decoding, differ from their more able peers primarily in their ability to engage in inferential thinking (e.g., Perfetti et al., 2005). The reasons for this difficulty are still being researched, but Yuill and Oakhill (1991) suggest several possibilities, including the notions that less skilled comprehenders (1) do not have the knowledge needed to make the necessary inferences, (2) do not know when it is appropriate to make inferences, and/or (3) have processing limitations that interfere with their ability to integrate text information with prior knowledge. Cain and Oakhill (1999) suggested that failure to make inferences may be attributable to a focus on accurately reading the words in the text rather than on deriving a coherent understanding of the text. Clearly, all of these possibilities could play a role in limiting comprehension, and most of them are at least partially amenable to instructional interventions. In what follows, we describe the types of knowledge sources that need to be developed and describe how interactions with texts can help to promote the type of active thinking about text that needs to be established in order to enable the inferential thinking that is so critical to comprehension.

Developing Comprehension Skills and Strategies through Interactive Read-Alouds

While the ultimate goal of reading instruction is that learners will comprehend texts that they read themselves, young learners will encounter more complex texts and more diverse vocabulary and language structures in read-aloud contexts than in the texts most are able to read on their own. Therefore, reading aloud to students provides an ideal context for developing an active approach to comprehension because strong listening comprehension can facilitate strong reading comprehension.

Knowledge and Comprehension

World/background knowledge is an essential component of reading comprehension because every text takes for granted the readers' familiarity with a whole range of unspoken and unwritten facts about the cultural and natural world (Hirsch, 2003).

When an individual listens to or reads a text, a complex interaction takes place between what the individual already knows and what is presented in the text. Thus, differences between individuals in the amount of text-relevant knowledge they bring will have a substantial influence on their ability to make the required inferences and to comprehend the text (e.g., Kendeou & O'Brien, 2016). For example, someone who has taken a college chemistry class will learn more from reading an article about some aspect of biochemical engineering than will someone who has little or no background in chemistry. In fact, if, on the one hand, someone with no background knowledge persists with the reading at all, the reader is likely to read the text quite passively and with little expectation of understanding. If, on the other hand, biochemical engineers were to read the article, they are likely to learn much more than the individual with only college chemistry because the engineers are more thoroughly versed in the terminology and concepts and in how various biochemical processes work. Before even beginning to read the article, though, the biochemical engineers are likely to consider the quality of the journal in which it was published and the credentials of the author(s) in order to determine whether the article is likely to provide trustworthy information and therefore warrant the time to read it. If the engineers do decide to read it, they are likely to read very actively and to begin forming hypotheses and questions about what will be learned even before they have finished reading the title (Anderson & Pearson, 1984). While reading, the engineers are likely to think actively about the content and to compare it to what they already know about the topic. If there are discrepancies between the engineers' knowledge and the information presented in the text, they may change their thinking on the topic, reject the new information, and/or decide that there is a need to seek further information so that they can be more confident in the interpretation of the topic of the text.

Types of Knowledge That Influence Comprehension

As illustrated above, how one interprets a text and what one learns from a text depend, to a great extent, on what one already knows. Several types of knowledge play a part in comprehension, including general world knowledge, topic-specific knowledge, schematic knowledge, genre knowledge, and, of course, language-based knowledge (vocabulary and syntax). Although the various types of knowledge clearly overlap, it is useful to consider them individually because they carry somewhat different instructional implications. Several knowledge types are discussed next (language-based knowledge was discussed in Chapter 15).

General Knowledge

General knowledge is sometimes referred to as *world knowledge* or *background knowledge*. This overarching term encompasses the other types of knowledge described here. General knowledge incorporates the facts and concepts that an individual "knows" and includes the interrelations among more isolated bits of knowledge. General knowledge accumulates over time, often in small increments. This type of knowledge would include the knowledge that readers draw on when they initially infer, in the *Max* example, that there is something potentially threatening about the building he is approaching: this type of knowledge is typically not explicitly taught. General knowledge would also include the knowledge that the engineer drew upon in evaluating the credentials of the author and the quality of the journal in which the article appeared. This kind of knowledge might or might not be taught explicitly.

In working with young children, teachers should be alert for general knowledge gaps that may interfere with children's ability to understand instructional interactions. Knowledge of word meanings is one general area in which this will be an issue. However, myriad other points of confusion can arise because children lack specific bits of information that teachers (and texts) assume they have.

Topic-Specific Knowledge

Topic-specific knowledge refers to knowledge that relates directly to the topic(s) addressed in a text. For example, the engineer had a good deal of topic-specific knowledge that would have been an advantage in reading a research article addressing a problem in biochemical engineering. The individual who had never taken a chemistry course, on the other hand, would probably have very little topic-specific knowledge to assist in understanding the article. The individual with just one course in chemistry is somewhere in between. As this example illustrates, having topic-specific knowledge is generally not an all-or-nothing matter. For a given topic, individuals vary along a continuum ranging from little or no knowledge to a level of expertise that requires a substantial investment of time and energy to acquire. Individuals can also possess incorrect knowledge. When this is the case, that knowledge can seriously interfere with one's ability to gain new, correct knowledge on the topic of interest (Kendeou & O'Brien, 2016).

During the elementary years and beyond, children are expected to become knowledgeable about many social studies and science topics. In the early primary grades, engaging children in read-alouds of informational books on topics and/ or those that include concepts that will be revisited in later grades will help to prepare them for content they will be expected to comprehend and use when they read texts related to that content. Indeed, in a recent study, Kaefer (2020) suggests that having previously established background knowledge to draw upon enables comprehension more readily than efforts to "establish" background knowledge during prereading activities. This likely is, in part, due to the fact that knowledge development is an incremental process. It is easier to learn more about something when you already know something about it.

Schematic Knowledge

Schematic knowledge refers to knowledge that is structured and organized. Because individuals encounter so many bits of information in a typical day, it would be impossible to store and retrieve much of the information unless it was organized in some way. An individual's *schemas* affect how one perceives, notices, and interprets information (Anderson, 1984). For example, most of us have a school schema that was probably activated in reading the *Max* example. Although each individual's school schema is likely somewhat unique, there are likely to be some commonalities for those who have experienced typical educational settings in the United States— such as a school having multiple classrooms, with each classroom having students of similar ages, a teacher, work surfaces and chairs, books, a white-board, computers, and so forth. Incorporated in the school schema are likely to be schemas for student and teacher, which were also activated in the *Max* example.

Having a schema related to the topic plays a big role in facilitating one's understanding of a text. For example, understanding the following text is challenging for most people:

> The procedure is actually quite simple. First, you arrange things into different groups. Of course, one pile may be sufficient depending on how much there is to do. If you have to go somewhere else due to lack of facilities, that is the next step; otherwise, you are pretty well set. It is important not to overdo things. That is, it is better to do too few things at once than too many. In the short run this may not seem important but complications can easily arise. A mistake can be expensive as well. At first, the whole procedure will seem complicated. Soon, however, it will

become just another fact of life. It is difficult to foresee any end to the necessity for this task in the immediate future, but then one can never tell. After the procedure is completed one arranges the materials into different groups again. Then they can be put into their appropriate places. Eventually they will be used once more and the whole cycle will then have to be repeated. However, that is a part of life. (Bransford & Johnson, 1972, p. 722)

The authors of the passage intended it to be ambiguous and challenging to understand in order to evaluate the extent to which schemas influence comprehension. And, indeed, most proficient readers find it difficult to retell or summarize the passage after reading it. However, readers who were given the title of the text, "Washing Clothes," activated the proper schema and found it much easier to comprehend. Thus, without any changes in the text, the reader who knew the title would know that the *things* and *materials* were items of clothing, and that *facilities* referred to washers and dryers. The expensive mistake is also perfectly comprehensible.

Clearly, having an appropriate schema that is relevant to the text and activating that schema are both important to the comprehension process. Book introductions can help children to activate relevant schemas (if they have them) and thus enable richer comprehension of a text. As noted in the example above, even just providing a descriptive title for a text can make a big difference in the reader's ability to integrate the information in the text and make the necessary inferences.

Genre Knowledge

Genre knowledge is a specific type of schematic knowledge that involves understanding the characteristics of different types of text. *Fiction* and *nonfiction* represent major subdivisions relative to text structures, and each type carries different expectations for the reader. For example, fiction is meant to entertain and not to be (necessarily) factual, whereas nonfiction is meant to be believed and may or may not have entertainment as a purpose.

Fictional texts are typically narrative in nature and, as such, follow the structure of a story grammar in which the author provides information about the setting, the characters, one or more problems, the characters' attempts to solve the problems, and the resolution(s). Children who are familiar with this genre and its characteristics are likely to (or may be guided to) listen to or read text with an expectation that these story elements will be provided by the author, and they are, therefore, apt to attend to the text in a more active way.

There are multiple common structures for nonfiction texts, which are often referred to as *informational texts*. Knowing the characteristics of informational texts would lead to a different set of learner expectations compared to the expectations for narrative texts. The Institute of Education Sciences' Practice Guide, focused on *Improving Reading Comprehension in Kindergarten through Third Grade* (Shanahan et al., 2010), recommends that students receive instruction on text structure to improve their comprehension. The accumulated research indicates that learners with knowledge of informational text structures and text features that signal those structures (such as titles, headings, etc.) recall more information from texts than do learners with less knowledge of text structures (Reutzel, Jones, Clark, & Kumar, 2016). Five of the most common structures of informational texts identified by Reutzel and colleagues (2016) are listed here, along with the *signal words* that alert readers to the structures:

1. *Description.* Signal words: *for example, most importantly, another kind, described as*
2. *Sequence.* Signal words: *first, second, next, finally, then, before, after, when, until,* and other signal words to indicate the sequence or process
3. *Problem–solution.* Signal words: *the question is, the problem is, therefore, if . . . then,* and other signal words to indicate questioning (5 *w*'s [*who, what, when, where, why*] and *how*)
4. *Cause–effect.* Signal words: *before, since, therefore, as a result, thus, hence,* and other signal words to indicate cause/effect
5. *Compare–contrast.* Signal words: *similarly, on the other hand, compared to, different from, same as,* and other signal words to indicate comparison

Familiarity with texts' genres provides an organizational structure that supports comprehension of those texts.

As teachers engage students in interactive read-alouds of informational texts, it is useful to identify and explain the structure, perhaps noting some of the signal words. When students are set to write their own versions of informational texts, they can be reminded of the structures and signals.

Considering/Assessing Learners' Knowledge and Knowledge Acquisition

Given the central role of knowledge in all aspects of comprehension, it is important to consider children's relative standing with regard to background knowledge as well as their ability to build new knowledge across instructional contexts. While it is, of course, not possible to explicitly evaluate these characteristics given the variation and breadth of knowledge across individuals, it is important for teachers to consider them. Doing so can, to an extent, guide instructional decision making in terms of both the degree and explicitness of preparation that may need to be offered when addressing instructional content. To that end, we include the group snapshot depicted in Figure 16.1. We recognize that teachers might not choose to make active use of this snapshot because of the vast array of knowledge types that need to be considered. We include it largely to emphasize the role knowledge plays in comprehension and the need to address knowledge development in order to enable comprehension in the short and the long term.

Group Snapshot—Background Knowledge and Knowledge Acquisition							
		Student names					
	Date						
Background knowledge relative to grade-level peers							
Knowledge acquisition—Learns and uses new information							

Key:

Background Knowledge
W—Well developed
A—Appropriately developed
N—Needs development

Knowledge Acquisition
E—Easy
S—Slow
V—Very slow

FIGURE 16.1. Group snapshot for knowledge.

Comprehension and Knowledge and Learning Standards

The Common Core State Standards (CCSS; National Governors Association Center for Best Practices & Council of Chief State School Officers [NGA & CCSSO], 2010) document clearly articulated the goal of systematically building knowledge to facilitate comprehension. As individual states have developed their own versions of standards, this purpose has remained central.

According to the CCSS:

> Building knowledge systematically in English language arts is like giving children various pieces of a puzzle in each grade that, over time, will form one big picture. . . . [T]exts—within and across grade levels—need to be selected around topics or themes that systematically develop the knowledge base of students. . . . [C]hildren in the early grades (particularly K–2) should participate in rich, structured conversations with an adult in response to the written texts that are read aloud, orally comparing and contrasting as well as analyzing and synthesizing, in the manner called for by the Standards. . . .
>
> Having students listen to read-alouds of informational texts in the early grades helps lay the necessary foundation for students' reading and understanding of increasingly complex texts on their own in subsequent grades (NGO & CCSSO, 2010, p. 33).

The commitment to build knowledge is also evident in the expectation that children in the primary grades will be exposed to much more informational text than was the tradition prior to adoption of the standards. In addition, the document includes speaking and listening standards that emphasize that comprehension and knowledge building is not an individual and isolated undertaking but rather a social practice that involves conversation with teachers, peers, and others and active processing and sharing of newly encountered information, including seeking clarification when comprehension is uncertain.

Comprehension and Knowledge and Multilingual Students

In a review of the research focused on instructional approaches to improving multilingual students' reading comprehension, Goldenberg (2020) concluded that approaches that work for students who speak only English also improve outcomes for MLs. However, he also noted that the factor that most strongly accounts for the weaker comprehension performance of MLs as compared to English only students is the English language proficiency of MLs. Goldenberg advocates for providing MLs with more opportunity to develop their English language proficiency, which, he argues, will increase their ability to comprehend texts written in English.

Gersten et al. (2007) also report that there is strong evidence in support of providing peer-assisted learning opportunities in which MLs are paired or grouped with native English-speaking or more English-proficient peers to work together on academic tasks several times a week. It is presumed that the benefits of such arrangements accrue through opportunities for the students to engage in the use of academic language for the purpose of accomplishing a shared academic goal. Goldenberg (2013) also points to the potential advantages of using the ML students' home language to support instruction. For example, the home language might be used to introduce key concepts and/or build background knowledge related to the content of texts that will be read. Alternatively, texts can be read in the home language (by a parent or the child, depending on the child's level of literacy in the home language) and then read again in English. As discussed in Chapter 15, the increasing recognition of the value of translanguaging has led to the publication of children's books that facilitate translanguaging by including two or more languages in a single text. Such texts invite and support discussion in multiple languages, thereby honoring cultural and linguistic diversity. Websites that identify texts that support translanguaging are provided in Chapter 15. Such texts would, ideally, be a frequent choice for interactive read-alouds in settings serving MLs.

Additional resources to support knowledge development among MLs include the International Children's Digital Library (*www.childrenslibrary.org*), which provides several such texts. Unite for Literacy (*www.uniteforliteracy.com*) offers free online books in English print but provides the option of having them read in multiple languages. *Diversebookfinder.org* also provides many books that celebrate multiculturalism.

Instruction and Knowledge Development

Because knowledge is so critical to comprehension, teachers need to consider whether children have the various types of knowledge that a particular text takes for granted. Taking this issue into consideration may mean that, in planning to read a book in which the setting is a farm, one teacher may need to explicitly tell children who are urban dwellers about farms and the function they serve, whereas a teacher using the same book in a rural farming community can reasonably assume that the children have at least the basics of a schema that would allow them to analyze and interpret the text. Similarly, teachers of children who have recently moved to a different country may need to carefully support the children's understanding and knowledge of cultural traditions and expectations relating to holidays, national heroes, and the like. If possible, they should help the children draw parallels between and among traditions in their former country and in their adopted country.

Differences in backgrounds can result in knowledge differences that impact students' abilities to comprehend texts encountered in classrooms. Development of the CCSS was driven in part by the concern that too little attention was being devoted to knowledge development in school, at least in the primary grades (Hirsch, 2006; Neuman, 2006). Children who have more knowledge of the topics of the texts they encounter will have stronger comprehension of those texts (Neuman, 2010). Children with less topical knowledge will need to learn what their peers already know *plus* what their peers are learning. Kaefer's (2020) study, cited above, speaks to this issue directly.

While there is no ready solution for addressing these knowledge differences (though experientially and academically rich summer programs would likely help), we encourage teachers to think carefully about the extent to which knowledge differences affect their students and to consider how they might begin to address them. For example, current technologies make many vehicles for knowledge development much more readily available than in the past. Most children have access to digital technologies via the Internet, at least at school, if not at home as well. A wealth of educational programming can be accessed and thus used to help expand children's knowledge. Teachers are encouraged to consider compiling a list of appropriate educational resources and to persuade children to view them at home, preferably with family members who will engage them in conversations about what they learn both during and after the viewing. Teachers are encouraged to investigate appropriate websites that will support the content focused on in their curriculum and to communicate their recommendations to the children's families.

Teachers also, of course, need to take responsibility for addressing the knowledge differences in their classrooms. Neuman (2006) is a staunch advocate of the need to address knowledge differences and has provided five research-based principles for improving the knowledge base of young children (pp. 35–36). Below we list Neuman's principles (in *italics*) and elaborate on each.

- *Children's learning benefits through integrated instruction* (p. 35). By this principle Neuman means that instruction should be organized around topics or projects that have coherence and depth and therefore provide children with the opportunity to develop concepts and apply them in new learning situations. Reading/listening to and discussing several books on the same or related topics will help children develop a depth of understanding that is not likely to occur when reading selections are not organized topically or thematically. As noted in Chapter 15, this will also help develop children's academic language skills.

- *Learning requires children's minds (not just their bodies) to be active* (p. 35). This principle relates back to a principle discussed in Chapter 1: Engagement leads to learning. We need to try to ensure that children's minds are engaged in the thinking that is intended. As we noted earlier, instruction should be goal oriented, not activity oriented. For example, if the goal is for students to learn about octopi, making a model of one using marshmallows and pipe cleaners might help children remember something about what an octopus looks like, but learning about its habitat and about how it sustains and defends itself would be critical to developing a rich and detailed knowledge base relative to this type of animal.

- *High levels of teacher interaction optimize children's learning* (p. 35). One of a teacher's major roles is to guide children's thinking by modeling ways of thinking about and analyzing situations and information and then supporting children as they begin to grow as strategic learners. Effective teachers interact with their students almost constantly—at times in whole-class contexts, at other times in small groups or one-to-one. For example, they may model the kinds of thinking that active and strategic comprehenders do when engaging with text.

For instance, they may engage learners in such things as wondering/predicting what will occur next in a text, discussing how one's thinking about a topic or an unfolding story changes as new information is encountered while reading/listening. In this instance, a frequent phase used during reading might be: "At first we thought . . . but now we've learned more and now we're thinking . . . because. . . . " This is the type of revision in thinking active comprehenders do, as illustrated in the earlier *Max* example.

• *Play supports children's learning* (p. 35). As long as the adults around them don't make it seem like work, much of what children are asked to do in the primary grades can be enjoyable and motivating, even if it is not play per se. For example, children can be given props related to a book they have just read or heard and can be allowed to "play" at reenacting the story. Such an activity has the advantage of engaging the children in thinking about the elements of narrative texts (e.g., story grammar). Another option would be to "play" teacher and (re)read a book to a couple of friends, lead a book discussion, respond to their classmates' writing, or explain and demonstrate the steps in a science experiment.

• *Developing competence enhances motivation and self-esteem* (p. 36). Successful learning experiences breed more successful learning experiences and the good feelings that go along with them. Unfortunately, for children who often have comparatively limited knowledge of a topic under consideration, success in school learning endeavors is less certain. Repeatedly finding oneself unable to understand central aspects of texts that one listens to or reads has the potential to reduce students' willingness to engage in learning activities, thereby increasing the likelihood of ongoing difficulty. Therefore, in planning to address major curricular themes, it is useful to develop thematic units composed of texts that are sequenced in such a way that simpler texts that introduce focal concepts related to the theme are read prior to more detailed and more sophisticated texts on the same theme (e.g., see Gelzheiser, Hallgren-Flynn, Connors, & Scanlon, 2014; Gelzheiser et al., 2019).

Comprehension Instruction

A good deal of research has focused on what "good" comprehenders do. We put the word *good* in quotation marks to signal our discomfort with it in this context: *Good* often serves as the opposite of *bad*, and certainly we don't want anyone who is not yet a *good* comprehender to be considered *bad*. Therefore, in what follows, we substitute the word *proficient*. In 2011, Duke, Pearson, Strachan, and Billman provided a summary of what "good" (proficient) readers do. Much of their summary was based on research in which competent adult readers were asked to *think aloud* as they read; that is, people were asked to describe their thinking as they read. There was a good deal of commonality in the reports that the participants provided. They tended to be very active as they read, used a large number of strategies, and were routinely monitoring their understanding. Figure 16.2 reproduces an adapted summary of what proficient readers do. We share this listing to

When Proficient Readers Read . . .

- They are active readers.
- From the outset, they have clear *goals* in mind for their reading. They constantly *evaluate* whether the text, and their reading of it, is meeting their goals.
- They typically *look over* the text before they read, noting such things as the *structure* of the text and text sections that might be most relevant to their reading goals.
- As they read, they frequently *make predictions* about what is to come.
- They read *selectively*, continually making decisions about their reading—what to read carefully, what to read quickly, what not to read, what to reread, and so forth.
- They *construct, revise,* and *question* the meanings they make as they read.
- They try to determine the meanings of *unfamiliar words and concepts* in the text, and they deal with inconsistencies or gaps as needed.
- They draw from, compare, and *integrate their prior knowledge* with material in the text.
- They think about the *authors* of the text, their style, beliefs, intentions, historical milieu, and so forth.
- They *monitor their understanding* of the text, making adjustments in their reading as necessary.
- They *evaluate the text's quality and value* and react to the text in a range of ways, both intellectually and emotionally.
- They *read different kinds of text differently.*
- When reading narrative, they attend closely to the setting and characters.
- When reading expository text, they frequently construct and revise summaries of what they have read.
- They process not only during "reading," but also during short breaks taken during reading and even after the reading has ceased.
- Comprehension is a consuming, continuous, and complex activity, but one that is both *satisfying and productive.*

FIGURE 16.2. Characteristics of proficient readers. Adapted from Duke et al. (2011). Copyright © 2011 The International Literacy Association. Adapted by permission.

emphasize how active and thoughtful proficient readers are and to show what the targeted endpoint for reading/comprehension development looks like.

The point of Figure 16.2 is certainly not to suggest that primary-grade learners would be expected to attain all of the competencies listed. Rather, the point is to help teachers develop insight into the very active way in which proficient readers interact with text and, thereby, to emphasize the goal of helping young learners engage in the comprehension process in very active ways and to view understanding of texts listened to or read as the major goal.

Comprehension Strategies

As the strategies used by proficient readers came to be understood, researchers began exploring whether it was possible to teach these strategies to people, including children, who were not using them and, if so, whether such strategy instruction would help to improve comprehension. The results of these studies indicated that a variety of approaches to comprehension strategy instruction are effective in helping children to learn and use the strategies and thereby improve their reading comprehension (e.g., Brown, Pressley, Van Meter, & Schuder, 1996; Fuchs, Fuchs,

& Burish, 2000; Guthrie et al., 2004; Klingner, Vaughn, & Schumm, 1998). However, most research on comprehension strategies instruction has focused on children beyond the primary grades, and, as Paris and Paris (2007) pointed out, when children in the early primary grades are included, the effects of comprehension strategy instruction can be confounded by differences in decoding skills. In confirmation of the point made by Paris and Paris (2007), Müller, Richter, Križan, Hecht, and Ennemoser (2015) found that when reading comprehension strategies were explicitly taught to second-grade children who demonstrated comprehension difficulties, children with adequate decoding skills benefited, whereas those with weak decoding skills did not. In fact, the latter group performed somewhat more poorly than the control group (with similarly weak decoding skills) that did not receive comprehension strategy instruction.

The Müller et al. (2015) study is the only study we know of that has looked at the impact of comprehension strategy instruction for readers with stronger versus weaker decoding skills. However, it is consistent with the approach we have taken to comprehension strategy instruction in the ISA studies, as discussed below. In developing the ISA, we were mindful of the studies of comprehension strategy instruction but leery of emulating their procedures with the young children who were our primary focus. We were concerned because we place considerable emphasis on strategic word solving (as discussed in Chapter 12), which, like using comprehension strategies, is a cognitively demanding enterprise. We did not want to overwhelm beginning and developing readers, particularly those who were experiencing difficulties with learning foundational skills, by asking them to be consciously strategic about *both* word solving and meaning construction. However, certainly we *did* want them to be involved in the process of meaning construction and to have meaning making as their primary purpose for reading and for listening to text.

Therefore, rather than explicitly teaching and practicing comprehension strategies, we opted to engage children in meaning construction by involving them in conversations about the texts they read and heard. In the context of these conversations, teachers modeled some of the most commonly taught comprehension strategies. Because some comprehension strategies are widely accepted as being useful to share with elementary-age children, we identified those strategies and encouraged teachers to become familiar with them. We urged teachers to use them to prompt and structure their conversations with students during read-alouds and shared and supported reading. Table 16.1 lists and briefly describes the strategies we encourage teachers to consider. The table also provides a brief commentary on what each strategy entails and why it is thought to be useful.

Inferencing and self-regulation skills also likely influence application of the comprehension strategies listed in Table 16.1. For example, to go back to the *Max* passage, *activation of prior knowledge* might lead the reader to *infer* that *Max* is a student in the second sentence, but, for readers who are monitoring their comprehension, the third sentence would lead them to modify their understanding in a way that incorporates the newly encountered information. This would constitute an instance of self-regulation.

TABLE 16.1. Comprehension Strategies Employed in the ISA While Engaging Children in Discussions of Texts

Strategy	What it involves	Why it is useful
Activation of prior knowledge	Thinking about what one already knows about a topic or concept	New information from the text will be easier to interpret if readers think about what they already know about a topic. That way, when something is read that doesn't fit with the existing schema or knowledge base, learners will be alert to that fact and will be more likely to take steps to clear up the discrepancies—for example by asking questions in a read-aloud context or by rereading or reading on for more information when they themselves are reading (which the teacher might do in a read-aloud context). Connecting information encountered in a text with existing knowledge is the essence of meaning construction.
Prediction	Anticipating what will occur in the text and then checking to see whether the prediction matches what is revealed in the text	Learners need to integrate prior knowledge with information from the text in order to make predictions. Generally, when learners have made a prediction, they become invested in determining whether their prediction is validated. This has the additional advantage of sustaining their interest in, and engagement with, the text.
Visualization	Imagining what events described in the text would look like if illustrated or made into a movie	To construct a visual image, learners must attend to the text in an active way, ideally modifying their envisionment as the text unfolds.
Summarization	Retelling the events from the text, typically using some sort of organizational structure, such as sequencing (*first, then, finally*) or story grammar (setting, characters, problem, resolution) for narrative texts and, for informational texts, using the organizational structure of the text (e.g., compare and contrast, sequence, problem solution)	When, after reading/listening to a text, readers reflect on it in such a way as to be able to summarize it, they will likely retain more of the information. Perhaps more importantly, over time, it is assumed that the practice of summarization will lead to more active engagement while listening to or reading texts because learners will use the summarization structures to guide their thinking as texts unfold. Teachers sometimes find it useful to provide learners with graphic organizers such as story maps or sequence charts *while* students are reading/listening rather than at the conclusion of the text.
Questioning	This is a very broad strategy that entails asking questions related to the content of the text and/or directed to the author of the text (e.g., "I wonder why . . . ," "Why didn't he . . . ?," "How come . . . ?")	When learners frequently generate questions they would like to ask the characters or author, they are likely to approach upcoming text with an eye toward answering those questions. Further, the questions that they generate often lead them back into previous parts of the text to seek clarification. Pressley et al. (1992) reported that teaching children to ask "why" questions is especially effective because children often have the necessary knowledge to understand a text, but they do not apply it.
Comprehension monitoring	Throughout engagement with a text, noticing whether it makes sense and, if not, taking steps to clarify the areas of confusion	To an extent, this strategy involves all of the others discussed above and can be considered a *metacognitive* strategy in that it involves individuals in thinking about their own thinking (Weinstein & Mayer, 1986). This strategy is particularly important to develop because it emphasizes the need for readers to take responsibility for determining whether the text makes sense to them and to take steps to clarify when comprehension breaks down. Comprehension monitoring is an example of self-regulation.

440

Conversations about Text

Our decision not to encourage *explicit* comprehension strategy instruction in the early primary grades was partly driven by the concern that teaching both word-identification strategies and comprehension strategies would overextend the cognitive capacities of young children. It was also motivated by our conviction that there are multiple less formalized ways of engaging children in meaning construction while reading or listening to texts. We suspected that these less formal forms of engagement could be more enjoyable and motivating for the children. Enjoyment and motivation struck us as particularly important elements for children who begin school with limited early literacy skills and limited literacy experiences more generally. The type of conversation-focused approach that we endorsed has been dubbed a "content" approach by McKeown, Beck, and Blake (2009) because it entails focusing most of the interaction around a text on constructing its meaning rather than on strategies that might be used to enable that construction. Although relatively little research has been done on the role of discussion in promoting comprehension in the primary grades, the research that does exist indicates that discussion about texts can promote problem solving, comprehension, and learning (Anderson, Chinn, Waggoner, & Nguyen, 1998; Cervetti et al., 2020; Nystrand, 1997; Taylor et al., 2000; Wegerif, Mercer, & Dawes, 1999). Roberts and Duke (2009) suggest that discussion of texts likely fosters comprehension owing to the "accountability inherent in saying something oneself and the opportunity to hear the interpretations of others" (p. 37).

Using Interactive Read-Alouds to Enhance Knowledge and Promote Engagement

Many of the books that primary-grade children are able to read provide limited comprehension challenges and few opportunities to build knowledge about the world. However, a good deal of comprehension-focused instruction and knowledge building can occur in the context of interactive read-alouds in the classroom. Further, classroom teachers can use classroom volunteers and other available personnel to address the knowledge and comprehension needs of the children about whom they have concerns.

Research evaluating the effects of reading frequently to children has demonstrated its value (Duke, 2021; McKeown & Beck, 2006). Marriott (1995) argued that "it is almost impossible to overemphasize the value of this activity for children of any age or reading level" (p. 65). Morrow and Gambrell (2000) and Snow et al. (1998) summarized the results of several studies that compared children from classrooms in which there were daily read-alouds with children from classrooms in which read-alouds occurred only occasionally. In general, these studies found that children who were read to often demonstrated greater motivation to read, greater gains in vocabulary, better comprehension of new stories they heard, greater familiarity with literary language, and better decoding skills.

KEEP IN MIND   Although this section focuses on read-alouds, many of the same types of interactions concerning the meanings of texts can occur in the context of a shared reading experience. In a shared reading activity, however, the teacher generally addresses several additional goals, including talking about the purposes and conventions of print and how the writing system is related to spoken language.

Similarly, as children begin to engage in reading texts themselves, both in supported reading groups and independently, the teacher needs to establish a specific focus on the meaning of the text. The events and/or information in the text should be discussed before, during, and after children read the text.

Implementing Interactive Read-Alouds

The effectiveness of read-alouds in supporting the development of active thinking during reading depends on the qualities of the interactions between the teacher and the children (see McKeown & Beck, 2006). As discussed briefly in the chapter on motivation (Chapter 3), the teacher's level of enthusiasm for the texts read and for reading in general are important. So too is the level of freedom children feel they have to initiate conversations about the texts. If reactions and questions have to wait until the end of the text or until the teacher initiates a discussion, then the children might well react less and comprehend less altogether. Virtually everyone has had the experience of missing a point midway through a passage while reading (or listening) and then having difficulty understanding everything that comes later. When children encounter a confusing part of a text, it would be ideal if they could clear up their confusion almost immediately by asking questions of the teacher or perhaps the other children in the group. We certainly expect older students to attempt some sort of "fix-up" when they realize that they are not comprehending what they are reading. Such active monitoring of one's understanding has been found to be vitally important to comprehension (Cain, Oakhill, & Bryant, 2004; see Baker & Beall, 2009, for a review). In the context of a read-aloud, the only option children have for addressing a breakdown of comprehension is to rely on someone else: they cannot go back and reread. So, teachers are strongly encouraged to make read-alouds as interactive as possible.

KEEP IN MIND   One of the major purposes of interactive read-alouds is to develop the belief that text should make sense and that, when it doesn't, listeners (and ultimately readers) should do something to clear up their confusion. If, in the context of read-alouds, children aren't allowed to seek clarification, they may come to believe that it is OK not to understand what is going on in a text. The development of that belief has the clear potential to carry over into the students' engagement in meaning construction when they are reading on their own.

In addition to answering questions as they arise, teachers can also be proactive, anticipating potential points of confusion and addressing them before a comprehension problem arises. In a study of exemplary literacy teachers at the kindergarten level, Block and Mangieri (2003) found that, when a portion of a book was probably unfamiliar to their students, exemplary teachers were likely to stop and rephrase the confusing aspect of the text or to create an example from students' life experiences.

Studies of the influences of reading aloud to children suggest that the greatest benefits accrue when the children are actively engaged during the course of the read-aloud (Beck & McKeown, 2001; Fisher, Flood, Lapp, & Frey, 2004; Hickman, Pollard-Durodola, & Vaughn, 2004; Santoro, Chard, Howard, & Baker, 2008). Participation can occur before, during, and after reading.

BEFORE READING

Participation *before reading* might include:

- Previewing the text through discussions of the title and the cover illustration.
- Discussions of the author and/or illustrator, particularly if the group is familiar with other texts by the author and/or illustrator.
- Making predictions about the text's content and discussing the basis for those predictions.
- Encouraging the children to think about the elements of genre and text structure in anticipating the book's content.
- Setting a purpose for listening, perhaps by relating it to a classroom theme or area of inquiry that the group is exploring.

DURING READING

Participation *during reading* should include spontaneous discussions of the text. Ideally, the discussions would be initiated by both the students and the teacher. Further, when the teacher initiates discussion, children should be encouraged to think beyond the literal level, and the teacher should model and prompt inferential and critical analysis of the text. This kind of guidance might include:

- Encouraging children to ask and answer questions and make comments as the text unfolds. Welcoming questions and comments in a conversational way will send the clear message that spontaneous reactions to the book are appropriate and that comprehension monitoring, making connections and inferences, and the like, are expected and valued.
  - "Ah, good question! Does anyone have any ideas about that?"
  - "Interesting question! Let's read to find out."
  - "Don't forget, if you are confused about something, listen a little longer to see if you can figure out what's going on. If not, you may want to ask a question."
  - "I agree. . . ."

- Noticing and discussing elements of story grammar.
  - "So, it looks like this story is set in the winter. Look at how they are all bundled up."
  - "What's the problem between our characters?"
  - "That is a solution I never would have guessed!"
  - "So, now we know what the problem is. Any ideas on how it will be resolved [solved]?"
- Comparing predictions to the events in the texts. Note that it is important to avoid talking about predictions as being either right or wrong, as some children really don't like to be wrong—and a prediction cannot really be wrong if it follows logically from what was known at the time it is made.
  - "That's just what Jared thought would happen."
  - "What did the author do that was different from what we expected [predicted]?"
- Making further predictions based on what has already happened in the text.
  - "Before we thought that. . . . But now we're thinking. . . ."
- Generating questions or comments relating to the text and/or the characters.
  - "I wonder why he didn't. . . ."
  - "Did you notice the look on his face? I bet he's. . . ."
  - "I wonder why the author. . . ."
  - "How do you think _____ is feeling right now?"
  - "Why do you think . . . ?"
  - "What do you notice . . . ?"
  - "If you could talk to the author right now, what would you ask?"
  - "Why . . . ?"
  - "Why . . . ?"
  - "Why . . . ?" (Research suggests that teaching children to ask and answer *why* questions is particularly helpful in getting them to apply their knowledge in interpreting text (Pressley et al., 1992). Graesser (2007) suggests that prompting students with *why* questions leads them to provide causal explanations—which is fundamental to strategic comprehension.
- Asking open-ended questions.
  - "Who has something they would like to say about this page?"
  - "What did you notice on this page?"
  - "Who would like to share their thinking about what we've learned so far?"
- Seeking clarifications.
  - "What do you think the author meant by. . . ."
  - "Let's think about this illustration. It may help us to figure out. . . ."
- Offering and eliciting personal reactions and connections.
  - "I just love the way he keeps. . . ."
  - "I really don't like the way. . . ."
  - "How would you feel if . . . ?"
  - "How would you handle this situation?"

- o "Does this book remind you of . . . ?"
- o "Did you ever . . . ?"
- Visualizing.
  - o "Just listen to this page as I read it and make a picture of what's happening in your head."
  - o "The illustrator didn't make a picture for that part. What do you think it would look like?"
- Comparing information in the current text with other texts with which the children are familiar.
  - o "This is sort of like the [text] we read."
  - o "This is the second book we've read where the. . . ."
  - o "Is this reminding you of another book we've read?"
    - "In what way?"
- Restating (perhaps using simpler vocabulary and/or sentence structures) any confusing portions of the text when they are encountered.

AFTER READING

- Participation *after reading* might include:
  - o Discussions of how predictions compared to the events in the text.
  - o Discussions of whether the purposes that were set were accomplished.
  - o Discussions of parts that may have been a bit confusing and then returning to those parts to reread for the purpose of clarification.
  - o Discussing or writing alternative endings (e.g., "What would have happened if . . . ?").
  - o Rereading the entire text with the specific purpose of clearing up points of confusion and/or simply for the sake of enjoying it.
  - o Encouraging children to draw a scene from the text as they envisioned it.
  - o Reflecting on what was learned and talking or writing about it.
  - o Reflecting on why the author might have written the book.
  - o Reenacting the story with the aid of story-related props.
  - o Retelling the stories for authentic purposes (e.g., retelling into an audio recorder for the benefit of a child who was absent or to share with family members).
  - o Reconstructing stories using pictures (for very beginning readers).

The comments and questions teachers use to foster conversations help children develop ways of thinking about and reacting to texts. The goal is that the children will ultimately internalize ways of thinking encouraged through these conversations, which will be useful to them when they are reading independently. In conducting these conversations, however, the teacher also needs to realize that too much talk can disrupt the flow of the text. As in all aspects of instruction, striking the right balance is important.

Using Informational (Nonfiction) Texts to Promote the Development of General World Knowledge

Although much can be learned from interactive read-alouds of storybooks, the wealth of knowledge that prepares children for later academic pursuits is most readily addressed through nonfiction books and other types of information-rich texts, such as historical fiction and fantastical science books such as the *Magic School Bus* series (published by Scholastic). Therefore, it is generally recommended that approximately 50% of the books children listen to or read be of the informational variety (NGO & CCSSO, 2010). Because children generally encounter greater amounts of new information with these types of text than with storybooks, they will likely need more teacher support to integrate the new information. This extra support might include:

- Reading simpler texts on a given topic before reading more challenging ones.
- Careful planning by the teacher, with the goal of anticipating the portions of the text that might confuse children and preparation of explanations that will help to clarify points or prevent the confusion altogether.
- Lengthier discussions before, during, and after reading the text.
- Frequent think-alouds in which the teacher models the kind of thinking that children will ultimately need to do.
- Extended discussions focused on specific concepts or causal relationships encountered in the text—often connecting new concepts to ideas familiar to children.
- Discussion of text structure (e.g., compare–contrast, cause–effect, sequence) as well as the signal words that can help children identify the structures (see the section on genre knowledge above, pp. 431–432).
- Periodic encouragement to summarize what has already been learned in the text; early on, children will typically need assistance with such summaries, including encouragement to organize summaries based on text structure.
- Rereading the entire book, perhaps more than once; each time children listen to (or read) a book, they are likely to understand the content at a deeper level and are therefore more likely to integrate the knowledge more effectively.
- Reconstructing processes using illustrations (e.g., stages of plant or animal development).

Comprehension Snapshots

Teachers have the opportunity to observe (and record) children's listening and reading comprehension skills, strategies, and attitudes across time. Those opportunities occur when the children are receiving instruction in a small-group context, when they are engaged in a whole-class reading or listening activities, and when they are engaged with texts more independently. Thus, observational data may be gathered throughout the day and not just when children are in their usual small groups. The teacher can nevertheless make use of the group snapshot to record impressions of individual children. Having data in one place for use during the course of small-group instruction allows the teacher to more effectively address the strategies and attitudes of the children in the instructional group. This is an important consideration because the instructional goals for children who are at different points in their literacy development may well differ across groups and can be most readily addressed in the small-group context.

Listening Comprehension Snapshot

Given that listening comprehension performance is highly predictive of and related to children's reading comprehension (Cervetti et al., 2020), it is important to attend to children's response to and ability to comprehend texts that are read aloud to them. Because children do not need to simultaneously attend to accurate word identification and the meaning of the text, their cognitive resources can be fully devoted to meaning construction. For that reason, it is useful to record observations of how children respond in the context of interactive read-alouds.

The characteristics/descriptors listed on the Listening Comprehension group snapshot in Figure 16.3 are premised on engaging children in interactive read-alouds. It is in such contexts that evidence of children's engagement in meaning construction would be most apparent. In a more passive read-aloud context in which the teacher reads and the children are expected to quietly listen, there would be very limited, if any, opportunity to observe how children are processing/thinking about the text as it unfolds. It is also important to note that some children will be much more (openly) active than others in responding to text during an interactive read-aloud. Therefore, to get a more comprehensive picture of the listening comprehension skills of some children, it may be necessary to occasionally engage them in interactive read-alouds in a small-group context.

The snapshot provides opportunities for teachers to record their observations/impressions on several dates—perhaps across the school year. Ideally, children who initially appear to not engage actively during read-aloud opportunities will become more engaged over time. Opportunities for such children to engage in interactive read-alouds in smaller group contexts or in one-to-one settings may support that development.

Comprehension Instruction/Focus
during Shared and Supported Reading

The discussion of the development of active comprehenders has largely focused on read-aloud interactions because the types of books that are read aloud to primary-grade children offer richer opportunities to focus on content than is possible with

(text resumes on p. 450)

Group Snapshot—Listening Comprehension						
	Dates	**Student names**				
Generally **U**nderstands texts read aloud						
Actively engages in meaning construction						
Makes **P**redictions						
Offers **R**eactions						
Asks **Q**uestions						
Makes **I**nferences						

(continued)

FIGURE 16.3. Group snapshot for listening comprehension.

	Dates	Student names				
Demonstrates understanding of text structures						
Narrative texts						
Informational texts						
Connects information in texts to . . .						
Own life						
Other texts						
Broader contexts						

Key:

YO—Yes—often and spontaneously

YS—Yes—sometimes but often needs prompting

NY—No—not yet

FIGURE 16.3. *(page 2 of 2)*

the types of texts that most young children are able to read. However, this focus on read-alouds should certainly not be taken to suggest that comprehension should be ignored during shared and supported reading. To the contrary, a major reason for encouraging active thinking during a read-aloud is that children are more inclined to be active thinkers when they themselves read.

Virtually all of the suggestions made relative to read-aloud situations can be applied to shared and supported reading situations. Texts should be discussed *before, during*, and *after* reading. The discussion should involve open-ended questions and reactions that prompt inferential and critical thinking. Discussions should give children the opportunity to think through what they are reading and to integrate it with what they already know. (See the discussion of supported reading in Chapter 17.)

Figure 16.4 presents the Reading Comprehension group snapshot for use when the students themselves are reading. Children are engaged in reading texts in three contexts:

• *Shared reading*, during which the children and their teacher read texts together and generally read the same text multiple times. Typically, teachers take the lead on the first reading or two and gradually reduce the prominence of their voices as the children gain familiarity with the text. Shared reading often occurs in a whole-class context and also in the context of small-group instruction. (See Chapter 2 for a discussion of the multiple instructional uses of shared reading.)

• *Supported reading*, during which the children themselves do the reading, with guidance and support from the teacher. This usually occurs in a small-group context,[1] which allows the teacher to more explicitly address instructional goals/objectives for individual children and/or the group. Ideally, in this context, children would not read in unison (and may not all be reading the same text). This encourages individual students to demonstrate their capabilities and allows the teacher to attend to the approaches that individuals take to both the word-solving and comprehension challenges encountered in the text. Supported reading is the context in which the teacher has the greatest opportunity to observe and note evidence of children's interest in and approach to meaning construction.

• *Buddy and independent reading*, during which children read a text with one or more partners or by themselves—without direct teacher support. This context for reading may occur during periods of the day when children have choices about how to spend their time or during a designated independent reading time. When children are reading, the teacher may periodically "listen in" to gather information about the children's approach to meaning construction. Alternatively, and especially for children who have learned various approaches to tracking their thinking as they read (see the section Writing to Enhance Reading Comprehension below),

---

[1] For children qualifying for Tier 3 intervention support, teachers may provide instruction in a one-to-one context.

Group Snapshot—Reading Comprehension						
		Student names				
	Date					
Chooses to read books and other texts						
Generally understands texts						
Actively engages in meaning construction						
Rereads or reads on to clear up confusion(s)						
Makes Predictions and reads on to verify/reject						
Offers Reactions						
Asks Questions and seeks answers in text						
Makes Inferences						

(continued)

FIGURE 16.4. Group snapshot for reading comprehension.

	Date	Student names			
Demonstrates understanding of text structures and features					
Narrative texts					
Informational texts					
Text features (e.g., bold print, glossary, graphics)					
Connects information in texts to . . .					
Own life					
Other texts					
Broader contexts					

Key:

YO—Yes—often and spontaneously

YS—Yes—sometimes but often needs prompting

NY—No—not yet

FIGURE 16.4. *(page 2 of 2)*

the teacher may conference with children to learn about their thinking about the texts they are reading.

Similar to the Listening Comprehension snapshot, the Reading Comprehension snapshot provides space for the teacher to record observations/impressions on multiple occasions across a period of weeks or months.

Additional Contributors to Reading Comprehension

High-Volume Reading

The amount of reading that children do is a strong predictor of their reading success (Allington & McGill-Franzen, 2021; Taylor et al., 2000). Although this may seem like a bit of a chicken–egg problem (Does reading more lead to reading success, or does being a successful reader lead one to read more?), Allington et al. (2010) found that simply increasing the availability of books over the summer break led to significant increases in the reading achievement of children living in high-poverty areas. This finding suggests that increased reading volume leads to improved reading achievement in areas where access to books tends to be limited. According to Allington and McGill-Franzen, the greatest impact of increased volume of reading is most evident once learners have developed foundational skills. This suggests that the volume of reading readers do has a *causal* impact on reading outcomes. Although this finding certainly comes as no surprise, we hope that it prompts teachers to consider how much reading their students do in the course of a typical school day and what their home reading expectations and options entail. Allington and McGill-Franzen (2013), for example, suggest that in some settings children read as little as 10 minutes in a typical 90-minute classroom reading block. Such limited reading is unlikely to help children to build the needed knowledge of words and of the world upon which reading comprehension depends.

Further, several studies have demonstrated that the reading achievement differences between children from low- versus higher-income backgrounds are largely attributable to losses in reading skills that occur over the summer for children living in poverty (see Allington & McGill-Franzen, 2013, and Kim & Quinn, 2013, for reviews). Based on the findings of the Allington et al. study (2010) cited above, this would seem to be largely due to lack of access to reading materials. This problem strikes us as a very fixable one for anyone with some grant-writing experience!

Of course, other issues influence the volume of reading that students do. One important factor is the difficulty level of the text. Children will read more (in terms of total words read and content covered) in a given period of time if the text is not too challenging. In addition, they will be more motivated to read when they can focus on the content of what they are reading rather than having to devote a great deal of their cognitive resources to the process of word solving. Further, Amendum, Conradi, and Hiebert (2018), in a synthesis of multiple studies of the relationship between text difficulty and reading comprehension, found that, as text difficulty increased, reading comprehension tended to decline. We have touched on concerns about text difficulty in some of the earlier chapters, and we repeat it here because we feel we can't stress it enough.

Writing to Enhance Comprehension and Knowledge Development

As children's literacy skills evolve, their comprehension can be supported through writing. For example, during independent reading, the children might:

- Use sticky notes to record their questions and thoughts and apply them to the appropriate pages. Later, when it is time to discuss the text, the children will have these reminders to help them participate in the discussion.

- Keep a reading journal wherein they record their reactions to, and learnings from, the texts they read. For example, they might draw a picture of how they envision a scene, write one or two of their predictions and whether the text matched them, or write questions they wish they could ask the author or main character(s) and read on to see if their questions are answered.

- Write book reviews to post as a way to encourage others to read particular books. (For example: "I recommend this book because . . .")

- Describe texts using structural formats such as story grammar (setting, characters, problem, and resolution of the story) or sequencing (*first, then, next, finally*).

- Keep a learning log in which they record information gleaned from nonfiction readings—perhaps using a *k*now–*w*ant to know–*l*earned (K-W-L) format (Ogle, 1986).

- Write their own texts (e.g., nonfiction books, short stories) modeled after books they've read and/or drawing on what they have learned through their reading.

KEY POINTS OF THIS CHAPTER

✓ Comprehension and knowledge development are the primary reasons for reading and learning to read.

✓ Learners' background knowledge and language skills have a strong influence on their ability to comprehend texts. Therefore, instruction to develop knowledge and language skills is critical.

✓ For young learners, interactive read-alouds provide the opportunity to model and engage children in the types of inferential and critical thinking characteristic of active and engaged comprehenders.

✓ The more children read, the more quickly they will gain proficiency in reading comprehension—assuming they understand that reading is about meaning making.

✓ Understanding the characteristics of different text structures, particularly informational text structures, can enhance comprehension.

✓ Readers need to monitor the coherence of their understanding of the texts they listen to and read and take action (e.g., ask a question, reread) when coherence is lacking.

PART V

Integration of the Goals
Putting It All Together

Introduction to Part V

In the foregoing chapters, we discussed the complexity of the reading process and how difficulties with any of the contributing components could lead to long-term reading difficulties. The major emphasis in this book is on the provision of effective instruction to prevent and help alleviate early difficulties with literacy learning. It is important that teachers have the knowledge and skills needed to identify and respond to the instructional needs of early literacy learners, especially those who experience difficulty. Teacher knowledge related to each of the instructional goals discussed in previous chapters has been a major focus of the book. In this final part of the book, we review and integrate some of the major ideas addressed in the preceding chapters.

In Chapter 17, we revisit Ehri's phase theory and discuss instructional implications based on the phase in which students are (primarily) performing. We also illustrate how multiple instructional goals might be addressed in the context of small-group supported reading lessons. In addition, we provide a Reflection Form (see Figure 17.1, pp. 474–476) that teachers have found useful for guiding their thinking about the instruction they offer during the portion of small-group lessons when children are engaged in reading a new book. In Chapter 18, we review the instructional principles that were first introduced in Chapter 2 and how these principles are related to one another and to the instructional goals discussed throughout the book. In this context, we focus primarily on comprehension and knowledge development, the ultimate goal of literacy instruction. This focus in Chapter 18 was driven by our concern that we may have led teachers to lose sight of this goal because so much of the book has been heavily focused on helping children learn to read words. We conclude Chapter 18 (and the book) by encouraging reflection on how some of the content covered in the text might usefully impact instructional practice.

Early in this text, we outlined a set of instructional goals for the purpose of demonstrating the multiple ways in which skills, abilities, knowledge sources, and attitudes and beliefs are interconnected and mutually supportive of literacy learning (see Chapter 1). In Part V, we revisit the complexity of the literacy (learning) process, with a particular focus on foundational skills and word-solving strategies in Chapter 17, as these are generally a major focus of small-group instruction in the primary grades. In Chapter 18, we also revisit some of the instructional principles introduced in Chapter 2, and we take the opportunity to emphasize, once again, the critical role that teachers, teachers' knowledge, and teachers' ability to utilize that knowledge in responsive ways can play in preventing long-term reading difficulties.

In Chapters 2–16, we discussed how instruction in whole-class contexts can be responsive to the variation in literacy skills in a typical primary-grade classroom. However, we also indicated that the most powerful setting for responsive instruction is the small-group context in which children with similar literacy skills are grouped together for instruction. In the primary grades, the most common, and probably the most productive, basis for forming small groups is the similarities in foundational skills among children (phonemic analysis skills, decoding and encoding skills, and high-frequency word knowledge). These foundational skills, coupled with lots of opportunity to read meaningful texts, enable learners to build their sight vocabularies, which, in turn, ultimately allows them to focus most of their cognitive resources on comprehending, learning from, and enjoying the texts they read.

We also advocated for intensifying instruction for children whose early literacy skills are limited relative to grade-level expectations. Intensification can be accomplished by providing small-group instruction more frequently, for longer periods of time, and/or in smaller groups. Indeed, for children who demonstrate the most limited skills, a combination of small-group instruction provided by the classroom teacher coupled with very small-group or even one-to-one intervention sessions beyond the classroom may be necessary to achieve the acceleration (growth) needed to meet grade-level expectations. This suggested intensification aligns with the response-to-intervention (RTI) framework introduced in Chapter 1.

In general, foundational skills are a major focus of instruction for children in the primary grades, and differences in these skills are often used to determine which children become involved in an RTI process. As noted above, we began this text with a focus on the complexity of the reading process and the central goal of reading instruction—comprehension and the development of knowledge (see Figure 1.2, p. 12) because the development of these skills is the reason we read and the reason to teach children to read. However, to comprehend text, readers must be able to effortlessly read the vast majority of words encountered in printed text, and they must have knowledge of the words' meanings and understand the sentence structures in which the words occur. While the ability to learn word meanings and understand complex sentence structures can be addressed in the context of whole-class read-alouds and conversations, skill with accurate identification of printed words can be most effectively accomplished in the context of small-group instruction. This allows for instruction to be tailored to the current skills and understandings of the students in the group. Indeed, we contend that responsive small-group instruction is *the* most effective way to respond to the variable print knowledge and skills that characterize children in most primary-grade classrooms.

In Chapter 12, we describe the primary process by which children build their sight vocabularies: effective word solving while reading. Figure V.1 illustrates the process. As depicted in the center vertical box, sight vocabulary is developed through a process of *word solving*, which, ideally, leads to accurate *word identification*, which, across multiple encounters with a given word, leads to *word learning* (that is, the ability to effortlessly and automatically identify printed words in all contexts). A reader's ability to solve an unfamiliar word encountered in the context of meaningful text depends on use of the code-based strategies listed in the box to the right of the center box. Foundational knowledge and skills (the code-based enablers depicted in the box to the right of the code-based strategies box) support learners' ability to utilize the code-based strategies to arrive at a likely pronunciation of an unfamiliar written word. The meaning-based strategies depicted to the left of the center box are used to determine whether an initial attempt at an unfamiliar word is a real word that fits the context in which it is encountered. The use of these meaning-based strategies depends on the knowledge sources identified in the meaning-based enablers box at the far left of the figure. Pearson (2022) suggests that both foundational skills (what we refer to as code-based enablers) and

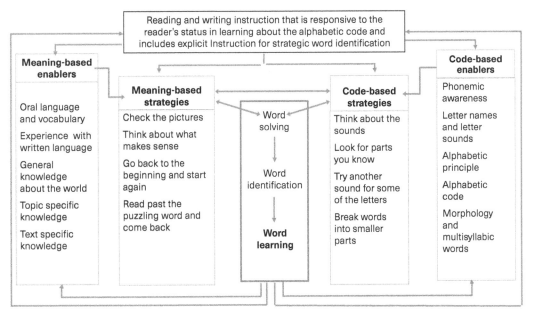

FIGURE V.1. Illustration of the complexity of the word-learning process. Adapted from Anderson and Scanlon (2020, p. 350). Copyright © 2020 The International Literacy Association. Adapted by permission.

efforts to construct meaning are necessary, but neither is sufficient when a reader "hits a bump in the road"—which is one way to construe the experience of encountering an unknown word in a text.

Examination of this graphic is in some ways reminiscent of Figure 1.2 (p. 12), which is our attempt to illustrate the complexity of the reading process, with comprehension and knowledge being the central focus. In the current graphic, we illustrate the complexity of the word-solving–word-identification–word-learning process more specifically. Obviously, readers cannot comprehend and gain knowledge from written text *unless* they can read the vast majority of the words in the text fairly effortlessly. While the meaning-based enablers can, to a great extent, be developed in whole-class instructional contexts and are typically developed both in and beyond the classroom and school, development of the code-based enablers (depicted in Figure V.1) is typically more dependent on in-school experiences, particularly for primary-grade children with limited early literacy skills.

The ultimate goals of literacy instruction are (1) to develop the knowledge base upon which comprehension depends, and (2) to encourage children to actively engage in meaning construction when listening to and reading texts. In the early primary grades, these purposes are served primarily, but not exclusively, through use of interactive read-alouds, especially of information-rich texts and, ideally, texts organized to support knowledge development. Effective text sets focused on science and/or social studies topics would, ideally, begin with easier, introductory texts on a given topic and gradually add texts that provide more complex and complete information on the topic.

While acknowledging that the ultimate goal of reading instruction is comprehension and knowledge development, in Chapter 17 we focus on small-group instruction which, in the primary grades, typically has a heavy focus on helping children learn to read and spell words—in and out of context. To this end, small-group instruction in the primary grades needs to focus largely, though not exclusively, on helping children develop foundational skills and word-solving strategies. These assets will enable them to effectively puzzle through, accurately identify, and ultimately learn to read unfamiliar printed words encountered while reading meaningful text. Once children become effective word learners, they can build the needed sight vocabulary that will enable them to focus their attention on understanding, learning from, and enjoying the texts they read—thereby accomplishing the major goals of reading instruction.

In the next chapter (Chapter 17), we illustrate how small-group supported reading instruction can be organized and delivered in ways that are responsive to the current capabilities and understandings of children who are at differing points in developing their literacy skills. In the final chapter (Chapter 18), we revisit the general principles for preventing reading difficulties that were introduced in Chapter 1. Those principles should now be more salient in the minds of our readers after having engaged with the content of the chapters on goals (Chapters 3–16).

CHAPTER 17

Small-Group Instruction

In this chapter, we describe the components of small-group supported reading instruction and how it would differ in response to children at different points in their literacy development. As we emphasized in the introduction to Part II, the development of sight vocabulary for young literacy learners is heavily dependent on the learning of several foundational skills, including print concepts and conventions, phonemic analysis, and the workings of the alphabetic and orthographic code. In relation to the alphabetic code, we presented Ehri's *phase theory* of word learning (Ehri, 2014), which provides useful guidance to support responsive instruction. The theory connects learners' knowledge and skill in relation to the writing system with how they approach word solving and the identification of unfamiliar printed words. Table 17.1 lists developmental phases identified by the theory, along with the characteristics of learners who are operating *primarily* at/in a particular phase. We also provide suggested instructional foci for learners whose primary approach to word learning is characteristic of a given phase. Note that Ehri's automatic phase is not reflected in the table because, for learners at this point in development, the primary instructional implication is to ensure the learners engage in large amounts of reading. There are no specific foci for word-solving instruction.

Supported Reading Lessons

In this section, we provide a general description of supported reading lessons. Such lessons may be provided by the classroom teacher during small-group time and, for those who need extra support, by intervention teachers. Ideally, children who are receiving more intensive tiers of intervention would participate in lessons provided by the classroom teacher as well as an intervention teacher. This approach provides the greatest potential to accelerate the progress of children who need more

TABLE 17.1. Ehri's (2014) Phase Theory: Phase Characteristics and Instructional Foci

Phase	Learner characteristics	Suggestions for instructional foci for learners at different phases of word learning
Prealphabetic	When learners attempt/pretend to read, they rely on nonalphabetic "cues" such as memory for a text previously read to them, the pictures in a text, and/or prominent visual features of words such as the length or shape of the word to identify the words. They may use the background in logos (e.g., they may "read" the word *Cheerios* on the box but not in any other context). Readers in this phase "rely primarily on visually salient cues and context cues but not letter–sound cues to read and write words" (Ehri, 2020, p. 6).	• Foundational print concepts such as the distinction between letters and words and the left-to-right and top-to-bottom sequencing of print (see Chapter 4). • Early phonemic analysis skills (see Chapter 5). • The names and forms of individual letters (see Chapter 6).
Partial (early) alphabetic	Learners attend to a limited amount of the alphabetic information in words when attempting to identify them. They rely on a combination of partial alphabetic information in combination with contextual information in attempts to identify words encountered in meaningful text.	• Continued attention to the development of phonemic analysis in the context of letter–sound instruction. • The most common sounds associated with individual letters and common consonant digraphs and the short sounds for individual vowel letters (see Chapter 7). • How to use the graphemes in one-syllable short-vowel words to build, read, and spell words in isolation (see Chapter 8). • How to decode and spell single-syllable short-vowel words encountered in meaningful texts. • Opportunities to read simple texts that help reinforce knowledge of explicitly taught grapheme–phoneme correspondences.
Full (later) alphabetic	Learners have relatively complete knowledge of the workings of the writing system. Readers who are at this phase will attempt to use all grapheme–phoneme information in unfamiliar words in attempts to identify words they cannot yet identify automatically. Reading unfamiliar words will likely be effortful and slow as learners may not yet be fluent in using some of the less common grapheme–phoneme relationships in the process of word identification.	• How to decode and spell words with complex vowel spellings (see Chapter 10). • Lots of opportunity to read meaningful text applying word-solving strategies to identify and learn unfamiliar printed words.
Consolidated	"Learners have accumulated fully analyzed spellings of many words in lexical memory and, as a result, have acquired knowledge of larger consolidated spelling patterns, representing spoken syllables and morphemes. These readers can use these larger units to decode multisyllabic words and to form connections to read and spell multisyllabic words from memory" (Ehri, 2020, p. 6).	• "Explicit instruction in using onset-rime units, syllabic units, and morphemic spelling-meaning units" (Ehri, 2020, p. 8) (see Chapters 8 and 11). • Lots of opportunity to read meaningful text applying word-solving strategies to identify and learn unfamiliar printed words.

opportunities to receive instruction, engage in practice, and receive guidance and feedback. Instructional groups would be composed of children at similar points in their literacy development, thereby allowing teachers to provide instruction that is more directly responsive to the children's current skills, strategies, and understanding of reading and writing processes.

In the ISA, small-group instruction typically involves five or six lesson segments, as outlined in Table 17.2. The table names the segments and describes the purpose of each of them. A more detailed discussion of each segment is provided next.

Supported Reading Lesson Segments

Below we describe each segment of the lesson in greater detail.

Rereading Book(s)

This segment of the lesson is intended to build fluency and confidence and thus addresses the following goals: motivation and engagement (Chapter 3), strategic word learning (Chapter 12), fluency (Chapter 14), and comprehension and knowledge (Chapter 16). During this segment, children independently read one or two books that were read in previous lessons. The teacher generally offers choices of books that, in the teacher's opinion, provide useful opportunities to reinforce skills and strategies and in which the child(ren) encountered some challenge on the prior reading. As needed, the teacher would remind the children of the elements they found challenging during the previous reading. The teacher might also remind children of any previously taught word-identification strategies they are not using reliably or independently. With regard to the comprehension and knowledge goal (Chapter 16), comprehension is enhanced because, on a reread, ideally, the reader would need to devote less attention to the word-solving process. This frees up cognitive resources to devote to comprehension and knowledge construction. Even a beginner-level text provides opportunities to add to a child's knowledge base through conversation about the text that may be (or has been) initiated/led by the teacher. Depending on the characteristics of the text, vocabulary and syntactic skills may also be enhanced through repeated exposure to the text.

Rereading, of course, helps to reinforce a variety of foundational skills as well. For example, for learners at the prealphabetic and partial alphabetic phases, rereading even a memorized text can reinforce important print concepts and conventions such as the difference between letters and words and the left-to-right and the top-to-bottom directionality of print (Chapter 4) and knowledge of high-frequency words. For learners at the full alphabetic phase of development, successful identification of words in the text can add to and reinforce their skills with the alphabetic code. For example, encountering a word in an orthographic word family that was previously taught and practiced will reinforce knowledge of the rime that is the center of that family, making other words in that family more accessible when encountered in other reading contexts.

TABLE 17.2. Small-Group Lesson Segments

Lesson segment	Description and purposes
Rereading texts from previous lessons	Rereading texts helps to reinforce the identities of words that learners may have needed to puzzle through on the first reading. It also enables learners to experience more fluent reading and to focus more on the meaning of the text because they need to devote less of their cognitive resources to puzzling through previously unfamiliar words. For children at early points in development, aspects of print concepts and conventions can be reviewed.
Phonemic analysis	For children who do not yet demonstrate skill in analyzing the sounds in spoken words, this element would involve them in sorting, blending, and segmenting spoken words, as detailed in Chapter 5. However, once children have learned several grapheme–phoneme correspondences, ongoing guidance in phonemic analysis can be incorporated into the phonics (decoding and encoding) portion of the lesson.
Decoding and encoding	Instruction focuses on decoding and encoding elements that will be encountered in the new text(s) to be read during the lesson as well as reviewing previously taught elements that need continued practice. Practice activities involve word building, word reading, and written spelling, as described in Chapters 8–11. The aspects of the alphabetic and orthographic code focused upon in this segment change in response to the learners' current (evolving) skills.
Reading new texts	Texts selected for this component would be those that provide some, but not too much, challenge in relation to word solving. High-frequency words that students do not yet know and that they do not yet have the decoding skills to puzzle through would be taught and briefly practiced in advance of reading the new text(s). Word-solving strategies would be taught and/or reviewed in advance of reading the new text(s), with particular emphasis placed on strategies that are (relatively) new for the students and/ or for which the students need additional instructional guidance and practice.
	As needed, students would be reminded of the resources available to support word solving, including:
	• Bb/Dd graphic (Chapter 6)
	• Key-word chart (Chapter 7 for consonant graphemes and short vowels)
	• Word-identification strategy chart (Chapter 12)
	• "Words We/I Know" chart (Chapter 13)
	As students advance and no longer demonstrate the need for one or more of the supports listed above, those supports can be retired and, as needed, replaced with one or both of the following:
	• Key words for vowel teams (Chapter 10)
	• Tips for breaking words apart (Chapter 11)
	Brief discussions of the meaning of the text would occur before, during, and after reading. This would include explanations of the meanings of words that may not be part of students' listening/spoken vocabularies.
Writing	One or two meaningful sentences would be written either in response to one of the books read during the lesson or related to a topic of interest to the student(s). The teacher would be fairly directive about what is written so as to maximize the time available for addressing aspects of conventional writing and spelling that are a current focus for the students. These foci might include print conventions (e.g., capitalization, spacing, punctuation) and/or use of resources to enable conventional spelling (e.g., key-word and high-frequency word charts, books in which intended words were encountered).
High-frequency words	Previously taught high-frequency words that are not yet part of readers' automatic sight vocabulary would be practiced with the goal of promoting automaticity in word identification. Various games involving word identification and written spelling are used to promote fluency (see Chapter 13).

One of the biggest advantages of rereading is the support it provides for word learning. When words that the learner needed to "solve" on the first encounter are revisited during rereading, it increases the likelihood that those will become part of the learner's sight vocabulary. At the very least, the child will likely need to do less thinking about the identity of the word because, in the process of solving the word on the first encounter, the reader is likely to have stored a fairly thorough orthographic representation of the word in memory.

Motivation for reading can also be enhanced via rereading. Young children tend to be very motivated by the ability to read "like a storyteller," which is much more likely to occur on second and subsequent readings of a given text. This clearly has the potential to build a sense of competence and confidence which will, in turn, help children sustain their efforts when engaging with challenging texts in the future.

Phonemic Analysis

As discussed in detail in Chapter 5, the ability to analyze (attend to and manipulate) the phonemes in spoken words is critical to the ability to connect those phonemes to their printed representations (their associated graphemes). Learners who are in Ehri's prealphabetic and partial alphabetic phases are often insensitive to the individual phonemes in spoken words. As noted in Chapter 5, individual phonemes can be difficult to detect both because there is no clear point of demarcation between one phoneme and the next and because, until children begin to learn about print, there may be little that would draw their attention to these sound components. However, in order for learners to develop skill with the alphabetic code (phonics), they need to be able to notice and manipulate phonemes.

Instruction that promotes the development of phonemic awareness includes sorting pictures by commonality in beginning, ending, and medial sounds, blending individual spoken sounds to form words, and segmenting the sounds in spoken words into their individual phonemes. When applied in the context of reading, blending is the last step in the word-solving process. When applied in the context of writing, segmenting is the first step in sound spelling.

Instruction in phonemic analysis is used for children at early points in the development of literacy skills—typically before and while children are learning about the names of printed letters and their associated sounds. As children gain skill with the workings of the alphabetic code, isolated phonemic analysis instruction is discontinued and instruction related to phonemic analysis/awareness occurs in the context of the decoding and encoding segment of the lesson.

Decoding and Encoding

The focus of this segment of a small-group lesson varies considerably based on the learners' knowledge and skills related to the writing system. Decisions about the appropriate focus of instruction for learners can be guided by the decision tree provided in Figure II.2 (p. 100) and the texts that the children are being prepared to read. In general, this segment of the lesson would focus on alphabetic or orthographic elements that can be applied/utilized in the next segment of the lesson which involves reading new text(s). Ideally, the texts used would provide the opportunity to systematically move learners from earlier acquired skills such as the names of letters and their sounds, as well as the sounds associated with common consonant digraphs, to texts that engage learners in decoding/reading words that require them to decode words with CVC patterns, followed by texts that include words with complex vowel patterns and words with more than one syllable and/or more than one meaningful part. Review of some of the previously taught reading and spelling elements that are not yet automatically applied/utilized by the learners might also be addressed during this segment.

For learners in the pre- and partial-alphabetic phases, the focus would be on helping children learn the names and most common sounds of individual letters and frequent consonant digraphs as well as the short sounds associated with vowel letters (as described in Chapters 6 and 7). Learning these grapheme–phoneme correspondences is supported by explicitly teaching key words and encouraging learners to reference them, as needed, when they can't recall the phoneme associated with particular graphemes (or, in the context of writing, the grapheme associated with a particular phoneme).

From the point at which letter sounds are first introduced, the major instructional activities involve word building—using movable letters/graphemes/morphemes, word reading—of words built by the teacher that focus on the same elements, and written spelling of words dictated by the teacher. We follow this word building–reading–writing sequence to encourage children to carefully attend to the phonic and orthographic elements under study and to help them gain a sense of mastery over these elements. The focus of these activities gradually increases the level of challenge encountered by learners. Common inflectional endings (i.e., *ed*, *ing*, *s,* or *es*) are introduced and practiced fairly early on because they come up early in the children's reading. For more advanced readers, this segment would also involve instruction on how to analyze, read, and spell words with more than one syllable including derivational morphemes (prefixes and suffixes).

Children at a beginning point in developing skills with the alphabetic code (those in the partial alphabetic phase) might first be asked to build words dictated by the teacher using a common rime and changing just the initial grapheme—for example, building *mat,* changing to *fat,* changing to *chat.* They would then read similar words built by the teacher and, afterward, write similar words. For learners moving from the partial to the full alphabetic phase, the focus would turn to instruction on building, reading, and spelling one-syllable short-vowel words, as described in Chapter 8. This would involve making changes to the beginnings and ends of one-syllable short-vowel words (e.g., making *lip,* changing to *lit* to *sit* to *sip* to *dip*). When students demonstrate skill with making changes in beginning and ending sounds, and once at least two short-vowel sounds have been explicitly taught, changes to medial sounds would be made as well (e.g., making *sit,* changing to *sat* to *bat* to *bit* to *hit* to *hat*).

As more short-vowel sounds are taught, they would be included in the building, reading, and writing activities (e.g., changing *sit* to *set* to *bet* to *bat* to *but* to *nut* to *net*). As learners demonstrate skill with changing just one phoneme at a time, they would be asked to make changes in multiple phonemes from one word to the next (e.g., making *bit*, changing to *cat* to *tap* to *net*).

Depending on the reading materials in use, children might also learn about orthographic word families, that is, words that share a common rime (as described in Chapter 9). In this case, once a new rime is introduced and practiced a little, previously taught rimes would be included in practice activities, as this encourages learners to more thoroughly attend to the spelling of the rime elements. For example, if the rimes *ight* and *all* had been taught, the word-building, word-reading, and written-spelling sequence might involve the words *night, fight, fall, tall, tight, bright*, and *ball*. (Note that the rimes for such an activity would be displayed on a single card.) Such a sequence requires learners to attend more carefully to the rime portion than they might if the rime didn't change from one word to the next (e.g., *night, fight, tight, sight, might*). As a result, learners are more likely to become sufficiently familiar with the rime to use it generatively in their reading and writing. To reinforce the utility of orthographic word families, teachers maintain a display containing the rimes that have been taught (see Figure 9.4, p. 224). Children are encouraged to refer to this display, as needed, when attempting to read and spell words that might belong to a particular family.

As learners continue to advance in their knowledge of the writing system, they would learn about more complex vowel spellings in this segment of the lesson— such as the silent-*e* generalization that often marks long-vowel sounds and decoding and spelling of vowel teams as described in Chapter 10. Learning about the more complex vowel spellings is especially useful in preparing learners to become fluent and flexible in decoding unfamiliar words encountered while reading increasingly challenging meaningful text. Flexibility with vowel sounds is important because every vowel letter commonly represents at least two vowel phonemes (the long and the short sounds), and because the pronunciation of vowel graphemes is substantially less reliable than the pronunciation of consonant graphemes. To promote this flexibility, once the long-vowel silent-*e* spelling has been introduced, practice activities involve building, reading, and written spelling of word sequences that involve changes between the long and short sounds. For example, learners might build words in the following sequence—*bit, bite, kite, kit, hit, him, dim, dime* (see Figure 10.4, pp. 245–246, for suggested word sequences).

Flexibility with vowel sounds is also useful when learners encounter words that do not follow the most common spelling patterns for long and short vowels— for example, in the words *give* and *cold* and for vowel teams that can be accurately decoded by trying different sounds for each letter in the team (e.g., *bead, head, break*). One word-solving strategy that is explicitly taught (as described in Chapter 12) encourages this flexibility: "Try different sounds for some of the letters, especially the vowels." This strategy would be applied in the context of reading meaningful text and can lead to more frequent accurate identification of unfamiliar words encountered in context.

This segment of the lesson also provides an opportunity to teach about ways to puzzle through words composed of more than one syllable and words composed of more than one morpheme, as described in Chapter 11. Some of these parts, such as past tense and plural endings, might be taught and practiced when children are at a fairly early point in development (partial and full alphabetic phases), as they tend to come up early in the texts children read. Chapter 11 also offers guidance on helping children to identify and spell words composed of more than one syllable.

Reading a New Book

Virtually all the instructional goals discussed in Chapters 3–16 can be addressed in this segment of a small-group lesson. However, in what follows, we focus especially on the word-solving/word-learning goal (Chapter 12) because, as we have emphasized frequently in this text, the vast majority of words that ultimately become part of a reader's sight vocabulary are not explicitly taught but, rather, are learned through effective word solving while reading meaningful text.

The language and meaning construction goals (Chapters 15 and 16) are also crucial in this segment of the lesson because new vocabulary and syntactic structures are apt to be encountered in new books. In addition, to check the accuracy of attempts to identify previously unfamiliar printed words, readers must attend to the meaning of the text they are reading to confirm that their attempted pronunciation is a real word that fits the context. If it is not, the reader should try different pronunciations for some of the letters/graphemes in an effort to settle on a real word that does fit the context. That is, when an attempt at a word does not result in a real word or a word that fits the context, it should prompt readers to draw on their set for variability—trying different pronunciations for some of the graphemes—especially the vowels. It is important to keep in mind, however, that it is really not possible to confirm a word's identity if the reader has never heard the word before. Although teachers may be able to anticipate and prepare learners for their encounters with unfamiliar words by explaining their meaning in advance of reading a text, it is likely that, at least on occasion, the lack of knowledge of word meanings will only become apparent when readers are unable to confirm that a word has been accurately pronounced (see the textbox).

Confirming the Identity of a Word for Which the Meaning Is Not Known

It is sometimes hard to anticipate which (spoken) words will not be in a learner's listening vocabulary. Therefore, it is important for teachers to be alert for occasions when learners signal uncertainty—which often occurs when the reader produces an accurate pronunciation of a word but with a rising intonation. As noted above, there is no way to confirm an accurate pronunciation if the meaning of the word is unknown. In such an instance, the teacher should step in, confirm the pronunciation (e.g., "Yes, that word is *bank*"), and offer a brief, context-specific definition (e.g., "The word *bank* has more than one meaning. Here *bank* means the edge of a river where the water and the land are touching. Read that sentence again and think about what the author is telling us.")

The word-identification strategies listed in Figure 12.2 (p. 306) are initially taught in preparation for reading a new book when readers have the foundational skills needed to utilize the strategy and when the new book/text presents opportunities to apply the strategy effectively.

When new strategies are taught, the teacher would employ a *gradual release of responsibility* process (Pearson & Gallagher, 1983) in which:

- The new strategy is explicitly explained.
- The use of the strategy is modeled by the teacher on multiple occasions as necessary—using a think-aloud procedure.
- Students have the opportunity to utilize/apply the strategy with teacher guidance and support.
- The teacher gradually reduces guidance and support as it becomes evident that students understand the application of the strategy.
- Students utilize the strategy with increasing independence across time and are periodically engaged in reflecting on the utility of the strategy and their effectiveness in employing it. This would occur especially early on when children begin to demonstrate independence in the application of particular strategies.

The new book segment of the lesson comprises three parts: before, during, and after reading.

BEFORE READING

Teachers are encouraged to select books that will provide children with some, but not too much, challenge. Reading books that are either too easy or too challenging will limit children's opportunity to be actively strategic and to receive guidance and feedback on their strategy use either because there will be too few words requiring word solving or so many that children will have limited ability to access the context needed to confirm attempts at word identification.

In selecting books, teachers who are using a familiar leveling system (such as Lexiles), as well as teachers using a sequenced core program, are encouraged to be mindful of the things that are not captured in the system or sequence that can make a book more or less challenging for particular children. These things include topical/background knowledge and interest in and motivation for learning about particular topics and, especially at early phases of reading development, the specific words and phonics elements that appear in the text.

Teachers are encouraged to thoughtfully prepare learners to read the text. The extent of preparation provided will impact the extent to which reading the new text will help to accomplish the instructional goals—especially the word-solving/word-learning goal. For example, if a teacher provides an extensive book introduction, including a detailed picture walk wherein successive pages are viewed and discussed, perhaps using some of the language in the book, the children may have little need of being strategic in relation to word solving while reading. Such conversations can lead readers to expect certain words and phrases and thereby require less interrogation of the print than might otherwise be the case. This may be all well and good if the goal is to help children to be fairly fluent on the first reading of the book. However, the potential downside is that, because the children will not need to look at the unfamiliar words thoroughly to puzzle them out, they may not store the words in memory with enough detail to make subsequent identification of the words, in other contexts, more certain and more automatic. As highlighted repeatedly throughout this book, the vast majority of words that become sight words for readers are learned in the context of reading meaningful text. Thus, careful analysis of unfamiliar printed words is an extremely important element of word learning. One of the most important purposes of small-group instruction, therefore, is to provide students with the instruction and support needed to engage in such analysis so that they will be prepared to engage in that analysis when reading independently. When children do not have the background knowledge, skills, and strategies needed to read a text they are, for some reason, expected to read, offering more thorough introductions to the text would, of course, be appropriate. In most contexts, however, we encourage teachers to offer a brief book introduction; to have already taught and provided practice with one or more of the decoding elements that will be useful in solving unfamiliar words in a given book; and, if need be, to explicitly teach and practice one or more new words that will be encountered in the book but that the children will be unable to solve given their current code-based skills and the available contextual supports. Caution regarding overly extensive book introductions applies to *meaning construction* as well: children will not have the need to "make sense" of what they read if the entire text has been discussed in detail prior to reading it.

Just before having learners begin to read the new book, the teacher would teach and/or revisit one or more of the word-solving strategies. Given that the ultimate goal is for children to internalize the strategies and to use them independently, teachers need to engage children in extensive amounts of strategy talk to support this development. For example, if most of the strategies have been explicitly taught but the children are not using them independently and reliably, the teacher might ask the children to name and discuss the strategies they can use to figure out a puzzling word. And/or the teacher might use a contrived bit of text to help children practice and discuss the usefulness of particular strategies (see the example of multiple strategy use in Chapter 12, p. 336).

When using such examples in preparation for reading a new text, particular emphasis would be placed on the decoding challenges that would be relatively novel for the students—for example, noticing and temporarily ignoring an affix or trying alternative pronunciations for some of the graphemes.

DURING READING

After all this preparation (which took much longer to describe than it would take to actually accomplish), the children would read the book, typically using a whisper voice—just loud enough for the teacher to hear, monitor, and, if need be, guide and support the word solving of individual readers. Sometimes children might read in pairs, coaching one another in the word-solving process by suggesting word-solving strategies that might help solve particular words. This useful practice helps children rehearse the strategies, making it more likely that the strategies will be available to them when they are reading on their own and when the strategy chart is not immediately available. The ultimate goal, of course, is to help children internalize the strategies and become automatic in their use and, therefore, no longer need to attend to the strategy chart and the icons that represent individual strategies.

The teacher's role as the children read is to scaffold their word-solving attempts, being careful to provide enough support so that readers are successful but not so much as to encourage heavy dependence on the teacher. This requires the teacher to consider the characteristics of the unfamiliar word, the supportiveness of the context, and the individual child's background knowledge, strategies, and decoding skills. Teachers encourage children to take responsibility for confirming that words have been accurately identified by checking whether the pronunciation settled upon based on the orthographic information provided in the printed word is a real word that makes sense in the context in which the word is encountered (recall Figure 12.1, p. 303). Also, as children read to the teacher or with one another, discussion of the meaning of the text should be encouraged. Because children at early points in learning to read need to devote substantial attention to the word-solving process, some of them will neglect thinking about the larger meaning of the text. Over time, this neglect may produce children who are competent with the word-reading aspect of reading but unable to comprehend the texts they read. As we've noted repeatedly, it is important that children are helped to view reading as a meaning-making enterprise from early on.

KEEP IN MIND Once word-solving strategies have been explicitly taught and practiced, the teacher's major role is to hand over responsibility for word solving to the children. See Table 12.3 (p. 341) for teacher moves that promote independence vs. dependence in word solving.

AFTER READING

The focus on meaning should continue as the children complete the book and share their thinking and what they learned, whether their initial thinking about what might happen matched the author's thinking, how they would have felt/reacted in situations described in the text, and so on. Meaning-focused conversations should not simply be "comprehension checks" but rather genuine conversations that convey to children that their thoughts matter and that different people may think about a given text in different ways. The intention is to build a foundation for the types of inferential and critical thinking about texts that will benefit children's comprehension as they encounter progressively more complex texts going forward.

After reading, teachers should also engage children in reflecting on the strategies they used and how well they worked. The purpose, here again, is to encourage children to view word solving as a strategic and useful process that is both doable and enjoyable. When children are routinely and effectively strategic in word solving, discussion of word-solving strategies before, during, and after reading can be gradually reduced and, ultimately, eliminated.

Writing

This segment of a small-group lesson addresses multiple instructional goals and may occur at different points in the lesson (e.g., immediately following the reading of any of the books read or at other points, depending on what is to be written). In support of comprehension and knowledge development, the writing segment often follows a reread or a new read and provides an opportunity for children to react in some way to text(s) read. In general, the writing segment does not have composition as one of its major objectives, but rather focuses on encoding oral language into print. To maintain a focus on encoding/spelling, teachers often construct or co-construct the message that will be captured in writing. Engaging children in writing also clearly helps to support multiple foundational skills that learners are developing. For example, in encouraging partial-alphabetic learners to write, teachers would draw children's attention to such things as the directionality of print, the concepts of letter and word, letter formation, and the function of spacing and common punctuation marks. For both partial- and full-alphabetic learners, the use of phonemic analysis to identify the phonemes in words and key words to select appropriate graphemes would come into play. For learners at the full and consolidated phases, segmenting multisyllabic words into their component syllables in preparing for spelling those syllables might also be addressed. For all learners for whom a "Words I/We Know" chart (see Figure 13.6, p. 371) has been developed, guidance in referencing that chart would also be addressed in the writing segment of the lesson. So too would encouragement to consult the books that were read for the book spellings of words used during writing.

As a portion of the writing that children do will occur somewhat independently (as the teacher's focus is on other children in the group), some of the children's writing will likely include (unconventional) sound spellings. Examination of these spellings can provide useful insights into the child's phonemic analysis skills (as illustrated in Table 5.1, pp. 128–130) as well as the skill with the alphabetic code and, thereby, inform future instruction. Understanding the origins of unconventional spellings and providing feedback on them, as described in Chapter 5 (pp. 126–130), can also help to move children forward.

High-Frequency Words

As noted in Chapter 13, the majority of words (approximately 70%) in any given text is composed of the 300 or so most frequently occurring words. Therefore, helping children learn these words to the point that they will be able to identify them automatically and in all contexts is extremely important to building reading proficiency. In small-group lessons, new high-frequency words are taught in preparation for reading new books in which they will be encountered as noted in the "Before Reading" discussion above. In the high-frequency word segment of a small-group lesson, the focus is on practicing and helping children to become automatic in identifying (and spelling) the accumulating set of high-frequency words that have been taught. This segment is a fairly short and playful part of a small-group lesson in which game-like activities that involve reading and written spelling of high-frequency words are employed. These activities are designed to help children attend to the internal structures of words and, therefore, help them to form stronger representations of those words in memory. For each small group or any student who is receiving one-to-one intervention, a "Words We/I Know" chart is developed that includes the words that the teacher believes the children can (should be able to) identify with some confidence. The chart can be used as a reference to enable conventional/book spelling of the words when children wish to use the words in their writing. An added value of the high-frequency word segment of the lesson is that, while some children can be set to playing a word game, the teacher may take the opportunity to work with one or more children in the group who need more individualized assistance with literacy learning. As noted in Chapter 13, some of the games used in the context of small-group instruction might also be used as center activities when children are not directly involved with the teacher.

Resources for Planning, Developing, and Documenting Small-Group Lessons

Lesson sheets to support planning, developing, and documenting students' performance during small-group lessons can be found on the book's companion website (see the box at the end of the table of contents). The website also provides guidance on the use of these forms. The lesson sheets included online are appropriate for use with students who are in the pre- and/or partial alphabetic (PPA) phases and with students in the full and/or consolidated alphabetic (FCA) phases of development. These tools are designed to help teachers provide instruction that is responsive to what children know and are able to do and that is consistent with the goals described throughout the text.

In addition, we provide a planning/reflection form in Figure 17.1 that is specifically focused on the portion of a small-group lesson involving children in reading a new book. This form was developed in response to teachers' observations that there are a lot of things to consider when engaging children in reading in this context. Teachers have found the form to be useful in reminding themselves of some of the guidance provided in this text relative to the interactions between students

(text resumes on p. 477)

TEACHER PLANNING AND REFLECTION FOR BEFORE, DURING AND AFTER READING A NEW BOOK IN A SMALL-GROUP LESSON

Before Reading	
Questions to Consider	**Thoughts and Plans**
Did I set a purpose (or help the students set a purpose) for reading the book and promote enthusiasm for reading?	
Did I choose a book that was at an appropriate level of challenge for the students in the group?	
Did I introduce and provide practice on one or two decoding elements that would be encountered in the text?	
Did I introduce and provide practice with a few high-frequency words that would be encountered in the text and that the students would be unlikely to figure out given their current skills and strategies?	
Did I provide a book introduction that made the text accessible to the students but still allowed opportunities for problem solving?	
Did I teach and/or review word-identification strategies that were appropriate for the children in the group?	
Did I discuss the meanings of important words for which the students might not know the meaning?	
During Reading	
Questions to Consider	**Thoughts and Plans**
Were the resources students might use during reading readily available (e.g., word wall or Words We Know chart, Bb/Dd chart, strategies chart, rime/word family list)?	

(continued)

FIGURE 17.1. Reflection form for ISA-supported reading of a new book.

Questions to Consider	Thoughts and Plans
Did the students approach reading as a meaning-making enterprise?	
Did the students rely too heavily on me when they encountered words they could not immediately identify?	
Did the students use both meaning-based and code-based strategies in mutually supportive ways?	
Was the support that I provided on puzzling words appropriate for these students at this point in time?	
When a student puzzled over a word, did I allow sufficient time before intervening?	
When students misidentified a word, did I wait for them to read far enough along to recognize that an error had occurred before I intervened?	
Was I careful to avoid confirming accurate word identification when individuals could do so on their own?	
Am I working toward encouraging independence in word solving?	
Do the students seem to construe word solving as "doable"?	
Was I careful not to take all the responsibility for noticing word-identification errors?	

(continued)

FIGURE 17.1. *(page 2 of 3)*

Questions to Consider	Thoughts and Plans
Did the students monitor their own comprehension?	
Was there sufficient conversation about the text to support and enhance the development of comprehension?	
Was meaning-focused discussion of the text collaborative and nonevaluative?	
Did the students enjoy their reading?	

After Reading	
Questions to Consider	**Thoughts and Plans**
Did the follow-up discussion initially focus on the meaning and enjoyment of the text?	
Did I help the children reflect on their word-solving strategies, and/or did the students do so spontaneously?	
Were the children able to articulate their word-solving strategies?	
What do I need to learn more about concerning the reading skills of these children?	
What knowledge or concepts do I see as needing attention?	

FIGURE 17.1. *(page 3 of 3)*

and the teacher during the book reading portion of a lesson. The form is worded as though it is completed following the lesson. Thus, it is identified as a *reflection form*. However, an important goal of the form is to provide teachers with a way to guide their thinking as they plan their lesson—thus the column entitled "Thoughts and Plans."

KEY POINTS OF THIS CHAPTER

✓ Small groups formed based on students' present levels of development across the foundational skills allow teachers to differentiate instruction based on students' current skills.

✓ Small-group lessons typically include five or six segments: rereading text(s), phonemic analysis, decoding and encoding, reading new text(s), writing, and high-frequency word practice. The phonemic analysis segment is dropped as a separate segment of the lesson when learners are able to connect phonemes to their written representations.

✓ Orthographic elements introduced and practiced during the decoding and encoding segment of the lesson should be selected based on the new text(s) that will be read during the lesson. Other elements that need additional practice can/should be included as well.

✓ Teachers should promote independence in the process of word solving/word learning by avoiding offering so much support that they limit the need for learners to be strategic.

✓ Text reading should always include attention to meaning construction and should be promoted through genuine conversations about what was read.

CHAPTER 18

Revisiting and Concluding

In concluding this text, we encourage teachers to revisit the discussion of the conceptual model of the reading and writing processes in Chapter 1 (beginning on p. 12) and to keep the complexity of the process of becoming literate in mind as they work with their young learners. Considering this complexity may help the teacher zero in on sources of difficulty for children who make limited progress. For example, when children don't understand the meaning of a passage, the reason could be that they were not motivated or were not sufficiently engaged.

Alternatively, the reason could be that they don't know the meanings of some of the important words in the passage or that the syntax was too unfamiliar; or it could be that the children don't have the requisite background knowledge and/or experience that the author of the text has taken for granted. Further, if children are reading rather than listening to the text, difficulties with comprehension could be due to their lack of experience with written language and/or skill with the orthography that they need to effectively puzzle through the unfamiliar words encountered. And, even if children do possess those skills, the unknown word may not be part of their listening/spoken vocabulary, and/or they may not have the language skills that would enable them to use sentence context to confirm that the word(s) have been accurately identified. The process is complex! In order to effectively guide young readers, the teacher needs to be mindful of all these possibilities (and more) to determine how to respond to difficulties.

General Principles for Early Literacy Instruction and Preventing Reading Difficulties

Following is a list of the principles for preventing reading difficulties that we discussed in some detail in Chapter 2. Here our goal is to remind readers of these principles and to discuss how the principles relate to one another and to the instructional goals more generally.

- Teach children to be effective and independent problem solvers.
- Ensure that students are actively engaged in learning.
- Strive to ensure culturally responsive and sustaining instruction.
- Set high expectations for all children.
- Integrate support services with the classroom program.
- Plan for success.
- Track student progress.

For the purpose of illustration, we consider how these principles apply in relation to comprehension and knowledge development, the central goal of reading and reading instruction. *Teaching children to be effective and independent problem solvers* relative to reading involves helping them to develop self-regulation skills. That involves helping them to realize when their comprehension has broken down; to understand that, when this happens, they must do something to resolve the problem; and to learn about and practice the kinds of things they might do to resolve their confusion. For example, their action could involve rereading and reading ahead in search of additional information, considering whether the words have been accurately identified, perhaps trying some alternative pronunciations, and so forth. In the context of listening to text read aloud, this would often involve asking a question. These are examples of the second principle listed above *ensuring that children are active and engaged learners*. To realize that their comprehension has broken down, children need to be really thinking about the text they are listening to or reading and they need to expect it to make sense.

In *striving to ensure culturally responsive and sustaining instruction*, teachers would offer texts that reflect the linguistic and cultural backgrounds of the students in the classroom and perhaps the school and larger community more generally. In discussions during and following listening to/reading a given text, students with knowledge of those backgrounds can help to enrich the comprehension of other students who don't share that background.

Teachers who *set high expectations* communicate their expectations in the texts they offer the children and in how they respond when students encounter difficulties. In the context of comprehension, if the teacher asks a question about a text that a child is unable to answer satisfactorily, a teacher who has high expectations for the child would explore the reasoning behind the child's response and perhaps spend some time guiding the child's thinking regarding the comprehension challenge posed. In contrast, a teacher with low expectations might simply move on to another child with the same question.

To *integrate support services with the classroom program*, classroom and intervention teachers would, ideally, share a common language in talking about certain comprehension processes (e.g., they might agree on talking about "visualizing" rather than "making a picture in your mind," or vice versa). *Planning for success*, in the context of comprehension and knowledge development, is largely about being thoughtful about the comprehension (and other types of) challenges a text will present. Teachers need to determine what can be done in advance of reading a text to increase the likelihood that children will understand it, while not doing so much preparation that the students do not need to actively engage in meaning construction. Here again, the principle of *ensuring culturally responsive and sustaining instruction* plays an important role. Depending on students' linguistic and cultural background, introductions to and discussions of texts need to be adjusted. The last of the principles listed, *track student progress*, is obviously related to a number of the other principles; it is critical, for example, in determining what aspects of comprehension need more thorough guidance (e.g., focusing on inference making, comprehension monitoring, etc.), as providing targeted instruction requires an understanding of where students are in relation to the learning objective.

There are numerous other ways in which abiding by the principles becomes mutually supportive toward the overarching goal of preventing reading difficulties. For example, by *teaching children to be effective, independent problem solvers*, we are essentially giving them the tools they need to grow as readers and writers; in this way, they are more likely to meet the *high expectations* we set for them and to be *active and engaged learners*. As another example, it is more likely that we will be able to teach children to be *active and independent problem solvers* if the *support services are integrated with the classroom program*. For instance, if teachers in support and intervention settings provide different guidance as to word solving and/or use different key words to remind students of grapheme–phoneme correspondences, children are less likely to become independent problem solvers, as they are receiving conflicting guidance. Students who are puzzling through words do not need the additional challenge of puzzling through conflicting guidance.

Of course, instruction can be guided by some of these principles and not others. For example, in conversations with teachers in our professional development offerings, we have frequently found that *support services are not integrated with the classroom program*. As a result, children receive very different and uncoordinated instruction in classroom and intervention settings. Research suggests, this will limit children's growth in literacy (e.g., Wonder-McDowell et al., 2011). It is also possible to be guided by a principle but in a less than productive way. For example, many schools have elected to *track student progress* in RTI implementation through frequent administration of measures of low-level skills (Scanlon et al., 2015). Among those measures are oral reading fluency measures, which provide little useful information to guide instruction (other than indicating that a child is or is not meeting grade-level expectations). As a result, teachers and children can lose time to assessment with no instructional benefit. This is a net loss for children. In contrast, in the ISA, we encourage teachers to *track progress* by documenting specific skills and developing abilities using snapshots that provide greater detail regarding what children know and are able to do, thereby providing information about what children are ready to learn next. This, in turn, enables teachers to *plan for success* as they know where students are in the learning process and where they need to go. And when that planning is successful and the children therefore experience a sense of success in their learning, this is likely to lead them to be *more engaged and active learners.*

Teachers as Reflective Practitioners

As we conclude this book, we wish to emphasize that one reason for revisiting the general principles is to encourage teachers to reflect on the instruction they provide on an ongoing basis and to consider whether and how they might want to modify their practices. In addition to the general principles discussed above, we have provided several resources throughout the text that may be useful tools for reflection. For example, Figure 1.2 (p. 12) portrays the complexity of the reading process and is intended to highlight the fact that comprehension and knowledge development is the central and ultimate goal of literacy instruction. Table 2.2 (pp. 46–49) illustrates how aspects of shared reading might be focused for children at different points along the continuum of literacy development. Table 2.3 (pp. 58–59) illustrates how small-group supported reading lessons would vary in relation to children's point in the development of literacy skills. Tables 3.1 and 3.2 (pp. 81–82) in the Motivation chapter offer examples of teacher responses to students' word-identification errors that are likely to have a positive impact on their sense of competence as readers—or not. Table 3.3 (p. 85) is intended to help teachers reflect on how comments they make to students may motivate their students' interest in literacy learning—or not.

In the introduction to Part II, Figure II.1 on p. 93 illustrates the progression that characterizes the development of skill with the English writing system. In addition, it is intended to highlight the importance of engaging children in reading and writing—even those at the preliterate/prealphabetic phase of development—for promoting literacy development. The decision tree provided in Figure II.2 on p. 100 is designed to help teachers consider appropriate next steps in instruction for children who demonstrate particular phonics skills. The figure also connects development of skill with the alphabetic code with the phonemic analysis skills that enable students to learn those skills. In addition, Figure II.2 connects the development of skill with the writing system with particular code-based word-solving strategies and the point at which children might be taught/expected to utilize them.

Figure 5.1 (p. 120) lists stretchable and stop consonant sounds. It is important for teachers of beginning readers to be thoughtful about how the use of stretchable phonemes (those that can be elongated without distortion) in early instruction makes it easier for children to isolate and focus on those phonemes. Figure 5.2 on p. 122 lists potentially confusable pairs of phonemes. Being aware of these sources of confusion can impact instructional decisions in various ways including how sound-sorting activities are constructed (by avoiding asking children to distinguish between confusable sounds early on) and how teachers provide feedback to children on their sound spellings (e.g., understanding why a child might use the letter *j* to represent the /ch/ sound). With regard to the latter point, Table 5.1 on pp. 128–130 provides more detail on what sound spellings reveal about a child's phonemic awareness and on how a teacher might respond to them.

As these examples show, the general point of the figures and tables in this book is to condense some of the detail presented in the narrative. Therefore, they may serve as useful tools for reflection—particularly for revisiting some of the concepts and details that were novel to readers when first encountered but that are relevant to the teacher's current teaching context.

Many of the goals chapters (Chapters 3–16) include *sample instructional dialogues* that may be helpful to teachers as they plan and reflect on how to teach particular skills, concepts, and strategies. Also, all the goals chapters include snapshots that, while presented as tools for documenting children's status and progress, can also serve as reflection forms for teachers even if teachers do not opt to use them as tools for documenting children's progress. Reflection on the snapshots can be useful as teachers consider whether they are addressing, or need to address, some of the skills, concepts, and dispositions listed. The reflection form provided in Figure 17.1 (pp. 474–476) is, of course, explicitly intended to support reflection on small-group supported reading lessons. Many teachers who have used the form in the past report that, while they may not routinely complete the form, they keep it available when they are planning lessons and they refer to it as needed—or, as some have reported, until they feel they have it internalized.

Finally, with regard to reflective teaching, the Key Points listed at the end of each chapter are intended to remind readers of some of the most important things discussed in the chapter and may lead them to revisit some of the content of the chapter.

Concluding Thoughts

Our goal in writing this book has been to share what has been learned about how to support children who are at early points in the literacy learning process, especially those who experience difficulty. The book focuses on a particular approach to early literacy instruction and intervention that we have found to be effective when implemented in intervention and classroom settings (Scanlon et al., 2005, 2008; Vellutino et al., 1996). In our studies, we focused on the critically important role of the teacher in identifying what children are ready to learn and in planning and delivering literacy instruction that will serve to move each individual forward. Because of the complexity of the reading process, and because each child brings a different mix of prior experiences and underlying aptitudes to the literacy learning context, teachers need a good deal of expertise to help all children succeed. In support of this perspective, our mantra across the last many years has become "Every child is ready to learn something, but they are not all ready to learn the same thing." Our job as educators is to figure out *what* individual children already know and what they are ready to learn next. Responsive instruction is key.

Glossary

Academic language	Language of the classroom or of schools; refers to the word-, sentence-, and discourse-level features commonly found in academic texts and discussions.
Academic vocabulary	Words that are commonly found in classrooms or academic texts, and are either discipline-specific (referring to only one academic discipline such as *hypotenuse* or *hibernation*) or general (referring to words such as *analyze* and *explain*) that are used across the disciplines.
Accuracy	Correct pronunciation of printed words.
Affix	Prefix- or suffix-bound morphemes that are added to base words.
Align/alignment	Correspondence among or agreement between instructional elements.
Alliteration	Repeated similar sounds at the beginning of words in a group or sentence (e.g., *big balloons bounce*).
Alphabetic code	The correspondence of phonemes (sounds) to graphemes (letters).
Alphabetic principle	The idea that the letters (graphemes) in printed words represent the sounds (phonemes) in spoken words.
Alphabetic processing	Use of individual graphemes to arrive at the pronunciation of an unfamiliar printed word.
Anaphor(a)	Use of a grammatical substitute, such as a pronoun, to refer to a word used earlier in a sentence or passage.
Articulatory feature	Characteristic of a speech sound based on its place or manner of articulation (e.g., voicing, position of the lips, tongue).
Attributions for success	Beliefs about the reasons for one's successful (or unsuccessful) performance (e.g., effort, ability, luck).

483

Author's chair   Opportunity for students to share their writing with classmates by reading it aloud.

Automatic/   Doing something quickly and effortlessly; for example, being able to
automaticity   immediately identify a word upon seeing it or spell it without hesitation.

Automatic phase   The last of Ehri's phases. The reader is largely fluent with identifying words and becomes more automatic with increased practice and exposure to diverse texts. Readers are considered "conventional."

Base word   An unbound morpheme that may stand alone. Note that unbound morphemes have often been referred to as *root* words. However, from a linguistics perspective, this term is inaccurate. (See the definition of *roots* below.)

Beginning reader/   Ehri's pre- to partial-alphabetic phase. Beginning readers (sometimes
emergent reader   referred to as emergent readers) have limited understanding of the role
(as used in this   played by print in the reading process. Beginning readers may know the
book)   names of few, if any, letters and have limited understanding of the most basic print conventions. When they attempt to read books intended for beginning readers, they rely primarily on the pictures and their memory of the text—if it has been read to them previously. They may or may not understand many other aspects of reading, such as that books tell stories and/or are sources of useful and interesting information.

Big book   A large book used in shared read-alouds with print large enough for the entire group to see with ease.

Blend (spoken   Say individual phonemes without pausing between them.
language)

Blend (written   A term sometimes used as a synonym for a consonant cluster. Examples
language)   include *st, bl,* and *fr.*

Blending   Putting sounds together (orally as in phonemic awareness tasks or with print when sounding out a word).

Book spelling   See *Conventional spelling.*

Bound morpheme   A unit of meaning (prefix or suffix) that is attached to a base word and that modifies the base word's meaning or role in a sentence. See also *Morpheme.*

Breve   A breve (pronounced brĕv) is a curved line above a vowel letter and is used to signal the short sound of a vowel letter (e.g., ă as in *apple).*

Buddy reading   Reading with a classmate or friend.

Centers   Classroom spaces designated for small-group, student-led engagements around literacy, science, social studies, or math. Students may be in centers, while teachers work directly with small groups.

Choral reading   A group of students simultaneously reading a text aloud at the same pace with similar intonation, typically led by or following a read-aloud by the teacher.

Coarticulation	The influence of the pronunciation of one phoneme on the sound of the phonemes that come before or after it due to the positions of the articulators (the mouth parts that move during pronunciation). Coarticulation makes it hard to identify individual phonemes that are coarticulated. For example, the sound of the phoneme associated with the letter *d* in a *dr* cluster is not discernible (*drop/jrop*).
Code-based information	The information in written materials provided by the graphemes and larger orthographic units that support the identification of an unfamiliar printed word.
Code-based strategy	A word-identification strategy that draws on alphabetic and orthographic information.
Coherence	Consistency in instructional guidance. Also, logical and consistent understanding of information presented in a text.
Comprehension	Occurs when the reader builds a mental representation of the texts they read (reading comprehension) or hear (listening comprehension) by drawing on what is stated in the text and their existing knowledge. See *Critical comprehension, Inferential comprehension,* and *Literal comprehension.*
Concept of letter	The understanding that a letter (grapheme) represents a sound in spoken language. Letters (graphemes) make up words.
Concept of word	The understanding that one spoken word aligns with one printed word (one-to-one match) and that letters (graphemes) make up words.
Concepts of print	Understanding that print is a form of communication, that it is composed of individual letters and groups of letters that form words, and that it is processed from left to right on a line and that multiple lines are processed from top to bottom of a page.
Confirm	To verify the accuracy of a printed word's identity/pronunciation.
Congruent instruction	Instruction across instructional contexts that works toward mutually supportive ends, such that students receiving specialized support outside of the classroom are receiving instruction that is aligned with classroom instruction. For example, the same key-word chart is used in all instructional settings (special education classrooms, general education classrooms, speech and language support, etc.).
Consolidated-alphabetic phase	Ehri's (2005/2014) term for the period of reading development wherein readers tend to rely less on individual grapheme–phoneme relations and more on larger orthographic "chunks" of print (syllables, prefixes and suffixes, rimes, and whole words). This is the phase just before a reader is considered to be in Ehri's final (automatic) phase. Readers may use analogy to recognize common patterns in words (e.g., using knowledge of the word *little* to identify the word *brittle).* They use various orthographic patterns to read words not seen before. The size of readers' sight word vocabularies grows substantially during this phase.
Consonant	A speech sound in which the air flow is momentarily stopped (e.g., /b/ and /k/) or partially obstructed (e.g., /f/ and /s/).

Consonant blend	Two or three consonant *phonemes* that occur together within a word or syllable in which each phoneme is at least somewhat discernible. (*Blend* and *cluster* are sometimes used interchangeably.)
Consonant cluster	Two or three consonant *letters* that occur adjacent to one another in a printed word or syllable, with each of the letters' sounds being at least somewhat discernible. (Blend and cluster are sometimes used interchangeably.)
Consonant digraph	Two consonant letters that together represent one phoneme (e.g., *ch*, *sh*, *th*).
Constrained skills	Skills that are learned over a relatively short time span and that are mastered by most students. In the context of literacy, the term is typically used in reference to decoding and encoding skills.
Context	Information provided in spoken or written text that helps to explain or verify information. For example, the context in which a written word appears can help the reader to determine whether a word has been accurately identified.
Continuant (consonant)	A consonant sound that can be elongated or stretched without distortion (e.g., the sounds for *f*, *m*, and *s*). Also referred to as a *stretchable consonant* in this text.
Conventional spelling	Also called *book spelling*. Accurate and traditional spelling.
Conventions of print	Print is used for communication and is read from left to right and from top to bottom, letters form words, there is one spoken word for each printed word (one-to-one match), punctuation conveys meaning within and across sentences, quotation marks denote speech, capitalization denotes proper nouns and the start of sentences. Knowledge of conventions of print facilitates reading.
Core vocabulary	The set of words that account for 90% of the words found in printed text (Hiebert et al., 2018).
Critical comprehension	Evaluating the information in the text relative to what it means to the reader and relative to the intentions, expertise, and/or perspective of the author.
Culturally responsive and sustaining instruction	Instruction that values students' home customs, beliefs, and language, for example, by inviting families in to share their traditions, languages, foods, and art, by offering books that represent diversity (and, when possible, having family members do read-alouds), and by allowing children to use their first language(s) in conversation and in writing.
CVC *words*	Words consisting of a consonant followed by a vowel letter representing a short-vowel sound and another consonant letter. Sometimes referred to as a syllable pattern.
CVCe *words*	Words consisting of a consonant, followed by a vowel letter representing its long-vowel sound, another consonant, and a final-*e*, which signals that the internal/first vowel will have its long sound.
Decode/decoding	Using the sounds of letters/graphemes and larger orthographic units to derive pronunciation of a word or nonsense word (for example, *frenick*).

Derivational morpheme	Prefixes or suffixes that change the part of speech or meaning of a base word. Examples include *un-, re-, -less, -ly*. See also *Morpheme*.
Developing reader (as used in this book)	Readers who have begun to learn something about the alphabet and the alphabetic principle (e.g., they know the names and sounds of most graphemes). When attempting to identify printed words, developing readers tend to rely on a combination of the alphabetic code and the context in which the word occurs, with the relative weight placed on one source of information, changing gradually from heavy reliance on context to greater reliance on the code. Developing readers may be able to identify many of the most frequently occurring words with relatively little effort.
Developmental spelling assessment	Assessment of knowledge of letter names, sounds, printing/formation, and learners' ability to apply letter–sound knowledge in encoding (spelling) attempts. Initial assessment of these early print-related skills can help to inform decision making for forming instructional groups of children who are at similar points in development.
Differentiated instruction	Instruction that is designed to meet the needs of each learner based on what the learner presently knows and is able to do.
Digraph	Two consonant letters that together represent one phoneme (e.g., *sh, ck, ph*). In some contexts, the term digraph is used to refer to vowel phonemes represented by two letters as well (e.g., *aw, oi*). In this text, we use the term *vowel team* to refer to such vowel combinations.
Diphthong	A vowel that changes sound quality due to changes in mouth position during pronunciation such as the long sound of a, the /ou/ in *shout*, and /oi/ in *toy*.
Disposition	Mindset or attitude about learning.
Ehri's phase theory	A theory that addresses how children develop word-reading proficiency. It includes prealphabetic, partial-alphabetic, full-alphabetic, consolidated-alphabetic, and automatic phases. (See p. 90.)
Elkonin boxes (sound squares/ boxes)	Boxes used to help students segment sounds in spoken words. Students move counters into empty squares/boxes to denote sounds in spoken words. Elkonin boxes may also be used for spelling tasks.
Embedded clause	A clause that modifies the noun that goes before it.
Encode	Writing, or translating oral language into written text.
Encoding	Translating words into their written representation (putting them into a written code).
English learner	A person who is learning English as an additional language.
Explicit instruction	Instruction that explains what is being learned, why it is useful/ important, and when/how the learner will use it. It involves presenting new information/concepts in small steps and providing guided practice with gradual release of responsibility (less guidance/support) as learners demonstrate increasing skill.
Extrinsic motivation	The desire to complete a task or goal for a reward (i.e., praise or something tangible).

Eye–voice span	The span of words between where the reader's eyes are focused and what the reader is reading/saying aloud. Readers with a broader eye–voice span are better able to apply more appropriate intonation and phrasing when reading aloud.
Feedback	Information about an action or process provided to a learner with the goal of improving performance or recognizing accomplishment.
Fiction	Stories that are at least partly imaginary, usually with characters, setting, and a plot.
Finger-point reading	Tracking text with one's finger while reading; pointing to each word consecutively as it is read.
Floss rule	Guidance for reminding children to double the final consonant in one-syllable short-vowel words ending in *f, l,* or *s* (the word *floss* contains these letters, hence the name). There are some exceptions to this rule (e.g., *gas* and *bus*).
Fluency	Accurate and quick reading of a text where words are grouped into meaningful phrases and read with appropriate intonation.
Foundational skills	Phonemic awareness/analysis, phonics, and high-frequency words.
Free morpheme	A morpheme that may stand alone; also called a base word.
Full-alphabetic phase	Ehri's (2005/2014) term for readers who have relatively complete alphabetic knowledge and are able to use grapheme–phoneme relationships in conjunction with contextual information to identify and confirm the identity of printed words that are initially unfamiliar to them. Reading in this phase is typically slow and requires substantial effort as readers tend to have relatively small numbers of words they can identify automatically and are not yet fluent with using grapheme–phoneme relationships for the purpose of word identification.
Genre	A category of text, such as fiction or nonfiction.
Gradual release of responsibility	The gradual removal of scaffolds or supports as learners' skills increase and thus allows them to become more independent learners.
Grammar/ grammatical	The structure of language that includes syntax, morphology, semantics and phonology. The term *grammatical* typically refers to following the rules of a language that govern the structure of sentences.
Grapheme	One to three letters that represent an individual phoneme (e.g., *t, sh, igh*).
Grapheme– phoneme association/ correspondence/ relationships	Also known as the alphabetic principle. Letters (graphemes) represent the sounds (phonemes) in spoken language.
High-frequency words	Words that occur with a high rate of frequency in print and spoken language. The 300 most frequently occurring words make up approximately 70% of any written text.

Independent reading	Reading alone without support. Students reading at an independent level can accurately identify approximately 95% or more of the words in the text and demonstrate strong comprehension. *Independent reading* is sometimes used to describe situations in which children read by themselves—without necessarily involving knowledge of the child's accuracy or comprehension.
Inferencing skills	Skills that allow the reader to bridge the information directly stated in the text with information that the reader already possesses. Effective readers draw on their knowledge to make inferences that fill in the gaps left by the author.
Inferential comprehension	Making inferences that bridge the information directly stated in the text with information the reader already possesses.
Inflectional morpheme	Suffixes that change the grammatical role of the word such as plural and tense markers, but do not change the word's part of speech or meaning. See also *Morpheme*.
Informational texts	Nonfiction texts that are intended to inform the reader about the natural and social world. These include biographies, encyclopedias, and other types of text that are assumed to provide accurate information about science and history and are intended to educate or inform.
Inhibitory control	The ability to inhibit (or stop) a dominant response in favor of a nondominant response. For example, the reader at an early point in development may be inclined to use the pictures to tell a story and must exhibit inhibitory control to read the print instead.
Interactive read-aloud	A read-aloud that includes extensive interaction between the teacher, who is reading the text aloud, and the students. The conversation is not all directed by the teacher, and includes rich conversations among the participants.
Interactive strategies	Code- and meaning-focused strategies used together for puzzling through unfamiliar printed words encountered while reading.
Intervention	Additional instructional supports.
Intonation	The rise and fall of one's voice while reading aloud.
Intrinsic motivation	The desire to complete a task because it is interesting or meaningful, not for an external reward. Intrinsically motivated learning tends to be more lasting.
Invented/ inventive spelling	See *Sound spelling*.
Justifiable letter	A letter that is a reasonable, but not necessarily an accurate, representation of a spoken sound. For example, spelling the short-*e* sound with the letter *a*.
Key word	A word associated with a picture intended to help children remember grapheme–phoneme relationships. For example, a picture of an apple to help children remember the short sound of the letter *a* or a picture of a chair to help them remember the sound of the *ch* digraph.

Key-word chart	Visual representations of mnemonics (key words) that help children remember grapheme–phoneme relationships.
Language experience chart (approach)	A text constructed collaboratively by teachers and children that typically captures some shared experience. Depending on children's point in development, teachers may engage the children in learning letter names and sounds, basic print conventions, meaning construction, and the like during the process of constructing the written message.
Language register	Setting-specific ways of using language. For example, how one speaks to friends may differ from how one speaks to teachers.
Letter formation	Printing letters.
Letter identification	The ability to name a printed letter. In an assessment context, the child is shown a letter and is asked to name it. The teacher notes whether the response is correct and, if so, whether it is fast (no hesitation).
Letter naming	Saying the name of the letter when presented with the grapheme in print.
Letter of the week	An instructional method in which students are taught one letter of the alphabet per week (its name, form, and sound, sometimes with the letters being presented in alphabetical order). This once common approach is no longer recommended.
Letter production	The child is asked to print the letter named by the teacher, and/or the teacher observes the child's printed messages to determine whether further guidance on letter-formation/production is called for.
Letter recognition	In an assessment context, the child is shown a small group of letters and is asked to point to the one named by the teacher. In an instructional context, children may be asked to find individual letters in meaningful text. The terms letter recognition and letter identification are used interchangeably in some contexts, in which case letter recognition is synonymous with letter identification.
Letter reversals/ confusions	Children sometimes confuse similar looking letters (e.g., *b* and *d*, *p* and *q*). This is not a problem with visual perception. Rather, it is due to not recalling the correct label for letters that differ only by their orientations.
Letter slide	A teacher-created instructional tool used to practice decoding skills. (See pp. 204–205.)
Letter–sound association	Grapheme–phoneme relation. Each letter (grapheme) represents one or more sounds (phonemes). The letter (grapheme) is a symbol of the sound (phoneme).
Lexicon	The body of words for which one knows the meaning. This is sometimes referred to as one's mental lexicon.
Linguistic diversity	Differences in language use (multiple languages, accents, dialects, or registers).
Linguistic register	Patterns of language content and form used in different social contexts.
Literal comprehension	Understanding the information stated directly in the text.

Long vowel (sound)	A vowel phoneme that is the same as the vowel letter's name. Letter digraphs and trigraphs can also sometimes represent long-vowel phonemes (e.g., *ay, igh*).
Lower-case letter	Shorter, smaller versions of letters that can be contrasted with larger, taller versions of letters (upper-case letters). For some letters, the lower- and upper-case versions of the letter look identical (or nearly so) (e.g., *Cc, Oo, Zz*). For other letters, the upper- and lower-case versions are quite different (e.g., *Aa, Ee, Gg*).
Macron	A macron (a straight line above a vowel letter [e.g., *ā*]) is used to signal the long sound of a vowel (as in *make*).
Maturing reader (as used in this book)	See *Full-alphabetic phase.*
Meaning-based information	Information provided by the context (including the phrase, sentence, and/or picture) which may support identification of an unfamiliar printed word.
Meaning construction	Building understanding or comprehension of texts read or heard.
Meaningful text	Written text that is meaningfully organized, generally composed of full sentences.
Meta-analysis	An analysis of multiple studies in an effort to provide more generalizable results than can be provided by one or only a few studies.
Mnemonic	A device to help remember information, for example, providing a key word to help link the letter sounds to letter names.
Morning meeting/ message	A time in the daily schedule when teachers bring the whole class together and outline the day. Teachers use this period to address literacy and other academic goals in many different ways (calendar, weather, jointly constructing a written message, etc.).
Morpheme	A unit of meaning (e.g., base word, prefix, suffix). There are two types of morphemes. Free morphemes can stand alone (e.g., base words such as *car, bus, run*), whereas bound morphemes must be attached to base words (e.g., prefixes and suffixes). Bound morphemes include inflectional morphemes (suffixes that change the grammatical role of the word such as plurals and tense markers, but do not change the word's part of speech or meaning) and derivational morphemes (prefixes or suffixes that change the part of speech or meaning such as *un-, re-, -less, -ly*).
Morphology	The study of words, how they are formed, and their relationship to other words in the same language.
Motivation	What gets one going, keeps one engaged, and moves one forward in any task that requires effort.
MTSS	See *Multi-tiered systems of support.*
Multilingual(ism)	Proficiency in multiple languages or a person who uses multiple languages to communicate (e.g., Mandarin and English).

Multi-tiered systems of support	An approach to responding to the needs of learners who experience academic and/or behavioral difficulties. It incorporates response to intervention's (RTI) focus on instructional concerns but takes a broader approach by attending to a greater range of factors (especially behavioral factors) that may be impacting children's ability to learn.
Nasal consonant	The sounds for *m, n,* and *ng* (which is a single phoneme) are nasal in that, when pronouncing the sound, the air flows through the nose (nasal passage) instead of the mouth.
Nonfiction text	Informational text designed to inform or instruct such as a biography, textbook, or encyclopedia or other forms of informational texts.
Nonsense word	Also called a pseudoword. Sometimes used to determine a child's ability to use decoding skills to read unfamiliar words.
Odd-one-out sorting	A phonemic awareness activity. In this activity, children are presented with groups of pictures, one group at a time. In each group, all of the pictures except one have the same sound in a specified part of the word. The children are asked to figure out which word doesn't have the same sound (does not belong).
Onset	The part of a syllable that comes before the vowel. For example, the onset in *pat* is /p/. Lunchbox has two onsets /l/ and /b/. Some words have no onset (e.g., *egg, ant*).
Oral reading fluency (ORF)	The calculation of the number of words read correctly per minute (WCPM), while a student reads text written at the student's grade level. Ideally, assessment of fluency would include measures of intonation and phrasing.
Orthographic mapping	Connecting a printed word's spelling, pronunciation, and meaning.
Orthographic processing	The use of familiar letter patterns to arrive at the pronunciation and spelling of initially unfamiliar words.
Orthographic unit	Letters of the alphabet (graphemes), or larger spelling patterns such as rimes.
Orthography	The conventional spelling system of a language.
Partial-alphabetic phase	Ehri's second phase of development (see *Ehri's phase theory*). Readers in this phase use partial or incomplete knowledge of letters and their sounds to puzzle through and attempt to identify printed words. Readers may attempt a word after identifying prominent letters (first and/or last, typically). Readers in this phase are not yet using all available alphabetic information to identify unknown words. The context in which a word appears, in this and the prior (prealphabetic) phase, can enable accurate word identification despite only partial (or almost no) alphabetically based analysis.
Passive voice	A sentence construction in which the subject has the action done to it (e.g., the paper was written).

Patterned text	Texts with a repeated pattern—generally across pages (e.g., "I see a house," "I see a flower," "I see a swing," "I see a boy"). In such texts, the pictures support the identification of the final word in each sentence. Also referred to as *predictable texts*.
Phoneme	The smallest unit of sound that distinguishes between words.
Phoneme blending	The teacher articulates/says individual sounds in words, and children blend the sounds together and say the whole word. Phoneme blending is also involved in efforts to identify unfamiliar printed words.
Phoneme segmentation	Separating a spoken word into its component phonemes. Phoneme segmentation is also involved in working out the spellings of words that have not been committed to memory.
Phonemic analysis	Analyzing spoken words to identify/isolate the individual sounds.
Phonemic awareness	Being aware that spoken words are composed of somewhat separable sounds and being able to manipulate those sounds. This includes sorting words by sound similarity, blending individual phonemes/sounds to form whole words, and segmenting (separating) the phonemes/sounds in spoken words.
Phonics	Learning the relationships between graphemes (letters) and their associated sounds/phonemes and between larger spelling patterns, such as rimes, and their pronunciation.
Phonogram	In some contexts, the term *phonogram* is used as a synonym for grapheme (the letter or letters that represent a single phoneme). In other contexts, the term *phonogram* is used as a synonym of rime—the vowel and what comes after it in a syllable.
Phonological awareness	The ability to analyze and manipulate the sounds in spoken words (onsets, rimes, syllables, and phonemes). Phonological awareness is an umbrella term that includes phonemic awareness as well as the ability to attend to larger units of sound—such as being able to identify rhyming words.
Phonological skills	Understanding and use of phonological elements (e.g., onset, rime, syllable, phoneme) in both their spoken and written form.
Phrasing	During oral reading, an effective reader pauses at logical places in a way that effectively conveys the author's meaning. Some readers have to pay so much attention to identifying individual words that they are unable to apply appropriate phrasing.
Prealphabetic phase	In the first of Ehri's phases, beginning readers use cues other than letters or words to "read." Often called emergent or pretend reading, this phase involves the use of visual cues such as illustrations, as well as familiarity with the text from having previously heard the text read aloud to retell the content. Learners may also identify individual written words by relying on the overall visual form of the words (see selective cues) but do not focus on individual letters or their associated sounds.

Predictable text (book)	See *Patterned text.*
Prefix	A bound morpheme that comes before the base word (*un-, re-, dis-*). See *Morpheme.*
Print concepts	See *Concepts of print.*
Print conventions	See *Conventions of print.*
Proficient reader (as used in this book)	A reader who is able to quickly analyze and identify unfamiliar words, even those that are composed of multiple syllables. Part of these readers' efficiency can be attributed to their strong *orthographic processing* skills, which have enabled them to store many larger orthographic units (e.g., *-tion, re-, -ly, -ing*) in memory. Thus, although they do not necessarily know how to read all of the printed words they encounter, they figure them out so quickly that they sound fluent. Proficient readers are able to devote virtually all of their thinking to interpreting and responding to the texts as they read. See also *Automatic phase.*
Progress monitoring	Regular assessment to determine whether students are making sufficient and expected growth. Assessment may be formal (quizzes) or informal (observations). In the primary grades, oral reading fluency measures are a common form of progress monitoring. The individual snapshots associated with the goals chapters of this book can also serve this purpose (see the online supplement).
Prosody/prosodic reading	"Reading texts with greater range and variation in pitch, grouping words into meaningful units or pausing at grammatically relevant junctures, and pausing for appropriate durations" (Kim et al., 2021, p. 719).
Pseudoword	See *Nonsense word.*
Purposes of print	Understanding that the purpose of print is to communicate; it can be used to tell stories and learn information, and it can be read or written.
Puzzle/puzzling	Determining the identity of an unfamiliar printed word by utilizing code-based strategies to arrive at a hypothesis about what a word is and then confirming (or disconfirming) by checking whether the word makes sense in the context in which it is encountered.
r-controlled vowel	Vowels that are influenced by the letter *r* that immediately follows them (*ar, er, ir, or, ur*). Neither the short nor long sound of the vowel can be distinctly heard.
Read-aloud	The teacher reads a text aloud to students.
Reading rope	Scarborough's (2001) effort to "unpack" the two major factors in Gough and Tunmer's (1986) simple view of reading (SVR) model. (See *Simple view of reading.*) It carries over the two major contributing factors in the SVR and unpacks each factor (see pp. 7–8).
Reliability	A statistical indicator of how consistently an assessment (measure) provides similar results across multiple administrations.

Response to intervention (RTI)	The process of identifying children who appear to be at risk of experiencing learning difficulties (ideally early in their schooling) to begin intervention in efforts to ameliorate those difficulties through a tiered system of supports. As commonly implemented, Tier 1 typically involves the core curriculum that meets the needs of at least 80% of students, Tier 2 provides additional support for those not making sufficient progress. Tier 3 provides intensive support, frequently through special education, for those not making sufficient progress with Tier 1 and Tier 2 supports. In the ISA, in the primary grades, we advocate providing intensive support (Tier 3) without necessarily concluding that a learner should be identified for special education services.
Responsive instruction	Instruction or teaching that targets a child's specific areas of need based on what the child presently knows and is able to do.
Rime	The vowel and what comes after it in a syllable (e.g., *ild*, *ap*, *ing*). The rime in *child* is *ild*. The word *children* has two rimes: *ild* and *en*.
Root	A meaningful part of a word that is not a stand-alone word. For example, the root *tele* (meaning distant) as in *tele*phone and *tele*vision and the root *vis* as in *vis*ion and *vis*able.
	The term *root word* has often been used instructionally to refer to *base* words (see entry of base word above). However, linguists consider this usage to be inaccurate.
Scaffold(ing)	The provision of various types of support that allow children to successfully accomplish a task that is too challenging for them to accomplish on their own.
Schema	A pattern of thought that organizes categories of information and the relationships among them. A schema is what the reader knows about a topic (prior knowledge) and enables the reader to more readily learn more about that topic.
Schwa sound	A vowel sound that is neither long nor short. It can be represented by any of the vowel letters and most typically occurs in unstressed syllables of multisyllabic words. Examples include the first vowel sound in the words *oven, balloon,* and *about* and the second vowel sound in the words *problem* and *pedal*.
Segmentation (phoneme)	See *Phoneme segmentation.*
Selective cue	Nonalphabetic sources of information (cues) used by prealphabetic/emergent readers to identify printed words. For example, a child may rely on the overall shape of the printed word or identify the word *yellow* by attending to the two "sticks" in the middle.
Self-regulation	The ability to independently notice and at least attempt to solve problems in social and cognitive contexts. In the context of reading, the reader uses self-regulation to solve word-identification and/or comprehension problems by noticing the issue and independently attempting to resolve the issue through strategy use.

Self-teaching	The ability to independently translate unfamiliar printed words into their spoken equivalents (Share, 1995) through the use of word-solving strategies.
Sense of efficacy	Self-confidence or the perceived capabilities for learning or performing actions at designated levels.
Set for variability	The ability to be flexible in decoding vowel and consonant sounds when a first attempt doesn't result in a real word that fits the context.
Shared reading	The teacher and student(s) reading a text aloud together.
Shared writing	The teacher and student(s) writing a text together.
Short vowel (sound)	The most common sound for a vowel letter—not the letter's name.
Side-by-side instruction	The teacher sitting next to the student to provide differentiated instruction that meets the student's needs.
Sight vocabulary	All the words a reader can effortlessly, immediately, and accurately identify on sight.
Sight word	A word the reader can effortlessly, immediately, and accurately identify upon sight in and out of context.
Simple view of reading (SVR)	The theory that reading comprehension (RC) is the product of listening/language comprehension (LC) and decoding (DC). This view is represented in the formula RC= LC × DC (Gough & Tunmer, 1986).
Sorting board	Charts that contain two or three columns, each headed by a picture that begins (ends, etc.) with a different sound. The children are then given a packet of pictures that have the same beginning (ending, etc.) sound as one of the pictures heading a column. One by one, children then place the pictures with the same sounds in the appropriate column. Letters rather than pictures may also be used as column headers when children are learning about letter–sound correspondences.
Sound spelling	The process of spelling words by analyzing the component phonemes/sounds and representing those sounds with letter(s). Such spellings are often unconventional. This process is often referred to as invented/inventive spelling. However, the term *sound spelling* is preferred as it conveys to children and their families what the process entails.
Spelling pattern	Two or more letters that are taught as orthographic units. These might include digraphs (e.g., th, ch), rimes (e.g., ight, ake), or common syllables (e.g., tion, ture).
Statistical learning	The process by which learners, through multiple encounters with given examples, learn patterns that are not explicitly taught. For example, they learn acceptable sequences for words in spoken sentences and aspects of printed language that help them derive acceptable versus unacceptable spellings. For instance, learners come to know that doubled consonants are, with rare exceptions, not acceptable at the beginning of printed English words. (See discussion on p. 96.)

Stop consonant/ phoneme	A phoneme that, when pronounced, cannot be elongated without distortion. The airflow is "stopped" or blocked by the closure of various parts of the vocal apparatus. Examples include the sounds for the letters b, k, and t.
Story grammar	A common structure of a narrative text in which the author provides information about the setting, the characters, one or more problems, the characters' attempts to solve the problem(s), and the resolution(s). An understanding of story grammar can enhance students' comprehension of narrative texts.
Strategy	A purposeful plan of action used to achieve a desired goal or outcome that can be applied across multiple contexts.
Stretchable sound/phoneme	A phoneme that, when pronounced in isolation, can be elongated without distortion. Also called a continuous or continuant phoneme. Examples include the sounds for f, m, and s.
Suffix	A bound morpheme that follows a base word *(e.g., -ed, -ly, -ness)*.
Supported reading lesson	A small-group or a one-to-one reading lesson that is carefully planned by the teacher to be responsive to children's current instructional needs. For small-group lessons, children with similar skills are grouped together. During the lesson, the teacher provides the level of support needed by the student(s) and notes areas of strength and needed foci for upcoming lessons.
Syllable	A unit of pronunciation having one vowel sound. Consonant sounds may or may not be included.
Syntax	The manner in which sentences and phrases are constructed from words.
Think-aloud	An instructional strategy through which teachers talk about their thinking as they demonstrate their approach to solving a cognitive problem. The purpose of thinking aloud is to help children learn about problem-solving processes.
Translanguaging	When speakers draw from all of their linguistic resources (multiple languages or ways of speaking) to create meaning.
Trigraph	Three letters that together represent one phoneme (e.g., *igh, tch, dge*).
Unvoiced phoneme	Phonemes for which the vocal cords do not vibrate during pronunciation (e.g., /p/, /t/, /f/).
Upper-case letter	Bigger, taller versions of letters. Also called capital letters. Their form may or may not be different from their lower-case counterparts (e.g., Bb, Ff, Pp, Ss).
Voiced phoneme	A sound (phoneme) that when produced involves the vibration of the vocal cords (e.g., /b/, /d/, /v/, /g/).
Vowel flexing	Trying out the different sounds for the vowel when decoding words (e.g., short, long, schwa) and alternative pronunciations for vowel teams such as *ow* and *oo*.

Vowel team	Two or three letters that together represent one vowel phoneme. The following are examples of vowel teams: *ai, ea, igh, oy, aw.*
Wide reading	Reading beyond what is explicitly required or assigned by the teacher—typically reading from a broad variety of texts to promote comprehension, knowledge development, and fluency.
Word building	Making words using movable letters/graphemes.
Word family chart	A chart depicting the rime portions of word families that have been explicitly taught.
Word family (morphological)	A group of words that share a common base (e.g., *do, doing, doable, undo*).
Word family (orthographic)	A group of (one-syllable) words that share a common rime (e.g., *sight, right, light, bright*).
Word identification/ solving strategies	Code- and meaning-focused strategies used for puzzling through unfamiliar words encountered in the context of meaningful text. (See Figure 12.2, p. 306.)
Word solving	Puzzling through a word by using code and meaning-based strategies in interactive and confirmatory ways.
Word wall/Words We Know chart	A display of high-frequency words that students are expected to know. The words are arranged alphabetically by first letter. Students are expected to spell the words conventionally when the chart is available for reference.
Zone of proximal development (ZPD)	What a learner is able to do with support or scaffolding from a more expert other. The zone of proximal development is just beyond what the learner can do independently.

References

Adams, M. J. (1990). *Beginning to read: Thinking and learning about print.* Cambridge, MA: MIT Press.

Afflerbach, P. (2022). *Teaching readers (not reading).* New York: Guilford Press.

Al Otaiba, S., Connor, C. M., Folsom, J. S., Wanzek, J., Greulich, L., & Wagner, R. K. (2014). To wait in Tier 1 or intervene immediately: A randomized experiment examining first-grade Response to Intervention in reading. *Exceptional Children, 81*(1), 11–27.

Allington, R. L., & Johnston, P. (1989). Coordination, collaboration, and consistency: The redesign of compensatory and special education interventions. In R. Slavin, N. Karweit, & N. Madden (Eds.), *Effective programs for students at risk* (pp. 220–263). Boston: Allyn & Bacon.

Allington, R. L., & McGill-Franzen, A. (2013). Summer reading loss. In R. L. Allington & A. McGill-Franzen (Eds.), *Summer reading: Closing the rich/poor reading achievement gap* (pp. 1–19). New York: Teachers College Press.

Allington, R. L., & McGill-Franzen, A. M. (2021). Reading volume and reading achievement: A review of recent research. *Reading Research Quarterly, 56*(1), S231–S238.

Allington, R. L., McGill-Franzen, A., Camilli, G., Williams, L., Graff, J., Zeig, J., . . . Nowak, R. (2010). Addressing summer reading setback among economically disadvantaged elementary students. *Reading Psychology, 31*(5), 411–427.

Amendum, S. J., Conradi, K., & Hiebert, E. (2018). Does text complexity matter in the elementary grades? A research synthesis of text difficulty and elementary students' reading fluency and comprehension. *Educational Psychology Review, 30*, 121–151.

Andersen, S. C., & Nielsen, H. S. (2016). Reading intervention with a growth mindset approach improves children's skills. *Proceedings of the National Academy of Sciences of the United States of America, 113*(43), 12111–12113.

Anderson, K. L. (2009). *The effects of professional development on early reading skills: A comparison of two approaches* (doctoral dissertation). Retrieved from ProQuest (ATT 3365837).

Anderson, K. L. (2023). Explicitly teach word solving strategies. *Literacy Today Magazine, January/February/March,* pp. 12–13.

Anderson, K. L., & Scanlon, D. M. (2020). The development of sight vocabulary. *The Reading Teacher, 74*(3), 346–352.

Anderson, R. C. (1984). The role of readers' schema in comprehension, learning, and memory. In R. C. Anderson, J. Osborn, & R. Tierney (Eds.), *Learning to read in American schools: Basal readers and content texts* (pp. 243–257). Hillsdale, NJ: Erlbaum.

Anderson, R. C., Chinn, C., Waggoner, M., & Nguyen, K. (1998). Intellectually stimulating story discussions. In J. Osborn & F. Lehr (Eds.), *Literacy for all: Issues in teaching and learning* (pp. 170–186). New York: Guilford Press.

Anderson, R. C., & Freebody, P. (1981). Vocabulary knowledge. In J. T. Guthrie (Ed.), *Comprehension and teaching: Research reviews* (pp. 77–117). Newark, DE: International Reading Association.

Anderson, R. C., & Pearson, P. D. (1984). A schema-theoretic view of basic processes in reading. In P. D. Pearson (Ed.), *Handbook of reading research* (pp. 255–291). New York: Longman.

Apel, K., Brimo, D., Diehm, E., & Apel, L. (2013). Morphological awareness intervention with kindergartners and first- and second-grade students from low socioeconomic status homes: A feasibility study. *Language, Speech, and Hearing Services in Schools, 44*, 161–173.

August, D., & Shanahan, T. (Eds.). (2006). *Developing literacy in second-language learners: Report of the National Literacy Panel on Language-Minority Children and Youth*. Mahwah, NJ: Erlbaum.

Baker, L., & Beall, L. C. (2009). Metacognitive processes and reading comprehension. In S. E. D. Israel (Ed.), *Handbook of research on reading comprehension* (pp. 373–388). New York: Routledge.

Ball, E., & Blachman, B. (1991). Does phoneme awareness training in kindergarten make a difference in early word recognition and developmental spelling? *Reading Research Quarterly, 26*(1), 49–66.

Balu, R., Zhu, P., Doolittle, F., Schiller, E., Jenkins, J., & Gersten, R. (2015). *Evaluation of response to intervention practices for elementary school reading*. Washington, DC: U.S. Department of Education, Institute of Education Sciences. Retrieved from *https://files. eric.ed.gov/fulltext/ED560820.pdf*.

Bandura, A. (1997). *Self-efficacy: The exercise of control*. New York: Freeman.

Barnes, E. M., Grifenhagen, J. F., & Dickinson, D. K. (2020). Mealtimes in Head Start prekindergarten classrooms: Examining language-promoting opportunities in a hybrid space. *Journal of Child Language, 47*(2), 337–357.

Barnes, E. M., Grifenhagen, J. F., & Dickinson, D. K. (2021). *From words to wisdom: Supporting academic language use in PreK–3rd grade*. New York: Teachers College Press.

Barnes, E. M., & Hadley, E. B. (2022). Participants, purpose, place: Planning for content-area talk. *The Reading Teacher, 76*(1), 14–22.

Bear, D. R., Invernizzi, M., Templeton, S., & Johnston, F. (2019). *Words their way: Word study for phonics, vocabulary, and spelling instruction* (6th ed.). Upper Saddle River, NJ: Prentice-Hall.

Beck, I. L., & McKeown, M. G. (2001). Text talk: Capturing the benefits of read-aloud experiences for young children. *The Reading Teacher, 55*, 10–20.

Beck, I. L., & McKeown, M. G. (2007). Increasing young low-income children's oral vocabulary repertoires through rich and focused instruction. *Elementary School Journal, 107*(3), 251–271.

Beck, I. L., McKeown, M. G., & Kucan, L. (2002). *Bringing words to life: Robust vocabulary instruction*. New York: Guilford Press.

Beck, I. L., McKeown, M. G., & Kucan, L. (2013). *Bringing words to life: Robust vocabulary instruction* (2nd ed.). New York: Guilford Press.

Berenhaus, M., Oakhill, J., & Rusted, J. (2015). When kids act out: A comparison of embodied methods to improve children's memory for a story. *Journal of Research in Reading, 38*(4), 331–343.

Bergelson, E. (2020). The comprehension boost in early word learning: Older infants are better learners. *Child Development Perspectives, 14*(3), 142–149.

Berko, J. (1958). The child's learning of English morphology. *Word, 14*, 150–217.

Berninger, V. W., Abbott, R. D., Nagy, W., & Carlisle, J. (2010). Growth in phonological, orthographic, and morphological awareness in grades 1 to 6. *Journal of Psycholinguistic Research, 39*, 141–163.

Biemiller, A. (2006). Vocabulary development and instruction: A prerequisite for school learning. In S. B. Neuman & D. K. Dickinson (Eds.), *Handbook of early literacy research* (Vol. 2, pp. 29–40). New York: Guilford Press.

Blachman, B. A., Ball, E. W., Black, R., & Tangel, D. M. (1994). Kindergarten teachers develop phoneme awareness in low-income, inner-city classrooms: Does it make a difference? *Reading and Writing: An Interdisciplinary Journal, 6*, 1–18.

Blachman, B., Schatschneider, C., Fletcher, J., Murray, M., Munger, K., & Vaughn, S. (2014). Intensive reading instruction in grade 2 or 3: Are there effects a decade later? *Journal of Educational Psychology, 106*(1), 46–57.

Block, C. C., & Mangieri, J. N. (2003). *Exemplary literacy teachers: Promoting success for all children in grades K–5*. New York: Guilford Press.

Bloom, P. (2000). *How children learn the meanings of words*. Cambridge, MA: MIT Press.

Borman, G. D., Wong, K. K., Hedges, L. V., & D'Agostino, J. V. (2001). Coordinating categorical and regular programs: Effects on Title I students' educational opportunities and outcomes. In G. D. Borman, S. C. Stringfield, & R. E. Slavin (Eds.), *Title I: Compensatory education at the crossroads* (pp. 79–116). Mahwah, NJ: Erlbaum.

Bowers, P. N., Kirby, J. R., & Deacon, S. H. (2010). The effects of morphological instruction on literacy skills: A systematic review of the literature. *Review of Educational Research, 80*, 144–179.

Bradley, L., & Bryant, P. (1991). Phonological skills before and after learning to read. In S. A. Brady & D. P. Shankweiler (Eds.), *Phonological processes in literacy: A tribute to Isabelle Y. Liberman* (pp. 37–45). Hillsdale, NJ: Erlbaum.

Brady, L. (2021). *Current knowledge about instruction in letter knowledge, phoneme awareness and handwriting: What to teach, when to start, and why to integrate*. Posted to The Reading League website. Retrieved from *https://learningally.org/Portals/6/Docs/white-papers/Current-Knowledge-About-Instruction_Brady.pdf*.

Brady, S. (2020). A 2020 perspective on research findings on alphabetics (phoneme awareness and phonics): Implications for instruction. *The Reading League Journal, 1*(3), 20–28.

Brady, S. A., Shankweiler, D., & Mann, V. (1983). Speech perception and memory coding in relation to reading ability. *Journal of Experimental Child Psychology, 35*, 346–367.

Bransford, J. D., & Johnson, M. (1972). Contextual prerequisites for understanding: Some investigations of comprehension and recall. *Journal of Verbal Learning and Behavior, 11*(6), 717–726.

Brown, R., Pressley, M., Van Meter, P., & Schuder, T. (1996). A quasi-experimental validation of transactional strategies instruction with low-achieving second graders. *Journal of Educational Psychology, 88*, 18–37.

Brown, W., Denton, E., Kelly, L., Outhred, L., & McNaught, M. (1999). RRs effectiveness: A five-year success story in San Louis Coastal Unified School District. *ERS Spectrum, 11*, 3–10.

Brown-Chidsey, R., & Steege, M. W. (2005). *Response to intervention: Principles and strategies for effective practice*. New York: Guilford Press.

Brueck, J. S., & Lenhart, L. A. (2015). E-books and TPACK. *The Reading Teacher, 68*(5), 373–376.

Bryant, P. E., MacLean, M., Bradley, L. L., & Crossland, J. (1990). Rhyme and alliteration, phoneme detection, and learning to read. *Developmental Psychology, 26*, 429–438.

Burns, M. K., Frederick, A., Helman, L., Pulles, S. M., McComas, J. J., & Aguilar, L. (2017). Relationship between language proficiency and growth during reading interventions. *Journal of Educational Research, 110*(6), 581–588.

Bus, A. G., Takacs, Z. K., & Kegel, C. A. T. (2015). Affordances and limitations of electronic storybooks for young children's emergent literacy. *Developmental Review, 35*, 79–97.

Buttaro, A., Jr., & Catsambis, S. (2019). Ability grouping in the early grades: Long-term consequences for educational equity in the United States. *Teachers College Record, 121(2)*, 1–50.

Butterfuss, R., & Kendeou, P. (2018). The role of executive functions in reading comprehension. *Educational Psychology Review, 30(3)*, 801–826.

Cain, K., & Oakhill, J. (1999). Inference ability and its relation to comprehension failure in young children. *Reading and Writing, 11*, 489–503.

Cain, K., & Oakhill, J. (2011). Matthew effects in young readers: Reading comprehension and reading experience aid vocabulary development. *Journal of Learning Disabilities, 44(5)*, 431–443.

Cain, K., Oakhill, J., & Bryant, P. (2004). Children's reading comprehension ability: Concurrent prediction by working memory, verbal ability, and component skills. *Journal of Educational Psychology, 96*, 31–42.

Carlisle, J. F., & Goodwin, A. P. (2014). Morphemes matter: How morphological knowledge contributes to reading and writing. In C. A. Stone, E. R. Silliman, B. J. Ehren, & G. P. Wallach (Eds.), *Handbook of language and literacy: Development and disorders* (2nd ed., pp. 265–282). New York: Guilford Press.

Castles, A., & Nation, K. (2006). How does orthographic learning happen? In S. Andrews (Ed.), *From inkmarks to ideas: Current issues in lexical processing* (pp. 151–179). Hove, UK: Psychology Press.

Castles, A., Rastle, K., & Nation, K. (2018). Ending the reading wars: Reading acquisition from novice to expert. *Psychological Science in the Public Interest, 19(1)*, 5–51.

Center, Y., Wheldall, K., Freeman, L., Outhred, L., & McNaught, M. (1995). An evaluation of Reading Recovery. *Reading Research Quarterly, 30*, 240–263.

Cervetti, G. N., Pearson, P. D., Palincsar, A. S., Afflerbach, P., Kendeou, P., Biancarosa, G., . . . Berman, A. I. (2020). How the reading for understanding initiative's research complicates the Simple View of Reading invoked in the science of reading. *Reading Research Quarterly, 55*, S161–S172.

Chall, J. S. (1967). *Learning to read: The great debate.* New York: McGraw-Hill.

Chapman, J. W., & Tunmer, W. E. (1995). Development of young children's reading self-concepts: An examination of emerging subcomponents. *Journal of Educational Psychology, 87(1)*, 154.

Chorzempa, B. F., & Graham, S. (2006). Primary-grade teachers' use of within-class ability grouping in reading. *Journal of Educational Psychology, 98(3)*, 529–541.

Clay, M. M. (1991). *Becoming literate: The construction of inner control.* Portsmouth, NH: Heinemann.

Clayton, F. J., West, G., Sears, C., Hulme, C., & Lervåg, A. (2020). A longitudinal study of early reading development: Letter-sound knowledge, phoneme awareness and RAN, but not letter-sound integration, predict variations in reading development. *Scientific Studies of Reading, 24(2)*, 91–107.

Clemens, N., Solari, E., Kearns, D. M., Fien, H., Nelson, N. J., Stelega, M., . . . Hoeft, F. (2021, December 14). They say you can do phonemic awareness instruction "in the dark," but should you? A critical evaluation of the trend toward advanced phonemic awareness training. *PsyArXiv.*

Clymer, T. (1963). The utility of phonic generalizations in the primary grades. *The Reading Teacher, 16*, 252–258.

Colenbrander, D., Kohnen, S., Beyersmann, E., Robidoux, S., Wegener, S., Arrow, T., . . . & Castles, A. (2022). Teaching children to read irregular words: A comparison of three instructional methods. *Scientific Studies of Reading, 26(6)*, 545–564.

Connor, C. M., Morrison, F. J., Schatschneider, C., Toste, J. R., Lundblom, E., Crowe, E. C., & Fishman, B. (2011). Effective classroom instruction: Implications of child characteristics by reading instruction interactions on first graders' word reading achievement. *Journal of Research on Educational Effectiveness, 4*, 173–207.

Coyne, M. D., McCoach, D. B., Loftus, S., Zipoli, R., & Kapp, K. (2009). Direct vocabulary instruction in kindergarten: Teaching for breadth versus depth. *Elementary School Journal, 110*(1), 1–18.

Coyne, M. D., Simmons, D. C., Hagan-Burke, S., Simmons, L. E., Kwok, O.-M., Kim, M., . . . Rawlinson, D. A. M. (2013). Adjusting beginning reading intervention based on student performance: An experimental evaluation. *Exceptional Children, 80*(1), 25–44.

Crosson, A. C., & Lesaux, N. K. (2010). Revisiting assumptions about the relationship of fluent reading to comprehension: Spanish-speakers' text-reading fluency in English. *Reading and Writing, 23,* 475–494.

Cunningham, A. E., & Stanovich, K. E. (1997). Early reading acquisition and its relation to reading experience and ability 10 years later. *Developmental Psychology, 33*(6), 934–945.

Curran, M. (2020). Complex sentences in an elementary science curriculum: A research note. *Language, Speech, and Hearing Services in Schools, 51*(2), 329–335.

Danielson, K., Wong, K. M., & Neuman, S. B. (2019). Vocabulary in educational media for preschoolers: A content analysis of word selection and screen-based pedagogical supports. *Journal of Children and Media, 13*(3), 345–362.

Dawson, H. C., & Phelan, M. (2016). *Language files: Materials for an introduction to language and linguistics (12th ed.).* Columbus: Ohio State University Press.

Dickinson, D. K. (2001). Book reading in preschool classrooms: Is recommended practice common? In D. K. Dickinson & P. O. Tabors (Eds.), *Beginning literacy with language: Young children learning at home and school* (pp. 175–203). Baltimore: Brookes.

Dickinson, D. K., McCabe, A., & Clark-Chiarelli, N. (2004). Preschool-based prevention of reading disability: Realities versus possibilities. In C. A. Stone, E. R. Silliman, B. J. Ehren, & K. Apel (Eds.), *Handbook of literacy and language: Development and disorders* (pp. 209–227). New York: Guilford Press.

Dickinson, D. K., McCabe, A., & Essex, M. J. (2006). A window of opportunity we must open to all: The case for preschool with high-quality language and literacy. In D. K. Dickinson & S. B. Neuman (Eds.), *Handbook of early literacy research* (Vol. 2, pp. 11–28). New York: Guilford Press.

Dickinson, D. K., McCabe, A., & Sprague, K. (2003). Teacher Rating of Oral Language and Literary Development (TROLL): Individualizing early literacy instruction with a standards-based rating tool. *The Reading Teacher, 56,* 554–569.

Dickinson, D. K., & Smith, M. W. (1994). Long-term effects of preschool teachers' book readings on low-income children's vocabulary and story comprehension. *Reading Research Quarterly, 29,* 104–122.

Dickinson, D. K., & Tabors, P. O. (Eds.). (2001). *Beginning with language: Young children learning at home and school.* Baltimore: Brookes.

Duffy, G. G. (2003). *Explaining reading: A resource for teaching concepts, skills, and strategies.* New York: Guilford Press.

Duffy, G. G., & Hoffman, J. V. (1999). In pursuit of an illusion: The flawed search for a perfect method. *The Reading Teacher, 53*(1), 10.

Duke, N. K. (2021). Nurturing curiosity: Using and creating informational texts. *Teaching Young Children, 13*(2), 24–25.

Duke, N. K., & Pearson, P. D. (2002). Effective practices for developing reading comprehension. In A. E. Farstrup & S. J. Samuels (Eds.), *What research has to say about reading instruction* (3rd ed., pp. 205–242). Newark, DE: International Reading Association.

Duke, N. K., Pearson, P. D., Strachan, S. L., & Billman, A. K. (2011). Essential elements of fostering and teaching reading comprehension. In S. J. Samuels & A. E. Farstrup (Eds.), *What research has to say about reading instruction* (4th ed., pp. 51–93). Newark, DE: International Reading Association.

Durrell, D. D. (1963). *Phonograms in primary grade words.* Boston: Boston University Press.

Dweck, C. (2017). The journey to children's mindsets—and beyond. *Child Development Perspectives, 11(2),* 139–144.

Ehri, L. C. (1998). Grapheme–phoneme knowledge is essential for learning to read words in English. In J. Metsala & L. C. Ehri (Eds.), *Word recognition in beginning literacy* (pp. 3–40). Mahwah, NJ: Erlbaum.

Ehri, L. C. (2005). Learning to read words: Theory, findings, and issues. *Scientific Studies of Reading, 9*(2), 167–188.

Ehri, L. C. (2014). Orthographic mapping in the acquisition of sight word reading, spelling memory, and vocabulary learning. *Scientific Studies of Reading, 18*(1), 5–21.

Ehri, L. C. (2020). The science of learning to read words: A case for systematic phonics instruction. *Reading Research Quarterly, 55*, S45–S60.

Ehri, L. C., Deffner, N. D., & Wilce, L. S. (1984). Pictorial mnemonics for phonics. *Journal of Educational Psychology, 76*, 880–893.

Ehri, L. C., Dreyer, L. G., Flugman, B., & Gross, A. (2007). Reading Rescue: An effective tutoring intervention model for language minority students who are struggling readers in first grade. *American Educational Research Journal, 44*(2), 414–448.

Elkonin, D. B. (1973). U.S.S.R. In J. Downing (Ed.), *Comparative reading* (pp. 551–579). New York: Macmillan.

Ellefson, M. R., Treiman, R., & Kessler, B. (2009). Learning to label letters by sounds or names: A comparison of England and the United States. *Journal of Experimental Child Psychology, 102*(3), 323–341.

Fisher, D., Flood, J., Lapp, D., & Frey, N. (2004). Interactive read alouds: Is there a common set of implementation practices? *The Reading Teacher, 58*, 8–17.

Fitzgerald, J., Elmore, J., Hiebert, E. H., Koons, H., Bowen, K., Sanford-Moore, E. E., & Stenner, A. J. (2016). Text complexity and the early grades: The fuss and how recent research can help. *Phi Delta Kappan, 97*(8), 60–66.

Flanigan, K. (2007). A concept of word in text: A pivotal event in early reading acquisition. *Journal of Literacy Research, 39*(1), 37–70.

Fletcher, J. M., Lyon, G. R., Fuchs, L. S., & Barnes, M. A. (2019). *Learning disabilities: From identification to intervention* (2nd ed.). New York: Guilford Press.

Fletcher, J. M., Savage, R., & Vaughn, S. (2021). A commentary on Bowers (2020) and the role of phonics instruction in reading. *Educational Psychology Review, 33*, 1249–1274.

Fletcher, J. M., Shaywitz, S. E., Shankweiler, D., Katz, I., Liberman, I., Steubing, K. K., . . . Shaywitz, B. A. (1994). Cognitive profiles of reading disability: Comparisons of discrepancy and low achievement definitions. *Journal of Educational Psychology, 86*, 6–23.

Flynn, E. E. (2021). "Rapunzel, Rapunzel, lanza tu pelo": Storytelling in a transcultural, translanguaging dialogic exchange. *Reading Research Quarterly, 56*(4), 643–658.

Foorman, B., Beyler, N., Borradaile, K., Coyne, M., Denton, C. A., Dimino, J., . . . Wissel, S. (2016). *Foundational skills to support reading for understanding in kindergarten through 3rd grade* (NCEE 2016-4008). Washington, DC: National Center for Education Evaluation and Regional Assistance (NCEE), Institute of Education Sciences, U.S. Department of Education. Retrieved from *https://ies.ed.gov/ncee/wwc/Docs/PracticeGuide/wwc_foundationalreading_040717.pdf*.

Foorman, B. R., Herrera, S., & Dombek, J. (2018). The relative impact of aligning Tier 2 intervention materials with classroom core reading materials in grades K–2. *Elementary School Journal, 118*(3), 477–504.

Fountas, I. C., & Pinnell, G. S. (2012). *The Fountas and Pinnell text level gradient: Revision to recommended grade-level goals*. Portsmouth, NH: Heinemann.

Francis, D. J., Shaywitz, S., & Steubing, K. (1996). Developmental lag versus deficit models of reading disability: A longitudinal, individual growth curves analysis. *Journal of Educational Psychology, 88*, 3–17.

Fry, E. (1999–2000). *1000 instant words*. Westminster, CA: Teacher Created Resources.

Fuchs, D., & Fuchs, L. S. (2006). Introduction to response to intervention: What, why, and how valid is it? *Reading Research Quarterly, 41*(1), 93–98.

Fuchs, D., Fuchs, L. S., & Burish, P. (2000). Peer-assisted learning strategies: An evidence-based practice to promote reading achievement. *Learning Disabilities Research and Practice, 15*, 85–91.

Fuchs, L. S., & Vaughn, S. (2012). Responsiveness-to-intervention: A decade later. *Journal of Learning Disabilities, 45,* 195–203.

Gallagher, A., Frith, U., & Snowling, M. J. (2000). Precursors of literacy delay among children at genetic risk of dyslexia. *Journal of Child Psychology and Psychiatry, 41,* 203–213.

Galloway, E. P., McClain, J. B., & Uccelli, P. (2020). Broadening the lens on the science of reading: A multifaceted perspective on the role of academic language in text understanding. *Reading Research Quarterly, 55*(S1), S331–S345.

García, O., & Kleifgen, J. (2020). Translanguaging and literacies. *Reading Research Quarterly, 55*(4), 553–571.

García, O., & Kleyn, T. (Eds.). (2016). *Translanguaging with multilingual students: Learning from classroom moments.* New York: Routledge.

Gelzheiser, L. M., Hallgren-Flynn, L., Connors, M., & Scanlon, D. M. (2014). Reading thematically related texts to develop knowledge and comprehension. *The Reading Teacher, 68*(1), 53–63.

Gelzheiser, L. M., Scanlon, D. M., Hallgren Flynn, L., & Connors, M. (2019). *Comprehensive reading intervention in grades 3–8: Fostering word learning, comprehension, and motivation.* New York: Guilford Press.

Gersten, R., Baker, S. K., Shanahan, T., Linan-Thompson, S., Collins, P., & Scarcella, R. (2007). *Effective literacy and English language instruction for English learners in the elementary grades: A practice guide* (NCEE 2007-4011). Washington, DC: U.S. Department of Education, Institute of Education Sciences, National Center for Education Evaluation and Regional Assistance. Retrieved from *http://ies.ed.gov/ncee/wwc/publications/practiceguides.*

Gersten, R., Compton, D., Connor, C. M., Dimino, J., Santoro, L., Linan-Thompson, S., & Tilly, W. D. (2008). *Assisting students struggling with reading: Response to intervention and multi-tier intervention for reading in the primary grades: A practice guide* (NCEE 2009-4045). Washington, DC: U.S. Department of Education, Institute of Education Sciences, National Center for Education Evaluation and Regional Assistance. Retrieved from *http://ies.ed.gov/ncee/wwc/publications/practiceguides.*

Gibson, E. J., & Levin, H. (1975). *The psychology of reading.* Cambridge, MA: MIT Press.

Goldenberg, C. (2013). Unlocking the research on English learners. *American Educator, 37*(2), 4–38.

Goldenberg, C. (2020). Reading wars, reading science, and English Learners. *Reading Research Quarterly, 55*(S1), S131–S144.

Gomez-Bellenge, F. X., Rogers, E., & Fullerton, S. K. (2003). *Reading recovery and Descubriendo la Lectura national report 2001–2002.* Columbus: Ohio State University Reading Recovery National Data Evaluation Center.

Goodman, K. S. (1967). Reading: A psycholinguistic guessing game. *Journal of the Reading Specialist, 6,* 126–135.

Goodwin, A., & Ahn, S. (2013). A meta-analysis of morphological interventions in English: Effects on literacy outcomes for school-age children. *Scientific Studies of Reading, 17*(4), 257–285.

Gottardo, A., Chen, X., & Huo, M. R. Y. (2021). Understanding within- and cross-language relations among language, preliteracy skills, and word reading in bilingual learners: Evidence from the science of reading. *Reading Research Quarterly, 56*(1), S371–S390.

Gough, P., Juel, C., & Griffith, P. (1992). Reading, spelling, and the orthographic cipher. In P. Gough, L. C. Ehri, & R. Treiman (Eds.), *Reading acquisition* (pp. 35–48). Hillsdale, NJ: Erlbaum.

Gough, P. B., & Tunmer, W. E. (1986). Decoding, reading, and reading disability. *Remedial and Special Education, 7,* 6–10.

Graesser, A. C. (2007). An introduction to reading comprehension. In D. S. McNamara (Ed.), *Reading comprehension strategies: Theories, interventions, and technologies* (pp. 3–26). New York: Psychology Press.

Graesser, A. C., McNamara, D. S., & Kulikowich, J. M. (2011). Coh-Metrix providing multilevel analyses of text characteristics. *Educational Researcher, 40*(5), 223–234.

Graham, S., Harris, K. R., & Fink, B. (2000). Is handwriting causally related to learning to write? Treatment of handwriting problems in beginning writers. *Journal of Educational Psychology, 92,* 620–633.

Guthrie, J. T., & Humenick, N. M. (2004). Motivating students to read: Evidence for classroom practices that increase reading motivation and achievement. In P. McCardle & V. Chhabra (Eds.), *The voice of evidence in reading research* (pp. 329–354). Baltimore: Brookes.

Guthrie, J. T., Wigfield, A., Barbosa, P., Perencevich, K. C., Taboada, A., Davis, M. H., . . . Tonks, S. (2004). Increasing reading comprehension and engagement through concept-oriented reading instruction. *Journal of Educational Psychology, 96*(3), 403–423.

Hadley, E. B., & Mendez, K. Z. (2021). A systematic review of word selection in early childhood vocabulary instruction. *Early Childhood Research Quarterly, 54,* 44–59.

Haimovitz, K., & Dweck, C. S. (2017). The origins of children's growth and fixed mindsets: New research and a new proposal. *Child Development, 88*(6), 1849–1859.

Halle, T., Hair, E., Wandner, L., McNamara, M., & Chien, N. (2012). Predictors and outcomes of early versus later English language proficiency among English language learners. *Early Childhood Research Quarterly, 27*(1), 1–20.

Hanno, E. C., Jones, S. M., McCoy, S. C. (2020). The joint development of literacy and self-regulation in early childhood: Implications for research and practice. In E. B. Moje, P. P. Afflerbach, P. Enciso, & L. K. Lesaux (Eds.), Handbook of reading research (Vol. 5, pp. 279–306). New York: Routledge.

Harris, J., Golinkoff, R., & Hirsh-Pasek, K. (2011). Lessons from the crib to the classroom: How children really learn vocabulary. In S. B. Neuman & D. K. Dickinson (Eds.), Handbook of early literacy research (Vol. 3, pp. 322–336). New York: Guilford Press.

Hasbrouck, J., & Tindal, G. A. (2017). *An update to compiled ORF norms* (Technical Report No. 1702). Eugene: Behavioral Research and Teaching, University of Oregon.

Hendricks, E. L., & Fuchs, D. (2020). Are individual differences in Response to Intervention influenced by the methods and measures used to define response? Implications for identifying children with learning disabilities. *Journal of Learning Disabilities, 53*(6), 428–443.

Hernandez, D. J. (2011). *Jeopardy: How third-grade reading skills and poverty influence high school graduation.* Report for the Annie E. Casey Foundation.

Hickman, P., Pollard-Durodola, S., & Vaughn, S. (2004). Storybook reading: Improving vocabulary and comprehension for English-language learners. *The Reading Teacher, 57,* 720–730.

Hiebert, E. H., Goodwin, A. P., & Cervetti, G. N. (2018). Core vocabulary: Its morphological content and presence in exemplar texts. *Reading Research Quarterly, 53*(1), 29–49.

Hiebert, E. H., & Tortorelli, L. S. (2022). The role of word-, sentence-, and text-level variables in predicting guided reading levels of kindergarten and first-grade texts. *Elementary School Journal, 122*(4), 557–590.

Hirsch, E. D. J. (2003). Reading comprehension requires knowledge of words and the world: Scientific insights into the fourth-grade slump and the nation's stagnant comprehension scores. *American Educator, 27*(1), 10–48.

Hirsch, E. D. (2006). *The knowledge deficit: Closing the shocking educational gap for American children.* Boston: Houghton Mifflin.

Honig, B., Diamond, L., & Gutlohn, L. (2018). *Teaching reading source book* (3rd ed.). Novato, CA: Arena Press.

Inhoff, A. W., Solomon, M., Radach, R., & Seymour, B. A. (2011). Temporal dynamics of the eye–voice span and eye movement control during oral reading. *Journal of Cognitive Psychology, 33,* 543–558.

Israelson, M. H. (2015). The app map: A tool for systematic evaluation of apps for early literacy learning. *The Reading Teacher, 69,* 339–349.

Johnston, F. R. (1999). The timing and teaching of word families. *The Reading Teacher, 53*(1), 64–75.

Johnston, P. H. (2004). *Choice words: How our language affects children's learning.* Portland, ME: Stenhouse.

Juel, C. (1988). Learning to read and write: A longitudinal study of 54 children from first through fourth grades. *Journal of Educational Psychology, 80*, 437–447.

Justice, L. M., & Piasta, S. B. (2011). Developing children's print knowledge through adult–child storybook reading interactions: Print referencing as an instructional practice. In S. B. Neuman & D. K. Dickinson (Eds.), *Handbook of early literacy research* (Vol. 3, pp. 200–213). New York: Guilford Press.

Kaefer, T. (2020). When did you learn it? How background knowledge impacts attention and comprehension in read-aloud activities. *Reading Research Quarterly, 55*, S173–S183.

Kearns, D. M. (2020). Does English have useful syllable division patterns? *Reading Research Quarterly, 55*(S1), S145–S160.

Kearns, D. M., & Whaley, V. M. (2019). Helping students with dyslexia read long words: Using syllables and morphemes. *Teaching Exceptional Children, 51*(3), 212–225.

Kelley, E. S., Goldstein, H., Spencer, T. D., & Sherman, A. (2015). Effects of automated tier 2 storybook intervention on vocabulary and comprehension learning in preschool children with limited oral language skills. *Early Childhood Research Quarterly, 31*, 47–61.

Kendeou, P., & O'Brien, E. J. (2016). Prior knowledge acquisition and revision. In P. Afflerbach (Ed.), *Handbook of individual differences in reading* (pp. 151–163). New York: Routledge.

Kessler, B., & Treiman, R. (2003). Is English spelling chaotic?: Misconceptions concerning its irregularity. *Reading Psychology, 24*, 267–289.

Kilpatrick, D. (2020). The study that prompted Tier 2 of RTI: Why aren't our results as good? *The Reading League Journal*, 28–31.

Kim, J. S., & Quinn, D. M. (2013). The effects of summer reading on low-income children's literacy achievement from kindergarten to grade 8: A meta-analysis of classroom and home interventions. *Review of Educational Research, 83*, 386–431.

Kim, Y.-S. G. (2022). Co-occurrence of reading and writing difficulties: The application of the interactive dynamic literacy model. *Journal of Learning Disabilities, 55*(6), 447–464.

Kim, Y.-S., Petscher, Y., Schatschneider, C., & Foorman, B. (2010). Does growth rate in oral reading fluency matter in predicting reading comprehension achievement? *Journal of Educational Psychology, 102*, 652–667.

Kim, Y.-S. G., Quinn, J. M., & Petscher, Y. (2021), What is text reading fluency and is it a predictor or an outcome of reading comprehension? A longitudinal investigation. *Developmental Psychology, 57*(5), 718–732.

Kim, Y.-S. G., & Wagner, R. K. (2015). Text (Oral) reading fluency as a construct in reading development: An investigation of its mediating role for children from grades 1 to 4. *Scientific Studies of Reading, 19*, 224–242.

Kintsch, W. (1998). *Comprehension: A paradigm for cognition*. Cambridge, UK: Cambridge University Press.

Klingner, J., Vaughn, S., & Schumm, J. S. (1998). Collaborative strategic reading during social studies in heterogeneous fourth-grade classrooms. *Elementary School Journal, 99*, 3–22.

Kolinsky, R., Navas, A. L., Vidigal de Paula, F., D., Ribeiro de Brito, N., de Medeiros Botechia, L., Bouton, S., & Semiclaes, W. (2021), The impact of alphabetic literacy on the perception of speech sounds. *Cognition, 213*, 104687.

Konstantopoulos, S., & Sun, M. (2012). Is the persistence of teacher effects in early grades larger for lower-performing students? *American Journal of Education, 188*, 309–339.

Koons, H., & Hiebert, E. H. (2019). *What do "levels" really mean? A closer look at text leveling*. Santa Cruz, CA: Text Project, Inc.

Kuhn, M. R., & Levy, L. (2015). *Developing fluent readers: Teaching fluency as a foundational skill*. New York: Guilford Press.

LaBerge, D., & Samuels, S. J. (1974). Toward a theory of automatic information processing in literacy. *Cognitive Psychology, 6*, 293–323.

Lems, K. (2022). A warm wELLcome for language learners: Arranged marriage or marriage of convenience? Oral reading fluency and English language learners. *Illinois Reading Council Journal, 50*(4), 75–79.

Lennox, S. (2013). Interactive read-alouds: An avenue for enhancing children's language for thinking and understanding: A review of recent research. *Early Childhood Education Journal, 41*(5), 381–389.

Levesque, K. C., Breadmore, H. L., & Deacon, S. H. (2021). How morphology impacts reading and spelling: Advancing the role of morphology in models of literacy development. *Journal of Research in Reading, 44*(1), 10–26.

Lobeck, A. (2019). Teaching linguistic diversity as the rule rather than the exception. In M. D. Devereaux & C. C. Palmer (Eds.), *Teaching language variation in the classroom: Strategies and models from teachers and linguists* (pp. 76–83). New York: Routledge.

Lou, Y., Abrami, P. C., & Spence, J. C. (2000). Effects of within-class ability grouping on student achievement: An exploratory model. *Journal of Educational Research, 94*, 101–112.

Ludwig, C., Guo, K., Georgiou, G. K. (2019). Are reading interventions for English Language Learners effective? A meta-analysis. *Journal of Learning Disabilities, 52*(3), 220–231.

Lyman, F. T. (1981). The responsive classroom discussion: The inclusion of all students. In A. Anderson (Ed.), *Mainstreaming digest* (pp. 109–113). College Park: University of Maryland Press.

Lyster, S. A. H., Snowling, M. J., Hulme, C., & Lervåg, A. O. (2021). Preschool phonological, morphological and semantic skills explain it all: Following reading development through a 9-year period. *Journal of Research in Reading, 44*(1), 175–188.

MacKay, E., Lynch, E., Duncan, T. S., & Deacon, S. H. (2021). Informing the Science of Reading: Students' awareness of sentence-level is important for reading comprehension. *Reading Research Quarterly, 56* (S1), S221–S230.

Maguire, M. J., Hirsh-Pasek, K., & Golinkoff, R. M. (2006). A unified theory of word learning: Putting verb acquisition in context. In K. Hirsh-Pasek & R. M. Golinkoff (Eds.), *Action meets word: How children learn verbs* (pp. 364–391). New York: Oxford University Press.

Marinak, B. A., Malloy, F. B., Gambrell, L. B., & Mazzoni, S. A. (2015). Me and my reading profile. *The Reading Teacher, 69*(1), 51–62.

Marriott, S. (1995). *Read on: Using fiction in the primary school.* London: Paul Chapman.

Mathes, P. G., Denton, C. A., Fletcher, J. M., Anthony, J. L., Francis, D. J., & Schatschneider, C. (2005). The effects of theoretically different instruction and student characteristics on the skills of struggling readers. *Reading Research Quarterly, 40*(2), 148–182.

McBreen, M., & Savage, R. (2021). The impact of motivational reading instruction on the reading achievement and motivation of students: A systematic review and meta-analysis. *Educational Psychology Review, 33*(3), 1125–1163.

McCoach, D. B., O'Connell, A. A., & Levitt, H. (2006). Ability grouping across kindergarten using an early childhood longitudinal study. *Journal of Educational Research, 99*(6), 339–346.

McGee, L. M., Kim, H., Nelson, K. S., & Fried, M. D. (2015). Change over time in first graders' strategic use of information at point of difficulty in reading. *Reading Research Quarterly, 50*(3), 263–291.

McGee, L. M., & Schickedanz, J. A. (2007). Repeated interactive read-alouds in preschool and kindergarten. *The Reading Teacher, 60*(8), 742–751.

McGeown, S. P., Osborne, C., Warhurst, A., Norgate, R., & Duncan, L. G. (2016). Understanding children's reading activities: Reading motivation, skill, and child characteristics as predictors. *Journal of Research in Reading, 39*(1), 109–125.

McKay, R., & Teale, W. H. (2015). *No more teaching a letter a week.* Portsmouth, NH: Heinemann.

McKenna, M. C., Kear, D. J., & Ellsworth, R. A. (1995). Children's attitude towards reading: A national survey. *Reading Research Quarterly, 30*, 934–956.

McKeown, M. G., & Beck, I. L. (2006). Encouraging young children's language interactions with stories. In D. K. Dickinson & S. B. Neuman (Eds.), *Handbook of early literacy research* (Vol. 2, pp. 281–294). New York: Guilford Press.

McKeown, M. G., Beck, I. L., & Blake, R. G. K. (2009). Rethinking reading comprehension instruction: A comparison of instruction for strategies and content approaches. *Reading Research Quarterly, 44*(3), 218–253.

Mellard, D. F., & Johnson, E. (2008). *RTI: A practitioner's guide to implementing response to intervention*. Thousand Oaks, CA: Corwin Press.

Mesmer, H. A. (2008). *Tools for matching readers to texts*. New York: Guilford Press.

Mesmer, H. A., & Williams, T. O. (2015). Examining the role of syllable awareness in a model of concept of word: Findings from preschoolers. *Reading Research Quarterly, 50*(4), 483–497.

Metsala, J. L. (2011). Lexical reorganization and the emergence of phonological awareness. In S. B. Neuman & D. K. Dickinson (Eds.), *Handbook of early literacy research* (Vol. 3, pp. 66–82). New York: Guilford Press.

Michaels, S. (1981). "Sharing time": Children's narrative styles and differential access to literacy. *Language in Society, 10*(3), 423–442.

Mol, S. E., Bus, A. G., DeJong, M. T., & Smeets, D. J. H. (2008) Added value of dialogic parent–child book readings: A meta-analysis. *Early Education and Development, 19*(1), 7–26.

Morgan, P. L., & Fuchs, D. (2007). Is there a bidirectional relationship between children's reading skills and reading motivation? *Exceptional Children, 73*(2), 165–183.

Morris, D., Bloodgood, J., Lomax, R. G., & Perney, J. (2003). Developmental steps in learning to read: A longitudinal study in kindergarten and first grade. *Reading Research Quarterly, 38*, 302–328.

Morris, R. D., Lovett, M. W., Wolf, M., Sevcik, R. A., Steinbach, K. A., Frijters, J. C., & Shapiro, M. B. (2012). Multiple component remediation for developmental reading disabilities: IQ, socioeconomic status, and race as factors in remedial outcome. *Journal of Learning Disabilities, 45*(2), 99–127.

Morrow, L. M., & Gambrell, L. B. (2000). Literature-based reading instruction. In M. L. Kamil, P. B. Mosenthal, P. D. Pearson, & R. Barr (Eds.), *Handbook of reading research* (Vol. 3, pp. 563–586). Mahwah, NJ: Erlbaum.

Mosenthal, J., Lipson, M., Torncello, S., Russ, B., & Mekkelsen, J. (2004). Contexts and practices of six schools successful in obtaining reading achievement. *Elementary School Journal, 104*(5), 343–367.

Mraz, M., Nichols, W., Caldwell, S., Beisley, R., Sargent, S., & Rupley, W. (2013). Improving oral reading fluency through Readers Theatre. *Reading Horizons, 52*(2), 163–179.

Müller, B., Richter, T., Križan, A., Hecht, T., & Ennemoser, M. (2015). Word recognition skills moderate the effectiveness of reading strategy training in grade 2. *Learning and Individual Differences, 40*, 55–62.

Nagy, W. E., & Anderson, R. C. (1984). How many words are there in printed school English? *Reading Research Quarterly, 19*, 357–366.

Nagy, W. E., & Herman, P. A. (1987). Breadth and depth of vocabulary knowledge: Implications for acquisition and instruction. In M. G. McKeown & M. E. Curtis (Eds.), *The nature of vocabulary acquisition* (pp. 19–36). Hillside, NJ: Erlbaum.

Nation, K. (2016). Nurturing a lexical legacy: Reading experience is critical for the development of word reading skill. *NPJ Science of Learning, 2*, 3.

National Assessment of Educational Progress. (2018/updated 2023). Oral reading fluency scale. Retrieved from *https://nces.ed.gov/nationsreportcard/studies/orf/scoring.aspx#scoring*.

National Association of State Directors of Special Education. (2005). *Response to intervention: Policy considerations and implementation*. Alexandria, VA: Author.

National Early Literacy Panel. (2008). *Developing early literacy*. Washington, DC: National Institute for Literacy.

National Governors Association Center for Best Practices & Council of Chief State School Officers. (2010). *Common Core State Standards for English language arts and literacy, history/social studies, science, and technical subjects*. Washington, DC: Author.

National Joint Committee on Learning Disabilities. (2020). *https://njcld.org*.

National Reading Panel. (2000). *Teaching children to read: An evidence-based assessment of the scientific research literature on reading and its implications for reading instruction: Reports of subgroups.* Washington, DC: National Institute of Child Health and Human Development.

Neuman, S. B. (2006). The knowledge gap: Implications for early education. In S. B. Neuman & D. K. Dickinson (Eds.), *Handbook of early literacy research* (Vol. 2, pp. 29–40). New York: Guilford Press.

Neuman, S. B. (2010). Lessons from my mother: Reflections on the National Early Literacy Panel Report. *Educational Researcher, 39*(4), 301–304.

Neuman, S. B. (2011). The challenge of teaching vocabulary in early education. In S. B. Neuman & D. K. Dickinson (Eds.), *Handbook of early literacy research* (Vol. 3, pp. 358–372). New York: Guilford Press.

Neuman, S. B., Wong, K., Flynn, R., & Kaefer, T. (2019). Learning vocabulary from educational media: The role of pedagogical supports for low-income preschoolers. *Journal of Educational Psychology, 111*, 32–44.

Neuman, S. B., & Wright, T. S. (2013). Supporting content-rich vocabulary instruction through book reading. In *All about words* (pp. 62–82). New York: Teachers College Press.

Nicholls, J. G. (1978). The development of the concepts of effort and ability, perception of academic attainment, and the understanding that difficult tasks require more than ability. *Child Development, 49*, 800–814.

Nicholls, J. G. (1990). What is ability and why are we mindful of it?: A developmental perspective. In R. Sternberg & J. Kolligian (Eds.), *Competence considered* (pp. 11–40). New Haven, CT: Yale University Press.

Niiya, Y., Crocker, J., & Bartmess, E. N. (2004). From vulnerability to resilience: Learning orientations buffer contingent self-esteem from failure. *Psychological Science, 15*, 801–805.

Nolen, S. B. (2001). Constructing literacy in the kindergarten: Task structure, collaboration, and motivation. *Cognition and Instruction, 19*, 95–142.

Nunes, T., & Bryant, P. (2006). *Improving literacy through teaching morphemes.* London: Routledge.

Nye, B., Konstantopolous, S., & Hedges, L. V. (2004). How large are teacher effects? *Educational Evaluation and Policy Analysis, 26*(3), 237–257.

Nystrand, M. (with Gamoran, A., Kachur, R., & Prendergast, C.). (1997). *Opening dialogue: Understanding the dynamics of language and learning in the English classroom.* New York: Teachers College Press.

O'Connor, R. E. (2000). Increasing the intensity of intervention in kindergarten and first grade. *Learning Disabilities Research and Practice, 15*(1), 43–54.

O'Connor, R. E., Harty, K. R., & Fulmer, D. (2005). Tiers of intervention in kindergarten through third grade. *Journal of Learning Disabilities, 38*(6), 532–538.

Ogle, D. (1986). K-W-L: A teaching model that develops action reading of expository text. *The Reading Teacher, 39*(6), 564–570.

Ouellette, G. P. (2006). What's meaning got to do with it?: The role of vocabulary in word reading and reading comprehension. *Journal of Educational Psychology, 98*(3), 554–566.

Ouellette, G. (2010). Orthographic learning in learning to spell: The roles of semantics and type of practice. *Journal of Experimental Child Psychology, 107*(1), 50–58.

Ouellette, G., Martin-Chang, S., & Rossi, M. (2017). Learning from our mistakes: Improvements in spelling lead to gains in reading speed. *Scientific Studies of Reading, 21*, 350–357.

Paivio, A. (1986). *Mental representations: A dual coding approach.* Oxford, UK: Oxford University Press.

Paris, A. H., & Paris, S. G. (2007). Teaching narrative comprehension strategies to first graders. *Cognition and Instruction, 25*(1), 1–44.

Paris, S. G. (2005). Reinterpreting the development of reading skills. *Reading Research Quarterly, 40*(2), 184–202.

Paris, S. G., Lipson, M., & Wixson, K. K. (1983). Becoming a strategic reader. *Contemporary Educational Psychology, 8*, 293–316.

Paul, R. (1981). Analyzing complex sentence development. In J. F. Miller (Ed.), *Assessing language production in children: Experimental procedures* (pp. 36–40). Baltimore: University Park Press.

Pearson, P. D. (2022). *The science of reading comprehension instruction.* Presentation for United States Institute of Education Sciences Reading Summit, June 8–9, 2021. Retrieved from *www.youtube.com/watch?v=9w_hkEh2cBo.*

Pearson, P. D., & Gallagher, M. (1983). The instruction of reading comprehension. *Contemporary Educational Psychology, 8,* 317–344.

Pearson, P. D., & Hiebert, E. H. (2014). The state of the field: Qualitative analyses of text complexity. *Elementary School Journal, 115(2),* 161–183.

Pearson, P. D., McVee, M. B., & Shanahan, L. E. (2019). In the beginning: The historical and conceptual genesis of the gradual release of responsibility. In M. B. McVee, E. Ortlieb, J. Reichenberg, & P. D. Pearson (Eds.), *The gradual release of responsibility in literacy research and practice* (pp. 1–21). Bingley, UK: Emerald Group.

Pearson, P. D., Palincsar, A. S., Biancarosa, G., & Berman, A. I. (Eds.). (2020). *Reaping the rewards of the reading for understanding initiative.* Washington, DC: National Academy of Education.

Perfetti, C. (2007). Reading ability: Lexical quality to comprehension. *Scientific Studies of Reading, 11(4),* 357–383.

Perfetti, C. A., Landi, N., & Oakhill, J. (2005). The acquisition of reading comprehension skill. In M. J. Snowling & C. Hulme (Eds.), *The science of reading: A handbook* (pp. 227–247). Malden, MA: Blackwell.

Perfetti, C., & Stafura, J. (2014). Word knowledge in a theory of reading comprehension. *Scientific Studies of Reading, 18,* 22–37.

Pfost, M., Hattie, J., Dörfler, T., & Artelt, C. (2014). Individual differences in reading development: A review of 25 years of empirical research on Matthew effects in reading. *Review of Educational Research, 84(2),* 203–244.

Phillips, B. M. (2014). Promotion of syntactical development and oral comprehension: Development and initial evaluation of a small-group intervention. *Child Language Teaching and Therapy, 30(1),* 63–77.

Phillips, L. M., Norris, S. P., Osmond, W. C., & Maynard, A. M. (2002). Relative reading achievement: A longitudinal study of 187 children from first through sixth grades. *Journal of Educational Psychology, 94(1),* 3–13.

Piasta, S. B., Petscher, Y., & Justice, L. M. (2012). How many letters should preschoolers in public programs know?: The diagnostic efficiency of various preschool letter-naming benchmarks for predicting first-grade literacy achievement. *Journal of Educational Psychology, 104(4),* 945–958.

Prawat, R. S. (1989). Promoting access to knowledge, strategy, and disposition in students: A research synthesis. *Review of Educational Research, 59(1),* 1–41.

Pressley, M. (2006). *Reading instruction that works: The case for balanced teaching* (3rd ed.). New York: Guilford Press.

Pressley, M., Wood, E., Woloshyn, V. E., Martin, V., King, A., & Menke, D. (1992). Encouraging mindful use of prior knowledge: Attempting to construct explanatory answers facilitates learning. *Educational Psychologist, 27,* 91–110.

Pressley, T., Allington, R. L., & Pressley, M. (2023). *Reading instruction that works: The case for balanced teaching* (5th ed.). New York: Guilford Press.

Price-Mohr, R., & Price, C. (2017). Gender differences in early reading strategies: A comparison of synthetic phonics only with a mixed approach to teaching reading to 4–5 year-old children. *Early Childhood Education Journal, 45(5),* 613–620.

Price-Mohr, R. M., & Price, C. B. (2018). Synthetic phonics and decodable instructional reading texts: How far do these support poor readers? *Dyslexia, 24,* 190–196.

Prochnow, J. E., Tunmer, W. E., & Chapman, J. W. (2013). A longitudinal investigation of the influence of literacy-related skills, reading self-perceptions, and inattentive behaviours on the development of literacy learning difficulties. *International Journal of Disability, Development and Education, 60(3),* 185–207.

Proctor, C. P., Silverman, R. D., Harring, J. R., Jones, R. L., & Hartranft, A. M. (2020).

Teaching bilingual learners: Effects of a language-based reading intervention on academic language and reading comprehension in grades 4 and 5. *Reading Research Quarterly, 55*(1), 95–122.

Pugh, A., Kearns, D. M., & Hiebert, E. H. (2023). Text types and their relation to efficacy in beginning reading interventions. *Reading Research Quarterly, 58*(4), 710–734.

Quinn, J. M., Spencer, M., & Wagner, R. K. (2015a). Individual differences in phonological awareness and their role in learning to read. In P. Afflerbach (Ed.), *Handbook of individual differences in reading: Reader, text, and context* (pp. 80–92). New York: Routledge.

Quinn, J. M., Wagner, R. K., Petscher, Y., & Lopez, D. (2015b). Developmental relations between vocabulary knowledge and reading comprehension: A latent change score modeling study. *Child Development, 86*(1), 159–175.

Quirk, M., & Beem, S. (2012). Examining the relations between reading fluency and reading comprehension for English Language learners. *Psychology in the Schools, 49*(6), 539–553.

Rasinski, T. V. (2004). Creating fluent readers. *Educational Leadership, 61*(6), 46–51.

Rasinski, T., Yates, R., Foerg, K., Greene, K., Paige, D., Young, C., & Rupley, W. (2020). Impact of classroom-based fluency instruction on grade one students in an urban elementary school. *Education Sciences, 10*(9), 227.

Rawlins, A., & Invernizzi, M. (2018). Reconceptualizing sight words: Building an early reading vocabulary. *The Reading Teacher, 72*(6), 711–719.

Rayner, K., Foorman, B. R., Perfetti, C. A., Pesetsky, D., & Seidenberg, M. S. (2001). How psychological science informs the teaching of reading. *Psychological Science in the Public Interest, 2*(2), 31–74.

Rayner, K., Foorman, B. R., Perfetti, C. A., Pesetsky, D., & Seidenberg, M. S. (2002). How should reading be taught? *Scientific American, 286*(3), 84–91.

Read, C. (1971). Preschool children's knowledge of English phonology. *Harvard Educational Review, 41*, 1–34.

Read, C., Zhang, Y. F., Nie, H. Y., & Ding, B. Q. (1986). The ability to manipulate speech sounds depends on knowing alphabetic writing. *Cognition, 24*, 270–292.

Reinking, D., & Reinking, S. L. (2022). Why phonics (in English) is difficult to teach, learn, and apply: What caregivers and teachers need to know. *The Journal of Reading Recovery, 22*(1), 5–19.

Reutzel, D. R., Jones, C. D., Clark, S. K., & Kumar, T. (2016). The Informational Text Structure Survey (ITS): An exploration of primary grade teachers' sensitivity to text structure in young children's informational texts. *Journal of Educational Research, 109*(1), 81–98.

Roberts, K. L., & Duke, N. K. (2009). Comprehension in the primary grades. In K. Ganske & D. Fisher (Eds.), *Comprehension across the curriculum: Perspectives and practices K–12* (pp. 23–45). New York: Guilford Press.

Roberts, T. A., & Sadler, C. D. (2019). Letter sound characters and imaginary narratives: Can they enhance motivation and letter sound learning? *Early Childhood Research Quarterly, 46*, 97–111.

Roberts, T. A., Vadasy, P. F., & Sanders, E. A. (2018). Preschoolers' alphabet learning: Letter name and sound instruction, cognitive processes, and English proficiency. *Early Childhood Research Quarterly, 44*, 257–274.

Rodgers, E., D'Agostino, J. V., Harmey, S. J., Kelly, R. H., & Brownfield, K. (2016). Examining the nature of scaffolding in an early literacy intervention. *Reading Research Quarterly, 51*(3), 345–360.

Samuels, S. J. (1979). The method of repeated reading. *The Reading Teacher, 32*, 403–408.

Samuels, S. J. (2006). Reading fluency: Its past, present, and future. In T. Rasinski, C. Blachowicz, & K. Lems (Eds.), *Fluency instruction: Research-based best practices* (pp. 7–20). New York: Guilford Press.

Santoro, L. E., Chard, D. J., Howard, L., & Baker, S. (2008). Making the very most of classroom read-alouds to promote comprehension and vocabulary. *The Reading Teacher, 61*(5), 396–408.

Saunders-Smith, G. (2003). *The ultimate guided reading how-to book: Building literacy through small-group instruction.* Tucson, AZ: Zephyr Press.

Savage, R., Georgiou, G., Parrila, R., & Maiorino, K. (2018). Preventative reading interventions teaching direct mapping of graphemes in texts and set-for-variability aid at-risk learners. *Scientific Studies of Reading, 22,* 225–247.

Scanlon, D. M. (2011). Response to intervention as an assessment approach. In A. McGill-Franzen & R. L. Allington (Eds.), *Handbook of reading disability research* (pp. 139–148). New York: Routledge.

Scanlon, D. M., & Anderson, K. L. (2010). Using the interactive strategies approach to preventing reading difficulties in an RTI context. In M. Y. Lipson & K. K. Wixson (Eds.), *Successful approaches to RTI: Collaborative practices for improving K–12 literacy* (pp. 20–65). Newark, DE: International Reading Association.

Scanlon, D. M., & Anderson, K. L. (2020). Using context as an assist in word solving: The contributions of 25 years of research on the interactive strategies approach. *Reading Research Quarterly, 55*(S1), S19–S34.

Scanlon, D. M., Anderson, K. L., Barnes, E. M., Morse, M., & Yurkewecz, T. (2024). *Helping your child become a reader.* Retrieved from *eltep.org/isa-parent-booklet.*

Scanlon, D. M., Anderson, K. L., & Goatley, V. (2015, December). *National RTI Survey.* Presented at the annual convention of the Literacy Research Association, Carlsbad, CA.

Scanlon, D. M., Anderson, K. L. & Sweeney, J. M. (2010). *Early intervention for reading difficulties,* New York: Guilford Press.

Scanlon, D. M., Anderson, K. L. & Sweeney, J. M. (2017). *Early intervention for reading difficulties* (2nd ed.). New York: Guilford Press.

Scanlon, D. M., Gelzheiser, L. M., Vellutino, F. R., Schatschneider, C., & Sweeney, J. M. (2008). Reducing the incidence of early reading difficulties: Professional development for classroom teachers versus direct interventions for children. *Learning and Individual Differences, 18*(3), 346–359.

Scanlon, D. M., & Vellutino, F. R. (1996). Prerequisite skills, early instruction, and success in first-grade reading: Selected results from a longitudinal study. *Mental Retardation and Developmental Disabilities Research Reviews, 2,* 54–63.

Scanlon, D. M., & Vellutino, F. R. (1997). A comparison of the instructional backgrounds and cognitive profiles of poor, average, and good readers who were initially identified as at risk for reading failure. *Scientific Studies of Reading, 1*(3), 191–215.

Scanlon, D. M., Vellutino, F. R., Small, S. G., Fanuele, D. P., & Sweeney, J. M. (2005). Severe reading difficulties—can they be prevented?: A comparison of prevention and intervention approaches. *Exceptionality, 13*(4), 209–227.

Scarborough, H. S. (2001). Connecting early language and literacy to later reading (dis)abilities: Evidence, theory, and practice. In S. B. Neuman & D. K. Dickinson (Eds.), *Handbook of early literacy research* (Vol. 1, pp. 97–110). New York: Guilford Press.

Scarborough, H. S., & Dobrich, W. (1994). On the efficacy of reading to preschoolers. *Developmental Review, 14,* 245–302.

Schilling, S. G., Carlisle, J. F., Scott, S. E., & Zeng, J. (2007). Are fluency measures accurate predictors of reading achievement? *Elementary School Journal, 107*(5), 429–448.

Schmidman, A., & Ehri, L. (2010). Embedded picture mnemonics to learn letters. *Scientific Studies of Reading, 14*(2), 159–182.

Schneider, W., Roth, E., & Ennemoser, M. (2000). Training phonological skills and letter knowledge in children at risk for dyslexia: A comparison of three kindergarten intervention programs. *Journal of Educational Psychology, 92,* 284–295.

Schultheiss, O. C., & Brunstein, J. C. (2005). An implicit motive perspective on competence. In A. J. Elliot & C. S. Dweck (Eds.), *Handbook of competence and motivation* (pp. 31–51). New York: Guilford Press.

Schunk, D. H., Pintrich, P. R., & Meece, J. L. (2008). *Motivation in education: Theory, research, and applications* (3rd ed.). Upper Saddle River, NJ: Pearson.

Schwanenflugel, P. J., & Kuhn, M. R. (2016). Reading fluency. In P. Afflerbach (Ed.), *Handbook of individual differences in reading: Text and context* (pp. 107–120). New York: Routledge.

Scott, C. M. (2009). A case for the sentence in reading comprehension. *Language, Speech, and Hearing Services in Schools, 40*(2), 184–191.

Seidenberg, M. S. (2017). *Language at the speed of sight.* New York: Basic Books.

Seidenberg, M. S. (2023). Phonemes, speech and reading. Retrieved September 12, 2023, from *https://seidenbergreading.net/wp-content/uploads/2023/03/part-1-phonemes-speech-and-reading-slides.pdf.*

Sénéchal, M., Ouellette, G., & Rodney, D. (2006). The misunderstood giant: On the predictive role of early vocabulary to future reading. In S. B. Neuman & D. K. Dickinson (Eds.), *Handbook of early literacy research* (Vol. 2, pp. 173–184). New York: Guilford Press.

Shahar-Yames, D., & Share, D. L. (2008). Spelling as a self-teaching mechanism in orthographic learning. *Journal of Research in Reading, 31*(1), 22–39.

Shanahan, T., Callison, K., Carriere, C., Duke, N. K., Pearson, P. D., Schatschneider, C., & Torgesen, J. (2010). *Improving reading comprehension in kindergarten through third grade* (NCEE 2010-4038). Washington, DC: Institute of Education Sciences. Retrieved from *https://files.eric.ed.gov/fulltext/ED512029.pdf.*

Share, D. L. (1995). Phonological recoding and self-teaching: Sine qua non of reading acquisition. *Cognition, 55,* 151–218.

Share, D. L. (2008). Orthographic learning, phonology and the self-teaching hypothesis. *Advances in Child Development and Behavior, 36,* 31–82.

Silverman, R. (2007a). A comparison of three methods of vocabulary instruction during read-alouds in kindergarten. *Elementary School Journal, 108*(2), 97–113.

Silverman, R. (2007b). Vocabulary development of English-language and English-only learners in kindergarten. *Elementary School Journal, 107,* 365–383.

Silverman, R., & Hines, S. (2009). The effects of multimedia-enhanced instruction on the vocabulary of English-language learners and non-English-language learners in prekindergarten through second grade. *Journal of Educational Psychology, 101*(2), 305–314.

Silverman, R. D., Speece, D. L., Harring, J. R., & Ritchey, C. D. (2013). Fluency has a role in the simple view of reading. *Scientific Studies of Reading, 17,* 108–133.

Simmons, D. (2015). Instructional engineering principles to frame the future of reading intervention research and practice. *Remedial and Special Education, 36*(1), 45–51.

Skar, G. B., Lei, P.-W., Graham, S., Aasen, A. J., Johansen, M. B., & Kvistad, A. H. (2022). Handwriting fluency and the quality of primary grade students' writing. *Reading & Writing, 35*(2), 509–538.

Smith, A. E., Jussim, L., & Eccles, J. (1999). Do self-fulfilling prophecies accumulate, dissipate, or remain stable over time? *Journal of Personality and Social Psychology, 77,* 548–565.

Smolkin, L. B., Yaden, D. B., Jr., Brown, L., & Hofius, B. (1992). The effects of genre, visual design choices, and discourse structure on preschoolers' responses to picture books during parent–child read-alouds. In C. K. Kinzer & D. J. Leu (Eds.), *Literacy research, theory, and practice: Views from many perspectives* (41st Yearbook of the National Reading Conference, pp. 291–301). Chicago: National Reading Conference.

Snow, C. E. (1990). The development of definitional skill. *Journal of Child Language, 17*(3), 697–710.

Snow, C. E., Burns, M. S., & Griffin, P. (1998). *Preventing reading difficulties in young children.* Washington, DC: National Academy Press.

Soemer, A., & Schiefele, U. (2018). Reading amount as a mediator between intrinsic reading motivation and reading comprehension in the early elementary grades. *Learning and Individual Differences, 67,* 1–11.

Spencer, M., & Wagner, R. K. (2018). The comprehension problems of children with poor reading comprehension despite adequate decoding: A meta-analysis. *Review of Educational Research, 88*(3), 366–400.

Stage, S., Sheppard, J., Davidson, M. M., & Browning, M. M. (2001). Prediction of first graders' growth in oral reading fluency using kindergarten letter fluency. *Journal of School Psychology, 29*(3), 225–237.

Stanovich, K. E. (1986). Matthew effects in reading: Some consequences of individual differences in the acquisition of literacy. *Reading Research Quarterly, 21*, 360–407.

Steacy, L. M., Edwards, A. A., Rigobon, V. M., Gutierrez, N., Marencin, N. C., Siegelman, N., . . . Compton, D. L. (2022). Set for Variability as a critical predictor of word reading: Potential implications for early identification and treatment of dyslexia. *Reading Research Quarterly, 58*(2), 1–14.

Steacy, L. M., Wade-Woolley, L., Rueckl, J. G., Pugh, K. R., Elliott, J. D., & Compton, D. L. (2019). The role of Set for Variability in irregular word reading: Word and child predictors in typically developing readers and students at-risk for reading disabilities. *Scientific Studies of Reading, 23*(6), 523–532.

Stenner, A. J., Burdick, H., Sanford, E. E., & Burdick, D. S. (2007). *The Lexile framework for reading technical report*. Durham, NC: Metametrics.

Storch, S. A., & Whitehurst, G. J. (2002). Oral language and code-related precursors to reading: Evidence from a longitudinal structural model. *Developmental Psychology, 38*, 934–947.

Swan, M., & Smith, B. (Eds.). (2001). *Learner English: A teacher's guide to interference and other problems* (2nd ed.). Cambridge, UK: Cambridge University Press.

Takacs, Z. K., Swart, E. K., & Bus, A. G. (2015). Benefits and pitfalls of multimedia and interactive features in technology-enhanced storybooks: A meta-analysis. *Review of Educational Research, 85*(4), 698–739.

Taylor, B. M., Pearson, P. D., Clark, K. M., & Walpole, S. (2000). Effective schools and accomplished teachers: Lessons about primary-grade reading instruction in low-income schools. *Elementary School Journal, 101*, 121–165.

Tivnan, T., & Hemphill, L. (2005). Comparing four literacy reform models in high-poverty schools: Patterns of first-grade achievement. *Elementary School Journal, 105*(5), 419–441.

Tomasello, M. (2001). First steps toward a usage-based theory of language acquisition. *Cognitive Linguistics, 11*(1–2), 61–82.

Torgesen, J. K., Alexander, A. W., Wagner, R. K., Rashotte, C. A., Voeller, K., & Conway, T. (2001). Intensive remedial instruction for students with severe reading disabilities: Immediate and long-term outcomes from two instructional approaches. *Journal of Learning Disabilities, 34*, 33–58.

Torgesen, J. K., & Burgess, S. R. (1998). Consistency of reading-related phonological processes throughout early childhood: Evidence from longitudinal-correlational and instructional studies. In J. L. Metsala & L. C. Ehri (Eds.), *Word recognition in beginning literacy* (pp. 161–188). Mahwah, NJ: Erlbaum.

Torgesen, J. K., Wagner, R. K., & Rashotte, C. (1994). Longitudinal studies of phonological processing and reading. *Journal of Learning Disabilities, 27*, 276–286.

Treiman, R., Sotak, L., & Bowman, M. (2001). The role of letter names and letter sounds in connecting print to speech. *Memory and Cognition, 29*, 860–873.

Tunmer, W. E., & Chapman, J. W. (1998). Language prediction skill, phonological recoding ability, and reading. In C. Hulme & R. M. Joshi (Eds.), *Reading and spelling: Development and disorders* (pp. 33–68). Mahwah, NJ: Erlbaum.

Tunmer, W. E., & Nicholson, T. (2011). The development and teaching of word recognition skill. In M. L. Kamil, P. D. Pearson, E. B. Moje, & P. P. Afflerbach (Eds.), *Handbook of reading research* (Vol. 4, pp. 405–431). New York: Routledge.

Turnbull, K. L. P., Bowles, R. P., Skibbe, L. E., Justice, L. M., & Wiggins, A. K. (2010). Theoretical explanations for preschoolers' lowercase alphabet knowledge. *Journal of Speech, Language, and Hearing Research, 53*(6), 1757–1768.

Valiandes, S. (2015). Evaluating the impact of differentiated instruction on literacy and reading in mixed ability classrooms: Quality and equity dimensions of education effectiveness. *Studies in Educational Evaluation, 45*, 17–26.

Vaughn, S., Linan-Thompson, S., & Hickman, P. (2003). Response to treatment as a means of identifying students with reading/learning disabilities. *Exceptional Children, 69*(4), 391–409.

Vaughn, S., Wanzek, J., Murray, C. S., & Roberts, G. (2012). *Intensive interventions for students struggling in reading and mathematics: A practice guide.* Portsmouth, NH: RMC Research Corporation, Center on Instruction.

Vellutino, F. R. (1987). Dyslexia. *Scientific American, 256*(3), 34–41.

Vellutino, F. R., Fletcher, J. M., Snowling, M. J., & Scanlon, D. M. (2004). Specific reading disability (dyslexia): What have we learned in the past four decades? *Journal of Child Psychology and Psychiatry, 45*(1), 2–40.

Vellutino, F. R., & Scanlon, D. M. (2002). The interactive strategies approach to reading intervention. *Contemporary Educational Psychology, 27*(4), 573–635.

Vellutino, F. R., Scanlon, D. M., Sipay, E. R., Small, S. G., Pratt, A., Chen, R., & Denckla, M. B. (1996). Cognitive profiles of difficult-to-remediate and readily remediated poor readers: Early intervention as a vehicle for distinguishing between cognitive and experiential deficits as basic causes of specific reading disability. *Journal of Educational Psychology, 88*(4), 601–638.

Vellutino, F. R., Scanlon, D. M., Zhang, H., & Schatschneider, C. (2008). Using response to kindergarten and first grade intervention to identify children at-risk for long-term reading difficulties. *Reading and Writing, 21,* 437–480.

Venezky, R. L. (1999). *The American way of spelling: The structures and origins of American English orthography.* New York: Guilford Press.

Verhallen, M., & Bus, A. G. (2010). Low-income immigrant pupils learning vocabulary through digital picture storybooks. *Journal of Educational Psychology, 102*(1), 54–61.

Verhallen, M., Bus, A. G., & de Jong, M. T. (2006). The promise of multimedia stories for kindergarten children at risk. *Journal of Educational Psychology, 98*(2), 410–419.

Vygotsky, L. S. (1978). *Mind in society: The development of higher psychological processes.* Cambridge, MA: Harvard University Press.

Wagner, R. K., Torgesen, J. K., & Rashotte, C. (1994). The development of reading related phonological processing abilities: New evidence of bidirectional causality from a latent variable longitudinal study. *Developmental Psychology, 30,* 73–78.

Walski, M. M. (2020). Leveled texts: How and when teachers should use them. *Illinois Reading Council Journal, 48*(2), 41–46.

Wanzek, J., Roberts, G., Al Otaiba, S., & Kent, S. C. (2014). The relationship of print reading in Tier I instruction and reading achievement for kindergarten students at risk of reading difficulties. *Learning Disability Quarterly, 37*(3), 148–160.

Wanzek, J., Stevens, E. A., Williams, K. J., Scammacca, N., Vaughn, S., & Sargent, K. (2018). Current evidence on the effects of intensive early reading interventions. *Journal of Learning Disabilities, 51*(6), 612–624.

Wanzek, J., & Vaughn, S. (2008). Response to varying amounts of time in reading intervention for students with low response to intervention. *Journal of Learning Disabilities, 42*(2), 126–142.

Washington, J. A., & Seidenberg, M. S. (2021). Teaching reading to African-American children: When home and school language differ. *American Educator, 45*(2), 26.

Wegerif, R., Mercer, N., & Dawes, L. (1999). From social interaction to individual reasoning: An empirical investigation of a possible socio-cultural model of cognitive development. *Learning and Instruction, 9*(6), 493–516.

Weinstein, C. F., & Mayer, R. F. (1986). The teaching of learning strategies. In M. C. Wittrock (Ed.), *Handbook of research on teaching* (pp. 315–327). New York: Macmillan

Welsch, J. G. (2008). Playing within and beyond the story: Encouraging book-related pretend play. *The Reading Teacher, 62*(2), 138–147.

Werker, J. F. & Hensch, T. K. (2015). Critical periods in speech perception: New directions. *Annual Review of Psychology, 66,* 173–196.

White, S., Sabatini, J., Park, B. J., Chen, J., Bernstein, J., & Li, M. (2021). *The 2018 NAEP Oral Reading Fluency Study* (NCES 2021-025). Washington, DC: Institute of Education

Sciences, National Center for Education Statistics. Retrieved from *https://nces.ed.gov/pubsearch/pubsinfo.asp?pubid=2021025*.

Willingham, D. T. (2018). Does tailoring instruction to "learning styles" help students learn? *American Educator, 42*(2), 28–36.

Wonder-McDowell, C., Reutzel, D. R., & Smith, J. A. (2011). Does instructional alignment matter?: Effects on struggling second graders' reading achievement. *Elementary School Journal, 112*(2), 259–279.

Wood, D., Bruner, J. S., & Ross, G. (1976). The role of tutoring in problem solving. *Journal of Child Psychology and Child Psychiatry, 17*(2), 89–100.

Yell, M. L., Shriner, J. G., & Katsiyannis, A. (2006). Individuals with Disabilities Education Improvement Act of 2004 and IDEA Regulations of 2006: Implications for educators, administrators, and teacher trainers. *Focus on Exceptional Children, 39*(1), 1–24.

Yopp, H. K. (1988). The validity and reliability of phonemic awareness tests. *Reading Research Quarterly, 23,* 159–199.

Yuill, N., & Oakhill, J. (1991). *Children's problems in text comprehension.* Cambridge, UK: Cambridge University Press.

Ziegler, J. C., & Goswami, U. (2005). Reading acquisition, developmental dyslexia and skilled reading across languages: A psycholinguistic grain size theory. *Psychological Bulletin, 131*(1), 3–29.

Zucker, T. A., Cabell, S. Q., & Pico, D. L. (2021). Going nuts for words: Recommendations for teaching young students academic vocabulary. *The Reading Teacher, 74*(5), 581–594.

Children's Books

Day, E. (1997). *Good dog Carl.* New York: Aladdin Paperbacks.

Dowd, N. (1996). *One bee got on the bus.* Parsippany, NJ: Modern Curriculum Press.

Hillert, M. (2017). *Not I, not I.* Chicago, IL: Norwood House Press.

Kosara, T. (2012). *Hibernation.* New York: Scholastic.

Lionni, L. (1963). *Swimmy.* New York: Knopf.

Mark, A. (1997). *Monster mop* (Celebration Press Ready Readers). Parsippany, NJ: Modern Curriculum Press.

Minkoff, M. (1996). *Where is the queen?* (Celebration Press Ready Readers). Parsippany, NJ: Modern Curriculum Press.

Pollock, P. (1996). *The turkey girl.* New York: Little, Brown.

Viorst, J. (1972). *Alexander and the horrible, terrible, no good very bad day.* New York: Atheneum.

Index

Note. *f, n,* or *t* following a page number indicates a figure, note, or a table.
Page references in **bold** indicate glossary entries.